Programming the 65816
Including the 6502,
65C02, and 65802

Programming the 65816 Including the 6502, 65C02, and 65802

David Eyes
Ron Lichty

A Brady Book
Published by Prentice Hall Press
New York, New York 10023

Programming the 65816 Including the 6502, 65C02, and 65802

Copyright © 1986 by Brady Communications Company, Inc.
All rights reserved
including the right of reproduction
in whole or in part in any form

A Brady Book
Published by Prentice Hall Press
A Division of Simon & Schuster, Inc.
Gulf + Western Building
One Gulf + Western Plaza
New York, New York 10023

PRENTICE HALL PRESS is a trademark of Simon & Schuster, Inc.

Manufactured in the United States of America

1 2 3 4 5 6 7 8 9 10

Library of Congress Cataloging in Publication Data

Eyes, David, 1955–
  Programming the 65816 including the 6502, 65C02, and 65802.

Includes index.
1. 65x series microprocessors—Programming.
2. Assembler language (Computer program language)
3. Computer architectures. I. Lichty, Ron. II. Title.
QA76.8.S633E95 1985   005.2'65   85-14892
ISBN 0-89303-789-3

To Carolyn and Althea

—David

To Marilou,
and to Mike and Jean

—Ron

Contents

Preface xiii

Acknowledgments xv

Foreword xvii

Introduction xx

Part I   Basics

1 Basic Assembly Language Programming Concepts   3

Binary Numbers 4/Grouping Bits into Bytes 4/Hexadecimal Representation of Binary 7/The ASCII Character Set 8/Boolean Logic 9/Signed Numbers 12/Storing Numbers in Decimal Form 13/Computer Arithmetic 15/Microprocessor Programming 15/Writing in Assembly Language 18/Basic Programming Concepts 18

Part II   Architecture

2 Architecture of the 6502   25

Microprocessor Architecture 26/The 6502 Registers 26/Addressing Modes 34/Instructions 36/The 6502 System Design 39/NMOS Process 43/Bugs and Quirks 43

3 Architecture of the 65C02   45

The 65C02 Architecture 46/Addressing Modes 46/Instructions 46/CMOS Process 47/Bugs and Quirks 48

4 Sixteen-Bit Architecture: The 65816 and the 65802   49

Power-On Status: 6502 Emulation Mode 50/The Full-Featured 65x Processor: The 65816 in Native Mode 51/The 65802 Native Mode 65/Emulation Mode 67/Switching Between 6502 Emulation and Native Modes 71/65802/65816 Bugs and Quirks 72

Part III   Tutorial

5 SEP, REP, and Other Details   75

The Assembler Used in This Book 78/Address Notation 81

6 First Examples: Moving Data   83

Loading and Storing Registers 85/Moving Data Using the Stack 89/Moving Data Between Registers 94/Storing Zero to Memory 103/Block Moves 103

7 The Simple Addressing Modes   107
Immediate Addressing 108/Absolute Addressing 111/Direct Page Addressing 114/Indexing 117/Absolute Indexed with X and Absolute Indexed with Y Addressing 120/Direct Page Indexed with X and Direct Page Indexed with Y Addressing 123/Accumulator Addressing 126/Implied Addressing 127/Stack 127/Direct Page Indirect Addressing 128/Absolute Long Addressing 130/Absolute Long Indexed with X Addressing 134/Direct Page Indirect Long 135/Block Move 137

8 The Flow of Control   139
Jump Instructions 140/Conditional Branching 143/Unconditional Branching 151

9 Built-In Arithmetic Functions   155
Increment and Decrement 156/Addition and Subtraction: Unsigned Arithmetic 161/Comparison 166/Signed Arithmetic 170/Signed Comparisons 174/Decimal Mode 176

10 Logic and Bit Manipulation Operations   179
Logic Functions 180/Bit Manipulation 187/Shifts and Rotates 189

11 The Complex Addressing Modes   197
Relocating the Direct Page 198/Assembler Addressing Mode Assumptions 200/Direct Page Indirect Indexed with Y Addressing 203/Direct Page Indexing Indirect Addressing 206/Absolute Indexed Indirect Addressing 210/Direct Page Indirect Long Indexed with Y Addressing 212/Stack Relative Addressing 213/Stack Relative Indirect Indexed Addressing 216/Push Effective Instructions 216

12 The Basic Building Block: The Subroutine   225
The Jump-to-Subroutine Instruction 226/The Return-from-Subroutine Instruction 226/JSR Using Absolute Indexed Indirect Addressing 230/The Long Jump to Subroutine 231/Return from Subroutine Long 232/Branch to Subroutine 232/Coding a Subroutine: How and When 235/Parameter Passing 237

13 Interrupts and System Control Instructions   249
Interrupts 250/Status Register Control Instructions 262/No Operation Instructions 263

Part IV Applications

14 Selected Code Samples 267
Multiplication 268/Division 272/Calling an Arbitrary 6502 Routine 277/ Testing Processor Type 284/Compiler-Generated 65816 Code for a Recursive Program 285
The Sieve of Eratosthenes Benchmark 293

15 DEBUG16—A 65816 Programming Tool 299
Declarations 302/LIST 305/FLIST 308/FRMOPRND 311/ POB 317/STEP 319/PUTHEX 321/CLRLN 324/UPDATE 325/ PRINTLN 328/TRACE 330/EBRKIN 332/CHKSPCL 339/ DUMPREGS 345/PUTREG8 347/Tables 348

16 Design and Debugging 361
Debugging Checklist 362/Generic Bugs: They Can Happen Anywhere 366/Top-Down Design and Structured Programming 368/Documentation 369

Part V Reference

17 The Addressing Mode 373
18 The Instruction Sets 421
19 Instruction Lists 527

Appendices

A 65x Signal Description 543
6502 Signals 545/65C02 Signals 546/ 65802 Signals 547/65816 Signals 547

B 65x Series Support Chips 551
The 6551 Serial Chip 552

C The Rockwell 65C02 561

D Instruction Groups 567
Group I Instructions 568/Group II Instructions 569

E W65C816 Data Sheet 573
F The ASCII Character Set 595
Index 599

Limits of Liability and Disclaimer of Warranty

The authors and publisher of this book have used their best efforts in preparing this book and the programs contained in it. These efforts include the development, research, and testing of the theories and programs to determine their effectiveness. The authors and publisher make no warranty of any kind, expressed or implied, with regard to these programs or the documentation contained in this book. The authors and publisher shall not be liable in any event for incidental or consequential damages in connection with, or arising out of, the furnishing, performance, or use of these programs.

Registered Trademarks

Apple and ProDOS are trademarks of Apple Computer, Inc. PIE is a trademark of SOFTWEST.

Preface

It is with great excitement that we present this book, which not only introduces the 65816 and the 65802 in complete detail for the first time, but also encompasses the 6502 and 65C02 in what is meant to provide a complete reference guide to the 65x family.

As 6502 enthusiasts, we believe the two new 16-bit microprocessors—the 65802 and the 65816—represent a great leap forward. We think they hold the potential in days ahead for advances in systems and software even greater than those realized by the 6502 in the early days of the microcomputer revolution. Because of their unique compatibility with the 6502 and 65C02, they bridge the past with the future in a way that no other microprocessor has done.

While this collaboration represents our first work of reference proportions in the computer science field, both of us have written extensively in this field and others, and both of us develop software professionally. It was our unalloyed enthusiasm for the subject that led us to this undertaking. We hope the thrill we experienced when we ran our first 65802 programs on beta copies of the processor plugged into our Apples will be yours to experience, too.

Both of us learned to program primarily through books and hands-on experimentation with personal computers rather than through formal training. Because of this, we share a high regard for the value of books in the learning process and have formed strong opinions about what is useful and what is not in learning how to use and program a new microprocessor. We hope what worked for us will work for you.

Ron Lichty
San Francisco, California

David Eyes
Lowell, Massachusetts

Acknowledgments

Many people have made contributions, directly and indirectly, to the development of this book. To begin with, we want to thank the designer of the 65816, 65802, and 65C02, Bill Mensch: first, for inviting us to be part of his vision; second, for sharing so much of his time to educate us in the details of the 65816 design during the two years in which it passed from first logic drawings to functional silicon; and finally, for providing us with copies of consecutive beta versions of 65802 and 65816 processors for us to test our routines and programs and to use.

It was Smokie Clenney who first got David to consider writing a computer book. Mike Violano wisely suggested he seek a coauthor about the time Ron realized he wanted to write this book and learned David had already started one.

Chris Williams, our editor, was among the first to understand the significance of the 65816. He further contributed to this book by encouraging us to deal with not only the 65802 and 65816 but the entire 65x family. We have appreciated his unflagging support throughout this effort.

Tom Crosley, Larry Hittel, Bill Judd, Bill Mensch, and Mike Westerfield all reviewed the entire manuscript for this work in a matter of weeks, providing many valuable suggestions for which we are grateful. Any errors remaining in this book were most likely introduced after they painstakingly proofed it. Their comments guided us as we sought to hone our facts and our presentation.

Tom Crosley, who at Softwest is Ron's employer, is also his mentor, and most important, his friend. He deserves special thanks both for his patience when Ron's attention wandered for days and weeks at a time back to the 65816 and for his guidance and advice, for which we are both thankful.

Mike Westerfield deserves to be commended for creating the first 65x assembler to work with the 65802 and 65816, ORCA/M. We certainly could not have developed the example programs and routines in this book in such a short time without it.

During David's early involvement with the 65816 project he worked for Bill Overholt. Bill provided much needed support and encouragement when there were those who said the chip would never happen. Bob Norby, recently of GTE Microcircuits, was a valuable resource and promoter of our book project. Mike Weinstock deserves special thanks for lending David an emergency printer during three of our most active writing months. Larry Hittel, who made one of the first of his Com Log Apple16 cards available, thereby gave us a complete 65816 test system. Hank Harrison provided David with much hospitality during frequent visits to California during the creation of the book. Bill Judd, currently of Apple computer, encouraged David through his friendship and eager anticipation of the finished book. Gus Andrade, also of Apple Computer, shared the results of his exhaustive analysis of the 65816 with us, pointing out some anomalies we had been unaware of. Thanks also to Bob Sander-Cederlof and Roger Wagner for providing us with versions of the S-C assembler and Glen Bredon's Merlin assembler.

Final thanks must go to our families—Marilou and Carolyn, and our children, Mike and Jean, and Althea. We appreciate their love and support and patience throughout.

This book was written on Apple // computers with Hayden Software's PIE Writer word processing system and The Speller spellchecker, Byte Works' ORCA/M assembler, Epson MX-80 and C.Itoh dot matrix printers, and, at David's end, the Sider hard disk. All performed marvelously.

Foreword

It was in July 1972, approximately one year after joining Motorola Semiconductor Products Division, Phoenix, Arizona, that I was first introduced to microprocessor design. Previously, I had worked on analog computers before graduating from Temple University in Philadelphia. While at the University of Arizona I worked on computer simulation of plasmas, simulating plasma reactions to radio frequency energy in search of a breakthrough enabling a nuclear fusion energy generation system (without radioactive waste) to become a reality. I graduated from the University of Arizona with a bachelor's degree in electrical engineering, majoring in digital semiconductor design with a minor in computer engineering.

Then in July 1972, I was faced with a major challenge. Rod Orgill and I were assigned the task that six engineers (two teams before us) had failed, which was to deliver a custom microprocessor to Olivetti of Italy. This was a very capable PMOS 8-bit microprocessor, which became a basis for the design approach of the Motorola 8-bit NMOS 6800. Rod (who now works for HP in Colorado) and I were successful; we were allowed to stay in design and become part of the 6800 design team. As you may be aware, the 6800 led to the 68000. As you may or may not be aware, it also led to the 6502.

In August of 1974, a few of us left Motorola and ended up at MOS Technology in Valley Forge, Pennsylvania. In September 1975 in the St. Francis Hotel in San Francisco, we introduced the NMOS 6502 with a purchase price of $25. Because of the price, Steve Wozniak and others could become familiar with this wonderful technology. At $375.00, (the price of the Intel 8080 and Motorola 6800), Steve and others would have bought a TV instead; with the 6502, we are talking about a computer chip selling for the price of an engineering textbook. And so the personal computer technology was born.

In May 1978, I founded the Western Design Center, Inc., in Mesa, Arizona. Our goal is to create the most affordable, highest performance, easiest to use, lowest power technology the world has seen. To this end we created the 65C02 in 1982 by using the low-power CMOS process (the same technology that lets a wristwatch run for a year off of a single battery). It is a direct replacement for the NMOS 6502. The 65C02 is destined to become the most used core microprocessor for a vast base of custom controller chips used in telephones, heart pacers, and more. The Apple //c was introduced in 1984 using the 65C02, and the Apple //e now uses it as well.

As Apple was introducing the Apple //c to the world, I was introducing to Apple the 16-bit version of the 65C02 known as the 65816. The

65816 will ultimately replace the 65C02 (as the 65C02 becomes used predominantly in one-chip microcomputers) and will become the mid-range computer chip. Features have been selected that allow for complete emulation of the 6502 and 65C02 using the E (emulation) bit. (Incidentally, it was David Eyes who first suggested the E bit.) This saves a lot of software from premature obsolescence.

Other features were picked for high-level languages, cache memory, and recursive and reentrant code, just like the "big systems." There will be other generations. The 65832, for example, will have 32-bit floating point operations, in addition to 8- and 16-bit operations. It will plug into a 65816 socket and, of course, will be fully compatible with the 65C02 and 65816.

As the technology improves over the next 10 years and the density of integration increases, we expect to have full-size personal computers on one chip with only memory off chip. The memory cycle time for cache operation should approach 100 MHz, the speed of multimillion dollar mainframes. The power of the 65C02, in the same time frame, should drop to under 1 micro amp (the same as a watch chip) running off a watch crystal. Because the technology is low-power CMOS, low-cost packages are available, and heat generated is very low; therefore, low-cost environments can be built. The cost of the basic microprocessor chip will be under $5.00. And so, this same technology that will power human beings in heart pacers will also power telephones, communication networks, personal computers, and desk-top work stations. It is my belief that this technology will fuel world peace.

This book, as I see it, is and will become the vehicle that WDC will use to communicate not only to the layman, but also to the engineer. Within this edition many of the details of the operation exist. I hope the success of this edition will provide the basis for future editions which will include new details about the chip and system usage gained from industry experience, as well as information about new versions of the processors.

The development of these processors is not the work of one man: many have contributed directly and indirectly. I would like to thank a few of the people who have helped me through the years: Rod Orgill, E. Ray Hirt (vice-president of WDC), and Chuck Peddle who have given me many good ideas over the years; Lorenz Hittel who has suggested many features used on the 65C02 and 65816; Desmond Sheahan, Ph.D. and Fran Krch who, while at GTE Microcircuits, were instrumental in having the 65C02 and 65816 second sourced by GTE—a key to the early success of these programs; Apple computer engineers who suggested features for the 65816; Mike Westerfield who created the ORCA/M macro assembler; David Eyes and Ron Lichty who not only have written this book, which promises to be a classic, but also helped in the debug process by running some of the first software exploring various modes of operation; Will Troxell who has developed a high-performance board for the Apple // and a high-performance operating system exploiting the potential of the 65816; my sister, Kathryn, Secretary of WDC, and WDC's layout design manager who laid out the entire 65816; and the entire staff at WDC.

A special thanks to my wife, Dolores (Treasurer of WDC), who has given me much love, support, encouragement, laid out chips, taught layout designers, and given me four, happy, healthy, beautiful children.

William D. Mensch, Jr.
Mesa, Arizona
June 1985

Introduction

For years, the 6502 stood alone as the original and sole member of the 65x series—or 6500 series, as the family was originally to be called. First shipped in 1975, the 6502 was, at its height, the most popular eight-bit microprocessor on the market, with tens of millions sold. It is found in such personal computers as those made by Acorn, Apple, Atari, Commodore, and Ohio Scientific—to name some of the leading manufacturers of past and present—as well as in video games and dedicated control applications. Currently the 6502 is manufactured by its original developer, MOS Technology, and also by Rockwell International.

The 65C02, first introduced in 1983, was intended as a replacement for the 6502. Using the CMOS fabrication process which became popular for microprocessor manufacturing in the early eighties, it strove for (and for most practical purposes achieved) complete compatibility with the 6502, and sought to differentiate itself in the market primarily by virtue of its CMOS fabrication. Nonetheless, it included several significant enhancements to the 6502 instruction set and fixed some of the known problems in the 6502 design. These minor extensions, it turned out, were intimations of the 65802 and 65816 to come.

The 65C02 was the design effort of William D. Mensch, Jr., who had been, at MOS Technology, the lead designer on the original 6502 development project. Mensch left MOS Technology to found his own company, The Western Design Center, where he designed the 65C02. In addition to being available from the Western Design Center, the 65C02 is also manufactured by GTE Microcircuits, NCR, Rockwell International, and Hyundai. The first notable adoption of the 65C02 was by Apple Computer for their portable Apple //c computer, in which the low power consumption and low heat generation that results from the CMOS process provides significant advantage over the 6502.

Almost immediately after completing the 65C02, Mensch and The Western Design Center began work on the 65816 and 65802 processors, sixteen-bit versions of the original 6502 design. In addition to the strengths they inherit from the 6502 and the set of powerful new extensions they implement, the 65802 and 65816 are unique among modern microprocessors in that they faithfully execute the object code of their eight-bit predecessors, the 6502 and 65C02.

Although they are two distinct products, the 65802 and 65816 are really just two versions of the same design, which is fully realized in the 65816, with its sixteen-megabyte address space. The 65802, on the other hand, provides compatibility with the 6502 not only on a software level but, incredibly, on a hardware level, too: it can replace a 6502 or 65C02 in an existing system and emulate the processor it replaces faithfully, even as it provides a broad range of new features like sixteen-bit registers; but all that compatibility leaves it confined to the earlier processors' 64K address space.

The hardware compatibility of the 65802 makes the 65816 architecture readily accessible to the thousands of users of existing personal computers. It will undoubtedly provide many users with their first exposure to the 65816.

How to Use this Book

The uniqueness of the 65802's and 65816's compatibility with the 6502 and 65C02 cried out for a unique approach to an assembly language book about them: an introduction not just to one of these microprocessors, but to the entire family of them.

How you approach this book will depend most of all on who you are. If you have little experience with assembly language, you should probably begin with Chapter One, **Basic Programming Concepts,** and read sequentially. You will find that it introduces you to the concepts essential to understanding everything that follows. It should also provide a useful and convenient review for more experienced readers.

If you understand assembly language, but have little or no experience with 65x family processors, you should begin with Part Two, **Architecture.** Each of the three chapters introduces the architecture of one of the three generations of 65x processors. Because the 65802 executes the same instruction set as the 65816 (as limited by the 65802's memory space restrictions), these two share a single chapter. Each chapter builds on the last, so you should read them in order: Since the 65816 is a superset of all of the other processors, each chapter describes a larger subset of the complete 65816 design. Furthermore, they illustrate the register set and other basics on which the tutorial section which follows is based.

If you know and have worked with the 6502 before, you may want to skip or lightly skim the 6502 architecture chapter and go right on to the 65C02 chapter. If you know the 65C02, you can go right on to the 65816/65802 chapter.

Part Three, **Tutorial,** is a teaching section, with code examples sprinkled throughout. It is devoted to a step-by-step survey of all 256 different instructions, grouped into six categories (moving data, flow of control, arithmetic, logic and bit manipulation, subroutines, and system control and interrupts), and all 25 different addressing modes, divided into two classes (simple and complex).

Those of you who either have no experience with assembly language or have no experience with the 65x family will find it especially helpful. Even if you're familiar with the 65x family, however, you may want to selectively read from this section.

Having built up to a concept of the 65816 by examining its predecessor designs, the tutorial section views the entire series from this vantage—that of the full 65816 architecture. Of course, the 65816 is a superset of all the other members of the 65x family, so a complete discussion of the 65816 is by definition a discussion of all the other processors as well.

Almost all of the examples in this section and the next are intended to be executed on a system with either a 65802 or 65816 processor, and more likely than not include 65816 instructions, although there are some examples which are intentionally restricted to either the 6502 or 65C02 instruction set for purposes of comparison.

As the 65816 is explored, however, care is taken to distinguish features, such as instructions or addressing modes, by the processors that they are common to. In this way, this book provides the only reference needed for the programmer faced with developing software for more than one of the different processors in the series.

The highlighting and contrasting of the differences between the processors in the series should also be helpful for the programmer already familiar with one processor who wants to learn another—both the 65816 programmer who needs to restrict his knowledge when programming for the 6502, as well as the 6502 programmer who wishes to learn the 65816.

If your interest is in writing applications for the 65x processors, you will find Part Four, **Applications,** of particular interest and use. From the selected code examples in Chapter 14 to the debugging tool in Chapter 15 to the debugging checklist in Chapter 16, this section should provide helpful, down-to-earth examples and how-to.

But even if your interest in the 65x family is strictly academic, you should study the examples in Chapter 14: The code for the sieve of Eratosthenes, for example, provides you the means of comparing the 65816/65802 with other processors, in design, size, and speed; multiply and divide routines for all three generations of 65x processors demonstrate what can be involved in conversion between them; there's a comparison between machine code created by a hypothetical compiler and assembly code written by a hypothetical programmer; and there are routines which deal with the likelihood that many readers will write 65802 programs to be run under 6502-based and 65C02-based operating systems.

Finally, Part Five, **Reference,** is designed so you can turn to it over and over for information and detail on how the various instructions and addressing modes work, their syntax, and their opcodes. You'll find fully illustrated addressing modes arranged alphabetically in Chapter 17; the instructions arranged alphabetically, with descriptions and tables of opcodes and syntax, in Chapter 18; and the instructions listed four ways—alphabetically, functionally, numerically, and mapped in a matrix—in Chapter 19.

If you're a whiz at assembly language or already know one of the 65x processors intimately, this section may be all you need to learn and use the entire 65x family (although we recommend looking over the architecture and applications sections for ideas and review; you may also want to use the Debug16 program in Chapter 15 as an aid for developing code).

If you need specialized information—hardware descriptions, data sheets, compatible I/O parts, cycle descriptions, instruction group breakdowns, deviant family members, and an ASCII chart (with high-bit both set and reset)—you'll find it in the appendix.

Programming the 65816
Including the 6502,
65C02, and 65802

Part I
Basics

1 | Basic Assembly Language Programming Concepts

This chapter reviews some of the key concepts that must be mastered prior to learning to program a computer in assembly language. These concepts include the use of the **binary** and **hexadecimal** number systems; **boolean logic**; how memory is **addressed** as **bytes** of data; how characters are represented as **ASCII** codes; **binary-coded decimal (BCD) number** systems, and more. The meaning of these terms is explained in this chapter. Also discussed is the use of an **assembler**, which is a program used to write machine-language programs, and programming techniques like **selection, loops,** and **subroutines.**

Since the primary purpose of this book is to introduce you to programming the 65816 and the other members of the 65x family, this single chapter can only be a survey of this information, rather than a complete guide.

Binary Numbers

In its normal, everyday work, most of the world uses the *decimal*, or *base ten*, number system, and everyone takes for granted that this system is the "natural" (or even the only) way to express the concept of numbers. Each place in a decimal number stands for a power of ten: ten to the 0 power is 1, ten to the 1st power is ten, ten to the 2nd power is 100, and so on. Thus, starting from a whole number's right-most digit and working your way left, the first digit is multiplied by the zero power of ten, the second by the first power of ten, and so on. The right-most digits are called the **low-order** or **least significant** digits in a **positional notation** system such as this, because they contribute least to the total magnitude of the number; conversely, the leftmost digits are called the **high-order** or **most significant** digits, because they add the most weight to the value of the number. Such a system is called a **positional notation** system because the position of a digit within a string of numbers determines its value.

Presumably, it was convenient and natural for early humans to count in multiples of ten because they had ten fingers to count with. But it is rather inconvenient for digital computers to count in decimal; they have the equivalent of only one finger, since the representation of numbers in a computer is simply the reflection of electrical charges, which are either on or off in a given circuit. The all or nothing nature of digital circuitry lends itself to the use of the **binary**, or **base two**, system of numbers, with one represented by "on" and zero represented by "off." A one or a zero in binary arithmetic is called a **binary digit**, or a **bit** for short.

Like base ten digits, base two digits can be strung together to represent numbers larger than a single digit can represent, using the same technique of positional notation described for base ten numbers above. In this case, each binary digit in such a base two number represents a power of two, with a whole number's right-most bit representing two to the zero power (ones), the next bit representing two to the first power (twos), the next representing two to the second power (fours), and so on (Figure 1.1).

Grouping Bits into Bytes

As explained, if the value of a binary digit, or bit, is a one, it is stored in a computer's memory by switching to an "on" or charged state, in which case the bit is described as being **set**; if the value of a given bit is a zero, it is marked in memory by switching to an "off" state, and the bit is said to be **reset**.

While memory may be filled with thousands or even millions of bits, a microprocessor must be able to deal with them in a workable size.

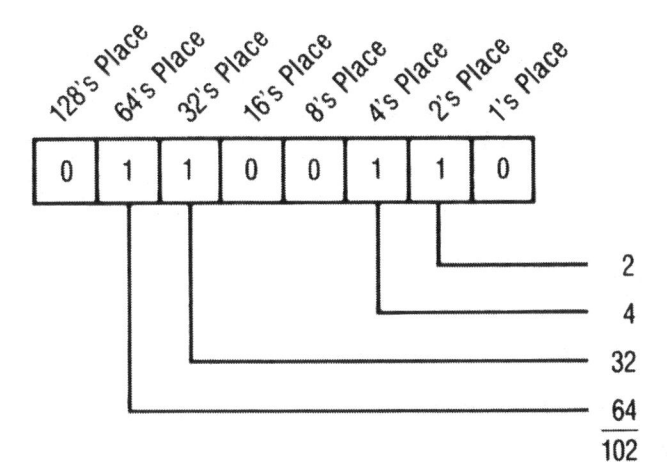

```
           128's 64's 32's 16's 8's  4's  2's  1's
           Place Place Place Place Place Place Place Place
          ┌────┬────┬────┬────┬────┬────┬────┬────┐
          │ 0  │ 1  │ 1  │ 0  │ 0  │ 1  │ 1  │ 0  │
          └────┴────┴────┴────┴────┴────┴────┴────┘
                                          │    │
                                          │    └──────  2
                                          └───────────  4
                                                       32
                                                       64
                                                      ───
                                                      102
```

Figure 1.1. Binary Representation.

The smallest memory location that can be individually referenced, or **addressed**, is usually, and always in the case of the 65x processors, a group of eight bits. This basic eight-bit unit of memory is known as a **byte**. Different types of processors can operate on different numbers of bits at any given time, with most microprocessors handling one, two, or four bytes of memory in a single operation. The 6502 and 65C02 processors can handle only eight bits at a time. The 65816 and 65802 can process either eight or sixteen bits at a time.

Memory is organized as adjacent, non-overlapping bytes, each of which has its own specific **address**. An address is the unique, sequential identifying number used to reference the byte at a particular location. Addresses start at zero and continue in ascending numeric order up to the highest addressable location.

As stated, the 65802 and 65816 can optionally manipulate two adjacent bytes at the same time; a sixteen-bit data item stored in two contiguous bytes is called a **double byte** in this book. A more common but misleading usage is to describe a sixteen-bit value as a **word**; the term word is more properly used to describe the number of bits a processor fetches in a single operation, which may be eight, sixteen, thirty-two, or some other number of bits depending on the type of processor.

It turns out that bytes—multiples of eight bits—are conveniently sized storage units for programming microprocessors. For example, a single byte can readily store enough information to uniquely represent all of the characters in the normal computer character set. An eight-bit binary value can be easily converted to two hexadecimal (base sixteen) digits; this fact provides a useful intermediate notation between the binary and decimal number systems. A double byte can represent the entire range of memory addressable by the 6502, 65C02, and 65802, and one complete **bank**—64K bytes—on the 65816. Once you've adjusted to it, you'll find that there is a consistent logic behind the organization of a computer's memory into eight-bit bytes.

Since the byte is one of the standard units of a computer system, a good question to ask at this point would be just how large a decimal number can you store in eight bits? The answer is 255. The largest binary number you can store in a given number of bits is the number represented by that many one-bits. In the case of the byte, this is 11111111, or 255 decimal (or $2^8 - 1$). Larger numbers are formed by storing longer bit-strings in consecutive bytes.

The size of a computer's memory is typically expressed in bytes, which makes sense because the byte is the smallest addressable unit. And since a byte is required to store the representation of a single alphanumeric character, you can get an easy visualization of about how much storage 64K of memory is by thinking of that many characters. The **K** stands for one thousand (from the Greek *kilo*, meaning thousand, as in kilogram or kilometer); however, since powers of two are always much more relevant when discussing computer memories, the symbol K in this context actually stands for 1024 bytes, the nearest power-of-two approximation of 1000, so 64K is 65,536 bytes, 128K is 131,072 bytes, and so on.

Within a given byte (or double byte) it is often necessary to refer to specific bits within the word. Bits are referred to by number. The low-order, or right-most bit, is called bit zero; this corresponds to the one's place. The next-higher-order bit is bit one, and so on. The high-order bit of a byte is therefore bit seven; of a double byte, bit fifteen. The convention of calling the low-order bit the "right-most" is consistent with the convention used in decimal positional notation; normal decimal numbers are read from left to right, from high-order to low-order. Figure 1.2 illustrates the bit numbers for bytes and double bytes, as well as the relative weights of each bit position.

Double-Byte

Byte

| 15 | 14 | 13 | 12 | 11 | 10 | 9 | 8 | 7 | 6 | 5 | 4 | 3 | 2 | 1 | 0 |

High-Order   Low-Order

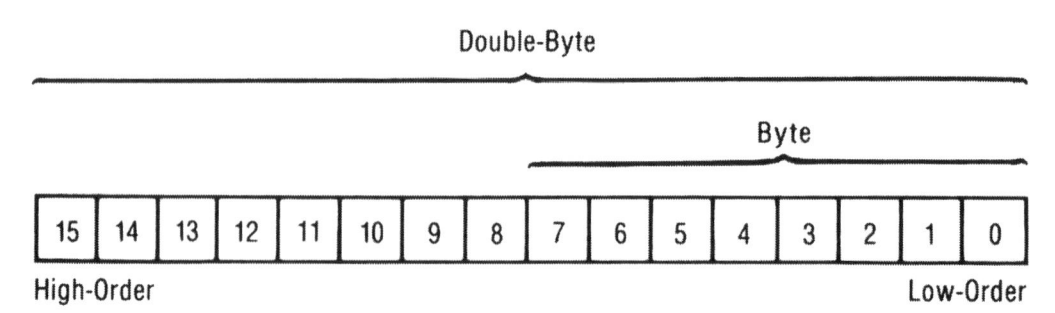

Figure 1.2. Bit Numbers.

Hexadecimal Representation of Binary

While binary is a convenient number system for computers to use, it is somewhat difficult to translate a series of ones and zeroes into a number that is meaningful. Any number that can be represented by eight binary bits can also be represented by two **hexadecimal** (or **hex** for short) digits. Hexadecimal numbers are base sixteen numbers. Since base two uses the digits zero through one, and base ten the digits zero through nine, clearly base sixteen must use digits standing for the numbers zero through fifteen. Table 1.1 is a chart of the sixteen possible four-bit numbers, with their respective decimal and hexadecimal representations.

Table 1.1. Decimal and Hex Numbers.

Binary	Decimal	Hexadecimal
0000	0	0
0001	1	1
0010	2	2
0011	3	3
0100	4	4
0101	5	5
0110	6	6
0111	7	7
1000	8	8
1001	9	9
1010	10	A
1011	11	B
1100	12	C
1101	13	D
1110	14	E
1111	15	F

Because the positional notation convention reserves only a single place for each multiplier of the power of that base, the numbers ten through fifteen must be represented by a single base-sixteen digit. Rather than create entirely new symbols for digits, the first six letters of the alphabet were chosen to represent the numbers ten through fifteen. Each of the sixteen hex digits corresponds to one of the possible combinations of four binary digits.

Binary numbers larger than 1111 are converted to hexadecimal by first separating the bits into groups of four, starting from the rightmost digit and moving left. Each group of four bits is converted into its corresponding hex equivalent. It is generally easier to work with a hexadecimal number like F93B than its binary counterpart

1111100100111011. Hexadecimal numbers are often used by machine language programming tools such as assemblers, monitors, and debuggers to represent memory addresses and their contents. The value of hexadecimal numbers is the ease with which they can be converted to and from their binary equivalents once the table has been memorized.

While a hexadecimal 3 and a decimal 3 stand for the same number, a hexadecimal 23 represents two decimal sixteen's plus 3, or 35 decimal. To distinguish a multiple-digit hex number from a decimal one, either the word hexadecimal should precede or follow it, or a '$' should prefix it, as in $23 for decimal 35, or $FF to represent 255. A number without any indication of base is presumed to be decimal. An alternative notation for hexadecimal numbers is to use the letter H as a suffix to the number (for example, FFH); however, the dollar-sign prefix is generally used by assemblers for the 65x processors.

The ASCII Character Set

Characters—letters, numbers, and punctuation—are stored in the computer as number values, and translated to and from readable form on input or output by hardware such as keyboards, printers, and CRTs. There are 26 English-language lower-case letters, another 26 upper-case ones, and a score or so of special characters, plus the ten numeric digits, any of which might be typed from a keyboard or displayed on a screen or printer, as well as stored or manipulated internally. Further, additional codes may be needed to tell a terminal or printer to perform a given function, such as cursor or print head positioning. These **control codes** include **carriage return**, which returns the cursor or print head to the beginning of a line; **line feed,** which moves the cursor or print head down a line; **bell,** which rings a bell; and **back space,** which moves the cursor or print head back one character.

The **American Standard Code for Information Interchange,** abbreviated **ASCII** and pronounced AS key, was designed to provide a common representation of characters for all computers. An ASCII code is stored in the low-order seven bits of a byte; the most significant bit is conventionally a zero, although a system can be designed either to expect it to be set or to ignore it. Seven bits allow the ASCII set to provide 128 different character codes, one for each English letter and number, most punctuation marks, the most commonly used mathematical symbols, and 32 control codes.

The use of different bit values, or numbers, to store character codes, is entirely analogous to the "decoder ring" type of cipher: the letter 'A' is one, 'B' is two, and so on; but in the case of the ASCII character set, the numbers assigned to the letters of the alphabet are different, and there are different codes for upper- and lower-case letters.

There is an ASCII chart in Appendix F of this book. Notice that since the decimal digits 0 through 9 are represented by $30 to $39, they can be easily converted between their binary representations and their actual values by the addition or subtraction of $30. The letters are arranged in alphabetical order, the capital letters from A through Z represented by $41 through $5A and the lower-case letters from a through z represented by $61 through $7A. This allows letters to be placed in alphabetical order by numerically sorting their ASCII values, and characters to be converted between upper- and lower-case by the addition or subtraction of $20. Finally, notice that the control characters from Ctrl-@ and Ctrl-A through Ctrl-Z and on to Ctrl-_ run from zero to $1F and allow easy conversion between the control characters and the equivalent printing characters by the addition or subtraction of $40.

To print a character on an output device, you must send it the ASCII value of the character: to print an 'A', you must send $41 to the screen, not $A, which is the ASCII code for a line feed; and to print an '8', you must send $38, not $8, which is the ASCII code for a back space. The space character, too, has an ASCII code: $20.

Since any memory value—take $41 for example—could represent either an ASCII code (for 'A' in this case) or a number (decimal 65), the interpretation of the data is defined by the code of the program itself and how it treats each piece of data it uses within a given context.

Boolean Logic

Logical operations interpret the binary on/off states of a computer's memory as the values **true** and **false** rather than the numbers one and zero. Since the computer handles data one or two bytes at a time, each logical operation actually manipulates a set of bits, each with its own position.

Logical operations manipulate binary "flags". There are three logical operations that are supported by 65x microprocessor instructions, each combining two operands to yield a logical (true or false) result: **and, or,** and **exclusive or.**

Logical And

The **AND** operator yields **true** only if *both* of the operands are themselves true; otherwise, it yields false. Remember, **true** is equivalent to one, and **false** equivalent to zero. Within the 65x processors, two strings of eight, or in the case of the 65816, eight or sixteen, individual logical values may be ANDed, generating a third string of bits; each bit in the third set is the result of ANDing the respective bit in each of the first two operands. As a result, the operation is called **bitwise**.

When considering bitwise logical operations, it is normal to use binary representation. When considered as a *numeric* operation on two binary numbers, the result given in Figure 1.3 makes little sense. By examining each bit of the result, however, you will see that each has been determined by ANDing the two corresponding operand bits.

```
              11011010   $DA
       AND    01000110   $45
              --------   ---
      equals  01000010   $42
```

Figure 1.3. ANDing Bits.

A **truth table** can be drawn for two-operand logical operations. You find the result of ANDing two bits by finding the setting of one bit on the left and following across until you're under the setting of the other bit. Table 1.2 shows the truth table for AND.

Table 1.2. Truth Table for AND.

	Second Operand	
	0	1
First Operand		
0	0	0
1	0	1

Logical Or

The OR operator yields a one or true value if either (or both) of the operands is true. Taking the same values as before, examine the result of the logical OR operation in Figure 1.4. The truth table for the OR function is shown in Table 1.3.

```
              11011010   $DA
       OR     01000110   $45
              --------   ---
      equals  11011110   $DE
```

Figure 1.4. ORing Bits.

Logical Exclusive Or

The **exclusive OR** operator is similar to the previously-described OR operation; in this case, the result is true only if one or the other of the

Table 1.3. Truth Table for OR.

	Second Operand	
First Operand	0	1
0	0	1
1	1	1

operands is true, but not if both are true or (as with OR) neither is true. That is, the result is true only if the operands are *different*, as Figure 1.5 illustrates using the same values as before. The truth table for exclusive OR is shown in Table 1.4.

```
              11011010   $DA
     EOR      01000110   $45
              --------   ---
   equals     10011100   $9C
```

Figure 1.5. EXCLUSIVE ORing Bits.

Table 1.4. Truth Table for EXCLUSIVE OR.

	Second Operand	
First Operand	0	1
0	0	1
1	1	0

Logical Complement

As Figure 1.6 shows, the logical **complement** of a value is its inverse: the complement of true is false, and the complement of false is true.

```
                    11011010   $DA
   COMPLEMENTED     --------   ---
       equals       00100101   $25
```

Figure 1.6. COMPLEMENTing Bits.

While the 65x processors have no complement or **not** function built in, **exclusive OR**ing a value with a string of ones ($FF or $FFFF) produces the complement, as Figure 1.7 illustrates.

```
                        11011010   $DA
              EOR       11111111   $FF
    equals Complement   00100101   $25
```

Figure 1.7. COMPLEMENTing Bits Using Exclusive OR.

Since complement has only one operand, its truth table, drawn in Table 1.5, is simpler than the other truth tables.

Table 1.5. Truth Table for COMPLEMENT.

operand	result
0	1
1	0

Signed Numbers

Many programs need nothing more than the whole numbers already discussed. But others need to store and perform arithmetic on both positive and negative numbers.

Of the possible systems for representing signed numbers, most microprocessors, among them those in the 65x family, use **two's complement**. Using two's-complement form, positive numbers are distinguished from negative ones by the most significant bit of the number: a zero means the number is positive; a one means it is negative.

To negate a number in the two's-complement system, you first complement each of its bits, then add one. For example, to negate one (to turn plus-one into minus-one):

```
00000001   To negate +1,
11111110   complement each bit
      +1   and add one.
```
```
11111111   The result is -1.
```

So $FF is the two's-complement representation of minus-one. When converting to two's complement by hand, an easier technique than the two-step process is to copy zeroes from the right (least significant bit) until the first one is reached; copy that one, and then change every zero to a one and every one to a zero as you continue to the left. Try it on the example above.

Now, instead of using eight bits to represent the integers from zero to 255, two's-complement arithmetic uses eight bits to represent signed numbers from -128 ($80) to +127 ($7F), as Table 1.6 shows. There is always one more negative than positive number in a two's-complement system.

Table 1.6. The Eight-Bit Range of Two's-Complement Numbers.

Decimal	Hexadecimal	Binary
+127	$7F	0111 1111
+126	$7E	0111 1110
+125	$7D	0111 1101
.	.	.
.	.	.
.	.	.
+1	1	0000 0001
0	0	0000 0000
−1	$FF	1111 1111
−2	$FE	1111 1110
−3	$FD	1111 1101
.	.	.
.	.	.
.	.	.
−126	$82	1000 0010
−127	$81	1000 0001
−128	$80	1000 0000

Another practical way to think of negative two's-complement numbers is to think of negative numbers as the (unsigned) value that must be added to the corresponding positive number to produce zero as the result. For example, in an eight-bit number system, the value that must be added to one to produce zero (disregarding the carry) is $FF; 1 + $FF = $100, or 0 if only the low-order eight bits is considered. $FF must therefore be the two's-complement value for minus one.

The introduction of two's-complement notation creates yet another possibility in interpreting the data stored at an arbitrary memory location. Since $FF could represent either the unsigned number 255 or the negative integer minus-one, it's important to remember that it is only the way in which a program interprets the data stored in memory that gives it its proper value—signed or unsigned.

Storing Numbers in Decimal Form

Computers use numbers in binary form most efficiently. But when a program calls for decimal numbers to be entered or output frequently, storing numbers in their decimal form—rather than converting them to binary and back—may be preferable. Further, converting floating-point decimal numbers to a binary floating-point form and back can introduce errors: for example, 8 minus 2.1 could result in 5.90000001 rather than the correct answer, 5.9.

As a result, some programs, such as accounting applications, store numbers in decimal form, each decimal digit represented by four bits, yielding two decimal digits per byte, as Table 1.7 shows. This form is called **binary coded decimal**, or **BCD**. BCD lies somewhere between the machine's native binary and abstractions such as the ASCII character codes for numbers.

Since four bits can represent the decimal numbers from zero to fifteen, using the same number of bits to represent only the numbers from zero through nine wastes six combinations of the binary digits. This less than optimal use of storage is the price of decimal accuracy and convenience.

Table 1.7. The First 16 BCD Numbers.

Binary	Hexadecimal	Decimal	BCD
0000 0000	0	0	0000 0000
0000 0001	1	1	0000 0001
0000 0010	2	2	0000 0010
0000 0011	3	3	0000 0011
0000 0100	4	4	0000 0100
0000 0101	5	5	0000 0101
0000 0110	6	6	0000 0110
0000 0111	7	7	0000 0111
0000 1000	8	8	0000 1000
0000 1001	9	9	0000 1001
0000 1010	A	10	0001 0000
0000 1011	B	11	0001 0001
0000 1100	C	12	0001 0010
0000 1101	D	13	0001 0011
0000 1110	E	14	0001 0100
0000 1111	F	15	0001 0101

The 65x processors have a special decimal mode which can be set by the programmer. When decimal mode is set, numbers are added and subtracted with the assumption that they are BCD numbers: in BCD mode, for example, 1001 + 1 (9 + 1) yields the BCD result of 0001 0000 rather than the binary result of 1010 (1010 has no meaning in the context of BCD number representation).

Obviously, in different contexts 0001 0000 could represent either 10 decimal or $10 hexadecimal (16 decimal); in this case, the interpretation is dependent on whether the processor is in decimal mode or not.

Computer Arithmetic

Binary arithmetic is just like decimal arithmetic, except that the highest digit isn't nine, it's one. Thus 1 + 0 = 1, while 1 + 1 = 0 with a carry of 1, or binary 10. Binary 10 is the equivalent of a decimal 2. And 1 − 0 = 1, while during the subtraction of binary 1 from binary 10, the 1 can't be subtracted from the 0, so a borrow is done, getting the 1 from the next position (leaving it 0); thus, 10 − 1 = 1.

Addition and subtraction are generally performed in one or more main processor registers, called accumulators. On the 65x processors, they can store either one or, optionally on the 65802 and 65816, two bytes. When two numbers are added that cause a carry from the highest bit in the accumulator, the result is larger than the accumulator can hold. To account for this, there is a special one-bit location, called a **carry bit**, which holds the carry out of the high bit from an addition. Very large numbers can be added by adding the low-order eight or sixteen bits (whichever the accumulator holds) of the numbers, and then adding the next set of bits plus the carry from the previous addition, and so on. Figure 1.8 illustrates this concept of multiple-precision arithmetic.

Microprocessor Programming

You have seen how various kinds of data are represented and, in general, how this data can be manipulated. To make those operations take place, a programmer must instruct the computer on the steps it must take to get the data, the operations to perform on it, and finally the steps to deliver the results in the appropriate manner. Just as a record player is useless without a record to play, so a computer is useless without a program to execute.

Machine Language

The microprocessor itself speaks only one language, its **machine language**, which inevitably is just another form of binary data. Each chip design has its own set of machine language instructions, called its **instruction set**, which defines the functions that it can understand and execute. Whether you program in machine language, in its corresponding assembly language, or in a higher level language like BASIC or Pascal, the instructions that the microprocessor ultimately executes are

Figure 1.8. Multiple-Precision Arithmetic.

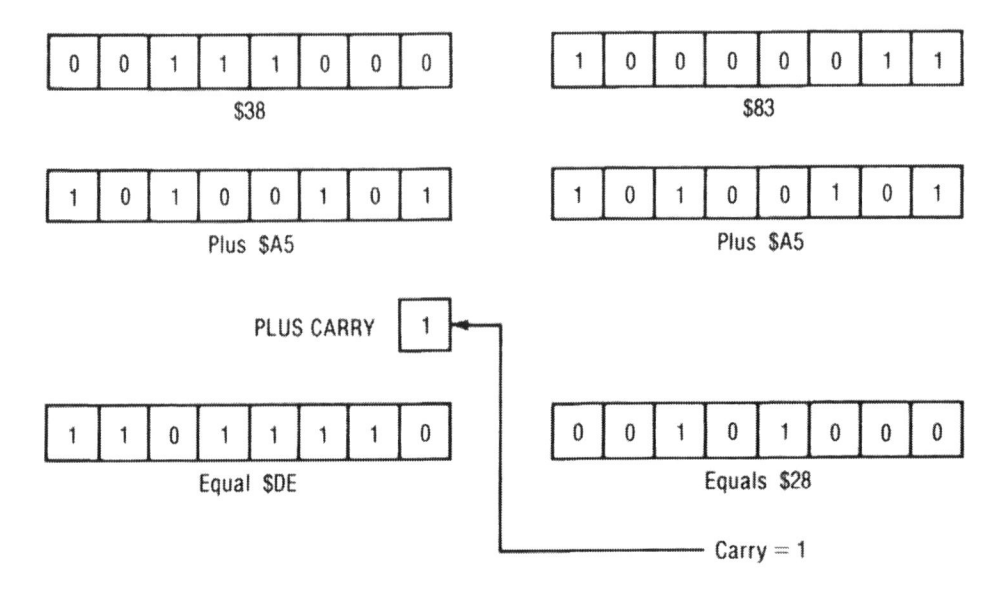

$3883 Plus $A5A5 Equals $DE28

always machine language instructions. Programs in assembly and higher-level languages are translated (by assemblers, compilers, and interpreters) to machine language before the processor can execute them.

Each machine language instruction in the 65x series of microprocessors is one to four bytes long. The first byte of each instruction is called the **operation code** (**opcode** for short); it specifies the operation the computer is to do. Any additional bytes in the instruction make up the **operand**, typically all or part of an address to be accessed, or a value to be processed.

Assembly Language

Writing long strings of hexadecimal or binary instructions to program a computer is obviously not something you would want to do if you could at all avoid it. The 65816's 256 different opcodes, for example, would be difficult to remember in hexadecimal form—and even harder in binary form. **Assembly language**, and programs which translate assembly language to machine code (called **assemblers**) were devised to simplify the task of machine programming.

Assembly language substitutes a short word—known as a **mnemonic** (which means memory aid)—for each binary machine code instruction.

So while the machine code instruction 1010 1010, which instructs the 65x processor to transfer the contents of the **A** accumulator to the **X** index register, may be hard to remember, its assembler mnemonic **TAX** (for "Transfer A to X") is much easier.

The entire set of 65x opcodes are covered alphabetically by mnemonic label in Chapter Eighteen, while Chapters Five through Thirteen discuss them in functional groups, introducing each of them, and providing examples of their use.

To write an assembly language program, you first use a text editing program to create a file containing the series of instruction mnemonics and operands that comprise it; this is called the **source program**, **source code** or just **source**. You then use this as the input to the assembler program, which translates the assembler statements into machine code, storing the generated code in an output file. The machine code is either in the form of **executable object code**, which is ready to be executed by the computer, or (using some development systems) a **relocatable object module**, which can be linked together with other assembled object modules before execution.

If this were all that assembly language provided, it would be enough to make machine programming practical. But just as the assembler lets you substitute instruction mnemonics for binary operation codes, it lets you use names for the memory locations specified in operands so you don't have to remember or compute their addresses. By naming routines, instructions which transfer control to them can be coded without having to know their addresses. By naming constant data, the value of each constant is stated only in one place, the place where it is named. If a program modification requires you to change the values of the constants, changing the definition of the constant in that one place changes the value wherever the name has been used in the program. These symbolic names given to routines and data are known as **labels.**

As your source program changes during development, the assembler will resolve each label reference anew each time an assembly is performed, allowing code insertions and deletions to be made. If you hard-coded the addresses yourself, you would have to recalculate them by hand each time you inserted or deleted a line of code.

The use of an assembler also lets you **comment** your program within the source file—that is, to explain in English what it is you intend the adjacent assembly statements to do and accomplish.

More sophisticated **macro assemblers** take symbol manipulation even further, allowing special labels, called **macro instructions** (or just **macros** for short), to be assigned to a whole series of instructions. *Macro* is a Greek word meaning *long*, so a macro instruction is a "long" instruction. Macros usually represent a series of instructions which will appear in the code frequently with slight variations. When you need the series, you can type in just the macro name, as though it were an instruction mnemonic; the assembler automatically "expands" the macro instruction to the previously-defined string of instructions. Slight variations in the expansion are provided for by a mechanism that allows macro instructions to have operands.

Writing in Assembly Language

In addition to understanding the processor you're working with, you must also have a good knowledge of the particular assembler you are using to program in assembly language. While the specific opcodes used are carved in the silicon die of the processor itself, the mnemonics for those opcodes are simply conventions and may vary slightly from one assembler to another (although the mnemonics proposed by a processor's manufacturer will tend to be seen as the standard). Varying even more widely are assembler **directives**—assembler options which can be specified in the midst of code. These options tell the assembler such things as where to locate the program in memory, which portions of the source listing to print, or what labels to assign to constants.

Nevertheless, most microcomputer assemblers have a great deal in common. They generally provide four columns, or **fields,** for different types of information about an operation: a label which can be used to symbolically identify the location of the code; the opcode; the operand; and space for comments. Figure 1.9 illustrates some typical assembler source code, with the different fields highlighted.

While an opcode or directive appears in every assembler statement, the operand field may or may not be required by any particular opcode, since there are several one-byte instructions which consist solely of an opcode. The label and comment field are optional, added to make the program easier to read, write, debug, and modify later.

During assembly, the assembler checks the fields to be sure the information there is complete, of the proper type, and not out of order, and issues error messages to warn you of problems. It also checks to be sure you have not tried to define the same label twice, and that you have not used a label you did not define.

Basic Programming Concepts

There are several concepts which, in general terms, characterize the different ways a program can execute.

The most obvious concept is that of **straight-line execution:** a program starts in low memory and steps a few bytes higher into memory with execution of each new instruction until it reaches the end, never

Label Field	Opcode Field	Operand Field	Comment Field
	REP	#$10	
	LONGI	ON	
	SEP	#$20	
	LONGA	OFF	
	LDY	#0	
LOOP	LDA	(1,S),Y	get character from first string
	BEQ	PASS	if zero, end of string: match
	CMP	(3,S),Y	compare to corresponding char in 2nd string
	BNE	FAIL	bra if not equal; probably failure
	INY		else do next pair
	BRA	LOOP	
;	matches shortest string		
PASS	PLP		they match up to shortest string;
	CLC		restore status, but clear carry
	BRA	EXIT	
FAIL	LDA	(3,S),Y	was last failure due to end of string2?
	BEQ	PASS	yes; let it pass
	PLP		restore status, but set carry (no match)
	SEC		

Figure 1.9. Typical Assembler Source Code.

doubling back or jumping forward. Straight-line execution is clean and clear: it begins at the beginning, executes every instruction in the program once, and ends at the end. This type of execution is the default execution mode. The 65x processors have a register called the **program counter**, which is automatically updated at the end of each instruction so that it contains the address of the next instruction to be executed.

Selection Between Paths

Real-life problems—the kind you want to write computer programs to solve—are seldom straight and simple. A computer would be very limited with only straight-line execution capability, that is, if it could not make choices between different courses of action based on the conditions that exist while it is executing. Selection between paths provides computers with their decision-making capabilities. The 65x microprocessors carry out selection between paths by means of **conditional branch instructions.**

An example of selection between paths would be a tic-tac-toe program. Playing second, the program must choose where to place its first token from eight different squares. If the opponent has taken the center square, the program must respond differently than if a side square were taken.

Execution still begins at the beginning and ends at the end, in a single pass through the code, but whole groups of instructions on paths not taken are not executed.

Looping

Let's say you write a program to convert a Fahrenheit temperature to Celsius. If you had only one temperature to convert, you wouldn't spend the time writing a program. What you want the program to do is prompt for a Fahrenheit temperature, convert it to Celsius, print out the result, then loop back and prompt for another Fahrenheit temperature, and so on—until you run out of temperatures to convert. This program uses a program concept called **looping** or **iteration,** which is simply the idea that the same code can be reexecuted repeatedly—with different values for key variables—until a given exit condition. In this case the exit condition might be the entry of a null or empty input string.

Often, it's not the whole program that loops, but just a portion of it. While a poker program could deal out 20 cards, one at a time, to four players, it would use much less program memory to deal out one card to each of the players, then loop back to do the same thing over again four more times, before going on to take bets and play the poker hands dealt.

Looping saves writing repetitive code over and over again, which is both tedious and uses up memory. The 65x microprocessors execute loops by means of **branch** and **jump** instructions.

Looping almost always uses the principle of selection between paths to handle exiting the loop. In the poker program, after each set of four cards has been dealt to the four players, the program must decide if that was the fifth set of four cards or if there are more to deal. Four times it will select to loop back and deal another set; the fifth time, it will select another path—to break out of the loop to begin prompting for bets.

Subroutines

Even with loops, programmers could find themselves writing the same section of code over and over when it appears in a program not in quick succession but rather recurring at irregular intervals throughout the program. The solution is to make the section of code a **subroutine,** which the program can **call** as many times and from as many locations as it needs to by means of a **jump-to-subroutine** instruction. The program, on encountering the subroutine call, makes note of its current location for purposes of returning to it, then jumps to the beginning of the subroutine code. At the end of the subroutine code, a **return-from-subroutine** instruction tells the program to return from the subroutine to the instruction after the subroutine call. There are several different types of calls and returns available on the different 65x processors; all of them have a basic call and return instruction in common.

Programmers often build up large **libraries** of general subroutines that multiply, divide, output messages, send bytes to and receive bytes from a communications line, output binary numbers in ASCII, translate numbers from keyboard ASCII into binary, and so on. Then when one of these subroutines is needed, the programmer can get a copy from the library or include the entire library as part of his program.

Part II
Architecture

2 Architecture of the 6502

This chapter, and the two which follow, provide overviews of the architecture of the four 65x family processors: the 6502, the 65C02, and the 65802/65816. Each chapter discusses the register set and the function of the individual registers, the memory model, the addressing modes, and the kinds of operations available for each respective processor. Because each successive processor is a superset of the previous one, each of the next two chapters will build on the material already covered. Much of what is discussed in this chapter will not be repeated in the next two chapters because it is true of *all* 65x processors. As the original 65x machine, the 6502 architecture is particularly fundamental, since it describes a great number of common architectural features.

Microprocessor Architecture

The number, kinds, and sizes of registers, and the types of operations available using them, defines the **architecture** of a processor. This architecture determines the way in which programming problems will be solved. An approach which is simple and straightforward on one processor may become clumsy and inefficient on another if the architectures are radically different.

A **register** is a special memory location within the processor itself, where intermediate results, addresses, and other information which must be accessed quickly are stored. Since the registers are within the processor itself, they can be accessed and manipulated much faster than external memory. Some instructions perform operations on only a single bit within a register; others on two registers at once; and others move data between a register within the processor and external memory. (Although the registers are indeed a special kind of memory, the term **memory** will be used only to refer to the addressable memory external to the microprocessor registers.)

The 6502 is not a **register-oriented** machine. As you will see, it has a comparatively small set of registers, each dedicated to a special purpose. The 6502 instead relies on its large number of addressing modes, particularly its direct-page indirect addressing modes, to give it power.

An **addressing mode** is a method, which may incorporate several intermediate calculations involving index registers, offsets, and base addresses, for generating an instruction's **effective address**—the memory address at which data is read or written. Many 6502 instructions, such as those for addition, have many alternate forms, each specifying a different addressing mode. The selection of the addressing mode by you, the programmer, determines the way in which the effective address will be calculated.

There are three aspects to learning how to program the 6502 or any processor. Learning the different addressing modes available and how to use them is a big part. Learning the available instructions and operations, such as addition, subtraction, branching and comparing, is another. But to make sense of either, you must begin by understanding what each of the different registers is and does, and how the memory is organized.

If you compare the different processors in the 65x family—the eight-bit 6502 and 65C02 and the sixteen-bit 65816 and 65802—you will find they all have a basic set of registers and a basic set of addressing modes in common: the 6502's.

The 6502 Registers

The 6502 registers are:
- The **accumulator**, or A register, is the primary user register and

generally holds one of the operands, as well as the result, of any of the basic data-manipulation instructions.
- The **X** and **Y** **index** registers are used chiefly in forming effective addresses for memory accesses and as loop counters.
- The **processor status**, or **P**, register contains bit-fields to indicate various conditions, modes, and results within the processor.
- The **stack pointer**, or **S** register, is a pointer to the next available location on the system stack, a special area of memory for temporary data storage. In addition to being available to the user, the stack pointer and stack are also used automatically every time a subroutine is called or an interrupt occurs to store return information.
- Finally, the **program counter**, or **PC**, is a pointer to the memory location of the instruction to be executed next.

These six basic 6502 registers are depicted in the **programmer model** diagrammed in Figure 2.1. Notice that, with the exception of the program counter (**PC**), all of them are eight-bit registers. Because they can contain only eight bits, or one byte, of data at a time, they can only perform operations, such as addition, on one byte at a time. Hence the 6502 is characterized as an "eight-bit" processor.

Although the user registers of the 6502 are only eight bits wide, all of the external addresses generated are sixteen bits. This gives the 6502 an **address space** of 64K (2^{16} = 65,536). In order to access data located anywhere in that 64K space with an eight-bit processor, one instruction operand in calculating effective addresses is almost always found in memory—either in the code itself following an instruction, or at a specified memory location—rather than in a register, because operands in memory have no such limits. All that is needed to make a memory operand sixteen bits are two adjacent memory locations to put them in.

To allow programs longer than 256 bytes, the program counter, which always points to the location of the next instruction to be executed, is necessarily sixteen bits, or two bytes, wide. You may therefore locate a 6502 program anywhere within its 64K address space.

Now each of the 6502 registers will be described in more detail.

The Accumulator

The accumulator (**A**) is the primary register in a 65x processor. Almost all arithmetic and most logical operations are performed on data in the accumulator, with the result of the operation being stored in the accumulator. For example, to add two numbers which are stored in memory, you must first load one of them into the accumulator. Then you add the other to it and the result is automatically stored in the accumulator, replacing the value previously loaded there.

6502 Programming Model

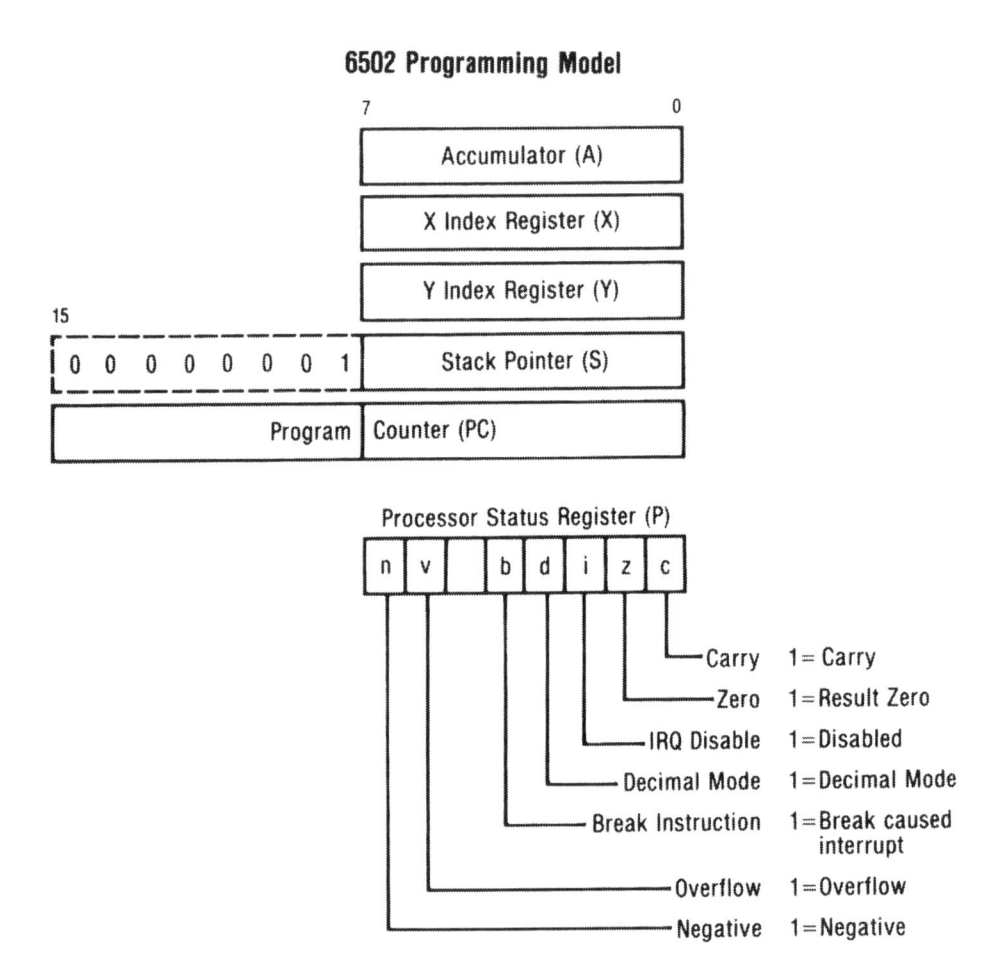

Figure 2.1. 6502 Programming Model.

Because the accumulator is the primary user register, there are more addressing modes for accumulator operations than for any other register.

The 6502 accumulator is an eight-bit register. Only one byte is ever fetched from memory when the accumulator is loaded, or for operations which use two values—one from memory and the other in the accumulator (as in the addition example above).

The X and Y Index Registers

The index registers are generally used either as components in generating effective addresses when any of the indexed addressing modes are used, or as loop counters. They can be easily **incremented** or **decre-**

mented; that is, the value in the index registers can, by means of a single instruction, be increased or decreased by the number one. They are, therefore, useful in accessing successive table locations, moving memory, and counting loop iterations. Unlike the accumulator, no logical or arithmetic operations (other than incrementing, decrementing, and comparing) may be performed upon them.

The use of indexing allows easy access to a continuous series of memory locations, such as a multiple-byte, binary floating-point number, or an array of many single- or multiple-byte objects. Indexing is performed by adding one of several forms of base addresses, specified in the operand field of an instruction, to the contents of an index register. While a constant operand is fixed when a program is created, the index registers are variable and their contents can be changed readily during the execution of a program. As a result, indexing provides an extremely flexible mechanism for accessing data in memory.

Although the X and Y index registers are basically similar, their capabilities are not identical. Certain instructions and addressing modes work only with one or the other of these registers. The **indirect indexed** addressing modes require the Y register. And while the X register is primarily used with **direct page indexed** and **absolute indexed** addressing, it has its own unique (though infrequently used) **indexed indirect** addressing mode. These differences will become clear as you learn more about the different addressing modes.

The Status Register

The status register (also called the P register, for **processor status**) contains a number of **flags** which describe, in part, the status of the microprocessor and its operations. A flag is, in this case, a single bit within the status register. Its value, set (a **one**) or reset (a **zero**), indicates one of two conditions. While the 6502's eight-bit status register could provide eight one-bit flags, only seven of them are used.

Figure 2.1 showed the 6502 P status register; Tables 2.1 and 2.2 describe the functions of its flags.

Table 2.1 describes the five status register **condition code** flags—**negative, zero, overflow, carry,** and **break.** Their values indicate various conditions that result from the execution of many 6502 instructions. Some instructions affect none of the condition code flags, others affect only some, and still others affect all. The effect that an instruction has on the condition flags is an important part of describing what the instruction does. These condition code flags are used to determine the success or failure of the **branch on condition** instructions.

Notice particularly the **zero** flag (z). It can sometimes confuse assembly programmers because a zero flag setting of one indicates a zero result while a zero flag setting of zero indicates a non-zero result.

Table 2.1. Status Register Condition Code Flags.

Name	Abbrev	Bit	Explicitly set or clear	Set or cleared to Reflect an operation result
negative	n	7	---	Reflects most significant bit of result (the sign of a two's-complement binary number): 0 = high bit clear (positive result) 1 = high bit set (negative result)
zero	z	1	---	Indicates zero or non-zero result: 0 = non-zero result 1 = zero result
overflow	v	6	Clear to reverse "set-overflow" hardware input	Indicates invalid carry into high bit of arithmetic result (two's-complement overflow): 0 = two's-complement result ok 1 = error if two's-complement arithmetic
carry	c	0	Clear before starting addition Set before starting subtraction	Arithmetic overflow: addition: carry out of high bit: 0 = no carry 1 = carry subtraction: borrow required to subtract: 0 = borrow required 1 = no borrow required Logic: receives bit shifted or rotated out; source of bit rotated in
break	b	4		Status register itself: no function; value unknown. Pushed status register after interrupt: indicates source of interrupt: 0 = hardware interrupt 1 = software interrupt (BRK instruction)

In connection with the carry flag, it is important to know that the 6502 add operation has been designed to always add in the carry, and the subtract operation to always use the carry as a borrow flag, making it possible to do multiple-precision arithmetic where you add successively higher sets of bytes plus the previous add's carry or subtract successively higher sets of bytes taking into the operation the previous subtract's borrow. The drawback to this scheme is that the carry must be zeroed before starting an add and set before starting a subtraction.

In the case of subtraction, the 6502's carry flag is an inverted borrow, unlike that of most other microprocessors. If a borrow occurred during the last operation, it is cleared; if a borrow did not result, it is set.

Finally, notice that in the status register itself, the break bit has no function. Only when an interrupt pushes the status register onto the stack is the break bit either cleared or set to indicate the type of interrupt responsible.

Table 2.2 describes the other two P register flags, the **mode select** flags: by explicitly setting or clearing them, you can change the operational modes of the processor.

Table 2.2. Status Register Mode Select Flags.

Name	Abbrev	Bit	Reason to explicitly set or clear
decimal	d	3	Determines mode for add & subtract (not increment/decrement, though): Set to force decimal operation (BCD) Clear to return to binary operation
interrupt	i	2	Enables or disables processor's IRQ interrupt line: Set to disable interrupts by masking the IRQ line Clear to enable IRQ interrupts

The **decimal mode** flag toggles add and subtract operations (but *not* increment or decrement instructions) between binary and decimal (BCD). Most processors require a separate decimal-adjust operation after numbers represented in decimal format have been added or subtracted. The 65x processors do on-the-fly decimal adjustment when the decimal flag is set.

The **IRQ disable** or **interrupt disable** flag, toggles between enabling and disabling interrupts. Typically, the interrupt mask is set during time-critical loops, during certain I/O operations, and while servicing another interrupt.

The Stack Pointer

The stack pointer (**S**) implements directly in hardware a data structure known as a **stack** or **push-down stack**. The **stack** is a dedicated area of memory which is accessed by the user via **push** and **pull** instructions. Push stores the contents of a register onto the stack; pull retrieves a data item from the stack, storing it into a register.

The 6502's stack is limited to 256 bytes by the eight-bit width of its stack pointer. The chip confines it in memory between $100 and $1FF by fixing the high-order byte of the stack address at $01. Software power-up routines generally initialize the 6502 stack pointer to $FF, resulting in an initial stack location of $1FF (*see* Figure 2.2).

Initializing the Stack Pointer to $FF:
Resulting Initial Stack of $1FF

Stack Pointer = $FF

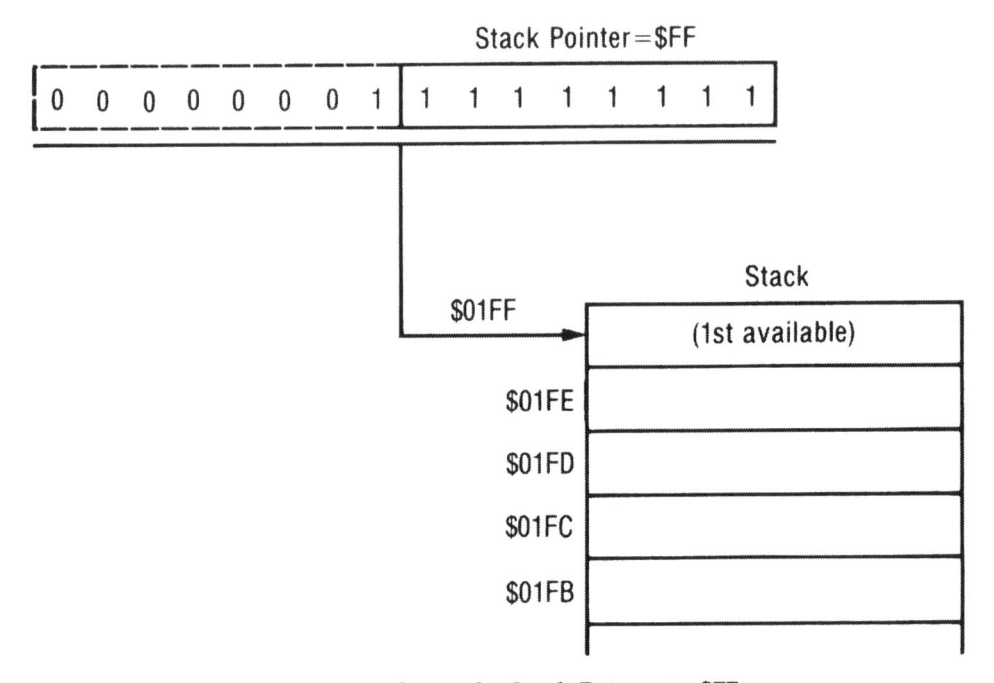

| 0 | 0 | 0 | 0 | 0 | 0 | 0 | 1 | 1 | 1 | 1 | 1 | 1 | 1 | 1 | 1 |

$01FF → Stack (1st available)

$01FE

$01FD

$01FC

$01FB

Figure 2.2. Initializing the Stack Pointer to $FF.

The push and pull instructions are one-byte instructions: the instruction itself specifies the register affected, and the value in the stack pointer register, added to $100, specifies the stack memory location to be accessed.

When a push instruction is executed, data is moved from the register specified by the instruction opcode to the stack address pointed to by the stack pointer. As Figure 2.3 shows, the value in the stack pointer is then decremented so that it points to the next lower memory location—the location to which the next push instruction encountered will store its data.

The pull instruction reverses the process and retrieves data from the stack. When a pull instruction is executed, first the stack pointer is incremented, then the register specified in the instruction opcode is loaded with the data at the incremented address pointed to by **SP**.

In addition to being available as a temporary storage area, the stack is also used by the system itself in processing interrupts, subroutine calls, and returns. When a subroutine is called, the current value of the program counter is pushed automatically onto the stack; the processor exe-

After Pushing the Accumulator

```
                        Stack Pointer=$FE
┌─────────────────────┬─────────────────────┐
│ 0  0  0  0  0  0  1 │ 1  1  1  1  1  1  0 │
└─────────────────────┴─────────────────────┘
```

Stack

$01FF	A A A A A A A A
$01FE	(next available)
$01FD	
$01FC	
$01FB	

Accumulator

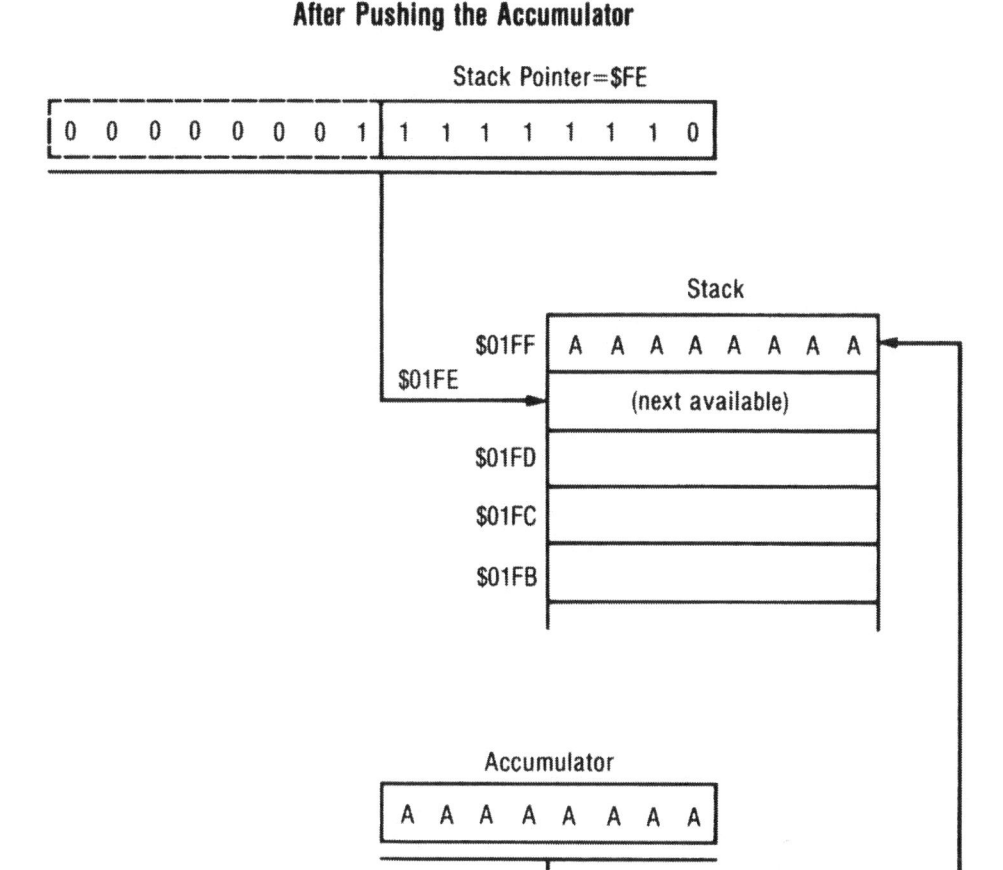

`A A A A A A A A`

Figure 2.3. After Pushing the Accumulator.

cutes a return instruction by reloading the program counter with the value on the top of the stack.

While data is pushed into subsequently lower memory locations on the 65x's stack, the location of the last data pushed is nonetheless referred to as the **top of the stack**.

The Program Counter

The program counter (PC) contains the address of the next byte in the instruction stream to fetch. Execution of a program begins when the program counter is set to the program's entry point (typically the address at which it was loaded). The processor fetches an instruction opcode from that location, and proceeds to execute it. Based on the given opcode, the processor will need to fetch zero, one, or two bytes of operand from the successive locations following the instruction. When the operand has been fetched, the instruction is executed. The program counter is normally incremented to point to the next instruction in memory, except in the case of jump, branch, and call instructions, which pass control to a new location within the program by storing the new location to the program counter.

The 6502 program counter is sixteen bits wide, allowing for programs of up to 64K bytes. If the program counter is incremented past $FFFF, it wraps around to $0000.

Addressing Modes

The fourteen different addressing modes that may be used with the 6502 are shown in Table 2.3. The availability of this many different addressing modes on the 6502 gives it much of its power: Each one allows a given instruction to specify its effective address—the source of the data it will reference—in a different manner.

Table 2.3. 6502 Addressing Modes.

Addressing Mode	Syntax Example	
	Opcode	Operand
Implied	DEX	
Accumulator	ASL	A
Immediate	LDA	#55
Absolute	LDA	$2000
Program Counter Relative	BEQ	LABEL12
Stack	PHA	
Zero Page	LDA	$81
Absolute Indexed with X	LDA	$2000,X
Absolute Indexed with Y	LDA	$2000,Y
Zero Page Indexed with X	LDA	$55,X
Zero Page Indexed with Y	LDX	$55,Y
Absolute Indirect	JMP	($1020)
Zero Page Indirect Indexed with Y (Postindexed)	LDA	($55),Y
Zero Page Indexed Indirect with X (Preindexed)	LDA	($55,X)

Not all addressing modes are available for all instructions; but each instruction provides a separate opcode for each of the addressing modes it supports.

For some of the 6502 addressing modes, the entire effective address is provided in the operand field of the instruction; for many of them, however, formation of the effective address involves an address calculation, that is, the addition of two or more values. The addressing mode indicates where these values are to come from and how they are to be added together to form the effective address.

Implied addressing instructions, such as **DEY** and **INX**, need no operands. The register that is the source of the data is named in the instruction mnemonic and is specified to the processor by the opcode. **Accumulator addressing,** in which data to be referenced is in the accumulator, is specified to the assembler by the operand **A**. **Immediate addressing,** used to access data which is constant throughout the execution of a program, causes the assembler to store the data right into the instruction stream. **Relative addressing** provides the means for conditional branch instructions to require only two bytes, one byte less than jump instructions take. The one-byte operand following the branch instruction is an offset from the current contents of the program counter. **Stack addressing** encompasses all instructions, such as push or pull instructions, which use the stack pointer register to access memory. And **absolute addressing** allows data in memory to be accessed by means of its address.

Like the 6800 processor, the 6502 treats the zero page of memory specially. A **page** of memory is an address range $100 bytes (256 decimal) long: the high bytes of the addresses in a given page are all the same, while the low bytes run from $00 through $FF. The **zero page** is the first page of memory, from $0000 through $00FF (the high byte of each address in the zero page is zero). **Zero page addressing,** a short form of absolute addressing, allows zero page operands to be referenced by just one byte, the low-order byte, resulting both in fewer code bytes and in fewer clock cycles.

While most other processors provide for some form of **indexing**, the 6502 provides some of the broadest indexing possibilities. Indexed effective addresses are formed from the addition of a specified base address and an index, as shown in Figure 2.4. Because the 6502's index registers (**X** and **Y**) can hold only eight bits, they are seldom used to hold index bases; rather, they are almost always used to hold the indexes themselves. The 6502's four simplest indexing modes add the contents of the X or Y register to an absolute or zero page base.

Indirection (Figure 2.5) is less commonly found in microprocessor repertoires, particularly among those microprocessors of the same design generation as the 6502. It lets the operand specify an address at which another address, the **indirect address**, can be found. It is at this second address that data will be referenced. The 6502 not only provides indirection for its jump instruction, allowing jumps to be vectored and revectored, but it also combines indirection with indexing to give it real power in accessing data. It's as though the storage cells for the indirect addresses are additional 6502 registers, massively extending the 6502's register set and possibilities. In one addressing mode, indexing is per-

Indexing: Base plus Index

For example:

Base = $2000
Index Register X = $ 03
Effective Address = $2003

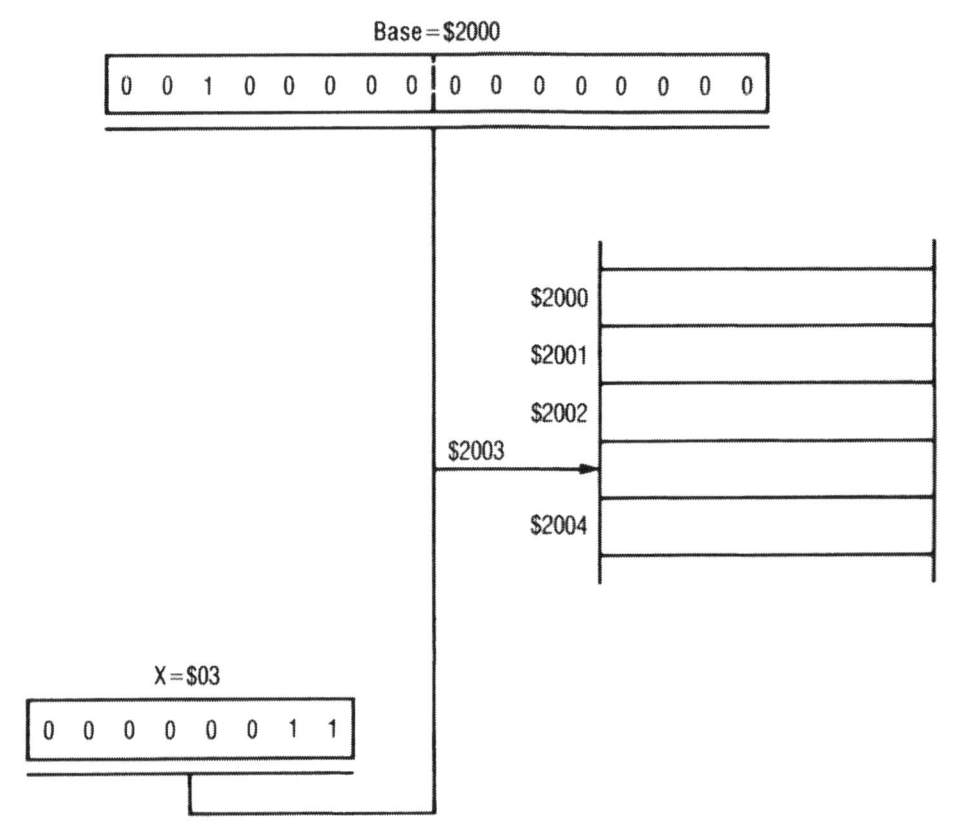

Base = $2000

```
0 0 1 0 0 0 0 0 | 0 0 0 0 0 0 0 0
```

$2000
$2001
$2002
$2003
$2004

X = $03

```
0 0 0 0 0 0 1 1
```

Figure 2.4. Indexing: Base Plus Index.

formed before indirection; in another, after. The first provides indexing into an array of indirect addresses and the second provides indexing into an array which is located by the indirect address.

The full set of 65x addressing modes are explained in detail in Chapters 7 and 11 and are reviewed in the Reference Section.

Instructions

The 6502 has 56 operation mnemonics, as listed in Table 2.4, which combine with its many addressing modes to make 151 instructions available to 6502 programmers.

Indirection: Operand Locates Indirect Address

For example: Zero Page Operand = $20
Data at $20.21 (Indirect Address) = $3458
Effective Address = $3458

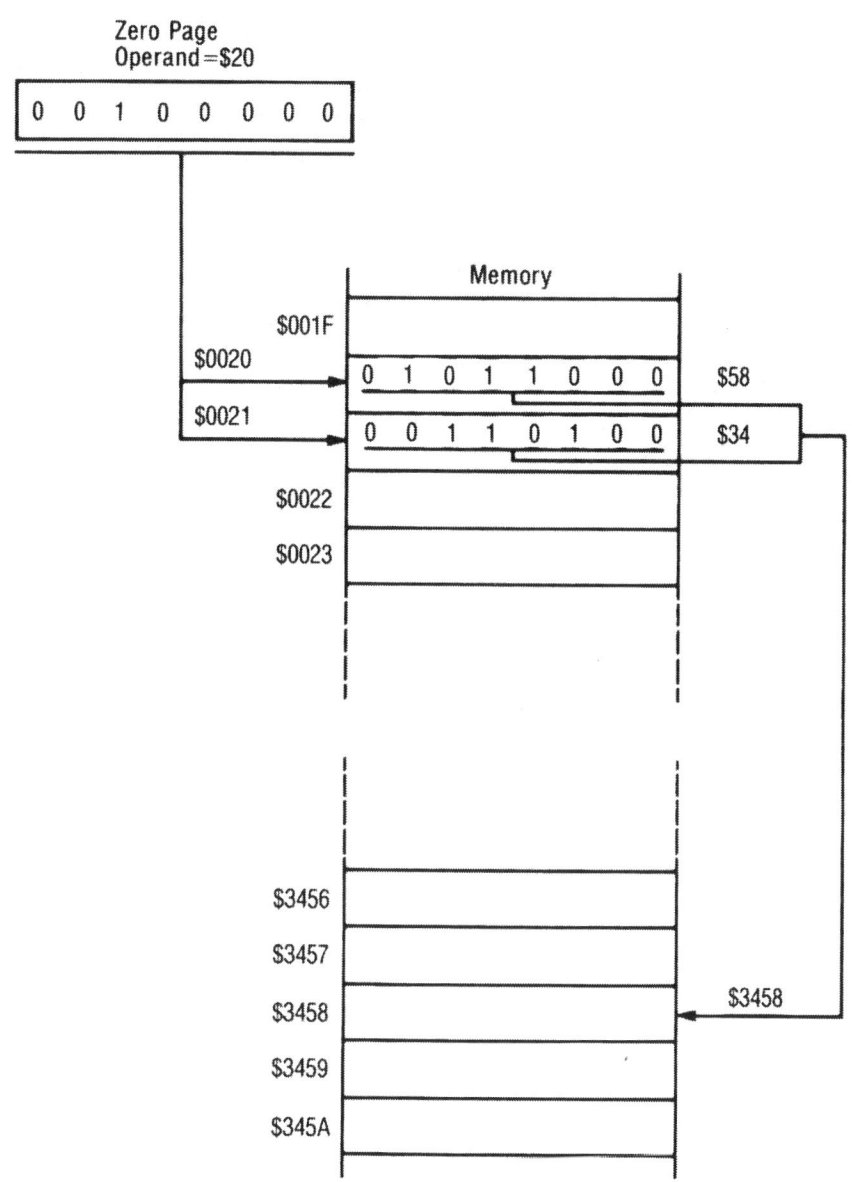

Figure 2.5. Indirection: Operand Locates Indirect Address.

Arithmetic instructions are available, including comparisons, increment, and decrement. But missing are addition or subtraction instruc-

Table 2.4. 6502 Instructions.

Instruction Mnemonic	Description
ADC	Add memory and carry to accumulator
AND	And accumulator with memory
ASL	Shift memory or accumulator left one bit
BCC	Branch if carry clear
BCS	Branch if carry set
BEQ	Branch if equal
BIT	Test memory bits against accumulator
BMI	Branch if negative
BNE	Branch if not equal
BPL	Branch if plus
BRK	Software break (interrupt)
BVC	Branch if overflow clear
BVS	Branch if overflow set
CLC	Clear carry flag
CLD	Clear decimal mode flag
CLI	Clear interrupt-disable flag
CLV	Clear overflow flag
CMP	Compare accumulator with memory
CPX	Compare index register X with memory
CPY	Compare index register Y with memory
DEC	Decrement
DEX	Decrement index register X
DEY	Decrement index register Y
EOR	Exclusive-OR accumulator with memory
INC	Increment
INX	Increment index register X
INY	Increment index register Y
JMP	Jump
JSR	Jump to subroutine
LDA	Load accumulator from memory
LDX	Load index register X from memory
LDY	Load index register Y from memory
LSR	Logical shift memory or accumulator right
NOP	No operation
ORA	OR accumulator with memory
PHA	Push accumulator onto stack
PHP	Push status flags onto stack
PLA	Pull accumulator from stack
PLP	Pull status flags from stack
ROL	Rotate memory or accumulator left one bit

Table 2.4. 6502 Instructions (Cont.).

Instruction Mnemonic	Description
ROR	Rotate memory or accumulator right one bit
RTI	Return from interrupt
RTS	Return from subroutine
SBC	Subtract memory with borrow from accumulator
SEC	Set carry flag
SED	Set decimal mode flag
SEI	Set interrupt-disable flag
STA	Store accumulator to memory
STX	Store index register X to memory
STY	Store index register Y to memory
TAX	Transfer accumulator to index register X
TAY	Transfer accumulator to index register Y
TSX	Transfer stack pointer to index register X
TXA	Transfer index register X to accumulator
TXS	Transfer index register X to stack pointer
TYA	Transfer index register Y to accumulator

tions which do not involve the carry; as a result, you must clear the carry before beginning an add and set it before beginning a subtraction.

Logic instructions available include shifts and rotates, as well as an instruction for bit comparing.

Branch instructions are entirely flag-based, not arithmetic-operation based, so there are no single branch-on-greater-than, branch-on-less-than-or-equal, or signed arithmetic branches. There is also no unconditional branch and no branch-to-subroutine. The unconditional branch can be imitated by first executing one of the 6502's many clear- or set-flag instructions, then executing a branch-on-that-flag's-condition instruction.

All three of the main user registers can be loaded from and stored to memory, but only the accumulator (not the index registers) can be pushed onto and pulled from the stack (although the flags can also be pushed and pulled). On the other hand, single instructions let the accumulator value be transferred to either index register or loaded from either index register. One more transfer instruction is provided for setting the value of the stack pointer to the value in the X index register.

The 6502 System Design

There are a number of other features of the 6502's design which make it unique and make systems designed with it stand apart from systems designed with other microprocessors.

Pipelining

The 65x microprocessors have the capability of doing two things at once: the 6502 can be carrying on an internal activity (like an arithmetic or logical operation) even as it's getting the next instruction byte from the instruction stream or accessing data in memory.

A processor is driven by a **clock** signal which synchronizes events within the processor with memory accesses. A cycle is a basic unit of time within which a single step of an operation can be performed. The speed with which an instruction can be executed is expressed in the number of cycles required to complete it. The actual speed of execution is a function both of the number of cycles required for completion and the number of timing signals provided by the clock every second. Typical clock values for 65x processors start at one million cycles per second and go up from there.

As a result of the 6502's capability of performing two different but overlapping phases of a task within a single cycle, which is called **pipelining**, the 65x processors are much faster than non-pipelined processors.

Take the addition of a constant to the 6502's eight-bit accumulator as an example. This requires five distinct steps:

Step 1: Fetch the instruction opcode ADC.
Step 2: Interpret the opcode to be ADC of a constant.
Step 3: Fetch the operand, the constant to be added.
Step 4: Add the constant to the accumulator contents.
Step 5: Store the result back to the accumulator.

Pipelining allows the 6502 to execute steps two and three in a single cycle: after getting an opcode, it increments the program counter, puts the new program address onto the address bus, and gets the next program byte, while simultaneously interpreting the opcode. The completion of steps four and five overlaps the next instruction's step one, eliminating the need for two additional cycles.

So the 6502's pipelining reduces the operation of adding a constant from five cycles to two!

The clock speed of a microprocessor has often been incorrectly presumed to be the sole determinant of its speed. What is most significant, however, is the memory cycle time. The 68000, for example, which typically operates at 6 to 12 megahertz (MHz, or millions of cycles per second) requires four clock periods to read or write data to and from memory. The 65x processors require only one clock period. Because the 6502 requires fewer machine cycles to perform the same functions, a one-megahertz 6502 has a throughput unmatched by the 8080 and Z80 processors until their clock rates are up to about four MHz.

The true measure of the relative speeds of various microprocessors can only be made by comparing how long each takes, in its own machine code, to complete the same operation.

Memory Order of Multiple-Byte Values

Multiple-byte values could be stored in memory in one of two ways: low-order byte first, followed by successively higher order bytes; or high-order byte first, followed by successively lower order bytes. The 6502, like the Intel and Zilog chips (the 8080, Z80, 8086, and so on), but unlike the Motorola chips (the 6800, 6809, 68000, and so on), puts the low-order byte first, into the lower memory address.

This seemingly unnatural order of the placement of multiple-byte values in memory can be disconcerting at first. The sixteen-bit value stored in memory as a $30 followed by $FE is not $30FE but rather $FE30. Multiple-byte values are written high-order first, to read from left to right; this is the opposite of how the bytes are placed in memory. This memory order, however, contributes to the success and speed of pipelining. Consider, as an example, the loading of the accumulator using absolute indexed addressing (two lines for a cycle indicate simultaneous operations due to pipelining):

Cycle 1: Fetch the instruction opcode, LDA.
Cycle 2: Fetch an operand byte, the low byte of an array base.
Interpret the opcode to be LDA absolute indexed.
Cycle 3: Fetch the second operand byte, the high array base byte.
Add the contents of the index register to the low byte.
Cycle 4: Add the carry from the low address add to the high byte.
Cycle 5: Fetch the byte at the new effective memory address.

(NOTE: The 6502 also does a fetch during Cycle 4, before it checks to see if there was any carry; if there is no carry into the high byte of the address, as is often true, then the address fetched from was correct and there is no cycle five; the operation is a four-cycle operation in this case. Absolute indexed writes, however, always require five cycles.)

The low–high memory order means that the first operand byte, which the 6502 fetches before it even knows that the opcode is LDA and the addressing mode is absolute indexed, is the low byte of the address base, the byte which must be added to the index register value first; it can do that add while getting the high byte.

Consider how high–low memory order would weaken the benefits of pipelining and slow the process down:

Cycle 1: Fetch the instruction opcode, LDA.
Cycle 2: Fetch an operand byte, the high byte of an array base.
Interpret the opcode to be LDA absolute indexed.

Cycle 3: Fetch the second operand byte, the low array base byte. Store the high byte temporarily.
Cycle 4: Add the contents of the index register to the low byte.
Cycle 5: Add the carry from the low address add to the high byte.
Cycle 6: Fetch the byte at the new effective memory address.

Memory-Mapped Input/Output

The 65x family (like Motorola's but unlike Zilog's and Intel's) accomplishes input and output not with special opcodes, but by assigning each input/output device a memory location, and by reading from or writing to that location. As a result, there's virtually no limit to the number of I/O devices which may be connected to a 65x system. The disadvantage of this method is that memory in a system is reduced by the number of locations which are set aside for I/O functions.

Interrupts

Interrupts tell the processor to stop what it is doing and to take care of some more pressing matter instead, before returning to where it left off in regular program code. An interrupt is much like a doorbell: having one means you don't have to keep going to the door every few minutes to see if someone is there; you can wait for it to ring instead.

An external device like a keyboard, for example, might cause an interrupt to present input. Or a clock might generate interrupts to toggle the processor back and forth between two or more routines, letting it do several tasks "at once." A special kind of interrupt is **reset** (the panic button), which is generally used out of frustration to force the processor into reinitialization. Reset generally does not return to the interrupted code after it has been served, however.

The 6502 has three **interrupt vectors**—memory addresses that hold the locations of routines which are automatically executed upon recognition of an interrupt by the processor. The first of these is used for reset.

The second vector is used both by **maskable interrupts**—those which you can force the processor to ignore, either temporarily or permanently, by setting the i interrupt bit in the status register—and by **software interrupts**—which are caused by the execution of the break instruction (**BRK**). If any hardware can cause a maskable interrupt, the **interrupt service routine** pointed to by this vector must determine the source of the interrupt. It must poll a status flag on each possible hardware source as well as check the stacked status register's **b** flag, which is set and pushed when a break instruction is executed. When it finds the source of the interrupt, it must then branch to a routine which will respond to the interrupt in a way appropriate to the source (getting a character from a communications port, for example).

The third vector is used by **nonmaskable interrupts,** those which interrupt regardless of the **i** bit in the status register. The non-maskable interrupt is usually reserved for a single high-priority or time-critical interrupt, such as refresh of a CRT screen or to warn of impending power failure.

The 6502 was designed to service interrupts as fast as possible. Because interrupts cannot be served until the current instruction is completed (so no data is lost), the worst case is the longest instruction time and the 6502's instructions each take very few cycles to execute. As a result, the 6502 and its successors have the lowest interrupt **latency**—the time between interrupt occurrence and interrupt-handling response—of any eight-bit or sixteen-bit processors.

NMOS Process

The 6502 is fabricated using the **NMOS** (pronounced "EN moss") process (for N-channel Metal-Oxide Semiconductor). Still one of the most common of the technologies used in large-scale and very-large-scale integrated circuits, NMOS was, at the time the 6502 was designed and for many years after, the most cost-efficient of the MOS technologies and the easiest process for implementation of relatively high-speed parts. This made NMOS popular among designers of microcomputers and other devices in which hardware cost was an important design factor.

Most of the current generation of 8-, 16-, and 32-bit processors were originally implemented in NMOS. Some, like the 6502, are still only available in NMOS process versions. Others, like all of the recently designed members of the 65x family (the 65C02, 65802, and 65816) were produced exclusively using the CMOS process.

Bugs and Quirks

The 6502 has a number of features which the less enthusiastic might be inclined to call bugs or quirks.

The one most clearly a bug involves using indirect addressing with the jump instruction, when its operand ends in $FF. To use an example,

```
JMP ($20FF)
```

should cause the program counter to get, as its new low byte, the contents of $20FF, and as its new high byte, the contents of $2100. However, while the 6502 increments the low byte of the indirect address from $FF to 00, it fails to add the carry into the high byte, and as a result gets the program counter's new high byte from $2000 rather than $2100.

You can also run into trouble trying to execute an unused opcode, of which the 6502 has many. The results are unpredictable, but can include causing the processor to "hang."

Finally, the decimal mode is not as easy to use as it might be. The negative, overflow, and zero flags in the status register are not valid in decimal mode and the setting of the decimal flag, which toggles the processor between binary and decimal math, is unknown after the processor has received a hardware "reset".

3 | Architecture of the 65C02

The 65C02 microprocessor is an enhanced version of the 6502, implemented using a silicon-gate CMOS process. The 65C02 was designed primarily as a CMOS replacement for the 6502. As a result, the significant differences between the two products are few. While the 65C02 adds 27 new opcodes and two new addressing modes (in addition to implementing the original 151 opcodes of the 6502), its register set, memory model, and types of operations remain the same.

The 65C02 is used in the Apple //c and, since early 1985, in the Apple //e, and it has been provided as an enhancement kit for earlier //e's.

Remember that even as the 65C02 is a superset of the 6502, the 65802 and 65816, described in the next chapter, are supersets of the 65C02. All of the enhancements found in the 65C02 are additionally significant in that they are intermediate to the full 65816 architecture. The next chapter will continue to borrow from the material covered in the previous ones, and generally what is covered in the earlier of these three architecture chapters is not repeated in the subsequent ones, since it is true for *all* 65x processors.

The 65C02 Architecture

Both the 65C02 and the 6502 are eight-bit processors, with a 64K address space and exactly the same register set.

The 65C02 features some small but highly desirable improvements in the use of the status register flags: it gives valid negative, overflow, and zero flags while in decimal mode, unlike the 6502; and it resets the decimal flag to zero after reset and interrupt.

The 65C02 has slightly different cycle counts on a number of operations from the 6502, some shorter and a few longer. The longer cycle counts are generally necessary to correct or improve operations from the 6502.

Addressing Modes

The 65C02 introduces the two new addressing modes shown in Table 3.1, as well as supporting all the 6502 addressing modes. All of them will be explained in detail in Chapters 7 and 11, and will be reviewed in the Reference Section.

Table 3.1. The 65C02's New Addressing Modes.

Addressing Mode	Syntax Example	
	Opcode	Operand
Zero Page Indirect	LDA	($55)
Absolute Indexed Indirect	JMP	($2000,X)

Zero page indirect provides an indirect addressing mode for accessing data which requires no indexing (the 6502's absolute indirect mode is available only to the jump instruction). 6502 programmers commonly simulate indirection by loading an index register with zero (losing its contents and taking extra steps), then using the preindexed or postindexed addressing modes to indirectly reference the data.

On the other hand, combining indexing and indirection proved so powerful for accessing data on the 6502 that programmers wanted to see this combination made available for tables of jump vectors. **Absolute indexed indirect**, available for the jump instruction only, provides this multi-directional branching capability, which can be very useful for *case* or *switch* statements common to many languages.

Instructions

While the 65C02 provides 27 new opcodes, there are only eight new operations. The 27 opcodes result from providing four different addressing modes for one of the new mnemonics and two for two others, and also from expanding the addressing modes for twelve 6502 instructions. The most significant expansion of a 6502 instruction by combining it with a 6502 addressing mode it did not previously use is probably the addition of accumulator addressing for the increment and decrement instructions.

The new 65C02 operations, shown in Table 3.2, answer many programmer's prayers: an unconditional branch instruction, instructions to push and pull the index registers, and instructions to zero out memory cells. These may be small enhancements, but they make programming the 65C02 easier, more straightforward, and clearer to document. Two more operations allow the 65C02 to set or clear any or all of the bits in a memory cell with a single instruction.

Table 3.2. New 65C02 Instructions.

Instruction Mnemonic	Description
BRA	Branch always (unconditional)
PHX	Push index register X onto stack
PHY	Push index register Y onto stack
PLX	Pull index register X from stack
PLY	Pull index register Y from stack
STZ	Store zero to memory
TRB	Test and reset memory bits against accumulator
TSB	Test and set memory bits against accumulator

CMOS Process

Unlike the 6502, which is fabricated in NMOS, the 65C02 is a **CMOS** (pronounced "SEE moss") part. CMOS stands for Complementary Metal-Oxide Semiconductor.

The most exciting feature of CMOS is its low power consumption, which has made portable, battery-operated computers possible. Its low power needs also result in lower heat generation, which means parts can be placed closer together and heat-dissipating air space minimized in CMOS-based computer designs.

CMOS technology is not a new process. It's been around for about as long as other MOS technologies. But higher manufacturing costs during the early days of the technology made CMOS impractical for the highly competitive microcomputer market until the mid 1980s, so process development efforts were concentrated on NMOS and not applied to CMOS until 1980 or 1981.

CMOS technology has reached a new threshold in that most of its negative qualities, such as the difficulty with which smaller geometries are achieved relative to the NMOS process, have been overcome. Price has become competitive with the more established NMOS as well.

Bugs and Quirks

The 65C02 fixes all of the known bugs and quirks in the 6502. The result of executing unused opcodes is now predictable—they do nothing (that is, they act like no-operation instructions). An interesting footnote is that, depending on the unimplemented instruction that is executed, the number of cycles consumed by the no-operation is variable between one and eight cycles. Also, the number of bytes the program counter is incremented by is variable. It is strongly recommended that this feature not be exploited, as its use will produce code incompatible with the next-generation 65802 and 65816.

The jump indirect instruction has been fixed to work correctly when its operand crosses a page boundary (although at the cost of an execution cycle). The negative, overflow, and zero flags have been implemented to work in decimal mode (also at the cost of an execution cycle). The decimal mode is now reset to binary after a hardware reset or an interrupt.

Finally, a fix which is generally transparent to the programmer, but which eliminates a possible cause of interference with memory-mapped I/O devices on the 6502, is the elimination of an invalid address read while generating an indexed effective address when a page boundary is crossed.

The quirk unique to the 65C02 results from trying to eliminate the quirks of the 6502. The timing improvements of a number of instructions and the bug fixes from the 6502 make the 65C02 an improvement over the 6502, but *not quite* fully compatible on a cycle-by-cycle basis. This is only a consideration during the execution of time-critical code, such as software timing loops. As a practical example, this has affected very little software being ported from the Apple //e to the //c.

4 | Sixteen-Bit Architecture: The 65816 and the 65802

While the 65C02 was designed more as a CMOS replacement for the 6502 than an enhancement of it, the 65802 and 65816 were created to move the earlier designs into the world of sixteen-bit processing. And although the eight-bit 6502 had been a speed demon when first released, its competition changed over the years as processing sixteen bits at a time became common, and as the memory new processors could address started at a megabyte.

The 65816 and the 65802 were designed to bring the 65x family into line with the current generation of advanced processors. First produced in prototypes in the second half of 1984, they were released simultaneously early in 1985. The 65816 is a full-featured realization of the 65x concept as a sixteen-bit machine. The 65802 is its little brother, with the 65816's sixteen-bit processing packaged with the 6502's pinout for compatibility with existing hardware.

The two processors are quite similar. They are, in fact, two different versions of the same basic design. In the early stages of the chip fabrication process they are identical and only assume their distinct "personalities" during the final (metalization) phase of manufacture.

The two processors provide a wealth of enhancements: another nine addressing modes, 78 new opcodes, a "hidden" second accumulator in eight-bit mode, and a zero page which, renamed the **direct page,** can be relocated to any contiguous set of $100 bytes anywhere within the first 64K of memory (which in the case of the 65802 is anywhere in its address space). The most dramatic of all the enhancements common to both 65802 and 65816, though, is the expansion of the primary user registers—the accumulator, index registers, and stack pointer—to sixteen-bit word size. The accumulator and index registers can be toggled to sixteen bits from eight, and back to eight when needed. The stack, pointed to by an expanded-to-sixteen-bit stack register, can be relocated from page one to anywhere in a 64K range.

The primary distinction between the two processors is the range of addressable memory: the 65816 can address up to sixteen megabytes; the 65802 is constrained by its 6502 pinout to 64K.

A secondary distinction between the two processors is that the 65816's new pinout also provides several significant new signals for the hardware designer. While outside the primary scope of this book, these new signals are mentioned in part in this chapter and described in some detail in Appendix C.

It is important to remember that the 65802 is in fact a 65816 that has been coerced to live in the environment designed originally for the 6502 and 65C02. Outside of the memory and signal distinctions just listed, the 65816 and the 65802 are identical. Both have a **native mode,** in which their registers can be used for either eight- or sixteen-bit operations. Both have a **6502 emulation mode,** in which the 6502's register set and instruction timings emulate the eight-bit 6502 (not the 65C02) *exactly* (except they correct a few 6502 bugs). *All* existing 6502 software can be run by the new processor—as can virtually all 65C02 software— even as most of the native mode's enhancements (other than sixteen-bit registers) are programmable in emulation mode, too.

To access sixteen megabytes, the signals assigned to the various pins of the 65816's 40-pin package are different from the 6502, the 65C02 and the 65802, so it cannot be installed in existing 65x computers as a replacement upgrade. The 65802, on the other hand, has a pinout that is identical to that of the 6502 and 65C02 and can indeed be used as a replacement upgrade.

This makes the 65802 a unique, pin-compatible, software-compatible sixteen-bit upgrade chip. You can pull a 6502 out of its socket in any existing 6502 system, and replace it with a 65802 because it powers-on in the 6502 emulation mode. It will run existing applications exactly the same as the 6502 did. Yet new software can be written, and 6502 programs rewritten, to take advantage of the 65802's sixteen-bit capabilities, resulting in programs which take up much less code space and which run faster. Unfortunately, even with a 65802 installed, an older system will remain unable to address memory beyond the original 64K limits of the 6502. This is the price of hardware compatibility.

The information presented in this chapter builds directly on the information in the previous two chapters; it should be considered as a continuous treatment of a single theme. Even in native mode with sixteen-bit registers, the 65802 and 65816 processors utilize many of the 6502 and 65C02 instructions, registers, and addressing modes in a manner which differs little from their use on the earlier processors. If you are already familiar with the 6502 or the 65C02, you will discover that the 65802 and 65816 logically expand on these earlier designs.

Power-On Status: 6502 Emulation Mode

When the 65816 and 65802 are powered on, they initialize themselves into **6502 emulation mode** in which, with the exception of fixing several

6502 bugs, they *exactly* emulate the 6502. The stack is confined to page one, just like the 6502 stack pointer. The registers are configured to eight bits, to model the 6502's registers. Every 6502 instruction is implemented identically. The timing of each instruction is exactly the same as on the original NMOS 6502. The direct page of the 65802 and 65816, which as you will learn can be relocated using the sixteen-bit direct page register, is initialized to page zero, making direct page addressing exactly equivalent to 6502 zero page addressing. The program and data bank registers, which as you will learn provide efficient access in the 65816 to any one or two 64K banks of memory at a time, are initialized to the zero bank.

Unlike the NMOS 6502, which has undefined results when unimplemented opcodes are executed, and the 65C02, which treats unimplemented opcodes as variously-timed and -sized no-operations, the 65802 instruction set implements every one of the 256 possible one-byte opcodes. These additional instructions are available in emulation mode as well as in native mode.

Among the newly implemented opcodes are ones that allow the processors to be switched to their native mode—sixteen-bit operation. While there is more to say about 6502 emulation mode, it will be easier to understand in the context of native mode.

The Full-Featured 65x Processor: The 65816 in Native Mode

The 65816 in its **native mode** (as opposed to its 6502 emulation mode) has it all: sixteen-bit registers, 24-bit addressing, and all the rest. The 65802's native mode is a subset of this, as are the emulation modes of both processors.

Figure 4.1 shows the programming model for the 65816 in native mode. While the accumulator is shown as a sixteen-bit register, it may be set to be either a single sixteen-bit accumulator (**A** or **C**) or two eight-bit accumulators, one accessible (**A**) and the other hidden but exchangeable (**B**). While the index registers are shown as sixteen-bit registers, they may be set, as a pair, to be either sixteen-bit registers or eight-bit registers—their high bytes are zeroed when they are set to eight bits. The obvious advantage of switching from a processor with eight-bit registers to one with sixteen-bit registers is the ability to write programs which are from 25 to 50 percent shorter, and which run 25 to 50 percent faster due to the ease with which sixteen-bit data is manipulated.

The feature that most clearly distinguishes the current generation of advanced microcomputer systems, however, is the ability to address

65816 Native Mode Programming Model
(16-bit accumulator & index register modes: m=0 & x=0)

```
23                    15                  7                    0
                      | Accumulator (B) (A or C) | Accumulator (A) |
| Data Bank Register (DBR) |
                      |       X Index | Register (X)     |
                      |       Y Index | Register (Y)     |
| 0 0 0 0 0 0 0 0 |   |        Direct | Page Register (D) |
| 0 0 0 0 0 0 0 0 |   |         Stack | Pointer (S)      |
| Program Bank Register (PBR) | Program | Counter (PC)    |
```

Processor Status Register (P)

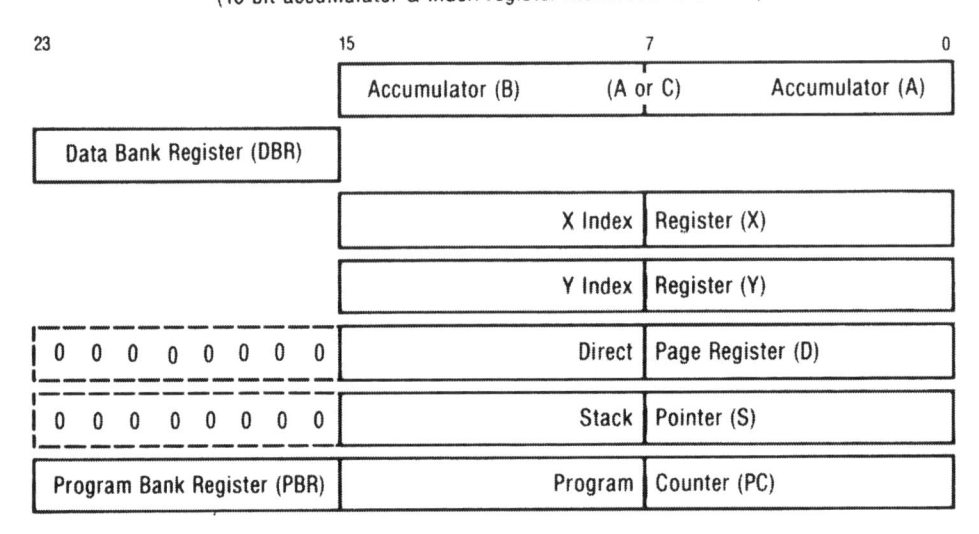

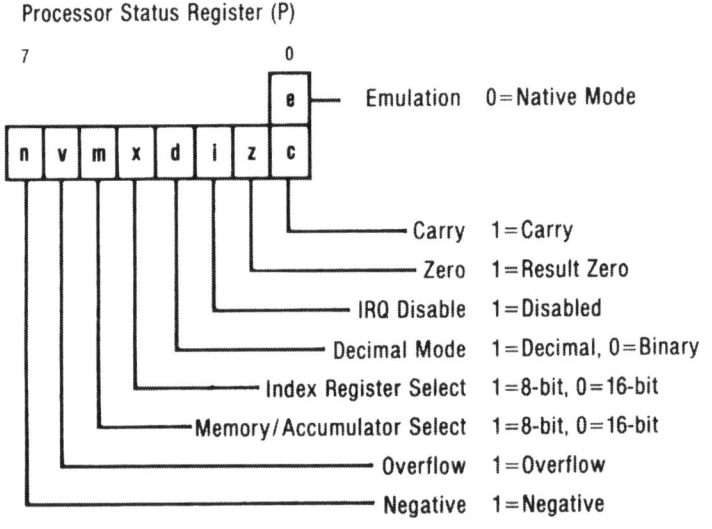

```
7                          0
                          e  — Emulation   0=Native Mode
| n | v | m | x | d | i | z | c |
                            └── Carry             1=Carry
                          └──── Zero              1=Result Zero
                      └──────── IRQ Disable       1=Disabled
                  └──────────── Decimal Mode      1=Decimal, 0=Binary
              └──────────────── Index Register Select   1=8-bit, 0=16-bit
          └──────────────────── Memory/Accumulator Select  1=8-bit, 0=16-bit
      └──────────────────────── Overflow          1=Overflow
  └──────────────────────────── Negative          1=Negative
```

Figure 4.1. 65816 Native Mode Programming Model.

lots of memory. It is this increased memory addressability which has ushered in the new era of microcomputer applications possibilities, such as large spreadsheets, integrated software, multi-user systems, and more. In this regard, the 65816 stands on or above par with any of the other high-performance microprocessors, such as the 68000, the 8086, or their successors.

There are two new eight-bit registers called **bank registers**. One, called the **data bank register**, is shown placed above the index registers and the other, called the **program bank register**, is appended to the program counter. The 65816 uses the two bank registers to provide 24-bit addressing.

A **bank** of memory is much like a **page**; just as a page is a range of memory that can be defined by eight bits (256 bytes), a bank is a range of memory that can be defined by sixteen bits (64K bytes). For processors like the 6502, which have only sixteen-bit addressing, a 64K bank is not a relevant concept, since the only bank is the one being currently addressed. The 65816, on the other hand, partitions its memory range into 64K banks so that sixteen-bit registers and addressing modes can be used to address the entire range of memory.

Bank zero, for example, is that 64K range for which, when addressed using 24 bits, the highest byte (also called the **bank byte**) is zero. Similarly, a highest byte of nine in a 24-bit address would address a location somewhere in bank nine. This highest byte is called the **bank byte** so that the term **high byte** can still be used to refer to the byte that determines the page address. In other words, "high byte" is used on the 65816 as it is on the 6502, 65C02 and 65802, where addresses are only sixteen bits.

Another new register shown in Figure 4.1 is the **direct page register**. Much like the 6800's special zero page became the 6809's direct page, the 6502's and 65C02's zero page has been transformed into the 65802's and 65816's direct page. This direct page is, as Figure 4.1 shows, limited to bank zero, shown in the programming model by the implied zero as its bank byte. The direct page register can be set to any 256-byte page starting on any byte boundary within bank zero. All of the 6502 instructions that use zero page addressing use an expanded form called direct page addressing on the 65816 and 65802; however, when the direct page register value is zero, the two modes are operationally identical.

Figure 4.1 also shows that the stack pointer has been unbound from page one to float anywhere in bank zero by making it a sixteen-bit register.

While Figure 4.1 doesn't show the interrupt vectors, they too are located in bank zero, and they point to interrupt handling routines which also must be located in bank zero.

Finally, the status register is different from the 6502's and 65C02's (compare Figure 4.1 with Figure 2.1 in Chapter 2). The first obvious difference is the single bit labelled **e** for emulation hanging off the top of the carry flag. Accessible only through the carry flag, its contents determine whether the processor is in native or 6502 emulation mode. Here it holds a zero to indicate the processor is in native mode. The second difference is the **m** and **x** flags replace the 6502's break and unused flags: **m** indicates the size of the accumulator (eight or sixteen bits) as well as the size of memory accesses; **x** indicates the size of the two index registers (eight or sixteen bits). Changing the contents of either of these two new flags toggles the size of the corresponding registers. The **b** flag is no longer necessary to distinguish the **BRK** software interrupt from hardware interrupts because native mode provides a new interrupt vector for software interrupts, separate from the hardware interrupt vector.

Native mode also provides one timing improvement over the 6502: one cycle is saved during a cross-page branch.

The Program Bank Register

The 65816's sixteen-bit program counter is concatenated to its eight-bit program counter bank register (**PBR**, or **K** when used in instruction mnemonics) to extend its instruction-addressing capability to 24 bits. When the 65816 gets an instruction from memory, it gets it from the location pointed to by the concatenation of the two registers. In many ways, the net effect is a 24-bit program counter; for example, when an interrupt occurs, all 24 bits (program counter plus program counter bank) are pushed onto the stack. Likewise, when a return-from-interrupt occurs, 24 bits (both registers) are pulled from the stack.

All previous instructions that jumped to sixteen-bit absolute addresses still work by staying within the same bank. Relative branches stay in the same bank; that is, you can't branch across bank boundaries. And program segments cannot cross bank boundaries; if the program counter increments past $FFFF, it rolls over to $0000 *without* incrementing the program counter bank.

New instructions and addressing modes were added to let you transfer control between banks: jump absolute long (jump to a specified 24-bit address), jump indirect long (the operand is an absolute address in bank zero pointing to a 24-bit address to which control is transferred), jump to subroutine long (to a specified 24-bit address, with the current program counter and program bank register pushed onto the stack first), and a corresponding return from subroutine long, which re-loads the bank register as well as the program counter. (The addressing modes are among those listed in Table 4.3, the instructions in Table 4.4.)

These instructions that specify a complete 24-bit address to go to, along with native mode's software interrupt and return from interrupt instructions, are the only ones that modify the value in the program bank register. The program bank can be pushed onto the stack so it can be pulled into another register and be examined or tested. But there is no instruction for pulling the program bank register from the stack, since that would change the bank the next instruction would come from—certain to be catastrophic. To avoid such "strange" branches across banks, the program counter bank register can only be changed when the program counter is changed at the same time.

The Data Bank Register

The data bank register (**DBR** or, when used as part of a mnemonic, **B**) defines the default bank to be used for reading or writing data whenever one of the addressing modes that specifies (only) a sixteen-bit address is used, such as the absolute, indirect, or indexed instructions found on the 6502. Such sixteen-bit effective addresses as used with the 6502 are concatenated with the value in the data bank register to form a 24-bit address, much as the program counter is concatenated with the program bank register. An important difference is that, unlike the program counter bank register, the data bank register can be *temporarily* incremented by instructions which use indexed addressing; in other words, bank boundaries do not confine indexing, which crosses them into the next bank.

As already mentioned, direct page and stack-based values are always accessed in bank zero, since the implied bank used with the direct page and stack is zero. But *indirect* addresses pulled out of the direct page or off the stack (when used with addressing modes that do not further specify the bank value) point to locations in the current data bank.

The existence of the data bank register on the 65816 provides a convenient way to access a large range of data memory without having to resort to 24-bit address operands for every operation.

The Direct Page Register

The direct page register (**D**) points to the beginning of direct page memory, which replaces zero page memory as the special page used for short-operand addressing. All of the 6502 instructions that use zero page addressing use an expanded form called direct page addressing on the 65816 and 65802. If the direct page register is set to zero, then direct page memory is the zero page, and direct page addressing is operationally identical to zero page addressing.

One effect of having a direct page register is that you can set up and alternate between multiple direct page areas, giving each subroutine or task its own private direct page of memory, which can prove both useful and efficient.

The Stack Pointer

The native mode stack pointer holds a sixteen-bit address value. This means it can be set to point to any location in bank zero. It also means the stack is no longer limited in length to just $100 bytes, nor limited to page one ($100 to $1FF). Page one therefore loses its character as a "special" memory area and may be treated like any other page while running the 65802 or 65816 in the native mode.

The Accumulator and the Index Registers

The key difference between the 65816/65802 and the earlier processors in the series is that the 65816's three primary user registers—the accumulator and the X and Y index registers—can be toggled between eight and sixteen bits. You can select which size (eight or sixteen bits) you wish to use by executing special control instructions that modify the new **m** and **x** flags.

This enhances the basic processing power of the chip tremendously. A simple subtraction of sixteen-bit numbers, for example, illustrates the difference. The eight-bit 6502 must be programmed to load the low byte of the first sixteen-bit number, subtract the low byte of the second number, then save the result, load the first number's high byte, subtract the second number's, and finally, save the high result. The sixteen-bit processors, on the other hand, can load one sixteen-bit value, subtract the other, then save the sixteen-bit result. Three steps replace six.

With its ability to change register size, the 65816 functions equally well with eight bits or sixteen. From the programmer's point of view, it is a dual word-size machine. The machine word size—the basic unit of data the machine processes in a given instruction cycle—may be either **byte** or **double byte**, that is, eight or sixteen bits.

In the terminology used in describing other sixteen-bit processors, the term *word* is used specifically to refer to sixteen-bit data, and *byte* to refer to eight-bit data. But other sixteen-bit processors generally have different mechanisms for selecting byte or double byte data to operate upon. The terminology appropriate to the 65802 and 65816 is to refer to sixteen-bit data as **double byte**, rather than **word**, since their word size alternates between eight bits and sixteen, and since they can operate in either byte mode or double byte mode with equal effectiveness. They are hybrid processors.

The width of the accumulator and the width of the index registers are independently controlled by setting and resetting the two special flag bits within the status register, the **index register select** (**x**) and **memory/accumulator select** (**m**) flags. When both are set, the eight-bit register architecture of the 6502 is in force. While very similar to the emulation mode, this eight-bit native mode is subtly different in important ways: a **BRK** vector is available in the native mode; interrupt processing is different between emulation and native mode in general; and of course sixteen-bit processing can be called up with a single instruction. Yet the 65802 and 65816 will execute a good deal of existing 6502 programs without modification in this mode.

Sixteen-Bit Architecture: The 65816 and the 65802

When either or both the index register select or memory select flags are cleared, the word size of the corresponding register(s) is expanded from eight bits to sixteen.

The four possible modes of operation are shown in Table 4.1.

Table 4.1. The Four Possible Native Mode Register Combinations.

eight-bit accumulator	(m bit is set)
eight-bit index registers	(x bit is set)
eight-bit accumulator	(m bit is set)
sixteen-bit index registers	(x bit is clear)
sixteen-bit accumulator	(m bit is clear)
eight-bit index registers	(x bit is set)
sixteen-bit accumulator	(m bit is clear)
sixteen-bit index registers	(x bit is clear)

When the opcode for a given instruction is fetched from memory during program execution, the processor may respond differently based upon the settings of the two register select flags. Their settings may be thought of as extensions to the opcode. For example, consider the following instruction:

```
object
 code      instruction
BD00B0     LDA $B000,X
```

which loads the accumulator with data from the effective address formed by the sum of $B000 and the contents of the X register. The X register contents can be either eight bits or sixteen, depending upon the value of the index select flag. Furthermore, the accumulator will be loaded from the effective address with either eight or sixteen bits of data, depending upon the value of the memory/accumulator select flag.

The instruction and addressing mode used in the example are found also on the 6502 and 65C02; the opcode byte ($BD) is identical on all four processors. The 65816's new mode flags greatly expand the scope of the 6502's instructions. For programmers already familiar with the 6502, the understanding of this basic principle—how one opcode can have up to four different effects based on the flag settings—is the single most important principle to grasp in moving to a quick mastery of the 65802 or 65816.

Switching Registers Between Eight and Sixteen Bits

The two register select flags are set or cleared by two new instructions provided for modifying the status register: one of the instructions, SEP, (set P) can be used to set any bit or bits in the P status register; the other, REP, (reset P) can be used to reset any bit or bits in the status register.

Figure 4.2 shows the results of changing the index registers and accumulator between eight and sixteen bits. When a sixteen-bit index register is switched to eight bits, the high byte is lost irretrievably and replaced by a zero. On the other hand, when an eight-bit index register is switched to sixteen bits, its unsigned value is retained by concatenating it to a zero high byte; that is, the eight-bit unsigned index already in the register is extended to sixteen bits.

Unlike the index operations, switching the accumulator's size in either direction is reversible. The accumulator is treated differently due to its function, not as an index register, but as the register of arithmetic and logic. In this role, it is often called upon to operate on eight-bit values with sixteen-bit ones and vice versa.

When the sixteen-bit A accumulator is switched to eight bits, the low byte becomes the new eight-bit A accumulator while the high byte becomes the eight-bit "hidden" B accumulator. B may be seen as an annex to the A accumulator, accessible only through a new instruction which exchanges the values in the two accumulators (making B useful for temporarily storing off the eight-bit value in A). Conversely, when the accumulator is switched from eight bits to sixteen, the new sixteen-bit A accumulator has, as its low byte, the previous eight-bit A accumulator and, as its high byte, the previous hidden B accumulator.

Certain instructions that transfer the accumulator to or from other sixteen-bit registers refer to the sixteen-bit accumulator as C to emphasize that all sixteen accumulator bits will be referenced regardless of whether the accumulator is set to eight- or sixteen-bit mode. Again, this is illustrated in Figure 4.2.

The Status Register

Because the emulation bit is a "phantom" bit, it cannot be directly tested, set, or cleared. The flag that it "phantoms" or overlays is the carry bit; there is a special instruction, XCE, that exchanges the contents of the two flags. This is the "trapdoor" through which the emulation mode is entered and exited.

Two status register bits were required for the two-flag eight-or-sixteen-bit scheme. While the 6502's status register has only one unused status register bit available, its break flag is used only for interrupt pro-

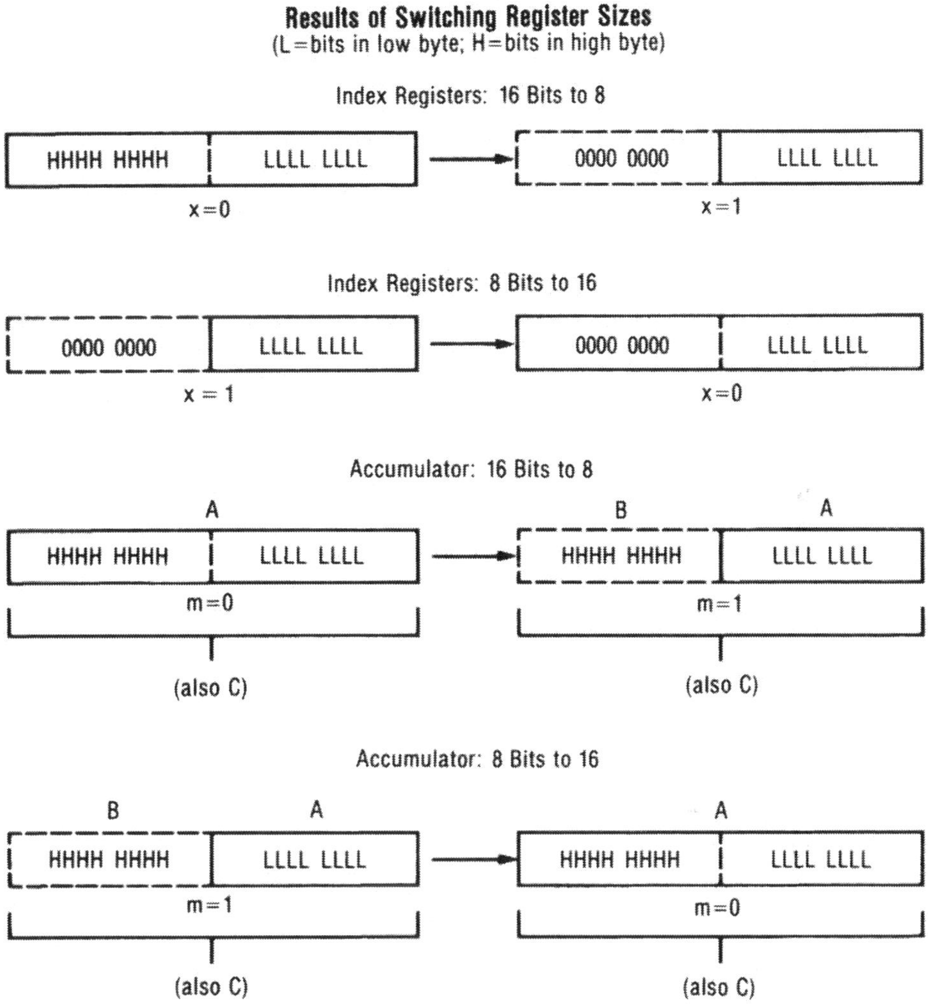

Results of Switching Register Sizes
(L=bits in low byte; H=bits in high byte)

Index Registers: 16 Bits to 8

| HHHH HHHH | LLLL LLLL | → | 0000 0000 | LLLL LLLL |

x=0   x=1

Index Registers: 8 Bits to 16

| 0000 0000 | LLLL LLLL | → | 0000 0000 | LLLL LLLL |

x=1   x=0

Accumulator: 16 Bits to 8

A: HHHH HHHH | LLLL LLLL → B: HHHH HHHH | A: LLLL LLLL

m=0   m=1
(also C)   (also C)

Accumulator: 8 Bits to 16

B: HHHH HHHH | A: LLLL LLLL → A: HHHH HHHH | LLLL LLLL

m=1   m=0
(also C)   (also C)

Figure 4.2. Results of Switching Register Sizes.

cessing, not during regular program execution, to flag whether an interrupt comes from a break instruction or from a hardware interrupt. By giving the break instruction its own interrupt vector in native mode, the 65816's designers made a second bit available for the **m** and **x** register select flags.

6502/65C02 Addressing Modes on the 65816

All of the 6502 and 65C02 addressing modes are available to the 65816/65802, but native mode's sixteen-bit features mean you need to expand your thinking about what they will do. For example, the 65816's direct page, which can be located anywhere in memory, replaces the earlier zero page as the special page for short-operand addressing modes. All 6502/65C02 zero page addressing modes become direct page addressing modes, as shown in Table 4.2.

Table 4.2. Addressing Modes: Zero Page vs. Direct Page.

6502/65C02 Zero Page Addressing Mode	65802/65816 Direct Page Addressing Mode	Syntax Example Common to Both Opcode Operand	
Zero Page	Direct Page	LDA	$55
Zero Page Indexed with X	Direct Page Indexed with X	LDA	$55,X
Zero Page Indexed with Y	Direct Page Indexed with Y	LDX	$55,Y
Zero Page Indirect Indexed with Y (Postindexed)	Direct Page Indirect Indexed with Y	LDA	($55),Y
Zero Page Indexed Indirect with X (Preindexed)	Direct Page Indexed Indirect with X	LDA	($55,X)
Zero Page Indirect	Direct Page Indirect	LDA	($55)

Notice in Table 4.2 that the assembler syntax for each direct page addressing mode (not to mention the object bytes themselves) is the same as its zero page counterpart. The names and the results of the addressing modes are what differ. Direct page addressing, like the 6502/65C02 zero page addressing, allows a memory location to be addressed using only an eight-bit operand. In the case of the 6502, a sixteen-bit zero page effective address is formed from an eight-bit offset by concatenating a zero high byte to it. In the 65802/65816, the direct page effective address is formed by adding the eight-bit offset to the sixteen-bit value in the direct page register. This lets you relocate the direct page anywhere in bank zero, on any byte boundary. Note, however, that it is most efficient to start the direct page on a page boundary because this saves one cycle for every direct page addressing operation.

When considering the use of 6502/65C02 zero page instructions as 65802/65816 direct page instructions, remember that a direct page address of $23 is located in memory at location $0023 only if the direct page register is set to zero; if the direct page register holds $4600, for example, then direct page address $23 is located at $4623. The direct page is essentially an array which, when it was the zero page, began at address zero, but which on the 65816 and 65802 can be set to begin at any location.

In the 6502/65C02, the effective address formed using zero page indexed addressing from a zero page base address of $F0 and an index of $20 is $10; that is, zero page indexed effective addresses wrap around to always remain in the zero page. In the emulation mode this is also true. But in native mode, there is no page wraparound: a direct page starting at $2000 combined with a direct page base of $20 and a sixteen-bit index holding $300 results in an effective address of $2320.

The three main registers of the 65802/65816 can, in native mode, be set to hold sixteen bits. When a register is set to sixteen bits, then the data to be accessed by that register will also be sixteen bits.

For example, shifting the accumulator left one bit, an instruction which uses the accumulator addressing mode, shifts sixteen bits left rather than eight if the accumulator is in sixteen-bit mode. Loading a sixteen-bit index register with a constant using immediate addressing means that a sixteen-bit value follows the instruction opcode. Loading a sixteen-bit accumulator by using absolute addressing means that the sixteen-bit value stored starting at the absolute address, and continuing into the location at the next address, is loaded into the accumulator.

Sixteen-bit index registers give new power to the indexed addressing modes. Sixteen-bit index registers can hold values ranging up to 64K; no longer must the double-byte base of an array be specified as a constant with the index register used for the index. A sixteen-bit index can hold the array base with the double-byte constant specifying the (fixed) index.

Finally, the 65816 has expanded the scope of 6502 and 65C02 instructions by mixing and matching many of them with more of the 6502/65C02 addressing modes. For example, the jump-to-subroutine instruction can now perform absolute indexed indirect addressing, a mode introduced on the 65C02 solely for the jump instruction.

New 65816 Addressing Modes

Not only do the 65802 and 65816 provide all the 6502 and 65C02 addressing modes, but they also offer nine new addressing modes of their own, in both emulation and native modes. They are shown in Table 4.3.

Table 4.3. The 65816/65802's New Addressing Modes.

Addressing Mode	*Syntax Example*	
	Opcode	*Operand*
Program Counter Relative Long	BRL	JMPLABEL
Stack Relative	LDA	3,S
Stack Relative Indirect Indexed with Y	LDA	(5,S),Y
Block Move	MVP	0,0
Absolute Long	LDA	$02F000
Absolute Long Indexed with X	LDA	$12D080,X
Absolute Indirect Long	JMP	[$2000]
Direct Page Indirect Long	LDA	[$55]
Direct Page Indirect Long Indexed with Y	LDA	[$55],Y

There are six new addressing modes that use the word "long", but with two very different meanings. Five of the "long" modes provide 24-bit addressing for interbank accesses. **Program counter relative long addressing**, on the other hand, provides an intrabank sixteen-bit form of relative addressing for branching. Like all the other branch instructions, its operand is an offset from the current contents of the program counter, but branch long's operand is sixteen bits instead of eight, which expands relative branching from plus 127 or minus 128 bytes to plus 32767 or minus 32768. This and other features greatly ease the task of writing position-independent code. The use of the word "long" in the description of this addressing mode means "longer than an eight bit offset," whereas the word "long" used with the other four addressing modes means "longer than sixteen bits."

Stack relative addressing and **Stack relative indirect indexed with Y addressing** treat the stack like an array and index into it. The stack pointer register holds the base of the array, while a one-byte operand provides the index into it. Since the stack register points to the next available location for data, a zero index is meaningless: data and addresses which have been pushed onto the stack start at index one. For stack relative, this locates the data; for stack relative indirect indexed, this locates an indirect address that points to the base of an array located elsewhere. Both give you the means to pass parameters on the stack in a clean, efficient manner. Stack relative addressing is a particularly useful capability, for example, in generating code for recursive high-level languages such as Pascal or C, which store local variables and parameters on a "stack frame."

Block move addressing is the power behind two new instructions that move a block of bytes—up to 64K of them—from one memory location to another all at once. The parameters of the move are held in the accumulator (the count), the index registers (the source and destination addresses), and a unique double operand (the source and destination addresses in the operand specify the source and destination banks for the move operation).

The five remaining "long" addressing modes provide an alternative to the use of bank registers for referencing the 65816's sixteen-megabyte address space. They let you temporarily override the data bank register value to address memory anywhere within the sixteen-megabyte address space. **Absolute long addressing**, for example, is just like absolute addressing except that, instead of providing a two-byte absolute address to be accessed in the data bank, you provide a three-byte absolute address which overrides the data bank. **Absolute long indexed with X**, too, is four bytes instead of three. On the other hand, it is the memory locations specified by **absolute indirect long**, **direct page indirect long**, and **direct page indirect long indexed with Y** that hold three-byte indirect addresses instead of two-byte ones. Three-byte addresses in memory appear in conventional 65x order; that is, the low byte is in the lower memory location, the middle byte (still referred to in 6502 fashion as the "high" byte) is in the next higher location, and the highest (bank) byte is in the highest location.

Instructions

There are 78 new opcodes put into use through the 28 new operations listed in Table 4.4, as well as through giving the previous processors' operations additional addressing modes.

Table 4.4. New 65816/65802 Instructions.

Instruction Mnemonic	Description
BRL	Branch always long
COP	Co-processor empowerment
JML	Jump long (interbank)
JSL	Jump to subroutine long (interbank)
MVN	Block move negative
MVP	Block move positive
PEA	Push effective absolute address onto stack
PEI	Push effective indirect address onto stack
PER	Push effective program counter relative address onto stack
PHB	Push data bank register onto stack
PHD	Push direct page register onto stack
PHK	Push program bank register onto stack
PLB	Pull data bank register from stack
PLD	Pull direct page register from stack
REP	Reset status bits
RTL	Return from subroutine long
SEP	Set status bits
STP	Stop the processor
TCD	Transfer 16-bit accumulator to direct page register
TCS	Transfer accumulator to stack pointer
TDC	Transfer direct page register to 16-bit accumulator
TSC	Transfer stack pointer to 16-bit accumulator
TXY	Transfer index registers X to Y
TYX	Transfer index registers Y to X
WAI	Wait for interrupt
WDM	Reserved for future two-byte opcodes
XBA	Exchange the B and A accumulators
XCE	Exchange carry and emulation bits

Five of the new push and pull instructions allow the new registers to be stored on the stack; the other three let you push constants and memory values onto the stack without having to first load them into a register. PER is unique in that it lets data be accessed relative to the program counter, a function useful when writing relocatable code.

There are also instructions to transfer data between new combinations of the registers, including between the index registers—a long-wished-for operation; to exchange the two bytes of the sixteen-bit accumulator; and to exchange the carry and emulation bits, the only method for toggling the processor between emulation and native modes.

There are new jump, branch, return, and move instructions already described in the section on addressing modes. There's a new software interrupt provided for sharing a system with a co-processor. There are two instructions for putting the processor to "sleep" in special low-power states. And finally, there's a reserved opcode, called **WDM** (the initials of the 65816's designer, William D. Mensch, Jr.), reserved for some future compatible processor as the first byte of a possible 256 *two-byte* opcodes.

Interrupts

Native mode supplies an entire set of interrupt vectors at different locations from the emulation mode (and earlier 6502/65C02) ones to service native mode and emulation mode interrupts differently. Shown in Table 4.5, all are in bank zero; in addition, the sixteen-bit contents of each vector points to a handling routine which must be located in bank zero.

Table 4.5. Interrupt Vector Locations.

	Emulation Mode	Native Mode
IRQ	FFFE,FFFF	FFEE,FFEF
RESET	FFFC,FFFD	-
NMI	FFFA,FFFB	FFEA,FFEB
ABORT	FFF8,FFF9	FFE8,FFE9
BRK	-	FFE6,FFE7
COP	FFF4,FFF5	FFE4,FFE5

All locations are in bank zero.

As discussed earlier in this chapter, native mode frees up the **b** bit in the status register by giving the break instruction its own vector. When a **BRK** is executed, the program counter and the status register are pushed onto the stack and the program counter is loaded with the address at $FFE6, the break instruction vector location.

The reset vector is only available in emulation mode because reset always returns the processor to that mode.

Sixteen-Bit Architecture: The 65816 and the 65802 **65**

The 65816/65802, in both emulation and native modes, also provides a new coprocessor interrupt instruction to support hardware coprocessing, such as by a floating point processor. When the **COP** instruction is encountered, the 65802's interrupt processing routines transfer control to the co-processor vector location.

Finally, the pinout on the 65816 provides a new **abort** signal. This lets external hardware prevent the 65816 from updating memory or registers while completing the current instruction, useful in sophisticated memory-management schemes. An interrupt-like operation then occurs, transferring control through the special abort vector.

The 65802 Native Mode

For all that the 65816 is, it is not pin-compatible with the 6502 and 65C02. You can't just replace the earlier chips with it. It is here that the other version of this chip, the 65802, comes into its glory. The price, of course, is that the 65802 has the same addressability limitations as the 6502 and 65C02.

Figure 4.3 shows the programming model for the 65802's native mode. The bank registers, while they exist, do not modify addressability, so they are shown as eight-bit entities. All registers have been scaled back to sixteen bits. There is only one bank a 65802 can address; since it holds the direct page, the stack pointer, and the interrupt vectors (bank-zero features on the 65816), you can consider the 65802's bank to be bank zero. Otherwise, the programming model is identical to the 65816's.

The bank registers are an anomaly. They have no function because the packaging provides no pins to connect them to. But they exist because, inside the packaging, the chip itself is a 65816. In fact, you can change their value just as you would on the 65816, with a pull instruction, a long jump or **JSR**, an interrupt, or a long return, either from subroutine or from interrupt. Furthermore, *every* interrupt and return from interrupt pushes the program bank byte onto the stack or pulls it off, just like the 65816 does. But the bank register values are ignored (stripped from 24-bit addresses when they're sent to the sixteen-bit output pins).

The long addressing modes also seem misplaced here. You can execute instructions using long addressing on the 65802, but the bank addresses are, again, ignored. They are certainly an inefficient method for undertaking intrabank accesses and transfers, since they take up extra bytes for the bank address, and use up extra cycles in translation. Still, they cause the 65802 no problems, as long as you understand that the bank value is disregarded and only the remaining sixteen bits of

65802 Native Mode Programming Model
(16-bit accumulator & index register modes: m=0 & x=0)

```
15                    7                    0
┌─────────────────────┬─────────────────────┐
│  Accumulator (B)    │    Accumulator (A)  │
│                (A or C)                   │
├─────────────────────┴─────────────────────┤
│         X Index      Register (X)         │
├───────────────────────────────────────────┤
│         Y Index      Register (Y)         │
├───────────────────────────────────────────┤
│         Direct       Page Register (D)    │
├───────────────────────────────────────────┤
│         Stack        Pointer (S)          │
├───────────────────────────────────────────┤
│         Program      Counter (PC)         │
└─────────────────────┬─────────────────────┘
                      │  Data Bank Register (DBR)  │
                      ├────────────────────────────┤
                      │ Program Bank Register (PBR)│
                      └────────────────────────────┘
```

Processor Status Register (P)

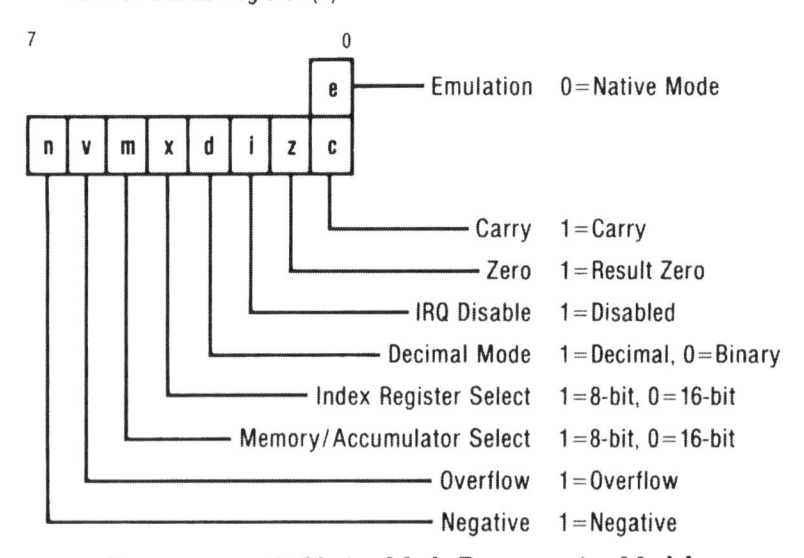

```
7                         0
                         ┌─┐
                         │e│ ── Emulation   0=Native Mode
┌─┬─┬─┬─┬─┬─┬─┬─┐        └─┘
│n│v│m│x│d│i│z│c│
└─┴─┴─┴─┴─┴─┴─┴─┘
```

- Carry   1=Carry
- Zero   1=Result Zero
- IRQ Disable   1=Disabled
- Decimal Mode   1=Decimal, 0=Binary
- Index Register Select   1=8-bit, 0=16-bit
- Memory/Accumulator Select 1=8-bit, 0=16-bit
- Overflow   1=Overflow
- Negative   1=Negative

Figure 4.3. 65802 Native Mode Programming Model.

Sixteen-Bit Architecture: The 65816 and the 65802

address are effective in pointing to an address in the 65802's single addressable bank of memory.

Finally, the bank bytes specified to the block move instructions are ignored, too. Block moves are by necessity entirely intrabank on the 65802.

Because the abort signal was designed into the 65816 by virtue of its redesigned pinout, its vector exists on the 65802 but has no connection to the outside world. Since there is no way to abort an instruction without using the external pin, the abort operation can never occur on the 65802.

In all other respects, the 65802 and 65816 are identical, so the 65802 can almost be thought of as a 65816 in a system with only 64K of physical memory installed. Table 4.6 summarizes the differences between the 65802 and 65816 native modes and the 6502 and 65C02.

Emulation Mode

That the 65802 provides a pinout the same as the 6502's and the 65C02's is not enough to run all the software written for the earlier two processors. For one thing, the eight-bit software expects interrupt handlers to distinguish break instructions by checking the stacked break flag, and the 65802's native mode has no break flag, having replaced both it and the 6502's unused flag with the **m** and **x** flags. For another, 6502 instructions that use eight-bit registers to set the stack would set only half of the sixteen-bit stack. The native mode interrupt vectors are different from their 6502/65C02 counterparts, as Table 4.5 showed. There are also little differences; for example, while the direct page can be set to the zero page, direct page indexed addresses can cross pages in native mode, but wrap on the 6502 and 65C02.

Reaching beyond hardware compatibility to software compatibility was clearly so important that the designers of the 65802 and 65816 devised the **6502 emulation mode** scheme. Both processors power-on in emulation mode, with the bank registers and the direct page register initialized to zero. As a result of both this and having the same pinout, a 65802 can be substituted for a 6502 in any application and will execute the existing software the same. Furthermore, it is possible to design second-generation 65816 systems compatible with existing 6502 designs which, provided the computer's designers do as good a job in providing compatibility as the 65816's designers have, could run all the existing software of the first generation system in emulation mode, yet switch into native mode for sixteen-bit power and 24-bit addressing.

It is important to realize, however, that 6502 emulation mode goes far beyond emulating the 6502. It embodies all the addressing mode and instruction enhancements of both the 65C02 and the 65802/65816; it has a fully relocatable direct page register; it provides the stack relative

Table 4.6. Major Differences Between Processors and Modes.

	6502	65C02	65802 Native	65802 Emulation	65816 Native	65816 Emulation
6502 pinout	yes	yes	yes	yes	no	no
6502 timing	yes	no	no	no	no	yes
abort signal	no	no	no	no	yes	yes
accumulator	8 bits	8 bits	16 or 8/8 bits	8/8 bits	16 or 8/8 bits	8/8 bits
addressing modes	14	16	25	25	25	25
address space	64K	64K	64K	64K	16M	16M
bank registers	none	none	not connected	not connected	yes	yes
block moves	none	none	yes	of little use	yes	of little use
break flag	yes	yes	no	yes	no	yes
decimal mode flags	N, V, Z invalid	N, V, Z valid	N, V, Z valid	N, V, Z valid	N, V, Z valid	N, V, Z valid
direct page indexed	wraps	wraps	crosses page	wraps	crosses page	wraps
flags after interrupt	D not modified	D = 0	D = 0	D not modified	D = 0	D not modified
flags after reset	D unknown	D = 0	D = 0	D not modified	D = 0	D not modified
index registers	8 bits	8 bits	8 or 16 bits	8 bits	8 or 16 bits	8 bits
instructions	151	178	256	256	256	256
interrupts	FFFA..FFFF	FFFA..FFFF	FFE4..FFEF	FFF4..FFFF	FFE4..FFEF	FFF4..FFFF
mnemonics	56	64	92	92	92	92
special page	zero page	zero page	direct page	direct page	direct page	direct page
stack	page 1	page 1	bank 0	page 1	bank 0	page 1
unused opcodes	could crash	NOP	none	none	none	none

addressing modes; and in the 65816's emulation mode, it can switch between banks to use 24-bit addressing. The primary differences between native and emulation modes are limitations placed on certain emulation mode registers and flags so that existing programs are not surprised (and crashed) by non-6502-like results. These differences are summarized in Table 4.6.

The pair of 65816 instructions that have little use in emulation mode are the block move instructions. Because the source and destination parameters for moves are passed to the instruction in the index registers, their eight-bit limits confine the instruction to the zero page: a block can only be moved from one zero page location to another.

Only in emulation mode do 65802/65816 interrupt vectors match their 6502/65C02 counterparts. Native mode interrupt vectors have their own locations, as Table 4.5 showed.

Emulation Mode Registers

The 65802/65816, under emulation mode, has the same six registers as the 6502/65C02. In addition, all of the new 65802/65816 registers are available in some form, although some of these on a limited basis. Figure 4.4 shows the result.

The primary accumulator **A** is always limited to eight bits by lack of an **m** flag, but the hidden eight-bit accumulator **B** is available, as with the native mode eight-bit accumulator setting. For certain register-transfer operations, the two are combined to form the sixteen-bit register **C**, just as in native mode. The index registers are limited to eight bits by lack of an **x** flag. The direct page register is fully functional, although direct page indexing wraps rather than crossing into the next page. The stack pointer is curtailed to page one, as on the 6502 and 65C02; if a sixteen-bit value is used to set it, the high byte is ignored. Finally, there are the two bank registers, which are initialized to zero, but which can be changed to point to other banks.

Now look at the **P** status register. In addition to the eight bits of the standard 6502/65C02 status register, you'll see the ninth "phantom" **e** bit, which contains a one; this setting puts the processor into its 6502 emulation mode.

The **A** and **B** registers, which together make up the native mode sixteen-bit accumulator, are used together in emulation mode as **C** solely for transferring values to and from the direct page register and the stack.

The direct page register (**D**) points to the beginning of direct page memory. You'll probably normally set it to zero in the emulation mode to make the direct page identical to 6502 zero page memory. This is particularly true if your 65802 program is running within a 6502 or 65C02

65816 Emulation Mode Programming Model

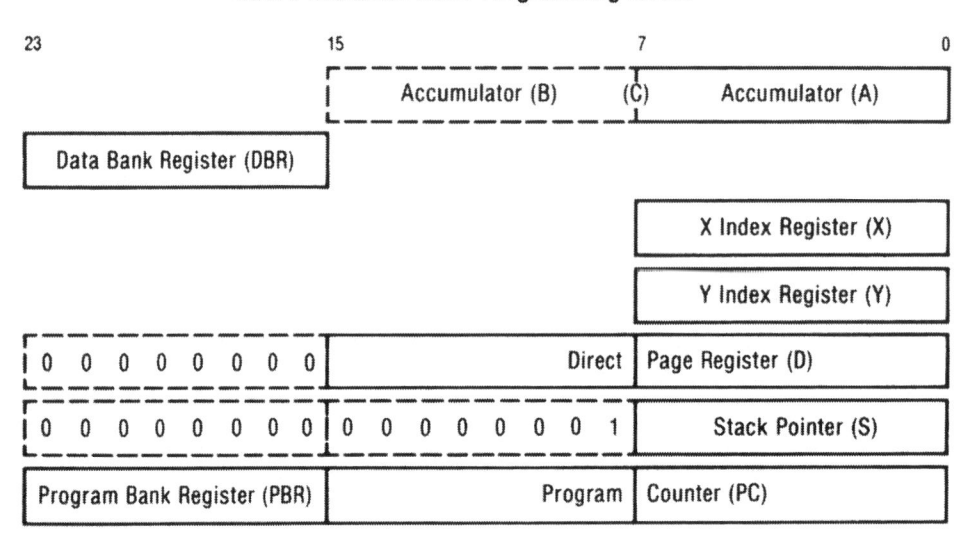

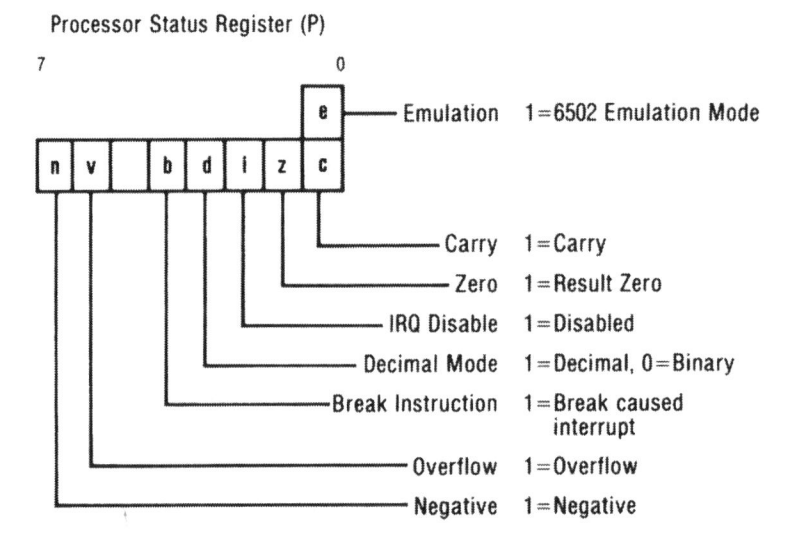

Figure 4.4. 65816 Emulation Mode Programming Model.

operating system. The operating system will have stored values to zero page memory; if you change the direct page to point to another page, then call an operating system routine, the operating system will load its information from the wrong direct page (any page other than the zero page) and fail miserably.

Switching Between 6502 Emulation and Native Modes

As you've seen, the native mode and the 6502 emulation mode embody a number of significant differences. When running the 65802 in an older machine, such as the Apple //c, //e, or II Plus, you will probably call your 65802 programs from a 6502 operating system or program. Your 65802 code can immediately switch the processor into native mode, so you can take advantage of the additional power. You must, however, switch back to emulation mode to use any I/O routines, or to call the 6502-based operating system.

Understanding the transitions between the two modes is critical, particularly in an environment where you are switching back and forth between 6502 systems programs and your own 65802 code.

Switching from Emulation to Native Mode

When the 65802 is switched from emulation to native mode, the value in the status register's carry bit winds up being toggled. Native mode is set by swapping a cleared carry bit with the current value in the emulation bit (which was a one if the processor was in emulation mode). The m and x flags in the status register are switched into place (replacing the b break flag) and the processor automatically forces the flags to one, which leaves the accumulator and index registers as eight-bit registers, the same as they were in emulation mode. The rest of the bits in the status register remain the same.

While the emulation mode stack pointer register is only an eight-bit register, it can be thought of as a sixteen-bit register with its high byte hard-wired to one, so that the emulation stack is always in page one. When the 65802 is switched from emulation to native mode, the sixteen-bit native mode stack pointer assumes the same value the emulation mode stack pointer has been pointing to—a page one address.

All other registers make the transition unchanged.

Switching from Native to Emulation Mode

Switching from native to emulation mode also toggles the carry. The carry bit is set, then exchanged with the emulation bit to force the processor back into emulation mode. Provided the processor was previously in native mode, the carry flag is cleared. The status register's m and x bits disappear, forcing the accumulator and index registers back to eight bits. If the index registers were in sixteen-bit mode, they keep their low bytes, but their high bytes are permanently lost. If, on the other hand, the accumulator was in sixteen-bit mode, the low byte remains in accumulator **A** while the high byte remains accessible as the hidden accumulator **B**. The **m** bit (bit five) returns to its emulation role as the break flag; the **x** bit (bit four) becomes once again an unused flag.

The stack is truncated from sixteen to eight bits, with its high byte forced to a one; that is, the stack is forced to page one. Any value in the high byte of the stack pointer register is permanently lost, which means you must be *very* careful not to "lose" a non-page-one stack. Solving this and other sticky problems involved with calling an emulation mode routine from native mode is the goal of one of the routines in Chapter 14.

All other registers make the transition unchanged.

65802/65816 Bugs and Quirks

As on the 65C02, the 6502's bugs are corrected by the 65802. Unlike the 65C02, however, the 65802 fixes the bug either only in native mode or without modifying the 6502's cycle counts (as the 65C02 in some cases does). There are no unused opcodes on the 65802, although there is an opcode which, while technically "used," is really reserved. If executed, it acts like a no-operation instruction.

The most anomolous feature of the 65816 is the behavior of new opcodes while in the 6502 emulation mode. While strict 6502 compatability is enforced for all 6502 and 65C02 opcodes, this is not the case with new opcodes. For example, although the high byte of the stack register is always set to one, wrapping of the stack during the execution of a single non-6502 instruction is not supported. These issues are discussed more fully in Chapter 16.

Because the 65802 fixes the 6502's bugs and quirks while leaving that chip's timing cycles untouched, the 65802 is in fact a hair more compatible as an upgrade chip than is the 65C02.

Part III
Tutorial

5 | SEP, REP, and Other Details

Part Three is devoted to a step by step survey of all 92 different 65816 instructions and the 25 different types of addressing modes which, together, account for the 256 operation codes of the 65802 and 65816. As a matter of course, this survey naturally embraces the instruction sets of the 6502 and 65C02 as well.

The instructions are grouped into six categories: data movement, flow of control, arithmetic, logical and bit manipulation, subroutine calls, and system control instructions. A separate chapter is devoted to each group, and all of the instructions in a group are presented in their respective chapter.

The addressing modes are divided into two classes, simple and complex. The simple addressing modes are those that form their effective address directly—that is, without requiring any, or only minimal, combination or addition of partial addresses from several sources. The complex addressing modes are those that combine two or more of the basic addressing concepts, such as indirection and indexing, as part of the effective address calculation.

Almost all of the examples found in this book are intended to be executed on a system with either a 65802 or 65816 processor, and most include 65816 instructions, although there are some examples that are intentionally restricted to either the 6502 or 65C02 instruction set for purposes of comparison.

Because of the easy availability of the pin-compatible 65802, there is a good chance that you may, in fact, be executing your first sample programs on a system originally designed as a 6502-based system, with system software such as machine-level monitors and operating systems that naturally support 6502 code only. All of the software in this book was developed and tested on just such systems (Apple // computers with either 65802s replacing the 6502, or with 65816 processor cards installed).

It is assumed that you will have some kind of support environment allowing you to develop programs and load them into memory, as well as a monitor program that lets you examine and modify memory, such as that found in the Apple // firmware. Since such programs were originally designed to support 6502 code, the case of calling a 65816 program from a 6502-based system program must be given special attention.

A 65802 or 65816 system is in the 6502 emulation mode when first initialized at power-up. This is quite appropriate if the system software you are using to load and execute the sample programs is 6502-based, as it would probably not execute correctly in the native 65816 mode.

Even though almost all of the examples are for the 65816 native mode of operation, the early examples assume that the direct page register, program counter bank register, and data bank register are all in their default condition—set to zero—in which case they provide an environment that corresponds to the 64K programming space and zero page addressing of the 6502 and 65C02. Aside from keeping the examples simple, it permits easy switching between the native mode and the emulation mode. If you have just powered up your 65816 or 65802 system, nothing need be done to alter these default values.

The one initialization you must do is to switch from the emulation to the native mode. To switch out of the 6502 emulation mode, which is the default condition upon powering up a system, the code in Fragment 5.1 must be executed once.

```
0000 18       CLC     clear carry flag
0001 FB       XCE     exchange carry with e bit (clears e bit)
```

Fragment 5.1.

This clears the special e flag, putting the processor into the 65816 native mode.

If you are using a 65802 processor in an old 6502 system, the above code needs to be executed each time an example is called. Further, before exiting a 65816 program to return to a 6502 calling program, the opposite sequence in Fragment 5.2 must be executed.

```
0000 38       SEC     set carry flag
0001 FB       XCE     exchange carry with e bit (sets e bit)
```

Fragment 5.2.

Even if you are running your test programs from a fully supported 65816 or 65802 environment, you should include the first mode-switching fragment, since the operating mode may be undefined on entry to a program. Execution of the second should be acceptable since the system program should reinitialize itself to the native mode upon return from a called program.

A further requirement to successfully execute the example programs is to provide a means for returning control to the calling monitor program. In the examples, the **RTS** (return from subroutine) instruction is used. The **RTS** instruction is not explained in detail until Chapter 12; however, by coding it at the end of each example, control will normally return to the system program that called the example program. So to exit a program, you will always code the sequence in Fragment 5.3.

```
0000 38        SEC     set carry flag
0001 FB        XCE     exchange carry with e bit (sets e bit)
0002 60        RTS
```

Fragment 5.3.

Some systems may have a mechanism other than **RTS** to return control to the system; consult your system documentation.

In addition to these two details, a final pair of housekeeping instructions must be mastered early in order to understand the examples.

These two instructions are **SEP** and **REP** (set P and reset P). Although they are not formally introduced until Chapter 13, their use is essential to effective use of the 65802 and 65816. The **SEP** and **REP** instructions have many uses, but their primary use is to change the value of the **m** and **x** flags in the status register. As you recall from Chapter 4, the **m** and **x** registers determine the size of the accumulator and index registers, respectively. When a flag is set (has a value of one), the corresponding register is eight bits; when a flag is clear, the corresponding register is sixteen bits. **SEP**, which *sets* bits in the status register, is used to change either the accumulator, or index registers, or both, to eight bits; **REP**, which *clears* bits, is used to change either or both to sixteen bits. Whenever a register changes size, all of the operations that move data in and out of the register are affected as well. In this sense, the flag bits are extensions to the opcode, changing their interpretation by the processor.

The operand following the **SEP** and **REP** instructions is a "mask" of the flags to be modified. Since bit five of the status register is the **m** memory/accumulator select flag, an instruction of the form:

REP #%00100000

makes the accumulator size sixteen bits; a **SEP** instruction with the same argument (or its hexadecimal equivalent, $20) would make it eight bits. The binary value for modifying the x flag is %00010000, or $10; the value for modifying both flags at once is %00110000, or $30. The sharp (#) preceding the operand signifies the operand is immediate data, stored in the byte following the opcode in program memory; the percent

(%) and dollar ($) signs are special symbols signifying either binary or hexadecimal number representation, respectively, as explained in Chapter 1.

Understanding the basic operation of **SEP** and **REP** is relatively simple. What takes more skill is to develop a sense of their appropriate use, since there is always more than one way to do things. Although there is an immediate impulse to want to use the sixteen-bit modes for everything, it should be fairly obvious that the eight-bit accumulator mode will, for example, be more appropriate to applications such as character manipulation. Old 6502 programmers should resist the feeling that if they're not using the sixteen-bit modes "all the time" they're not getting full advantage from their 65802 or 65816. The eight-bit accumulator and index register size modes, which correspond to the 6502 architecture, can be used to do some of the kinds of things the 6502 was doing successfully before the *option* of using sixteen-bit registers was provided by the 65816. Even in eight-bit mode, the 65802 or 65816 will provide numerous advantages over the 6502.

What is most important is to develop a sense of rhythm; it is undesirable to be constantly switching modes. Since the exact order in which a short sequence of loosely related instructions is executed is somewhat arbitrary, try to do as many operations in a single mode as possible before switching modes. At the same time, you should be aware that the point at which an efficiency gain is made by switching to a more appropriate mode is reached very quickly. By examining the various possibilities, and experimenting with them, a sense that translates into an effective rhythm in coding can be developed.

Finally, a word about the examples as they appear in this book. Two different styles are used: Code Fragments, and complete Code Listings.

Code Fragments are the kinds of examples used so far in this chapter. Code Listings, on the other hand, are self-contained programs, ready to be executed. Both appear in boxes, and are listed with the generated object code as produced by the assembler. Single-line listings are included in the text.

The Assembler Used in This Book

The assembly syntax used in this book is that recommended by the Western Design Center in their data sheet (*see* Appendix F). The assembler actually used is the ProDOS ORCA/M assembler for the Apple // computer, by Byteworks, Inc. Before learning how to code the 65816, a few details about some of the assembler directives need to be explained.

Full-line comments are indicated by starting a line with an asterisk or a semicolon.

If no starting address is specified, programs begin by default at $2000. That address can be changed by using the origin directive, **ORG**. The statement

               ORG $7000

when included in a source program, will cause the next byte of code generated to be located at memory location $7000, with subsequently generated bytes following it.

Values can be assigned labels with the global equate directive, **GEQU**. For example, in a card-playing program, spades might be represented by the value $7F; the program is much easier to code (and read) if you can use the label **SPADE** instead of remembering which of four values goes with which of the four suits, as seen in Fragment 5.4.

```
0000            SPADE     GEQU   $7F
0000            HEART     GEQU   $FF
0000            CLUB      GEQU   $3F
0000            DIAMOND   GEQU   $1F
```

Fragment 5.4.

Now rather than loading the **A** accumulator by specifying a hard-to-remember value,

A97F   LDA   #$7F

you can load it by specifying the easier-to-remember label:

A900   LDA   #SPADE

Once you have defined a label using **GEQU**, the assembler automatically substitutes the value assigned whenever the label is encountered.

The **#** sharp or pound sign is used to indicate that the accumulator is to be loaded with an immediate constant.

In addition to being defined by **GEQU** statements, labels are also defined by being coded in the label field—starting in the first column of a source line, right in front of an instruction or storage-defining directive. When coded in front of an instruction:

A905   BEGIN   LDA   #5

the label defines an entry point for a branch or jump to go to; when an instruction such as

4C0400   JMP   BEGIN

is assembled, the assembler automatically calculates the value of **BEGIN** and uses that value as the operand of the **JMP** instruction.

Variable and array space can be set aside and optionally labelled with the define storage directive, **DS**. In the example in Fragment 5.5, the first **DS** directive sets aside one byte at $1000 for the variable FLAG1; the second **DS** directive sets aside 20 bytes starting at $1001 for ARRAY1.

```
0000                    ORG     $1000
0000           MAIN     START
0000 00        FLAG1    DS      1
0001 00000000  ARRAY1   DS      20
0015                    END
```

Fragment 5.5.

The value stored at FLAG1 can be loaded into the accumulator by specifying FLAG1 as the operand of the **LDA** instruction:

```
AD0010         LDA     FLAG1
```

Program constants, primarily default values for initializing variables, prompts, and messages, are located in memory and optionally given a label by the declare constant directive, **DC**. The first character(s) of its operand specifies a type (A for two-byte addresses, I1 for one-byte integers, H for hex bytes and C for character strings, for example) followed by the value or values to be stored, which are delimited by single quotes.

Fragment 5.6 gives an example. The first constant, DFLAG1, is a default value for code in the program to assign to the variable FLAG1. You may realize that DFLAG1 could be used as a variable; with a label, later values of the flag could be stored here and then there would be no need for any initialization code. But good programming practice suggests otherwise: once another value is stored into DFLAG1, its initial value is lost, which keeps the program from being restarted from memory. On the other hand, using a **GEQU** to set up DFLAG1 would prevent you from patching the location with a different value should you change your mind about its initial value after the code has been assembled.

```
0000 FE        DFLAG1   DC      I1'$FE'
0001 0010      COUNT    DC      A'$1000'
0003 496E7365  PROMPT   DC      C'Insert disk into drive 1'
001B 00                 DC      I1'0'
```

Fragment 5.6.

Defining **COUNT** as a declared constant allows it, too, to be patched in object as well as edited in source.

PROMPT is a message to be written to the screen when the program is running. The assembler lists only the first four object bytes generated ('496E7365') to save room, but generates them all. The zero on the next line acts as a string terminator.

Sometimes it is useful to define a label at a given point in the code, but not associate it with a particular source line; the **ANOP** (assembler no-operation) instruction does this. The value of the label will be the location of the code resulting from the next code-generating source line. One use of this feature is to define two labels with the same value, as shown in Fragment 5.7.

```
0000            BLACK   ANOP
0000 0000       WHITE   DS      2
```

Fragment 5.7.

The two bytes of variable storage reserved may now be referred to as either **BLACK** or **WHITE**; their value is the same.

Address Notation

The 16-megabyte address space of the 65816 is divided into 256 64K banks. Although it is possible to treat the address space in a linear fashion—the range of bytes from $000000 to $FFFFFF—it is often desirable and almost always easier to read if you distinguish the bank component of a 24-bit address by separating it with a colon:

```
$00:FFF0
$xx:1234
$01:xxxx
```

In these examples, the x characters indicate that that address component can be any legal value; the thing of interest is the specified component.

Similarly, when specifying direct page addresses, remember that a direct page address is only an offset; it must be added to the value in the direct page register:

```
dp:$30
$1000:30
```

The **dp** in the first example is used to simply indicate the contents of the direct page register, whatever it may be; in the second case, the value in the direct page register is given as $1000. Note that this notation is distinguished from the previous one by the fact that the address to the left of the colon is a sixteen-bit value, the address on the right is eight. Twenty-four-bit addresses are the other way around.

A third notation used in this book describes ranges of address. Whenever two addresses appear together separated by a single dot, the entire range of memory location between and including the two addresses is being referred to. For example, **$2000.2001** refers to the double-byte starting at $2000. If high bytes of the second address are omitted, they are assumed to have the same value as the first address. Thus, **$2000.03** refers to the addresses between $2000 and $2003 inclusive.

6 First Examples: Moving Data

Most people associate what a computer does with arithmetic calculations and computations. That is only part of the story. A great deal of compute time in any application is devoted to simply moving data around the system: from here to there in memory, from memory into the processor to perform some operation, and from the processor to memory to store a result or to temporarily save an intermediate value. Data movement is one of the easiest computer operations to grasp and is ideal for learning the various addressing modes (there are more addressing modes available to the data movement operations than to any other class of instructions). It, therefore, presents a natural point of entry for learning to program the 65x instruction set.

On the 65x series of processors—the eight-bit 6502 and 65C02 and their sixteen-bit successors, the 65802 and 65816—you move data almost entirely using the microprocessor registers.

This chapter discusses how to load the registers with data and store data from the registers to memory (using one of the simple addressing modes as an example), how to transfer and exchange data between registers, how to move information onto and off of the stack, and how to move blocks (or strings) of data from one memory location to another (*see* Table 6-1).

Table 6.1. Data Movement Instructions.

Mnemonic	Available on: 6502	65C02	65802/816	Description
Load/Store Instructions:				
LDA	x	x	x	load the accumulator
LDX	x	x	x	load the X index register
LDY	x	x	x	load the Y index register
STA	x	x	x	store the accumulator
STX	x	x	x	store the X index register
STY	x	x	x	store the Y index register
Push Instructions:				
PHA	x	x	x	push the accumulator
PHP	x	x	x	push status register (flags)
PHX		x	x	push X index register
PHY		x	x	push Y index register
PHB			x	push data bank register
PHK			x	push program bank register
PHD			x	push direct page register
Push Instructions Introduced:				
PEA			x	push effective absolute address
PEI			x	push effective indirect address
PER			x	push effective relative address
Pull Instructions:				
PLA	x	x	x	pull the accumulator
PLP	x	x	x	pull status register (flags)
PLX		x	x	pull X index register
PLY		x	x	pull Y index register
PLB			x	pull data bank register
PLD			x	pull direct page register
Transfer Instructions:				
TAX	x	x	x	transfer A to X
TAY	x	x	x	transfer A to Y
TSX	x	x	x	transfer S to X
TXS	x	x	x	transfer X to S
TXA	x	x	x	transfer X to A
TYA	x	x	x	transfer Y to A
TCD			x	transfer C accumulator to D
TDC			x	transfer D to C accumulator
TCS			x	transfer C accumulator to S

(Continued)

Table 6.1. Data Movement Instructions (Cont.).

Mnemonic	6502	65C02	65802/816	Description
TSC			x	transfer S to C accumulator
TXY			x	transfer X to Y
TYX			x	transfer Y to X
Exchange Instructions:				
XBA			x	exchange B & A accumulators
XCE			x	exchange carry & emulation bits
Store Zero to Memory:				
STZ		x	x	store zero to memory
Block Moves:				
MVN			x	move block in negative direction
MVP			x	move block in positive direction

When programming the 6502, whether you're storing a constant value to memory or moving data from one memory location to another, one of the registers is always intermediate. The same is generally true for the other 65x processors, with a few exceptions: the 65816's two block move instructions, three of its push instructions, and an instruction first introduced on the 65C02 to store zero to memory.

As a result, two instructions are required for most data movement: one to load a register either with a constant value from program memory or with a variable value from data memory; the second to store the value to a new memory location.

Most data is moved via the accumulator. This is true for several reasons. First, the accumulator can access memory using more addressing modes than any of the other registers. Second, with a few exceptions, it's only in the accumulator that you can arithmetically or logically operate on data (although the index registers, in keeping with their role as loop counters and array pointers, can be incremented, decremented, and compared). Third, data movement often takes place inside of loops, program structures in which the index registers are often dedicated to serving as counters and pointers.

Loading and Storing Registers

To provide examples of the six basic data-movement instructions—**LDA, LDX, LDY** (load accumulator or index registers) and **STA, STX,** and **STY** (store accumulator or index registers)—requires introducing at least one of the 65x addressing modes. Except for certain instructions—such as push and pull, which use forms of stack addressing—the **absolute** addressing mode will generally be used in this chapter. Absolute addressing, available on all four 65x processors, is one of the simplest modes to understand. It accesses data at a known, fixed memory location.

For example, to move a byte from one absolute memory location to another, load a register from the first location, then store that register to the other location. In Listing 6.1, the eight-bit value $77 stored at the absolute location identified by the label **SOURCE** is first loaded into the accumulator, then saved to the absolute location labeled **DEST**. Note the inclusion of the mode-switching code described in the previous chapter.

The code generated by the assembler, when linked, will begin at the default origin location, $2000. The example generates 13 ($0D) bytes of actual code (the address of the **RTS** instruction is at memory location $200C). The assembler then automatically assigns the next available memory location, $200D, to the label on the following line, **SOURCE**. This line contains a **DC** (**define constant**) assembler directive, which causes the hexadecimal value $77 to be stored at that location in the code file ($200D). Since only one byte of storage is used, the data storage location reserved for the label **DEST** on the next line is $200E.

The syntax for absolute addressing lets you code, as an instruction's operand, either a symbolic label or an actual value. The assembler converts a symbolic operand to its correct absolute value, determines from its context that absolute addressing is intended, and generates the correct opcode for the instruction using absolute addressing. The assembler-generated hexadecimal object code listed to the left of the source code shows that the assembler filled in addresses $000D and $000E as the operands for the **LDA** and **STA** instructions, respectively (they are, of course, in the 65x's standard low-high order and relative to the $0000 start address the assembler assigns to its relocatable modules; the linker will modify these addresses to $200D and $200E when creating the final loadable object).

As Chapter 4 explained, the 65816's accumulator can be toggled to deal with either eight-bit or sixteen-bit quantities, as can its index registers, by setting or resetting the **m** (memory/accumulator select) or **x** (index register select) flag bits of the status register. You don't need to execute a **SEP** or **REP** instruction before every instruction or every memory move, *provided* you know the register you intend to use is already set correctly. But always be careful to avoid making invalid assumptions about the modes currently in force, particularly when transferring control from code in one location to code in another.

6 First Examples: Moving Data

```
0001  0000                      KEEP  KL.6.1
0002  0000                      65816 ON
0003  0000
0004  0000           MAIN       START
0005  0000
0006  0000             ;        code to switch from 6502 emulation to native mode
0007  0000
0008  0000 18                   CLC              clear carry flag
0009  0001 FB                   XCE              exchange carry with E bit (clear E bit)
0010  0002
0011  0002             ;        main example code
0012  0002
0013  0002 E220                 SEP #%00100000   set 8-bit data mode
0014  0004 AD0D00               LDA SOURCE       load byte from memory location SOURCE
0015  0007 8D0E00               STA DEST         store byte to memory location DEST
0016  000A
0017  000A             ;        code to return to 6502 emulation mode
0018  000A
0019  000A 38                   SEC              set carry flag
0020  000B FB                   XCE              exchange carry with E bit (set E bit)
0021  000C             ;
0022  000C 60                   RTS
0023  000D
0024  000D 77         SOURCE    DC    H'77'
0025  000E 00         DEST      DS    1
0026  000F
0027  000F                      END
```

Listing 6.1.

The load and store instructions in Listing 6.1 will as easily move a double byte as they did a byte, if the register you use is in sixteen-bit mode, as in Listing 6.2.

Note that the source data in the define constant statement is now two bytes long, as is storage reserved by the define storage statement that follows. If you look at the interlisted hexadecimal code generated by the assembler, you will see that the address of the label **DEST** is now $200F. The assembler has automatically adjusted for the increase in the size of the data at **SOURCE**, which is the great advantage of using symbolic labels rather than fixed addresses in writing assembler programs.

The load and store instructions are paired here to demonstrate that, when using identical addressing modes, the load and store operations are symmetrical. In many cases, though, a value loaded into a register

```
0001  0000                            KEEP   KL.6.2
0002  0000                            65816 ON
0003  0000
0004  0000              MAIN   START
0005  0000
0006  0000                     ;      switch from 6502 emulation to native mode
0007  0000 18                         CLC
0008  0001 FB                         XCE
0009  0002                     ;
0010  0002 C220                       REP    #%00100000      reset accumulator to 16-bit mode
0011  0004 AD0D00                     LDA    SOURCE          load double byte from memory location SOURCE
0012  0007 8D0F00                     STA    DEST            store double byte to memory location DEST
0013  000A
0014  000A                     ;      switch back to emulation mode
0015  000A 38                         SEC
0016  000B FB                         XCE
0017  000C                     ;
0018  000C 60                         RTS
0019  000D                     ;
0020  000D 7F7F          SOURCE DC     A'$7F7F'
0021  000F 0000          DEST   DS     2
0022  0011                             END
```

Listing 6.2.

will be stored many instructions later, or never at all, or stored using an addressing mode different from that of the load instruction.

Effect of Load and Store Operations on Status Flags

One of the results of the register load operations—LDA, LDY, and LDX—is their effect on certain **status flags** in the status register. When a register is loaded, the **n** and **z** flags are changed to reflect two conditions: whether the value loaded has its high bit set (is negative when considered as a signed, two's-complement number); and whether the number is equal to zero. The **n** flag is set when the value loaded is negative and cleared otherwise. The **z** flag is set when the value loaded is zero and cleared otherwise. How you use these status flags will be covered in detail in Chapter 8, Flow of Control.

The store operation does *not* change any flags, unlike the Motorola 68xx store instructions. On the other hand, Intel 808x programmers will discover the 65x processors use load and store instructions instead of the 808x's all-encompassing **MOV** instruction. The 808x move instruction changes no flags whatsoever, unlike the 65x load instruction, which does.

Moving Data Using the Stack

All of the 65x processors have a single stack pointer. (This is a typical processor design, although there are designs that feature other stack implementations, such as providing separate stack pointers for the system supervisor and the user.) This single stack is therefore used both by the system for automatic storage of address information during subroutine calls and of address and register information during interrupts, and by user programs for temporary storage of data. Stack use by the system will be covered in later chapters.

As the architecture chapters in Part II discussed, the S register (stack pointer) **points to** the next available stack location; that is, S *holds* the address of the next available stack location. Instructions using stack addressing locate their data storage either at or relative to the next available stack location.

The stack pointers of the 6502 and 65C02 are only eight bits wide; the eight-bit value in the stack pointer is added to an implied base of $100, giving the actual stack memory of $100 to $1FF; the stack is confined to page one. The 65816's native mode stack pointer, on the other hand, is sixteen bits wide, and may point to any location in bank zero (the first 64K of memory). The difference is illustrated in Figure 6.1.

Push

Push instructions store data, generally located in a register, onto the stack. Regardless of a register's size, the instruction that pushes it takes only a single byte.

When a byte is pushed onto the stack, it is stored to the location pointed to by the stack pointer, after which the stack pointer is automatically decremented to point to the next available location.

When double-byte data or a sixteen-bit address is pushed onto the stack, first its high-order byte is stored to the location pointed to by the stack pointer, the stack pointer is decremented, the low byte is stored to the new location pointed to by the stack pointer, and finally the stack pointer is decremented once again, pointing *past* both bytes of pushed data. The sixteen-bit value ends up on the stack in the usual 65x memory order: low byte in the lower address, high byte in the higher address.

In both cases, the stack grows downward, and the stack pointer points to the next available (unused) location at the end of the operation.

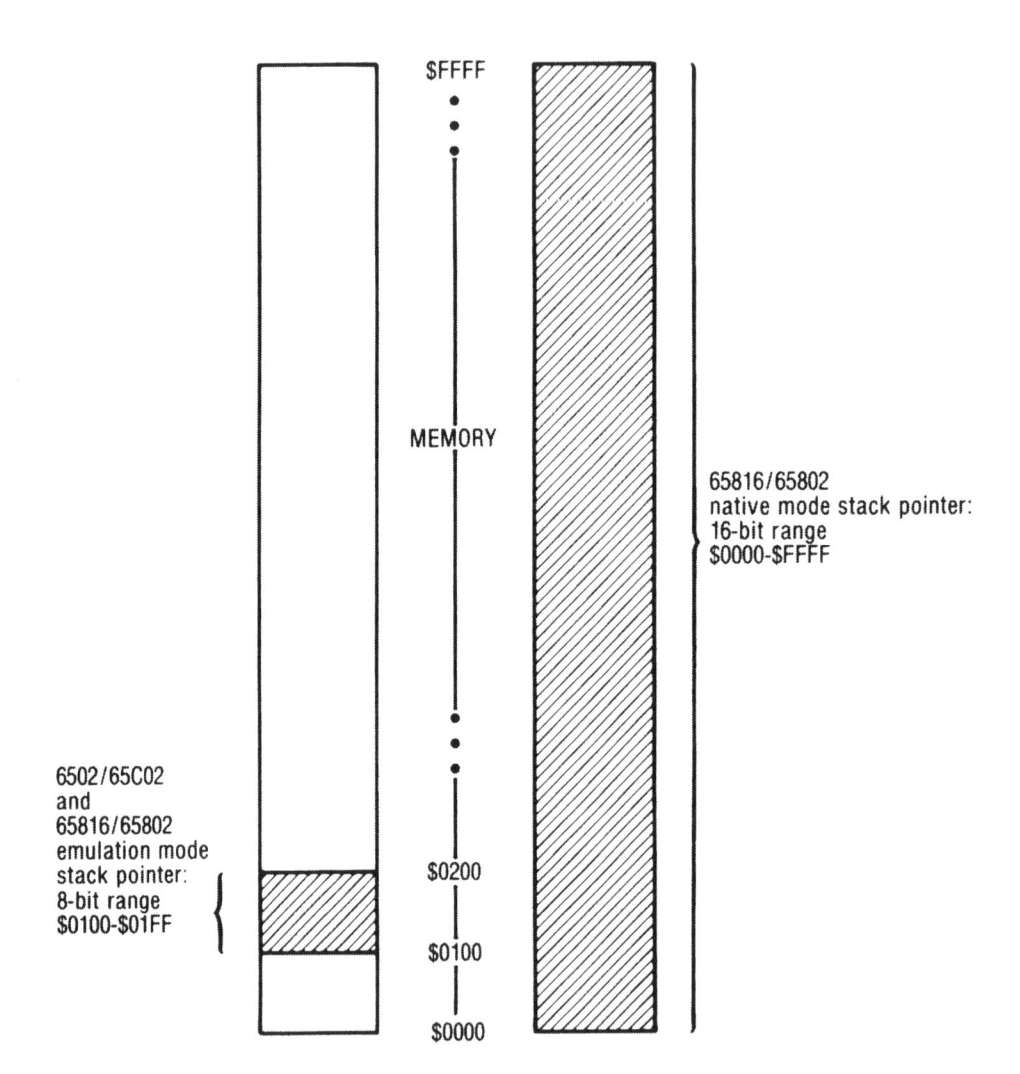

Figure 6.1. Stack Memory.

Pushing the Basic 65x Registers

On the 6502, only the contents of the accumulator and the status register can be pushed directly onto the stack in a single operation, using the PHA and PHP instructions, respectively. The 65C02 adds instructions to push the index registers onto the stack: **PHX** and **PHY**.

The 65816 and 65802 let double-byte data as well as single bytes be pushed onto the stack. Figure 6.2 shows the results of both. In the case of the accumulator and index registers, the size of the data pushed onto the stack depends on the settings of the m memory/accumulator select and x index register select flags. Since the accumulator and index registers are of variable size (eight bits or sixteen), the PHA, PHX, and PHY instructions have correspondingly variable effects.

Pull

Pull instructions reverse the effects of the push instructions, but there are fewer pull instructions, all of them single-byte instructions that pull a value off the stack into a register. Unlike the Motorola and Intel processors (68xx and 808x), the 65x pull instructions set the n and z flags. So programmers used to using pull instructions between a test and a branch on the other processors should exercise caution with the 65x pull instructions.

Pulling the Basic 65x Registers

The 6502 pull instructions completely complement its push instructions. **PLP** increments the stack pointer, then loads the processor status register (the flags) from the page one address pointed to by the offset in the stack pointer (of course, this destroys the previous contents of the status register). **PLA** pulls a byte from the stack into the accumulator, which affects the n and z flags in the status register just as a load accumulator instruction does.

As instructions for pushing the index registers were added to the 65C02, complementary pull instructions were added, too—that is, **PLX** and **PLY**. The pull index register instructions also affect the n and z flags.

On the 65802 and 65816, the push and pull instructions for the primary user registers—A, X, and Y—have been augmented to handle sixteen-bit data when the appropriate select flag (memory/accumulator or index register) is clear. Code these three pull instructions carefully since the stack pointer will be incremented one or two bytes per pull depending on the current settings of the m and x flags.

Pushing and Pulling the 65816's Additional Registers

The 65816 adds one-byte push instructions for all its new registers, and pull instructions for all but one of them. In fact, the bank registers can only be accessed using the stack.

PHB pushes the contents of the data bank register, an eight-bit register, onto the stack. **PLB** pulls an eight-bit value from the stack into the

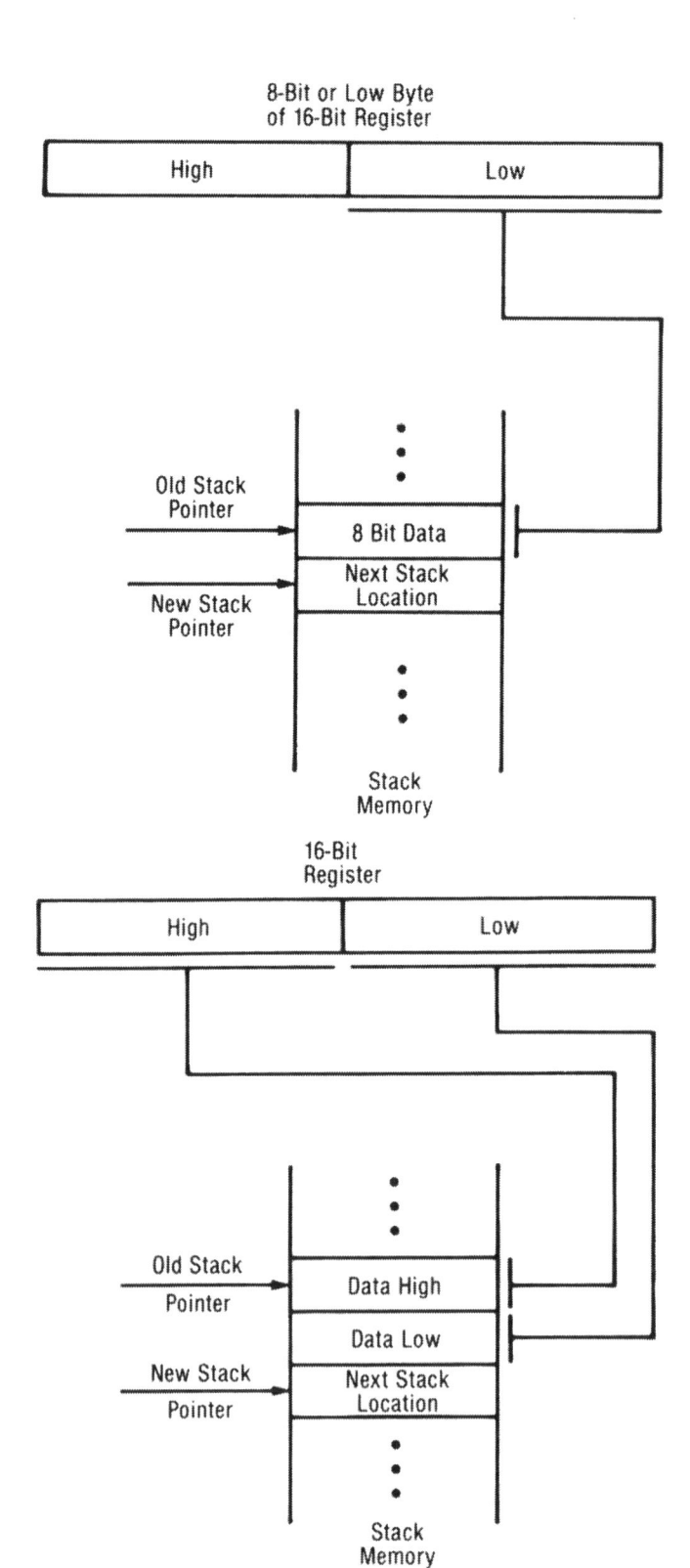

Figure 6.2. Push.

data bank register. The two most common uses for **PHB** are, first, to let a program determine the currently active data bank, and second, to save the current data bank prior to switching to another bank.

Fragment 6.1 is a 65816 code fragment which switches between two data banks. While **OTHBNK** is declared just once, it represents two different memory cells, both with the same sixteen-bit address of $FFF3, but in two different 64K banks: one is in the data bank that is current when the code fragment is entered; the second is in the data bank switched to by the code fragment. The code fragment could be executed a second time and the data bank would be switched back to the original bank.

```
0000            OTHBNK  GEQU    $FFF3           location of other bank stored here
0000
0000                    .
0000                    .
0000                    .
0000 E220               SEP     #%00100000      set accumulator to 8-bit mode
0002
0002 ADF3FF             LDA     OTHBNK          get location of bank to switch to
0005
0005 8B                 PHB                     push current data bank onto stack
0006 48                 PHA                     push other data bank onto stack
0007
0007 AB                 PLB                     pull data bank: make other data bank current
0008 68                 PLA                     get original data bank into accum
0009
0009 8DF3FF             STA     OTHBNK          store it in 2nd bank so can be restored
000C                    .
000C                    .
000C                    .
000C
```

Fragment 6.1.

Similar to **PHB**, the **PHK** instruction pushes the value in the eight-bit program counter bank register onto the stack. Again, the instruction can be used to let you locate the current bank; this is useful in writing bank-independent code, which can be executed out of any arbitrarily assigned bank.

You're less likely to use **PHK** to preserve the current bank prior to changing banks (as in the case of **PHB** above) because the **jump to subroutine long** instruction automatically pushes the program counter bank as it changes it, and because there is no complementary pull instruction.

The only way to change the value in the program counter bank register is to execute a long jump instruction, an interrupt, or a return from subroutine or interrupt. However, you can use **PHK** to synthesize more complex call and return sequences, or to set the data bank equal to the program bank.

Finally, the **PHD** instruction pushes the sixteen-bit direct page register onto the stack, and **PLD** pulls a sixteen-bit value from the stack into the direct page register. **PHD** is useful primarily for preserving the direct page location before changing it, while **PLD** is an easy way to change or restore it. Note that **PLB** and **PLD** also affect the n and z flags.

Pushing Effective Addresses

The 65816 also provides three instructions which can push data onto the stack without altering any registers. These three **push effective address** instructions—PEA, PEI, and PER—push absolute, indirect, and relative sixteen-bit addresses or data directly onto the stack from memory. Their use will be explained when their addressing modes are presented in detail in Chapter 11 (Complex Addressing Modes).

Other Attributes of Push and Pull

The types of data that can be pushed but not pulled are effective addresses and the K (or more commonly **PBR**) program bank register.

PLD and **PLB** are typically used to restore values from a previous state.

Finally, you should note that even though the push and pull operations are largely symmetrical, data that is pushed onto the stack from one register does not need to be pulled off the stack into the same register. As far as the processor is concerned, data pulled off the stack does not have to be the same size as was pushed onto it. But needless to say, the stack can quickly become garbled if you are not extremely careful.

Moving Data Between Registers

Transfers

The accumulator is the most powerful of the user registers, both in the addressing modes available to accumulator operations and in its arithmetic and logic capabilities. As a result, addresses and indexes that must be used in one of the index registers must often be calculated in the accumulator. A typical problem on the 6502 and 65C02, since their registers are only eight bits wide, is that sixteen-bit values such as addresses must be added or otherwise manipulated eight bits at a time. The other half of the value, the high or low byte, must meanwhile be stored away for easy retrieval and quick temporary storage of register contents in a currently unused register is desirable.

For these reasons as well as to transfer a value to a register where a different operation or addressing mode is available, all 65x processors implement a set of one-byte implied operand instructions which transfer data from one register to another:

TAX transfers the contents of the accumulator to the X index register
TAY transfers the contents of the accumulator to the Y index register
TSX transfers the contents of the stack pointer to the X index register
TXS transfers the contents of the X index register to the stack pointer
TXA transfers the contents of the X index register to the accumulator
TYA transfers the contents of the Y index register to the accumulator

Like the load instructions, all of these transfer operations except **TXS** set both the n and z flags. (TXS does not affect the flags because setting the stack is considered an operation in which the data transferred is fully known and will not be further manipulated.)

The availability of these instructions on the 65802/65816, with its dual-word-size architecture, naturally leads to some questions when you consider transfer of data between registers of different sizes. For example, you may have set the accumulator word size to sixteen bits, and the index register size to eight. What happens when you execute a **TAY** (transfer A to Y) instruction?

The first rule to remember is that the nature of the transfer is determined by the *destination* register. In this case, only the low-order eight bits of the accumulator will be transferred to the eight-bit Y register. A second rule also applies here: when the index registers are eight bits (because the index register select flag is set), the high byte of each index register is always forced to zero upon return to sixteen-bit size, and the low-order value of each sixteen-bit index register contains its previous eight-bit value.

Listing 6.3 illustrates these rules with **TAY**. In this example, the value stored at the location **DATA2** is $0033; only the low order byte has been transferred from the accumulator, while the high byte has been zeroed.

The accumulator, on the other hand, operates differently. When the accumulator word size is switched from sixteen bits to eight, the high-order byte is preserved in a "hidden" accumulator, **B**. It can even be accessed without changing modes back to the sixteen-bit accumulator size by executing the **XBA** (exchange B with A) instruction, described in the following section. Listing 6.4 illustrates this persistence of the accumulator's high byte. After running it, the contents of locations **RESULT**. RESULT + 1 will be $7F33, or 33 7F, in low-high memory order. In other words, the value in the high byte of the sixteen-bit accumulator, $7F, was preserved across the mode switch to eight-bit word size.

```
0001  0000                         KEEP   KL.6.3
0002  0000
0003  0000                         65816 ON
0004  0000
0005  0000
0006  0000          MAIN  START
0007  0000            ;           switch-to-native-mode code
0008  0000 18                      CLC            clear carry flag
0009  0001 FB                      XCE            exchange carry with e bit (clear e bit)
0010  0002
0011  0002 C220                    REP    #$20    set accum to 16
0012  0004 E210                    SEP    #$10    set index to 8
0013  0006 AD1200                  LDA    DATA
0014  0009 A8                      TAY
0015  000A C210                    REP    #$10    set index to 16
0016  000C 8C1400                  STY    DATA2
0017  000F
0018  000F            ;           return to 6502 emulation mode
0019  000F 38                      SEC            set carry flag
0020  0010 FB                      XCE            exchange carry with e bit (set e bit)
0021  0011
0022  0011 60                      RTS
0023  0012
0024  0012 33FF      DATA  DC     A'$FF33'
0025  0014 0000      DATA2 DS     2
0026  0016
0027  0016                         END
```

Listing 6.3.

Now consider the case where the sixteen-bit Y register is transferred to an eight-bit accumulator, as shown in Listing 6.5. The result in this case is $33FF, making it clear that the high byte of the Y register has not been transferred into the inactive high-order byte of the accumulator. The rule is that operations on the eight-bit A accumulator affect only the low-order byte in A, not the hidden high byte in B. Transfers into the A accumulator fall within the rule.

Figure 6.3 summarizes the effects of transfers between registers of different sizes.

There are also rules for transfers from an eight-bit to a sixteen-bit register. Transfers out of the eight-bit accumulator into a sixteen-bit index register transfer both eight-bit accumulators.

In Listing 6.6, the value saved to RESULT is $7FFF, showing that not only is the eight-bit A accumulator transferred to become the low byte

6 First Examples: Moving Data

```
0001 0000                         KEEP    KL.6.4
0002 0000                         65816 ON
0003 0000
0004 0000            MAIN         START
0005 0000
0006 0000                  ;      switch-to-native-mode code
0007 0000 18                      CLC             clear carry flag
0008 0001 FB                      XCE             exchange carry with e bit (clear e bit)
0009 0002
0010 0002 C230                    REP     #$30    set accum and index size to 16
0011 0004 AD1400                  LDA     DATA16  load accum with 16-bit value at DATA16
0012 0007 E220                    SEP     #$20    set accum to eight bits
0013 0009 AD1600                  LDA     DATA8   load 8-bit value at DATA8
0014 000C C220                    REP     #$20    make accum 16 again
0015 000E 8D1700                  STA     RESULT  save accum lo.hi in RESULT.RESULT+1
0016 0011
0017 0011                  ;      return to 6502 emulation mode
0018 0011 38                      SEC             set carry flag
0019 0012 FB                      XCE             exchange carry with e bit (set e bit)
0020 0013
0021 0013 60                      RTS
0022 0014
0023 0014 FF7F     DATA16         DC      A'$7FFF'
0024 0016 33       DATA8          DC      H'33'
0025 0017 0000     RESULT         DS      2
0026 0019
0027 0019                         END
```

Listing 6.4.

of the sixteen-bit index register, but the hidden B accumulator is transferred to become the high byte of the index register. This means you can form a sixteen-bit index in the eight-bit accumulator one byte at a time, then transfer the whole thing to the index register without having to switch the accumulator to sixteen bits first. However, take care not to inadvertently transfer an unknown hidden value when doing transfers from the eight-bit accumulator to a sixteen-bit index register.

Transfers from an eight-bit index register to the sixteen-bit accumulator result in the index register being transferred into the accumulator's low byte while the accumulator's high byte is zeroed. This is consistent with the zeroing of the high byte when eight-bit index registers are switched to sixteen bits.

In Listing 6.7, the result is $0033, demonstrating that when an eight-bit index register is transferred to the sixteen-bit accumulator, a zero is concatenated as the high byte of the new accumulator value.

```
0001  0000                        KEEP   KL.6.5
0002  0000                        65816 ON
0003  0000
0004  0000          MAIN  START
0005  0000
0006  0000                ;     switch to native mode
0007  0000
0008  0000 18                    CLC             clear carry flag
0009  0001 FB                    XCE             exchange carry with e bit (clear e bit)
0010  0002
0011  0002 C230                  REP    #$30     set accum, index size to 16
0012  0004 AC1500                LDY    DATA16   load Y-reg with 16-bit value at DATA16
0013  0007 AD1700                LDA    DATA2    load accum with 16-bit value at DATA2
0014  000A E220                  SEP    #$20     set accum to eight bits
0015  000C 98                    TYA             transfer Y register's value to A
0016  000D C220                  REP    #$20     make accum 16 again
0017  000F 8D1900                STA    RESULT   save accum lo.hi in RESULT.RESULT+1
0018  0012
0019  0012                ;     return to 6502 emulation mode
0020  0012
0021  0012 38                    SEC             set carry flag
0022  0013 FB                    XCE             exchange carry with e bit (set e bit)
0023  0014
0024  0014 60                    RTS
0025  0015
0026  0015 FF7F         DATA16   DC     A'$7FFF'
0027  0017 4433         DATA2    DC     A'$3344'
0028  0019 0000         RESULT   DS     2
0029  001B
0030  001B                       END
```

Listing 6.5.

In the 65816, transfers between index registers and the stack also depend on the setting of the *destination* register. For example, transferring the sixteen-bit stack to an eight-bit index register, as in Fragment 6.2, results in the transfer of just the low byte. Obviously, though, you'll find few reasons to transfer only the low byte of the sixteen-bit stack pointer. **As always, you need to be watchful of the current modes in force in each of your routines.**

The 65816 also adds new transfer operations to accommodate direct transfer of data to and from the new 65816 environment-setting registers (the direct page register and the sixteen-bit stack register), and also to complete the set of possible register transfer instructions for the basic 65x user register set:

6 First Examples: Moving Data 99

(L=bits in low byte; H=bits in high byte; P=previous bits unmodified by transfer)

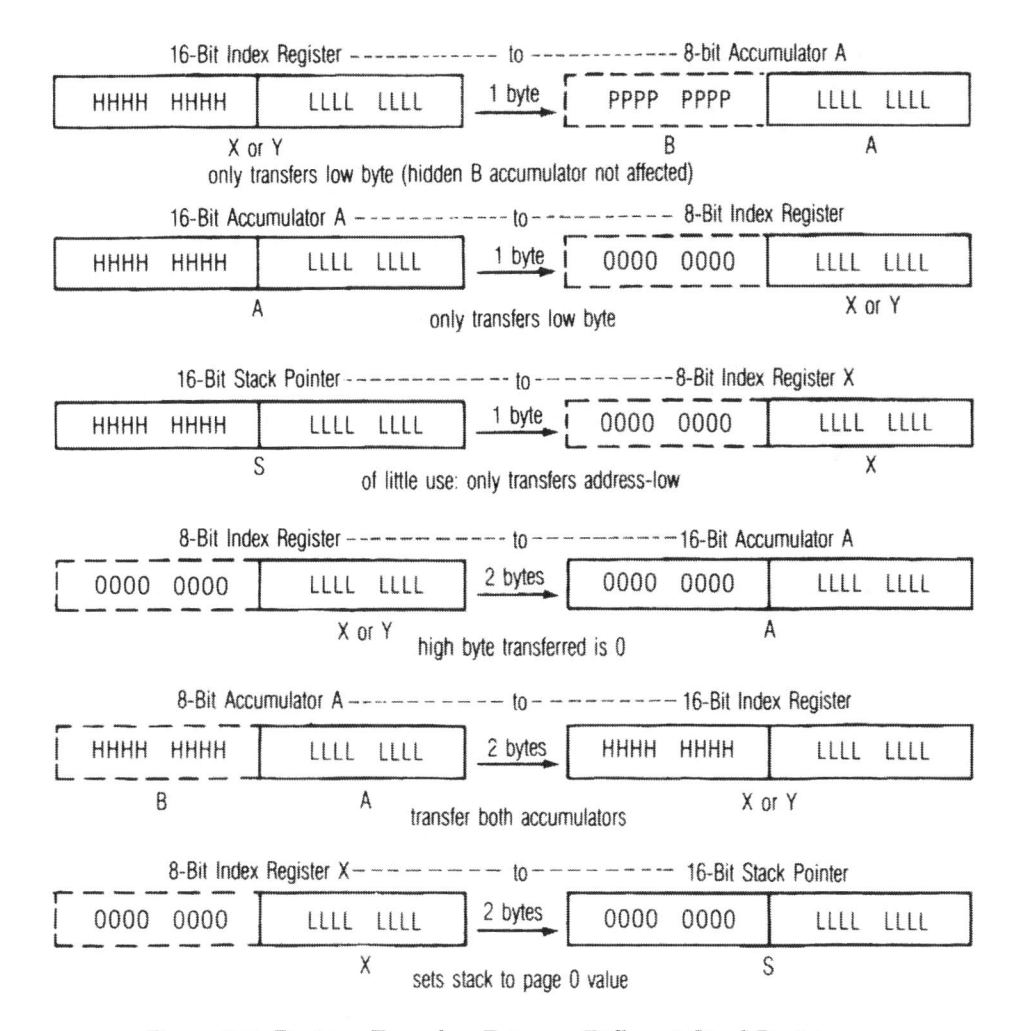

```
         16-Bit Index Register ------------ to ----------- 8-bit Accumulator A
    ┌─────────────┬─────────────┐         ┌─────────────┬─────────────┐
    │ HHHH  HHHH  │ LLLL  LLLL  │ 1 byte  │ PPPP  PPPP  │ LLLL  LLLL  │
    └─────────────┴─────────────┘   ───▶  └─────────────┴─────────────┘
              X or Y                             B             A
         only transfers low byte (hidden B accumulator not affected)

         16-Bit Accumulator A ------------ to ----------- 8-Bit Index Register
    ┌─────────────┬─────────────┐         ┌─────────────┬─────────────┐
    │ HHHH  HHHH  │ LLLL  LLLL  │ 1 byte  │ 0000  0000  │ LLLL  LLLL  │
    └─────────────┴─────────────┘   ───▶  └─────────────┴─────────────┘
                A                                         X or Y
                   only transfers low byte

         16-Bit Stack Pointer ----------- to ---------- 8-Bit Index Register X
    ┌─────────────┬─────────────┐         ┌─────────────┬─────────────┐
    │ HHHH  HHHH  │ LLLL  LLLL  │ 1 byte  │ 0000  0000  │ LLLL  LLLL  │
    └─────────────┴─────────────┘   ───▶  └─────────────┴─────────────┘
                S                                           X
                   of little use: only transfers address-low

         8-Bit Index Register ----------- to ---------- 16-Bit Accumulator A
    ┌─────────────┬─────────────┐         ┌─────────────┬─────────────┐
    │ 0000  0000  │ LLLL  LLLL  │ 2 bytes │ 0000  0000  │ LLLL  LLLL  │
    └─────────────┴─────────────┘   ───▶  └─────────────┴─────────────┘
              X or Y                                      A
                         high byte transferred is 0

         8-Bit Accumulator A ----------- to ---------- 16-Bit Index Register
    ┌─────────────┬─────────────┐         ┌─────────────┬─────────────┐
    │ HHHH  HHHH  │ LLLL  LLLL  │ 2 bytes │ HHHH  HHHH  │ LLLL  LLLL  │
    └─────────────┴─────────────┘   ───▶  └─────────────┴─────────────┘
          B             A                               X or Y
                         transfer both accumulators

         8-Bit Index Register X -------- to --------- 16-Bit Stack Pointer
    ┌─────────────┬─────────────┐         ┌─────────────┬─────────────┐
    │ 0000  0000  │ LLLL  LLLL  │ 2 bytes │ 0000  0000  │ LLLL  LLLL  │
    └─────────────┴─────────────┘   ───▶  └─────────────┴─────────────┘
                X                                         S
                       sets stack to page 0 value
```

Figure 6.3. Register Transfers Between Different-Sized Registers.

TCD transfers the contents of the sixteen-bit accumulator C to the D direct page register. The use of the letter C in this instruction's mnemonic to refer to the accumulator indicates that this operation is always a sixteen-bit transfer, regardless of the setting of the memory select flag. For such a transfer to be meaningful, of course, the high-order byte of the accumulator must contain a valid value.

TDC transfers the contents of the D direct page register to the sixteen-bit accumulator. Again, the use of the letter C in the

```
0001  0000                       KEEP    KL.6.6
0002  0000                       65816 ON
0003  0000
0004  0000           MAIN        START
0005  0000
0006  0000              ;        switch to native mode
0007  0000
0008  0000 18                    CLC             clear carry flag
0009  0001 FB                    XCE             exchange carry with e bit (clear e bit)
0010  0002
0011  0002 C230                  REP     #$30    set accum, index size to 16 bits
0012  0004 AD1300                LDA     DATA16  load accum with 16-bit value at DATA16
0013  0007 AC1500                LDY     DATA2   load Y-reg with 16-bit value at DATA2
0014  000A E220                  SEP     #$20    set accum to eight bits
0015  000C A8                    TAY             transfer accum to Y
0016  000D 8C1700                STY     RESULT  save 16-bit index into RESULT,RESULT+1
0017  0010
0018  0010              ;        return to 6502 emulation mode
0019  0010
0020  0010 38                    SEC             set carry flag
0021  0011 FB                    XCE             exchange carry with e bit (set e bit)
0022  0012
0023  0012 60                    RTS
0024  0013
0025  0013
0026  0013 FF7F      DATA16      DC      A'$7FFF'
0027  0015 4433      DATA2       DC      A'$3344'
0028  0017 0000      RESULT      DS      2
0029  0019
0030  0019                       END
```

Listing 6.6.

mnemonic to name the accumulator indicates that the sixteen-bit accumulator is always used, regardless of the setting of the memory select flag. Thus, sixteen bits are always transferred, even if the accumulator size is eight bits, in which case the high byte is stored to the hidden B accumulator.

TCS transfers the contents of the sixteen-bit C accumulator to the S stack pointer register, thereby relocating the stack. Since sixteen bits will be transferred regardless of the accumulator word size, the high byte of the accumulator must contain valid data.

TSC transfers the contents of the sixteen-bit S stack pointer register to the sixteen-bit accumulator, C, regardless of the accumulator word size.

6 First Examples: Moving Data

```
0001 0000                    KEEP   KL.6.7
0002 0000                    65816  ON
0003 0000
0004 0000
0005 0000         MAIN       START
0006 0000
0007 0000           ;        switch-to-native-mode code
0008 0000
0009 0000 18                 CLC              clear carry flag
0010 0001 FB                 XCE              exchange carry with e bit (clear e bit)
0011 0002
0012 0002 E210               SEP    #$10      set index size to 8 bits
0013 0004 C220               REP    #$20      set accum to 16 bits
0014 0006 AD1300             LDA    DATA16    load accum with 16-bit value at DATA16
0015 0009 AC1500             LDY    DATA8     load Y-reg with 8-bit value at DATA8
0016 000C 98                 TYA              transfer Y to accumulator
0017 000D 8D1600             STA    RESULT    save 16-bit accum into RESULT.RESULT+1
0018 0010
0019 0010           ;        return to 6502 emulation mode
0020 0010
0021 0010 38                 SEC              set carry flag
0022 0011 FB                 XCE              exchange carry with e bit (set e bit)
0023 0012
0024 0012 60                 RTS
0025 0013
0026 0013
0027 0013 FF7F    DATA16     DC     A'$7FFF'
0028 0015 33      DATA8      DC     H'33'
0029 0016 0000    RESULT     DS     2
0030 0018
0031 0018                    END
```

Listing 6.7.

```
0000 E210              SEP    #%00010000   set index mode to 8 bits
0002 BA                TSX                 transfer low byte of stack ptr to 8-bit X
```

Fragment 6.2.

TXY transfers the contents of the X index register to the Y index register. Since X and Y will always have the same register size, there is no ambiguity.

TYX transfers the contents of the Y index register to the X index register. Both will always be the same size.

Transfer instructions take only one byte, with the source and destination both specified in the opcode itself. In all transfers, the data remains intact in the original register as well as being copied into the new register.

Using **TCS** and **TCD** can be dangerous when the accumulator is in eight-bit mode, unless the accumulator was recently loaded in sixteen-bit mode so that the high byte, hidden when the switch was made to eight-bit mode, is still known. Transferring an indeterminate hidden high byte of the accumulator along with its known low byte into a sixteen-bit environment register such as the stack pointer will generally result in disaster.

As always, you need to be watchful of the modes currently in force in each of your routines.

Exchanges

The 65802 and 65816 also implement two exchange instructions, neither available on the 6502 or 65C02. An exchange differs from a transfer in that two values are swapped, rather than one value being copied to a new location.

The first of the two exchange instructions, **XBA**, swaps the high and low bytes of the sixteen-bit accumulator (the **C** accumulator).

The terminology used to describe the various components of the eight-or-sixteen bit accumulator is: to use **A** to name the accumulator as a register that may be optionally eight or sixteen bits wide (depending on the **m** memory/accumulator select flag); to use **C** when the accumulator is considered to be sixteen bits regardless of the setting of the **m** flag; and, when **A** is used in eight-bit mode to describe the low byte only, to use **B** to describe the hidden high byte of the sixteen-bit accumulator. In the latter case, when the accumulator size is set to eight bits, only the **XBA** instruction can directly access the high byte of the sixteen-bit "double accumulator", **B**. This replacement of **A** for **B** and **B** for **A** can be used to simulate two eight-bit accumulators, each of which, by swapping, "shares" the actual **A** accumulator. It can also be used in the sixteen-bit mode for inverting a double-byte value. The **XBA** instruction is exceptional in that the **n** flag is always set on the basis of bit seven of the resulting accumulator **A**, even if the accumulator is sixteen bits.

The second exchange instruction, **XCE**, is the 65816's only method for toggling between 6502 emulation mode and 65816 native mode. Rather than exchanging register values, it exchanges two bits—the carry flag, which is bit zero of the status register, and the **e** bit, which should be considered a kind of appendage to the status register and which determines the use of several of the other flags.

Fragment 6.3 sets the processor to 6502 emulation mode. Conversely, native mode can be set by replacing the **SEC** with a **CLC** clear carry instruction.

```
0010 38            SEC
0011 FB            XCE
```

Fragment 6.3.

Because the exchange stores the previous emulation flag setting into the carry, it can be saved and restored later. It can also be evaluated with the branch-on-condition instructions to be discussed in Chapter 8 (Flow of Control) to determine which mode the processor was just in. A device driver routine that needs to set the emulation bit, for example, can save its previous value for restoration before returning.

The selection of the carry flag for the e bit exchange instruction is in no way connected to the normal use of the carry flag in arithmetic operations. It was selected because it is easy to set and reset, it is less frequently used than the sign and zero flags, and there are branch-on-condition instructions which test it. The primary use of the **SEC** and **CLC** instructions for arithmetic will be covered in upcoming chapters.

Storing Zero to Memory

The **STZ** instruction, introduced on the 65C02, lets you clear either a single or double byte memory word to zero, depending, as usual, on the current memory/accumulator select flag word size. Zero has long been recognized as one of the most commonly stored values, so a "dedicated" instruction to store zero to memory can improve the efficiency of many 65x programs. Furthermore, the **STZ** instruction lets you clear memory without having to first load one of the registers with zero. Using **STZ** results in fewer bytes of code, faster execution, and undisturbed registers.

Block Moves

The two block move instructions, available only on the 65802 and the 65816, let entire blocks (or strings) of memory be moved at once.

Before using either instruction, all three user registers (**C, X, and Y**) must be set up with values which serve as parameters.

The C accumulator holds the count of the number of bytes to be moved, *minus one*. It may take some getting used to, but this "count" is numbered from zero rather than one. The C accumulator is always sixteen bits: if the **m** mode flag is set to eight bits, the count is still the sixteen-bit value in C, the concatenation of B and A.

X and Y specify either the top or the bottom addresses of the two blocks, depending on which of the two versions of the instruction you choose. In Listing 6.8, $2000 bytes of data are moved from location $2000 to $4000.

```
0001  0000                      KEEP   KL.6.8
0002  0000                      65816  ON
0003  0000
0004  0000          MAIN        START
0005  0000
0006  0000 18                   CLC
0007  0001 FB                   XCE
0008  0002
0009  0002 C230                 REP    #$30           reset data and index mode to 16 bits
0010  0004                      LONGA  ON
0011  0004                      LONGI  ON
0012  0004
0013  0004 AD1300               LDA    COUNT          load 16-bit C accum with # bytes to be moved
0014  0007 AE1500               LDX    SOURCE         load 16-bit X reg with address of source
0015  000A AC1700               LDY    DEST           load 16-bit Y reg with address of destination
0016  000D
0017  000D 540000               MVN    0,0
0018  0010
0019  0010 38                   SEC
0020  0011 FB                   XCE
0021  0012 60                   RTS
0022  0013
0023  0013 FF1F    COUNT        DC     A'$1FFF'
0024  0015 0020    SOURCE       DC     A'$2000'
0025  0017 0040    DEST         DC     A'$4000'
0026  0019
0027  0019                      END
```

Listing 6.8.

The **MVN** instruction uses X and Y to specify the bottom (or beginning) addresses of the two blocks of memory. The first byte is moved from the address in X to the address in Y; then X and Y are incremented, C is decremented, and the next byte is moved, and so on, until the number of bytes specified by the value in C is moved (that is, until C reaches $FFFF). If C is zero, a single first byte is moved, X and Y are each incremented once, and C is decremented to $FFFF.

The MVP instruction assumes X and Y specify the top (or ending) addresses of the two blocks of memory. The first byte is moved from the address in X to the address in Y; then X, Y and C are decremented, the next byte is moved, and so on, until the number of bytes specified by the value in C is moved (until C reaches $FFFF).

The need for two distinct block move instructions becomes apparent when the problem of **memory overlap** is considered. Typically, when a block of memory starting at location X is to be moved to location Y, the intention is to replace the memory locations from Y to Y + C with the identical contents of the range X through X + C. However, if these two ranges overlap, it is possible that as the processor blindly transfers memory one byte at a time, it may overwrite a value in the source range before that value has been transferred.

The rule of thumb is, when the destination range is a lower memory address than the source range, the MVN instruction should be used (thus "Move Next") to avoid overwriting source bytes before they have been copied to the destination. When the destination range is a higher memory location than the source range, the MVP instruction should be used ("Move Previous").

While you could conceivably move blocks with the index registers set to eight bits (your only option in emulation mode), you could only move blocks in page zero to other page zero locations. For all practical purposes, you must reset the x mode flag to sixteen bits before setting up and executing a block move.

Notice that assembling an MVN or MVP instruction generates not only an opcode, but also two bytes of operand. The operand bytes specify the 64K bank from which and to which data is moved. When operating in the 65816's sixteen-megabyte memory space, this supports the transfer of up to 64K of memory from one bank to another. In the object code, the first byte following the opcode is the bank address of the destination and the second byte is the bank address of the source.

But while this order provides microprocessor efficiency, assembler syntax has always been the more logical left to right, source to destination (TAY, for example, transfers the accumulator to the Y index register). As a result, the recommended assembler syntax is to follow the mnemonic first with a 24-bit source address then with a 24-bit destination address—or more commonly with labels representing code or data addresses. The assembler strips the bank byte from each address (ignoring the rest) and inserts them in the correct object code sequence. (Destination bank, source bank.) For example:

```
440102    MVP SOURCE,DEST    move from bank of source(02) to bank of dest(01)
```

The bank byte of the label **SOURCE** is 02 while the bank byte of the label **DEST** is 01. As always, the assembler does the work of converting the more human-friendly assembly code to the correct object code format for the processor.

If the source and destination banks are not specified, some assemblers will provide a user-specified default bank value.

The assembler will translate the opcode to object code, then supply its bank value for both of the operand bytes:

```
440000    MVP
```

If either bank is different from the default value, both must be specified.

7 The Simple Addressing Modes

The term **addressing mode** refers to the method by which the processor determines where it is to get the data needed to perform a given operation. The data used by a 65x processor may come either from memory or from one or another of the processor's registers. Data for certain operations may optionally come from either location, some from only one or the other. For those operations which take one of their operands from memory, there may be several ways of specifying a given memory location. The method best suited in a particular instance is a function of the overall implementation of a chosen problem-solving algorithm. Indeed, there are so many addressing modes available on the 65x processors that there is not necessarily a single "correct" addressing mode in each situation.

This chapter deals with those addressing modes which may be described as the "simple" addressing modes. You have already seen some of these used in the examples of the previous chapter; the simple addressing modes are listed in Table 7.1. Each of these addressing modes is straightforward. Those addressing modes that require more than a simple combination of values from several memory locations or registers are described as "complex modes" in Chapter 11.

Table 7.1. List of Simple Addressing Modes.

Available on all 65x processors:	Example Syntax
immediate	LDA #$12
absolute	LDA $1234
direct page (zero page)	LDA $12
accumulator	ASL A
implied	TAY
stack	PHA

Available on the 65C02, 65802 and 65816 only:	
direct page (zero page) indirect	LDA ($12)

Available on the 65802 and 65816 only:	
absolute long	LDA $123456
direct page indirect long	LDA [$12]
block move	MVN SOURCE,DEST

In addition to solving a given problem, the processor must spend a great deal of its time simply calculating effective addresses. The simple addressing modes require little or no effective address computation, and therefore tend to be the fastest executing. However, the problem-solving and memory efficiencies of the complex addressing modes, which will be described in subsequent chapters, can make up for their effective address calculation overhead. In each case, the nature of the problem at hand determines the best addressing mode to use.

Immediate Addressing

Immediate data is data found embedded in the instruction stream of a program itself, immediately following the opcode which uses the data. Because it is part of the program itself, it is always a constant value, known at assembly time and specified when you create the program. Typically, small amounts of constant data are handled most efficiently by using the immediate addressing mode to load either the accumulator or an index register with a specific value. Note that the immediate addressing mode is not available with any of the store instructions (**STA**, **STX**, or **STY**), since it makes no sense to *store* a value to the operand location within the code stream.

To specify the immediate addressing mode to a 65x assembler, prefix the operand with a # (pound or sharp) sign. The constant operand may be either data or an address.

For example,

```
A912            LDA     #$12
```

loads the hexadecimal value $12 into the accumulator.

The 6502 and 65C02, their registers limited to only eight bits, permit only an eight-bit operand to follow the load register immediate opcodes. When the constant in an assembly source line is a sixteen-bit value, greater-than and less-than signs are used to specify whether the high- or low-order byte of the double-byte value are to be used. A less-than indicates that the low byte is to be used, and thus:

```
A234            LDX     #<$1234
```

causes the assembler to generate the LDX opcode followed by a one-byte operand, the low byte of the source operand, which is $34. It's equivalent to:

```
A234            LDX     #$34
```

The use of a greater-than sign would cause the value $12 to be loaded. If neither the less-than nor greater-than operator is specified, most assemblers will default to the low byte when confronted with a double-byte value.

When assembling 65816 source code, the problem becomes trickier. The 6502 and 65C02 neither have nor need an instruction to set up the eight-bit mode because they are always in it. But the 65816's accumulator may be toggled to deal with either eight- or sixteen-bit quantities, as can its index registers, by setting or resetting the **m** (memory/accumulator select) or **x** (index select) flag bits of the status register. Setting the **m** bit puts the accumulator in eight-bit mode; resetting it puts it in sixteen-bit mode. Setting the **x** bit puts the index registers in eight-bit mode; resetting it puts them in sixteen-bit mode.

The **m** and **x** flags may be set and reset many times throughout a 65816 program. But while assembly code is assembled from beginning to end, it rarely executes in that fashion. More commonly, it follows a circuitous route of execution filled with branches, jumps, and subroutine calls. Except for right after the **m** or **x** flag has been explicitly set or reset, the assembler has no way of knowing the correct value of either: your program may branch somewhere, and reenter with either flag having either value, quite possibly an incorrect one.

While the programmer must always be aware of the proper values of these two flags, for most instructions the assembler doesn't need to know their status in order to generate code. Most instructions generated are the same in both eight- or sixteen-bit mode. Assembling a load accumulator absolute instruction, for example, puts the same opcode value and the same absolute address into the code stream regardless of accumulator size; it is at execution time that the **m** bit setting makes a difference between whether the accumulator is loaded with one or two bytes from the absolute address.

But a load register immediate instruction is followed by the constant to be loaded. As Figure 7.1 shows, if the register is set to eight-bit mode at the point the instruction is encountered, the 65816 expects a one-byte constant to follow before it fetches the next opcode. On the other hand, if the register is set to sixteen-bit mode at the point the instruction is encountered, the 65816 expects a double-byte constant to follow before it fetches the next opcode. The assembler must put either a one-byte or two-byte constant operand into the code following the load register immediate opcode based on the status of a flag which it doesn't know.

Immediate Addressing: 8 bits vs. 16

8-Bit Data (all processors): Data: Operand byte.

Instruction:

Opcode	Data=Operand

16-Bit Data (65802/65816, native mode, applicable mode flag m or x =0):

Data High: Second operand byte.

Data Low: First operand byte.

Instruction:

Opcode	Data Low = Operand Low	Data High = Operand High

Figure 7.1. Immediate Addressing: 8 vs. 16 bits.

Two assembler directives have been designed to tell the assembler which way to go: LONGA and LONGI, each followed with the value ON or OFF. LONGA ON indicates the accumulator is in sixteen-bit mode, LONGA OFF in eight-bit mode. LONGI ON tells the assembler that the index registers are in sixteen-bit mode, LONGI OFF that they are in eight-bit mode. Load register immediate instructions are assembled on the basis of the last LONGA or LONGI directive the assembler has seen—that is, the one most immediately preceding it in the source file. For example,

```
LONGA ON
LONGI ON
```

tells the assembler that both accumulator and index registers are set to sixteen bits. Now, if it next encounters the following two instructions

```
A93412          LDA     #$1234
A05600          LDY     #$56
```

then the first puts a **LDA** immediate opcode followed by the constant $1234 into the code, and the second a **LDY** immediate opcode followed by the constant $0056, again two bytes of operand, the high byte padded with zero.

On the other hand,

```
        LONGA OFF
        LONGI OFF
```

tells the assembler that both accumulator and index registers are set to eight bits. Now,

```
A934            LDA     #$1234
A056            LDY     #$56
```

puts a **LDA** immediate opcode followed by the constant $34 into the code, and the second a **LDY** immediate opcode followed by the constant $56, each one byte of operand.

Like the flags themselves, of course, one directive may be **ON** and the other **OFF** at any time. They also do not need to both be specified at the same time.

The settings of the **LONGA** and **LONGI** directives to either **ON** or **OFF** simply represent a promise by you, the programmer, that the flags will, in fact, have these values at execution time. The directives do nothing by themselves to change the settings of the actual m and x flags; this is typically done by using the **SEP** and **REP** instructions, explained earlier. (Note, incidentally, that these two instructions use a special form of the immediate addressing mode, where the operand is always eight bits.) Nor does setting the flags change the settings of the directives. You must therefore exercise caution to set the **LONGA** and **LONGI** flags to correctly represent the settings of the m and x flags, and to be sure never to branch into the code with the m or x flag set differently. If, for example, the assembler generated a **LDA #$1234** instruction with **LONGA** set **ON**, only to have the m accumulator flag set to eight bits when the code is executed, the processor would load the accumulator with $34, then see the $12 which follows as the next opcode and try to execute it, resulting in program failure.

Absolute Addressing

There are two categories of simple addressing modes available for accessing data in a known memory location: absolute and direct page.

The first of these, absolute addressing, is used to load or store a byte to or from a fixed memory location (within the current 64K data bank on the 65816, which defaults to bank zero on power up). You specify the sixteen-bit memory location in the operand field (following the opcode) in your assembly language source line, as Figure 7.2 shows.

For example, Fragment 7.1 loads the eight-bit constant $34 into the accumulator, then stores it to memory location $B100 in the current data bank.

```
0000 E220          SEP     #%00100000    set 8-bit accumulator/memory mode
0002               LONGA   OFF           tell assembler the accumulator mode
0002 A934          LDA     #$34          load constant $34 as immediate data
0004 8D00B1        STA     $B100         store byte to memory location $B100
```

Fragment 7.1.

The same memory move could be done with either of the index registers, as shown in Fragment 7.2 using the **X** register. Symbolic labels in the operand fields provide better self-documentation and easier program modification.

```
0000         NUM1   GEQU    $34           give this data byte a symbolic label
0000         DATA   GEQU    $B100         give this data byte a symbolic label
0000
0000 E210           SEP     #%00010000    set index registers to 8-bit mode
0002                LONGI   OFF           tell assembler the index mode is 8-bit
0002 A234           LDX     #NUM1         load constant $34 as immediate data
0004 8E00B1         STX     DATA          store byte to memory location $B100
```

Fragment 7.2.

As you have seen, the 65816's accumulator may be toggled to deal with either eight- or sixteen-bit quantities, as can its index registers, by setting or resetting the **m** or **x** flag bits of the status register. Naturally, you don't need to execute a **SEP** or **REP** instruction nor a **LONGA** or **LONGI** assembler directive before every routine, provided you know the register you intend to use is already set correctly, and the assembler correctly knows that setting. But you must always exercise extreme care when developing 65816 programs to avoid making invalid assumptions about the modes currently in force or taking unintentional branches from code in one mode to code in another.

Effective Address:

```
23    15    7    0
[Bank][High][Low]
```

Instruction:

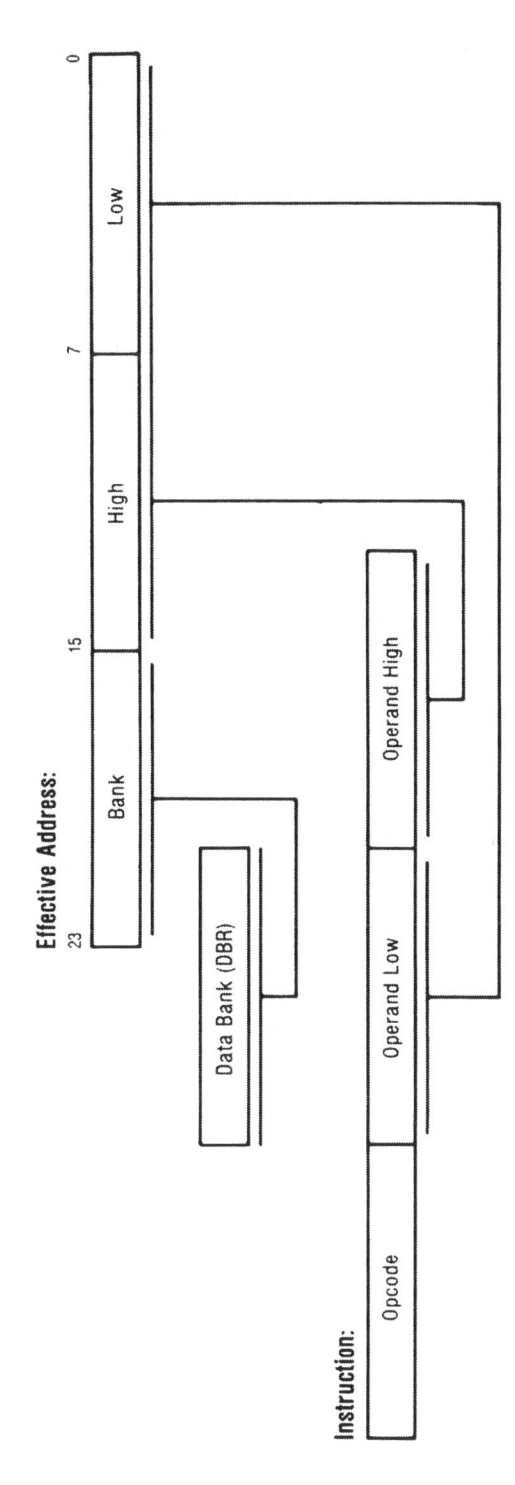

```
[Opcode][Operand Low][Operand High]
```

[Data Bank (DBR)]

Figure 7.2. Absolute Addressing.

As Fragment 7.3 shows, the load and store instructions above will as easily move sixteen bits of data as they did eight bits; all that's needed is to be sure the register used is in sixteen-bit mode, and that the assembler has been alerted to the setting.

```
0000             DATA    GEQU    $B100           give this location a symbolic label
0000
0000 C210                REP     #%00010000      reset index registers to 16-bit mode
0002                     LONGI   ON              tell assembler
0002 A23412              LDX     #1234           load 16-bit constant $1234 immediate
0005 8E00B1              STX     DATA            store double byte to memory loc $B100
```

Fragment 7.3.

As indicated, absolute addresses are sixteen-bit addresses. On the 6502, 65C02, and 65802, with memory space limited to 64K, sixteen bits can specify any fixed location within the entire address space of the processor. Therefore, the term **absolute addressing** was appropriate.

The 65816, on the other hand, with its segmentation into 256 possible 64K banks, requires a 24-bit address to specify any fixed location within its address space. However, the same opcodes that generated sixteen-bit absolute addresses on the 6502 and 65C02 generate 24-bit addresses on the 65816 by concatenating the value of the data bank register with the sixteen-bit value in the operand field of the instruction. (Instructions that transfer control, to be discussed in Chapter 8, substitute the program bank register value for the data bank register value.)

Absolute addressing on the 65816 is therefore actually an offset from the base of the current bank; nevertheless, the use of the term absolute addressing has survived on the 65816 to refer to sixteen-bit fixed addresses within the current 64K data bank.

So long as the programmer needs to access only the contents of the current data bank, (sixteen-bit) absolute addressing is the best way to access data at any known location in that bank.

Direct Page Addressing

One of the most powerful and useful features of the 6502 and 65C02 processors is their zero page addressing modes. A **page** of memory on a 65x processor consists of 256 memory locations, starting at an address which is an integer multiple of $100 hexadecimal, that is, $0000, $0100, $0200, and so on. Generally, pages are numbered in hexadecimal, so their range within a 64K bank is $00 through $FF. **Zero page** addressing is made even more powerful and generalized as **direct page addressing** on the 65802 and 65816.

The zero page is the first of the 256 pages found within the 64K address space of the 6502 and 65C02—memory addresses $0000 to $00FF. These addresses may be accessed one byte cheaper than absolute memory accesses. Whereas loading or storing data from an absolute location will require three bytes of code, loading or storing a byte from a zero page location requires only two bytes, as Figure 7.3 shows.

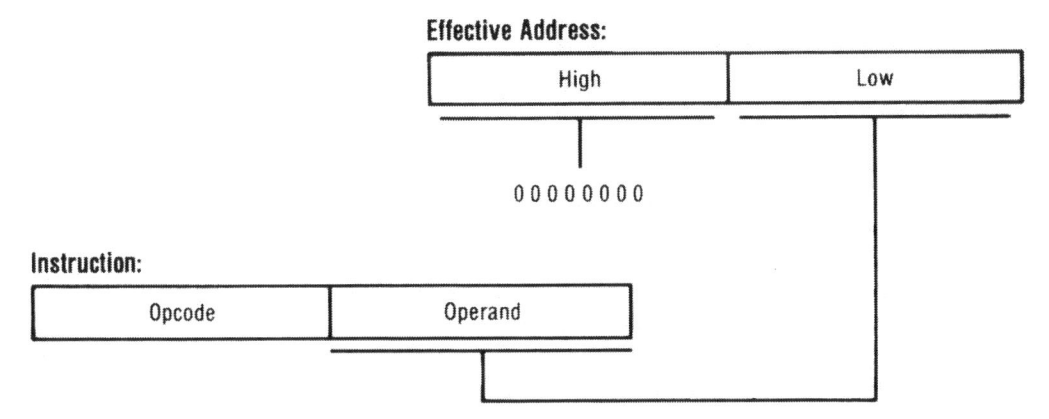

Figure 7.3. Zero Page Addressing.

Since all of the addresses in the zero page are less than $0100 (such as $003F, for example) it follows that, if the computer knew enough to assume two leading hexadecimal zeroes, a zero page address could be represented in only one byte, saving both space and time. But if absolute addressing is used, the processor has to assume that two bytes follow an instruction to represent the operand, regardless of whether the high-order byte is zero or not.

This concept of expressing a zero page address with a single-byte operand was implemented on the 6502 and 65C02 by reserving separate opcodes for the various instructions using zero page addressing. Since an instruction's opcode for using zero page addressing is unique (as opcodes are for all of the different addressing modes of a given instruction), the processor will fetch only one operand byte from the code stream, using it in effect as a displacement from a known base ($0000, in the case of the 6502 and 65C02). Since only one byte need be fetched from the instruction stream to determine the effective address, the execution time is faster by one cycle. The result is a form of addressing that is shorter, both in memory use and execution time, than regular sixteen-bit absolute addressing.

Clearly, locating your most often accessed variables in zero page memory results in considerably shorter code and faster execution time.

The limitation of having this special area of memory available to the zero page addressing mode instructions is that there are only 256 bytes of memory available for use in connection with it. That is, there are only 256 zero page addresses. Resident system programs, such as operating systems and language interpreters, typically grab large chunks of page zero for their own variable space; applications programmers must carefully step around the operating system's variables, limiting assignment of their own program's zero page variables to some fraction of the zero page.

This problem is overcome on the 65816 by letting its direct page be set up anywhere within the first 64K of system memory (bank zero), under program control. No longer limited to page zero, it is referred to as **direct page addressing.** The result is, potentially, multiple areas of 256 ($100) bytes each, which can be accessed one byte and one cycle cheaper than absolute memory. Setting the direct page anywhere is made possible by the 65816's **direct page register,** which serves as the base pointer for the direct page area of memory. Expressed in terms of the 65816's direct page concept, it can be said that on the 6502 (and 65C02), the direct page is fixed in memory to be the zero page.

So 6502 and 65C02 zero page addressing opcodes become direct page opcodes on the 65802 and 65816; and when they are executed, the "zero page address"—the single byte that the processor fetches immediately after the opcode fetch—becomes instead a **direct page offset.** This means that instead of simply pointing to a location in the range $0000 to $00FF as it would on the 6502 and 65C02, the direct page offset is added to the sixteen-bit value in the direct page register to form the **effective direct page address,** which can be anywhere in the range $00:0000 to $00:FFFF.

For purposes of this chapter, however, the discussion of direct page addressing will be limited to the default case, where the value in the direct page register is zero, making it functionally identical to the 6502 and 65C02 zero page addressing mode. Since it requires the effective address to be computed, relocation of the direct page will be considered as a form of complex addressing, and will be covered in future chapters. While "direct page offset" is more correct, it is also more abstract; the term **direct page address** is most commonly used. However, it is essential to remember that it is, in fact, an offset relative to a previously established direct page value (again, as used in this chapter, $0000).

An example of the use of direct page addressing to store a constant value to memory is as follows:

```
A9F0          LDA     #$F0
8512          STA     $12
```

This stores the one-byte value $F0 at address $0012. Note that the object code generated for the store requires only one byte for the opcode and one for operand.

```
A9F0                LDA    #$F0
8D00B1              STA    $B100
```

stores the same one-byte value at the address $B100. In this case, the store requires one byte for the opcode and *two* bytes for the operand.

Notice how the assembler automatically assumes that if the value of the operand can be expressed in eight bits—if it is a value less than $100, whether coded as $34 or $0034 or $000034—the address is a direct page address. It therefore generates the opcode for the direct page addressing form of the instruction, and puts only a one-byte operand into the object code. For example, in the first of the two examples above, the direct page address to store to is $12. One result of the assembler's assumption that values less than $100 are direct page offsets is that physical addresses in the range $xx:0000 to $xx:00FF cannot be referenced normally when either the bank (the "xx") register is other than zero or the direct page register is set to other than $0000. For example, assembler syntax like:

```
A4F0                LDY    $F0
```

or

```
A4F0                LDY    $00F0
```

is direct page syntax. It will not access absolute address $00F0 if the direct page register holds a value other than zero; nor will it access $00F0 in another bank, even if the data bank register is set to the other bank. Both are evaluated to the same $F0 offset in the direct page. Instead, to access physical address $xx:00F0, you must force absolute addressing by using the vertical bar or exclamation point in your assembler source line:

```
ACF000              LDY    !$F0    load Y absolute (not direct page) from $00F0
```

Indexing

An **array** is a table or list in memory of sequentially stored data items of the same type and size. Accessing any particular item of data in an array requires that you specify both the location of the base of the array and the item number within the array. Either your program or the processor must translate the item number into the byte number within the array (they are the same if the items are bytes) and add it to the base location to find the address of the item to be accessed (*see* Figure 7.4).

Sometimes an array might be a table of addresses, either of data to be accessed or of the locations of routines to be executed. In this case, the size of each item is two bytes; the first address is at locations zero and one within the array, the second at locations two and three, the third at locations four and five, and so on. You must double the item number,

Indexing: Base plus Index

For example:

Base = $2000
Index Register X = $ 03
Effective Address = $2003

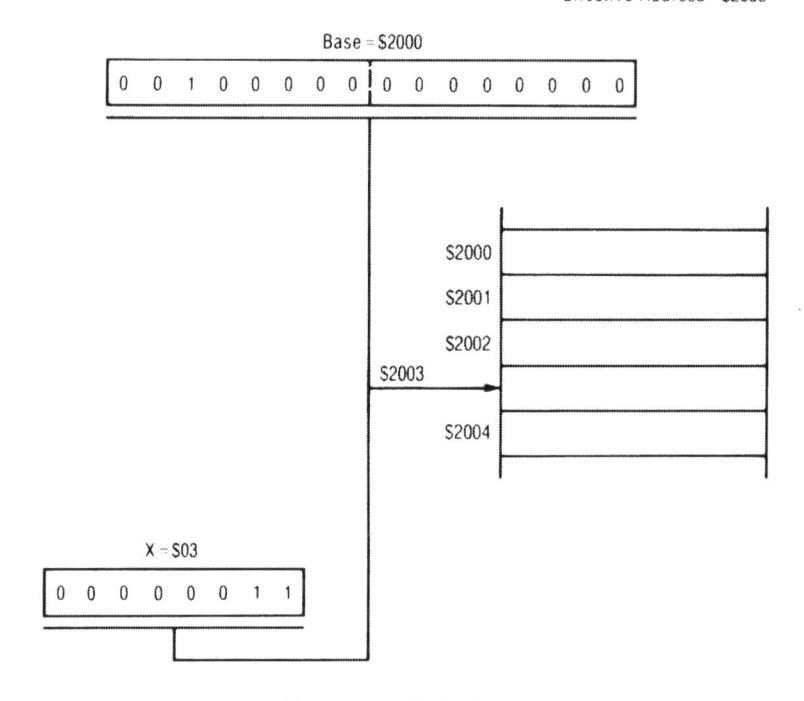

Figure 7.4. Indexing.

resulting in the values 0, 2, 4, . . . from the array indices 0, 1, 2, . . . , and so on, to create an index into this array of two-byte data items.

The 65x processors provide a wide range of **indexed addressing modes** that provide automatic indexing capability. In all of them, a value in one of the two index registers specifies the unsigned (positive integer) index into the array, while the instruction's operand specifies either the base of the array or a pointer to an indirect address at which the base may be found. Each addressing mode has a special operand field syntax for specifying the addressing mode to the assembler. It selects the opcode that will correctly instruct the processor where to find both the base and index.

Some early processors (the 6800, for example) had only one index register; moving data from one array to another required saving off the first index and loading the second before accessing the second array, then incrementing the second index and saving it before reloading the first index to again access the first array. The 65x processors were designed with two index registers so data can be quickly moved from an array indexed by one to a second array indexed by the other.

7 The Simple Addressing Modes

Often, the index registers are used simultaneously as indexes and as counters within loops in which consecutive memory locations are accessed.

The 65802 and 65816 index registers can optionally specify sixteen-bit offsets into an array, rather than eight-bit offsets, if the x index register select flag is clear when an indexed addressing mode is encountered. This lets simple arrays and other structured data elements be as large as 64K.

On the 6502, 65C02, and 65802, if an index plus its base would exceed $FFFF, it wraps to continue from the beginning of the 64K bank zero; that is, when index is added to base, any carry out of the low-order sixteen bits is lost. (*See* Figure 7.5.)

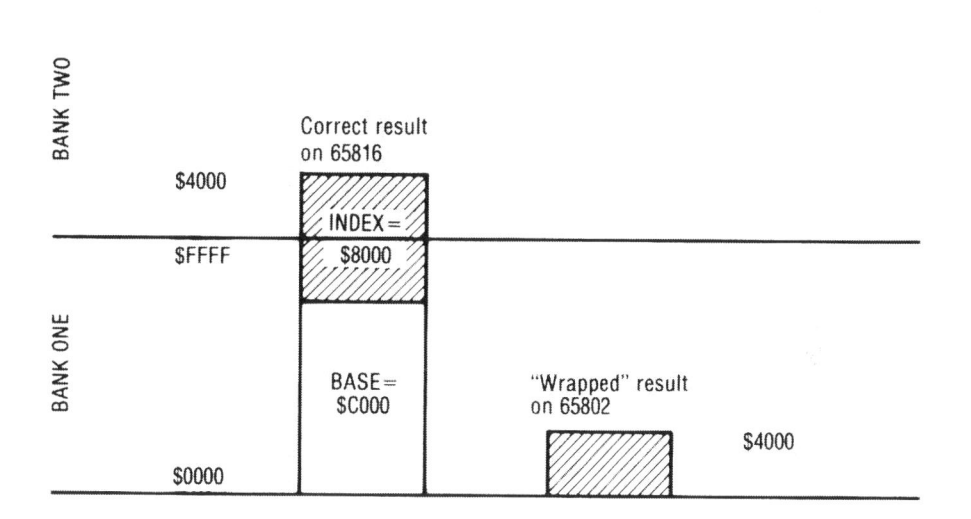

Figure 7.5. Indexing Beyond the End of the Bank.

On the 65816, the same is true of direct page indexing: because the direct page is always located in bank zero, any time the direct page, plus an offset into the direct page, plus an index exceeds $FFFF, the address wraps to remain in bank zero.

But as Figure 7.5 shows, whenever a 65816 base is specified by a 24-bit (long) address, or the base is specified by sixteen bits and assumes the data bank as its bank, then, if an index plus the low-order sixteen bits of its base exceeds $FFFF, it will temporarily (just for the current instruction) increment the bank. The 65816 assumes that the array being accessed extends into the next bank.

Absolute Indexed with X and Absolute Indexed with Y Addressing

Absolute addresses can be indexed with either the X (referred to as **Absolute,X** addressing) or the Y (referred to as **Absolute,Y** addressing) index register; but indexing with X is available to half again as many instructions as indexing with Y.

The base in these modes is specified by the operand, a sixteen-bit absolute address in the current data bank (Figure 7.6). The index is specified by the value in the X or Y register; the assembler picks the correct opcode on the basis of which index register the syntax specifies.

In Fragment 7.4, the X register is used to load the accumulator from $2200 plus 5, or $2205. If run on the 65816 in native mode, then if the accumulator is set to sixteen-bit mode, two bytes will be loaded from $2205 and $2206 in the current data bank.

```
0000 A20500      LDX     #5          load an index value of five
0003 BD0022      LDA     $2200,X     load the accumulator from $2205
```

Fragment 7.4.

If the 65816 is in native mode and the index registers are set to sixteen-bit mode, indexes greater than $FF can be used, as Fragment 7.5 illustrates.

```
0000 A00501      LDY     #$105       load an index value of $105
0003 B90022      LDA     $2200,Y     load the accumulator from $2305
```

Fragment 7.5.

If the index register plus the constant base exceeds $FFFF, the result will continue beyond the end of the current 64K data bank into the next bank (the bank byte of the 24-bit address is temporarily incremented by one). So an array of any length (up to 64K bytes) can be started at any location and absolute indexed addressing will correctly index into the array, even across a bank boundary. 65802 arrays, however, wrap at the 64K boundary, since effectively there is only the single 64K bank zero.

Loading the index register with an immediate constant, as in the previous two examples, is of limited use: if, when writing a program, you

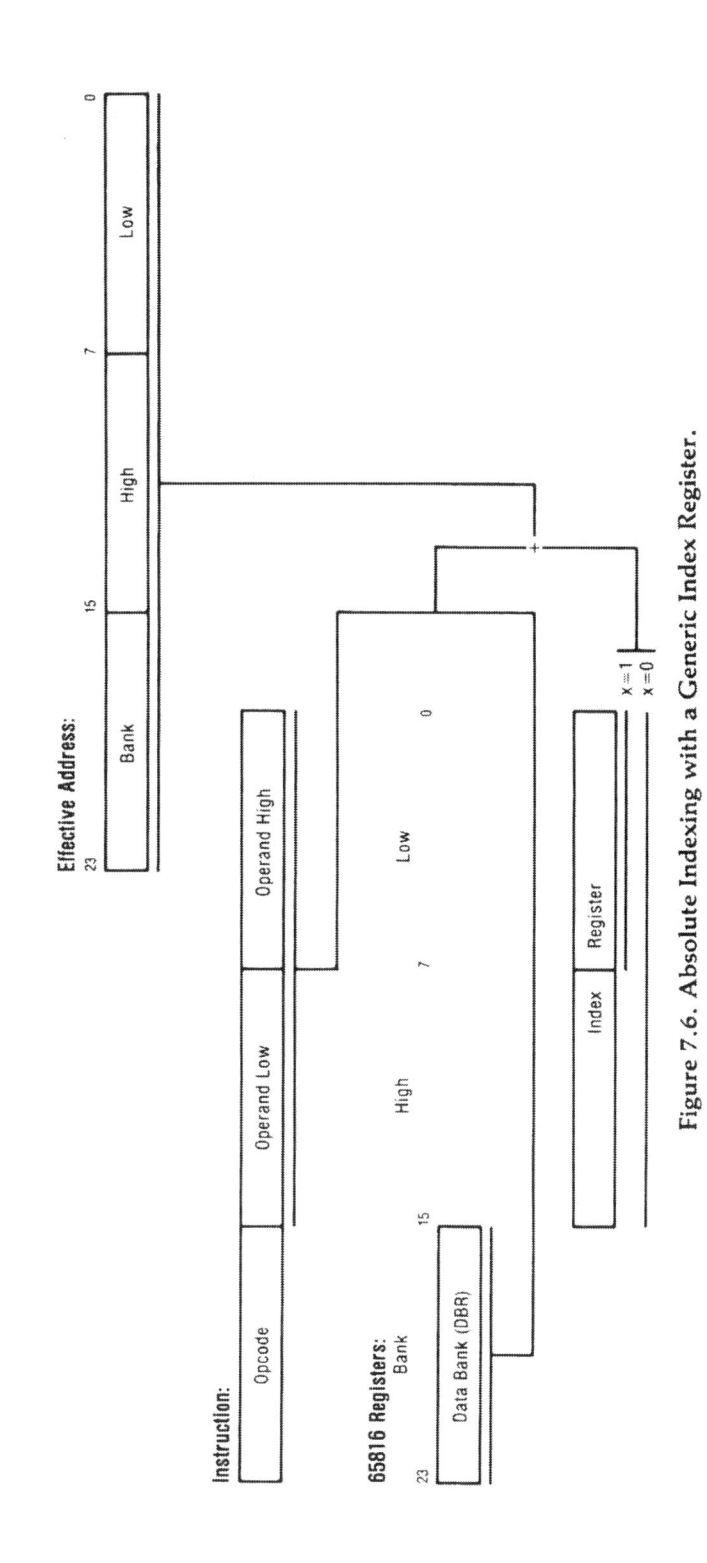

Figure 7.6. Absolute Indexing with a Generic Index Register.

know that you want to load the accumulator from $2305, you will generate far fewer bytes by using absolute addressing:

```
AD0523          LDA     $2305   load the accumulator from $2305
```

The usefulness of indexed addressing becomes clear when you don't know, as you write a program, what the index into the array will be. Perhaps the program will select among indexes, or calculate one, or retrieve it from a variable, as in Fragment 7.6.

```
0000 AE0600          LDX     INDEX     get previously calculated index from memory
0003 BD0022          LDA     $2200,X   load the accumulator from the array,X
0006                 .
0006                 .
0006                 .
0006 0000    INDEX   DS      2
```

Fragment 7.6.

It can be useful to be able to put the base of an array into the index register and let it vary, while keeping the index into the array constant. This is seldom possible with the eight bits of the 6502's and 65C02's index registers, since they limit the base addresses they can hold to the zero page, but it is a useful capability of the 65802 and 65816.

For example, suppose, as in Fragment 7.7, you're dealing with dozens (or hundreds) of records in memory. You need to be able to update the fifth byte (which is a status field) of an arbitrary record. By loading the base address of the desired record into an index register, you can use a constant to access the status field. The index into the array, five, is fixed; the array base varies.

Because the index is less than $100, the assembler would normally generate direct page indexing. To force the assembler to generate absolute indexing, not direct page indexing, you must use the vertical bar (or exclamation point) in front of the five, as Fragment 7.7 shows. That way, the five is generated as the double-byte operand $0005, an absolute address to which the address in the index register is added to form the absolute effective address.

Had the Y index register been used instead of X in Fragment 7.7, the vertical bar would have been acceptable but not necessary; direct page,Y addressing, as you will learn in the next section, can only be used with the LDX and STX instructions, so the assembler would have been forced to use absolute,Y addressing regardless.

Both absolute,X and absolute,Y can be used by what are called the eight Group I instructions, the memory-to-accumulator instructions

```
0000                STATUS  GEQU    5
0000                OK      GEQU    1
0000                BAD     GEQU    0
0000
0000 18                     CLC
0001 FB                     XCE
0002
0002 C210                   REP     #$10            set index registers to 16 bits
0004                        LONGI   ON
0004
0004 E220                   SEP     #$20
0006                        LONGA   OFF
0006
0006 AE0E00                 LDX     REC             get location of record to update
0009 A901                   LDA     #OK             load A with ok status token
000B 9D0500                 STA     !STATUS,X       store to status field
000E        ;                                       force absolute,X addressing
000E        .
000E        .
000E        .
000E
000E 0030   REC             DC      A'$3000'        loc of 1st record (in data bank)
```

Fragment 7.7.

which can use more addressing modes than any others: **LDA**, **STA**, **ADC**, **SBC**, **CMP**, **AND**, **ORA**, and **EOR**. In addition, absolute,X can be used for shifting data in memory, incrementing and decrementing data in memory, loading the Y register, and for other instructions; but absolute,Y has only one other use—to load the X register.

Direct Page Indexed with X and Direct Page Indexed with Y Addressing

Arrays based in the direct page (the zero page on the 6502 and 65C02) can be indexed with either the X register (called **Direct Page,X** addressing) or the Y register (called **Direct Page,Y** addressing). However, direct page,Y addressing is available only for the purpose of loading and storing the X register, while direct page,X is full-featured.

As is standard with indexed addressing modes, the index, which is specified by the index register, is added to the array base specified by the operand. Unlike the absolute indexed modes, the array always starts in the direct page. So the array base, a direct page offset, can be specified with a single byte. The sum of the base and the index, a direct page offset, must be added to the value in the direct page register to find its absolute address, as shown in Figure 7.7.

In Fragment 7.8, the accumulator is loaded from a direct page offset base of $32 plus index of $10, or an offset of $42 from the direct page register's setting.

```
0000 A21000    LDX    #$10        set up an index of $10
0003 B532      LDA    $32,X       load accumulator from dp:$42
```

Fragment 7.8.

Remember that the effective address is an offset of $42 from the direct page register and is always in bank zero. It will correspond to an absolute address of $0042 only when the direct page register is equal to zero (the default here in this chapter). Chapter 11, which covers the complex addressing modes, details relocation of the direct page.

When the index registers are set to eight bits, you can code the index and the array base interchangeably—they are both the same size. So the index, if it is a constant, may be specified as the operand, with the array base in the index register. Using the last example, the $10 in the index register could be the direct page base of the array; the operand, $32, would then be the index into an array in the direct page which begins at the direct page offset $10.

On the 6502 and the 65C02, and in the 6502 emulation modes of the two sixteen-bit processors, indexing past the end of the direct page wraps to the beginning of the direct page, as Fragment 7.9 shows. The index and the direct page array base are added, but only the low eight bits of the sum specify the direct page offset of the effective address. So in Fragment 7.9, while the base of $32 plus the index of $F0 equals $122, only the $22 is kept, and the accumulator is loaded from dp:$22.

```
A2F0      LDX    #$F0        set up an index of $F0
B532      LDA    $32,X       load accumulator from dp:$22
```

Fragment 7.9.

In 65802 and 65816 native mode, however, indexes can be sixteen bits, so direct page indexing was freed of the restriction that the effective

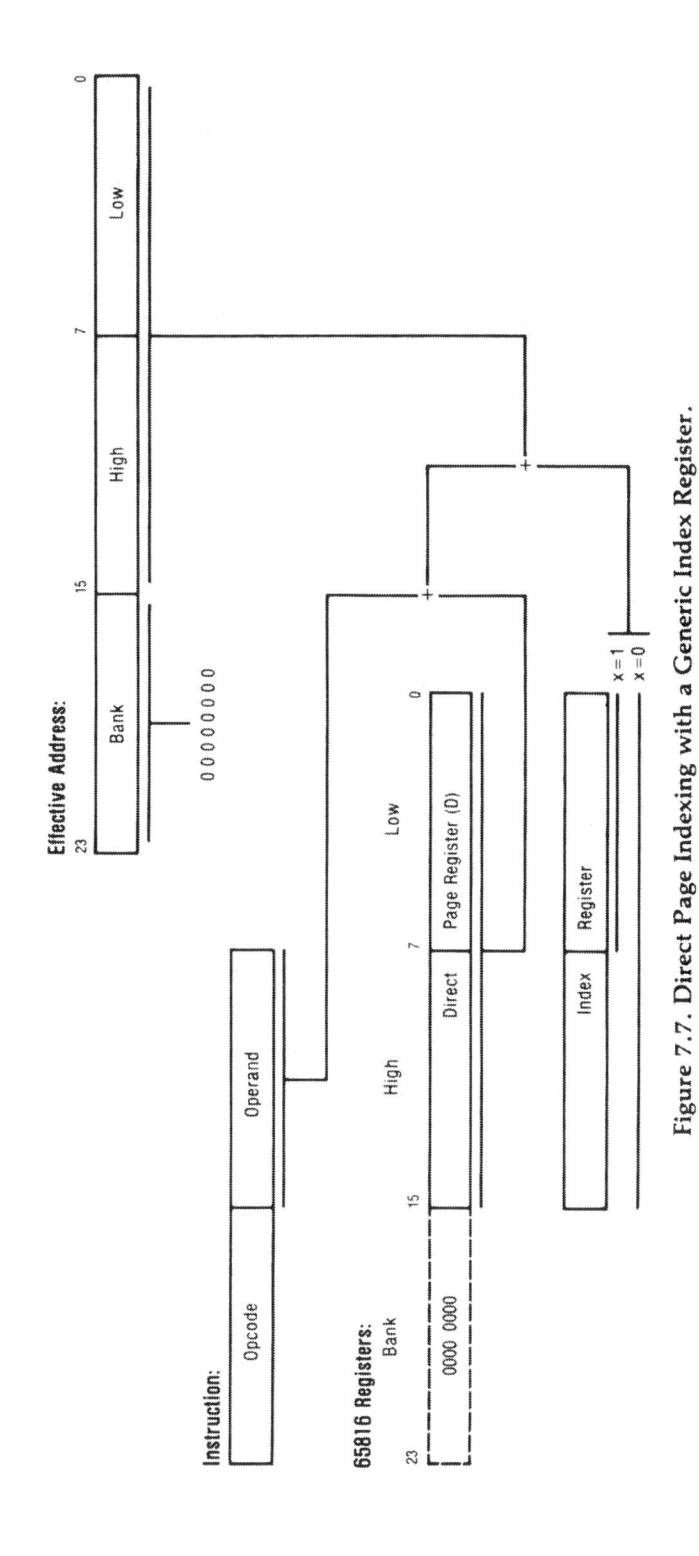

Figure 7.7. Direct Page Indexing with a Generic Index Register.

address be within the direct page. Arrays always start in the direct page, but indexing past the end of the direct page extends on through bank zero, except that it wraps when the result is greater than $FFFF to remain in bank zero (unlike absolute indexing, which temporarily allows access into the next higher bank).

In Fragment 7.10, the accumulator is loaded from the value in the direct page register plus the direct page base of $12 plus index of $FFF0, or dp:$0002. Note this is in bank zero, not bank one.

```
0000 C230       REP    #$30         set index and accumulator 16-bit modes
0002            LONGA  ON
0002            LONGI  ON
0002
0002
0002 A2F0FF     LDX    #$FFF0
0005 B512       LDA    $12,X        load accum from $0002
```

Fragment 7.10.

If the index registers are set to sixteen bits and the array indexes you need to use are all known constants less than $100, then you can use direct page indexing to access arrays beginning, not just in the direct page, but anywhere in bank zero memory: load the index register with the sixteen-bit base of the array and specify the index into the array as the operand constant. This technique would generally only be useful if the direct page register has its default value of zero.

Accumulator Addressing

Accumulator addressing is only available for the read-modify-write instructions such as shifts and rotates. The instructions themselves will be explained in subsequent chapters, and the use of accumulator addressing with them will be reviewed in detail.

As a simple addressing mode, accumulator addressing is included in this chapter for the sake of completeness even though the instructions which use it have not yet been introduced.

Generally, most operations take place upon two operands, one of which is stored in the accumulator, the other in memory, with the result being stored in the accumulator. Read-modify-write instructions, such as the shifts and rotates, are "unary" operations; that is, they have only a single operand, which in the case of accumulator addressing, is located in the accumulator. There is no reference to external memory in the accumulator addressing modes. As usual, the result is stored in the accumulator.

The syntax for accumulator addressing, using the **ASL** (arithmetic shift left) instruction as an example, is:

```
0A              ASL     A
```

Implied Addressing

In implied addressing, the operand of the instruction is implicit in the operation code itself; when the operand is a register, it is specified in the opcode's mnemonic. Implied operand instructions are therefore single-byte instructions consisting of opcode only, unlike instructions that reference external memory and as a result must have operands in subsequent bytes of the instruction.

You have already encountered implied addressing in the previous chapter in the form of the register transfer instructions and exchanges. Since there are a small number of registers, it is possible to dedicate an opcode to each specific register transfer operation. Other instructions that use implied addressing are the register increments and decrements.

As one-byte instructions, there is no assembler operand field to be coded: You simply code the assembler mnemonic for the given instruction, as below:

```
7B              TDC     transfer direct page register to double accumulator
AA              TAX     transfer A to X
9B              TXY     transfer X to Y
```

Stack

Stack addressing references the memory location pointed to by the stack register. Typical use of the stack addressing mode is via the push and pull instructions, which add or remove data to or from the stack area of memory and which automatically decrement or increment the stack pointer. Examples of the use of push and pull instructions were given in the previous chapter.

Additionally, the stack is used by the jump to subroutine, return from subroutine, interrupt, and return from interrupt instructions to automatically store and retrieve return addresses and in some cases also the status register. This form of stack addressing will be covered in Chapter 12, Subroutines, and Chapter 13, System Control.

The assembler syntax of the push and pull instructions is similar to that of implied instructions; no operand field is coded, since the operation will always access memory at the stack pointer location.

Direct Page Indirect Addressing

Direct page indirect addressing, or, as it is known on the 65C02, **zero page indirect**, is unavailable on the 6502; it was first introduced on the 65C02.

Indirect addressing was designed for the 65C02 as a simplification of two often-used complex forms of addressing available on the 6502 known as zero page indirect indexed and zero page indexed indirect addressing (these forms of addressing on the 65816 are of course *direct page* indirect indexed or indexed indirect addressing; they are explained in Chapter 11, Complex Addressing Modes). It was found that programmers were tolerating the overhead inherent in these two complex addressing modes to simulate simple indirection.

The concept of simple indirect addressing lies on the borderline between the simple and complex addressing modes. An understanding of it forms the basis for understanding several of the more complex indexed modes which use indirection as well.

An **indirect address** is an address stored in memory which points to the data to be accessed; it is located by means of the operand, an address which points to the indirect address, as shown in Figure 7.8. Except in the case of indirect jump instructions, explained in Chapter 8, Flow of Control, this pointer is always a direct page address.

The use of indirect addresses brings great flexibility to the addressing options available to you. There is, however, a penalty in execution speed, imposed by the fact that, in addition to the operand fetch from the code stream, the actual effective address must also be fetched from memory before the data itself can be accessed. For this reason, direct page addresses are used as the pointers to the indirect addresses since, as you will remember from the discussion of direct page addressing, the direct page offset itself can be determined with only a single memory fetch.

The syntax for indirect addressing is to enclose in parentheses, as the operand, the direct page pointer to the indirect address.

```
B280            LDA       ($80)
```

This means, as Figure 7.8 illustrates, "go to the direct page address $80 and fetch the absolute (sixteen-bit) address stored there, and then load the accumulator with the data at that address." The low-order byte of the indirect address is stored at dp:$80, the high-order byte at dp:$81—typical 65x low/high fashion. Remember, in the default case where **DP** equals $0000, the direct page address equals the zero page address, namely $00:0080.

As explained above, the indirect address stored at the direct page location (pointed to by the instruction operand) is a sixteen-bit address.

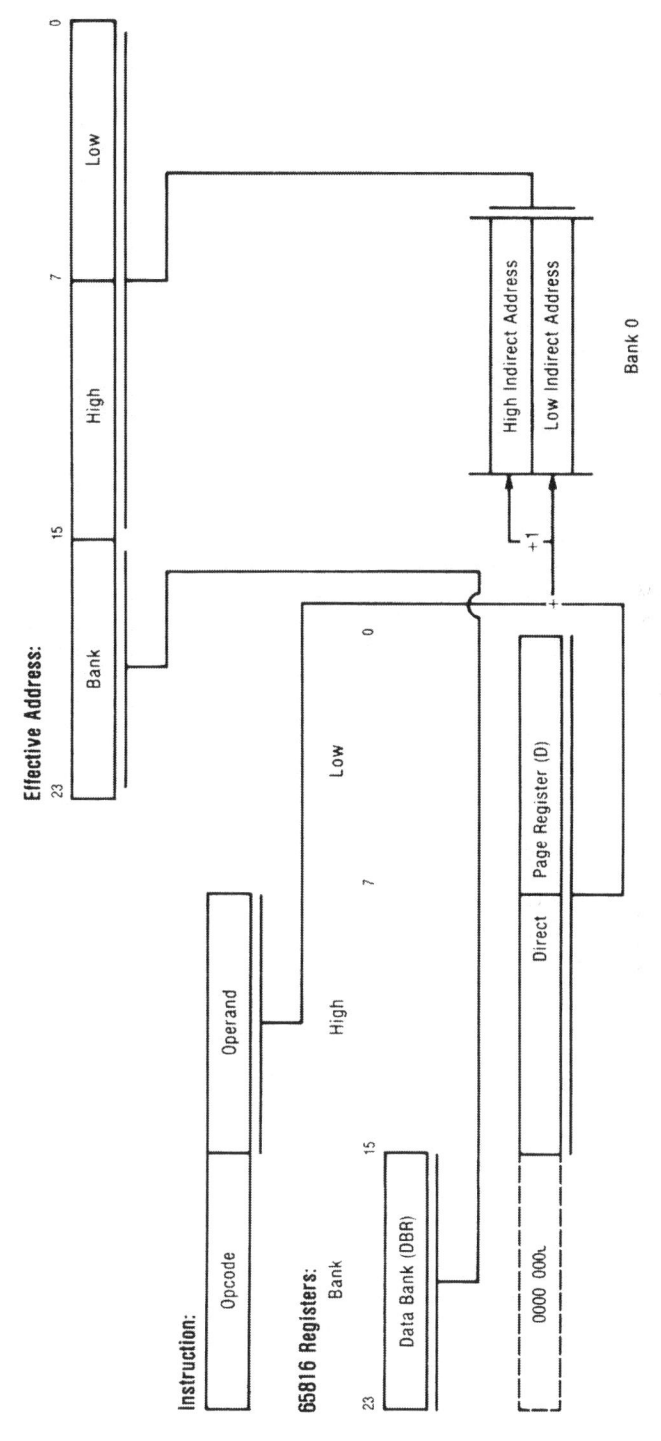

Figure 7.8. Direct Page Indirect Addressing.

The general rule for the 65816 is that when an addressing mode only specifies sixteen bits of the address, then the bank byte (bits 16-23) of the address is provided by the data bank register. This rule applies here; but you must first note that the direct page offset which *points* to the indirect address is itself always located in bank zero because the direct page itself is *always* located in bank zero. The examples, however, were simplified to assume both the data bank and the direct page register to be zero.

The use of indirect addressing allows an address that is referenced numerous times throughout a routine and is subject to modification—for example, a pointer to a data region—to be modified in only one location and yet alter the effective address of many instructions.

In Listing 7.1, the data $1234 is moved from location **VAR1** to **VAR2**. Note that the load and store instructions had the same operand: the symbol **DPA**, which had been given a value of $80. The indirect address stored at that location was different in each case, however, resulting in the data being copied from one location to another. While this example in itself is an inefficient way to move a double-byte word to another location, it does illustrate the basic method of indirect addressing, which will become quite useful as looping and counting instructions are added to your working set of 65x instructions.

Absolute Long Addressing

This is the first of the simple addressing modes that are available only on the 65816 and 65802 processors.

Absolute long addressing is an extension of (sixteen-bit) absolute addressing—that is, addressing at a known location. Remember that on the 6502 and 65C02, address space is limited to 64K, and any location within the entire memory range can be specified with a sixteen-bit address. This is not the case with the 65816, which can address up to sixteen megabytes of memory. Thus 24 bits are required to specify a given memory location.

In general, there are two ways by which a 24-bit data address is generated. In the case of sixteen-bit absolute addressing, a 64K memory context is defined by the value of the data bank register; the bank byte of the 24-bit address is derived directly from that register via simple concatenation (connecting together) of the data bank value and the sixteen-bit address. The alternative method is to specify a complete 24-bit effective address for a given instruction. The absolute long addressing mode is one of the means for doing this.

As the name should imply, this addressing mode specifies a known, fixed location within the sixteen-megabyte addressing space of the 65816, just as sixteen-bit absolute addressing specifies a known, fixed

```
0001 0000                         KEEP  KL.7.1
0002 0000
0003 0000                         65816 ON
0004 0000
0005 0000           MAIN  START
0006 0000
0007 0000           DPA   EQU   $80           give memory cell at $80 a label
0008 0000
0009 0000                 ;     switch from 6502 emulation to native mode
0010 0000
0011 0000 18              CLC                 clear carry flag
0012 0001 FB              XCE                 exchange carry with e bit (clear e bit)
0013 0002
0014 0002 C230            REP   #$30          set 16-bit registers
0015 0004           LONGA ON
0016 0004           LONGI ON
0017 0004
0018 0004 A01500          LDY   #VAR1         get the address where $1234 is stored
0019 0007 8480            STY   DPA             and store it as an indirect address at $80
0020 0009 B280            LDA   (DPA)         now load $1234 indirectly
0021 000B A01700          LDY   #VAR2         change the indirect address in DPA
0022 000E 8480            STY   DPA             to point to VAR2
0023 0010 9280            STA   (DPA)         and store $1234 by overwriting the $0000 there
0024 0012
0025 0012                 ;     return to 6502 emulation mode
0026 0012
0027 0012 38              SEC                 set carry flag
0028 0013 FB              XCE                 exchange carry with e bit (set e bit)
0029 0014
0030 0014 60              RTS
0031 0015
0032 0015 3412      VAR1  DC    A'$1234'
0033 0017 0000      VAR2  DC    A'0000'
0034 0019
0035 0019                 END
```

Listing 7.1.

location within either the 64K space of the 6502, 65C02, or 65802, or else the 64K data space determined by the 65816's data bank register. Just as the sixteen-bit absolute addressing operations are three-byte instructions, consisting of opcode, address low, and address high, the instructions that use the 24-bit absolute long addressing mode are four-byte instructions, comprised of opcode, low byte of address, high byte of address, and bank byte of address, as shown in Figure 7.9. The value in bits 8–15 of the effective address is described as the high byte, and

16-23 as the bank byte, because this most clearly reflects both the parallels with the 6502 and 65C02 and the bank-oriented memory segmentation of the 65816 architecture.

When absolute long addressing is used, the bank address in the operand of the instruction temporarily overrides the value in the data bank register *for the duration of a single instruction*. Thus, it is possible to directly address any memory location within the entire sixteen-megabyte address space.

You will likely find, however, that this form of addressing is one of the less frequently used. There are two reasons for this: first, it is more efficient to use the shorter sixteen-bit addressing modes, provided that the data bank register has been appropriately set; second, it is generally undesirable to hard code fixed 24-bit addresses into an application, as this tends to make the application dependent on being run in a fixed location within a fixed bank. (An exception to this is the case where the address referenced is an I/O location, which is fixed by the given system hardware configuration.)

The 65x processors, in general, do not lend themselves to writing entirely position-independent code, although the 65816 certainly eases this task compared to the 6502 and 65C02. There is, however, no reason why code should not be written on the 65816 and 65802 to be **bank-independent**—that is, capable of being executed from an arbitrary memory bank. But using absolute long addressing will tend to make this difficult if not impossible.

If you are using a 65802 in an existing system, it is important to note that although the address space of the 65802 is limited to 64K at the hardware level, internally the processor still works with 24-bit addresses. One thing this means is that it is legal to use the long addressing modes such as absolute long. But using them is futile, even wasteful: an extra address byte is required for the bank, but the bank address generated is ignored. There are cases where use of forms of long addressing other than absolute long should be used if you are targeting your code for both the 65802 and the 65816. But generally there is little reason to use the absolute long addressing mode on the 65802, except perhaps for fine-tuning a timing loop (the absolute long addressing mode requires an extra cycle to execute in order to fetch the bank address in the fourth byte of the instruction).

The assembler syntax to indicate the absolute long addressing mode is simply to code a value in the operand field greater than $FFFF. To force long addressing for bank zero addresses ($00:0000 to $00:FFFF), use the greater-than sign (>) as a prefix to the operand (similar to the use of the vertical bar to force sixteen-bit absolute addressing) as shown in Fragment 7.11.

Note that the first **STA** instruction in Fragment 7.11 generates a four-

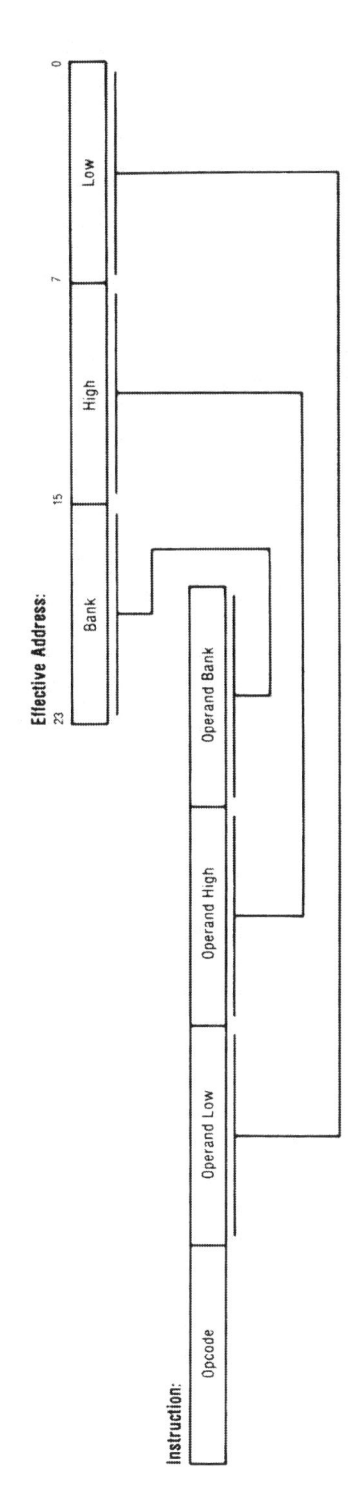

Figure 7.9. Absolute Long Addressing.

byte instruction to store the accumulator to a bank zero address, while the second STA instruction generates a three-byte instruction to store the accumulator to the same sixteen-bit displacement but within bank two, the current data bank. Also note that for both the load and the first store instructions, absolute long addressing causes the current data bank register, which is set to two, to be overridden.

```
0000  E220              SEP     #$20        set 8 bit accumulator
0002                    LONGA   OFF
0002
0002  A902              LDA     #$02        set data bank
0004  48                PHA                 to bank two
0005  AB                PLB
0006
0006  AF9DA303          LDA     $03A39D     absolute long at $03:A39D
000A  8F7F2E00          STA     >$2E7F      store data to $00:2E7F
000E  8D7F2E            STA     $2E7F       store data to $02:2E7F
```

Fragment 7.11.

Absolute Long Indexed with X Addressing

Absolute long indexed with X, or **absolute long indexed,** uses the X register for its index, and an absolute long address as its base. It lets you index into an array located in a bank other than the data bank.

Instructions using absolute long indexed addressing are four bytes in length, since three bytes are needed to express 24-bit absolute-long operands. The bank byte, being the highest byte in the operand, is the fourth byte of the instruction. The contents of the X index register are added to the absolute-long operand to form the 24-bit effective address at which data will be accessed.

For example, Fragment 7.12 gets a character from a text buffer starting at $3000 in bank zero and stores it into buffers starting at $1000 in bank two and at $E000 in bank three. Because the character to be loaded is in bank zero, its long address is expressed in sixteen bits. You must preface a reference to it with the greater-than sign to override the assembler assumption that a sixteen-bit operand is in the data bank, and force the assembler to instead use long addressing. The next instruction stores to the data bank, requiring only absolute indexing; the assembler assumes simple sixteen-bit operands are located in the data bank. Finally, storing into bank three requires no special specification: since $03E000 cannot be expressed in sixteen bits, long addressing is assumed.

```
0000 E220              SEP    #$20           set accumulator to 8 bits
0002                   LONGA  OFF
0002 C210              REP    #$10           set indexes to 16 bits
0004                   LONGI  ON
0004
0004 A902              LDA    #2             set the data bank to bank 2
0006 48                PHA
0007 AB                PLB
0008
0008 AE0080            LDX    BUFIDX         get 16 bit buffer index
000B BF003000          LDA    >$3000,X       force long indexed addr:bank0
000F 9D0010            STA    $1000,X        store into data bank(bank 2)
0012 9F00E003          STA    $03E000,X      store into bank 3
```

Fragment 7.12.

Direct Page Indirect Long

Direct page indirect long is another case of long (24-bit) addressing, where the effective address generated temporarily overrides the current value in the data bank register. Unlike the previous two long addressing modes, however, the 24-bit address is not contained in the operand itself. The instruction is two bytes long, much like regular direct page indirect addressing. The operand of the instruction is, like its non-long counterpart, a direct page offset acting as an indirect pointer; the difference in this case is that rather than pointing to a sixteen-bit address in the data bank, it points to a 24-bit address. If, for example, the direct page address is $80, as in Figure 7.10, the processor will fetch the low byte of the effective address from dp:$80, the high byte from dp:$81, and the bank byte from dp:$82. The bank byte temporarily overrides the value in the data bank register.

Fragment 7.13 shows the use of both direct page indirect addressing and direct page indirect long, using the latter to access the data as set up in Figure 7.10. The syntax for indirect long addressing is similar to that for direct page indirect, except left and right square brackets rather than parentheses enclose the direct page address to indicate the indirect address is long.

In this example, a sixteen-bit accumulator size is used with eight-bit index registers. The simultaneous availability of both an eight-bit and a sixteen-bit register in this mode simplifies the manipulation of long addresses. First, a value of $04 is loaded into the eight-bit Y register using immediate addressing. Since the **LONGI OFF** directive has been coded, the assembler automatically generates an eight-bit operand for

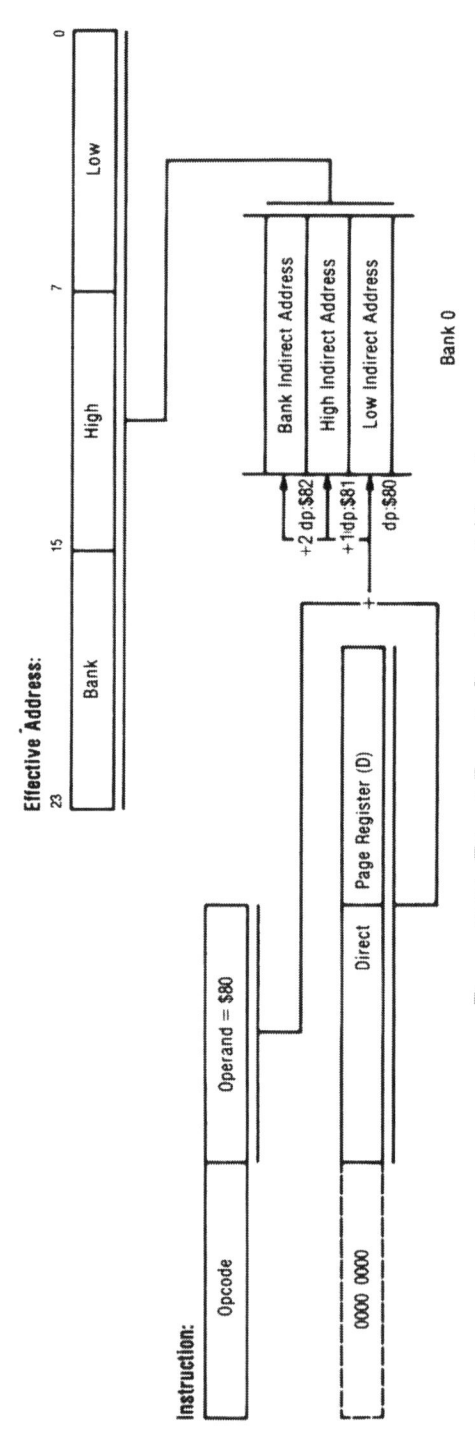

Figure 7.10. Direct Page Indirect Long Addressing.

```
0000 C220              REP     #$20           set accum/memory size to 16 bits
0002                   LONGA   ON
0002
0002 E210              SEP     #$10           set index size to eight bits
0004                   LONGI   OFF
0004
0004 A004              LDY     #$04           set data bank
0006 5A                PHY                    to bank 4
0007 AB                PLB
0008           ;
0008 A002              LDY     #$02           bank of indirect address
000A 8482              STY     $82
000C           ;
000C A90020            LDA     #$2000         high/low of indirect address
000F 8580              STA     $80
0011           ;
0011 B280              LDA     ($80)          load indirect from $04:2000
0013 8780              STA     [$80]          store indirect long to $02:2000
```

Fragment 7.13.

this instruction. This is pushed onto the stack, and then pulled into the bank register. Next, Y is loaded with #$02, the bank component of the indirect long address, which is stored to dp:$82. The sixteen-bit accumulator is then used to load an immediate $2000 (high/low of the indirect and the indirect long addresses), which is stored at dp:$80. This results in the following values in memory: at dp:$80 is $00, at dp:$81 is $20, and at dp:$82 is $02. The data bank register contains $04. The memory at locations dp:$80.81 contains the indirect address $2000, while the memory at locations dp:$80.82 contains the indirect long address $02:2000. The load indirect instruction uses the data bank register to form the bank address, and so loads double-byte data from $04:2000. The store indirect long stores the double-byte data at $02:2000. The overlapping of the low and high bytes of the indirect address in locations dp:$80 and dp:$81 highlights the difference in the source of the bank byte using the two addressing modes.

Block Move

Block move addressing is a dedicated addressing mode, available only for two instructions, **MVN** and **MVP**, which have no other addressing modes available to them. These operations were explained in the previous chapter.

8 | The Flow of Control

Flow of control refers to the way in which a processor, as it executes a program, makes its way through the various sections of code. Chapter 1 discussed four basic types of execution: straight-line, selection between paths, looping, and subroutines. This chapter deals with those instructions that cause the processor to jump or branch to other areas of code, rather than continuing the default straight-line flow of execution. Such instructions are essential to selection and looping.

The jump and branch instructions alter the default flow of control by causing the **program counter** to be loaded with an entirely new value. In sequential execution, on the other hand, the program counter is incremented as each byte from the code stream—opcode or operand—is fetched.

The 65x processors have a variety of branch and jump instructions, as shown in Table 8.1. Of these, when coding in the larger-than-64K environment of the 65816, only the three jump-long instructions (jump indirect long, jump absolute long, and jump to subroutine long) and the return from subroutine long instruction are capable of changing the program bank register—that is, of jumping to a segment of code in another bank. All of the other branch or jump instructions simply transfer within the current bank. In fact, the interrupt instructions (break, return from interrupt, and coprocessor instructions) are the only others which can change the program bank; there is no direct way to modify the program counter bank without at the same time modifying the program counter register because the program counter would still point to the next instruction in the old bank.

Table 8.1. Branch and Jump Instructions.

Mnemonic	Available on: 6502	65C02	65802/816	Description
BEQ	x	x	x	branch on condition instructions (eight)
JMP	x	x	x	jump absolute
JMP	x	x	x	jump indirect
JSR	x	x	x	jump to subroutine absolute
RTS	x	x	x	return from subroutine
BRA		x	x	branch always (unconditional)
JMP		x	x	jump absolute indexed indirect
BRL			x	branch long always (unconditional, 64K range)
JSR			x	jump to subroutine absolute indexed indirect
JMP			x	jump indirect long (interbank)
JMP			x	jump absolute long (interbank)
JSL			x	jump to subroutine long (interbank)
RTL			x	return from subroutine long (interbank)

As you may have noticed, all of the flow-of-control instructions (except the return instructions) can be divided into two categories: jump-type instructions and branch-type instructions. This division is based on addressing modes: branch instructions use program counter relative addressing modes; jump instructions don't.

Jump instructions can be further split into two groups: those which transfer control to another section of code, irreversibly, and those which transfer control to a subroutine, a section of code which is meant to eventually return control to the original (calling) section of code, at the instruction following the jump-to-subroutine instruction.

The jump instructions will be covered in this chapter first, then the branches; jump-to-subroutine instructions will be discussed in Chapter 12, which deals with subroutines.

Jump Instructions

The jump instruction (JMP) can be used with any one of five different 65816 addressing modes (only two of these are available on the 6502, a third is available on the 65C02) to form an effective address; control then passes to that address when the processor loads the program counter with it. For example,

```
4C0020          JMP     $2000   jump absolute to the code at location $2000
```

uses absolute addressing, a mode available to all 65x processors, to pass control to the code located at $2000 in the current program bank. (Notice that using absolute addressing to access data in the last chapter used the data bank in place of the program bank.)

In addition to absolute addressing, all of the 65x processors provide a jump instruction with absolute indirect addressing. While this form of indirect addressing is unique to the jump instruction, it is quite similar to the direct page indirect addressing mode described in Chapter 7. In this case, the sixteen-bit operand is the address of a double-byte variable located in bank zero containing the effective address; the effective address is loaded into the program counter. As with absolute addressing, the program bank remains unchanged (Figure 8.1).

For example, the jump instruction in Fragment 8.1 causes the processor to load the program counter with the value in the double-byte variable located at $00:2000. Unlike direct page indirect addressing, the operand is an absolute address rather than a direct page offset. Furthermore, this form of absolute addressing is unusual in that it *always* references a location in bank zero, *not* the current data bank.

```
0000                    LONGA   ON
0000 C220               REP     #$20       set 16-bit accumulator
0002 A93412             LDA     #$1234     load sixteen-bit accumulator with $1234
0005 8F002000           STA     >$2000     store long to location $00:2000
0009 6C0020             JMP     ($2000)    jump to location $1234 in program bank
```

Fragment 8.1.

The 65C02 added the absolute indexed indirect addressing mode to those available to the jump instruction. This mode is discussed further in Chapter 12, The Complex Addressing Modes. Although its effective address calculation is not as simple as the jump absolute or jump absolute indirect, its result is the same: a transfer of control to a new location.

The 65802 and 65816 added long (24-bit) versions of the absolute and indirect addressing modes. The absolute long addressing mode has a three-byte operand; the first two bytes are loaded into the program counter as before, while the third byte is loaded into the program bank register, giving the jump instruction a full 24-bit absolute addressing mode. For example,

```
5C4423FF                JMP     $FF2344
```

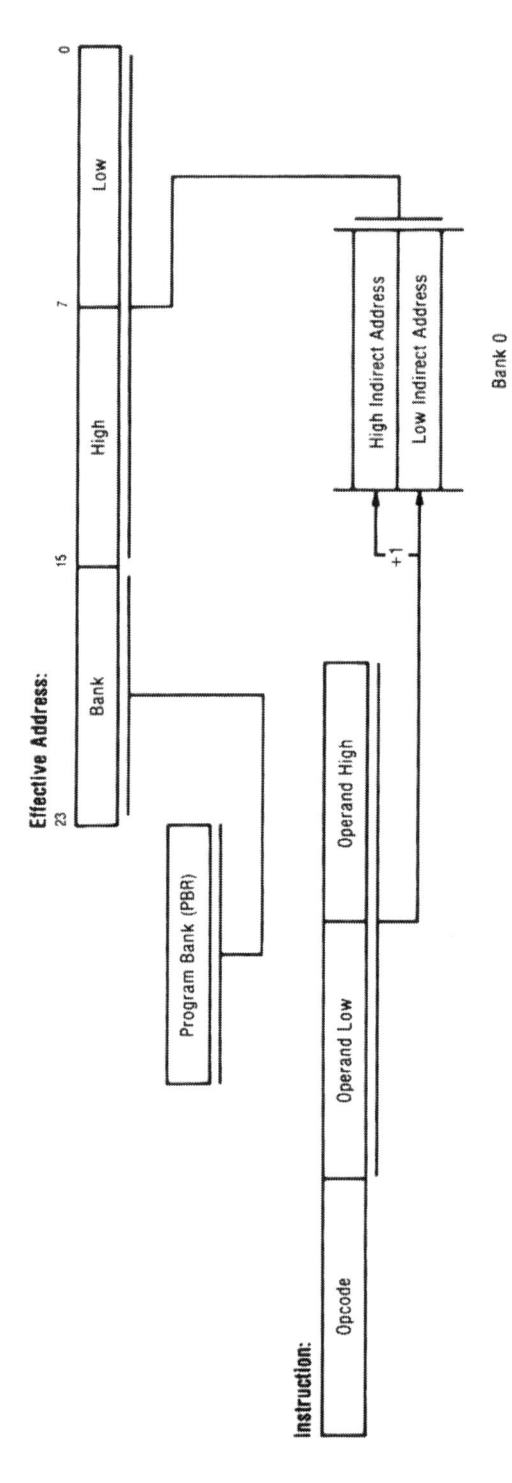

Figure 8.1. Jump's Absolute Indirect Addressing Mode.

causes the program counter to be loaded with $2344 and the program bank counter with $FF. Note that on the 65802, even though the bank register is modified by the long jump instruction, the bank address is effectively ignored; the jump is to the same location as the equivalent (sixteen-bit) absolute jump.

When the target of a long jump is in bank zero, say to $00A030, then the assembler has a problem. It assumes a jump to any address between zero and $FFFF (regardless of whether it's written as $A030 or $00A030) is a jump within the current program bank, not to another bank, so it will generate an absolute jump, not a long jump. There are two solutions. One is to use the greater-than sign (>) in front of the operand, which forces the assembler to override its assumptions and use long addressing:

```
5C30A000    JMP    >$A030    long jump from the current program bank to $00:A030
```

The alternative is to use the JML alias, or alternate mnemonic, which also forces a jump to be long, even if the value of the operand is less than $10000:

```
5C30A000    JML    $A030    jump from the current bank to $00:A030
```

The final form of the jump instruction is a 24-bit (long) jump using absolute indirect addressing. In the instruction,

```
DC0020    JMP    [$2000]    jump to the 24-bit address stored at $00:2000
```

the operand is the bank zero double-byte address $2000, which locates a *triple-byte* value; the program counter low is loaded with the byte at $2000 and the program counter high with the byte at $2001; the program bank register is loaded with the byte at $2002. A standard assembler will allow the JML (jump long) alias here as well.

Notice that absolute indirect long jumps are differentiated from absolute indirect jumps within the same bank by using parentheses for absolute indirect and square brackets for absolute indirect long. In both cases the operand, an absolute address, points to a location in bank zero.

The jump instructions change no flags and affect no registers other than the program counter.

Conditional Branching

While the jump instructions provide the tools for executing a program made up of disjoined code segments or for looping, they provide no way to conditionally break out of a loop or to select between paths. These are the jobs of the conditional branch instructions.

The jump instruction requires a minimum three bytes to transfer control anywhere in a 64K range. But selection between paths is needed so frequently and for the most part for such short hops that using three bytes per branch would tend to be unnecessarily costly in memory usage. To save memory, branches use an addressing mode called program counter relative, which requires just two bytes; the branch opcode is followed by a one-byte operand—a signed, two's-complement offset from the current program location.

When a conditional branch instruction is encountered, the processor first tests the value of a status register flag for the condition specified by the branch opcode. If the branch condition is false, the processor ignores the branch instruction and goes on to fetch and execute the next instruction from the next sequential program location. If, on the other hand, the branch condition is true, then the processor transfers control to the effective address formed by adding the one-byte signed operand to the value currently in the program counter (Figure 8.2).

As Chapter 1 notes, positive numbers are indicated by a zero in the high bit (bit seven), negative numbers by a one in the high bit. Branching is limited by the signed one-byte operands to 127 bytes forward or 128 bytes backward, counting from the end of the instruction. Because a new value for the program counter must be calculated if the branch is taken, an extra execution cycle is required. Further, the 6502 and 65C02 (and 65802 and 65816 in emulation mode) require an additional cycle if the branch crosses a page boundary. The native mode 65802 and 65816 do not require the second additional cycle, because they use a sixteen-bit (rather than eight-bit) adder to make the calculation.

The program counter value to which the operand is added is *not* the address of the branch instruction but rather the address of the opcode *following* the branch instruction. Thus, measured from the branch opcode itself, branching is limited to 129 bytes forward and 126 bytes backward. A conditional branch instruction with an operand of zero will continue with the next instruction regardless of whether the condition tested is true or false. A branch with an operand of zero is thus a two-byte no-operation instruction, with a variable (by one cycle) execution time, depending on whether the branch is or isn't taken.

The 65x processors have eight instructions which let your programs branch based on the settings of four of the condition code flag bits in the status register: the zero flag, the carry flag, the negative flag, and the overflow flag.

None of the conditional branch instructions change any of the flags, nor do they affect any registers other than the program counter, which they affect only if the condition being tested for is true. The most recent flag value always remains valid until the next flag-modifying instruction is executed.

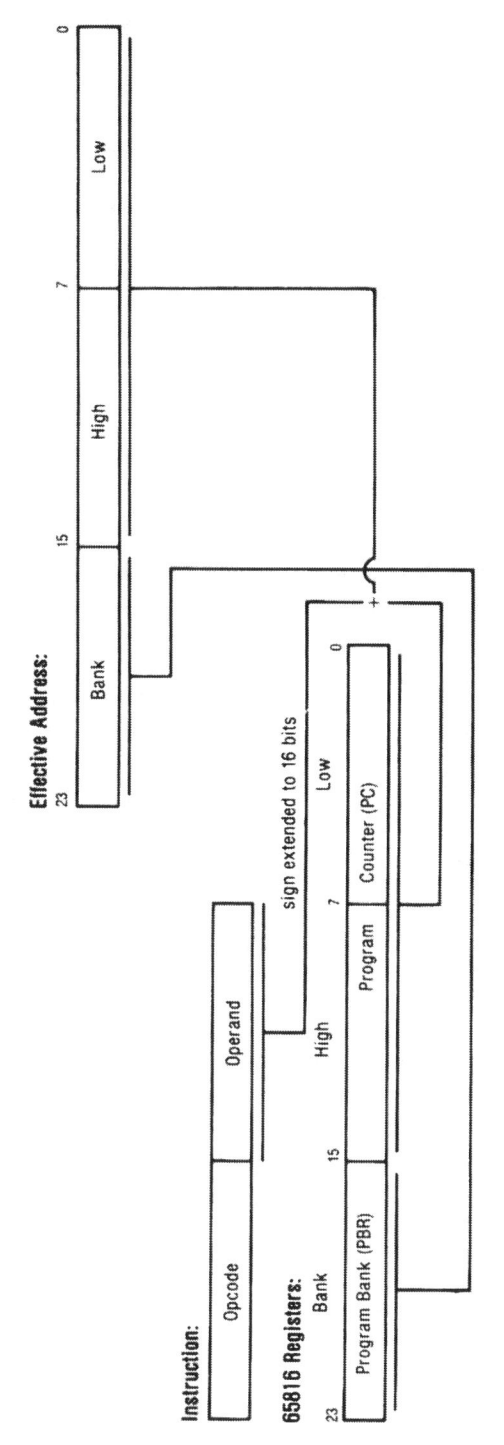

Figure 8.2. Relative Branch Calculation.

Branching Based on the Zero Flag

The zero bit in the status register indicates whether or not the result of an arithmetic, logical, load, pull, or transfer operation is zero. A zero result causes the bit to be set; a non-zero result causes the bit to be reset.

The **BEQ** instruction is used to branch when a result is zero—that is, when the zero bit is set. Its mnemonic meaning, that of **branch if equal (to zero)**, describes what the processor does. Alternatively, it may be considered a mnemonic for **branch if (comparison) equal** because it is often used after two values are compared or subtracted; if the two values are equal, then the result of the comparison (subtraction) is zero (no difference), and the branch is taken.

The **BNE** instruction is used to branch when a result is not zero. Also, any non-zero value which is loaded into a register will clear the zero flag. It is a mnemonic for **branch if not equal**; it too is used to branch after a comparison or subtraction if the two values are not equal.

Zero is often used as a terminator, indicating the end of a list, or that a loop counter has counted down to the end of the loop. Fragment 8.2 is a short routine to search for the end of a linked list of records, and then insert a new element at the end. Each element in the list contains a pointer to the next element in the chain. The last element in the chain contains a zero in its link field, indicating that the end of the list has been reached.

```
0000             ;      traverse linked list searching for end of chain
0000
0000 AC0080             LDY    NEXTNODE      nextnode contains address of next
0003             ;                           data element to be inserted.
0003 A90080             LDA    #ROOT         ROOT contains the address of
0006             ;                           the link field of the first
0006             ;                           record in the chain.
0006 AA     LOOP         TAX                 use fetched address to get next link
0007 B500               LDA    0,X
0009 D0FB               BNE    LOOP          if not zero, use value to go to next
000B             ;                           record
000B 98                 TYA
000C 9500               STA    0,X           store address of next record
000E             ;                           in link field of current record
000E AA                 TAX
000F 7400               STZ    0,X           now store zero to link field of
0011             ;                           new record, which is now end
```

Fragment 8.2.

The routine hinges on the **BNE** instruction found half-way through the code; until the zero element is reached, the processor continues looping through as many linked records as exist. Notice that the routine has no need to know how many elements there are or to count them as it adds a new element. Figure 8.3 pictures such a linked list.

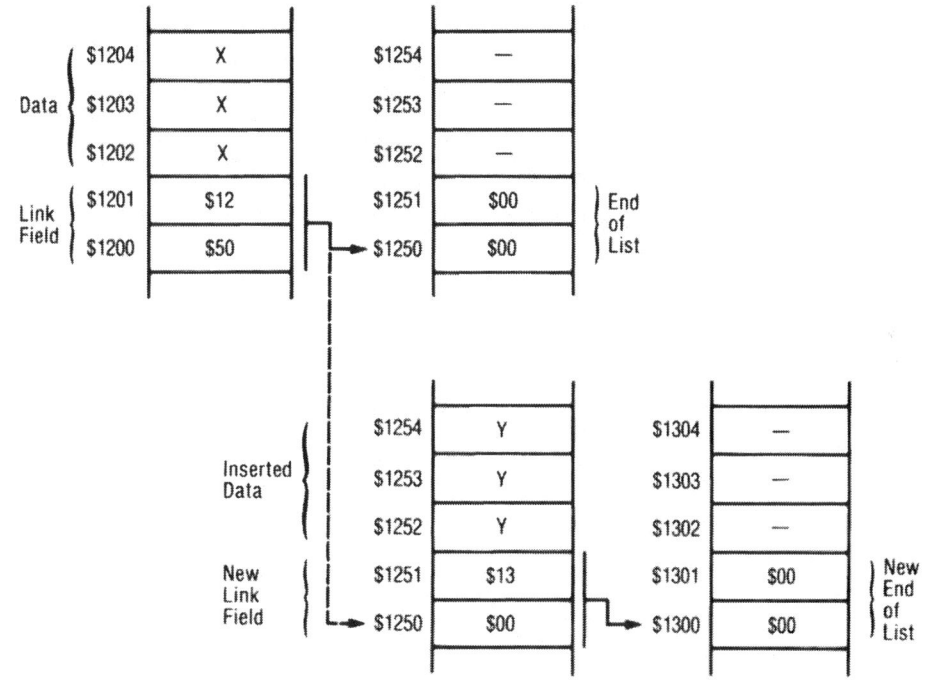

Figure 8.3. Linked List.

The two conditional branch instructions that check the zero flag are also frequently used following a subtraction or comparison to evaluate the equality or inequality of two values. Their use in arithmetic, logical, and relational expressions will be covered in more detail, with examples, in the next few chapters.

Branching Based on the Carry Flag

The carry flag in the status register is affected by addition, subtraction, and shift instructions, as well as by two implied-addressing instructions that explicitly set or clear the carry (**SEC** and **CLC**) and, on the 65802/65816, by the emulation and carry swapping **XCE** instruction, and the **SEP** and **REP** instructions.

The **BCC** instruction (branch on carry clear) is used to branch when the carry flag is a zero. The **BCS** instruction (branch on carry set) is used to branch when the carry flag is a one.

The carry flag bit is the only condition code flag for which there are explicit instructions both to clear and to set it. (The decimal flag, which can also be set and cleared explicitly, is a mode-setting flag; there are no instructions to branch on the status of the decimal flag.) This can come in handy on the 6502, which has no branch-always instruction (only the non-relocatable absolute jump): branch-always can be faked by setting the carry, then branching on carry set:

```
38              SEC             set carry bit in status register
B0EB            BCS     NEWCODE always document a BCS being used as branch-always
```

Since the code which follows this use of the **BCS** instruction will never be executed due to failure of the condition test, it should be documented as acting like a branch-always instruction.

The 6502 emulation mode of the 65802 and 65816 can be toggled on or off only by exchanging the carry bit with the emulation bit; so the only means of testing whether the processor is in emulation mode or native mode is to exchange the emulation flag with the carry flag and test the carry flag, as in Fragment 8.3. Note that **CLC**, **XCE**, and **BCS** instructions themselves always behave the same regardless of mode.

```
0000            .
0000            .
0000 18         CLC             shift to native mode
0001 FB         XCE             swap previous emulation bit value into carry
0002 B0FC       BCS     EMHAND  if was emulation, branch to emulation handler
0004            .
0004            .               else processor in native mode
0004            .
0004
```

Fragment 8.3.

Arithmetic and logical uses of branching based on the carry flag will be discussed in the next two chapters.

Branching Based on the Negative Flag

The negative flag bit in the status register indicates whether the result of an arithmetic, logical, load, pull, or transfer operation is negative or positive when considered as a two's-complement number. A negative result causes the flag to be set; a zero or positive result causes the flag to be cleared. The processor determines the sign of a result by checking to see if the high-order bit is set or not. A two's-complement negative number will always have its high-order bit set, a positive number always has it clear.

The **BMI** (branch-minus) instruction is used to branch when a result is negative, or whenever a specific action needs to be taken if the high-order (sign) bit of a value is set. Execution of the **BPL** (branch-plus) instruction will cause a branch whenever a result is positive or zero—that is, when the high-order bit is clear.

The ease with which these instructions can check the status of the high order-bit has not been lost on hardware designers. For example, the Apple // keyboard is read by checking a specific memory location (remember, the 65x processors use memory-mapped I/O). Like most computer I/O devices, the keyboard generates ASCII codes in response to keypresses. The code returned by the keyboard only uses the low-order seven bits; this leaves the eighth bit free to be used as a special flag to determine if a key has been pressed since the last time a key was retrieved. To wait for a keypress, a routine (*see* Fragment 8.4) loops until the high-order bit of the keyboard I/O location is set.

```
0000            KEYBD   GEQU    $C000
0000            KSTRB   GEQU    $C010
0000
0000            ;       wait until a character is pressed at the keyboard
0000
0000 E230               SEP     #$30    eight-bit words are used for I/O
0002
0002 AD00C0     LOOP    LDA     KEYBD
0005 10FB               BPL     LOOP    loop until high order bit is set
0007 8D10C0             STA     KSTRB   got one; reset keyboard
000A                    .
000A                    .               continue execution having fetched key
000A                    .               from keyboard
000A
```

Fragment 8.4.

The **STA KSTRB** instruction that follows a successful fetch is necessary to tell the hardware that a key has been read; it clears the high-order bit at the **KEYBD** location so that the next time the routine is called, it will again loop until the next key is pressed.

Remember that the high-order or sign bit is always bit seven on a 6502 or 65C02 or, on the 65802 or 65816, if the register loaded is set to an eight-bit mode. If a register being used on the 65802 or 65816 is set to sixteen-bit mode, however, then the high bit—the bit that affects the negative flag—is bit fifteen.

Branching Based on the Overflow Flag

Only four instructions affect the overflow (v) flag on the 6502 and 65C02: adding, subtracting, bit-testing, and an instruction dedicated to explicitly clearing it. The 65802/65816's **SEP** and **REP** instructions can set and clear the overflow flag as well. The next chapter will discuss the conditions under which the flag is set or cleared.

The **BVS** instruction is used to branch when a result sets the overflow flag. The **BVC** instruction is used to branch when a result clears the overflow flag.

Additionally, there is a hardware input on the 6502, 65C02, and 65802 that causes the overflow flag to be set in response to a hardware signal. This input pin is generally left unconnected in most personal computer systems. It is more likely to be useful in dedicated control applications.

Limitations of Conditional Branches

If you attempt to exceed the limits (+127 and −128) of the conditional branches by coding a target operand that is out of range, an error will result when you try to assemble it. If you should need a conditional branch with a longer reach, one solution is to use the inverse branch; if you would have used **BNE**, test it instead for equal to zero using **BEQ**. If the condition is true, target the next location past a jump to your real target. For example, Fragment 8.5 shows the end of a fairly large section of code, at the point at which it is necessary to loop back to the top (**TOP**) of the section if the value in location **CONTROL** is not equal to zero. You would use the code like Fragment 8.5 if **TOP** is more than 128 bytes back.

```
0000 AD0080              LDA    CONTROL
0003 F003                BEQ    DONE        done processing; skip over loop back
0005 4C0080              JMP    TOP         control not equal to zero; loop again
0008         DONE        ANOP               go on to next phase of processing
0008                     .
0008                     .
```

Fragment 8.5.

The price of having efficient two-byte short branches is that you must use five bytes to simulate a long conditional branch.

Many times it is possible and sensible to branch to another nearby flow of control statement and use it to puddle-jump to your final target. Sometimes you will find the branch or jump statement you need for puddle jumping already within your code because it's not unusual for two or more segments of code to conditionally branch to the same place. This method costs you no additional code, but you should document the intermediate branch, noting that it's being used as a puddle-jump. Should you change it later, you won't inadvertently alter its use by the other branch.

Each of the 65x branch instructions is based on a single status bit. Some arithmetic conditions, however, are based on more than one flag being changed. There are no branch instructions available for the relations of *unsigned greater than* and *unsigned less than or equal to*; these relations can only be determined by examining more than one flag bit. There are also no branch instructions available for *signed* comparisons, other than *equal* and *not equal*. How to synthesize these operations is described in the following chapter.

Unconditional Branching

The 65C02 introduced the **BRA** branch always (or unconditional branch) instruction, to the relief of 6502 programmers; they had found that a good percentage of the jump instructions coded were for short distances within the range of a branch instruction.

Having an unconditional branch available makes creating relocatable code easier. Every program must have a starting address, or origin, specified, which tells the assembler where in memory the program will be loaded. This is necessary so that the assembler will be able to generate the correct values for locations defined by labels in the source code.

Consider Fragment 8.6, the beginning of a program that specifies an origin of $2000. In order to make patching certain variables easier, they have been located right at the beginning of the program. When this program is assembled, location $2000 holds a jump instruction, and the assembler gives its operand the value of the location of **BEGCODE**, that is, $2005. If this program were then loaded at $2200, instead of $2000 as was "promised" by the **ORG** directive, it would fail because the very first instruction executed, at $2200, would be the jump to $2005. Since the program has now been loaded at $2200, the contents of $2005 are no longer as expected, and the program is in deep trouble.

By substituting an unconditional branch instruction for the jump, as in Fragment 8.7, the operand of the branch is now a relative displacement (the value two), and the branch instruction will cause two to be added to the current value of the program counter, whatever it may be. The result is that execution continues at **BEGCODE**, the same relative location the jump instruction transferred control to in the fixed-position version.

The code is now one byte shorter. Most importantly, though, this sec-

```
0000                ORG     $2000
0000        MAIN    START
0000 4C0500         JMP     BEGCODE       jump around data to beginning code
0003 77     DATA1   DC      H'77'
0004 88     DATA2   DC      H'88'
0005        BEGCODE ANOP
0005                .
0005                .
0005                .
```

Fragment 8.6.

tion of the program is now position-independent. If executed at $2000, the branch is located at $2000; the program counter value before the branch's operand is added is $2002; the result of the addition is $2004, the location of **BEGCODE**. Load and execute the program instead at $2200, and the branch is located at $2200; the program counter value before the branch operand is added is $2202; the result of the addition is $2204, which is the new location of **BEGCODE**.

```
0000                ORG     $2000
0000        MAIN    START
0000 8002           BRA     BEGCODE       branch around data to beginning code
0002 77     DATA1   DC      H'77'
0003 88     DATA2   DC      H'88'
0004 AD0200 BEGCODE LDA     DATA1
0007                .
0007                .
0007                .
0007
```

Fragment 8.7.

Because the operand of a branch instruction is always relative to the program counter, its effective address can only be formed by using the program counter. Programs that use branches rather than jumps may be located anywhere in memory.

6502 programmers in need of relocatability get around the lack of an unconditional branch instruction by using the technique described earlier of setting a flag to a known value prior to executing a branch-on-that-condition instruction.

Even with the unconditional branch instruction, however, relocatability can still be a problem if the need for branching extends beyond the limits imposed by its eight-bit operand. There is some help available on the 6502 and 65C02 in the form of the absolute indirect jump, which can be loaded with a target that is calculated at run time.

The 65802 and 65816 introduce the **BRL** unconditional branch long instruction. This is the only 65x branch instruction which does not take an eight-bit operand: its operand, being sixteen bits, lets it specify a target anywhere within the current 64K program bank. It is coded like any other branch, except that the target label can be outside the range of the other branches. Obviously, a two-byte displacement is generated by the assembler, making this branch a three-byte instruction. If the effective address that results when the sixteen-bit displacement is added to the current program counter would extend beyond the 64K limit of the current program bank, then it **wraps around** to remain within the current program bank.

The **BRL** instruction can replace entirely the absolute **JMP** instruction in a relocatable program; the price is an extra execution cycle per branch.

9 | Built-In Arithmetic Functions

With this chapter you make your first approach to the heart of the beast: the computer as automated calculator. Although their applications cover a broad range of functions, computers are generally associated first and foremost with their prodigious calculating abilities. Not without reason, for even in character-oriented applications such as word processing, the computer is constantly calculating. At the level of the processor itself, everything from instruction decoding to effective address generation is permeated by arithmetic or arithmetic-like operations. At the software implementation level, the program is constantly calculating horizontal and vertical cursor location, buffer pointer locations, indents, page numbers, and more.

But unlike dedicated machines, such as desk-top or pocket calculators, which are *merely* calculators, a computer is a flexible and generalized system which can be programmed and reprogrammed to perform an unlimited variety of functions. One of the keys to this ability lies in the computer's ability to implement control structures, such as loops, and to perform comparisons and select an action based on the result. Because this chapter introduces comparison, the elements necessary to demonstrate these features are complete. The other key element, the ability to branch on condition, was presented in the previous chapter. This chapter therefore contains the first examples of these control structures, as they are implemented on the 65x processors.

Armed with the material presented in Chapter 1 about positional notation as it applies to the binary and hexadecimal number systems, as well as the facts concerning two's-complement binary numbers and binary arithmetic, you should possess the background required to study the arithmetic instructions available on the 65x series of processors.

Consistent with the simple design approach of the 65x family, only elementary arithmetic functions are provided, as listed in Table 9.1, leaving the rest to be synthesized in software. There are, for example, no built-in integer multiply or divide. More advanced examples presented in later chapters will show how to synthesize these more complex operations.

Table 9.1. Arithmetic Instructions.

Mnemonic	Available on: 6502	65C02	65802/816	Description
Increment Instructions:				
DEC	x	x	x	decrement
DEX	x	x	x	decrement index register X
DEY	x	x	x	decrement index register Y
INC	x	x	x	increment
INX	x	x	x	increment index register X
INY	x	x	x	increment index register Y
Arithmetic Instructions:				
ADC	x	x	x	add with carry
SBC	x	x	x	subtract with borrow
Compare with Memory Instructions:				
CMP	x	x	x	compare accumulator
CPX	x	x	x	compare index register X
CPY	x	x	x	compare index register Y

Increment and Decrement

The simplest of the 65x arithmetic instructions are **increment** and **decrement**. In the case of the 65x processors, all of the increment and decrement operations add or subtract **one** to a number. (Some other processors allow you to increment or decrement by one, two, or more.)

There are several reasons for having special instructions to add or subtract one to a number, but the most general explanation says it all: the number one tends to be, by far, the most frequently added number in virtually any computer application. One reason for this is that **indexing** is used so frequently to access multi-byte data structures, such as address tables, character strings, multiple-precision numbers, and most forms of record structures. Since the items in a great percentage of such data structures are byte or double-byte wide, the index counter **step value** (the number of bytes from one array item to the next) is usually one or two. The 65x processors, in particular, have many addressing modes that feature indexing; that is, they use a value in one of the index registers as part of the effective address.

All 65x processors have four instructions to increment and decrement the index registers: **INX, INY, DEX,** and **DEY.** They are single-byte implied operand instructions and either add one to, or subtract one from, the X or Y register. They execute quite quickly—in two cycles—because they access no memory and affect only a single register.

9 Built-In Arithmetic Functions

All 65x processors also have a set of instructions for incrementing and decrementing memory, the **INC** and **DEC** instructions, which operate similarly. They too are unary operations, the operand being the data stored at the effective address specified in the operand field of the instruction. There are several addressing modes available to these two instructions. Note that, unlike the register increment and decrement instructions, the **INC** and **DEC** instructions are among the slowest-executing 65x instructions. That is because they are **Read-Modify-Write** operations: the number to be incremented or decremented must first be fetched from memory; then it is operated upon within the processor; and, finally, the modified value is written back to memory. Compare this with some of the more typical operations, where the result is left in the accumulator. Although read-modify-write instructions require many cycles to execute, each is much more efficient, both byte- and cycle-wise, than the three instructions it replaces—load, modify, and store.

In Chapter 6, you saw how the load operations affected the **n** and **z** flags depending on whether the loaded number was negative (that is, had its high bit set), or was zero. The 65x arithmetic functions, including the increment and decrement operations, also set the **n** and **z** status flags to reflect the **result** of the operation.

In Fragment 9.1, one is added to the value in the Y register, $7FFF. The result is $8000, which, since the high-order bit is turned on, may be interpreted as a negative two's-complement number. Therefore the **n** flag is set.

```
0000 C230            REP     #$30            16-bit registers
0002                 LONGA   ON
0002                 LONGI   ON
0002 A0FF7F          LDY     #$7FFF          $7FFF is a positive number
0005 C8              INY                     $8000 is a negative number;n=1
```

Fragment 9.1.

In a similar example, Fragment 9.2, the Y register is loaded with the highest possible value which can be represented in sixteen bits (all bits turned on).

```
0000 C230            REP     #$30
0002                 LONGA   ON
0002                 LONGI   ON
0002 A0FFFF          LDY     #$FFFF
0005 C8              INY                     z = 1 in status register
```

Fragment 9.2.

If one is added to the unsigned value $FFFF, the result is $10000:

```
                          1   one to be added
        + 1111 1111 1111 1111   binary equivalent of $FFFF
          1 0000 0000 0000 0000   result is $10000
```

Since there are no longer any extra bits available in the sixteen-bit register, however, the low order sixteen bits of the number in Y (that is, zero) does not represent the actual result. As you will see later, addition and subtraction instructions use the **carry flag** to reflect a carry out of the register, indicating that a number larger than can be represented using the current word size (sixteen bits in the above example) has been generated. While increment and decrement instructions do not affect the carry, a zero result in the Y register after an increment (indicated by the z status flag being set) shows that a carry has been generated, even though the carry flag itself does not indicate this.

A classic example of this usage is found in Fragment 9.3, which shows the technique commonly used on the eight-bit 6502 and 65C02 to increment a sixteen-bit value in memory. Note the branch-on-condition instruction, **BNE**, which was introduced in the previous chapter, is being used to indicate if any overflow from the low byte requires the high byte to be incremented, too. As long as the value stored at the direct page location **ABC** is non-zero following the increment operation, processing continues at the location **SKIP**. If **ABC** is zero as a result of the increment operation, a page boundary has been crossed, and the high order byte of the value must be incremented as well. If the high-order byte were not incremented, the sixteen-bit value would "wrap around" within the low byte.

```
0000 EE0080    TOP      INC    ABC       increment low byte
0003 D0FB               BNE    SKIP      if no overflow, done
0005 EE0180             INC    ABC+1     if overflow: increment high byte, too
0008           SKIP     .                continue
0008                    .
0008                    .
0008                    .
```

Fragment 9.3.

Such use of the z flag to detect carry (or borrow) is peculiar to the increment and decrement operations: if you could increment or decrement by values other than one, this technique would not work consistently, since it would be possible to cross the "threshold" (zero) without actually "landing" on it (you might, for example, go from $FFFF to $0001 if the step value was 2).

A zero result following a decrement operation, on the other hand, indicates that the *next* decrement operation will cause a borrow to be generated. In Fragment 9.4, the Y register is loaded with one, and then one is subtracted from it by the DEY instruction. The result is clearly zero; however, if Y is decremented again, $FFFF will result. If you are treating the number as a signed, two's-complement number, this is just fine, as $FFFF is equivalent to a sixteen-bit, negative one. But if it is an unsigned number, a borrow exists.

```
0000 C230        REP      #$30       16-bit registers
0002             LONGA    ON
0002             LONGI    ON
0002 A00100      LDY      #$0001     z = 0 in the status register
0005 88          DEY                 z = 1 in the status register
```

Fragment 9.4.

Together with the branch-on-condition instructions introduced in the previous chapter, you can now efficiently implement one of the most commonly used control structures in computer programming, the program loop.

A rudimentary loop would be a zero-fill loop; that is, a piece of code to fill a range of memory with zeroes. Suppose, as in Listing 9.1, the memory area from $4000 to $5FFF was to be zeroed (for example, to clear hi-res page two graphics memory in the Apple //). By loading an index register with the size of the area to be cleared, the memory can be easily accessed by indexing from an absolute base of $4000.

The two lines at **BASE** and **COUNT** assign symbolic names to the starting address and length of the fill area. The **REP** instruction puts the processor into the long index/long accumulator mode. The long index allows the range of memory being zeroed to be greater than 256 bytes; the long accumulator provides for faster zeroing of memory, by clearing two bytes with a single instruction.

The loop is initialized by loading the X register with the value **COUNT**, which is the number of bytes to be zeroed. The assembler is instructed to subtract two from the total to allow for the fact that the array starts at zero, rather than one, and for the fact that two bytes are cleared at a time.

```
0001 0000
0002 0000                      KEEP    KL.9.1
0003 0000                      65816   ON
0004 0000          L91         START
0005 0000
0006 0000 18                   CLC
0007 0001 FB                   XCE
0008 0002
0009 0002
0010 0002          BASE    GEQU    $4000       starting address of fill area
0011 0002          COUNT   GEQU    $2000       number of bytes to clear
0012 0002
0013 0002 C230             REP     #$30        turn 16-bit modes on
0014 0004
0015 0004                  LONGA   ON
0016 0004                  LONGI   ON
0017 0004
0018 0004 A2FE1F            LDX    #COUNT-2    get the number of bytes to clear into X
0019 0007          ;                              minus two
0020 0007
0021 0007 9E0040  LOOP       STZ    BASE,X      store zero to memory
0022 000A CA                 DEX
0023 000B CA                 DEX
0024 000C 10F9               BPL    LOOP        repeat loop again if not done
0025 000E
0026 000E 38     DONE        SEC
0027 000F FB                 XCE
0028 0010 60                 RTS
0029 0011
0030 0011                    END
```

Listing 9.1.

The loop itself is then entered for the first time, and the **STZ** instruction is used to clear the memory location formed by adding the index register to the constant **BASE**. Next come two decrement instructions; two are needed because the **STZ** instruction stored a double-byte zero. By starting at the end of the memory range and indexing down, it is possible to use a single register for both address generation and loop control. A simple comparison, checking to see that the index register is still positive, is all that is needed to control the loop.

Another concrete example of a program loop is provided in Listing 9.2, which toggles the built-in speaker in an Apple // computer with increasing frequency, resulting in a tone of increasing pitch. It features an outer driving loop (**TOP**), an inner loop that produces a tone of a

```
0001  0000                    KEEP    KL.9.2
0002  0000                    65816   ON
0003  0000
0004  0000            L92     START
0005  0000 18                 CLC
0006  0001 FB                 XCE
0007  0002 E230               SEP     #$30            set 8-bit modes
0008  0004                    LONGA   OFF
0009  0004                    LONGI   OFF
0010  0004            BELL    GEQU    $C030
0011  0004
0012  0004 A200               LDX     #0
0013  0006 8A                 TXA                     X, now in A, initializes the delay loop
0014  0007
0015  0007 9B      TOP        TXY                     initialize X & Y to 0
0016  0008
0017  0008 8D30C0  LOOP       STA     BELL            accessing the tone generator pulses it
0018  000B
0019  000B 8A                 TXA                     dimininishing delay loop
0020  000C
0021  000C 3A      DELAY      DEC     A
0022  000D D0FD               BNE     DELAY           loop 256 times before continuing
0023  000F
0024  000F
0025  000F 88                 DEY
0026  0010 D0F6               BNE     LOOP
0027  0012
0028  0012 CA                 DEX
0029  0013 D0F2               BNE     TOP
0030  0015
0031  0015 38                 SEC
0032  0016 FB                 XCE
0033  0017 60                 RTS
0034  0018                    END
```

Listing 9.2.

given pitch, and an inner-most delay loop. The pitch of the tone can be varied by using different initial values for the loop indices.

Addition and Subtraction: Unsigned Arithmetic

The 65x processors have only two dedicated general purpose arithmetic instructions: add with carry, **ADC**, and subtract with carry, **SBC**. As will be seen later, it is possible to synthesize all other arithmetic functions using these and other 65x instructions.

As the names of these instructions indicate, the carry flag from the status register is involved with the two operations. The role of the carry flag is to "link" the individual additions and subtractions that make up multiple-precision arithmetic operations. The earlier example of the 6502 sixteen-bit increment was a special case of the multiple-precision arithmetic technique used on the 65x processors, the link provided in that case by the **BNE** instruction.

Consider the addition of two decimal numbers, 56 and 72. You begin your calculation by adding six to two. If you are working the calculation out on paper, you place the result, eight, in the right-most column, the one's place:

```
  56
  72
  ──
   8
```

Next you add the ten's column; 5 plus 7 equals 12. The two is placed in the tens place of the sum, and the one is a **carry** into the 100's place. Normally, since you have plenty of room on your worksheet, you simply pencil in the one to the left of the two, and you have the answer.

The situation within the processor when it adds two numbers is basically similar, but with a few differences. First, the numbers added and subtracted in a 65x processor are normally binary numbers (although there is also a special on-the-fly decimal adjust mode for adding and subtracting numbers in binary-coded decimal format). Just as you began adding, the processor starts in the right-most column, or one's place, and continues adding columns to the left. The augend (the number added to) is always in the accumulator; the location of the addend is specified in the operand field of the instruction. Since a binary digit can only be a zero or a one, the addition of 2 ones results in a zero in the current column and a carry into the next column. This process of addition continues until the highest bit of the accumulator has been added (the highest bit being either bit seven or, alternatively on the 65802/65816, bit fifteen, if the **m** flag is cleared). But suppose that $82 is added to $AB in the eight-bit accumulator:

```
    1     1    carry digits from previous addition to right
    1000 0010  binary equivalent of $82
  + 1010 1011  binary equivalent of $AB
    ─────────
    0010 1101
```

If you begin by adding the binary digits from the right and marking the sum in the proper column, and then placing any carry that results at the top of the next column to the left, you will find that a carry results when the ones in column seven are added together. However, since the accumulator is only eight bits wide, there is no place to store this value; the result has "overflowed" the space allocated to it. In this case, the final carry is stored in the carry flag after the operation. If there had been no carry, the carry flag would be reset to zero.

The automatic generation of a carry flag at the end of an addition is complemented by a second feature of this instruction that is executed at the beginning of the instruction: the **ADC** instruction itself always adds the previously generated one-bit carry flag value with the right-most column of binary digits. Therefore, it is always necessary to explicitly clear the carry flag before adding two numbers together, unless the numbers being added are succeeding words of a multi-word arithmetic operation. By adding in a previous value held in the carry flag, and storing a resulting carry there, it is possible to chain together several limited-precision (each only eight or sixteen bits) arithmetic operations.

First, consider how you would represent an unsigned binary number greater than $FFFF (decimal 65,536)—that is, one that cannot be stored in a single double-byte cell. Suppose the number is $023A8EF1. This would simply be stored in memory in four successive bytes, from low to high order, as follows, beginning at $1000:

```
1000 - F1
1001 - 8E
1002 - 3A
1003 - 02
```

Since the number is greater than the largest available word size of the processor (double byte), any arithmetic operations performed on this number will have to be treated as multiple-precision operations, where only one part of a number is added to the corresponding part of another number at a time. As each part is added, the intermediate result is stored; and then the next part is added, and so on, until all of the parts of the number have been added.

Multiple-precision operations always proceed from low-order part to high-order part because the carry is generated from low to high, as seen in our original addition of decimal 56 to 72.

Listing 9.3 is an assembly language example of the addition of multiple-precision numbers $023A8EF1 to $0000A2C1. This example begins by setting the accumulator word size to sixteen bits, which lets you process half of the four-byte addition in a single operation. The carry flag is then cleared because there must be no initial carry when an add operation begins. The two bytes stored at **BIGNUM** and **BIGNUM + 1** are loaded into the double-byte accumulator. Note that the **DC I4** assembler directive automatically stores the four-byte integer constant value in memory in low-to-high order. The **ADC** instruction is then executed, adding $8EF1 to $A2C1.

```
0001 0000                   KEEP  KL.9.3
0002 0000                   65816 ON
0003 0000
0004 0000         L93       START
0005 0000 18               CLC
0006 0001 FB               XCE
0007 0002 C220             REP   #$20           use sixteen-bit accumulator
0008 0004                   LONGA ON
0009 0004 18               CLC                  make sure carry is clear to start
0010 0005 AD1A00           LDA   BIGNUM         load low-order two bytes
0011 0008 6D1E00           ADC   NEXTNUM        add to low-order two bytes of NEXTNUM
0012 000B 8D2200           STA   RESULT         save low-order result
0013 000E AD1C00           LDA   BIGNUM+2       now load high-order two bytes
0014 0011 6D2000           ADC   NEXTNUM+2      add to high order of NEXTNUM with carry
0015 0014 8D2400           STA   RESULT+2       save result
0016 0017 38               SEC
0017 0018 FB               XCE
0018 0019 60               RTS
0019 001A F18E3A02  BIGNUM  DC    I4'$023A8EF1'
0020 001E C1A20000  NEXTNUM DC    I4'$0000A2C1'
0021 0022 00000000  RESULT  DS    4
0022 0026                   END
```

Listing 9.3.

Examine the equivalent binary addition:

```
1   1 11 1       1   carry from addition of column to right
 1000 1110 1111 0001 $8EF1
 1010 0010 1100 0001 $A2C1
 0011 0001 1011 0010 $31B2
```

The sixteen-bit result found in the accumulator after the ADC is executed is $31B2; however, this is clearly incorrect. The correct answer, $131B2, requires seventeen bits to represent it, so an additional result of the ADC operation in this case is that the carry flag in the status register is set. Meanwhile, since the value in the accumulator consists of the correct low-order sixteen bits, the accumulator is stored at RESULT and RESULT + 1.

With the partial sum of the last operation saved, the high-order sixteen bits of BIGNUM are loaded (from BIGNUM + 2) into the accumulator, followed immediately by the ADC NEXTNUM + 2 instruction, which is not preceded by CLC this time. For all but the first addition of a multiple-precision operation, the carry flag is not cleared; rather, the setting of the carry flag from the previous addition is allowed to be

9 Built-In Arithmetic Functions

automatically added into the next addition. You will note in the present example that the high-order sixteen bits of **NEXTNUM** are zero; it almost seems unnecessary to add them. At the same time, remember that there was a carry left over from the first addition; when the **ADC NEXTNUM + 2** instruction is executed, this carry is automatically added in; that is, the resulting value in the accumulator is equal to the carry flag (1) plus the original value in the accumulator ($023A) plus the value at the address **NEXTNUM + 2** ($0000), or $023B. This is then stored in the high-order bytes of **RESULT**, which leaves the complete, correct value stored in locations **RESULT** through **RESULT + 3** in low-high order:

```
RESULT    - B2
RESULT+1  - 31
RESULT+2  - 3B
RESULT+3  - 02
```

Reading from high to low, the sum is $023B31B2.

This type of multiple precision addition is required constantly on the eight-bit 6502 and 65C02 processors in order to manipulate addresses, which are sixteen-bit quantities. Since the 65816 and 65802 provide sixteen-bit arithmetic operations when the **m** flag is cleared, this burden is greatly reduced. If you wish, however, to manipulate long addresses on the 65816, that is, 24-bit addresses, you will similarly have to resort to multiple precision. Otherwise, it is likely that multiple-precision arithmetic generally will only be required on the 65802 or 65816 in math routines to perform number-crunching on user data, rather than for internal address manipulation.

An interesting footnote to the multiple-precision arithmetic comparison between the 6502 and the 65816 is to observe that since the 6502 only has an eight-bit adder, even those instructions that automatically perform sixteen-bit arithmetic (such as branch calculation and effective address generation) require an additional cycle to perform the addition of the high-order byte of the address. The presence of a sixteen-bit adder within the 65802 and 65816 explains how it is able to shave cycles off certain operations while in native mode, such as branching across page boundaries, where an eight-bit quantity is added to a sixteen-bit value. On the 6502, if a page boundary isn't crossed, the high byte of the sixteen-bit operand is used as-is; if a carry is generated by adding the two low bytes, a second eight-bit add must be performed, requiring an additional machine cycle. On the 65816, the addition is treated as a single operation.

Subtraction on the 65x processors is analogous to addition, with the borrow serving a similar role in handling multiple-precision subtractions. On the 65x processors, the carry flag is also used to store a subtraction's borrow. In the case of the addition operation, a one stored in the carry flag indicates that a carry exists, and the value in the carry flag will be added into the next add operation. The borrow stored in the carry flag is actually an inverted borrow: that is, the carry flag cleared to zero means that there is a borrow, while carry set means that there is none. Thus prior to beginning a subtraction, the carry flag should be *set* so that no borrow is subtracted by the **SBC** instruction.

Although you can simply accept this rule at face value, the explanation is interesting. The simplest way to understand the inverted borrow of the 65x series is to realize that, like most computers, a 65x processor has no separate subtraction circuits as such; all it has is an adder, which serves for both addition and subtraction. Obviously, addition of a negative number is the same as subtraction of a positive. To subtract a number, then, the value which is being subtracted is inverted, yielding a one's-complement negative number. This is then added to the other value and, as is usual with addition on the 65x machines, the carry is added in as well.

Since the add operation automatically adds in the carry, if the carry is set prior to subtraction, this simply converts the inverted value to two's complement form. (Remember, two's complement is formed by inverting a number and adding one; in this case the added one is the carry flag.) If, on the other hand, the carry was clear, this has the effect of subtracting one by creating a two's-complement number which is one greater than if the carry had been present. (Assuming a negative number is being formed, remember that the more negative a number is, the greater its value as an unsigned number, for example, $FFFF = -1, $8000 = -32767.) Thus, if a borrow exists, a value which is more negative by one is created, which is added to the other operand, effectively subtracting a carry.

Comparison

The comparison operation—is **VALUE1** equal to **VALUE2**, for example—is implemented on the 65x, as on most processors, as an implied subtraction. In order to compare **VALUE1** to **VALUE2**, one of the values is subtracted from the other. Clearly, if the result is zero, then the numbers are equal.

This kind of comparison can be made using the instructions you already know, as Fragment 9.5 illustrates. In this fragment, you can see that the branch to **TRUE** will be taken, and the **INC VAL** instruction never executed, because $1234 minus $1234 equals zero. Since the results of subtractions condition the z flag, the **BEQ** instruction (which literally means "branch if result equal to zero"), in this case, means "branch if the compared values are equal."

```
0000 C230              REP    #$30          16-bit registers
0002                   LONGA  ON
0002                   LONGI  ON
0002
0002 9C1200            STZ    VAL           clear double-byte at VAL
0005 A93412            LDA    #$1234        get one value
0008 38                SEC
0009 E93412            SBC    #$1234        subtract another
000C F003              BEQ    TRUE          if they are the same, leave VAL zero
000E EE1200            INC    VAL           if they are different, set VAL
0011 60         TRUE   RTS
0012 0000       VAL    DS     2
```

Fragment 9.5.

There are two undesirable aspects of this technique, however, if comparison is all that is desired rather than actual subtraction. First, because the 65x subtraction instruction expects the carry flag to be set for single precision subtractions, the **SEC** instruction must be executed before each comparison using **SBC**. Second, it is not always desirable to have the original value in the accumulator lost when the result of the subtraction is stored there.

Because comparison is such a common programming operation, there is a separate compare instruction, **CMP**. Compare subtracts the value specified in the operand field of the instruction from the value in the accumulator *without* storing the result; the original accumulator value remains intact. Status flags normally affected by a subtraction—z, n, and c—are set to reflect the result of the subtraction just performed. Additionally, the carry flag is automatically set before the instruction is executed, as it should be for a single-precision subtraction. (Unlike the **ADC** and **SBC** instructions, **CMP** does not set the overflow flag, complicating signed comparisons somewhat, a problem which will be covered later in this chapter.)

Given the flags that are set by the **CMP** instruction, and the set of branch-on-condition instructions, the relations shown in Table 9.2 can be easily tested for. A represents the value in the accumulator, DATA is the value specified in the operand field of the instruction, and Bxx is the branch-on-condition instruction that causes a branch to be taken (to the code labelled TRUE) if the indicated relationship is true after a comparison.

Because the action taken after a comparison by the **BCC** and **BCS** is not immediately obvious from their mnemonic names, the recommended assembler syntax standard allows the alternate mnemonics

Table 9.2. Equalities.

BEQ	TRUE	branch if A = DATA
BNE	TRUE	branch if A < > DATA
BCC	TRUE	branch if A < DATA
BCS	TRUE	branch if A > = DATA

BLT, for "branch on less than," and **BGE**, for "branch if greater or equal," respectively, which generate the identical object code.

Other comparisons can be synthesized using combinations of branch-on-condition instructions. Fragment 9.6 shows how the operation "branch on greater than" can be synthesized.

```
0000 F002            BEQ   SKIP         branch to TRUE if
0002 B0FC            BGE   TRUE           A > DATA
0004        SKIP     ANOP
```

Fragment 9.6.

Fragment 9.7 shows "branch on less or equal."

```
0000 F0FE            BEQ   TRUE         branch if
0002 90FC            BCC   TRUE           A <= DATA
```

Fragment 9.7.

Listing 9.4 features the use of the compare instruction to count the number of elements in a list which are less than, equal to, and greater than a given value. While of little utility by itself, this type of comparison operation is just a few steps away from a simple sort routine. The value the list will be compared against is assumed to be stored in memory locations $88.89, which are given the symbolic name **VALUE** in the example. The list, called **TABLE**, uses the **DC I** directive, which stores each number as a sixteen-bit integer.

```
0001 0000                  KEEP  KL.9.4
0002 0000                        65816 ON
0003 0000
0004 0000           L94    START
0005 0000
0006 0000
0007 0000           LESS   GEQU  $82      counter
```

Listing 9.4. *Continued on next page*

```
0008  0000                  SAME    GEQU    $84         counter
0009  0000                  MORE    GEQU    $86         counter
0010  0000
0011  0000                  VALUE   GEQU    $88         value for list to be compared against
0012  0000
0013  0000 18                       CLC
0014  0001 FB                       XCE
0015  0002 C230                     REP     #$30        turn on both 16-bit modes
0016  0004
0017  0004                          LONGA ON
0018  0004                          LONGI ON
0019  0004
0020  0004
0021  0004 6482                     STZ     LESS        zero the counters
0022  0006 6484                     STZ     SAME
0023  0008 6486                     STZ     MORE
0024  000A
0025  000A
0026  000A A588                     LDA     VALUE       get the comparison value
0027  000C A01A00                   LDY     #LAST-TABLE get a counter to # of list items
0028  000F
0029  000F
0030  000F D92700          TOP      CMP     TABLE,Y     compare accum to first list item
0031  0012 F006                     BEQ     ISEQ
0032  0014 9008                     BLT     ISMORE
0033  0016 E682                     INC     LESS        VALUE is less, bump LESS
0034  0018 8006                     BRA     LOOP
0035  001A E684           ISEQ      INC     SAME        value is same; bump SAME
0036  001C 8002                     BRA     LOOP
0037  001E E686           ISMORE    INC     MORE        VALUE is greater; bump MORE
0038  0020
0039  0020 88             LOOP      DEY                 move pointer to next list item
0040  0021 88                       DEY
0041  0022 10EB                     BPL     TOP         continue if there are any list items
0042  0024              ;                               left to compare
0043  0024
0044  0024 38                       SEC
0045  0025 FB                       XCE
0046  0026 60                       RTS
0047  0027
0048  0027 0C000900       TABLE     DC      I'12,9,302,956,123,1234,98'
0049  0035 04116300                 DC      I'4356,99,11,40000,23145,562'
0050  0041 0F27           LAST      DC      I'9999'
0051  0043
0052  0043                          END
```

Listing 9.4 (Cont.).

After setting the mode to sixteen-bit word/index size, the locations that will hold the number of occurrences of each of the three possible relationships are zeroed. The length of the list is loaded into the Y register. The accumulator is loaded with the comparison value.

The loop itself is entered, with a comparison to the first item in the list; in this and each succeeding case, control is transferred to counter-incrementing code depending on the relationship that exists. Note that equality and less-than are tested first, and greater-than is assumed if control falls through. This is necessary since there is no branch on greater-than (only branch on greater-than-or-equal). Following the incrementing of the selected relation-counter, control passes either via an unconditional branch, or by falling through, to the loop-control code, which decrements Y twice (since double-byte integers are being compared). Control resumes at the top of the loop unless all of the elements have been compared, at which point Y is negative, and the routine ends.

In addition to comparing the accumulator with memory, there are instructions for comparing the values in the two index registers with memory, **CPX** and **CPY**. These instructions come in especially handy when it is not convenient or possible to decrement an index to zero—if instead you must increment or decrement it until a particular value is reached. The appropriate compare index register instruction is inserted before the branch-on-condition instruction either loops or breaks out of the loop. Fragment 9.8 shows a loop that continues until the value in X reaches $A0.

```
0000         LOOP    ANOP              work to be done in the loop goes here
0000                 .
0000                 .
0000                 .
0000 E8              INX
0001 E0A000          CPX     #$A0
0004 D0FA            BNE     LOOP      continue incrementing X until
0006                 ANOP              X = $A0, so loop ended
```

Fragment 9.8.

Signed Arithmetic

The examples so far have dealt with unsigned arithmetic—that is, addition and subtraction of binary numbers of the same sign. What about signed numbers?

As you saw in Chapter 1, signed numbers can be represented using **two's-complement** notation. The two's complement of a number is formed by inverting it (one bits become zeroes, zeroes become ones) and then adding one. For example, a negative one is represented by forming the two's complement of one:

```
0000 0000 0000 0001   —binary one in sixteen-bit word
1111 1111 1111 1110   —complement word
0000 0000 0000 0001   —add one to complement
1111 1111 1111 1111   —result is two's-complement
                       representation of minus one
```

Minus one is therefore equivalent to a hexadecimal $FFFF. But as far as the processor is concerned, the unsigned value $FFFF (65,535 decimal) and the signed value minus-one are equivalent. They both amount to the same stream of bits stored in a register. It's the interpretation of them given by the programmer which is significant—an interpretation that must be consistently applied across each of the steps that perform a multi-step function.

Consider all of the possible signed and unsigned numbers that can be represented using a sixteen-bit register. The two's complement of $0002 is $FFFE—as the positive numbers increase, the two's-complement (negative) numbers decrease (in the unsigned sense). Increasing the positive value to $7FFF (%0111 1111 1111 1111), the two's complement is $8001 (%1000 0000 0000 0001); except for $8000, all of the possible values have been used to represent the respective positive and negative numbers between $0001 and $7FFF.

Since their point of intersection, $8000, determines the maximum range of a signed number, the high-order bit (bit fifteen) will always be one if the number is negative, and zero if the number is positive. Thus the range of possible binary values (%0000 0000 0000 0000 through %1111 1111 1111 1111, or $0000 .. $FFFF), using two's-complement form, is divided evenly between representations of positive numbers, and representations of the corresponding range of negative numbers. Since $8000 is also negative, there seems to be one more possible negative number than positive; for the purposes here, however, zero is considered positive.

The high-order bit is therefore referred to as the **sign bit.** On the 6502, with its eight-bit word size (or the 65816 in an eight-bit register mode), bit seven is the sign bit. With sixteen-bit registers, bit fifteen is the sign bit. The n or negative flag in the status register reflects whether or not the high-order bit of a given register is set or clear after execution of operations which affect that register, allowing easy determination of the sign of a signed number by using either the **BPL** (branch on plus) or **BMI** (branch if minus) instructions introduced in the last chapter.

Using the high-order bit as the sign bit sacrifices the carry flag's normal (unsigned) function. If the high-order bit is used to represent the sign, then the addition or subtraction of the sign bits (plus a possible carry out of the next-to-highest bit) results in a sign bit that may be invalid and that will erroneously affect the carry flag.

To deal with this situation, the status register provides another flag bit, the v or **overflow** flag, which is set or reset as the result of the **ADC** and **SBC** operations. The overflow bit indicates whether a signed result is too large (or too small) to be represented in the precision available, just as the carry flag does for unsigned arithmetic.

Since the high-order bit is used to store the sign, the penultimate bit (the next-highest bit) is the high-order bit as far as magnitude representation is concerned. If you knew if there was a carry out of this bit, it would obviously be helpful in determining overflow or underflow.

However, the overflow flag is not simply the carry out of bit six (if $m = 1$ for eight-bit mode) or bit fourteen (if $m = 0$ for sixteen-bit mode). Signed generation of the v flag is not as straightforward as unsigned generation of the carry flag. It is not automatically true that if there is a carry out of the penultimate bits that overflow has occurred, because it could also mean that the sign has changed. This is because of the circular or wraparound nature of two's-complement representation.

Consider Fragment 9.9. Decimal values with sign prefixes are used for emphasis (and convenience) as the immediate operands in the source program; their hexadecimal values appear in the left-hand column which interlists the generated object code (opcode first, low byte, high byte). You can see that -10 is equivalent to $FFF6 hexadecimal, while 20 is hexadecimal $0014. Examine this addition operation in binary:

```
0000 C230        REP     #$30         16-bit registers
0002             LONGA   ON
0002             LONGI   ON
0002
0002 A9F6FF      LDA     #-10
0005 18          CLC
0006 691400      ADC     #20
```

Fragment 9.9.

Two things should become clear: that the magnitude of the result (10 decimal) is such that it will easily fit within the number of bits available for its representation, and that there is a carry out of bit fourteen:

```
  1 1111 1111 111  1      carry from previous bit
    1111 1111 1111 0110   -10 decimal
    0000 0000 0001 0100   +20 decimal
  ─────────────────────
  1 0000 0000 0000 1010   result is +10 decimal
```

In this case, the overflow flag is not set, because the carry out of the penultimate bit indicates **wraparound** rather than overflow (or underflow). Whenever the two operands are of different signs, a carry out of the next-to-highest bit indicates wraparound; the addition of a positive and a negative number (or *vice versa*) can never result in a number too large (try it), but it may result in wraparound.

Conversely, overflow exists in the addition of two negative numbers if **no** carry results from the addition of the next-to-highest (penultimate) bits. If two negative numbers are added without overflow, they will always wrap around, resulting in a carry out of the next-to-highest bit. When wraparound has occurred, the sign bit is set due to the carry out of the penultimate bit. In the case of two negative numbers being added (which always produces a negative result), this setting of the sign bit results in the correct sign. In the case of the addition of two positive numbers, wraparound never occurs, so a carry out of the penultimate bit always means that the overflow flag will be set.

These rules likewise apply for subtraction; however, you must consider that subtraction is really an addition with the sign of the addend inverted, and apply them in this sense.

In order for the processor to determine the correct overflow flag value, it exclusive-or's the carry out of the penultimate bit with the carry out of the high-order bit (the value that winds up in the carry flag), and sets or resets the overflow according to the result. By taking the exclusive-or of these two values, the overflow flag is set according to the rules above.

Consider the possible results:

- *If both values are positive*, the carry will be clear; if there is no penultimate carry, the overflow flag, too, will be clear, because 0 **XOR** 0 equals 0; the value in the sign bit is zero, which is correct because a positive number plus a positive number always equals a positive number. On the other hand, if there is a penultimate carry, the sign bit will change. While there is still no final carry, overflow is set. The final carry (clear) **xor** penultimate carry (set) equals one. Whenever overflow is set, the sign bit of the result has the wrong value.
- *If the signs are different*, and there is a penultimate carry (which means wraparound in this case), there will be a final carry. But when this is exclusive-or'd with the penultimate carry, it is canceled out, resulting in overflow being cleared. If, though, there were no penultimate carry, there would be no final carry; again, 0 **XOR** 0 = 0, or overflow clear. If the sign bit is cleared by the addition of a penultimate carry and the single negative sign bit, since wraparound in this case implies the transition from a negative to a positive number, the sign (clear) is correct. If there was

no wraparound, the result is negative, and the sign bit is also correct (set).
- Finally, *if both signs are negative,* there will always be a carry out of the sign bit. A carry out of the penultimate bit means wraparound (with a correctly negative result), so carry (set) XOR penultimate carry (set) equals zero and the overflow flag is clear. If, however, there is no carry, overflow (or rather, underflow) has occurred, and the overflow is set because carry XOR no carry equals one.

The net result of this analysis is that, with the exception of overflow detection, signed arithmetic is performed in the same way as unsigned arithmetic. Multiple-precision signed arithmetic is also done in the same way as unsigned multiple-precision arithmetic; the sign of the two numbers is only significant when the high-order word is added.

When overflow is detected, it can be handled in three ways: treated as an error, and reported; ignored; or responded to by attempting to extend the precision of the result. Although this latter case is not generally practical, you must remember that, in this case, the value in the sign bit will have been inverted. Having determined the correct sign, the precision may be expanded using **sign extension**, if there is an extra byte of storage available and your arithmetic routines can work with a higher-precision variable. The method for extending the sign of a number involves the bit manipulation instructions described in the next chapter; an example of it is found there.

Signed Comparisons

The principle of signed comparisons is similar to that of unsigned comparisons: the relation of one operand to another is determined by subtracting one from the other. However, the 65x **CMP** instruction, unlike **SBC**, does not affect the v flag, so does not reflect signed overflow/underflow. Therefore, signed comparisons must be performed using the **SBC** instruction. This means that the carry flag must be set prior to the comparison (subtraction), and that the original value in the accumulator will be replaced by the difference. Although the value of the difference is not relevant to the comparison operation, the sign is. If the sign of the result (now in the accumulator) is positive (as determined according to rules outlined above for proper determination of the sign of the result of a signed operation), then the value in memory is less than the original value in the accumulator; if the sign is negative, it is greater. If, though, the result of the subtraction is zero, then the values were equal, so this should be checked for first.

The code for signed comparisons is similar to that for signed subtraction. Since a correct result need not be completely formed, however, overflow can be tolerated since the goal of the subtraction is not to generate a result that can be represented in a given precision, but only to determine the relationship of one value to another. Overflow must still be taken into account in correctly determining the sign. The value of the sign bit (the high-order bit) will be the correct sign of the result unless overflow has occurred. In that case, it is the inverted sign.

Listing 9.5 does a signed comparison of the number stored in **VAL1** with the number stored in **VAL2**, and sets **RELATION** to minus one, zero, or one, depending on whether VAL1 < VAL2, VAL1 = VAL2 or VAL1 > VAL2, respectively:

```
0001 0000                     KEEP    KL.9.5
0002 0000                     65816 ON
0003 0000
0004 0000       COMPARE START
0005 0000
0006 0000 18                  CLC
0007 0001 FB                  XCE
0008 0002 C230                REP     #$30            turn 16-bit modes on
0009 0004
0010 0004                     LONGA ON
0011 0004                     LONGI ON
0012 0004
0013 0004 9C2500              STZ     RELATION        clear result cell
0014 0007 AD2100              LDA     VAL1
0015 000A 38                  SEC
0016 000B ED2300              SBC     VAL2
0017 000E F00E                BEQ     SAME
0018 0010 7007                BVS     INVERT          if v set, invert meaning of sign
0019 0012 3007                BMI     LESS            bra if VAL1 is less than VAL2
0020 0014 EE2500   GREATER    INC     RELATION        VAL1 is greater than VAL2
0021 0017 8005               BRA     SAME
0022 0019 30F9    INVERT      BMI     GREATER         invert: bra if minus: minus=greater
0023 001B CE2500  LESS        DEC     RELATION
0024 001E 38      SAME        CLC
0025 001F FB                  XCE
0026 0020 60                  RTS
0027 0021
0028 0021 0000    VAL1        DS      2
0029 0023 0000    VAL2        DS      2
0030 0025 0000    RELATION DS  2
0031 0027
0032 0027                     END
```

Listing 9.5.

Decimal Mode

All of the examples in this chapter have dealt with binary numbers. In certain applications, however, such as numeric I/O programming, where conversion between ASCII and binary representation of decimal strings is inconvenient, and business applications, in which conversion of binary fractions to decimal fractions results in approximation errors, it is convenient to represent numbers in decimal form and, if possible, perform arithmetic operations on them directly in this form.

Like most processors, the 65x series provides a way to handle decimal representations of numbers. Unlike most processors, it does this by providing a special **decimal mode** that causes the processor to use decimal arithmetic for **ADC**, **SBC**, and **CMP** operations, with automatic "on the fly" decimal adjustment. Most other microprocessors, on the other hand, do all arithmetic the same, requiring a second "decimal adjust" operation to convert back to decimal form the binary result of arithmetic performed on decimal numbers. As you remember from Chapter 1, binary-coded-decimal (BCD) digits are represented in four bits as binary values from zero to nine. Although values from $A to $F (ten to fifteen) may also be represented in four bits, these bit patterns are illegal in decimal mode. So when $03 is added to $09, the result is $12, not $0C as in binary mode.

Each four-bit field in a BCD number is a binary representation of a single decimal digit, the rightmost being the one's place, the second the ten's, and so on. Thus, the eight-bit accumulator can represent numbers in the range 0 through 99 decimal, and the sixteen-bit accumulator can represent numbers in the range 0 through 9999. Larger decimal numbers can be represented in multiple-precision, using memory variables to store the partial results and the carry flag to link the component fields of the number together, just as multiple-precision binary numbers are.

Decimal mode is set via execution of the **SED** instruction (or a **SEP** instruction with bit three set). This sets the **d** or decimal flag in the status register, causing all future additions and subtractions to be performed in decimal mode until the flag is cleared.

The default mode of the 65x processors is the binary mode with the decimal flag clear. It is important to remember that the decimal flag may accidentally be set by a wild branch, and on the NMOS 6502, it is not cleared on reset. The 65C02, 65802, and 65816 do clear the decimal flag on reset, so this is of slightly less concern. Arithmetic operations intended to be executed in binary mode, such as address calculations, can produce totally unpredictable results if they are accidentally executed in decimal mode.

Finally, although the carry flag is set correctly in the decimal mode allowing unsigned multiple-precision operations, the overflow flag is not, making signed decimal arithmetic, while possible, difficult. You must create your own sign representation and logic for handling arithmetic based on the signs of the operands. Borrowing from the binary two's-complement representation, you could represent negative numbers as those (unsigned) values which, when added to a positive number result in zero if overflow is ignored. For example, 99 would equal -1, since 1 plus 99 equals 100, or zero within a two-digit precision. 98 would be -2, and so on. The different nature of decimal representation, however, does not lend itself to signed operation quite as conveniently as does the binary two's-complement form.

10 | Logic and Bit Manipulation Operations

The logical operations found in this chapter are the very essence of computer processing; even the arithmetic functions, at the lowest level, are implemented as combinations of logic gates. Logic, or more accurately, **boolean logic**, is concerned with the determination of "true" and "false."

Computers can represent simple logical propositions and relationships as binary states: the bit-value used to represent "1" in a given computer is considered equivalent to true; the bit-value which stands for "0" is considered equivalent to false. This designation is in fact arbitrary, and the values could easily be reversed. What matters is the consistent application of the convention. Alternative terms are "set" and "reset" (or "clear"), "on" and "off," "high" and "low," "asserted" and "negated." There is a tendency to equate all of these terms; this is generally acceptable except when you are concerned with the actual hardware implementation of these values, in which case the issue of positive logic ("on" means "true") vs. negative logic ("off" means "true") becomes a consideration. But the intuitive assumption of a positive logic system ("1" equals "on" equals "true") seems the most natural, and may be considered conventional, so the terms listed above as equivalent will be used interchangeably, as appropriate for a given context.

Before discussing these functions, it is important to remember the bit-numbering scheme described in Chapter 1: bits are numbered right to left from least significant to most significant, starting with zero. So a single byte contains bits zero through seven, and a double byte contains bits zero through fifteen. Bit zero always stands for the "one's place." Bit seven stands for the "128ths place" and bit fifteen stands for the "32768ths place," except that the high bit of a signed number is, instead, the sign bit. A single bit (or string of bits smaller than a byte or double byte) is sometimes called a **bit-field**, implying that the bits are just a part of a larger data element like a byte or double byte.

You'll find two types of instructions discussed in this chapter: the basic **logic** functions, and the **shifts** and **rotates**. They're listed in Table 10.1.

Table 10.1. Logic Instructions.

Mnemonic	Available on:			Description
	6502	65C02	65802/816	
Logic Instructions:				
AND	x	x	x	logical and
EOR	x	x	x	logical exclusive-or
ORA	x	x	x	logical or (inclusive or)
Bit Manipulation Instructions:				
BIT	x	x	x	test bits
TRB		x	x	test and reset bits
TSB		x	x	test and set bits
Shift and Rotate Instructions:				
ASL	x	x	x	shift bits left
LSR	x	x	x	shift bits right
ROL	x	x	x	rotate bits left
ROR	x	x	x	rotate bits right

Logic Functions

The fundamental logical operations implemented on the 65x processor are **and, inclusive or,** and **exclusive or.** These are implemented as the **AND, ORA,** and **EOR** machine instructions. These three logical operators have two operands, one in the accumulator and the second in memory. All of the addressing modes available for the **LDA, STA, ADC, SBC,** and **CMP** instructions are also available to the logical operations. The truth tables for these operations are found in Chapter 1 and are repeated again in the descriptions of the individual instructions in Chapter 18.

In addition to these instructions, there are also bit testing instructions that perform logical operations; these are the **BIT** (test memory bits), **TSB** (test and set bits), and **TRB** (test and reset bits) instructions. These three instructions set status flags or memory values based on the result of logical operations, rather than affecting the accumulator.

The logical and bit manipulation instructions are broadly useful: for testing for a condition using boolean logic (for example, *if* this is true *and* that is true *then* do this); for **masking** bit fields in a word, forcing them to be on or off; for performing quick, simple multiplication and division functions, such as multiplying by two or taking the modulus of a power of two (finding the remainder of a division by a power of two); for controlling I/O devices; and for a number of other functions.

The most typical usage of the boolean or logical operators is probably where one of the two operands is an immediate value. Immediate values will generally be used in these examples. Additionally, operands will usually be represented in binary form (prefixed by a percent sign—%), since it makes the bit-pattern more obvious. All of the logical operations are performed **bitwise**; that is, the result is determined by applying the logical operation to each of the respective bits of the operands.

Logical AND

Consider, for example, the eight-bit **AND** operation illustrated in Figure 10.1.

```
        bit number
        7 6 5 4 3 2 1 0
        0 1 1 1 0 1 1 0            $76
    and 1 1 0 0 1 0 1 1        and $CB
        0 1 0 0 0 0 1 0            $42 result
```

Figure 10.1. The AND Operation.

The result, $42 or %0100 0010, is formed by **AND**ing bit zero of the first operand with bit zero of the second to form bit zero of the result; bit one with bit one; and so on. In each bit, a one results only if there is a one in the corresponding bit-fields of both the first operand **and** the second operand; otherwise zero results.

An example of the use of the **AND** instruction would be to **mask** bits out of a double-byte word to isolate a character (single-byte) value. A mask is a string of bits, typically a constant, used as an operand to a logic instruction to single out of the second operand a given bit or bit-field by forcing the other bits to zeroes or ones. Masking characters out of double bytes is common in 65802 and 65816 applications where a "default" mode of sixteen-bit accumulator and sixteen-bit index registers has been selected by the programmer, but character data needs to be accessed as well. For some types of character manipulation, it is quicker to simply mask out the extraneous data in the high-order byte than to switch into eight-bit mode. The code in Listing 10.1 is fragmentary in the sense that it is assumed that the core routine is inserted in the middle of other code, with the sixteen-bit accumulator size already selected.

It may seem to be splitting hairs, but this routine, which compares the value in a string of characters pointed to by the value in the memory variable **CHARDEX** to the letter 'e' is two machine cycles faster than the alternative approach, which would be to switch the processor into the eight-bit accumulator mode, compare the character, and then switch back into the sixteen-bit mode.

```
0001  0000                     KEEP    KL.10.1
0002  0000                     65816 ON
0003  0000
0004  0000         MAIN        START
0005  0000         PTR         GEQU    $80
0006  0000
0007  0000 18                  CLC
0008  0001 FB                  XCE
0009  0002
0010  0002 C230                REP     #$30              assume operation in 16-bit modes
0011  0004                     LONGA ON
0012  0004                     LONGI ON
0013  0004
0014  0004 AC4C00              LDY     CHARDEX           get index pointing to desired char
0015  0007 B91A00   LOOP       LDA     STRING,Y          get the char & the one after it
0016  000A 29FF00              AND     #%0000000011111111    AND out the "next" char
0017  000D C96500              CMP     #'e'              cmp low byte to 'e', high 0 byte to 0
0018  0010 D004                BNE     NOMATCH
0019  0012
0020  0012 38                  SEC                       return to emulation mode
0021  0013 FB                  XCE
0022  0014
0023  0014 38                  SEC                       set carry indicates successful match
0024  0015 60                  RTS
0025  0016
0026  0016 38       NOMATCH    SEC                       return to emulation mode
0027  0017 FB                  XCE
0028  0018
0029  0018 18                  CLC                       clear carry indicates unsuccessful match
0030  0019 60                  RTS
0031  001A
0032  001A 54686573 STRING     DC      C'These characters'
0033  002A 61726520            DC      C'are all packed next to'
0034  0040 65616368            DC      C'each other'
0035  004A 0000                DC      H'0000'
0036  004C 0000     CHARDEX    DS      2                 index to a particular char in STRING
0037  004E                     END
```

Listing 10.1.

Each time the program is executed with a different value for **CHARDEX**, a different adjacent character will also be loaded into the high byte of the accumulator. Suppose the value in **CHARDEX** were four; when the **LDA STRING,Y** instruction is executed, the value in the low byte of the accumulator is $65, the ASCII value for a lower-case 'e'.

The value in the high byte is $20, the ASCII value for the space character (the space between "These" and "characters"). Even though the low bytes match, a comparison to 'e' would fail, because the high byte of the **CMP** instruction's immediate operand is zero, not $20 (the assembler having automatically generated a zero as the high byte for the single-character operand 'e').

However, by **AND**ing the value in the accumulator with %0000000011111111 ($00FF), *no matter what the original value in the accumulator,* the high byte of the accumulator is zeroed (since none of the corresponding bits in the immediate operand are set). Therefore the comparison in this case will succeed, as it will for **CHARDEX** values of 2, 13, 18, 28, 32, 38, and 46, even though their adjacent characters, automatically loaded into the high byte of the accumulator, are different.

The **AND** instruction is also useful in performing certain multiplication and division functions. For example, it may be used to calculate the **modulus** of a power of two. (The modulus operation returns the remainder of an integer division; for example, 13 **mod** 5 equals 3, which is the remainder of 13 divided by 5.) This is done simply by **AND**ing with ones all of the bits to the right of the power of two you wish the modulus of and masking out the rest. A program fragment illustrating this will be provided later in this chapter, where an example of the use of the **LSR** instruction to perform division by powers of two will also be given.

In general, the **AND** operation is found in two types of applications: selectively turning bits off (by **AND**ing with zero), and determining if two logical values are both true.

Logical OR

The **ORA** instruction is used to selectively turn bits on by ORing them with ones, and to determine if either (or both) of two logical values is true. A character-manipulation example (Listing 10.2) is used—this time writing a string of characters, the high bit of each of which must be set, to the Apple // screen memory—to demonstrate a typical use of the **ORA** instruction.

Since the video screen is memory-mapped, outputting a string is basically a string move. Since normal Apple video characters must be stored in memory with their high-order bit turned on, however, the **ORA** #%10000000 instruction is required to do this if the character string, as in the example, was originally stored in normal ASCII, with the high-order bit turned off. Note that it clearly does no harm to **OR** a character with $80 (%10000000) even if its high bit is already set, so the output routine does not check characters to see if they need to have set the high bit, but rather routinely ORs them all with $80 before writing them to the screen. When each character is first loaded into the eight-bit accu-

```
0001  0000                    KEEP  KL.10.2
0002  0000                    65816 ON
0003  0000
0004  0000           L102     START
0005  0000                    MSB   OFF
0006  0000          SCREEN    GEQU  $400           start of Apple // screen memory
0007  0000
0008  0000 18                 CLC
0009  0001 FB                 XCE
0010  0002
0011  0002 C210               REP   #$10           16-bit index registers
0012  0004                    LONGI ON
0013  0004
0014  0004 E220               SEP   #$20           8-bit accum
0015  0006                    LONGA OFF
0016  0006
0017  0006 A00000             LDY   #0             starting index into string & screen = 0
0018  0009
0019  0009 B91900    TOP      LDA   STRING,Y       get char from string
0020  000C F008               BEQ   DONE           branch if at 0 terminator
0021  000E 0980               ORA   #%10000000     set the high bit
0022  0010 990004             STA   SCREEN,Y       store the char into screen memory
0023  0013
0024  0013 C8                 INY
0025  0014 80F3               BRA   TOP
0026  0016
0027  0016 38        DONE     SEC
0028  0017 FB                 XCE
0029  0018 60                 RTS
0030  0019
0031  0019 48656C6C  STRING   DC    C'Hello'
0032  001E 00                 DC    H'00'
0033  001F
0034  001F                    END
```

Listing 10.2.

mulator from **STRING**, its high bit is off (zero); the **ORA** instruction converts each of the values—$48, $65, $6C, $6C, $6F—into the corresponding high-bit-set ASCII values—$C8, $E5, $EC, $EC, and $EF, before storing them to screen memory, where they will be displayed as normal, non-inverse characters on the video screen. In this case, the same effect (the setting of the high-order bit) could have been achieved if $80 had been added to each of the characters instead; however, the **OR** operation differs from addition in that even if the high bit of the character already had a value of one, the result would still be one, rather than zero plus a carry as would be the case if addition were used. (Further a **CLC** operation would also have been required prior to the addition, making **ORA** a more efficient choice as well.)

Logical Exclusive-OR

The third logical operation, **Exclusive-OR,** is used to invert bits. Just as inclusive-OR **(ORA)** will yield a true result if either or both of the operands are true, exclusive-or yields true only if one operand is true and the other is false; if both are true or both are false, the result is false. This means that by setting a bit in the memory operand of an **EOR** instruction, you can invert the corresponding bit of the accumulator operand (where the result is stored). In the preceding example, where the character constants were stored with their high bits off, an **EOR #$80** instruction would have had the same effect as **ORA #$80**; but like addition, if some of the characters to be converted already had their high-order bits set, the **EOR** operation would clear them.

Two good examples of the application of the **EOR** operation apply to signed arithmetic. Consider the multiplication of two signed numbers. As you know, the sign of the product is determined by the signs of the multiplier and multiplicand according to the following rule: if both operands have the same sign, either positive or negative, the result is always positive; if the two operands have different signs, the result is always negative. You perform signed multiplication by determining the sign of the result, and then multiplying the absolute values of both operands using the same technique as for unsigned arithmetic. Finally, you consider the sign of the result: if it is positive, your unsigned result is the final result; if it is negative, you form the final result by taking the two's complement of the unsigned result. Because the actual multiplication code is not included, this example is given as two fragments, 10.1 and 10.2.

Fragment 10.1 begins by clearing the memory location **SIGN**, which will be used to store the sign of the result. Then the two values to be multiplied are exclusive-OR'd, and the sign of the result is tested with the **BPL** instruction. If the sign bit of the result is negative, you know that the sign bits of the two operands were different, and therefore the result will be negative; a negative result is preserved by decrementing the variable **SIGN**, making its value $FFFF.

Next, the two operands are converted to their absolute values by two's complementing them if they are negative. The technique for forming the two's complement of a number is to invert it, and then add one. The **EOR** operation is used again to perform the inversion; the instruction **EOR #$FFFF** will invert all of the bits in the accumulator: ones become zeroes, and zeroes become ones. An **INC A** instruction adds

```
0000 0000           NUM1   DS    2
0002 0000           NUM2   DS    2
0004
0004 C230                  REP   #$30         16-bit modes
0006                       LONGA ON
0006                       LONGI ON
0006
0006 9C0080                STZ   SIGN         clear the sign
0009 AD0000                LDA   NUM1
000C 4D0200                EOR   NUM2         exclusive-or: check sign
000F 1003                  BPL   OK
0011 CE0080                DEC   SIGN         negative: sign=$FFFF
0014 AD0200         OK     LDA   NUM2
0017 1007                  BPL   OK1
0019 49FFFF                EOR   #$FFFF       minus: get absolute value
001C 1A                    INC   A
001D 8D0200                STA   NUM2
0020 AD0000         OK1    LDA   NUM1
0023 1004                  BPL   OK2
0025 49FFFF                EOR   #$FFFF
0028 1A                    INC   A
0029                OK2    ANOP
```

Fragment 10.1.

one. In the case of **NUM2**, this result must be saved to memory before the accumulator is reloaded with **NUM1**, which is also two's complemented if negative.

At this point, the unsigned multiplication of the accumulator and **NUM2** can be performed. The code for the multiplication itself is omitted from these fragments; however, an example of unsigned multiplication is found in Chapter 14. The important fact for the moment is that the multiplication code is assumed to return the unsigned product in the accumulator.

```
0000 AE0080                LDX   SIGN
0003 1004                  BPL   DONE
0005 49FFFF                EOR   #$FFFF       if should be neg,
0008 1A                    INC   A            two's complement the result
0009 60          DONE      RTS
000A
```

Fragment 10.2.

10 Logic and Bit Manipulation Operations

What remains is to adjust the sign of the result; this code is found in Fragment 10.2. By testing the sign of **SIGN**, it can be determined whether or not the result is negative; if it is negative, the actual result is the two's complement of the unsigned product, which is formed as described above.

Bit Manipulation

You have now been introduced to the three principal logical operators, **AND, ORA,** and **EOR.** In addition, there are three more specialized bit-manipulating instructions that use the same logical operations.

The first of these is the **BIT** instruction. The **BIT** instruction really performs two distinct operations. First, it directly transfers the highest and next to highest bits of the memory operand (that is, seven and six if **m** = 1, or fifteen and fourteen if **m** = 0) to the **n** and **v** flags. It does this without modifying the value in the accumulator, making it useful for testing the sign of a value in memory without loading it into one of the registers. An exception to this is the case where the immediate addressing mode is used with the **BIT** instruction: since it serves no purpose to test the bits of a constant value, the **n** and **v** flags are left unchanged in this one case.

BIT's second operation is to logically AND the value of the memory operand with the value in the accumulator, conditioning the **z** flag in the status register to reflect whether or not the result of the ANDing was zero or not, but *without* storing the result in the accumulator (as is the case with the **AND** instruction) or saving the result in any other way. This provides the ability to test if a given bit (or one or more bits in a bit-field) is set by first loading the accumulator with a mask of the desired bit patterns, and then performing the **BIT** operation. The result will be non-zero only if at least one of the bits set in the accumulator is likewise set in the memory operand. Actually, you can write your programs to use either operand as the mask to test the other, except when immediate addressing is used, in which case the immediate operand is the mask, and the value in the accumulator is tested.

A problem that remained from the previous chapter was **sign extension,** which is necessary when mixed-precision arithmetic is performed—that is, when the operands are of different sizes. It might also be used when converting to a higher precision due to overflow. The most typical example of this is the addition (or subtraction) of a signed eight-bit and a signed sixteen-bit value. In order for the lesser-precision number to be converted to a signed number of the same precision as the larger number, it must be **sign-extended** first, by setting or clearing all of the high-order bits of the expanded-precision number to the same value as the sign bit of the original, lesser-precision number.

In other words, $7F would become $007F when sign-extended to sixteen bits, while $8F would become $FF8F. A sign-extended number evaluates to the same number as its lesser precision form. For example, $FF and $FFFF both evaluate to -1.

You can use the **BIT** instruction to determine if the high-order bit of the low-order byte of the accumulator is set, even while in the sixteen-bit accumulator mode. This is used to sign extend an eight-bit value in the accumulator to a sixteen-bit one in Listing 10.3.

```
0001  0000                KEEP  KL.10.3
0002  0000                65816 ON
0003  0000
0004  0000          L103  START
0005  0000 18             CLC
0006  0001 FB             XCE
0007  0002
0008  0002 C230           REP   #$30        turn 16-bit modes on
0009  0004                LONGA ON
0010  0004                LONGI ON
0011  0004
0012  0004 A500           LDA   0           get value to sign extend
0013  0006
0014  0006 29FF00         AND   #$FF        zero out any garbage in high byte
0015  0009 898000         BIT   #$80        test high bit of low byte
0016  000C F003           BEQ   OK          number is positive; leave as is
0017  000E 0900FF         ORA   #$FF00      turn on high bits
0018  0011
0019  0011 8500      OK   STA   0           save sign-extended value
0020  0013
0021  0013 38             SEC
0022  0014 FB             XCE
0023  0015 60             RTS
0024  0016                END
```

Listing 10.3.

The pair of "test-and-set" instructions, **TSB** and **TRB**, are similar to the **BIT** instruction in that they set the zero flag to represent the result of ANDing the two operands. They are dissimilar in that they do not affect the n and v flags. Importantly, they also set (in the case of **TSB**) or reset (in the case of **TRB**) the bits of the memory operand according to the bits that are set in the accumulator (the accumulator value is a mask). You should recognize that the mechanics of this involve the logical functions described above: the **TSB** instruction ORs the accumulator with the memory operand, and stores the result to memory; the TRB inverts the value in the accumulator, and then ANDs it with the memory operand. Unlike the **BIT** instruction, both of the test-and-set operations are read-modify-write instructions; that is, in addition to performing an operation on the memory value specified in the operand field of the instruction, they also store a result to the same location.

The test-and-set instructions are highly specialized instructions intended primarily for control of memory-mapped I/O devices. This is evidenced by the availability of only two addressing modes, direct and absolute, for these instructions; this is sufficient when dealing with memory-mapped I/O, since I/O devices are always found at fixed memory locations.

Shifts and Rotates

The second class of bit-manipulating instructions to be presented in this chapter are the **shift** and **rotate** instructions: **ASL, LSR, ROL** and **ROR**. These instructions copy each bit value of a given word into the adjacent bit to the "left" or "right." A shift to the left means that the bits are shifted into the next-higher-order bit; a shift to the right means that each is shifted into the next-lower-order bit. The bit shifted out of the end—that is, the original high-order bit for a left shift, or the original low-order bit for a right shift—is copied into the carry flag.

Shift and rotate instructions differ in the value chosen for the origin bit of the shift or rotate. The shift instructions write a zero into the origin bit of the shift—the low-order bit for a shift left or the high-order bit for a shift right. The rotates, on the other hand, copy the original value of the carry flag into the origin bit of the shift. Figure 10.2a. and Figure 10.2b. illustrate the operation of the shift and rotate instructions.

The carry flag, as Fragment 10.3 illustrates, is used by the combination of a shift followed by one or more rotate instructions to allow multiple-precision shifts, much as it is used by **ADC** and **SBC** instructions to enable multiple-precision arithmetic operations.

In this code fragment, the high-order bit in **LOC1** is shifted into the carry flag in the first **ASL** instruction and a zero is shifted into the low-order bit of **LOC1**; its binary value changes from

1010101010101010

to

0101010101010100   carry=1

The next instruction, **ROL**, shifts the value in the carry flag (the old high bit of **LOC1**) into the low bit of **LOC2**. The high bit of **LOC2** is shifted into the carry.

ASL-Before

| 1 | 0 | 1 | 1 | 0 | 0 | 1 | 1 |

X
CARRY FLAG

Rol-Before

| 1 | 0 | 1 | 1 | 0 | 0 | 1 | 1 |

X
CARRY FLAG

ASL

| 1 | 0 | 1 | 1 | 0 | 0 | 1 | 1 | ← 0

X
Carry Flag

ROL

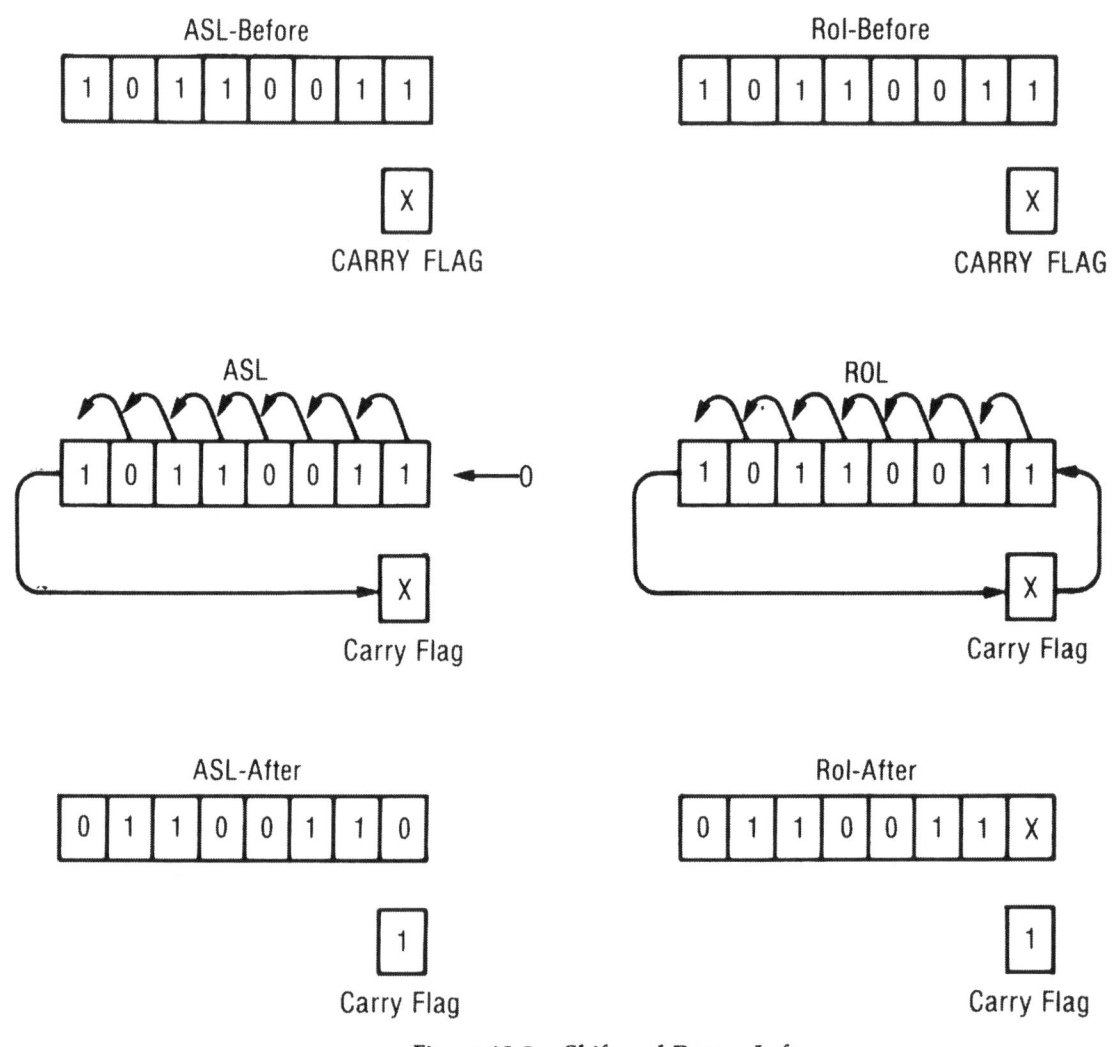

| 1 | 0 | 1 | 1 | 0 | 0 | 1 | 1 |

X
Carry Flag

ASL-After

| 0 | 1 | 1 | 0 | 0 | 1 | 1 | 0 |

1
Carry Flag

Rol-After

| 0 | 1 | 1 | 0 | 0 | 1 | 1 | X |

1
Carry Flag

Figure 10.2a. Shift and Rotate Left.

```
0000  A9AAAA         LDA    #%1010101010101010
0003  8D0080         STA    LOC1
0006  A9AAAA         LDA    #%1010101010101010
0009  8D0080         STA    LOC2
000C  0E0080         ASL    LOC1
000F  2E0080         ROL    LOC2
```

Fragment 10.3.

10 Logic and Bit Manipulation Operations

LSR-Before

| 1 | 0 | 1 | 1 | 0 | 0 | 1 | 1 |

X Carry Flag

LSR

| 1 | 0 | 1 | 1 | 0 | 0 | 1 | 1 | → X

Carry Flag

LSR-After

| 0 | 1 | 0 | 1 | 1 | 0 | 0 | 1 |

1 Carry Flag

ROR-Before

| 1 | 0 | 1 | 1 | 0 | 0 | 1 | 1 |

X Carry Flag

ROR

| 1 | 0 | 1 | 1 | 0 | 0 | 1 | 1 | → X

ROR-After

| X | 1 | 0 | 1 | 1 | 0 | 0 | 1 |

1

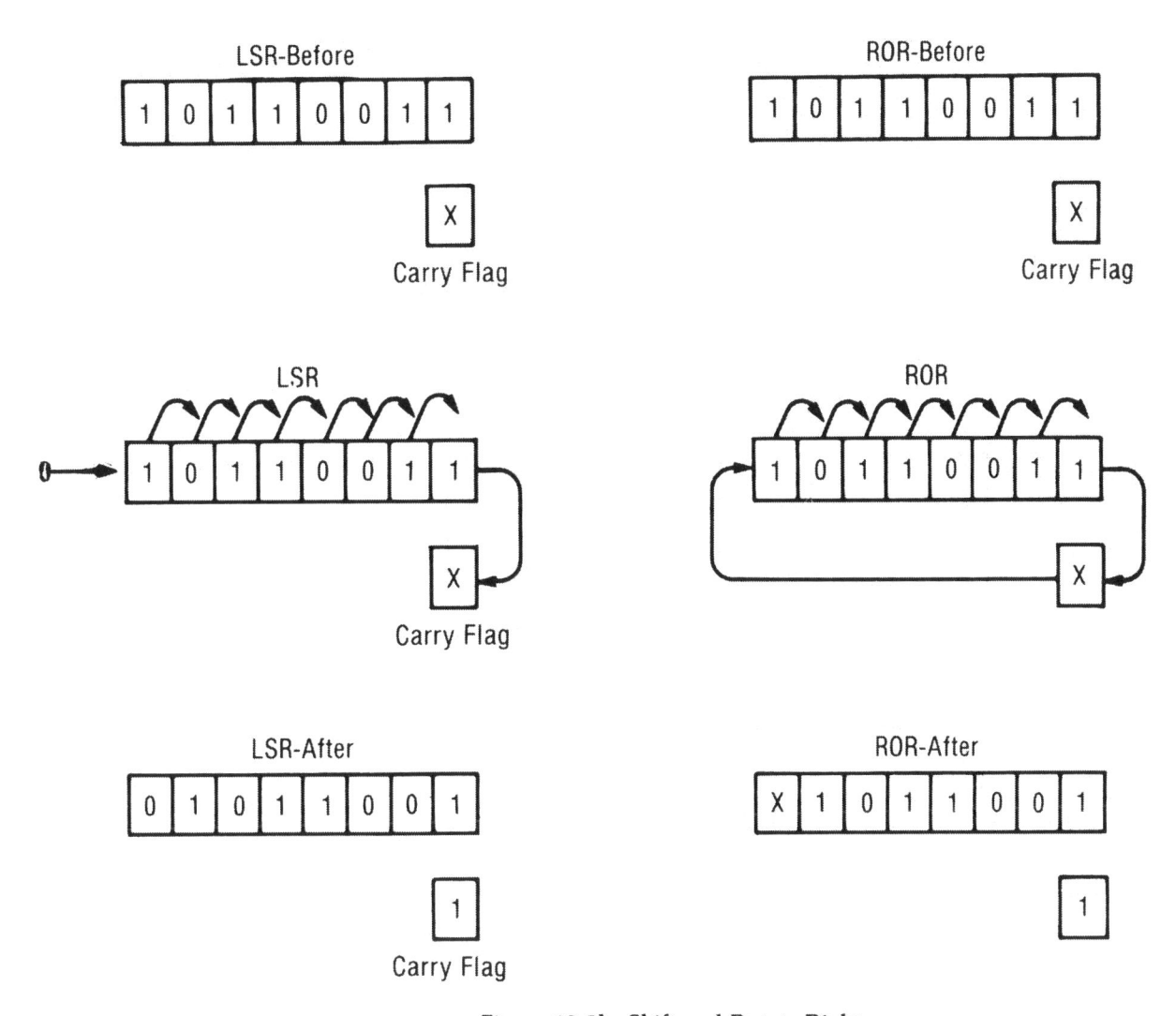

Figure 10.2b. Shift and Rotate Right.

```
1010101010101010
```

becomes

```
0101010101010101    carry=1
```

A double-precision shift left has been performed.

What is the application of the shift and rotate instructions? There are two distinct categories: multiplication and division by powers of two, and generalized bit-manipulation.

Left shifts multiply the original value by two. Right shifts divide the original value by two. This principal is inherent in the concept of positional notation; when you multiply a value by ten by adding a zero to the end of it, you are in effect shifting it left one position; likewise when you divide by ten by taking away the right-most digit, you are shifting right. The only difference is the number base of the digits, which in this case is base two.

Shifting is also useful, for the same reason, in a generalized multiply routine, where a combination of shift and add operations are performed iteratively to accomplish the multiplication. Sometimes, however, it is useful to have a dedicated multiplication routine, as when a quick multiplication by a constant value is needed. If the constant value is a power of two—such as four, the constant multiplier in Fragment 10.4—the solution is simple: shift left a number of times equal to the constant's power of two (four is two to the two power, so two left shifts are equivalent to multiplying by four).

```
0000 A93423       LDA    #$2334
0003 0A           ASL    A         times 4 (2 to the 2nd power)
0004 0A           ASL    A
```

Fragment 10.4.

The result in the accumulator is $2334 times four, or $8CD0. Other "quickie" multiply routines can be easily devised for multiplication by constants that are not a power of two. Fragment 10.5 illustrates multiplication by ten: the problem is reduced to a multiplication by eight plus a multiplication by two.

```
0000 A9D204       LDA    #1234
0003 0A           ASL    A         multiply by 2
0004 8D0080       STA    TEMP      save intermediate result
0007 0A           ASL    A         times 2 again = times 4
0008 0A           ASL    A         times 2 again = times 8
0009 18           CLC
000A 6D0080       ADC    TEMP      = times 10
```

Fragment 10.5.

After the first shift left, which multiplies the original value by two,

10 Logic and Bit Manipulation Operations

the intermediate result (1234 * 2 = 2468) is stored at location **TEMP**. Two more shifts are applied to the value in the accumulator, which equals 9872 at the end of the third shift. This is added to the intermediate result of 1234 times 2, which was earlier stored at location **TEMP**, to give the result 12,340, or 1234 * 10.

Division using the shift right instructions is similar. Since bits are lost during a shift right operation, just as there is often a remainder when an integer division is performed, it would be useful if there were an easy way to calculate the remainder (or modulus) of a division by a power of two. This is where the use of the **AND** instruction alluded to earlier comes into play.

```
0000 A91FE2         LDA  #$E21F
0003 48             PHA                 save accumulator
0004 4A             LSR  A              divide by 2
0005 4A             LSR  A              divide by 2 again = divide
0006 8D0080         STA  QUO            save quotient
0009 68             PLA                 recover original value
000A 290300         AND  #$3
000D 8D0080         STA  MOD            save modulus
```

Fragment 10.6.

Consider Fragment 10.6. In this case, $E21F is to be divided by four. As with multiplication, so with division: two shifts are applied, one for each power of two, this time to the right. By the end of the second shift, the value in the accumulator is $3887, which is the correct answer. However, two bits have been shifted off to the right. The original value in the accumulator is recovered from the stack and then ANDed with the divisor minus one, or three. This masks out all but the bits that are shifted out during division by four, the bits which correspond to the remainder or modulus; in other words, the original value can be reconstructed by multiplying the quotient times four, and then adding the remainder.

The second use for the shift instructions is for general bit manipulation. Since the bit shifted out of the word always ends up in the carry flag, this is an easy way to quickly test the value of the high- or low-order bit of a word. Listing 10.4 gives a particularly useful example: a short routine to display the value of each of the flags in the status register. This routine will, one by one, print the letter-name of each of the status register flags if the flag is set (as tested by the **BCS** instruction), or else print a dash if it is clear.

```
0001  0000                    KEEP  KL.10.4
0002  0000                    65816 ON
0003  0000
0004  0000
0005  0000         PRINTP  START
0006  0000         PREG    GEQU  $80
0007  0000         PTR     GEQU  $82
0008  0000
0009  0000
0010  0000 08              PHP                save (on the stack)
0011  0001              ;                     the status reg to be displayed
0012  0001
0013  0001 18              CLC
0014  0002 FB              XCE
0015  0003
0016  0003 C2FF            REP   #$FF         16-bit index regs; reset all flags
0017  0005 E220            SEP   #$20         8-bit accum
0018  0007                 LONGI ON
0019  0007                 LONGA OFF
0020  0007
0021  0007 68              PLA                pull status reg to display into accum
0022  0008 8580            STA   PREG           then store to memory location PREG
0023  000A A23000          LDX   #FLAGS       load 16-bit X with ptr to flag string
0024  000D 8682            STX   PTR            and store to PTR
0025  000F A20800          LDX   #8           load X with counter (# of flag bits)
0026  0012
0027  0012 0680    LOOP    ASL   PREG         shift high bit of PREG -> carry
0028  0014 B004            BCS   DOFLAG       branch if set
0029  0016 A92D            LDA   #'-'         if flag not set, output '-'
0030  0018 8002            BRA   SKIP
0031  001A B282    DOFLAG  LDA   (PTR)        get flag letter from FLAGS
0032  001C 200080  SKIP    JSR   COUT         output flag letter or '-'
0033  001F E682            INC   PTR          16-bit
0034  0021 D002            BNE   OK             increment
0035  0023 E683            INC   PTR+1          (incr hi byte if low rolls over)
0036  0025 CA      OK      DEX                decrement counter
0037  0026 D0EA            BNE   LOOP         dontinue thru all 8 bits of status reg
0038  0028 A90D            LDA   #$0D         output cr after all 8 flags
0039  002A 200080          JSR   COUT
0040  002D
0041  002D 38              SEC
0042  002E FB              XCE
0043  002F 60              RTS
0044  0030
```

Listing 10.4.

```
0045  0030 6E766D78    FLAGS   DC    c'nvmxdizc'
0046  0038
0047  0038                     END



SKIP         00001C



0048  0000
0049  0000
0050  0000              COUT   START
0051  0000              ECOUT  GEQU  $FDED         COUT IN APPLE // MONITOR
0052  0000 48                  PHA
0053  0001 DA                  PHX
0054  0002 5A                  PHY
0055  0003 08                  PHP
0056  0004 38                  SEC
0057  0005 FB                  XCE
0058  0006 20EDFD              JSR   ECOUT
0059  0009 18                  CLC
0060  000A FB                  XCE
0061  000B 28                  PLP
0062  000C 7A                  PLY
0063  000D FA                  PLX
0064  000E 68                  PLA
0065  000F 60                  RTS
0066  0010                     END
```

Listing 10.4. (Cont.)

11 | The Complex Addressing Modes

Chapter 7 defined the term **addressing mode** and introduced the set of simple 65x addressing modes, those which involve at most a minimum of calculating combined values from multiple locations.

This chapter continues and expands the discussion of one of those modes, the direct page addressing mode, for those cases where the direct page register value is other than zero. It discusses the basis for selection by the assembler among the direct page, absolute, and long addressing modes, and how you can explicitly override those assumptions. And it discusses the set of complex addressing modes available on the 6502, the 65C02, the 65802, and the 65816, those which require the effective address to be calculated from several sources (Table 11.1). The understanding of these modes also provides the context within which to discuss several more complex push instructions that were previously deferred to this chapter (Table 11.2).

Table 11.1. Complex Addressing Modes.

Available on all 65x processors:	*Example Syntax*
absolute indexed with X	LDA $2234,X
absolute indexed with Y	LDA $2234,Y
direct page (zero page) indexed with X	LDA $17,X
direct page (zero page) indexed with Y	LDX $17,Y
direct page (zero page) indirect indexed with Y	LDA ($17),Y
direct page (zero page) indexed indirect with X	LDA ($17,X)
Available on the 65C02, 65802 and 65816 only:	
absolute indexed indirect	JMP ($7821,X)
Available on the 65802 and 65816 only:	
non-zero direct page	LDA $17
absolute long indexed with X	LDA $654321,X
direct page indirect long indexed with Y	LDA [$17],Y
stack relative	LDA $29,S
stack relative indirect indexed with Y	LDA ($29,S),Y

Table 11.2. Complex Push Instructions.

Mnemonic	Available on: 6502	65C02	65802/816	Description
PEA			x	push effective absolute address
PEI			x	push effective indirect address
PER			x	push effective relative address

Relocating the Direct Page

Chapter 7 discussed zero page addressing as found on the 6502 and 65C02 and introduced direct page addressing, the 65816's enhancement to zero page addressing. The 65816 lets the zero page addressing modes use a direct page that can be located and relocated anywhere in the first 64K of memory. But Chapter 7 left the direct page set to page zero so it could be discussed as a simple addressing mode—that is, so no calculation of direct page register base plus direct page offset needed to be done and so the operand, a direct page offset, could be thought of as an absolute address with a high-order byte of zero.

Relocating the direct page from page zero, to which it is initialized on power-up, can be accomplished in either of two ways. The first would let a new value be pulled off the stack into the direct page register with the PLD instruction, as found in Fragment 11.1.

```
0000            ;                 set direct page register to $3400
0000 A20034     LDX    #$3400     get $3400 into a register
0003 DA         PHX               and push it onto the stack,
0004 2B         PLD               then pull it into direct page reg
```

Fragment 11.1.

Fragment 11.2 illustrates the second method. The direct page register can be set to the value in the sixteen-bit C accumulator by use of the TCD instruction, which transfers sixteen bits from accumulator to direct page register.

```
0000            ;                 set direct page register to $FE00
0000 A900FE     LDA    #$FE00     get $FE00 into sixteen-bit accum
0003 5B         TCD               and transfer from C accum into direct pg
```

Fragment 11.2.

Both methods of setting the direct page register give it a sixteen-bit value. Since sixteen bits are only capable of specifying an address within a 64K range, its bank component must be provided in another manner; this has been done by limiting the direct page to bank zero. The direct page can be located anywhere in 64K but the bank address of the direct page is always bank zero.

Chapter 7, which limited the use of the direct page to page zero, used the example shown in Fragment 11.3 to store the one-byte value $F0 at address $0012, which is the direct page offset of $12 added to a direct page register value of zero. If instead the direct page register is set to $FE00, then $F0 is stored to $FE12; the direct page offset of $12 is added to the direct page register value of $FE00.

```
0000  A9F000           LDA     #$F0
0003  8512             STA     $12         store accumulator to dp:$12
```

Fragment 11.3.

While it is common to speak of a **direct page address** of $12, $12 is really an *offset* from the base value in the direct page register ($FE00 in the last example). The two values are added to form the **effective direct page address** of $FE12.

But while Chapter 7 defined a **page** of memory as $100 locations starting from a page boundary (any multiple of $100), the direct page does not have to start on a page boundary; the direct page register can hold *any* sixteen-bit value. If the code in Fragment 11.4 is executed, running the code in Fragment 11.3 stores the one-byte value $F0 at address $1025: $1013 plus $12.

```
0000              ;             set direct page register to $1013
0000  A91310      LDA   #$1013  get $1013 into sixteen-bit accum
0003  5B          TCD           transfer $1013 from C into direct pg reg
```

Fragment 11.4.

You will for the most part, however, want to set the direct page to begin on a page boundary: it saves one cycle for every direct page addressing operation. This is because the processor design includes logic that, when the direct page register's low byte is zero, concatenates the direct page register's high byte to the direct page offset—instead of adding the offset to the entire direct page register—to form the effective direct page address; concatenation saves a cycle over addition.

One of the benefits of the direct page concept is that programs, and even parts of programs, can have their own $100-byte direct pages of variable space separate from the operating system's direct page of variable space. A routine might set up its own direct page with the code in Fragment 11.5.

```
0000        ;                   set up direct page for this routine at $0300
0000 0B             PHD                 first save current direct page location
0001 A90003         LDA     #$300       load sixteen-bit accumulator with $300
0004 5B             TCD                 transfer $300 into direct page reg
```

Fragment 11.5.

To end the routine and restore the direct page register to its previous value, simply execute a **PLD** instruction.

As discussed in Chapter 7, having a direct page makes accessing zero page addresses in any bank require special assembler syntax. Since the zero page is no longer special, absolute addressing must be used; but since the assembler normally selects direct page addressing for operands less than $100, the standard syntax requires that you prefix a vertical bar or exclamation point to the operand to force the assembler to use absolute addressing. This is just one of the potential assembler misassumptions covered in the next section.

Assembler Addressing Mode Assumptions

When the assembler encounters an address in the operand field of an instruction, it must decide whether the address is a direct page offset, a sixteen-bit absolute address, or a 24-bit long address and generate opcode and operand values which are appropriate. Its decision is based on the operand's size—not the number of digits in the operand, but whether the value of the operand is greater than $FF or greater than $FFFF. For example, the assembler will interpret the operand $3F to be a direct page offset regardless of whether it is written as $3F, $003F, or $00003F, because its value is less than 100 hex.

As a result, there are several areas of memory in 65802 and 65816 systems that the assembler will not access without entering the special syntax shown in Table 11.3 to override the assembler's assumptions.

Table 11.3. Assembler Syntax for Complete Memory Access.

Syntax	Description

8-bit operand (less than $100):

  Normal direct page addressing:
    LDA $32   load accum from: bank zero:direct page:$32

  Force absolute addressing: zero page in data bank:
    LDA   !$32   load accum from: data bank:$0032

  Force long addressing: zero page in bank zero:
    LDA   >$32   load accum from: $00:0032

16-bit operand (from $100 through $FFFF):

  Normal absolute addressing:
    LDA $7512   load accum from: data bank:$7512

  Force direct page addressing:
    LDA   <$7512   load accum from: bank zero:direct page:$12

  Force long addressing:
    LDA   >$7512   load accum from: $00:7512

24-bit operand (over $FFFF):

  Normal long addressing:
    LDA $123456   load accum from: $12:3456

  Force absolute addressing:
    LDA   !$123456 load accum from: data bank:$3456

  Force direct page addressing:
    LDA   <$123456 load accum from: bank zero:direct page:$56

The first is zero page memory. Page zero has no special meaning in the 65802 and 65816: its special attributes have been usurped by the direct page, so accessing it requires use of absolute addressing just like any other absolute location. But the assembler assumes addresses less than $100 are direct page *offsets*, not zero page *addresses*; it will not generate code to access the zero page (unless the direct page is set to the zero page so that the two are one and the same) without explicit direction. And even if the direct page is set to the zero page, 65816 systems have a zero page not only in bank zero but also in every other bank, and those other page zeroes cannot ever be accessed by absolute addressing without special direction.

The syntax to force the assembler to use absolute addressing is to precede an operand with a vertical bar or exclamation point as shown in Fragment 11.6.

```
0000 C220        REP     #$20      set accumulator/memory to sixteen
0002             LONGA   ON
0002 A90032      LDA     #$3200    get new direct page location
0005 5B          TCD               and set up direct page at $3200
0006 E210        SEP     #$10      set index registers to eight-bit
0008             LONGI   OFF
0008 A202        LDX     #2        set new data bank location to bank 2
000A DA          PHX               push 2 on stack
000B AB          PLB               and pull it off into data bank
000C A532        LDA     $32       load accumulator from dp:$32 in bank 0
000E 8D3200      STA     !$32      store accum at $02:0032 (data bank)
0011 8F320000    STA     >$32      store accum at $00:0032 (long address)
```

Fragment 11.6.

Notice the use of another symbol, the greater-than sign (>), to force long addressing. This solves another problem: The assembler assumes absolute addresses are in the data bank; if the value in the data bank is other than zero, then it similarly will not generate code to access bank zero without special direction. The greater-than sign forces the assembler to use a long addressing mode, concatenating zero high bits onto the operand until it's 24 bits in length. This usage is shown in Fragment 11.7, where the greater-than sign forces absolute long addressing, resulting in the assembler generating an opcode using absolute long addressing to store the accumulator, followed by the three absolute long address bytes for $00:0127, which are, in 65x order, $27, then $01, then $00.

The **ASL** instruction in Fragment 11.7 makes use of the third assembler override syntax: prefixing an operand with the less-than sign (<) forces direct page addressing. It's not likely you'll use this last syntax often, but it may come in handy when you've assigned a label to a value that you need the assembler to truncate to its low-order eight bits so it will be used as a direct page offset.

Note that this override syntax is the recommended standard syntax. As Chapter 1 (Basic Concepts) pointed out, even mnemonics can vary from one assembler to another, so assembler syntax such as this can differ as well.

```
0000 E210             SEP    #$10         use 8 bit index registers
0002                  LONGI  OFF
0002
0002 A202             LDX    #2           get new data bank value
0004 DA               PHX                   push it on stack
0005 AB               PLB                   pull into data bank
0006 AD2701           LDA    $127         from B:$0127 ($02:0127)
0009 8F270100         STA    >$127        store at $00:0127
000D 0627             ASL    <$127        shift word at dp:$27
```

Fragment 11.7.

Direct Page Indirect Indexed with Y Addressing

Direct page indirect indexed addressing or **postindexing**, which uses the Y register, is one of two ways indirect addressing can be combined with indexing (the other will be described in the next section). In postindexing, the processor goes to the location the direct page operand specifies and adds the index to the indirect address found there.

Like direct page indirect addressing, which was discussed in Chapter 7 (The Simple Addressing Modes), postindexing gives you the freedom to access a memory location which is not determined until the program is executing. As you also learned from Chapter 7, direct page indirect lets your program store the absolute address of a data bank location you want to access (this address is called the indirect address) into any two consecutive bytes in the direct page. This makes those two bytes perform as though they are an extra sixteen-bit register in the microprocessor itself. Further, it leaves the processor's registers unobstructed, and it allows data at the location stored in the direct page "register" to be accessed at any time.

Postindexing differs in that the absolute address you store into the direct page "register" is not one location but the base of an array; you can then access a particular byte in the array by loading its array index into the Y register and specifying, as your operand, the direct page "register" (the location of the indirect base of the array). As Figure 11.1 shows, the processor goes to the direct page offset, gets the absolute memory location stored there, then adds the contents of the Y register to get the absolute memory location it will access. The direct page offset, being in the direct page, is in bank zero on the 65816; the array, on the other hand, is in the data bank.

Effective Address:

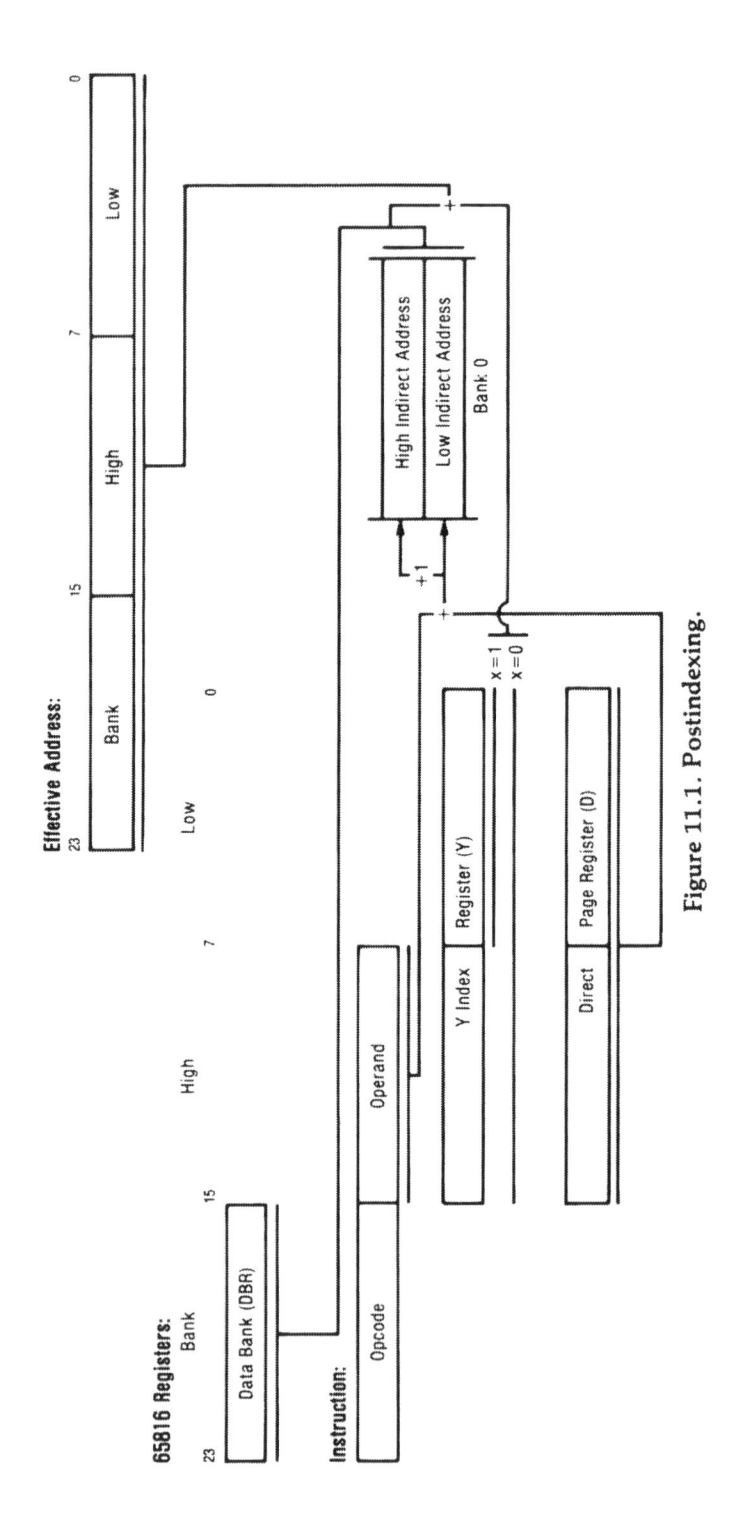

Bank	High	Low
23	15 7	0

65816 Registers:

Bank	High	Low
Data Bank (DBR)		
23 15	7	0

Instruction:

Opcode | Operand

Y Index Register (Y)

Direct Page Register (D)

High Indirect Address / Low Indirect Address — Bank 0

Figure 11.1. Postindexing.

This addressing mode is called postindexing because the Y index register is added *after* the indirect address is retrieved from the direct page.

For example, suppose that your program needs to write a dash (hyphen) character to a location on the Apple //'s 40-column screen that will be determined while the program is running. Further suppose your program picks a screen location at column nine on line seven. The Apple // has a firmware routine (called **BASCALC**) which, when presented with the number of a line on the screen, calculates the address of the leftmost position in the line and returns it in zero page location **BASL**, located at memory locations $0028 and $0029.

If you wanted to write your hyphen to the *first* position on the line, you could, after calling **BASCALC** and loading the character to print into the accumulator, use the 65C02's indirect addressing mode:

```
9228            STA     (BASL)
```

The 6502 has no simple indirect addressing mode, but Fragment 11.8 illustrates what 6502 programmers long ago learned: you can use postindexing to the same effect as simple indirect by loading the Y register with zero.

```
0000            BASL    EQU     $28
0000 A92D               LDA     #'-'            write a dash
0002 A000               LDY     #0
0004 9128               STA     (BASL),Y        to (BASL)
0006                    .
0006                    .
0006                    .
```

Fragment 11.8.

But you want to write the hyphen character to column nine (the leftmost position being column zero), not column zero. After calling **BASCALC**, you load the Y register with nine and write your character indirect through **BASL** indexed by the nine in Y as seen in Fragment 11.9. If **BASCALC** calculates line seven on the screen to start at location $780, and as a result stores that address at **BASL**, then the routine in Fragment 11.9 will write a dash to location $789 (column nine on line seven).

```
0000 A92D               LDA     #'-'            write a dash
0002 A009               LDY     #9              to col 9
0004 9128               STA     (BASL),Y        on the line with its base i
```

Fragment 11.9.

You could write a line of dashes from column nine through column sixteen simply by creating the loop coded in Listing 11.1. This kind of routine has been used for years on the 6502-based Apple //.

```
0001 0000                    KEEP  KL.11.1
0002 0000                    65816 OFF
0003 0000            ;       6502 example
0004 0000
0005 0000            L111    START
0006 0000
0007 0000            BASL    GEQU  $28
0008 0000            LINE7   GEQU  $780
0009 0000
0010 0000 A980               LDA   #LINE7
0011 0002 8528               STA   BASL
0012 0004 A907               LDA   #>LINE7
0013 0006 8529               STA   BASL+1
0014 0008 A92D               LDA   #'-'            write a dash
0015 000A A009               LDY   #9              to col 9
0016 000C 9128       LOOP    STA   (BASL),Y        on the line with its base in BASL
0017 000E C8                 INY                   incr pointer to next column position
0018 000F C011               CPY   #17
0019 0011 90F9               BCC   LOOP            (BLT): write another dash up to col. 17
0020 0013 60                 RTS
0021 0014
0022 0014                    END
```

Listing 11.1.

Finally, note that, like absolute indexed addressing, the array of memory accessible to the indirect indexed addressing mode can extend beyond the current 64K data bank into the next 64K bank, if the index plus the array base exceeds $FFFF.

Direct Page Indexing Indirect Addressing

As the introduction to the last section pointed out, you can combine indexing with indirection in two ways. Postindexing, discussed in the last section, is one. The other is called **direct page indexed indirect addressing** or **preindexing** and uses the X register. It adds the index to the operand (a direct page base) to form a direct page offset at which the indirect address (the address of the data to be accessed) is located.

In effect, preindexing lets you index into a double-byte array of absolute memory addresses based in the direct page to choose the memory location to access; the array begins at the direct page offset specified by the operand.

Since the array base is a direct page location, adding the direct page register value yields the absolute location in bank zero. The processor then adds the value in the X register, which is the index into the array of memory locations. Now the processor finally has an address that holds the memory location you want to access; it now gets the location and accesses the data at that location. This is shown in Figure 11.2. Since indexing is done in order to find the indirect address, this addressing mode is also called **preindexing.**

You'll find preindexing useful for writing routines which need to access data in a number of different locations in exactly the same way. For example, a tic-tac-toe game drawn on the screen has nine boxes to which an 'O' or an 'X' might be written. The tic-tac-toe program might keep internal arrays of information about the content of each of the nine boxes, as well as arrays of data for working its win-seeking algorithms, using indexes from 0 to 8 to represent the locations.

When it comes time for the program to write an 'X' to a chosen square, you could, of course, write nine nearly identical routines which differ only in the address to which the 'X' will be written; you would also have to write a tenth routine to select which one of the routines needs to be called, based on the value of the box index (from zero to eight).

A faster and less wasteful method of writing the 'X' would be to use preindexing. In the section of code which initially draws the tic-tac-toe grid, you would determine the nine addresses where characters are to be written and store them into a direct page array, perhaps starting at direct page offset $50; this puts the 0 location at $50 and $51 (stored, in 65x fashion, low byte in $50 and high byte in $51), the 1 location at $52 and 53, and so on. The nine addresses use 18 bytes of memory.

When an 'X' is to be stored to one of the nine screen locations, only one routine is necessary: you multiply the box number by two (using the **ASL** instruction). Remember that each indirect address takes up two bytes in the direct page array. Transfer it to the X register. Then load an 'X' character into the accumulator and write it to the box on the screen using preindexing as Fragment 11.10 shows.

```
0000 AD0080   WRITEX   LDA   BOXNUMBR   get which box to write an 'X' to
0003 0A                ASL   A          multiply by two to get index
0004 AA                TAX              and transfer index to X register
0005 A958              LDA   #'X'       write 'X' character
0007 8150              STA   ($50,X)    to scrn location at (dp:$50, index reg)
```

Fragment 11.10.

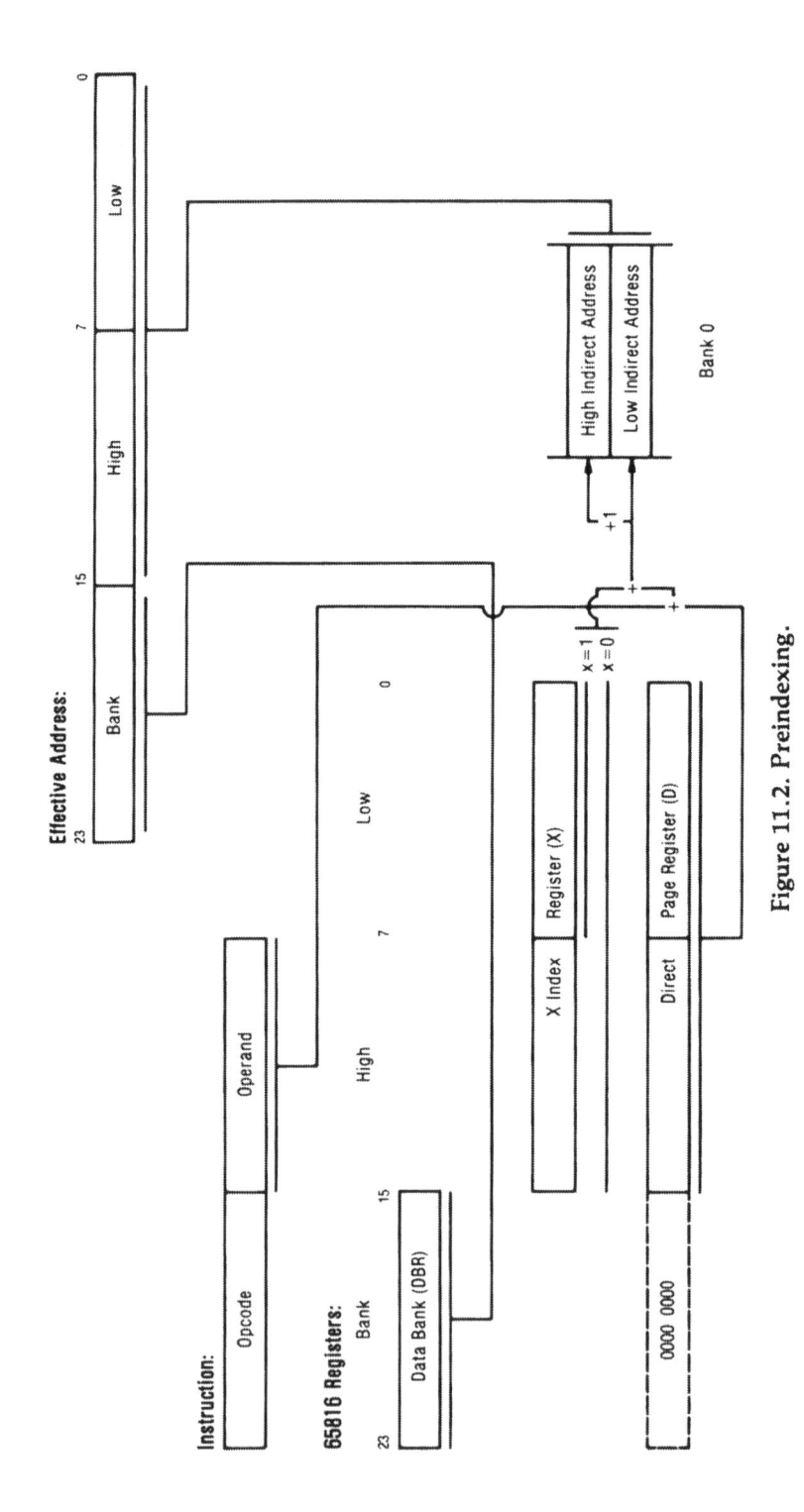

Figure 11.2. Preindexing.

Notice the differing syntax: postindexing looked like this:

```
9128            STA         (BASL),Y
```

In postindexed, the operand locates the indirect address, so it's in parentheses to indicate indirection. The ",Y" is not in parentheses, since the index register is not part of finding the indirect address—it's added to the indirect address once it is found.

On the other hand, with preindexing:

```
8150            STA         ($50,X)
```

both the operand and the index register are involved in locating the indirect address, so both are in parentheses.

A very different application for preindexing enables the 65x to read from (or write to) several I/O peripherals "at once." Obviously, a microprocessor can only read from one device at a time, so it polls each device: provided each device uses the same I/O controller chip (so that a single routine can check the status of all devices and read a character from each of them identically), your program can poll the various status locations using preindexing. Begin by storing an array of all the status locations in the direct page. Specify the base of the array as the operand to a preindexed instruction. Load the X index with 0 and increment it by two until you've checked the last device. Finally, restore it to zero and cycle through again and again.

If a status check reveals a character waiting to be read, your program can branch to code that actually reads the character from the device. This time, you'll use preindexing to access a second direct page array of the character-reading addresses for each device; the index in the X register from the status-checking routine provides the index into the character-reading routine.

On the 6502, the 65C02, and the 6502 emulation modes, the entire array set up for preindexing must be in the direct page. (On the 6502 and 65C02, this means the array must be entirely in the zero page which, unfortunately, severely limits the use of preindexing due to the competition for zero page locations.) If the specified direct page offset plus the index in X exceeds $FF, the array wraps around within the direct page rather than extending beyond it. That is,

```
A21A            LDX         #$1A
```

followed by

```
A1F0            LDA         ($F0,X)
```

would load the accumulator from the indirect address in location $0A, not $10A.

On the 65802 and 65816 (in native mode), the array must still start in the direct page but wraps, not at the end of the direct page, but at the end of bank zero, when the array base plus the D direct page setting plus the X index exceeds $00:FFFF.

On the 65816, the data that is ultimately accessed (after the indirection) is always in the *data bank*.

Absolute Indexed Indirect Addressing

The 65C02 introduced a new addressing mode, **absolute indexed indirect addressing**, which is quite similar to direct page indexed indirect. (It is also preindexed using the X index register, but indexes into absolute addressed memory rather than the direct page to find the indirect address.) This new addressing mode is used only by the jump instruction and, on the 65802 and 65816, the jump-to-subroutine instruction.

Absolute indexed indirect provides a method for your program, not to *access* data in scattered locations by putting the locations of the data into a table and indexing into it, but to *jump* to routines at various locations by putting those locations into a table, indexing into it, and jumping to the location stored in the table at the index. Figure 11.3 shows what happens.

A menu-driven program, for example, could ask users to respond to a prompt by pressing a number key from '0' through '7'. Your program would convert the key's value to an index by subtracting the ASCII value of '0' and doubling the result (to reflect the fact that each table entry is an address and thus takes two bytes in the table) (Fragment 11.11). It would then jump indexed indirect to a routine appropriate to the menu choice.

```
0000              ;              get menu choice into accumulator
0000
0000 38                    SEC                 set carry before subtract
0001 E93000                SBC    #'0'         convert '0'-'7' to 0-7
0004 0A                    ASL    A            times 2 = index
0005 AA                    TAX                 transfer index to X
0006 7C0900                JMP    (TABLE,X)    jump to address TABLE + X
0009
0009 0080      TABLE       DC     A'ROUTIN0'   routine for response '0'
000B 0080                  DC     A'ROUTIN1'     menu response '1'
000D 0080                  DC     A'ROUTIN2'     menu response '2'
000F 0080                  DC     A'ROUTIN3'     menu response '3'
0011 0080                  DC     A'ROUTIN4'     menu response '4'
0013 0080                  DC     A'ROUTIN5'     menu response '5'
0015 0080                  DC     A'ROUTIN6'     menu response '6'
0017 0080                  DC     A'ROUTIN7'     menu response '7'
```

Fragment 11.11.

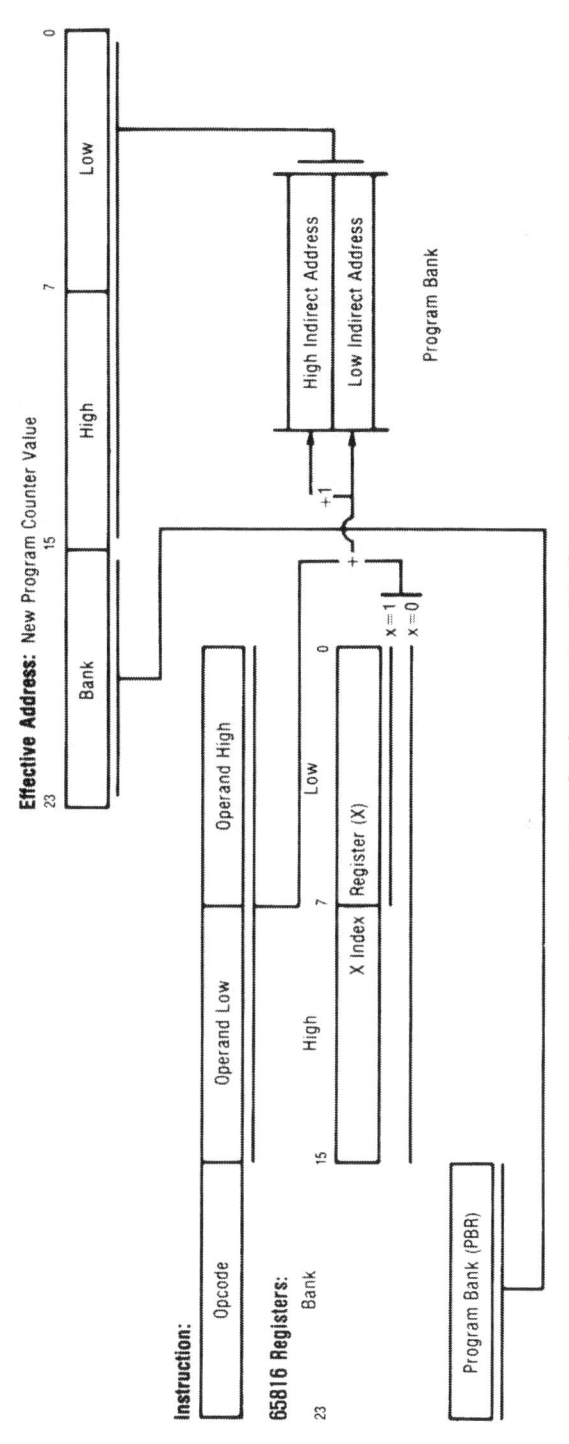

Figure 11.3. Absolute Indexed Indirect.

Because both the operand (the absolute address of the base of the table) and the index register are involved in determining the indirect address, both are within the parentheses.

On the 65816, a jump-indirect operand is in bank zero, but a jump-indexed-indirect operand is in the *program* bank. There is a different assumption for each mode. Jump indirect assumes that the indirect address to be jumped to was stored by the program in a variable memory cell; such variables are generally in bank zero. Jump indexed indirect, on the other hand, assumes that a table of locations of routines would be part of the program itself and would be loaded, right along with the routines, into the bank holding the program. So,

```
6C3412    JMP    ($1234)      jump to address stored at $00:1234.1235
```

assumes $1234 is in a double-byte cell in bank zero. But

```
7C3412    JMP    ($1234,X)    jump to address stored at pb:$1234,X
```

assumes $1234 is in the program bank, the bank in which the code currently being executed resides.

The indirect addresses stored in the table are absolute addresses also assumed to be in the current program bank.

Direct Page Indirect Long Indexed with Y Addressing

The 65816 can access sixteen megabytes of memory, yet lets you access most data (data located in the current data bank) with just two bytes. Nevertheless, there are times when data must be accessed in a bank other than the current data bank when it would be inconvenient to change the data bank, then change it back. As Chapter 7 pointed out, this problem is solved by the "long" addressing modes, which allow three bytes (the bank in addition to the address within the bank) to specify a full 24-bit address. This solution lets you access the 65816's full sixteen-megabyte address space. Probably the most useful way to reference data outside of the current data bank is via the **direct page indirect long indexed with Y**, or **postindexed long**, addressing mode. This is the long version of direct page indirect indexed addressing, discussed earlier in this chapter.

Instructions are two bytes in length, as shown in Figure 11.4: The opcode is followed by a single byte, which is a direct page offset in bank zero. The indirect address stored in the direct page (to which the operand points) is, in the long version, three bytes (a full 24-bit address); the byte at the direct page offset is the low byte of the 24-bit address, the byte in the next direct page location the middle byte of the 24-bit address, and the byte in the third location the bank byte of the 24-bit address. The contents of the Y index register are added to this 24-bit address to form the 24-bit effective address at which data will be accessed.

The syntax for postindexed long is:

```
B715          LDA     [$15],Y
```

The square brackets are used to indicate the indirect address is long.

So, like its sixteen-bit counterpart, indirect long indexed addressing allows you to index into an array of which neither the base nor the index need be determined until the program is executing. Unlike its sixteen-bit counterpart, it allows you to access an array in *any* bank, not just the current data bank.

Stack Relative Addressing

Possibly the most exciting new addressing method introduced by the 65802 and 65816 is stack relative. This is the first 65x method for directly accessing a stack byte other than the last data item pushed.

Stack relative addressing lets you easily access any byte or address in the last $FF bytes stacked. Instructions using stack relative addressing are two bytes long, the operand a single byte that is an index into the stack. As Figure 11.5 shows, the stack is treated as an array with its base the address in the stack pointer. The operand is added to the stack pointer value to form the bank zero effective address which will be accessed.

This can be especially useful when one part of a program needs to send data to another part of the program, such as a multiply routine. The two sixteen-bit values to be multiplied are pushed onto the stack in one part of the program. Later, the multiply routine loads one of the operands using stack relative addressing, leaving both the other operand and the stack pointer undisturbed:

```
A303          LDA     3,S         load first operand
```

or

```
A301          LDA     1,S         load second operand
```

Notice that accessing the last data put on the stack requires an index of 1, not of 0. This is because the stack pointer always points to the *next available* location, which is one byte below the last byte pushed onto the stack. An index of zero would generally be meaningless, except perhaps to re-read the last byte *pulled off* the stack! (The latter would also be extremely dangerous since, should an interrupt occur, the left-behind byte would be overwritten by interrupt-stacked bytes.)

Effective Address:

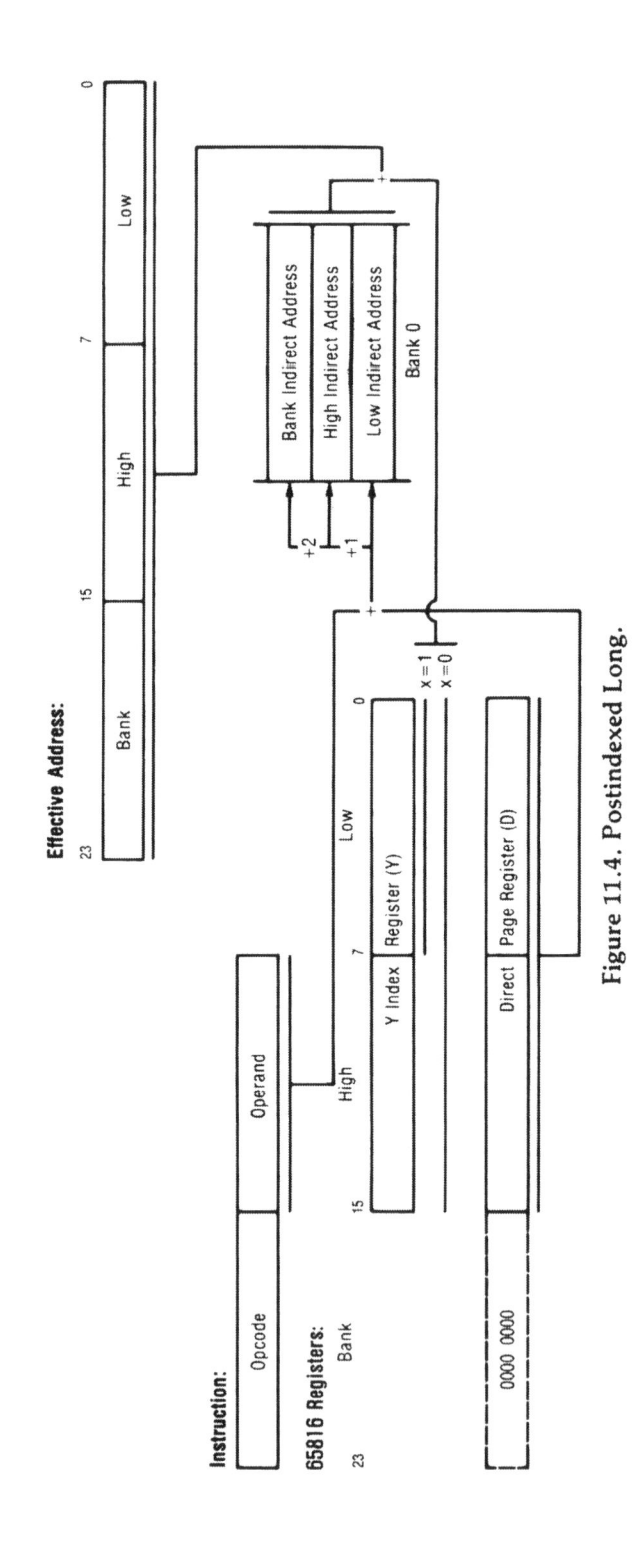

| Bank | High | Low |

Bank Indirect Address
High Indirect Address
Low Indirect Address

Bank 0

+2
+1

x = 1
x = 0

Y Index | Register (Y)

Direct Page Register (D)

Instruction:

Opcode | Operand

High

65816 Registers:

Bank

0000 0000

Figure 11.4. Postindexed Long.

Effective Address:

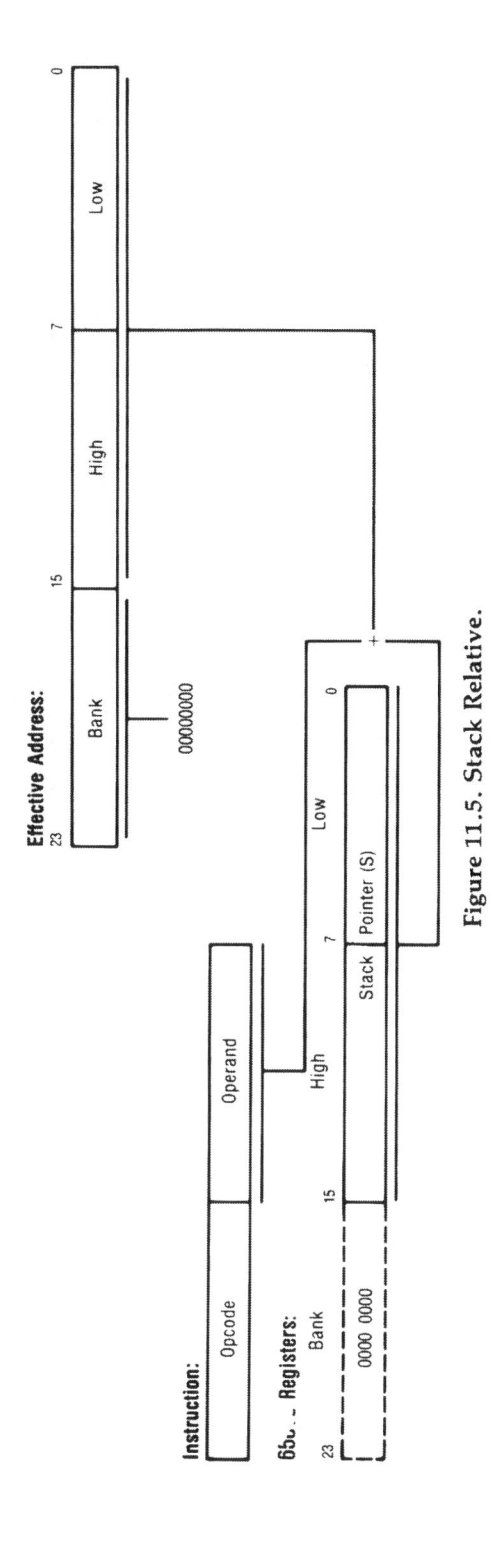

Bank	High	Low
23 15	15 7	7 0

00000000

Instruction:

Opcode	Operand

Registers:

Bank: 0000 0000 (23 — 15)

Stack Pointer (S): High | Low (15 — 7 — 0)

Figure 11.5. Stack Relative.

Stack Relative Indirect Indexed Addressing

While the stack relative addressing mode serves to access data on the stack, the stack relative indirect indexed addressing mode lets you access data indirectly through *addresses* that have been pushed onto the stack.

Change the previous example: Instead of stacking the two sixteen-bit values to be multiplied, the values are found in memory cells in the data bank, one after the other (occupying four consecutive bytes), and it's the address of the first that is pushed onto the stack. Now, as Fragment 11.12 shows, either value can be loaded using the stacked indirect address:

```
0000 A00000         LDY     #0
0003 B301           LDA     (1,S),Y     load first 16-bit multiply operand
0005 AA             TAX                 save first value
0006 A00200         LDY     #2
0009 B301           LDA     (1,S),Y     load second 16-bit multiply operand
```

Fragment 11.12.

The 1,S is the stack location where the indirect address was pushed. (Actually, 1,S points to the stack location of the low byte of the indirect address; the high byte is in 2,S, the next higher stack location.) To this indirect address, the value in Y is added: the indirect address plus 0 locates the first value to be multiplied; the indirect address plus 2 locates the second. Finally the accumulator is loaded from this indirect indexed address. Figure 11.6 illustrates the sequence.

This mode, very similar to direct page indirect indexing (also called postindexing), might be called "stack postindexing." The operand which indexes into the stack is very similar to a direct page address; both are limited to eight bits and both are added to a sixteen-bit base register (D or S). In both cases, the indirect address points to a cell or an array in the data bank. In both cases, Y must be the index register. And in both cases in the 65816, the postindexed indirect address about to be accessed may extend out of the data bank and into the next bank if index plus address exceeds $FFFF; that is, if the indirect address is the base of an array, the array can extend into the next bank.

Push Effective Instructions

The 65802 and the 65816 provide three instructions which push, not registers, but absolute, indirect, and relative addresses straight onto the

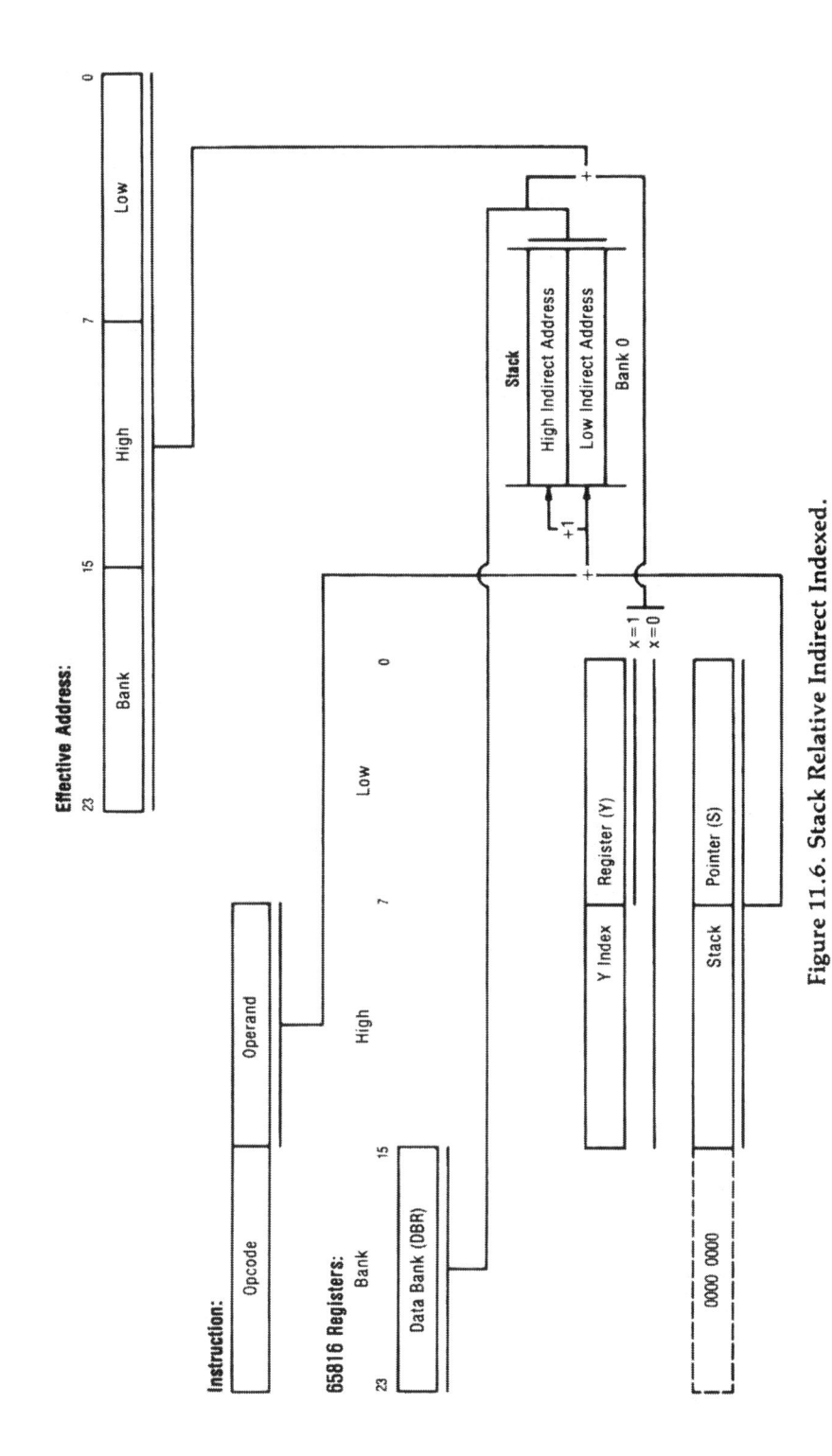

Figure 11.6. Stack Relative Indirect Indexed.

stack. These three instructions are **PEA**, **PEI**, and **PER**, the **push effective address** instructions. Addresses so pushed might be accessed, for example, using the stack relative indirect indexed addressing mode just discussed. Chapter 6, which introduced the push instructions in the context of data movement, deferred discussion of these three instructions to this chapter. Except for the block move instructions, these are the only instructions that move data directly from one memory location to another.

As Figure 11.7 shows, the **PEA** (push effective absolute address) instruction pushes the operand, a 16-bit absolute address or immediate data word, onto the stack. For example,

```
F43421          PEA     $2134       push $2134 onto the stack
```

pushes what may be either sixteen-bit immediate data or a sixteen-bit address onto the stack. The operand pushed by the **PEA** instruction is always 16 bits regardless of the settings of the **m** memory/accumulator and **x** index mode select flags.

The **PEI** (push effective indirect address) instruction has, as an operand, a direct page location: it's the sixteen-bit value stored at the location that is pushed onto the stack. Figure 11.8 shows that this has the effect of pushing either an indirect address or sixteen bits of direct page data onto the stack. For example, if you had stored the value or indirect address $5678 at direct page location $21, then

```
D421            PEI     ($21)       push two bytes at dp:$21 and dp:$22
```

would get the $5678 from the direct page location and push it onto the stack. Like the **PEA** instruction, the **PEI** instruction always pushes sixteen bits regardless of the settings of the **m** memory/accumulator and **x** index mode select flags.

The **PER** (push effective relative) instruction pushes an effective program counter relative address onto the stack, a capability helpful in writing relocatable code. The operand you specify to the assembler is a location in the program, for example, of a data area; the operand the assembler generates is a sixteen-bit relative displacement, the difference between the next instruction's address and the operand address. Figure 11.9 shows that when the instruction is executed, the displacement is added to the next instruction's *run-time* address to form the address at which the data is now located; it is this address which is pushed onto the stack. If the data location precedes the **PER** instruction, the assembler generates a very large sixteen-bit displacement which, when added to the program counter value, will wrap around within the program bank to reach the data.

The operation of the **PER** instruction is similar to the operation of the **BRL** (branch long) instruction: the branch long operand you specify to

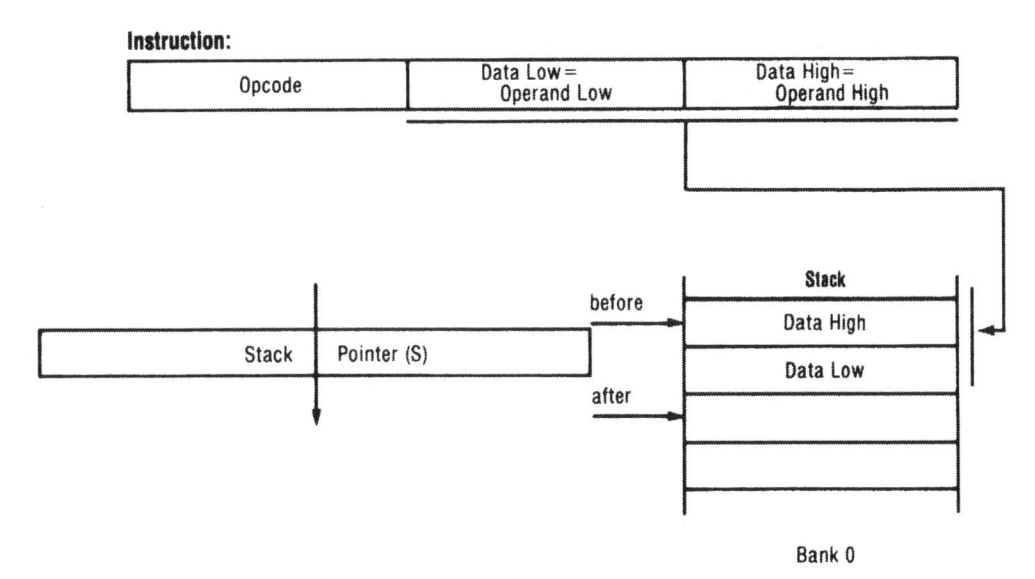

Figure 11.7. PEA Addressing.

Effective Address:

Bank	High	Low
23 15	15 7	7 0

0000 0000

Instruction:

Opcode	Operand

65816 Registers:

Bank	Direct	Page Register (D)
23 15	15 7	7 0

0000 0000

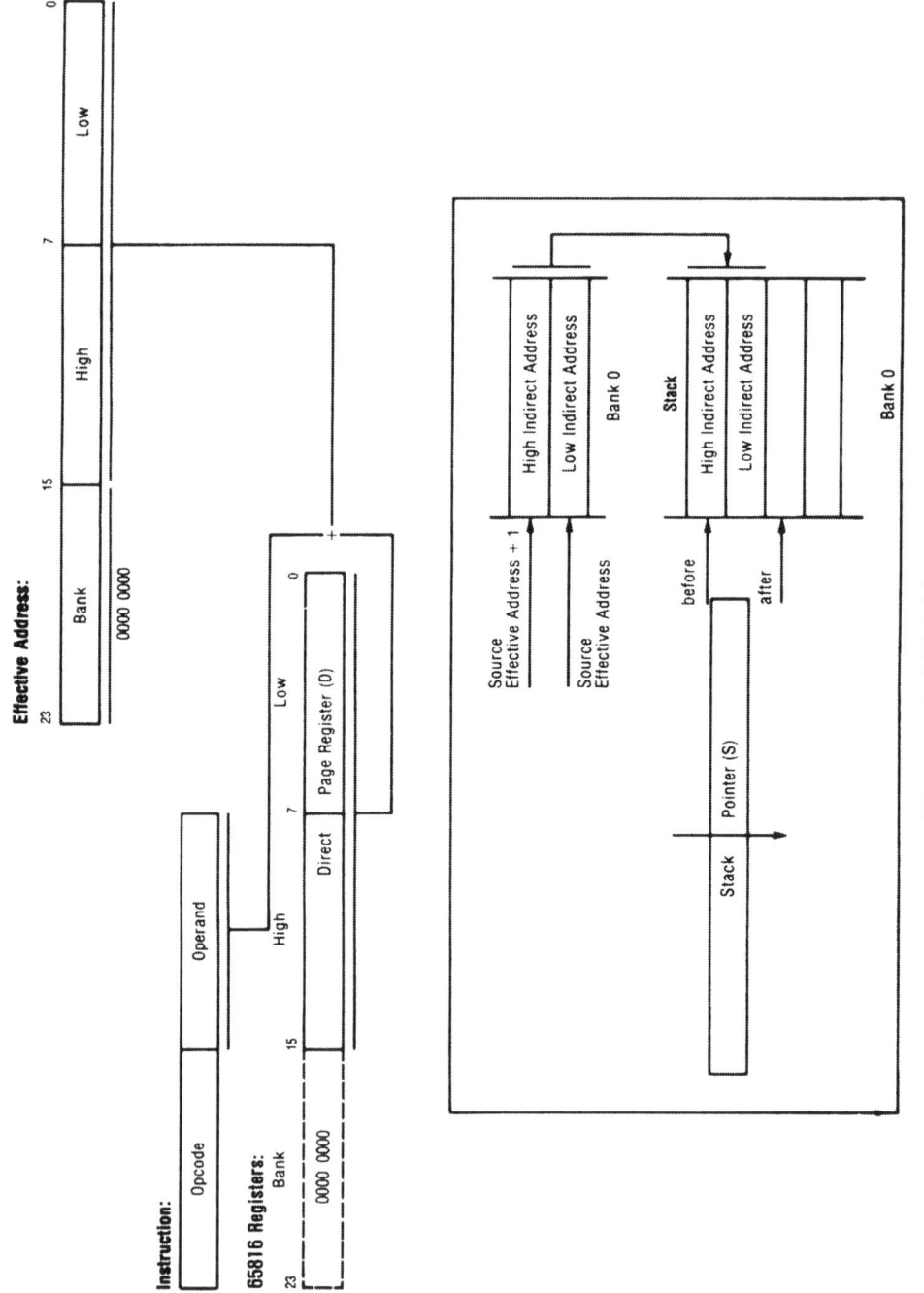

Figure 11.8. PEI Addressing.

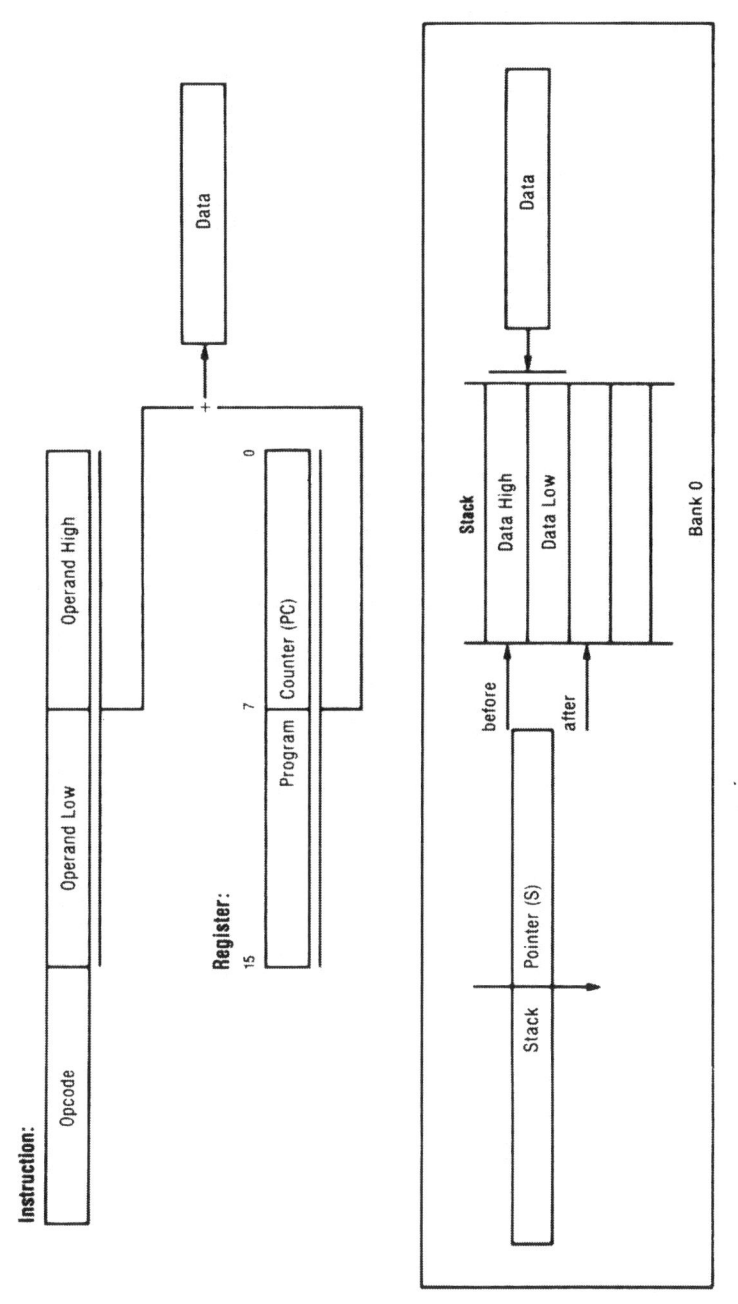

Figure 11.9. PER Addressing.

the assembler is also a location in the program; the operand the assembler generates is also a sixteen-bit displacement; and when the instruction is executed, the displacement is added to the next instruction's run-time address to form the address to which the program will branch.

To understand the use of the **PER** instruction, together with the relative branches, in writing a program that will run at *any* address, suppose that your relocatable program is assembled starting at location $2000. There's a data area starting at location $2500 called **DATA0**. A section of program code at $2200 needs to access a byte three bytes past, called **DATA1**. A simple **LDA $2503** would work, but only if the program were intended to always begin at location $2000. If it's meant to be relocatable, you might load the program at $3000, in which case the data is at $3503 and a **LDA $2503** loads the accumulator with random information from what is now a non-program address. Using the instruction

```
62E17F          PER     DATA3       push address of DATA3 relative to PC
```

in your source program causes the assembler to calculate the offset from $2203 (from the instruction following the **PER** instruction at $2200) to **DATA1** at $2503, an offset of $300. So the assembler generates object code of a **PER** opcode followed by $300. Now if the code is loaded at $3000, execution of the **PER** instruction causes the processor to calculate and stack the current absolute address of **DATA1** by adding the operand, $300, to the current program counter location; the result is $3503, so it's $3503 that's stacked. Once on the stack, provided the program and data banks are the same, the data can be accessed using stack relative indirect indexed addressing. Fragment 11.13 contains the example code.

Once the address of **DATA1** is on the stack, the values at **DATA2** and **DATA3** can be accessed as well simply by using values of one and two, respectively, in the Y index register.

```
0000                    ORG     $2200
0000        ACCESS      START
0000
0000 62FD7F             PER     DATA1       push run-time address of DATA1 onto stack
0003 E220               SEP     #$20        set accum to 8-bit mode
0005 A00000             LDY     #0          zero index: DATA1 is cell, not array
0008 B301               LDA     (1,S),Y     load accum from DATA1 in data ban
000A        ;                               (address of DATA1 @ 1,S & 2,S)
000A                    .
000A                    .
000A                    .
000A
000A                    END


0000
0000                    ORG $2500
0000        DATA0       START
0000 2A2A2A             DC      C'***'
0003 FF     DATA1       DC      H'FF'
0004 F7     DATA2       DC      H'F7'
0005 E3     DATA3       DC      H'E3'
0006
0006                    END
```

Fragment 11.13.

12 | The Basic Building Block: The Subroutine

The feature essential to any processor to support efficient, compact code, as well as modular or top-down programming methods, is a means of defining a **subroutine**. A subroutine is a block of code that can be entered (called) repeatedly from various parts of a main program, and that can automatically return control to the instruction following the calling instruction, wherever it may be. The 65x jump-to-subroutine instruction provides just such a capability.

When a jump-to-subroutine, or **JSR**, instruction is encountered, the processor first pushes its current location onto the stack for purposes of returning, then jumps to the beginning of the subroutine code. At the end of the subroutine code, a return-from-subroutine (**RTS**) instruction tells the processor to return from the subroutine to the instruction after the subroutine call, which it locates by pulling the previously saved return location from the stack.

Because subroutines let you write a recurring section of program code just once and call it from each place that it's needed, they are the basis of top-down, structured programming. Common subroutines are often collected together by programmers to form a **library**, from which they can be selected and reused as needed.

Chapter 8, Flow of Control, introduced the 65x jump instructions—those flow-of-control instructions which do *not* use the stack for return purposes. But discussion of the jump-to-subroutine instructions was put off to this chapter.

Table 12.1 lists the instructions to be explained in this chapter. In addition, this chapter will use the simple example of a negation routine to illustrate how library routines (and routines in general) are written and documented, and it examines the question of when to code a subroutine and when to use in-line code. Finally, methods of passing information (or **parameters**) to and from subroutines are compared and illustrated.

Table 12.1. Subroutine Instructions.

Mnemonic	Available on:			Description
	6502	65C02	65802/816	
65x Subroutine Instructions:				
JSR	x	x	x	jump to subroutine
RTS	x	x	x	return from subroutine
JSL			x	long jump to subroutine
RTL			x	long return from subroutine

The Jump-to-Subroutine Instruction

There is just one addressing mode available to the JSR instruction on the 6502 and 65C02—absolute addressing. This mode lets you code a subroutine call to a known location. When used on the 65816, that location must be within the current *program* bank. It uses the absolute addressing syntax introduced earlier:

```
200020      JSR     $2000     jump to subroutine located at pb:$2000
```

or

```
200080      JSR     SUBR1     jump to subroutine SUBR1 in program bank
```

In the second case, the assembler determines the address of subroutine **SUBR1**.

The processor, upon encountering a jump-to-subroutine instruction, first saves a return address. The address saved is the address of the *last byte* of the JSR instruction (the address of the last byte of the operand), not the address of the next instruction as is the case with some other processors. The address is pushed onto the stack in standard 65x order—the low byte in the lower address, the high byte in the higher address—and done in standard 65x fashion—the first byte is stored at the location pointed to by the stack pointer, the stack pointer is decremented, the second byte is stored, and the stack pointer is decremented again. Once the return address has been saved onto the stack, the processor loads the program counter with the operand value, thus jumping to the operand location, as shown in Figure 12.1. Jumping to a subroutine has no effect on the status register flags.

The Return-from-Subroutine Instruction

At the end of each subroutine you write, the one-byte **RTS**, or **return-from-subroutine**, instruction must be coded. When the return-from-subroutine instruction is executed, the processor pulls the stored

12 The Basic Building Block: The Subroutine

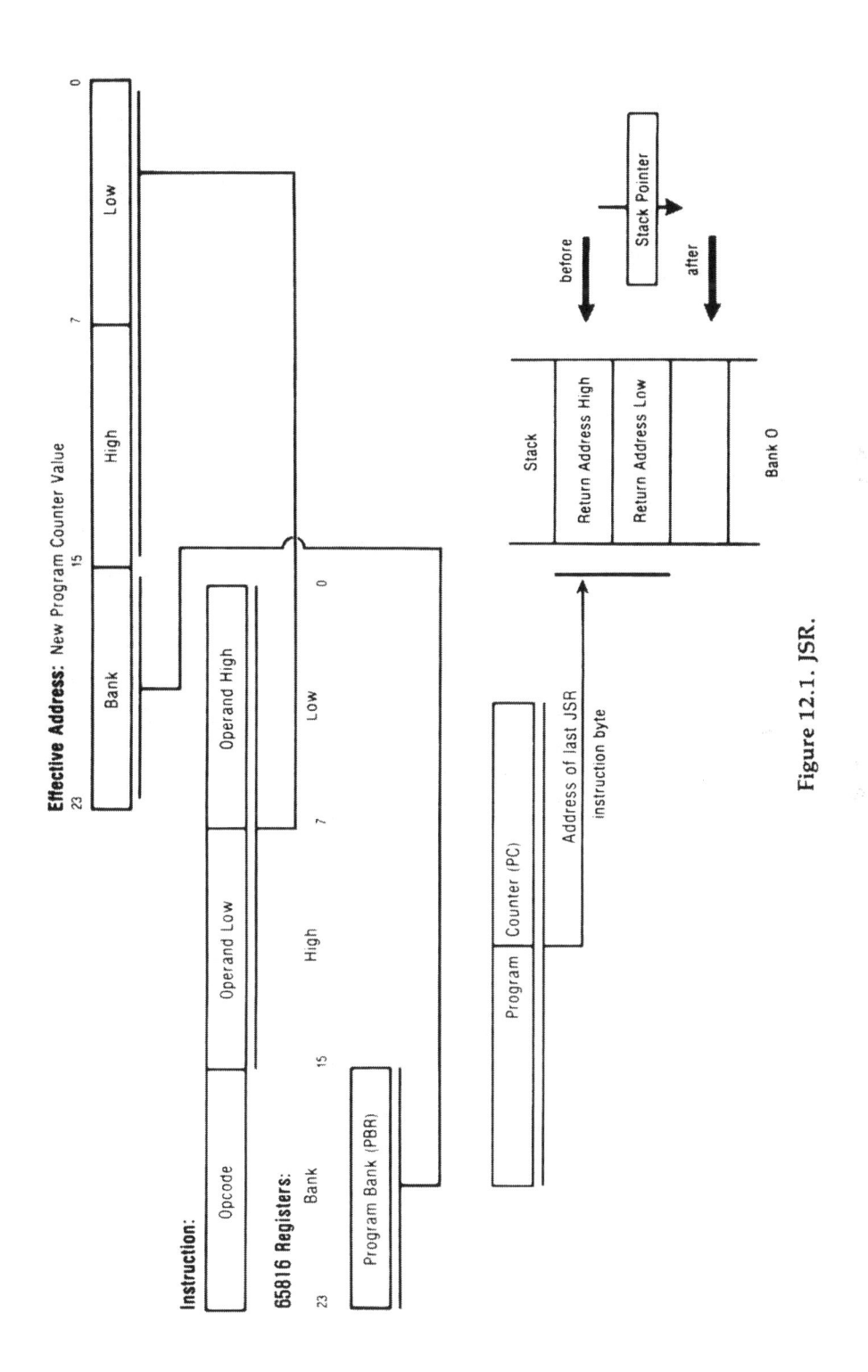

Figure 12.1. JSR.

address from the stack, incrementing the stack pointer by one before retrieving each of the two bytes to which it points. But the return address that was stored on the stack was the address of the *third byte of the JSR instruction*. When the processor pulls the return address off the stack, it automatically increments the address by one so that it points to the instruction following the JSR instruction which should be executed when the subroutine is done. The processor loads this incremented return address into the program counter and continues execution from the instruction following the original JSR instruction, as Figure 12.2 shows.

The processor *assumes* that the two bytes at the top of the stack are a return address stored by a JSR instruction and that these bytes got there as the result of a previous JSR. But as a result, if the subroutine used the stack and left it pointing to data other than the return address, the RTS instruction will pull two irrelevant data bytes as the address to return to. Cleaning up the stack after using it within a subroutine is therefore imperative.

The useful side of the processor's inability to discern whether the address at the top of the stack was pushed there by a JSR instruction is that you can write a reentrant indirect jump using the RTS instruction. First formulate the address to be jumped to, then decrement it by one (or better, start with an already-decremented address), push it onto the stack (pushing first high byte, then low byte, so that it is in correct 65x order on the stack) and, finally, code an RTS instruction. The return-from-subroutine pulls the address back off the stack, increments it, and loads the result into the program counter to cause a jump to the location, as Fragment 12.1 illustrates.

```
0000              ; 16-bit accumulator holds address of code to jump to
0000 3A      DEC    A     DEST-1: address of byte before target
0001 48      PHA          push it; now address is stacked as tho JSR
0002 60      RTS          pull address; increment it; transfer control
```

Fragment 12.1.

Reentrancy is the ability of a section of code to be interrupted, then executed by the interrupting routine, and still execute properly both for the interrupting routine and for the original routine when control is returned to it. The interruption may be a result of a hardware interrupt (as described in the next chapter), or the result of the routine calling itself, in which case the routine is said to be **recursive**. The keys to reentrancy are, first, to be sure you save all important registers before

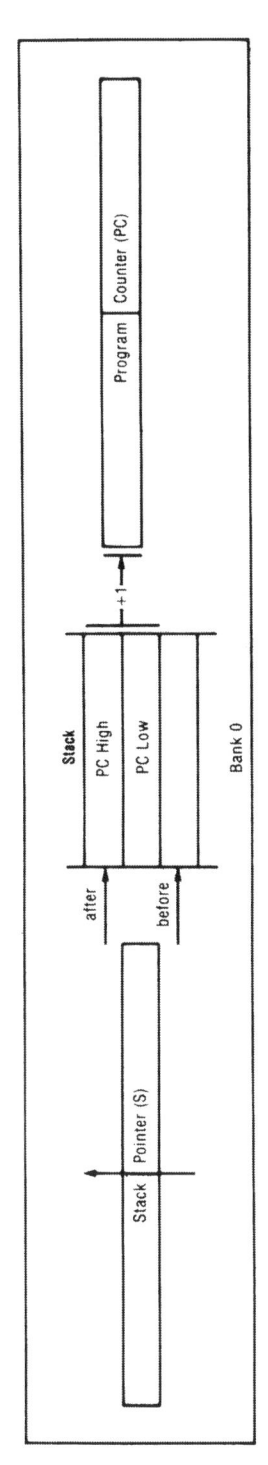

Figure 12.2. RTS.

reentering and, second, to use no fixed memory locations in the reentrant code. (There will be more on interrupts and reentrancy in the next chapters.)

The indirect jump using RTS qualifies for reentrancy: While normally you would code an indirect jump by forming the address to jump to and storing it to an absolute address, then jumping indirect through the address, this jump by use of RTS uses only registers and stack.

A subroutine can have more than one RTS instruction. It's common for subroutines to return from internal loops upon certain error conditions, in addition to returning normally from one or more locations. Some structured programming purists would object to this practice, but the efficiency of having multiple exit points is unquestionable.

Returning from a subroutine does not affect the status flags.

JSR Using Absolute Indexed Indirect Addressing

The 65802/65816 gives JSR another addressing mode—absolute indexed indirect (covered in the last chapter) which lets your program select, on the basis of the index in the X register, a subroutine location from a table of such locations and call it:

```
FC0080          JSR     (TABLE,X)    JSR to indirect address in (TABLE at X)
```

The array TABLE must be located in the program bank. The addressing mode assumes that a table of locations of routines would be part of the program itself and would be loaded, right along with the routines, into the bank holding the program. The indirect address (the address with which the program counter will be loaded), a sixteen-bit value, is concatenated with the program bank register, resulting in a transfer within the current program bank. If the addition of X causes a result greater than $FFFF, the effective address will wrap, remaining in the current program bank, unlike the indexing across banks that occurs for data accesses.

This addressing mode also lets you do an indirect jump-to-subroutine through a single double-byte cell by first loading the X register with zero. You must remember in coding this use for the 65816, however, that the cell holding the indirect address is in the program bank, *not* bank zero as with absolute indirect jumps.

The indexed indirect jump-to-subroutine is executed in virtually the same manner as the absolute jump-to-subroutine: the processor pushes the address of the final byte of the instruction onto the stack as a return address; then the address in the double-byte cell pointed to by the sum of the operand and the X index register is loaded into the program counter.

There is no difference between returning from a subroutine called by this instruction and returning from a subroutine called by an absolute JSR. You code an RTS instruction which, when executed, causes the address on the top of the stack to be pulled and incremented to point to the instruction following the JSR, then to be loaded into the program counter to give control to that instruction.

The Long Jump to Subroutine

A third jump-to-subroutine addressing mode is provided for programming in the 16-megabyte address space of the 65816—absolute long addressing. Jump-to-subroutine absolute long is a four-byte instruction, the operand a 24-bit address in standard 65x order (the low byte of the 24-bit address is in the lowest memory location immediately following the opcode and the high byte is next, followed by the bank byte):

```
22563412       JSR     $123456    jump to subroutine at $3456 in bank $12
```

This time a three-byte (long) return address is pushed onto the stack. Again it is not the address of the next instruction but rather the address of the last byte of the JSR instruction which is pushed onto the stack (the address of the fourth byte of the JSR instruction in this case). As Figure 12.3 shows, the address is pushed onto the stack in standard 65x order: low byte in the lower address, high byte in the higher address, bank byte in the highest address (which also means the bank byte is the first of the three pushed, the low byte last).

Jumping long to a bank zero subroutine requires the greater-than (>) sign, as explained in the last chapter:

```
22563400       JSR     >$3456     long jump to subroutine at $3456 in bank 0
```

The greater-than sign forces long addressing to bank zero, voiding the assembler's normal assumption to use absolute addressing to jump to a subroutine at $3456 in the current program bank.

To avoid this confusion altogether, there is an equivalent standard mnemonic for jump-to-subroutine long—JSL:

```
22563400       JSL     $3456      long jump to subroutine at $3456 in bank 0
```

or

```
22563402       JSL     $023456    long jump to subroutine at $3456 in bank 2
```

Using an alternate mnemonic is particularly appropriate for jump-to-subroutine long, since this instruction *requires* you to use an entirely different return-from-subroutine instruction—RTL, or **return-from-subroutine long**.

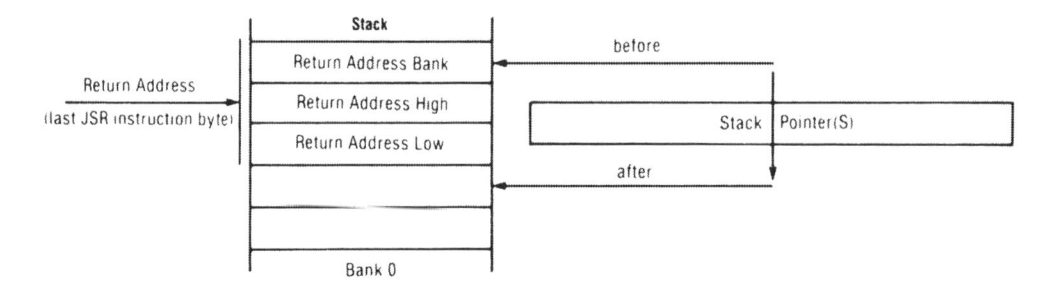

```
                    Stack
                ┌──────────────────┐         before
                │ Return Address Bank │ ◄─────────
Return Address  ├──────────────────┤
(last JSR instruction byte)
                │ Return Address High │                    Stack  Pointer(S)
                ├──────────────────┤
                │ Return Address Low  │
                ├──────────────────┤         after
                │                  │ ◄─────────
                │                  │
                │     Bank 0       │
                └──────────────────┘
```

Figure 12.3. JSL.

Return from Subroutine Long

The return from subroutine instruction pops two bytes off the stack as an absolute address, increments it, and jumps there. But the jump to subroutine long instruction pushes a *three-byte* address onto the stack— a *long* return address that points to the original code, and is typically in a bank different from the subroutine bank.

So the 65816 provides a return from subroutine long instruction, **RTL**. This return instruction first pulls, increments, and loads the program counter, just as **RTS** does; then it pulls and loads a third byte, the program bank register, to jump long to the return address. This is illustrated in Figure 12.4.

Branch to Subroutine

One of the glaring deficiencies of the 6502 was its lack of support for writing relocatable code; the 65802 and 65816 address this deficiency, but still lack the branch-to-subroutine instruction some other processors provide. There is no instruction that lets you call a subroutine with an operand that is program counter relative, not an absolute address. Yet, to write relocatable code easily, a **BSR** instruction is required: suppose a relocatable program assembled at $0 has an often-called multiply subroutine at $07FE; if the program is later loaded at $7000, that subroutine is at $77FE; obviously, a JSR to $07FE will fail.

The 65802 and 65816 can synthesize the **BSR** function using their **PER** instruction. You use **PER** to compute and push the current run-time

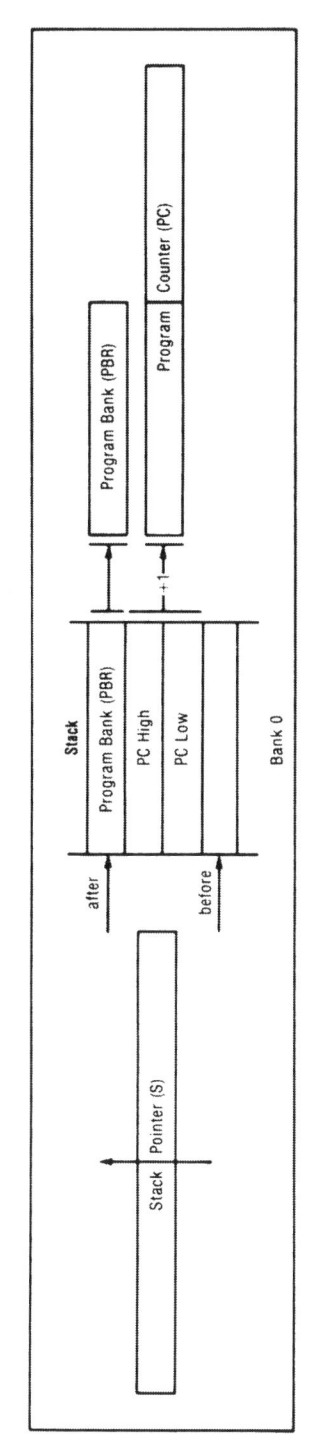

Figure 12.4. RTL.

return address; since its operand is the return address' relative offset (from the current address of the PER instruction), PER provides relocatability. As Fragment 12.2 shows, once the correct return address is on the stack, a BRA or BRL completes the synthesized BSR operation.

```
0000                      .
0000                      .
0000
0000  62FC7F         PER   RETURN-1    push run-time return address
0003  82FA7F         BRL   SUBR1       intra-bank relative branch is BSR
0006         RETURN  .                 continue processing here
0006                      .
0006                      .
0006                      .
0006                      
0006         SUBR1   .
0006                      .            execute subroutine function
0006                      .
0006                      .
0006  60             RTS               return from subroutine
```

Fragment 12.2.

In this case, you specify as the assembler operand the symbolic location of the routine you want to return to *minus one*. Remember that the return address on the stack is pulled, *then incremented*, before control is passed to it. The assembler transforms the source code operand, RETURN-1, into the instruction's object code operand, a relative displacement from the next instruction to RETURN-1. In this case, the displacement is $0002, the difference between the first byte of the BRL instruction and its last byte. (Remember, PER works the same as the BRL instruction; in both cases, the assembler turns the location you specify into a relative displacement from the program counter.) When the instruction is executed, the processor adds the displacement ($0002, in this case) to the current program counter address (the address of the BRL instruction); the resulting sum is the current absolute address of RETURN-1, which is what is pushed onto the stack.

If at run-time the PER instruction is at $1000, then the BRL instruction will be at $1003, and RETURN at $1006. Execution of PER pushes $1005 onto the stack, and the program branches to SUBR1. The RTS at the end of the subroutine causes the $1005 to be pulled from the stack, incremented to $1006 (the address of RETURN), and loaded into the program counter.

If, on the other hand, the instructions are at $2000, $2003, and $2006, then $2005 is pushed onto the stack by execution of **PER**, then pulled off again when **RTS** is encountered, incremented to $2006 (the current runtime address of **RETURN**), and loaded into the program counter.

If a macro assembler is available, synthetic instructions such as this are best dealt with by burying this code in a single macro call.

Coding a Subroutine: How and When

The uses of subroutines are many. At the simplest level, they let you compact in a single location instructions that would otherwise be repeated if coded in-line. Programmers often build up libraries of general subroutines from which they can pluck the routine they want for use in a particular program; even if the routine is only called once, this allows quick coding of commonly used functions.

The next few pages will look at a simple logic function for the 65x processors—forming the negation (two's complement) of eight- and sixteen-bit numbers—and how such a routine is written. Also covered is how subroutines in general (and library routines in particular) should be documented.

The 65x processors have no negate instruction, so the two's complement is formed by complementing the number (one's complement) and adding one.

6502 Eight-Bit Negation—A Library Example

If the value to be negated is an eight-bit value, the routine in Listing 12.1 will yield the desired result.

```
0001  0000                    KEEP    KL.12.1
0002  0000
0003  0000           ; NEGACC --
0004  0000           ;
0005  0000           ; Negate the 8-bit value in the accumulator
0006  0000           ; On entry:  Value to be negated is in accumulator
0007  0000           ; On exit:   Value now negated is in accumulator
0008  0000
0009  0000           NEGACC   START
0010  0000 49FF               EOR     #%11111111     form one's complement
0011  0002 18                 CLC                    prepare to add one
0012  0003 6901               ADC     #1             add one
0013  0005 60                 RTS                    return
0014  0006                    END
```

Listing 12.1.

It is extremely important to clearly document library routines. Perhaps the best approach is to begin with a block comment at the head of the routine, describing its name, what the routine does, what it expects as input, what direct page locations it uses during execution, if the contents of any registers or any memory special locations are modified during execution, and how and where results are returned.

By documenting the entry and exit conditions as part of the header, as in the example, when the routine is used from a library you won't have to reread the code to get this information. Although this example is quite simple, when applied to larger, more complex subroutines, the principle is the same: Document the entry and exit conditions, the function performed, and any side effects.

As a subroutine, this code to negate the accumulator takes six bytes. Each JSR instruction takes three. So calling it twice from a single program requires 12 bytes of code; if called three times, 15 bytes; if four, 18 bytes.

On the other hand, if this code were in-line once, it would take only five bytes, but each additional time it is needed would require another five bytes, so using it twice takes 10 bytes, three times takes 15, and four times takes 20. You can see that only if you need to negate the accumulator four or more times does calling this code as a subroutine make sense in view of object byte economy.

65C02, 65802, and 65816 Eight-Bit Negation

The addition of the accumulator addressing mode for the INC increment instruction on the 65C02, 65802, and 65816 means no subroutine is required for negating an eight-bit value in the accumulator on these processors: the in-line code in Fragment 12.3 takes only three bytes.

```
0000 49FF         EOR    #%11111111  form one's complement of accum
0002 1A           INC    A           increment the accum by one
```

Fragment 12.3.

Since the in-line code takes the same number of bytes as the JSR instruction, you would lose four bytes (the number in the subroutine itself) by calling it as a subroutine.

6502 Sixteen-Bit Negation

Negating sixteen-bit values makes even more sense as a subroutine on the 6502. One method, given the previously-coded routine NEGACC, is shown in Listing 12.2.

```
0001  0000                        KEEP    KL.12.2
0002  0000
0003  0000
0004  0000           ; Negate the 16-bit value in registers X-A (hi-lo)
0005  0000           ; On entry:  Value to be negated is in X-A (hi-lo)
0006  0000           ; On exit:   Value now negated is in A-Y (hi-lo)
0007  0000           ;            X is unchanged
0008  0000           ;            must be linked with NEGACC
0009  0000
0010  0000           NEGXA    START
0011  0000           ; first call the 8-bit negation routine defined a few pages back
0012  0000 200080             JSR     NEGACC        negate the low 8 bits in the accum
0013  0003           ; then get and negate the high 8 bits
0014  0003 A8                 TAY
0015  0004 8A                 TXA                   get high 8 bits into accum
0016  0005 49FF               EOR     #%11111111    form one's complement
0017  0007 6900               ADC     #0            add carry from adding 1 to low byte
0018  0009 60                 RTS                   return
0019  000A                    END
```

Listing 12.2.

Here, one subroutine (NEGXA) calls another (the subroutine described previously that negates eight bits).

65802 and 65816 Sixteen-Bit Negation

Fragment 12.4 shows that on the 65802 and 65816, the sixteen-bit accumulator can be negated in-line in only four bytes. As a result, a subroutine to negate the sixteen-bit accumulator would be inefficient, requiring five calls to catch up with the one-byte difference; in addition, you should note that there is a speed penalty associated with calling a subroutine—the time required to execute the JSR and RTS instructions.

```
0000 49FFFF          EOR     #$FFFF        form one's complement of accum
0003 1A              INC     A             increment the accum by one
```

Fragment 12.4.

Parameter Passing

When dealing with subroutines, which by definition are generalized pieces of code used over and over again, the question of how to give the subroutine the information needed to perform its function must be considered. Values passed to or from subroutines are referred to as the **parameters** of the subroutine. Parameters can include values to be acted upon, such as two numbers to be multiplied, or may be information that defines the context or range of activity of the subroutine. For example, a subroutine parameter could be the address of a region of memory to work on or in, rather than the actual data itself.

The preceding examples demonstrated one of the simplest methods of parameter-passing, by using the registers. Since many of the operations that are coded as subroutines in assembly language are primitives that operate on a single element, like "print a character on the output device" or "convert this character from binary to hexadecimal," passing parameters in registers is probably the approach most commonly found.

A natural extension of this approach, which is particularly appropriate for the 65802 and 65816, but also possible on the 6502 and 65C02, is to pass the address of a parameter list in a register (or, on the 6502 and 65C02, in *two* registers). Listing 12.3 gives an example.

```
0001  0000                         KEEP   KL.12.3
0002  0000                         65816 ON
0003  0000
0004  0000            L123         START
0005  0000 18                      CLC
0006  0001 FB                      XCE
0007  0002
0008  0002 E220                    SEP    #$20         8-bit accumulator
0009  0004                         LONGA  OFF
0010  0004
0011  0004 C210                    REP    #$10         16-bit index registers
0012  0006                         LONGI  ON
0013  0006
0014  0006 A21500                  LDX    #STRING1     pass the address of STRING1 to PRSTRNG
0015  0009 200080                  JSR    PRSTRNG      print STRING1
0016  000C
0017  000C A22800                  LDX    #STRING2     pass the address of STRING2 to PRSTRNG
0018  000F 200080                  JSR    PRSTRNG      print STRING2
0019  0012
0020  0012 38                      SEC
0021  0013 FB                      XCE
0022  0014 60                      RTS
0023  0015
0024  0015 54686973   STRING1      DC     C'This is string one',H'00'
0025  0028 54686973   STRING2      DC     C'This is string two',H'00'
0026  003B
```

```
0027 003B                    END
0028 0000
0029 0000          ; print a string of characters terminated by a 0 byte
0030 0000          ; on entry: X register holds location of string
0031 0000
0032 0000          PRSTRNG  START
0033 0000 BD0000   TOP      LDA   !0,X        get char at index position in string
0034 0003 F006              BEQ   DONE        if character is 0, return
0035 0005 200080            JSR   COUT        print character in accum
0036 0008 E8                INX               point to next char
0037 0009 80F5              BRA   TOP         loop thru string
0038 000B 60       DONE     RTS
0039 000C
0040 000C                   END
0041 0000
0042 0000          ;        COUT
0043 0000          ;        machine-dependent routine to output a character
0044 0000          ;
0045 0000          COUT     START
0046 0000          ECOUT    GEQU  $FDED       Apple // COUT
0047 0000 48                PHA               Save registers
0048 0001 DA                PHX
0049 0002 5A                PHY
0050 0003 08                PHP               and status,
0051 0004 38                SEC               switch to emulation
0052 0005 FB                XCE
0053 0006 20EDFD            JSR   ECOUT       call 6502 routine
0054 0009 18                CLC
0055 000A FB                XCE               restore native mode
0056 000B 28                PLP               restore status
0057 000C 7A                PLY               restore registers
0058 000D FA                PLX
0059 000E 68                PLA
0060 000F 60                RTS
0061 0010                   END
```

Listing 12.3.

By loading the **X** register with the address of a string constant, the subroutine **PRSTRNG** has all the information it needs to print the string at that address each time it is called. The data at the address passed in a register could also be a more complex data structure than a string constant.

On the 6502 and 65C02, a sixteen-bit address has to be passed in two registers. Because of this, parameters are often passed in fixed memory locations. Typically, these might be direct page addresses. Listing 12.4 gives an example of this method.

```
0001  0000                              KEEP    KL.12.4
0002  0000
0003  0000
0004  0000              ;       6502/65C02 example
0005  0000
0006  0000              PEX     START
0007  0000
0008  0000              PARAM   GEQU    $80
0009  0000
0010  0000 A200                 LDX     #>STRING1       load high byte of STRING1's address
0011  0002 8681                 STX     PARAM+1         store to high byte of direct page cell
0012  0004 A20C                 LDX     #<STRING1       load low byte of STRING1's address
0013  0006 8680                 STX     PARAM           store to low byte of direct page cell
0014  0008 200080               JSR     PRSTRNG         print STRING1
0015  000B 60                   RTS
0016  000C
0017  000C 54686973     STRING1 DC      C'This is string one',H'00'
0018  001F
0019  001F                      END
0020  0000
0021  0000              ; print a string of characters terminated by a 0 byte
0022  0000              ; on entry: direct page location PARAM holds address of string
0023  0000
0024  0000              PRSTRNG START
0025  0000              COUT    GEQU    $FDED           Apple // output routine
0026  0000
0027  0000 A000                 LDY     #0              start at string position zero
0028  0002 B180         LOOP    LDA     (PARAM),Y       get char at index position in string
0029  0004 F006                 BEQ     DONE            if character is 0, return
0030  0006 20EDFD               JSR     COUT            print character in accum
0031  0009 C8                   INY                     point to next char
0032  000A D0F6                 BNE     LOOP            loop thru string: must be < 256
0033  000C 60           DONE    RTS
0034  000D
0035  000D
0036  000D                      END
```

Listing 12.4.

Unfortunately, it takes eight bytes to set up **PARAM** each time **PRSTRNG** is called. As a result, a frequently used method of passing parameters to a subroutine is to code the data in-line, immediately following the subroutine call. This technique (*see* Fragment 12.5) uses no registers and no data memory, only program memory.

12 The Basic Building Block: The Subroutine 241

```
0000                  .
0000                  .
0000 200080      JSR      PRSTRNG    print the following string
0003 54686520    DC       C'The string to be printed',H'00'
001C             RETURN   .          execution continues here
001C                      .
001C                      .
001C                      .
001C                      .
```

Fragment 12.5.

This method looks, at first glance, bizarre. Normally, when a subroutine returns to the calling section of code, the instruction immediately following the JSR is executed. Obviously, in this example, the data stored at that location is not executable code, but string data. Execution should resume instead at the label RETURN, which is exactly what happens using the PRSTRNG coded in Listing 12.5. The return address pushed onto the stack by the JSR is *not* a return address at all; it is, rather, the parameter to PRSTRNG.

```
0001 0000                     KEEP  KL.12.5
0002 0000                     65816 ON
0003 0000
0004 0000       PRSTRNG START
0005 0000
0006 0000 18                  CLC
0007 0001 FB                  XCE
0008 0002
0009 0002 E220                SEP   #$20     8-bit accum
0010 0004                     LONGA OFF
0011 0004
0012 0004 C210                REP   #$10     16-bit index regs
0013 0006                     LONGI ON
0014 0006
0015 0006 FA                  PLX            pull return address
0016 0007 E8                  INX            and increment to point past JSR to string
0017 0008 BD0000  LOOP        LDA   !0,X     get char at index position in string
0018 000B F006                BEQ   DONE     if character is 0, return
0019 000D 200080              JSR   COUT     print char in accum
0020 0010 E8                  INX            point to next char
0021 0011 80F5                BRA   LOOP     loop thru string
```

```
0022 0013
0023 0013                     ; push pointer to zero-terminator as return addr (RETURN-1)
0024 0013
0025 0013 DA        DONE      PHX
0026 0014 60                  RTS             return to label RETURN
0027 0015                     END
0028 0000
0029 0000
0030 0000         ;   COUT
0031 0000         ;   machine-dependent routine to output a character
0032 0000         ;
0033 0000         COUT   START
0034 0000         ECOUT  GEQU  $FDED         Apple // COUT
0035 0000 48             PHA                 Save registers
0036 0001 DA             PHX
0037 0002 5A             PHY
0038 0003 08             PHP                 and status,
0039 0004 38             SEC                 switch to emulation
0040 0005 FB             XCE
0041 0006 20EDFD         JSR   ECOUT         call 6502 routine
0042 0009 18             CLC
0043 000A FB             XCE                 restore native mode
0044 000B 28             PLP                 restore status
0045 000C 7A             PLY                 restore registers
0046 000D FA             PLX                 return
0047 000E 68             PLA
0048 000F 60             RTS
0049 0010               END
```

Listing 12.5.

The parameter address on the stack need only be pulled and incremented once, and the data can then be accessed in the same manner as in the foregoing example. Since the loop terminates when the zero end-of-string marker is reached, pushing its address in the X register onto the stack gives **RTS** a correct return value—**RETURN-1**—the byte before the location where execution should resume. Note that the data bank is assumed to equal the program bank.

The advantage of this method is in bytes used: there is no need for any explicit parameter-passing by the calling code, and the JSR mechanism makes the required information available to the subroutine automatically. In fact, for most applications on all four 65x microprocessors, this method uses fewer bytes for passing a single parameter than any other.

12 The Basic Building Block: The Subroutine

One slight disadvantage of this method is that if the string is to be output more than once, it and its preceding **JSR** must be made into a subroutine that is called to output the string.

A second disadvantage to this method comes in calling routines to which more than one parameter must be passed. This last example demonstrated how a parameter (the address of the string) can be implicitly passed on the stack. But there is no way to extend the principle so two parameters could be implicitly passed, for instance, to a routine that compares two strings. On the other hand, parameters can also be explicitly passed on the stack. The push effective address instructions and stack-relative addressing modes make this all the easier, as Fragment 12.6 and Listing 12.6 show.

```
0000 F40080      PEA    STRING1    push address of STRING1 onto stack
0003 F40080      PEA    STRING2    push address of STRING2 onto stack
0006 200080      JSR    COMPARE    compare the two
0009            .                  return and continue processing
0009            .
0009            .
```

Fragment 12.6.

```
0001  0000                   KEEP   KL.12.6
0002  0000                   65816 ON
0003  0000
0004  0000         ; compare two strings of characters, each terminated by a 0 byte
0005  0000         ; on entry: locs of strings are stacked just below the return addr
0006  0000         ; on exit:  carry clear if chars match up to len of shortest string
0007  0000         ;           else carry set for no match
0008  0000
0009  0000         COMPARE START
0010  0000
0011  0000 08              PHP              assume native mode; save status
0012  0001
0013  0001 C210            REP    #$10
0014  0003                 LONGI  ON
0015  0003 E220            SEP    #$20
0016  0005                 LONGA  OFF
0017  0005
0018  0005 A00000          LDY    #0
0019  0008 B303    LOOP    LDA    (3,S),Y   get character from first string
0020  000A F007            BEQ    PASS      if zero, end of string: match
0021  000C D305            CMP    (5,S),Y   compare to corresponding char in 2nd string
0022  000E D006            BNE    FAIL      branch if not equal; probably failure
0023  0010 C8              INY              else do next pair
0024  0011 80F5            BRA    LOOP
0025  0013
0026  0013
0027  0013         ;        matches shortest string: ok
0028  0013
0029  0013 28      PASS    PLP              restore previous status
0030  0014 18              CLC              but clear carry
0031  0015 60              RTS
0032  0016
0033  0016 B305    FAIL    LDA    (5,S),Y   was last failure due to end of string2?
0034  0018 F0F9            BEQ    PASS      yes; let it pass
0035  001A
0036  001A 28              PLP              restore previous status
0037  001B 38              SEC              sorry, no good
0038  001C 60              RTS
0039  001D
0040  001D                 END
```

Listing 12.6.

12 The Basic Building Block: The Subroutine

This example, which compares two strings to see if they are equal up to the length of the shorter of the two strings, uses parameters that have been explicitly passed on the stack. This approach, since it explicitly passes the addresses of the strings, lets them be located anywhere and referred to any number of times. Its problem is that when the subroutine returns, the parameters are left on the stack. Clearly, the subroutine should clean up the stack before returning; however, it can't simply pull the parameters off, because the return address is sitting on top of the stack (which explains why stack offsets of three and five, rather than one and three, are used).

Perhaps the cleanest way to pass parameters on the stack prior to a subroutine call is to decompose the **JSR** instruction into two: one to push the return address, the other to transfer to the subroutine. The push effective address instructions again come in handy. Fragment 12.7 shows how the parameters to the routine in Listing 12.7 are passed.

```
0000                 .
0000                 .
0000  F4FF7F    PEA    RETURN-1   push return addr before parameters
0003  F40080    PEA    STRING1    push address of STRING1 onto stack
0006  F40080    PEA    STRING2    push address of STRING2 onto stack
0009  4C0080    JMP    COMPARE    compare them
000C       RETURN .                continue processing
000C                 .
000C                 .
000C
```

Fragment 12.7.

```
0001  0000                        KEEP    KL.12.7
0002  0000                        65816 ON
0003  0000
0004  0000         ; compare two strings of characters, each terminated by a 0 byte
0005  0000         ; on entry: locs of strings are at top of stack
0006  0000         ;           return address is stacked just beneath
0007  0000         ; on exit:  carry clear if chars match up to len of shortest string
0008  0000         ;           else carry set for no match
0009  0000
0010  0000         COMPARE START
0011  0000
0012  0000 08              PHP                assume native mode; save status
0013  0001
0014  0001 C210            REP     #$10
0015  0003                 LONGI ON
0016  0003
0017  0003 E220            SEP     #$20
0018  0005                 LONGA OFF
0019  0005
0020  0005 A00000          LDY     #0
0021  0008 B301   LOOP     LDA     (1,S),Y    get character from first string
0022  000A F007            BEQ     PASS       if zero, end of string: match
0023  000C D303            CMP     (3,S),Y    compare to corresponding char in 2nd string
0024  000E D007            BNE     FAIL       bra if not equal; probably failure
0025  0010 C8              INY                else do next pair
0026  0011 80F5            BRA     LOOP
0027  0013
0028  0013         ;       matches shortest string
0029  0013
0030  0013 28     PASS     PLP                they match up to shortest string;
0031  0014 18              CLC                restore status, but clear carry
0032  0015 8006            BRA     EXIT
0033  0017
0034  0017 B303   FAIL     LDA     (3,S),Y    was last failure due to end of string2?
0035  0019 F0F8            BEQ     PASS       yes; let it pass
0036  001B 28              PLP                restore status, but set carry (no match)
0037  001C 38              SEC
0038  001D
0039  001D FA     EXIT     PLX                clean up stack: remove both 16-bit params
0040  001E FA              PLX
0041  001F 60              RTS                now return
0042  0020
0043  0020                 END
```

Listing 12.7.

12 The Basic Building Block: The Subroutine

Since the return address was pushed first, the parameter addresses on the stack are accessed via offsets of one and three. Before returning, two pull instructions pop the parameters off the stack, then the **RTS** is executed, which returns control to the main program with the stack in order.

Passing parameters on the stack is particularly well-suited for both recursive routines (routines that call themselves) and reentrant routines (routines that can be interrupted and used successfully both by the interrupting code and the original call) because new memory is automatically allocated for parameters for each invocation of the subroutine. This is the method generally used by most high-level languages that support recursion.

Fragment 12.8 sets up multiple parameters implicitly passed on the stack by coding after the **JSR**, not data, but pointers to data. The routine called is in Listing 12.8.

```
0000                   .
0000                   .
0000 200080    JSR     COMPARE    compare two strings; addresses follow
0003 0080      DC      A'STRING1' address of STRING1
0005 0080      DC      A'STRING2' address of STRING2
0007 RETURN    .                  continue processing
0007                   .
0007                   .
0007
```

Fragment 12.8.

While this subroutine, unlike the previous one, uses a dozen bytes just getting itself ready to start, each call requires only seven bytes (three for the **JSR**, and two each for the parameters), while each call to the previous routine required twelve bytes (three **PER**s at three bytes each plus three for the **JMP**).

Apple Computer's ProDOS operating system takes this method a step further: all operating system routines are called via a **JSR** to a single ProDOS entry point. One of the parameters that follows the **JSR** specifies the routine to be called, the second parameter specifies the address of the routine's parameter block. This method allows the entry points of the internal ProDOS routines to "float" from one version of ProDOS to the next; user programs don't need to know where any given routine is located.

```
0001  0000                      KEEP  KL.12.8
0002  0000                      65816 ON
0003  0000
0004  0000         ; compare two strings of characters, each terminated by a 0 byte
0005  0000         ; on entry:  increment address at top of stack: pts to loc of 1st str
0006  0000         ;            incr twice more to point to loc of 2nd str
0007  0000
0008  0000         COMPARE  START
0009  0000
0010  0000 C210             REP   #$10         caller must save and
0011  0002                   LONGI ON                restore mode status
0012  0002
0013  0002 E220             SEP   #$20
0014  0004                   LONGA OFF
0015  0004
0016  0004 7A               PLY
0017  0005 C8               INY                points to indirect address of 1st str
0018  0006 B90000            LDA   !0,Y        load accum with address of 1st string
0019  0009 C8               INY
0020  000A C8               INY                point Y to indirect addr of 2nd string
0021  000B BE0000            LDX   !0,Y        load X with address of 2nd string
0022  000E C8               INY                point Y to RETURN-1 for RTS
0023  000F 5A               PHY                  and push it onto stack for RTS
0024  0010 A8               TAY                load Y with address of 1st string
0025  0011
0026  0011 B90000   LOOP    LDA   !0,Y         get character from first string
0027  0014 F009             BEQ   PASS         if zero, end of string: match
0028  0016 DD0000            CMP   !0,X        compare to corresponding char in 2nd string
0029  0019 D006             BNE   FAIL         bra if not equal; probably failure
0030  001B C8               INY                else do next pair
0031  001C E8               INX
0032  001D 80F2             BRA   LOOP
0033  001F 18       PASS    CLC                they match up to shortest string;
0034  0020 60               RTS
0035  0021 BD0000   FAIL    LDA   !0,X         was last failure due to end of string2?
0036  0024 F0F9             BEQ   PASS           yes; let it pass
0037  0026 38               SEC                sorry, no good
0038  0027 60       EXIT    RTS                now return!
0039  0028
0040  0028                   END
```

Listing 12.8.

13 | Interrupts and System Control Instructions

This is the last chapter that introduces new instructions; almost the entire 65816 instruction set, and all of the addressing modes, have been presented. The only instructions remaining are the interrupt and status register control instructions, listed in Table 13.1. This chapter introduces interrupt processing, as well.

Most of the system control functions described are of practical interest only if you are implementing systems programs for the 65x processors, such as operating systems or device handling routines. It is quite possible that if you are programming on an existing machine, with full operating system support, you will have little cause to use many of the system control instructions.

Table 13.1. Interrupt and System Control Instructions.

	Available on:			
Mnemonic	6502	65C02	65802/816	Description
BRK	x	x	x	Break (software interrupt)
RTI	x	x	x	Return from Interrupt
NOP	x	x	x	No operation
SEC	x	x	x	Set carry flag
CLC	x	x	x	Clear carry flag
SED	x	x	x	Set decimal mode
CLD	x	x	x	Clear decimal mode
SEI	x	x	x	Set interrupt disable flag
CLI	x	x	x	Clear interrupt disable flag
CLV	x	x	x	Clear overflow flag
SEP			x	Set status register bits
REP			x	Clear status register bits
COP			x	Co-processor or software interrupt
STP			x	Stop the clock
WAI			x	Wait for interrupt
WDM			x	Reserved for expansion

Interrupts

An **interrupt**, as the name implies, is a disruption of the normal sequential flow of control, as modified by the flow-altering statements such as branches and jump instructions encountered in the stream of code.

Hardware interrupts are generated when an external device causes one of the interrupt pins, usually the **IRQ'** or **interrupt request** pin, to be electrically pulled low from its normally high signal level. The typical application of 65x interrupts is the implementation of an interrupt-driven I/O system, where input-output devices are allowed to operate **asynchronously** from the processor. This type of system is generally considered to be superior to the alternative type of I/O management system, where devices are polled at regular intervals to determine whether or not they are ready to send or receive data; in an interrupt-driven system, I/O service only claims processor time when an I/O operation is ready for service. Figure 13.1 illustrates how processor time is spent under either system.

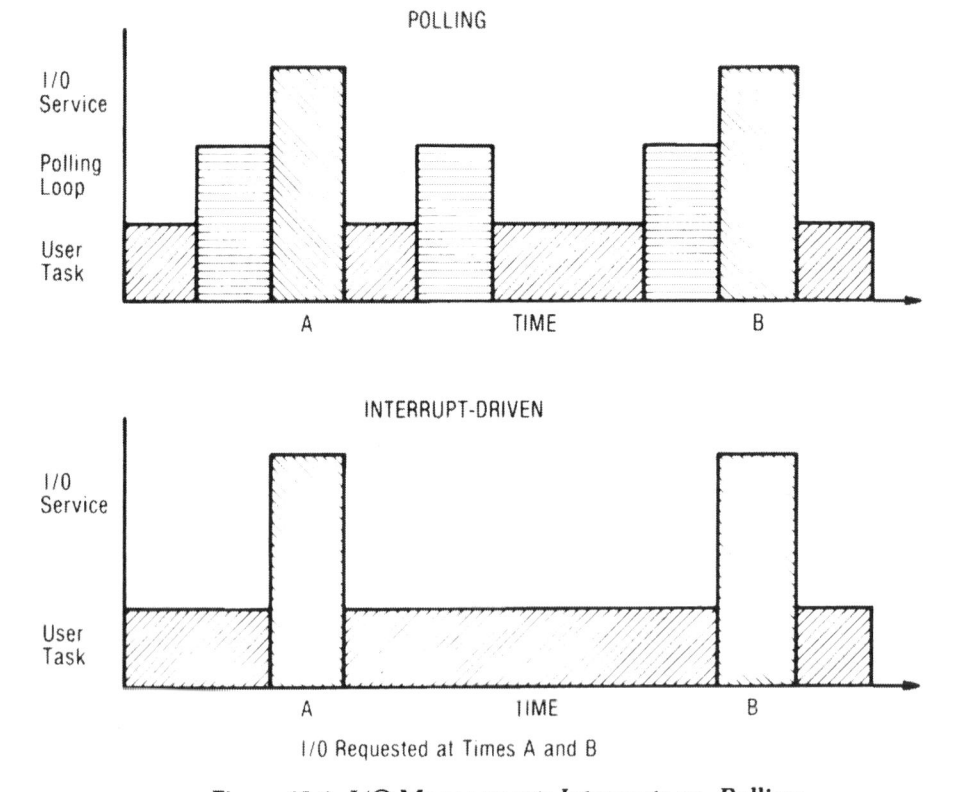

Figure 13.1. I/O Management: Interrupts vs. Polling.

Software interrupts are special instructions that trigger the same type of system behavior as occurs during a hardware interrupt.

When an interrupt signal is received, the processor loads the program counter with the address stored in one of the sixteen-bit **interrupt vectors** in page $FF of bank zero memory, jumping to the (bank zero) routine whose address is stored there. (In the case of the 6502, 65C02, and 65802, "bank zero" refers to the lone 64K bank of memory addressable by these processors.) The routine that it finds there must determine the nature of the interrupt and handle it accordingly.

When an interrupt is first received, the processor finishes the currently executing instruction and pushes the double-byte program counter (which now points to the instruction following the one being executed when the interrupt was received) and the status flag byte onto the stack. Since the 6502 and 65C02 have only a sixteen-bit program counter, only a sixteen-bit program counter address is pushed onto the stack; naturally, this is the way the 65802 and 65816 behave when in emulation mode as well. The native-mode 65802 and 65816 must (and do) also push the program counter bank register, since it is changed to zero when control is transferred through the bank zero interrupt vectors.

As Figure 13.2 shows, in native mode the program bank is pushed onto the stack first, before the program counter and the status register; but in emulation mode it is lost. This means that if a 65816 program is running in emulation mode in a bank other than zero when an interrupt occurs, there will be no way of knowing where to return to after the interrupt is processed because the original bank will have been lost.

This unavoidable but fairly esoteric problem can be dealt with in two ways. The first is simply never to run in emulation mode outside bank zero. The second solution, which is to store the value of the program counter bank register in a known location before entering the emulation mode with a non-zero program counter bank register, is described later in this chapter.

In addition to pushing the status and program counter information onto the stack, the **d** decimal flag in the status register is cleared (except on the 6502), returning arithmetic to binary mode. The **i** interrupt disable flag is set, preventing further interrupts until your interrupt-service routine resets it (it may do this as soon as it is finished saving the previous context) or the routine is exited (with an **RTI** return-from-interrupt instruction). Indeed, if the interrupt flag had already been set, the first interrupt would have been ignored as well.

This last feature of disabling interrupts, however, does not apply to a second type of hardware interrupt, called the non-maskable interrupt (or **NMI'**) for the very reason that it cannot be ignored, even if the **i** flag is set. **NMI'** is triggered by a separate pin on a 65x processor; its use is usually reserved for a single high priority interrupt, such as power failure detection.

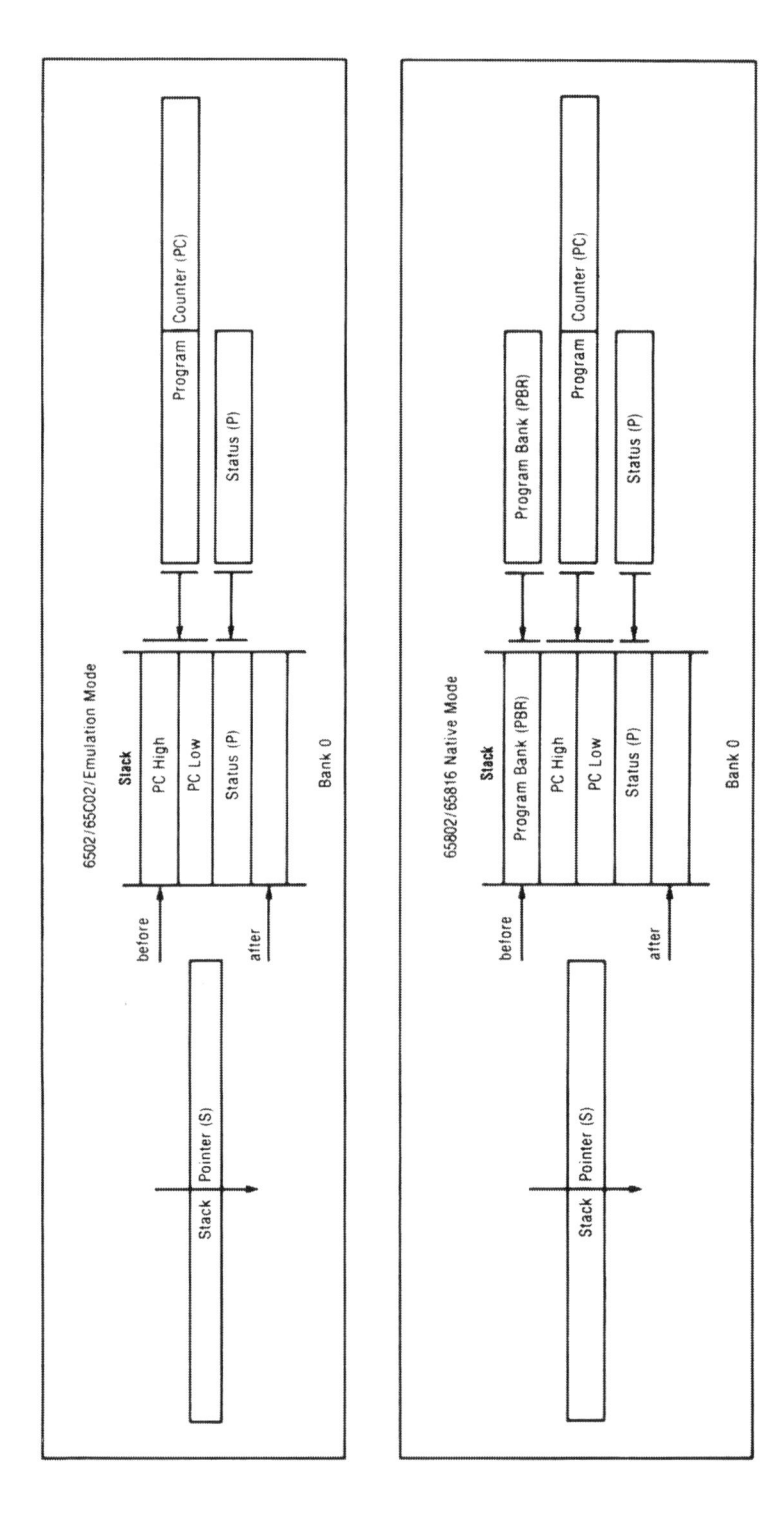

Figure 13.2. Interrupt Processing.

Just as the two types of interrupt have their own signals and pins, they also have their own vectors—locations where the address of the interrupt-handling routine is stored. As Table 13.2 shows, on the 65802 and 65816 there are two sets of interrupt vectors: one set for when the processor is in emulation mode, and one set for when the processor is in native mode. Needless to say, the locations of the emulation mode vectors are identical to the locations of the 6502 and 65C02 vectors.

Table 13.2. Interrupt Vectors.

Emulation mode, $e = 1$			Native mode, $e = 0$		
00FFFE,FF	—	IRQ/BRK	00FFEE,EF	—	IRQ
00FFFC,FD	—	RESET			
00FFFA,FB	—	NMI	00FFEA,EB	—	NMI
00FFF8,F9	—	ABORT	00FFE8,E9	—	ABORT
			00FFE6,E7	—	BRK
00FFF4,F5	—	COP	00FFE4,E5	—	COP

As you can see in Table 13.2, there are several other vector locations named in addition to IRQ' and NMI'. Note that there is no native mode RESET' vector: RESET' always forces the processor to emulation mode. Also note that the IRQ' vector among the 6502 vectors is listed as IRQ'/BRK, while in the 65802/65816 native mode list, each has a separate vector.

The **BRK** and **COP** vectors are for handling **software interrupts**. A software interrupt is an instruction that imitates the behavior of a hardware interrupt by stacking the program counter and the status register, and then branching through a vector location. On the 6502 and 65C02, the location jumped to in response to the execution of a **BRK** (a software interrupt) and the location to which control is transferred after an **IRQ'** (a hardware interrupt) is the same; the interrupt routine itself must determine the source of the interrupt (that is, either software or hardware) by checking the value of bit five of the processor status register pushed onto the stack. On the 6502 and 65C02 (and the 6502 emulation mode of the 65802 and 65816), bit five is the **b** break flag. Note first that this is not true of the 65816 native mode, since bit five of its status register is the **m** memory select flag. Secondly, notice that it is the *stacked* status byte which must be checked, *not* the current status byte.

Suppose, for example, that the **IRQ'/BRK** vector at $00:FFFE.FF contains the address $B100 (naturally, in the low-high order all 65x addresses are stored in), and the code in Fragment 13.1 is stored starting at $B100. When a **BRK** instruction is executed, this routine distinguishes it from a hardware interrupt and handles each uniquely.

```
0000                    ORG     $B100
0000
0000         IRQBRKIN   START
0000 8D1000             STA     SAVEA       save original accumulator
0003 68                 PLA                 copy p register
0004 48                 PHA                 return it to stack
0005 2920               AND     #%00010000  look at bit four only
0007 D0F7               BNE     ISBRK       bra if bit 4 set:
0009         ;                                  BRK caused interrupt
0009         .                              else caused by IRQ'
0009         .
0009         .
0009         .
0009 4C0C00             JMP     RETURN      reload accum and return
000C
000C         ; handle interrupt caused by BRK instruction
000C
000C         ISBRK      .                   do BRK handling code
000C                    .
000C                    .
000C AD1000  RETURN     LDA     SAVEA       reload saved accumulator
000F 40                 RTI                 return
0010
0010 00      SAVEA      DS      1
0011
0011                    END
```

Fragment 13.1.

The RTI, or **return-from-interrupt** instruction is similar to the RTS (return-from-subroutine) instruction. RTI returns control to the location following the instruction that was interrupted by pulling the return address off the stack. Unlike the RTS instruction, however, since the status register was also pushed onto the stack in response to the interrupt, it too is restored, returning the system to its prior state. Further, in the 65802/65816 native mode the RTI instruction behaves like an RTL (return from subroutine long), in that the program counter bank register is also pulled off the stack. This difference makes it critical that the processor always be in the same state when the RTI instruction is executed as it was when it was interrupted. The fact that the 65816 has separate vector groups for native and emulation modes makes this easier to achieve.

There is another key difference between the RTI and the RTS or RTL: RTS and RTL increment the return address after pulling it off the stack and before loading it into the program counter; RTI on the other hand loads the program counter with the stacked return address unchanged.

RTI will probably not function correctly in the special case where an interrupt occurred while code was executing in the emulation mode in a non-zero bank: RTI will try to return control to an address within the bank the RTI is executed in, which will probably not be the correct bank because (as on the 6502 and 65C02) the bank address is not stacked. As mentioned earlier, the only way to deal with this is to save the bank address prior to entering emulation mode. When the interrupt handler returns, it should use this saved bank address to execute a long jump to an RTI instruction stored somewhere within the return bank; the long jump will preset the program bank address to the correct value before the RTI is executed.

The interrupt handler itself should enter the native mode if interrupts are to be reenabled before exiting in order to avoid the same problem, then return to emulation mode before exiting via the long jump to the RTI instruction.

Concerning the **BRK** instruction, you should also note that although its second byte is basically a "don't care" byte—that is, it can have any value—the **BRK** (and **COP** instruction as well) is a two-byte instruction; the second byte sometimes is used as a **signature byte** to determine the nature of the **BRK** being executed. When an RTI instruction is executed, control always returns to the *second byte past* the **BRK** opcode. Figure 13.3 illustrates a stream of instructions in hexadecimal form, the **BRK** instruction, its signature byte, and the location an **RTI** returns to. The **BRK** instruction has been inserted in the middle; after the **BRK** is processed by a routine (such as the skeleton of a routine described above), control will return to the **BCC** instruction, which is the second byte past the **BRK** opcode.

The fact that the opcode for the **BRK** instruction is 00 is directly related to one of its uses: **patching** existing programs. Patching is the process of inserting instruction data in the middle of an existing program in memory to modify (usually to correct) the program without reassembling it. This is a favored method of some programmers in debugging and testing assembly language programs, and is quite simple if you have a good machine-level monitor program that allows easy examination and modification of memory locations. However, if the program to be patched is stored in **PROM** (programmable read-only memory), the only way to modify a program that has already been "burned-in" is to change any remaining one bits to zeroes. Once a PROM bit has been "blown" to zero, it cannot be restored to a one. The only way to modify the flow of control is to insert **BRK** instructions—all zeroes—at the patch location and to have the **BRK** handling routine take control from there.

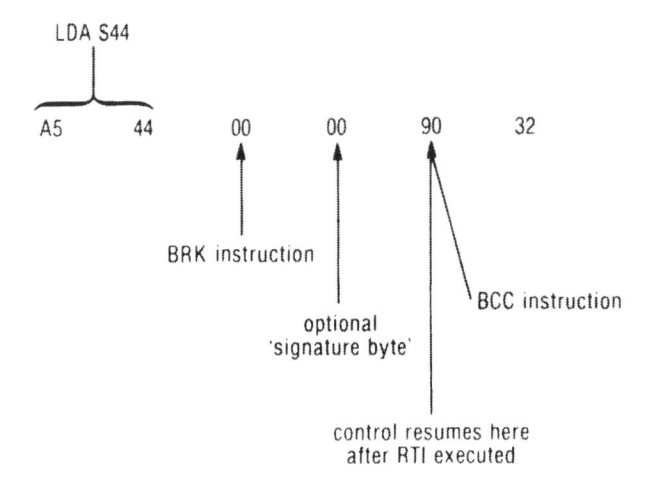

```
              LDA S44
         ┌──────┴──────┐
    A5       44       00        00        90         32
                       ↑         ↑         ↑
                       │         │         │
                  BRK instruction         BCC instruction
                              optional
                           'signature byte'

                           control resumes here
                            after RTI executed
```

Figure 13.3. Break Signature Byte Illustration.

Processing Interrupts

Before an interrupt handling routine can perform a useful task, it must first know what is expected of it. The example of distinguishing a **BRK** from an **IRQ** is just a special case of the general problem of identifying the source of an interrupt. The fact that different vectors exist for different types of interrupts—for example, **NMI** would usually be reserved for some catastrophic type of interrupt, like "power failure imminent", which demanded immediate response—solves the problem somewhat. Typically, however, in an interrupt-driven system there will be multiple sources of interrupts through a single vector. The 65802 and 65816, when in native mode, eliminate the need for a routine to distinguish between **IRQ** and **BRK**, such as the one above, by providing a separate **BRK** vector, as indicated in Table 13.2. Although this does simplify interrupt processing somewhat, it was done primarily to free up bit five in the status register to serve as the native mode memory select flag, which determines the size of the accumulator.

The interrupt source is generally determined by a software technique called **polling**: when an interrupt occurs, all of the devices that are known to be possible sources of interrupts are checked for an indication that they were the source of the interrupt. (I/O devices typically have a status bit for this purpose.) A hardware solution also exists, which is to externally modify the value that is apparently contained in the vector location depending on the source of interrupt. The 65816 aids the implementation of such systems by providing a **VECTOR PULL** signal,

13 Interrupts and System Control Instructions 257

which is asserted whenever the interrupt vector memory locations are being accessed in response to an interrupt.

A simple example of the polling method could be found in a system that includes the 6522 Versatile Interface Adapter as one of its I/O controllers. The 6522 is a peripheral control IC designed for hardware compatibility with the 65x processor family. The 6522 includes two parallel I/O ports and two timer/counters. It can be programmed to generate interrupts in response to events such as hardware handshaking signals, indicating that data has been read or written to its I/O ports, or to respond to one of its countdown timers reaching zero. The 6522 contains sixteen different control and I/O registers, each of which is typically mapped to an adjacent address in the 65x memory space. When an interrupt occurs, the processor must poll the **interrupt flag register**, shown in Figure 13.4, to determine the cause of the interrupt.

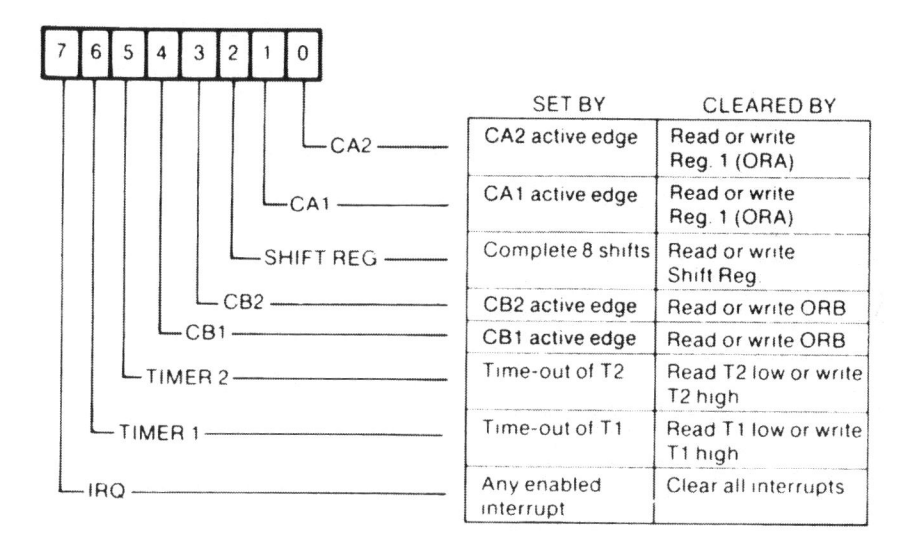

Bit	Label	SET BY	CLEARED BY
0	CA2	CA2 active edge	Read or write Reg. 1 (ORA)
1	CA1	CA1 active edge	Read or write Reg. 1 (ORA)
2	SHIFT REG	Complete 8 shifts	Read or write Shift Reg.
3	CB2	CB2 active edge	Read or write ORB
4	CB1	CB1 active edge	Read or write ORB
5	TIMER 2	Time-out of T2	Read T2 low or write T2 high
6	TIMER 1	Time-out of T1	Read T1 low or write T1 high
7	IRQ	Any enabled interrupt	Clear all interrupts

Figure 13.4. 6522 VIA Interrupt Flag Register.

If register zero of the 6522 is mapped to location $FF:B080 of a 65816 system, for example, the interrupt flag register would normally be found at $FF:B08D. The polling routine in Fragment 13.2 would be needed whenever an interrupt occurred. To keep the example simple, assume that only the two timer interrupts are enabled (for example, timer 1 to indicate, in a multi-tasking system, that a given process' time-slice has expired and the next process must be activated; timer 2, on the other hand, to maintain a time-of-day clock).

```
0000                IRQIN   START
0000 E220                   SEP     #$20            8-bit accumulator
0002                        LONGA   OFF
0002
0002 8D1B00                 STA     SAVEA           save the accumulator
0005 AF8DB0FF               LDA     $FFB08D         device interrupt register
0009 10F5                   BPL     NEXTDEV         branch if bit 7 clear
000B 0A                     ASL     A               check bits 6 & 5
000C 0A                     ASL     A               bit 6 to carry, 5 to sign
000D 30F1                   BMI     TIMER2          if 5 set, timer2 caused
000F                ;                                 interrupt
000F
000F                ; timer2 didn't cause interrupt; timer1?
000F
000F 90EF                   BCC     ERROR           interrupt source unknown
0011
0011                ; bit 6 set: timer1 caused interrupt
0011
0011                TIMER1  .                       timer 1 handler code
0011                        .
0011                        .
0011
0011 8004                   BRA     RETURN
0013
0013                ; bit 5 set: timer2 caused interrupt
0013
0013                TIMER2  .                       timer 2 handler code
0013                        .
0013                        .
0013 8002                   BRA     RETURN
0015
0015                ; interrupt not caused by 6522: check other devices
0015
0015                NEXTDEV .                       code to poll next device
0015                        .
0015                        .
0015 8000                   BRA     RETURN
0017
0017                ERROR   .                       error handling code
0017                        .
0017                        .
0017
0017 AD1B00      RETURN     LDA     SAVEA           reload saved accumulator
001A 40                     RTI                     and return
001B
001B 00          SAVEA      DS      1
001C                        END
```

Fragment 13.2.

When the interrupt flag register is loaded into the accumulator, the first thing checked is whether or not bit seven is set; bit seven is set if any 6522 interrupt is enabled. If it is clear, then the interrupt handler branches to the location **NEXTDEV**, which polls all other connected I/O devices looking for the source of the interrupt.

If the 6522 was the source of the interrupt, then two shifts move the flag register's bit six into the carry and bit five into bit seven of the accumulator. Since bit five is set by the time-out of timer 2, if the high-order bit of the accumulator is set (minus), then the source of the interrupt must be timer 2. If timer 2 did not cause the interrupt, then the carry flag is checked; if it's set, then timer 1 caused the interrupt; if it's clear, then timer 1 didn't cause it either, so there has been some kind of error.

Control is thus assigned to the correct routine to handle the specific source of interrupt.

It is important to note that in both examples in this chapter, the accumulator was saved in memory prior to its use within the interrupt-handling routine. You should further note that in the second example, which is specific to the 65816, only the low-order byte of the accumulator was stored, because the **STA SAVEA** instruction was executed after the **SEP #$20** instruction, which set the accumulator size to eight bits. When the **RTI** instruction is executed at the end of the interrupt service routine, the **m** status flag will be restored to whatever value it had prior to the interrupt. If **m** was clear and the accumulator was in sixteen-bit mode, the high-order byte will have been preserved throughout the interrupt routine provided that none of the interrupt handling routines switch into sixteen-bit mode; if they do, the high-order part of the accumulator must be saved first, then restored before execution of the **RTI**.

An important concept related to interrupt handling is that of **reentrancy**; a reentrant program can be interrupted and literally reentered by the interrupt handling routine and return correct values for both the original invocation and the reentrant call from the interrupt handler. Reentrancy is normally achieved by using no addressable memory—only registers, which may be saved and restored on the stack on entry and exit, and variable storage dynamically allocated on the stack each time the routine is entered. The stack relative addressing modes simplify the writing of reentrant routines considerably.

Interrupt Response Time

By saving only the essentials—the program counter, program counter bank in 65802/65816 native mode, and status register—and shifting the burden of saving and restoring user registers (those that are actually used) to the programmer of the interrupt-handler, the 65x processors provide maximum flexibility and efficiency. It is quite possible for an interrupt routine to do useful work—such as checking the status of something within the system at periodic intervals—without using *any* registers.

At either seven or eight cycles per interrupt—the time required to stack the program counter, pc bank, and status register, and then jump through the interrupt vectors—the interrupt response cycle is among the longest-executing 65x instructions. Since an interrupt always lets the current instruction complete execution, there is a possible seven-cycle delay between the receipt of an interrupt and the servicing of one; this delay is called the **interrupt latency.** Small as the delay is, it can be significant in the servicing of data acquisition and control devices operating in real time, systems in which it is important that interrupts be disabled as little as possible.

It has been the goal of the designers of the 65x series to keep interrupt latency to a minimum. To further reduce interrupt latency, the 65802 and 65816 introduced a special new instruction, the **WAI** or **wait for interrupt** instruction. In an environment where the processor can be dedicated to serving interrupts—that is, where the interrupts provide timing or synchronization information, rather than being used to allow asynchronous I/O operations to be performed—the processor can be put into a special state where it sits and waits for an interrupt to happen. This lets any of the user registers be saved before the interrupt occurs, and eliminates the latency required to complete an existing instruction. Upon execution of a **WAI** instruction, the processor goes into a very low-power state, signals the outside world that it is waiting by pulling the bi-directional **RDY** signal low, and sits idle until an interrupt is received. When that occurs, response is immediate since no cycles are wasted completing an executing instruction.

There are two responses to an interrupt after the **WAI** instruction is executed. The first, as you might expect, is to release the waiting condition and transfer control to the appropriate interrupt vector, as normally takes place whenever interrupts are serviced. The second response is if maskable interrupts (on the **IRQ'** line) have been disabled, in which case the normal interrupt processing does not occur. However, since the waiting condition is released, execution continues with the instruction following the **WAI** opcode. This means that specialized interrupt-synchronization routines can be coded with a one-cycle latency between receipt of interrupt and response.

A second, similar 65802/65816 instruction is the **STP** or **stop the clock** instruction. The **STP** instruction reduces on-chip power consumption to a very low level by stopping the phase two clock input. Since power consumption of CMOS circuits increases with operating frequency, by halting the clock input the **STP** instruction is able to reduce the power consumption of the 65816 to its lowest possible value. Like the WAI instruction, the STP idles the processor after being executed. Further, the processor I/O buffers are disabled, making the bus available. The processor is powered back up in response to a RESET' signal being asserted.

The RESET' pin is an input similar to the IRQ' and NMI' inputs. It is used to perform system initialization or reinitialization. When a 65x system is first powered up, RESET' must be asserted by external power-up circuitry. It can also be used to let the user force the system into a known state, for example, to break out of an infinite loop.

When RESET' is asserted, the processor is forced to emulation mode and the registers and status flags are initialized as shown in Table 13.3. Note that the initialization of the index register high bytes to zero is really a function of x being forced to one; $x = 1$ always clears the high byte of the index registers.

Table 13.3. Reset Initialization.

Stack High	01
Direct Page Register	0000
X Register High	00
Y Register High	00
Program Bank Register	00
Data Bank Register	00
Status Register	$m = 1, x = 1, d = 0, i = 1$
Emulation Flag	1

In addition to the BRK, IRQ', RESET' and NMI' vectors discussed, there are two remaining interrupt-like vectors. These are the COP (co-processor) and ABORT' vectors. The COP vector is essentially a second software interrupt, similar to BRK, with its own vector. Although it can be used in a manner similar to BRK, it is intended particularly for use with co-processors, such as floating-point processors. Like BRK, it is a two-byte instruction with the second available as a signature byte.

The ABORT' vector contains the address of the routine which gains control when the 65816 ABORT' signal is asserted. Prior to transferring control through the ABORT' vector, the current instruction is completed but *no registers are modified.* The pc bank, program counter, and status register are pushed onto the stack in the same manner as an interrupt. The ABORT' signal itself is only available on the 65816; although the 65802 has an ABORT' vector, it is ineffective since no ABORT' signal can be generated because of the need for the 65802 to be pin-compatible with the 6502. Typical application of the abort instruction feature is the implementation of hardware memory-management schemes in more sophisticated 65816 systems. When a memory-bounds violation of some kind is detected by external logic, the ABORT' signal is asserted, letting the operating system attempt to correct the memory-management anomaly before resuming execution.

Status Register Control Instructions

There are nine instructions that directly modify the flags of the status register; two of them are available only on the 65802 and 65816. These last two are the SEP (set the P status register) and REP (reset P) instructions, which you are already familiar with from their use in the examples to set or reset the m and x flags in the status register. They can be used to set or clear any of the flags in the status register. For each bit in the immediate byte that follows the opcode, the corresponding bit in the status register is set or cleared (depending on whether SEP or REP, respectively, was used).

The other seven flag instructions set or clear individual flags in the status register. The pair SEC and CLC set and clear the carry flag when executed. These should be familiar to you from the chapter on arithmetic, where the CLC is always used before the first of a series of ADC instructions, and SEC before the first of a series of SBC instructions. Likewise, the SED and CLD modes should also be familiar from the same chapter's discussion of decimal-mode arithmetic; these two instructions set or clear the decimal mode. Note that reset can also affect the decimal flag: it is always initialized to zero on reset on the 65C02, 65802, and 65816; on the other hand, its value is indeterminate after reset on the 6502.

The SEI (set interrupt disable flag) and CLI (clear interrupt disable flag) instructions are new to this chapter: they are used to enable or disable the processor's response to interrupt requests via the IRQ' signal. If the SEI instruction has been executed, interrupts are disabled; a CLI interrupt instruction may be used to reenable interrupts. Note that the interrupt disable flag is set automatically in response to an interrupt request, whether a software interrupt or IRQ', NMI', or RESET'; this "locks out" other interrupts from occurring until the current one has been serviced. Similarly, the interrupt disable flag is cleared automatically upon return from an interrupt via RTI due to reloading of the stacked status register, which was pushed with i clear.

The SEI lets interrupts be locked out during critical routines which should not be interrupted. An example would be a device controller that depended on software timing loops for correct operation; interrupts must be locked out for the duration of the timing loop. It is important in an environment where interrupts are supported that they not be locked out for long periods of time. Although the CLI instruction will explicitly clear the interrupt disable flag, it is rarely used because typically the processor status is saved before execution of an SEI instruction as in

Fragment 13.3, which reclears the flag by restoring the entire processor status register.

```
0000 08              PHP            save status
0001 78              SEI            disable interrupts
0002                  .
0002                  .             execute time-critical code
0002                  .
0002 28              PLP            done—restore status, enable interrupts
```

Fragment 13.3.

Since the interrupt disable flag was clear when the **PHP** instruction was executed, the **PLP** instruction restores the cleared flag. This same technique is also useful when mixing subroutine calls to routines with different default modes for accumulator and index register sizes; since saving the status with **PHP** is a common operation between subroutine calls anyway, the **PLP** instruction can be used to conveniently restore operating modes as well as status flags.

Finally, there is a **CLV** (clear overflow flag). There is no corresponding set overflow instruction, and, as you will recall from the chapter on arithmetic, the overflow flag does not need to be explicitly cleared before a signed operation. The arithmetic operations always change the overflow status to correctly reflect the result. The reason for including an explicit **CLV** instruction in the 65x repertoire is that the 6502, 65C02, and 65802 have a **SET OVERFLOW** input signal; external hardware logic can set the overflow flag of the status register by pulling the **SET OVERFLOW** input low. Since there is no corresponding clear overflow input signal, the overflow must be cleared in software in order to regain susceptibility to the **SET OVERFLOW** signal.

The practical application of the **SET OVERFLOW** signal is generally limited to dedicated control applications; it is rarely connected on general-purpose, 6502-based computer systems. On the 65816, there is no **SET OVERFLOW** input; it was sacrificed to make room for some of the more generally useful new signals available on the 65816 pin configuration.

No Operation Instructions

The final two instructions to complete the 65816 instruction set are the **no operation** instructions. These do exactly what they sound like: nothing. They are used as place holders, or time-wasters; often they are used to patch out code during debugging. The **NOP** instruction—with a hexadecimal value of $EA—is the standard no operation.

As mentioned in the earlier architecture chapters, the 6502 and 65C02 have a number of unimplemented instructions—the same opcodes which, on the 65802 and 65816, correspond to the new instructions. On the 6502, the operation of the processor when these "instructions" are executed is undefined; some of them cause the processor to "hang up." On the 65C02, these are all "well-behaved" no-operations of either one, two, or more cycles. On the 65802 and 65816, there is only one unimplemented instruction, defined as **WDM;** this is reserved for future systems as an **escape** prefix to expand the instruction set with sixteen-bit opcodes. For this reason, it should not be used in your current programs, as it will tend to make them incompatible with future generations of the 65816.

Part IV
Applications

14 | Selected Code Samples

This chapter contains five different types of example programs, which are examined in detail. Each focuses on a different topic of interest to the 65x programmer: multiplication and division algorithms; a 65802-to-6502 mode-switching *tour de force*; a quick utility routine to determine which 65x processor a program is running under; high-level languages; and a popular performance benchmark.

Multiplication

Probably the most common multiply routine written for eight-bit applications is to multiply one sixteen-bit number by another, returning a sixteen-bit result. While multiplying two large sixteen-bit numbers would yield a 32-bit result, much of systems programming is done with positive integers limited to sixteen bits, which is why this multiply example is so common. Be aware that a result over sixteen bits cannot be generated by the examples as coded—you'll have to extend them if you need to handle larger numbers.

There are several methods for the sixteen-by-sixteen multiply, but all are based on the multiplication principles for multi-digit numbers you were taught in grade school: multiply the top number by the right-most digit of the bottom number; move left, digit by digit, through the bottom number, multiplying it by the top number, each time shifting the resulting product left one more space and adding it to the sum of the previous products:

```
         2344
    ×   12211
         2344
         2344
        4688
       4688
      2344
     28622584
```

Or to better match the description:

```
         2344
    ×   12211
         2344
    +    2344
        25784   sum of products so far
    +   4688
       494584   sum of products so far
    +  4688
      5182584   sum of products so far
    + 2344
     28622584   final product (sum of all single-digit multiplies)
```

Binary multiplication is no different, except that, since each single-digit multiply is by either zero or one, each resulting single-digit product is either the top number itself or all zeroes.

```
       101
    x 1010
       000         5
       101      x 10
      000         0
     101          5
    110010       50 decimal
```

To have the computer do it, you have it shift the bottom operand right; if it shifts out a zero, you need do nothing, but if it shifts out a one, you add the top number to the partial product (which is initialized at zero). Then you shift the top number left for the possible add during the next time through this loop. When there are no more ones in the bottom number, you are done.

6502 Multiplication

With only three eight-bit registers, you can't pass two sixteen-bit operands to your multiply routine in registers. One solution, the one used below, is to pass one operand in two direct page (zero page) bytes, while passing the other in two more; the result is returned in two of the 6502's registers. All this is carefully documented in the header of the routine in Listing 14.1.

This 6502 multiply routine takes 33 bytes.

65C02 Multiplication

With the same three eight-bit registers as the 6502, and an instruction set only somewhat enhanced, the 65C02 multiply routine is virtually the same as the 6502s. Only one byte can be saved by the substitution of an unconditional branch instruction for the jump instruction, for a total byte count of 32.

65802 and 65816 Multiplication

The 65802 and 65816, when running in native mode, have three registers, all of which can be set to sixteen bits, in addition to having many more addressing modes. As you might expect, a multiply routine for these processors is considerably shorter than the 6502 and 65C02. What you might not expect is how much shorter: the multiply routine in Listing 14.2 for the 65802 and 65816 takes only 19 bytes—its length is less than 60 percent of each of the other two routines!

Notice the additional documentation at the beginning of the routine. The processor must have both its index registers and its accumulator in sixteen-bit modes *before* calling this routine.

```
0001  0000                          KEEP  KL.14.1
0002  0000
0003  0000
0004  0000           ;    16 by 16 = 16-bit multiply for 6502 microprocessor
0005  0000           ;    operand 1: sixteen bits in direct page loc MCAND1/MCAND1+1
0006  0000           ;    operand 2: sixteen bits in direct page loc MCAND2/MCAND2+1
0007  0000           ;    result:    returned in X-Y (hi-lo)
0008  0000           ;               all original register values are destroyed
0009  0000
0010  0000           MULT    START
0011  0000           MCAND1  GEQU  $80
0012  0000           MCAND2  GEQU  $82
0013  0000
0014  0000 A200              LDX   #0            initialize result (hi)
0015  0002 A000              LDY   #0            initialize result (lo)
0016  0004
0017  0004 A580      MULT1   LDA   MCAND1        operand 1 (lo)
0018  0006 0581              ORA   MCAND1+1      operand 1 (hi); if 16-bit operand 1 is 0, done
0019  0008 F016              BEQ   DONE
0020  000A 4681              LSR   MCAND1+1      get right bit, operand 1
0021  000C 6680              ROR   MCAND1
0022  000E 9009              BCC   MULT2         if clear, no addition to previous products
0023  0010 18                CLC                 else add oprd 2 to partial result
0024  0011 98                TYA
0025  0012 6582              ADC   MCAND2
0026  0014 A8                TAY
0027  0015 8A                TXA
0028  0016 6583              ADC   MCAND2+1
0029  0018 AA                TAX
0030  0019
0031  0019 0682      MULT2   ASL   MCAND2        now shift oprd 2 left for poss. add next
                                                 iteration
0032  001B 2683              ROL   MCAND2+1
0033  001D 4C0400            JMP   MULT1
0034  0020
0035  0020 60        DONE    RTS
0036  0021
0037  0021                   END
```

Listing 14.1.

14 Selected Code Samples

```
0001 0000                    KEEP  KL.14.2
0002 0000                    65816 ON
0003 0000
0004 0000          ;    16 by 16 = 16 multiply
0005 0000          ;    for 65802/65816 microprocessors in native mode with
0006 0000          ;       index registers and accumulator already set to 16 bits
0007 0000          ;    operand 1: sixteen bits in direct page location MCAND1
0008 0000          ;    operand 2: sixteen bits in direct page location MCAND2
0009 0000          ;    result:    sixteen bits returned in accumulator
0010 0000
0011 0000   MULT   START
0012 0000   MCAND1 GEQU  $80
0013 0000   MCAND2 GEQU  $82
0014 0000
0015 0000 18       CLC
0016 0001 FB       XCE
0017 0002 C230     REP   #$30
0018 0004
0019 0004          LONGA ON             tell assembler about
0020 0004          LONGI ON             index & accum settings
0021 0004
0022 0004 A90000   LDA   #0             initialize result
0023 0007
0024 0007 A680 MULT1  LDX  MCAND1       get operand 1
0025 0009 F00B       BEQ  DONE          if operand 1 is zero, done
0026 000B 4680       LSR  MCAND1        get right bit, operand 1
0027 000D 9003       BCC  MULT2         if clear, no addition to previous products
0028 000F 18         CLC                else add oprd 2 to partial result
0029 0010 6582       ADC  MCAND2
0030 0012
0031 0012 0682 MULT2  ASL  MCAND2       now shift oprd 2 left for poss add next time
0032 0014 80F1       BRA  MULT1
0033 0016
0034 0016 38   DONE  SEC
0035 0017 FB         XCE
0036 0018 60         RTS
0037 0019            END
```

Listing 14.2.

Along the same lines, notice that the first two lines of the subroutine are the mode directives—**LONGA ON** and **LONGI ON**—which inform the assembler that all three registers have been set to sixteen bits. That way, when the accumulator is loaded with immediate zero, the assembler will generate a sixteen-bit operand rather than an incorrect eight-bit one, which would cause program failure when executed.

The **RTS** instruction is the intra-bank return instruction. An **RTL** instruction could be substituted if the subroutine were intended to be called *only* by long jump-to-subroutine instructions, whether by code outside the bank or by code within it. You should document such a requirement in the routine's introductory comments.

Division

Probably the most common division routine written for eight-bit applications is the converse of the multiply routine just covered—to divide one sixteen-bit number by another sixteen-bit number, returning both a sixteen-bit quotient and a sixteen-bit remainder.

There are several methods for doing this, but all are based on the division principles for multi-digit numbers that you learned in grade school. Line up the divisor under the left-most set of digits of the dividend, appending an imaginary set of zeroes out to the right, and subtract as many times as possible. Record the number of successful subtractions; then shift the divisor right one place and continue until the divisor is flush right with the dividend, and no more subtractions are possible. Any unsubtractable value remaining is called the remainder.

```
              12211 remainder 1
        2344 ⌐28622585
             -2344
              5182585
             -2344
              2838585
             -2344
               494585
              -2344
               260185
              -2344
                25785
               -2344
                 2345
                -2344
                    1
```

Binary division is even easier since, with only ones and zeroes, subtraction is possible at each digit position either only once or not at all:

```
            1100 remainder 1         12 remainder 1
     101 ⟌ 111101                 5 ⟌ 61
           -101                       -5
           10101                      11
           -101                       -5
              01                       6
                                      -5
                                       1
```

Many programs calling this division routine will need only the quotient or only the remainder, although some will require both. The routines here return both.

6502 Division

The 6502, with its three eight-bit registers, handles passing parameters to and from a division routine even less smoothly than to and from a multiplication routine: not only do you need to pass it two sixteen-bit values, but it needs to pass back two sixteen-bit results.

The solution used in Listing 14.3 is to pass the dividend and the divisor in two direct page double bytes, then pass back the remainder in a direct page double byte and the quotient in two registers.

```
0001  0000                    KEEP    KL.14.3
0002  0000
0003  0000
0004  0000           ; 16 divided by 16 = 16 divide for 6502 microprocessor
0005  0000           ; divide DIVDND / DIVSOR -> XA (hi-lo); remainder in DIVDND
0006  0000           ; DIVDND and DIVSOR are direct page double byte cells
0007  0000           ; no special handling for divide by zero (returns $FFFF quotient)
0008  0000
0009  0000   DIV     START
0010  0000   DIVDND  GEQU    $80
0011  0000   DIVSOR  GEQU    $82
0012  0000
0013  0000 A900              LDA     #0
0014  0002 AA                TAX             initialize quotient (hi)
0015  0003 48                PHA             initialize quotient (lo)
0016  0004 A001              LDY     #1      initialize shift count =1
0017  0006 A582              LDA     DIVSOR  get high byte of divisor
0018  0008 300B              BMI     DIV2    bra if divisor can't be shifted left
0019  000A
```

```
0020  000A C8         DIV1    INY                     else shift divisor to leftmost position
0021  000B 0682               ASL     DIVSOR
0022  000D 2683               ROL     DIVSOR+1        test divisor
0023  000F 3004               BMI     DIV2            done if divisor in leftmost position
0024  0011 C011               CPY     #17             max count (all zeroes in divisor)
0025  0013 D0F5               BNE     DIV1            loop if not done
0026  0015
0027  0015 38         DIV2    SEC                     now do division by subtraction
0028  0016 A580               LDA     DIVDND          subtract divisor from dividend
0029  0018 E582               SBC     DIVSOR          low bytes first
0030  001A 48                 PHA                     save lo difference temporarily on stack
0031  001B A581               LDA     DIVDND+1        then subtract high bytes
0032  001D E583               SBC     DIVSOR+1
0033  001F 9006               BCC     DIV3            bra if can't subtract divisor from dividend
0034  0021                    ; else carry is set to shift into quotient
0035  0021 8581               STA     DIVDND+1        store high byte of difference
0036  0023 68                 PLA                     get low subtract result from stack
0037  0024 8580               STA     DIVDND
0038  0026 48                 PHA                     restore low subtract result->stack for pull
0039  0027 68         DIV3    PLA                     throw away low subtract result
0040  0028 68                 PLA                     get quotient low byte from stack
0041  0029 2A                 ROL     A               shift carry->quotient (1 for divide, 0 for not)
0042  002A 48                 PHA                     put back on stack
0043  002B 8A                 TXA                     get quotient high byte
0044  002C 2A                 ROL     A               continue shift->quotient (high)
0045  002D AA                 TAX                     put back in x
0046  002E 4683               LSR     DIVSOR+1        shift divisor right for next subtract
0047  0030 6682               ROR     DIVSOR
0048  0032 88                 DEY                     decrement count
0049  0033 D0E0               BNE     DIV2            branch unless done (count is 0)
0050  0035
0051  0035 68         DONE    PLA                     get quotient (lo)
0052  0036 60                 RTS
0053  0037
0054  0037                    END
```

Listing 14.3.

The label **DONE** is not needed (there is no branch to the location), but was added for clarity.

The routine at **DIV2** may seem curious. The 6502 has no sixteen-bit compare; to compare two sixteen-bit numbers, you must actually subtract them (setting the carry first, as is required before a subtract using the 65x **SBC** instruction). So the divisor is subtracted from the dividend, with the low result saved on the stack. If the carry is clear, the divisor is too large to be subtracted from the dividend. Thus a branch is taken to **DIV3**, where the low result is pulled but not used and the cleared carry is rolled into the quotient to acknowledge the unsuccessful subtraction. If the carry is set, then the high result, still in the accumulator, is stored, and the low result is pulled from the stack, stored, then restacked to be repulled at **DIV3**; since the carry is known to be set, it does not need to be explicitly set before rolling it into the quotient to acknowledge the successful subtraction.

The quotient is returned in registers **X** and **A**.

This 6502 divide routine takes 55 bytes.

65C02 Division

The 65C02 routine is virtually the same; only three early instructions (shown in Fragment 14.1) in the 6502 routine are changed to the code in Fragment 14.2, for a net savings of one byte, because the 65C02 has instructions to push the index registers. This 65C02 divide routine takes 54 bytes, one byte fewer than the 6502 divide routine takes.

```
0000 A900         LDA     #0
0002 AA           TAX
0003 48           PHA
```

Fragment 14.1.

```
0000 A200         LDX     #0
0002 DA           PHX
```

Fragment 14.2.

65802/65816 Division

The 65802 and 65816 processors, with their registers extendable to sixteen bits, can handle sixteen-bit division with ease. In the divide routine in Listing 14.4, the dividend and the divisor are passed in sixteen-bit registers X and A respectively; the quotient is passed back in a sixteen-bit direct page location and the remainder in X.

```
0001 0000              KEEP  KL.14.4
0002 0000              65816 ON
0003 0000
```

```
0004  0000            ; 16 divided by 16 = 16 divide for 65802/65816 microprocessor
0005  0000            ; 16-bit divide: X / A -> QUOTNT; remainder in X
0006  0000            ; QUOTNT is a 16-bit direct page cell
0007  0000            ; native mode: all registers set to 16-bit modes
0008  0000            ; no special handling for divide by zero (returns $FFFF quotient)
0009  0000
0010  0000     DIV    START
0011  0000     QUOTNT GEQU  $80
0012  0000
0013  0001
0014  0002
0015  0004
0016  0004            LONGA ON              tell assembler about 16-bit
0017  0004            LONGI ON              index & accumulator settings
0018  0004
0019  0004 6480       STZ   QUOTNT          initialize quotient to 0
0020  0006 A00100     LDY   #1              initialize shift count to 1
0021  0009
0022  0009 0A   DIV1  ASL   A               shift divisor: test leftmost bit
0023  000A B006       BCS   DIV2            branch when get leftmost bit
0024  000C C8         INY                   else increment shift count
0025  000D C01100     CPY   #17             max count (all zeroes in divisor)
0026  0010 D0F7       BNE   DIV1            loop if not done
0027  0012
0028  0012 6A   DIV2  ROR   A               put shifted-out bit back
0029  0013
0030  0013            ; now divide by subtraction
0031  0013 48   DIV4  PHA                   push divisor
0032  0014 8A         TXA                   get dividend into accumulator
0033  0015 38         SEC
0034  0016 E301       SBC   1,S             subtract divisor from dividend
0035  0018 9001       BCC   DIV3            bra if can't subtract; dividend still in X
0036  001A AA         TAX                   store new dividend; carry=1 for quotient
0037  001B
0038  001B 2680 DIV3  ROL   QUOTNT          shift carry->quotient (1 for divide, 0 for not)
0039  001D 68         PLA                   pull divisor
0040  001E 4A         LSR   A               shift divisor right for next subtract
0041  001F 88         DEY                   decrement count
0042  0020 D0F1       BNE   DIV4            branch to repeat unless count is 0
0043  0022
0044  0022
0045  0023
0046  0024 60         RTS
0047  0025            END
```

Listing 14.4.

This divide routine for the 65802 and 65816 generates only 31 bytes, little more than half the bytes the 6502 and 65C02 divide routines generate.

As the introductory comments note, it requires the processor to be in native mode and the **m** and **x** memory select flags to be in sixteen-bit modes *before* the routine is called; these requirements become doubly obvious when you see in another of the comments that the values passed in the accumulator and an index register are sixteen bits, with one of the two sixteen-bit results being passed back in one of the same registers. Assemblers, however, do not read comments; they only read instructions and directives. That's the reason for the **LONGA ON** and **LONGI ON** directives at the beginning of the routine.

Calling an Arbitrary 6502 Routine

Particularly during the early phases of the processor's life cycle, you might wish to mix existing 6502 code with your 65816 applications. The routine provided below provides a general purpose way of doing this. Additionally, the context-saving code illustrated here could prove useful in other applications. You'll find similar code in the debugger in the next chapter, where it is needed to save the context between instructions of the user program being traced.

The simplest way to call a 6502 routine from the 65802 or 65816 is found in Fragment 14.3.

```
0000 38              SEC
0001 FB              XCE
0002 200080          JSR      D06502
```

Fragment 14.3.

Although this will work fine in *some* cases, it is not guaranteed to. In order to be assured of correct functioning of an existing 6502 routine, the direct page register must be reset to zero and the stack pointer must be relocated to page one. Although a 6502 program that uses zero page addressing will technically function correctly if the direct page has been relocated, the possibility that the zero page may be addressed using some form of absolute addressing, not to mention the probability that an existing 6502 monitor or operating system routine would expect to use values previously initialized and stored in the zero page, requires that this register be given its default 6502 value.

If the stack has been relocated from page one, it will be lost when the switch to emulation mode substitutes the mandatory stack high byte of one. So first, the sixteen-bit stack pointer must be saved. Second, if the 65802/65816 program was called from a 6502 environment, then there may be 6502 values on the original 6502 page-one stack; such a program must squirrel away the 6502 stack pointer on entry so it can be restored on exit, as well as used during temporary incursions, such as this routine, into the 6502 environment.

The goal, then, is this: provide a mechanism whereby a programmer may simply pass the address of a resident 6502 routine and any registers required for the call to a utility which will transfer control to the 6502 routine; the registers should be returned with their original (potentially sixteen-bit) values intact, except as modified by the 6502 routine; and finally the operating mode must be restored to its state before the call.

When loading the registers with any needed parameters, keep in mind that only the low-order values will be passed to a 6502 subroutine, even though this routine may be entered from either eight- or sixteen-bit modes.

The call itself is simple; you push the address of the routine to be called, *minus one*, onto the stack, typically using the **PEA** instruction. Then you call the routine, which executes the subroutine call and manages all of the necessary housekeeping. Fragment 14.4 gives an example of calling the routine.

```
0000 A94100           LDA      #'A'         character to be printed
0003 F4ECFD           PEA      $FDED-1      routine to be called
0006 200080           JSR      JSR6502
```

Fragment 14.4.

$FDED is the address of an existing Apple // routine to print characters, and **JSR6502** is the routine described in Listing 14.5.

```
0001 0000                        KEEP    KL.14.5
0002 0000                        65816 ON
0003 0000
0004 0000           JSR6502      START
0005 0000
0006 0000
0007 0000                        ; used by 65816 program called by 6502 code before moving stack
0008 0000
0009 0000 08                     PHP           save flags, including register sizes
0010 0001
```

```
0011  0001 C230                REP    #$30          set all registers to 16 bits
0012  0003                     LONGA  ON
0013  0003                     LONGI  ON
0014  0003
0015  0003 DA                  PHX                  then push them
0016  0004 5A                  PHY                  push index regs
0017  0005 0B                  PHD                  push direct page base
0018  0006 48                  PHA                  push accum
0019  0007
0020  0007          ; set up page-1 stack ptr, saving 65802 stack ptr in DP & on new stack
0021  0007 38                  TSC                  save old stack pointer in
0022  0008 5B                  TCD                  direct page register
0023  0009 2900FF              AND    #$FF00        mask stack pointer to examine high byte
0024  000C C90001              CMP    #$100
0025  000F F004                BEQ    USESTK        branch if stack already in page 1
0026  0011 AD4F00              LDA    STK6502       else retrieve safe 6502 stack pointer
0027  0014 1B                  TCS                  and load stack pointer with it
0028  0015 0B         USESTK   PHD                  push old stack pointer onto new stack
0029  0016
0030  0016          ; set up a return-to-this-code return address on new stack
0031  0016          ; (direct page register points to old stack with orig accum at 1)
0032  0016
0033  0016 F42700              PEA    RETURN-1      push local return address (out exit code)
0034  0019 D40C                PEI    (12)          push routine addr from prev stack onto this one
0035  001B A50A                LDA    10            shuffle return address
0036  001D 850C                STA    12            to bottom of old stack
0037  001F A501                LDA    1             restore accum from prev stack using dp reg
0038  0021
0039  0021          ; set direct page to zero page
0040  0021 F40000              PEA    0             set direct page
0041  0024 2B                  PLD                  to zero page
0042  0025
0043  0025          ; switch to emulation mode
0044  0025 38                  SEC
0045  0026 FB                  XCE                  switch to emulation mode
0046  0027                     LONGA  OFF
0047  0027                     LONGI  OFF
0048  0027
0049  0027          ; and call 6502 routine
0050  0027 60                  RTS                  JSR (via RTS) to 6502 routine @ stacked addr
0051  0028
0052  0028          ;
0053  0028          ; 6502 routine returns here
0054  0028 08         RETURN   PHP                  now save returned flag results from 6502 code
0055  0029 EB                  XBA                  save returned A accum in B accum
0056  002A 68                  PLA                  get flags into A accum
```

```
0057  002B 2B              PLD              get old stack pointer
0058  002C
0059  002C         ; address old stack values as direct page:
0060  002C         ; dp (stack) offset 12.13 = return address back to 65802/65816 code
0061  002C         ;                   10.11 = unused (orig held addr of 6502 routine)
0062  002C         ;                       9 = orig P flags
0063  002C         ;                     7.8 = orig 16-bit X
0064  002C         ;                     5.6 = orig 16-bit Y
0065  002C         ;                     3.4 = orig DP
0066  002C         ;                     1.2 = orig 16-bit accum
0067  002C         ;                       0 = was next available stack location
0068  002C
0069  002C         ; combine returned condition flags with 65802/816 mode flags
0070  002C 29CF            AND    #%11001111   mask out m & x flags
0071  002E 850B            STA    11           save for a minute; dp:11 is free
0072  0030 A509            LDA    9            get orig P value
0073  0032 2930            AND    #%00110000   mask out all but m & x flags
0074  0034 050B            ORA    11           combine new condition flags with old m & x
0075  0036 850B            STA    11           store new P @ 11
0076  0038         ; 9.10 in old stack now free
0077  0038
0078  0038         ; save registers returned from 6502 routine
0079  0038 EB              XBA              swap: 6502 accum back to A
0080  0039 8501            STA    1            save returned accumulator low
0081  003B 8405            STY    5            save returned Y low
0082  003D 8607            STX    7            save returned X low
0083  003F
0084  003F 18              CLC
0085  0040 FB              XCE              restore native mode
0086  0041
0087  0041 C230            REP    #$30         extend register size back to 16 bits
0088  0043            LONGA ON
0089  0043            LONGI ON
0090  0043
0091  0043 0B              PHD
0092  0044 FA              PLX
0093  0045 9A              TXS              restore old stack pointer
0094  0046
0095  0046         ; but still address old stack via direct page
0096  0046
0097  0046 68              PLA              copy accum to free stack bytes @ dp:9.10
0098  0047 8509            STA    9
0099  0049         ; stack was moved by PLA, but DP was not
0100  0049
0101  0049         ; pull registers from stack
0102  0049 2B              PLD              restore old direct page
```

```
0103  004A 7A              PLY
0104  004B FA              PLX
0105  004C 68              PLA            load accumulator again
0106  004D 28              PLP            get 6502 condition flags; 65802/816 modes
0107  004E
0108  004E 60              RTS            done!
0109  004F
0110  004F 8001  STK6502 DC  A'$180'      arbitrary 'safe' stack in page one
0111  0051         ;                      smart user will store last page one
0112  0051         ;                      stack value here before switching stack
0113  0051         ;                      out of page one
0114  0051
0115  0051              END
```

Listing 14.5.

The routine is entered with the return address on the top of the stack, and the go-to address of the 6502 routine at the next location on the stack. Since you want to be able to restore the m and x mode flags, the first thing the routine does is push the status register onto the stack. The **REP #$30** instruction, which follows, puts the processor into a known state, since the routine can be called from any of the four possible register-size modes. The long accumulator, long index mode is the obvious choice because it encompasses all the others. The user registers, including the direct page register, are saved on the stack, and then the stack pointer itself is saved to the direct page register via the accumulator. This has two benefits: it preserves the value of the old stack pointer across a relocation of the stack, and provides a means of accessing all of the data on the old stack after it has been relocated. This technique is of general usefulness, and should be understood clearly. Figure 14.1, which shows the state of the machine after line 0034 (the PEI instruction), helps make this clear.

The stack must be relocated to page one only if it is not already there. If it is elsewhere, then the last 6502 page-one stack pointer should be restored from where it was cubbyholed when the 65802/65816 program took control and moved the stack elsewhere. If there is no previous 6502 stack to avoid, any page one address could be used to initialize the temporary 6502 stack needed.

The first item that goes onto the new stack is the value of the old stack pointer, now found in the direct page register. Next, a local return address must be pushed on the stack for when the called 6502 routine executes an **RTS**.

While the direct page register was pushed onto the new stack, it

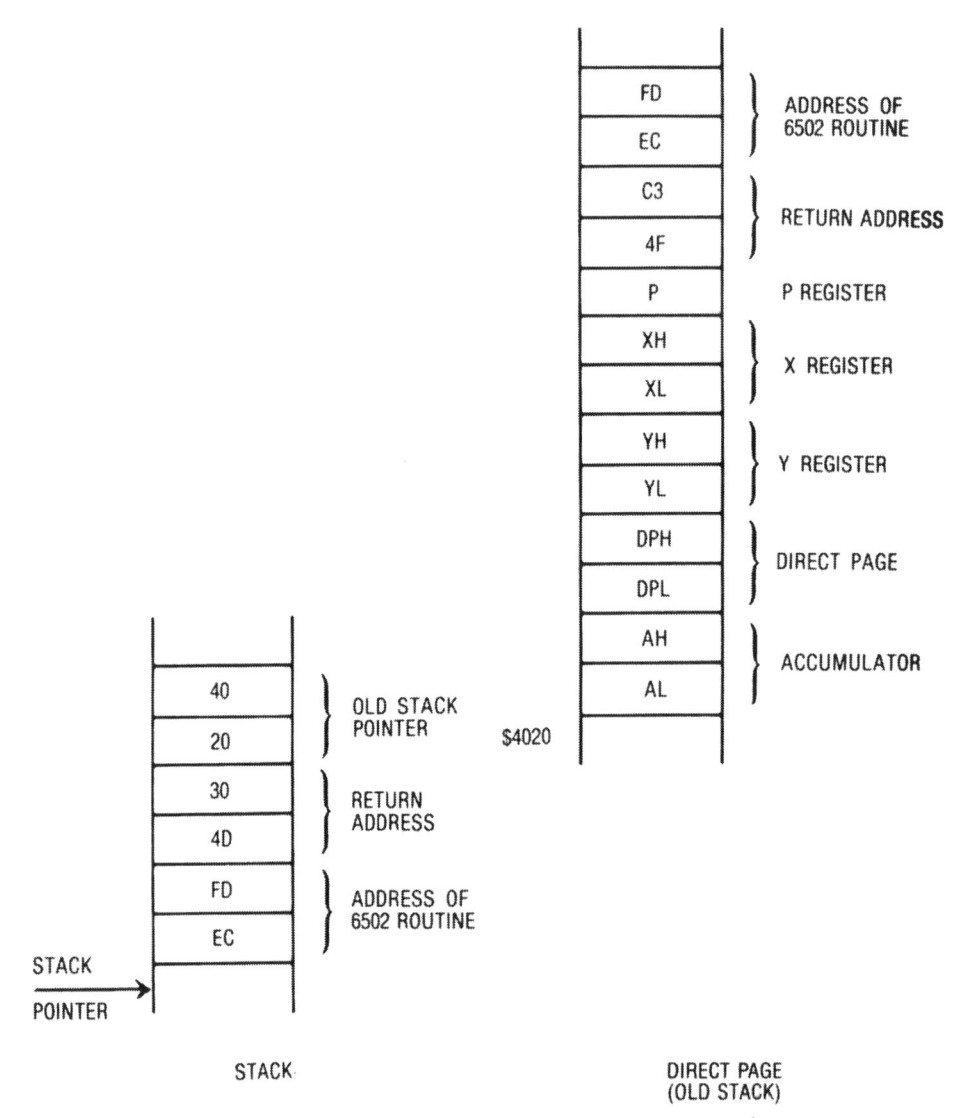

Figure 14.1. Stack Snapshot after PEI (12) Instruction.

retains its value, and still points to the old stack; so although the stack pointer has been relocated, you still have access to the values on the old stack via direct page addressing. One of the needed items is the go-to address, the address of the 6502 routine to be called. Since the size of all of the elements pushed on the stack is known, by referencing the direct page location 12, this value is retrieved. A **PEI** (push indirect) instruction is used to transfer the routine to be called from the old stack (now being referenced via the direct page) to the new stack. This frees up the double byte on the old stack at dp:12.13, the bottom of the old stack; the return address is shuffled in from dp:10.11, freeing those two bytes.

The accumulator was used during these operations, and must be restored because it may contain one of the parameters required by the 6502 routine. Like the go-to address, the accumulator is loaded from the old stack using direct page addressing.

Having restored the accumulator, all that remains is to set the direct page register to zero; since no registers can be modified at this point, this is accomplished by pushing a zero onto the stack, and then pulling it into the direct page register.

When you switch the processor into emulation mode, the environment is as it should be; the new stack is now set up to transfer control to the 6502 subroutine via the execution of an **RTS** instruction which, rather than exiting the JSR6502 routine, performs a kind of jump indirect to the value on top of the stack, the go-to address. The use of the **RTS** to transfer control to the 6502 routine is the reason the address *minus one* is put on the stack to begin with. This requirement could be eliminated if the go-to address was decremented before being pushed on the page one stack; but this would require the execution of two additional instructions, one to load it into a register, and one to decrement. **PEI** moves the value directly onto the stack from the direct page.

When control returns from the 6502 routine, the flags, representing the 6502 routine's results, are pushed, then pulled into the eight-bit **A** accumulator after its value has been saved by transferring it to the **B** accumulator with an **XBA**. The only other item left on the new stack is the old stack pointer. This is pulled into the direct page register, which immediately restores access to all of the values pushed onto the old stack.

The condition code bits in the returned status register are merged with the mode flags in the original status register. The eight-bit result is stored in the location immediately below the return address.

The register values upon return are saved into the locations where the registers were originally pushed on the stack. Since the processor is still in emulation mode, only the low bytes are stored; the high bytes of any of the 65802/65816 registers are always preserved (which means that if a low byte is unchanged, then the entire double-byte value is preserved).

The native mode is restored. The registers are extended to sixteen bits. The stack pointer is restored from the direct page register.

There remains a gap on the stack; the value of the accumulator is copied there. The registers are now restored, with the accumulator being pulled a second time from its new location.

Control is now back with the calling 65816 program, the processor never the wiser for having been transformed into a 6502.

This coding presumes that the calling code, the switching routine, and the 6502 routine are all located in the same bank, bank zero. It also assumes a data bank of zero. Should the 6502 routine be in a non-zero bank, then you should save its program bank to a safe location prior to the switch to emulation mode so that it cannot be lost in case of interrupt. You should also check your emulation mode interrupt service routines to be sure they restore the program bank from the safe location prior to returning.

Finally, should the calling code be in a bank different from the 6502 routine, you'll have to locate the switching code in the same bank with the 6502 routine (its return will be an **RTS**); call the switching code with a **JSL**; move the pushed program bank down two bytes to the bottom of the stack before relocating the return address; and return to the calling code via an **RTL**.

Testing Processor Type

A related utility routine (Listing 14.6) checks the processor type, allowing code targeted for the large 6502 installed-base to take advantage of a 65C02 or 65802/65816 if available. The processor is assumed to be in emulation mode if it is a 65816 or 65802.

This routine takes advantage of the fact that the 65C02 and 65816 set the sign flag correctly in the decimal mode, while the 6502 does not. The sign flag is set (minus) after loading $99 (a negative two's-complement number). When one is added to BCD 99, the result is BCD 0, a positive two's-complement number. On the 6502, adding one in decimal mode does not affect the sign flag. On the 65C02 and 65816, the sign flag is cleared to reflect that adding one results in a positive value (zero).

Having distinguished between the 65C02 and the 6502, the code further distinguishes between the 65C02 and 65816 by trying to execute one of the new 65816 instructions—specifically, the **XCE** instruction. If a 65C02 is in use, the execution of **XCE** has no effect; it simply performs a no-op, and the carry flag remains clear. On a 65816 in emulation mode, the carry flag would be set after exchanging.

```
0001  0000                    KEEP    KL.14.6
0002  0000                    65816 ON
0003  0000
0004  0000                    LONGA OFF
0005  0000                    LONGI OFF    generate '6502' code
0006  0000
0007  0000            ;       CHECK --
0008  0000            ;       CHECK PROCESSOR TYPE
0009  0000            ;          MINUS = 6502
0010  0000            ;          CARRY CLEAR = 65C02
0011  0000            ;          CARRY SET = 65816
0012  0000
0013  0000    CHECK   START
0014  0000 F8         SED                  Trick with decimal mode used
0015  0001 A999       LDA     #$99         set negative flag
0016  0003 18         CLC
0017  0004 6901       ADC     #$01         add 1 to get new accum value of 0
0018  0006 3006       BMI     DONE         branch if 0 does not clear negative flag: 6502
0019  0008
0020  0008            ; else 65C02 or 65802 if neg flag cleared by decimal-mode arith
0021  0008
0022  0008 18         CLC
0023  0009 FB         XCE                  OK to execute unimplemented C02 opcodes
0024  000A 9002       BCC     DONE         branch if didn't do anything: 65C02
0025  000C FB         XCE                  switch back to emulation mode
0026  000D 38         SEC                  set carry
0027  000E D8   DONE  CLD                  binary
0028  000F 60         RTS
0029  0010            END
```

Listing 14.6.

Compiler-Generated 65816 Code for a Recursive Program

Although it is not directly relevant to assembly-language programming per se, a look at how a compiler might generate 65816 code provides another angle on 65816 program design. You may also find it helpful when you are writing in a high-level language to have some idea as to what kind of code your compiler might be generating.

For the brief example presented here, an integer-only subset of the C programming language—such as the dialect known as "small C"—is used. To understand C, it is important to understand the concept of the **pointer**. Effectively, a pointer is a variable that holds the address of another data structure. C programmers are particularly known for their liberal use of pointers, primarily because they provide a method to manipulate data structures that is very close to the machine level. The concept of the variable itself is an abstraction which generally results in additional overhead.

The most notable thing about the use of pointers in the example is that they are limited to sixteen bits, even though the 65816 has an address space of sixteen megabytes. The sixteen-bit machine word size was chosen both for pointers and for the storage type **int**; this lets many operations be implemented using one or two 65816 instructions. As a consequence, the memory model used with this compiler limits data storage to 64K; program storage is also limited to 64K. If the loader for this hypothetical compiler supports loading of constant data and program code into separate banks, a total of 128K memory would be available to the program.

The first line of the program, shown in Listing 14.7, is the declaration of the function **main**. By convention, the function **main** is always called as the entry point to a program; it typically (but not necessarily) is the first routine coded, as it is in this example.

The curly braces define the function block; the first statement in the block is the declaration of **y**, which is a pointer to a character; an asterisk before an identifier indicates that it is a pointer variable. In C, pointers are typed by the type of the data object to which they point.

```
main ();
{
  char *y;
  y = "A string to invert";
  invert(y);
}

invert(yy) char *yy;
{
  if (*yy)
  {
    invert(yy+1);
    putchar(*yy);
  }
}
```

Listing 14.7.

The first executable statement is the assignment of the string constant "A string to invert" to the variable **y**. In this context, the **y** appears without the asterisk, because the variable is being given a value—an address—rather than the string it points to. The C compiler always returns the address of a string and zero-terminates it when it encounters a string constant.

The next statement is a call to the function **invert** with a parameter of **y** (which is the variable that just received a value in the preceding statement). Invert is the function that actually does the work of this program, which, as you may have guessed by now, prints an inverted (backwards) string.

After the closing brace for **main** comes the declaration of the function **invert. Invert** takes a parameter—a pointer to a character. When **invert** is called from **main** with **y** as the parameter, **yy** assumes the value of **y**.

The code of **invert** tests the value *pointed to* by **yy;** the first time **invert** is called, this will be the letter "A", the first character in the string constant. The test is whether or not the value "at yy" is non-zero or not; if it is non-zero, the statements within the braces will be executed. If (or when) the value is equal to zero, the code within the braces is skipped.

Looking at the first of the pair of lines contained within the braces, you will find that it is a call to **invert**—the same function presently being defined. This calling of a routine from within itself is called *recursion*, and programming languages such a C or Pascal, which allocate their local variables on the stack, make it easy to write recursive programs such as this one. The merits of using recursion for any given problem are the subject for another discussion; however, as seen in the example, it seems quite useful for the task at hand. What happens when this function calls itself will be explored in a moment, as the generated code itself is discussed.

The last executable line of the program calls the routine **putchar,** an I/O routine that outputs the value passed it as a character on the standard (default) output device.

Returning to the top of the program, Listing 14.8 shows the code generated by the compiler to execute the C program; it is inter-listed with the source code—each line of compiler source appears as an assembler-source comment.

Before the first statement is compiled, the compiler has already generated some code: a jump to a routine labeled **CCMAIN. CCMAIN** is a library routine that performs the "housekeeping" necessary to provide the right environment for the generated code to run in. At the very least, **CCMAIN** must make sure the processor is in the native mode, and switch into the default (for the compiler) sixteen-bit index and accumulator word sizes. If the operating system supports it, it should also initialize the variables **argc** and **argv,** which allow the programmer access to command-line parameters, although they are not used in this example. Finally, **CCMAIN** will call **main** to begin execution of the user-written code itself.

```
0001  0000                          KEEP  A.OUT
0002  0000                          65816 ON
0003  0000
0004  0000            CC0   START
0005  0000 4C0080           JMP   CCMAIN
0006  0003                  END



0007  0000            ;main ();
0008  0000            main  START
0009  0000            ;{
0010  0000            ;   char *y;
0011  0000            ;   y = "A string to invert";
0012  0000 DA                PHX
0013  0001 A90080           LDA   #CCC0+0
0014  0004 8301             STA   1,S
0015  0006            ;   invert(y);
0016  0006 A301             LDA   1,S
0017  0008 48               PHA
0018  0009 200080           JSR   invert
0019  000C FA               PLX
0020  000D            ;}
0021  000D FA               PLX
0022  000E 60               RTS
0023  000F                  END



0024  0000            ;invert(yy) char *yy;
0025  0000            invert START
0026  0000            ;{
0027  0000            ;   if (*yy)
0028  0000 A00000           LDY   #0
0029  0003 B303             LDA   (3,S),Y
0030  0005 29FF00           AND   #$FF
0031  0008 D003             BNE   *+5
0032  000A 4C1F00           JMP   CC3
0033  000D            ;   {
0034  000D            ;     invert(yy+1);
0035  000D A303             LDA   3,S
0036  000F 1A               INC   A
0037  0010 48               PHA
0038  0011 200080           JSR   invert
0039  0014 FA               PLX
0040  0015            ;     putchar(*yy);
```

```
0041  0015 A00000              LDY   #0
0042  0018 B303                LDA   (3,S),Y
0043  001A 48                  PHA
0044  001B 200080              JSR   putchar
0045  001E FA                  PLX
0046  001F             ;  }
0047  001F             ;}
0048  001F 60          CC3     RTS
0049  0020                     END



0050  0000
0051  0000           CCC0      START
0052  0000 41207374            DC    I1'$41,$20,$73,$74,$72,$69,$6E,$67'
0053  0008 20746F20            DC    I1'$20,$74,$6F,$20,$69,$6E,$76,$65'
0054  0010 727400              DC    I1'$72,$74,$00'
0055  0013                     END



0056  0000
0057  0000           ;         'LIBRARY' ROUTINES -- AS IF TO BE LINKED TO
0058  0000           ;         SOURCE PROGRAM
0059  0000
0060  0000           CCMAIN    START
0061  0000 18                  CLC
0062  0001 FB                  XCE
0063  0002 C230                REP   #$30
0064  0004 200080              JSR   MAIN
0065  0007 38                  SEC
0066  0008 FB                  XCE
0067  0009 60                  RTS
0068  000A                     END



0069  0000
0070  0000
0071  0000           PUTCHAR   START
0072  0000           COUT      GEQU  $FDED           Apple // character output
0073  0000
0074  0000
0075  0000 A303                LDA   3,S             get parameter from stack
0076  0002
0077  0002 08                  PHP
```

```
0078  0003 38              SEC
0079  0004 FB               XCE
0080  0005 20EDFD          JSR    COUT
0081  0008 18              CLC
0082  0009 FB               XCE
0083  000A
0084  000A 28              PLP
0085  000B 60              RTS
0086  000C                 END
```

Listing 14.8.

The declaration of **main** causes an assembler **START** statement to be output; this simply defines the beginning of the subroutine or function. The declaration **char *y** will cause the **PHX** instruction to be generated after the first line of executable code is generated; this reserves space for one variable (the pointer y) on the stack. That first executable code line is the assignment y = "A string to invert". This causes *the address* of the string constant, which will be temporarily stored at the end of the generated program, to be loaded into the accumulator. The address just loaded into the accumulator is now stored on the stack in the memory reserved for it by the **PHX** instruction; the value of X that was pushed onto the stack was meaningless in itself.

The next statement to be compiled is a call to the function **invert** with the variable y as the parameter. This causes the value stored on the stack to be loaded back into the accumulator, where it is then pushed onto the stack. All parameters to function calls are passed on the stack.

Note that the accumulator already contained the value stored on the top of the stack; the **LDA 1,S** instruction was redundant. However, the hypothetical compiler in this example does not optimize across statements, so the potential optimization—elimination of the load instruction—cannot be realized. Once the parameter is on the top of the stack, the function itself is called via a **JSR** instruction. Since the program space is limited to 64K, only a sixteen-bit subroutine call is used. After the call returns, the **PLX** instruction removes the no-longer-needed parameter from the stack. The right bracket indicating the end of the function **main** causes the compiler to generate another **PLX** to remove the variable storage, an **RTS** instruction, and an assembler **END** statement.

Invert is defined as having one parameter, the character pointer yy. By declaring the function in this way, the compiler knows to generate code to look for the variable yy on top of the stack whenever a reference to it is made. You can see how this is done by looking at the code generated for the first line, which tests the value *at* yy (rather than the value *of* yy) to see whether it is *true*, that is, not equal to zero. To get this value, the stack relative indirect indexed addressing mode is used. First the Y register is loaded with zero, so that the first element pointed to by the indirect value on the stack is accessed. The stack offset used is three, rather than one, because when the subroutine call was made, after the parameter was pushed onto the stack, the return address was pushed onto the stack, on top of the parameter.

After the value is loaded, it must be ANDed with $FF to mask out the high-order contents, since this is a character (one-byte) type of variable.

If the character is not equal to zero, as it is not the first time through, the JMP CC3 instruction is skipped, and execution continues with the code generated for the C source statements inside the braces.

The first statement is the recursive call to **invert**. Similar to the call from **main**, a parameter is pushed onto the stack. Since an expression (yy + 1) is being passed, however, it must first be evaluated. First the value of **yy** is loaded from the stack, and then one is added to it. Although this hypothetical compiler does not optimize across statements, it apparently does a pretty good job within them, for it has optimized the addition of one to a single increment instruction.

Invert is then called again. If you start counting them, you will find that more pushes than pulls will have been made at this point; in other words, the stack is growing. When **invert** is reentered, the value it finds on the stack is the starting address of the string literal *plus one*; in other words, the second element is being addressed. As long as the value pointed to by the parameter passed to **invert** is non-zero, **invert** will continue to be called recursively, and the stack will continue to grow. When the last element (with the value of zero) is reached, the recursive function "bottoms out"; the jump to **CC3** that occurs when the value at **yy** is equal to zero jumps directly to an RTS instruction. This causes control to return to the next statement after the call to **invert**. The value of **yy** in the most recently called invocation (the value at 3,S) will be a pointer to the last character in the string; it is this character that is first loaded into the accumulator, then pushed, output via a call to the routine **putchar**, then pulled again.

Upon return from **putchar**, control falls through to the RTS instruction, and the next set of values on the stack are processed. This continues until all of the characters pointed to by the values on the stack have been printed, in the reverse order in which they were found. Finally, the last return executed pulls the address of the return address in **main** off the stack, and the program terminates.

The Same Example Hand-Coded in Assembly Language

A distinctive characteristic of the preceding high-level language programming example was that the algorithm employed involved recursion. Consider Listing 14.9, which is the same algorithm hand-coded in assembly language; it is much more efficient than the compiler-generated example.

```
0001  0000                        KEEP    KL.14.9
0002  0000                        65816   ON
0003  0000
0004  0000          MAIN    START
0005  0000 18               CLC
0006  0001 FB               XCE
0007  0002
0008  0002 C210             REP     #$10        16-bit index registers
0009  0004                  LONGI   ON
0010  0004 E220             SEP     #$20        8-bit accumulator
0011  0006                  LONGA   OFF
0012  0006
0013  0006 A21900           LDX     #STRING
0014  0009
0015  0009 B500     INVERT  LDA     0,X
0016  000B F009             BEQ     DONE
0017  000D 48               PHA
0018  000E E8               INX
0019  000F 200900           JSR     INVERT
0020  0012 68               PLA
0021  0013 200080           JSR     COUT
0022  0016
0023  0016 38       DONE    SEC
0024  0017 FB               XCE
0025  0018 60               RTS
0026  0019
0027  0019 41207374 STRING  DC      C'A string to invert',H'00'
0028  002C                  END


0029  0000
0030  0000
0031  0000             ;    COUT
0032  0000             ;    machine-dependent routine to output a character
0033  0000             ;
0034  0000          COUT    START
0035  0000          ECOUT   GEQU    $FDED       Apple // COUT
0036  0000 48               PHA                 Save registers
0037  0001 DA               PHX
0038  0002 5A               PHY
0039  0003 08               PHP                 and status,
```

```
0040  0004  38         SEC                switch to emulation
0041  0005  FB         XCE
0042  0006  20EDFD     JSR   ECOUT        call 6502 routine
0043  0009  18         CLC                restore native mode
0044  000A  FB         XCE
0045  000B  28         PLP                restore status
0046  000C  7A         PLY                restore registers
0047  000D  FA         PLX
0048  000E  68         PLA
0049  000F  60         RTS                return
0050  0010             END
```

Listing 14.9.

Because the more elaborate parameter-passing and variable-allocation requirements of the C language can be bypassed, the example here is much more efficient. (Although some further optimization of the compiler-generated code, as noted, is possible, the code in the example would probably be a typical result.)

To start with, a more intelligent decision about the mode flags is made right from the start, rather than coping with the default sixteen-bit accumulator size of the compiler code by masking out the high-order byte whenever a character is loaded.

Secondly, full use of the index register is made, both to access the data and as the parameter-passing mechanism. Rather than push successive pointers to the inverted character string on the stack, the character itself is stored.

If this routine will be used to invert a single, known string (as opposed to making **INVERT** a subroutine for inverting *any* string, the beginning character of which is pointed to by the X register), then any assembly language programmer would simply write the code found in Listing 14.10. When the assembler evaluates the **LDX** instruction's operand, the "L:" function determines the length of **STRING**.

The Sieve of Eratosthenes Benchmark

With all of the different factors that affect system performance, it is difficult to find a clear criterion by which to judge a processor's performance. Rightly or wrongly, the speed with which a processor runs a standard "benchmark" program is often used in forming a judgement of it. One of the most commonly used (and cited) benchmarks is the Sieve of Eratosthenes algorithm. The use of the Sieve program first gained popularity as the result of articles written by Jim Gilbreath and Gary

```
0001  0000                     KEEP    KL.14.10
0002  0000                     65816   ON
0003  0000
0004  0000           MAIN      START
0005  0000
0006  0000 C210               REP     #$10          16-bit index registers
0007  0002                    LONGI   ON
0008  0002 E220               SEP     #$20          8-bit accumulator
0009  0004                    LONGA   OFF
0010  0004
0011  0004 A21700             LDX     #L:STRING-1   get length of string less one
0012  0007
0013  0007 BD1100   INVERT    LDA     STRING,X      get a char from end of string
0014  000A 200080             JSR     COUT              and output it
0015  000D CA                 DEX                   point to previous char
0016  000E 10F7                BPL    INVERT            and loop through all characters
0017  0010 60       DONE      RTS
0018  0011 41207374 STRING    DC      C'A string to invert',H'00'
0019  0024                    END


0020  0000
0021  0000
0022  0000            ;
0023  0000            ;         COUT
0024  0000            ;         machine-dependent routine to output a character
0025  0000           COUT      START
0026  0000           ECOUT     GEQU    $FDED         Apple // COUT
0027  0000 48                  PHA                   Save registers
0028  0001 DA                  PHX
0029  0002 5A                  PHY
0030  0003 08                  PHP                   and status,
0031  0004 38                  SEC
0032  0005 FB                  XCE                   switch to emulation
0033  0006 20EDFD              JSR     ECOUT         call 6502 routine
0034  0009 18                  CLC
0035  000A FB                  XCE                   restore native mode
0036  000B 28                  PLP                   restore status
0037  000C 7A                  PLY                   restore registers
0038  000D FA                  PLX
0039  000E 68                  PLA                   return
0040  000F 60                  RTS
0041  0010                     END
```

Listing 14.10.

Gilbreath, appearing in *BYTE* magazine (September 1980, page 180), and updated in January 1983 (page 283).

The Sieve program calculates the prime numbers between 3 and 16,381; it is based on an algorithm originally attributed to the Greek mathematician Eratosthenes. The basic procedure is to eliminate every *n*th number after a given number *n*, up to the limit of range within which primes are desired. Presumably the range of primes is itself infinite.

As well as providing a common yardstick with which to gauge the 65816, the Sieve program in Listing 14.11 provides an opportunity to examine performance-oriented programming; since the name of the game is performance, any and all techniques are valid in coding an assembly-language version of a benchmark.

Four variable locations are defined for the program. ITER counts down the number of times the routine is executed; to time it accurately, the test is repeated 100 times. COUNT holds the count of primes discovered. K is a temporary variable. And PRIME is the value of the current prime number.

The variable I has no storage reserved for it because the Y register is used; it is an index counter. Y is used instead of X because certain indexed operations need the absolute,X addressing mode.

The constant SIZE is equal to one-half of the range of numbers within which the primes are to be discovered; this algorithm ignores all even numbers (even numbers being non-prime). The first element in the array represents 3, the second 5, the third 7, and so on.

```
0001  0000                KEEP    KL.14.11
0002  0000                65816   ON
0003  0000
0004  0000      ERATOS    START
0005  0000
0006  0000      SIZE      GEQU    8192
0007  0000
0008  0000      ITER      GEQU    $80
0009  0000      COUNT     GEQU    $82
0010  0000      K         GEQU    $84
0011  0000      PRIME     GEQU    $86
0012  0000      FLAGS     GEQU    $4000
0013  0000
0014  0000 18             CLC                     enter native mode
0015  0001 FB             XCE
0016  0002 C230           REP     #$30            with 16-bit A and X
0017  0004                LONGI   ON
0018  0004                LONGA   ON
```

```
0019   0004
0020   0004
0021   0004 A96400              LDA   #100         do one hundred iterations
0022   0007 8580                STA   ITER         in order to time
0023   0009
0024   0009 6482      AGAIN     STZ   COUNT        zero count (# of primes)
0025   000B
0026   000B A0FF1F              LDY   #SIZE-1      for I = 0 to size
0027   000E A9FFFF              LDA   #$FFFF
0028   0011 8D0040              STA   FLAGS        (handle zero case)
0029   0014
0030   0014 990040    LOOP      STA   FLAGS,Y
0031   0017 88                  DEY                flags[I] = TRUE
0032   0018 88                  DEY
0033   0019 10F9                BPL   LOOP
0034   001B
0035   001B A00000              LDY   #0           for i = 0 to size
0036   001E         ;                              ("i" stored in Y)
0037   001E
0038   001E
0039   001E B9FF3F    MAIN      LDA   FLAGS-1,Y    if flags[I] then
0040   0021 101E                BPL   SKIP         minus-one offset: to see
0041   0023         ;                              high bit in long a mode
0042   0023 98                  TYA
0043   0024 0A                  ASL   A            prime = I + I + 3
0044   0025 1A                  INC   A
0045   0026 1A                  INC   A
0046   0027 1A                  INC   A
0047   0028 8586                STA   PRIME
0048   002A
0049   002A 98                  TYA
0050   002B 18                  CLC
0051   002C 6586                ADC   PRIME        k = i + prime
0052   002E
0053   002E C90120    TOP       CMP   #SIZE+1      while k <= size
0054   0031 B00C                BGE   SKIP2
0055   0033
0056   0033 AA                  TAX                flags[k] = FALSE
0057   0034
0058   0034 E220                SEP   #$20         clear only
0059   0036 9E0040              STZ   FLAGS,X      one byte
0060   0039 C221                REP   #$21         clears carry as well
0061   003B
0062   003B 6586                ADC   PRIME        k = k + prime
0063   003D 80EF                BRA   TOP          (end while k <= size)
0064   003F
```

```
0065  003F E682       SKIP2   INC     COUNT
0066  0041
0067  0041 C8         SKIP    INY             (end for i = 0 to size)
0068  0042 C00120             CPY     #SIZE+1
0069  0045 D0D7               BNE     MAIN
0070  0047
0071  0047 C680               DEC     ITER
0072  0049 D0BE               BNE     AGAIN
0073  004B
0074  004B 38                 SEC
0075  004C FB                 XCE
0076  004D 60                 RTS
0077  004E
0078  004E
0079  004E               END
```

Listing 14.11.

The program begins by entering the native mode and extending the user registers to sixteen bits. **ITER** is initialized for 100 iterations. An array (starting at **FLAGS**) of memory of size **SIZE** is initialized to $FF's, two bytes at a time.

The routine proper now begins. Y is initialized with zero, and control falls into the main loop. The high-order bit of each cell of the array **FLAGS** is tested. Initially, they are all set, but the algorithm iteratively clears succeeding non-prime values before they are tested by this code. If the high bit is clear, this number has already been eliminated by the algorithm; it is non-prime. Notice that the high-order bit of the **FLAG[I]** (or **FLAG[Y]**) array is desired; however, since the processor is in sixteen-bit mode, the high bit will be loaded from the memory location at the effective address *plus one*. To overcome this, the base of the array is specified as the actual base minus one; this calculation is performed by the assembler during generation of the object code.

If the current value has not been cleared, the algorithm calls for the number which is two times the current index value plus three (this converts the index to the array values of 3, 5, 7 . . .) to be the next value for **PRIME**. This prime number is generated quickly by transferring the Y index register into the accumulator, shifting it left once to multiply by two, and incrementing it three times. Remember, this number is generated from the current index only if the index value has not already been eliminated as being non-prime.

This prime number is then added to the current index, and the array elements at this offset, and at all succeeding indices every **PRIME** value apart are eliminated from the array as being non-prime. They have the current prime number as one of their factors. The most significant thing to note here in the code is that only one byte can be cleared; the accumulator must temporarily be switched into the eight-bit mode to accomplish this. However, since the next operation is an addition, an optimization is available: both the sixteen-bit mode can be restored and the carry cleared in a single **REP** operation.

The program now loops, checking to see if the next index value has been eliminated; this process continues until the index reaches the limit of **SIZE**.

You may be wondering what the result is: at 4 MHz, ten iterations are completed in 1.56 seconds, which is twice as fast as a 4 MHz 6502. The January, 1983 *BYTE* article cites results of 4.0 seconds for a 5 MHz 8088, 1.90 seconds for an 8 MHz 8086, and .49 seconds for an 8 MHz 68000; an 8 MHz 65816 would yield .78 seconds.

15 | DEBUG16—A 65816 Programming Tool

This chapter consists of a complete 65816 application example and a detailed discussion of its dozen or so routines. Where possible, different programming techniques have been employed in an effort to illustrate some of the different methods of coding that are available.

The program, **DEBUG16**, is a rudimentary step-and-trace debugger. A **debugger** is a tool used during software development to isolate and reveal sources of error in the program being tested. In other words, it helps the programmer eliminate the **bugs** in a program, hence the name. A **step-and-trace** function lets the program be halted after the execution of each single instruction and the registers and possibly other memory locations to be examined. This effectively provides a "view" into the otherwise invisible internals of the processor.

The ability to trace programs in this manner can be extremely useful: uninitialized variables, wild branches, infinite loops—all of the common flaws that normally result in your program going away to never-never land with little clue to their reasons for departure—are made visible. In addition to displaying the register contents, a tracer will also list the opcode mnemonic and display the operand using the same syntax as originally specified in the source program. This process is called **disassembly**. Although the tracing program can accurately regenerate an approximation of the source line that resulted in a given instruction, it cannot determine any of the symbolic labels that might have been given to the addresses found by the tracer in the assembler source program. More sophisticated debuggers called *symbolic debuggers* let you load a program's symbol table created by either the link editor or assembler; the debugger's disassembly routine looks up each address in a disassembly in the symbol table and inserts labels in place of addresses wherever a correspondence is found.

DEBUG16 also has a **LIST** entry point, at which its disassembler can be used apart from its tracer; this lets you re-create a listing of a program without having the source code available. Again, there is no symbolic information (labels) available. Additionally, the disassembler in its current form does not deal with variable lengths of immediate operands when in the LIST mode.

The tracer can display the disassembled instruction and register values either one instruction at a time, or allow the trace to execute in free-running mode. When only one instruction is disassembled at a time, the tracer is said to be **single-stepping**; pressing a key lets the next instruction be executed. Pressing **RETURN** toggles the tracer into free-running mode. While free-running, a single key press will pause the trace. Pressing any key except **RETURN** resumes tracing; **RETURN** switches back to single-stepping.

The basic theory of operation of the tracer is simple. Starting with the first program instruction, the tracer calculates the length of the instruction by first determining the addressing mode associated with the opcode, and then referring to a table that gives the instruction lengths for the different addressing modes. It can therefore determine the location of the next instruction that follows the current one. It places a **BRK** instruction at that location, having first saved the original value stored there. Next, it executes (via a **JMP** instruction) the current instruction. As soon as that instruction completes, the program counter increments to the next instruction, where it encounters the inserted **BRK**. **BRK** initiates an interrupt cycle that returns control back to the tracer, saves copies of all of the processor's register contents to memory, then calls a routine which displays them, along with the disassembled instruction.

When the next step (next instruction) is to be executed, the **BRK** instruction is replaced with its original value, and the cycle is repeated. In this way the program is able to gain control of the processor "in between" the execution of each instruction.

The exception to this method is whenever an instruction (such as a branch or jump) is encountered which can change the flow of control; in these cases, the target location must be determined (by examining the operand of the instruction), and a **BRK** inserted at that location instead.

The disassembly output looks like Figure 15.1.

```
00:2000   4CCB22    JMP    $22CB
00:2003   08        PHP
00:2004   18        CLC
00:2005   FB        XCE
00:2006   08        PHP
00:2007   0B        PHD
00:2008   F40003    PEA    $0300
00:200B   2B        PLD
00:200C   C220      REP    #$20
00:200E   E210      SEP    #$10
```

Figure 15.1. Disassembly Output.

And the tracer output looks like Figure 15.2.

```
00:5000    A905       LDA     #$05
A= 15 05 X= 00 11 Y= 00 13 S= 01 AA D= 00 00 B= 00 P= 7D E:1
00:5002    AB         TAY
A= 15 05 X= 00 11 Y= 00 05 S= 01 AA D= 00 00 B= 00 P= 7D E:1
00:5003    990060     STA     $600,Y
A= 15 05 X= 00 11 Y= 00 05 S= 01 AA D= 00 00 B= 00 P= 7D E:1
00:5006    88         DEY
A= 15 05 X= 00 11 Y= 00 04 S= 01 AA D= 00 00 B= 00 P= 7D E:1
00:5007    D0FA       BNE     $5003
A= 15 05 X= 00 11 Y= 00 04 S= 01 AA D= 00 00 B= 00 P= 7D E:1
00:5003    990060     STA     $600,Y
A= 15 05 X= 00 11 Y= 00 04 S= 01 AA D= 00 00 B= 00 P= 7D E:1
00:5006    88         DEY
A= 15 05 X= 00 11 Y= 00 03 S= 01 AA D= 00 00 B= 00 P= 7D E:1
00:5007    D0FA       BNE     $5003
A= 15 05 X= 00 11 Y= 00 03 S= 01 AA D= 00 00 B= 00 P= 7D E:1
00:5003    990060     STA     $6000,Y
A= 15 05 X= 00 11 Y= 00 03 S= 01 AA D= 00 00 B= 00 P= 7D E:1
00:5006    88         DEY
A= 15 05 X= 00 11 Y= 00 02 S= 01 AA D= 00 00 B= 00 P= 7D E:1
```

Figure 15.2. Tracer Output.

This example was developed and tested using an Apple //e with a 65816 processor card installed; the calls to machine-dependent locations have been isolated and are clearly identified as such. **DEBUG16 uses the native BRK vector.** On an Apple //, this location ($FFE6.FFE7) normally contains ROM data, which varies between monitor ROM versions. Since there is no way to patch ROM, the solution opted for here is for **DEBUG16** to try to patch the location pointed to by the data that is stored there. For current ROMs, these are RAM locations that happen to be more or less livable. Check the location pointed to by your ROMs, and make sure that neither your own code nor the debugger are loaded into that area. **DEBUG16** will automatically read whatever value is stored there and store a vector to that address to regain control after a **BRK**.

Both programs are executed by putting the starting address of the routine to list or trace (which has been loaded into memory) at **DPAGE + 80.82** ($380.82) in low - high - bank order, and then calling either the **TRACE** entry point at $2000, or the **LIST** entry at $2003.

Declarations

The listing begins with the declaration of global values by way of **GEQU** statements. Almost all of these are addresses of direct page memory locations that will be used; one notable exception is the label **DPAGE**, a sixteen-bit value that defines the beginning of the direct page memory to be used by this program. Because a 65816 debugger is by definition a 6502 debugger, it is wise to relocate the direct page out of the default zero page, since it will be used by 6502 programs, and you want to avoid conflicting memory usage between the debugger and the program being debugged. In the listing, a value of $300 is used; on an Apple //, this relocates the direct page to page three, which is a convenient page to use.

Many of the direct page locations are used to store the register contents of the user program when the debugger is executing. All of the registers are represented. As you will see in the code, the adjacent positioning of some of the registers is important and must be maintained.

In addition to the direct page locations used for register storage, one general-purpose temporary variable is used, called **TEMP**. Three other variables—**ADDRMODE, MNX,** and **OPLEN** (for *address mode, mnemonic index,* and *operation length,* respectively)—are used primarily to access the tables used in disassembling an instruction.

The variable **CODE** contains the instruction opcode currently being executed in the user program. The variable **NCODE** contains the *next* instruction opcode to be executed, saved there before being replaced with the **BRK** instruction inserted in the code. **OPRNDL, OPRNDH,** and **OPRNDB** contain the three (possible) values of the operand of a given instruction.

```
0001  0000
0002  0000                KEEP    DEBUG16
0003  0000
0004  0000                65816 ON
0005  0000                MSB   ON
0006  0000                LONGA OFF
0007  0000                LONGI OFF
0008  0000
0009  0000        ****************************************
0010  0000        *                                      *
0011  0000        *       DEBUG16                        *
0012  0000        *       A 65816 DEBUGGER               *
0013  0000        *                                      *
0014  0000        *                                      *
0015  0000        ****************************************
0016  0000
0017  0000                ORG     $8000
0018  0000
0019  0000        MAIN    START
0020  0000
0021  0000                USING MN
0022  0000                USING ATRIBL
0023  0000
0024  0000
0025  0000        DPAGE   GEQU    $300            LOCATION OF THIS APPLICATION'S
0026  0000        ;                                 DIRECT PAGE
0027  0000
0028  0000        ;       DIRECT PAGE STORAGE
0029  0000        ;       TRACE REGISTERS
0030  0000        ;
0031  0000
0032  0000        PCREG   GEQU    $80             PROGRAM COUNTER
0033  0000        PCREGH  GEQU    PCREG+1
0034  0000        PCREGB  GEQU    PCREGH+1        INCLUDING BANK
0035  0000
0036  0000        NCODE   GEQU    PCREGB+1        NEXT CODE TO BE TRACED
0037  0000
0038  0000        OPCREG  GEQU    NCODE+1         OLD PROGRAM COUNTER VALUE
0039  0000        OPCREGH GEQU    OPCREG+1
0040  0000        OPCREGB GEQU    OPCREGH+1
0041  0000
0042  0000        CODE    GEQU    OPCREGB+1       CURRENT CODE TO BE TRACED
0043  0000
0044  0000        OPRNDL  GEQU    CODE+1          OPERANDS OF CURRENT
0045  0000        OPRNDH  GEQU    OPRNDL+1          INSTRUCTION
0046  0000        OPRNDB  GEQU    OPRNDH+1
```

```
0047  0000
0048  0000
0049  0000        XREG      GEQU  OPRNDB+1    X REGISTER
0050  0000        XREGH     GEQU  XREG+1
0051  0000
0052  0000        YREG      GEQU  XREGH+1     Y REGISTER
0053  0000        YREGH     GEQU  YREG+1
0054  0000
0055  0000        AREG      GEQU  YREGH+1     ACCUMULATOR
0056  0000        AREGH     GEQU  AREG+1
0057  0000
0058  0000        STACK     GEQU  AREGH+1     STACK POINTER
0059  0000        STACKH    GEQU  STACK+1
0060  0000
0061  0000
0062  0000        DIRREG    GEQU  STACKH+1    DIRECT PAGE REGISTER
0063  0000        DIRREGH   GEQU  DIRREG+1
0064  0000
0065  0000        DBREG     GEQU  DIRREGH+1   DATA BANK REGISTER
0066  0000
0067  0000        PREG      GEQU  DBREG+1     P STATUS REGISTER
0068  0000
0069  0000        EBIT      GEQU  PREG+1      E BIT
0070  0000
0071  0000        TEMP      GEQU  EBIT+2      TEMPORARY
0072  0000        TEMPH     GEQU  TEMP+1
0073  0000        TEMPB     GEQU  TEMPH+1
0074  0000
0075  0000
0076  0000        ADDRMODE  GEQU  TEMPB+1     ADDRESS MODE OF CURRENT OPCODE
0077  0000
0078  0000        MNX       GEQU  ADDRMODE+1  MNEMONIC INDEX
0079  0000        ;                           FROM ATTRIBUTE TABLE
0080  0000
0081  0000        OPLEN     GEQU  MNX+2       LENGTH OF OPERATION,
0082  0000        ;                           INCLUDING INSTRUCTION
0083  0000
0084  0000        CR        GEQU  $8D         CARRIAGE RETURN
0085  0000
0086  0000
0087  0000        M         GEQU  $20         SYMBOLIC NAMES FOR
0088  0000        X         GEQU  $10           STATUS REGISTER BITS
0089  0000        C         GEQU  $01
0090  0000
0091  0000
0092  0000
0093  0000 4C0080           JMP   TRACE
```

LIST

The program has two entry points, defined in the first routine. One is for listing (disassembling) a program, the other for tracing. The first entry point, at the program's origin (default $8000), is a jump to the actual entry point of the trace routine; the second, immediately past it (at $8003), is the beginning of the code for the disassembler.

Since this is a bare-bones disassembler, intended to be expanded and perhaps integrated with a general purpose machine language monitor, parameters such as the start address of the program to be traced are entered by modifying the values of the register variables; for example, to begin disassembly of a program stored at $800, the values $00, $08, and $00 are stored starting at **PCREG**. Since the direct page is relocated to page three, the absolute location of this variable is $380.

Starting at the **LIST** entry, some basic initialization is performed: saving the status register, switching to native mode, and then saving the previous operating mode (emulation/native) by pushing the status register a second time (the carry flag now containing the previous contents of the e bit). Thus this program may be called from either native or emulation mode.

The current value of the direct page is saved in program memory, and then the new value—**DPAGE**—is stored to the direct page register. The native mode is entered.

Control now continues at **TOP**, the beginning of the main loop of the disassembler. The mode is set to long accumulator, short index. This combination allows simple manipulation of both byte and double-byte values. The value of **PCREG** is copied to **OPCREG** (old pcreg). **OPCREG** will contain the starting location of the current instruction throughout the loop; **PCREG** will be modified to point to the next instruction. However, it hasn't been modified yet, so it is used to load the accumulator with the opcode byte. Indirect long addressing is used, so code anywhere within the sixteen-megabyte address space may be disassembled. Since the accumulator is sixteen bits, a second byte is fetched as well, but ignored; the next instruction transfers the opcode to the X register and then stores it at the location **CODE**.

The utility routine **UPDATE** is called next. This is common to both the disassembler and the tracer, and determines the attributes of this instruction by looking the instruction up in a table; it also increments the program counter to point to the next instruction.

The routines **FLIST**, **FRMOPRND**, and **PRINTLN** form the disassembled line and display it. After each line is printed, the routine **PAUSE** is called to check the keyboard to see if a key has been pressed, signalling a pause. If **PAUSE** returns with the carry clear, it means the user has signalled to quit, and control falls through to **QUIT**; otherwise, the program loops to **TOP** again, where it repeats the process for the next instruction.

```
0094  0003
0095  0003              ;.................................................
0096  0003              ;
0097  0003              ; LIST
0098  0003              ; MAIN LOOP OF DISASSMBLER FUNCTION
0099  0003              ;
0100  0003              ;.................................................
0101  0003              ;
0102  0003
0103  0003
0104  0003       LIST    ENTRY
0105  0003 08            PHP              SAVE ORIGINAL FLAGS
0106  0004 18            CLC
0107  0005 FB            XCE              SET NATIVE MODE
0108  0006 08            PHP              SAVE PREVIOUS MODE
0109  0007
0110  0007 0B            PHD              SAVE CURRENT DP
0111  0008 F40003        PEA    DPAGE
0112  000B 2B            PLD              SET TO NEW DP
0113  000C
0114  000C       TOP     ANOP
0115  000C
0116  000C C220          REP    #M
0117  000E E210          SEP    #X
0118  0010                LONGA ON
0119  0010                LONGI OFF
0120  0010
0121  0010 649D          STZ    MNX       CLEAR MNEMONIC INDEX
0122  0012 A580          LDA    PCREG     MOVE PROGRAM COUNTER
0123  0014 8584          STA    OPCREG     TO 'OLD PROGRAM COUNTER'
0124  0016 A682          LDX    PCREGB     INCLUDING BANK
0125  0018 8686          STX    OPCREGB
0126  001A A780          LDA    [PCREG]   GET NEXT INSTRUCTION
0127  001C AA            TAX
0128  001D 8687          STX    CODE      SAVE AS 'CODE'
0129  001F
0130  001F 200080        JSR    UPDATE    UPDATE ATTRIBUTE VARIABLES
0131  0022
0132  0022 200080        JSR    FLIST     FORM OBJECT CODE, MNEMONIC
0133  0025 200080        JSR    FRMOPRND  FORM OPERAND FIELD
0134  0028 200080        JSR    PAUSE     CHECK FOR USER PAUSE
0135  002B 9005          BCC    QUIT
0136  002D 200080        JSR    PRINTLN   PRINT IT
0137  0030
0138  0030 80DA          BRA    TOP       LOOP TIL END
```

```
0139  0032
0140  0032 2B      QUIT    PLD           RESTORE ENVIRONMENT,
0141  0033 28              PLP           RETURN TO CALLER
0142  0034 FB              XCE
0143  0035 28              PLP
0144  0036 60              RTS
0145  0037              END
0146  0037



Local  Symbols

LIST        000003  QUIT    000032  TOP      00000C
```

FLIST

FLIST is called by both the disassembler and the tracer. This routine displays the current program counter value, the object code of the instruction being disassembled in hexadecimal, and the mnemonic for the opcode. The code required to do this is basically the same for any instruction, the only difference being the length of the instruction, which has already been determined by UPDATE.

The first thing the code does is to blank the output buffer by calling CLRLN. Particularly since 6502 emulation-mode I/O routines are used, it is more efficient to build an output line first, then display it all at once, rather than output the line "on the fly." Characters are stored in the output buffer LINE via indexed absolute addressing; the Y register contains a pointer to the current character position within the line, and is incremented every time a character is stored. Since character manipulation is the primary activity in this routine, the accumulator is set to eight bits for most of the routine.

The flow of the program proceeds to generate the line from left to right, as it is printed; the first characters stored are therefore the current program counter values. Since UPDATE has already modified the program counter variable to load the operands of the instruction, the value in the variable OPCREG is used. The hex conversion routine, PUTHEX, converts the data in the accumulator into the two ASCII characters that represent the number's two hexadecimal digits, storing each character at the location pointed to by LINE,Y, and then incrementing Y to point to the next character. A colon is printed between the bank byte and the sixteen-bit program counter display to aid readability.

Next, some spaces are skipped by loading the Y register with a higher value, and the object code bytes are displayed in hexadecimal. These values have already been stored in direct page memory locations CODE and OPRNDL, OPRNDH, and OPRNDB by the UPDATE routine, which also determined the length of the instruction and stored it at OPLEN. The length of the operand controls a loop that outputs the bytes; note that a negative displacement of one is calculated by the assembler so that the loop is not executed when OPLEN is equal to one.

All that remains is to print the instruction mnemonic. The characters for all of the mnemonics are stored in a table called MN; at three characters per mnemonic (which as you may have noticed is the standard length for all 65x mnemonics), the mnemonic index (MNX) determined by UPDATE from the instruction attribute table must be multiplied by three. This is done by shifting left once (to multiply by two), and adding the result to the original value of MNX. Note that this type of "custom" multiplication routine is much more efficient than the generalized multiplication routines described in the previous chapter. The characters in the mnemonic table are copied into the output line using the MVN instruction; the result just calculated is transferred into the X register as the source of the move. It is the line-buffered output that allows use of the block-move instruction; on-the-fly output would have required each character to be copied out of the mnemonic table in a loop.

```
0147  0000                        ;
0148  0000                        ; FLIST - FORM IMAGE OF PROGRAM COUNTER,
0149  0000                        ; OBJECT CODE, AND MNEMONIC IN 'LINE'
0150  0000                        ;
0151  0000                        ; REQUIRES ATTRIBUTE VARIABLES TO BE PREVIOUSLY INITIALIZED
0152  0000                        ;.........................................................
0153  0000                        ;
0154  0000
0155  0000            FLIST   START
0156  0000                    USING MN
0157  0000
0158  0000 200080             JSR     CLRLN       BLANK 'LINE' VARIABLE
0159  0003
0160  0003 E230               SEP     #M+X        SHORT REGISTERS
0161  0005                    LONGA OFF
0162  0005                    LONGI OFF
0163  0005
0164  0005 A000               LDY     #0
0165  0007 A586               LDA     OPCREGB     GET BANK BYTE, FORM AS HEX
0166  0009 200080             JSR     PUTHEX        STRING
0167  000C A9BA               LDA     #':'        BANK DELIMITER
0168  000E 990080             STA     LINE,Y
0169  0011 C8                 INY
0170  0012 A585               LDA     OPCREGH     GET BYTES OF PROGRAM COUNTER
0171  0014 200080             JSR     PUTHEX        FORM AS HEX STRING IN
0172  0017 A584               LDA     OPCREG        LINE
0173  0019 200080             JSR     PUTHEX
0174  001C
0175  001C A00A               LDY     #10
0176  001E A587               LDA     CODE        STORE OPCODE AS HEX STRING
0177  0020 200080             JSR     PUTHEX
0178  0023 A201               LDX     #1
0179  0025
0180  0025 E49F       MORE    CPX     OPLEN       LIST OPERANDS, IF ANY
0181  0027 F008               BEQ     DONE
0182  0029 B587               LDA     OPRNDL-1,X
0183  002B 200080             JSR     PUTHEX
0184  002E E8                 INX
0185  002F 80F4               BRA     MORE
0186  0031
```

```
0187  0031 C230      DONE    REP     #M+X
0188  0033                   LONGA   ON
0189  0033                   LONGI   ON
0190  0033
0191  0033 A59D              LDA     MNX                 GET MNEMONIC INDEX,
0192  0035 0A                ASL     A                   MULTIPLY BY THREE
0193  0036 18                CLC                         (TIMES TWO PLUS SELF)
0194  0037 659D              ADC     MNX
0195  0039 18                CLC
0196  003A 690080            ADC     #MN
0197  003D AA                TAX                         INDEX INTO MNEMONIC TABLE
0198  003E A01480            LDY     #LINE+20            COPY INTO 'LINE'
0199  0041 A90200            LDA     #2
0200  0044             MOVE  ENTRY
0201  0044 540000            MVN     0,0
0202  0047
0203  0047 60                RTS
0204  0048                   END


Local Symbols

DONE       000031   MORE    000025   MOVE    000044
```

FRMOPRND

This routine is the second part of the line-disassembly pair. It performs the address-mode specific generation of the disassembled operand field; the result is similar to the address mode specification syntax of a line of 65x source code.

The Y register is loaded with the starting destination in **LINE**, and the attribute stored at **ADDRMODE** is multiplied by two to form an index into a jump table. There is a separate routine for each addressing mode; the address of that routine is stored in a table called **MODES** in the order that corresponds to the attributes given them from the attribute table.

The **JMP** indirect indexed instruction is used to transfer control through the jump table **MODES** to the appropriate routine, whose index, times two, has been loaded into the X register.

Each of the routines is basically similar; they output any special characters and print the address of the operand found in the instruction stream. There are three related routines, **POB, PODB,** and **POTB** (for put operand byte, put operand double byte, and put operand triple byte) which output direct page, absolute, and absolute long addresses.

The two routines **FPCR** and **FPCRL**, which handle the program counter relative instructions, however, must first calculate the destination address (which is how an assembler would specify the operand, so this is how they are disassembled) by adding the actual operand, a displacement, to the current program counter. The operand of a short program counter relative instruction is sign-extended before adding, resulting in a sixteen-bit signed displacement which is added to the program counter to find the destination address.

```
0205  0000
0206  0009            ;..............................................................
0207  0000            ;
0208  0000            ; FRMOPRND --
0209  0000            ; FORMS OPERAND FIELD OF DISASSEMBLED INSTRUCTION
0210  0000            ;
0211  0000            ; OPLEN, ADDRMODE, AND OPRND MUST HAVE BEEN
0212  0000            ; INITIALIZED BY 'UPDATE'
0213  0000            ;..............................................................
0214  0000            ;
0215  0000
0216  0000            FRMOPRND START
0217  0000                     USING MODES
0218  0000 E230                SEP     #M+X
0219  0002                     LONGA OFF
0220  0002                     LONGI OFF
0221  0002
0222  0002 A01C                LDY     #28         OFFSET INTO 'LINE' FOR OPERAND
0223  0004            ;                            TO BEGIN
0224  0004 A59C                LDA     ADDRMODE    GET ADDRESS MODE, MULTIPLY BY
0225  0006 0A                  ASL     A           TWO, JUMP THROUGH ADDRESS
0226  0007 AA                  TAX                 MODE JUMP TABLE TO PROPER
0227  0008 7C0080              JMP     (MODES,X)   HANDLER
0228  000B
0229  000B
0230  000B           FIMM      ENTRY               IMMEDIATE MODE --
0231  000B A9A3                LDA     #'#'        OUTPUT POUND SIGN,
0232  000D 990080              STA     LINE,Y      ONE OR TWO
0233  0010 C8                  INY                 OPERAND BYTES, DEPENDING
0234  0011 A59F                LDA     OPLEN       ON OPLEN
0235  0013 C902                CMP     #2
0236  0015 F003                BEQ     GOSHORT
0237  0017 4C0080              JMP     PODB
0238  001A 4C0080   GOSHORT    JMP     POB
0239  001D
0240  001D           FABS      ENTRY               ABSOLUTE MODE --
0241  001D 4C0080              JMP     PODB        JUST OUTPUT A DOUBLE BYTE
0242  0020
0243  0020           FABSL     ENTRY               ABSOLUTE LONG --
0244  0020 4C0080              JMP     POTB        OUTPUT A TRIPLE BYTE
0245  0023
0246  0023           FDIR      ENTRY               DIRECT MODE --
0247  0023 4C0080              JMP     POB         OUTPUT A SINGLE BYTE
0248  0026
0249  0026           FACC      ENTRY               ACCUMULATOR --
0250  0026 A9C1                LDA     #'A'        JUST AN A
```

```
0251   0028 990080                   STA    LINE,Y
0252   002B 60                       RTS
0253   002C
0254   002C           FIMP    ENTRY         IMPLIED --
0255   002C 60                       RTS             NO OPERAND
0256   002D
0257   002D           FINDINX ENTRY         INDIRECT INDEXED --
0258   002D 20B600                   JSR    FIND       CALL 'INDIRECT', THEN FALL
0259   0030           ;                                THROUGH TO INDEXED BY Y
0260   0030
0261   0030           FINY    ENTRY         INDEXED BY Y MODES --
0262   0030 A9AC                     LDA    #','       TACK ON A 'COMMA, Y'
0263   0032 990080                   STA    LINE,Y
0264   0035 C8                       INY
0265   0036 A9D9                     LDA    #'Y'
0266   0038 990080                   STA    LINE,Y
0267   003B 60                       RTS
0268   003C
0269   003C           FINDINXL ENTRY        INDIRECT INDEXED LONG --
0270   003C 20C600                   JSR    FINDL      CALL 'INDIRECT LONG', THEN
0271   003F 4C3000                   JMP    FINY       EXIT THROUGH INDEXED BY Y
0272   0042
0273   0042           FINXIND ENTRY         INDEX INDIRECT --
0274   0042 A9A8                     LDA    #'('       PARENTHESIS
0275   0044 990080                   STA    LINE,Y
0276   0047 C8                       INY
0277   0048 200080                   JSR    POB        A SINGLE BYTE --
0278   004B 206000                   JSR    FINX       COMMA, X
0279   004E A9A9                     LDA    #')'       CLOSE.
0280   0050 990080                   STA    LINE,Y
0281   0053 60                       RTS
0282   0054
0283   0054           FDIRINXX ENTRY        DIRECT INDEXED BY X --
0284   0054 200080                   JSR    POB        OUTPUT A BYTE,
0285   0057 4C6000                   JMP    FINX       TACK ON COMMA,X
0286   005A
0287   005A           FDIRINXY ENTRY        DIRECT INDEXED BY Y --
0288   005A 200080                   JSR    POB        OUTPUT A BYTE,
0289   005D 4C3000                   JMP    FINY       TACK ON COMMA,Y
0290   0060
0291   0060           FINX    ENTRY         INDEXED BY X --
0292   0060 A9AC                     LDA    #','       TACK ON A
0293   0062 990080                   STA    LINE,Y     COMMA,X
0294   0065 C8                       INY              (USED BY SEVERAL
0295   0066 A9D8                     LDA    #'X'       MODES)
0296   0068 990080                   STA    LINE,Y
```

```
0297  006B C8                    INY
0298  006C 60                    RTS
0299  006D
0300  006D         FABSX  ENTRY           ABSOLUTE INDEXED BY X --
0301  006D 200080         JSR    PODB     OUTPUT A DOUBLE BYTE,
0302  0070 4C6000         JMP    FINX     TACK ON A COMMA,X
0303  0073
0304  0073         FABSLX ENTRY           ABSOLUTE LONG BY X --
0305  0073 200080         JSR    POTB     OUTPUT A TRIPLE BYTE,
0306  0076 4C6000         JMP    FINX     TACK ON COMMA, X
0307  0079
0308  0079         FABSY  ENTRY           ABSOLUTE Y --
0309  0079 200080         JSR    PODB     OUTPUT A DOUBLE BYTE,
0310  007C 4C3000         JMP    FINY     TACK ON COMMA,Y
0311  007F
0312  007F         FPCR   ENTRY           PROGRAM COUNTER RELATIVE --
0313  007F A9FF           LDA    #$FF     SIGN EXTEND OPERAND
0314  0081 EB             XBA
0315  0082 A588           LDA    OPRNDL
0316  0084 C221           REP    #M+C
0317  0086                LONGA  ON
0318  0086 3003           BMI    OK
0319  0088 297F00         AND    #$7F
0320  008B 6584    OK     ADC    OPCREG   ADD TO PROGRAM COUNTER
0321  008D 1A             INC    A        ADD TWO, WITHOUT CARRY
0322  008E 1A             INC    A
0323  008F 8588           STA    OPRNDL   STORE AS NEW 'OPERAND'
0324  0091
0325  0091 E220           SEP    #M
0326  0093                LONGA  OFF
0327  0093
0328  0093 4C0080         JMP    PODB     NOW JUST DISPLAY A DOUBLE BYTE
0329  0096
0330  0096         FCPRL  ENTRY           PROGRAM COUNTER RELATIVE LONG
0331  0096
0332  0096 C221           REP    #M+C
0333  0098                LONGA  ON
0334  0098
0335  0098 A588           LDA    OPRNDL   JUST ADD THE OPERAND
0336  009A 6584           ADC    OPCREG
0337  009C 18             CLC             BUMP BY THREE, PAST INSTRUCTION
0338  009D 690300         ADC    #3
0339  00A0 8588           STA    OPRNDL   STORE AS NEW 'OPERAND'
0340  00A2
0341  00A2 E220           SEP    #M
0342  00A4                LONGA  OFF
0343  00A4
```

15   DEBUG16—A 65816 Programming Tool

```
0344  00A4 4C0080                JMP   PODB         PRINT A DOUBLE BYTE
0345  00A7
0346  00A7           FABSIND  ENTRY                 ABSOLUTE INDIRECT
0347  00A7 A9A8                 LDA   #'('          SURROUND A DOUBLE BYTE
0348  00A9 990080                STA   LINE,Y         WITH PARENTHESES
0349  00AC C8                   INY
0350  00AD 200080                JSR   PODB
0351  00B0 A9A9                 LDA   #')'
0352  00B2 990080                STA   LINE,Y
0353  00B5 60                   RTS
0354  00B6
0355  00B6           FIND     ENTRY                 INDIRECT --
0356  00B6 A9A8                 LDA   #'('          SURROUND A SINGLE BYTE
0357  00B8 990080                STA   LINE,Y         WITH PARENTHESES
0358  00BB C8                   INY
0359  00BC 200080                JSR   POB
0360  00BF A9A9                 LDA   #')'
0361  00C1 990080                STA   LINE,Y
0362  00C4 C8                   INY
0363  00C5 60                   RTS
0364  00C6
0365  00C6           FINDL    ENTRY                 INDIRECT LONG --
0366  00C6 A9DB                 LDA   #'['          SURROUND A SINGLE BYTE
0367  00C8 990080                STA   LINE,Y         WITH SQUARE BRACKETS
0368  00CB C8                   INY
0369  00CC 200080                JSR   POB
0370  00CF A9DD                 LDA   #']'
0371  00D1 990080                STA   LINE,Y
0372  00D4 C8                   INY
0373  00D5 60                   RTS
0374  00D6
0375  00D6           FABSINXIND ENTRY               ABSOLUTE INDIRECT INDEXED
0376  00D6 A9A8                 LDA   #'('
0377  00D8 990080                STA   LINE,Y       SURROUND A CALL TO 'ABSOLUTE
0378  00DB C8                   INY                  INDEXED' WITH PARENTHESES
0379  00DC 206D00                JSR   FABSX
0380  00DF A9A9                 LDA   #')'
0381  00E1 990080                STA   LINE,Y
0382  00E4 60                   RTS
0383  00E5
0384  00E5           FSTACK   ENTRY                 STACK -- IMPLIED
0385  00E5 60                   RTS
0386  00E6
0387  00E6           FSTACKREL ENTRY                STACK RELATIVE
0388  00E6 202300                JSR   FDIR         JUST LIKE
0389  00E9 A9AC                 LDA   #','         DIRECT INDEXED, BUT WITH
0390  00EB 990080                STA   LINE,Y        AN 'S'
```

```
0391  00EE C8                   INY
0392  00EF A9D3                 LDA    #'S'
0393  00F1 990080               STA    LINE,Y
0394  00F4 C8                   INY
0395  00F5 60                   RTS
0396  00F6
0397  00F6
0398  00F6         FSRINDINX ENTRY              STACK RELATIVE INDIRECT INDEX
0399  00F6 A9A8                 LDA    #'('
0400  00F8 990080               STA    LINE,Y    SURROUND STACK RELATIVE WITH
0401  00FB C8                   INY                PARENTHESES, THEN
0402  00FC 20E600               JSR    FSTACKREL
0403  00FF A9A9                 LDA    #')'
0404  0101 990080               STA    LINE,Y
0405  0104 C8                   INY
0406  0105 4C3000               JMP    FINY      TACK ON A COMMA,Y
0407  0108
0408  0108
0409  0108          FBLOCK  ENTRY              BLOCK MOVE
0410  0108
0411  0108 C220                 REP    #M
0412  010A A588                 LDA    OPRNDL    MAKE HUMAN-READABLE:
0413  010C EB                   XBA              SWAP SOURCE, DEST
0414  010D 8588                 STA    OPRNDL
0415  010F E220                 SEP    #M
0416  0111
0417  0111 200080               JSR    POB       OUTPUT THE SOURCE
0418  0114 A9AC                 LDA    #','      THEN COMMA
0419  0116 990080               STA    LINE,Y
0420  0119 C8                   INY
0421  011A EB                   XBA              SWAP DEST INTO OPRNDL
0422  011B 8588                 STA    OPRNDL    THEN PRINT ONE BYTE
0423  011D 4C0080               JMP    POB
0424  0120
0425  0120
0426  0120                      END

Local Symbols

FABS      00001D   FABSIND    0000A7   FABSINXIND 0000D6   FABSL      000020
FABSLX    000073   FABSX      00006D   FABSY      000079   FACC       000026
FBLOCK    000108   FDIR       000023   FDIRINXX   000054   FDIRINXY   00005A
FIMM      00000B   FIMP       00002C   FIND       0000B6   FINDINX    00002D
FINDINXL  00003C   FINDL      0000C6   FINX       000060   FINXIND    000042
FINY      000030   FPCR       00007F   FPCRL      000096   FSRINDINX  0000F6
FSTACK    0000E5   FSTACKREL  0000E6   GOSHORT    00001A   OK         00008B
```

POB

This routine (put operand byte), with three entry points, outputs a dollar sign, followed by either one, two, or three operand bytes in hexadecimal form; it calls the routine **PUTHEX** to output the operand bytes. It is called by **FRMOPRND**.

Depending on the entry point, the X register is loaded with 0, 1, or 2, controlling the number of times the loop at **MORE** is executed; on each iteration of the loop, an operand byte is loaded by indexing into **OPRNDL** and then printed by **PUTHEX**.

```
0427  0000
0428  0000           ;.............................................................
0429  0000           ;
0430  0000           ; POB, PODB, POTB
0431  0000           ; PUT OPERAND (DOUBLE, TRIPLE) BYTE
0432  0000           ;
0433  0000           ; PUTS OPRNDL (OPRNDH, OPRNDB) IN LINE AS HEX VALUE
0434  0000           ; WITH '$' PREFIX
0435  0000           ;
0436  0000           ; ASSUMES SHORT ACCUMULATOR AND INDEX REGISTERS
0437  0000           ; (CALLED BY FOPRND)
0438  0000           ;.............................................................
0439  0000           ;
0440  0000
0441  0000
0442  0000
0443  0000           POB     START
0444  0000                   LONGA OFF
0445  0000                   LONGI OFF
0446  0000
0447  0000           ;                           PRINT:
0448  0000 A200              LDX   #0            ONE OPERAND BYTE
0449  0002 8006              BRA   IN              SKIP
0450  0004           PODB    ENTRY
0451  0004 A201              LDX   #1            TWO OPERAND BYTES
0452  0006 8002              BRA   IN              SKIP
0453  0008           POTB    ENTRY
0454  0008 A202              LDX   #2            THREE OPERAND BYTES
0455  000A           ;                             FALL THROUGH
0456  000A A9A4      IN      LDA   #'$'          PRINT LEAD-IN
0457  000C 990080            STA   LINE,Y
0458  000F C8                INY
0459  0010
0460  0010 B588      MORE    LDA   OPRNDL,X      LOOP THROUGH OPERAND
```

```
0461   0012 200080        JSR    PUTHEX        HIGH TO LOW
0462   0015 CA            DEX
0463   0016 10F8          BPL    MORE
0464   0018 60            RTS
0465   0019               END



Local Symbols

IN         00000A   MORE     000010   PODB     000004   POTB     000008
```

STEP

This routine also contains the **PAUSE** entry point called by **LIST**; **STEP** waits until a keypress, **PAUSE** simply checks to see if a key has been pressed, and waits only if there has been an initial keypress. In both cases, the wait loop continues until the next keypress. If the keypress that exits the wait loop was the **ESCAPE** key, the carry is cleared, signalling the calling program that the user wants to quit rather than continue. If it was **RETURN,** the overflow flag is cleared; the tracer uses this toggle between tracing and single stepping. Any other keypress causes the routine to return with both flags set.

The code in this listing is machine-dependent; it checks the keyboard locations of the Apple //. Since this is a relatively trivial task, in-line code is used rather than a call to one of the existing 6502 monitor routines; therefore, the processor remains in the native mode while it performs this I/O operation.

Like all utility routines, **STEP** saves and restores the status on entry and exit.

```
0466  0000
0467  0000
0468  0000
0469  0000                    APPEND DB.UTILITY
0470  0000
0471  0000
0472  0000          ;..........................................
0473  0000          ;
0474  0000          ;  STEP -- CHECKS FOR USER PAUSE SIGNAL
0475  0000          ;  (KEYSTROKE)
0476  0000          ;
0477  0000          ;  CONTAINS MACHINE-DEPENDENT CODE
0478  0000          ;  FOR APPLE //
0479  0000          ;..........................................
0480  0000          ;
0481  0000
0482  0000          STEP    START
0483  0000          KEYBD   EQU    $C000
0484  0000          KEYSTB  EQU    $C010
0485  0000          ESC     EQU    $9B           ESCAPE KEY (HIGH BIT SET)
0486  0000          V       EQU    $40           MASK FOR OVERFLOW FLAG
0487  0000                  LONGA  OFF
0488  0000                  LONGI  OFF
0489  0000
0490  0000 08               PHP                  SAVE MODES
0491  0001 E230             SEP    #M+X
```

```
0492  0003  800B            BRA     WAIT
0493  0005
0494  0005          PAUSE   ENTRY                   ENTRY FOR 'PAUSE' CALL
0495  0005  08              PHP
0496  0006  E230            SEP     #M+X
0497  0008  AD00C0          LDA     KEYBD           CHECK FOR KEYPRESS

0498  000B  101B            BPL     RETNCR          NONE; DON'T PAUSE
0499  000D  8D10C0          STA     KEYSTB          CLEAR STROBE
0500  0010          ;                               IF KEYSTROKE
0501  0010  AD00C0  WAIT    LDA     KEYBD           LOOP FOR NEXT KEY
0502  0013  10FB            BPL     WAIT
0503  0015  8D10C0          STA     KEYSTB          CLEAR STROBE
0504  0018  C99B            CMP     #ESC            IF ESC RETURN WITH

0505  001A  D004            BNE     RETNESC
0506  001C
0507  001C  28      RETEQ   PLP                     CARRY CLEAR (QUIT)

0508  001D  EA              NOP
0509  001E  18              CLC
0510  001F  60              RTS
0511  0020
0512  0020  C98D    RETNESC CMP     #CR
0513  0022  D004            BNE     RETNCR
0514  0024  28              PLP
0515  0025  E241            SEP     #C+V
0516  0027  60              RTS
0517  0028
0518  0028  8D10C0  RETNCR  STA     KEYSTB
0519  002B  28              PLP                     ELSE SET
0520  002C  38              SEC
0521  002D  B8              CLV
0522  002E  60              RTS             (CONTINUE)
0523  002F                  END


Local Symbols

ESC      00009B  KEYBD   00C000  KEYSTB  00C010  PAUSE   000005
RETEQ    00001C  RETNCR  000028  RETNESC 000020  V       000040
WAIT     000010
```

PUTHEX

This utility routine, already referred to in several descriptions, is called whenever a hexadecimal value needs to be output. It converts the character in the low byte of the accumulator into two hexadecimal characters, and stores them in the buffer **LINE** at the position pointed to by the Y register.

PUTHEX calls an internal subroutine, **MAKEHEX**, which does the actual conversion. This call (rather than in-line code) allows **MAKEHEX** to first call, then fall through into, an internal routine, **FORMNIB**.

When **MAKEHEX** returns, it contains the two characters to be printed in the high and low bytes of the accumulator; **MAKEHEX** was processed with the accumulator eight bits wide, so the sixteen-bit mode is switched to, letting both bytes be stored in one instruction. The Y register is incremented twice, pointing it to the space immediately past the second character printed.

FORMNIB is both called (for processing the first nibble) and fallen into (for processing the second). Thus the **RTS** that exits **FORMNIB** returns variously to either **MAKEHEX** or **PUTHEX.** This technique results in more compact code than if **FORMNIB** were called twice.

The conversion itself is done by isolating the respective bits, and then adding the appropriate offset to form either the correct decimal or alphabetic (A-F) hexadecimal character.

Like all utility routines, the status is saved and restored on entry and exit.

```
0524  0000
0525  0000
0526  0000              ;............................................................
0527  0000              ;
0528  0000              ; PUTHEX
0529  0000              ;
0530  0000              ; CONVERTS NUMBER IN ACCUMULATOR TO HEX STRING
0531  0000              ; STORED AT LINE,Y
0532  0000              ;
0533  0000              ; SAVES AND RESTORES MODE FLAGS
0534  0000              ;............................................................
0535  0000              ;
0536  0000
0537  0000
0538  0000
0539  0000       PUTHEX    START
0540  0000 08              PHP                    SAVE MODE FLAGS
0541  0001 200D00          JSR    MAKEHEX         GET ASCII CODES IN A, B
0542  0004 C220            REP    #M
0543  0006            LONGA ON
0544  0006 990080          STA    LINE,Y          PUT TWO BYTES AT LINE
0545  0009 C8              INY                    INCREMENT Y PAST THEM
0546  000A C8              INY
0547  000B 28              PLP                    RESTORE MODE
0548  000C 60              RTS                    RETURN
0549  000D
0550  000D E230   MAKEHEX  SEP    #M+X            ALL EIGHT BIT
0551  000F            LONGA OFF
0552  000F            LONGI OFF
0553  000F
0554  000F 48              PHA                    SAVE VALUE TO BE CONVERTED
0555  0010 290F            AND    #$0F            MASK OFF LOW NIBBLE
0556  0012 201B00          JSR    FORMNIB         CONVERT TO HEX
0557  0015 EB              XBA                    STORE IN B
0558  0016 68              PLA                    RESTORE VALUE
0559  0017 4A              LSR    A               SHIFT HIGH NIBBLE
0560  0018 4A              LSR    A                 TO LOW NIBBLE
0561  0019 4A              LSR    A
0562  001A 4A              LSR    A
0563  001B           ;                            FALL THROUGH TO CONVERT
0564  001B
0565  001B C90A   FORMNIB  CMP    #$A             IF GREATER THAN OR EQUAL TO
0566  001D B004            BGE    HEXDIG          10, USE DIGITS A .. F
0567  001F 18              CLC                    ELSE SIMPLY ADD '0' TO
0568  0020 69B0            ADC    #'0'              CONVERT TO ASCII
0569  0022 60              RTS
```

```
0570  0023
0571  0023 69B6      HEXDIG   ADC   $'A'-11      SUBTRACT 11, ADD 'A'
0572  0025 60                 RTS                (SORT OF)
0573  0026
0574  0026                    END




Local Symbols

FORMNIB    00001B  HEXDIG    000023  MAKEHEX    00000D
```

CLRLN

CLRLN performs the very straightforward task of clearing the output buffer, LINE, to blanks. It also contains the global storage reserved for LINE.

Like the other utility routines, CLRLN saves and restores the status.

```
0575  0000
0576  0000           ;..........................................................
0577  0000           ;
0578  0000           ; CLRLN
0579  0000           ;
0580  0000           ; CLEARS 'LINE' WITH BLANKS
0581  0000           ;
0582  0000           ; SAVES AND RESTORES MODE FLAGS
0583  0000           ;
0584  0000           ;..........................................................
0585  0000           ;
0586  0000
0587  0000
0588  0000             CLRLN   START
0589  0000 08                  PHP
0590  0001 C230               REP     #M+X
0591  0003                    LONGA ON
0592  0003                    LONGI ON
0593  0003
0594  0003 A9A0A0             LDA     #' '
0595  0006 A24400             LDX     #68
0596  0009
0597  0009 9D1200     LOOP    STA     LINE,X
0598  000C CA                 DEX
0599  000D CA                 DEX
0600  000E 10F9               BPL     LOOP
0601  0010 28                 PLP
0602  0011 60                 RTS
0603  0012
0604  0012
0605  0012       LINE    ENTRY
0606  0012 A0A0A0A0            DC      70C' '
0607  0058 8D00                DC      H'8D00'
0608  005A                     END


Local Symbols

LINE      000012   LOOP      000009
```

UPDATE

This routine, common to both the disassembler and the tracer, updates the program counter and other direct page variables—the address mode attribute (**ADDRMODE**) and the length (**OPLEN**)—and, using the length, reads the instruction operands into direct page memory.

The address mode and length attributes are stored in a table called **ATRIBL**, two bytes per instruction. Since there are 256 different opcodes, the table size is 512 bytes. The current opcode itself, fetched previously, is used as the index into the table. Since the table entries are two bytes each, the index is first multiplied by two by shifting left. Since the sixteen-bit accumulator was used to calculate the index, both attribute bytes can be loaded in a single operation; since their location in direct page memory is adjacent, they can be stored in a single operation as well.

Normally, the value of **OPLEN** loaded from the attribute table is the correct one; in the case of the immediate addressing mode, however, the length varies with the setting of the **m** and **x** flags. The opcodes for the immediate instructions are trapped using just three comparisons, an **AND**, and four branches to test the opcode bits. Note that the immediate operands are multiplied times two because the opcode already happens to be shifted left once. If the current instruction uses immediate addressing, the stored value of the status register is checked for the relevant flag setting; if **m** or **x**, as appropriate, is clear, then **OPLEN** is incremented. The routines that output the immediate operand now know the correct number of operand bytes to print, and the tracer knows where the next instruction begins.

The status is saved on entry and restored on exit.

```
0609  0000
0610  0000
0611  0000          ;..............................................
0612  0000          ;
0613  0000          ;   UPDATE
0614  0000          ;
0615  0000          ;   UPDATES ATTRIBUTE VARIABLES BASED ON OPCODE
0616  0000          ;   PASSED IN ACCUMULATOR BY LOOKING IN ATTRIBUTE
0617  0000          ;   TABLES
0618  0000          ;
0619  0000          ;   SAVES AND RESTORES MODE FLAGS
0620  0000          ;..............................................
0621  0000          ;
0622  0000
0623  0000
0624  0000      UPDATE   START
0625  0000               USING   ATRIBL
0626  0000
0627  0000
0628  0000      LDYI     EQU     $A0*2           OPCODE VALUE TIMES TWO
0629  0000      LDXI     EQU     $A2*2
0630  0000
0631  0000 08            PHP                     SAVE STATE
0632  0001 C230          REP     #M+X
0633  0003               LONGA   ON
0634  0003               LONGI   ON
0635  0003
0636  0003 29FF00        AND     #$FF            MASK HIGH BYTE
0637  0006 0A            ASL     A               TIMES TWO
0638  0007
0639  0007 A8            TAY
0640  0008 B90080        LDA     ATRIBL,Y        INDEX INTO ATTRIBUTE TABLE
0641  000B EB            XBA                     SWAP ORDER OF ENTRIES
0642  000C 859C          STA     ADDRMODE        SAVE ADDRMODE, MNEMONIC INDEX
0643  000E
0644  000E AA            TAX                     ADDRMODE TO X (LOW)
0645  000F 98            TYA                     OPCODE * 2 TO ACCUM
0646  0010 E210          SEP     #X
0647  0012               LONGI   OFF
0648  0012
0649  0012 BCFF7F        LDY     LENS-1,X        GET LENGTH OF OPERATION
0650  0015 849F          STY     OPLEN
0651  0017
0652  0017
0653  0017 A697          LDX     EBIT            EMULATION MODE?
0654  0019 E001          CPX     #1              TEST BIT ZERO
0655  001B F02E          BEQ     SHORT           YES--ALL IMMEDIATE ARE
```

```
0656   001D              ;                          SHORT
0657   001D 892000              BIT     #$20        IS MSD*2 EVEN?
0658   0020 D029                BNE     SHORT       NO, CAN'T BE IMMEDIATE
0659   0022 C94401              CMP     #LDXI       IS IT LDX #?
0660   0025 F00A                BEQ     CHKX
0661   0027 891E00              BIT     #$F*2       IS LSD*2 ZERO?
0662   002A D00E                BNE     CHKA        CHECK ACCUMULATOR OPCODES
0663   002C C94001              CMP     #LDYI       MUST = LDY# OR GREATER
0664   002F 9009                BLT     CHKA        NO, MAYBE ACCUMULATOR
0665   0031 A596                LDA     PREG        IF IT IS, WHAT IS FLAG SETTING?
0666   0033 291000              AND     #X
0667   0036 F011                BEQ     LONG        CLEAR - 16 BIT MODE
0668   0038 D011                BNE     SHORT       SET - 8 BIT
0669   003A
0670   003A 291E00      CHKA    AND     #$0F*2      MASK OUT MSD
0671   003D C91200              CMP     #$9*2       IS LSD = 9?
0672   0040 D009                BNE     SHORT
0673   0042 A596                LDA     PREG        WHAT IS FLAG SETTING?
0674   0044 292000              AND     #M
0675   0047 D002                BNE     SHORT       NO, 8 BIT MODE
0676   0049
0677   0049 E69F        LONG    INC     OPLEN       LONG IMMEDIATE -- LENGTH IS
0678   004B              ;                          ONE MORE THAN FOUND IN TABLE
0679   004B
0680   004B A000        SHORT   LDY     #0
0681   004D 8005                BRA     LOOPIN
0682   004F
0683   004F A780        LOOP    LDA     [PCREG]     LOAD 16 BITS --16 BIT MODE
0684   0051              ;                          USED TO BUMP PCREG EASILY
0685   0051 AA                  TAX                 TRUNCATE TO EIGHT BITS
0686   0052 9687                STX     ORPNDL-1,Y  SAVE
0687   0054
0688   0054 E680        LOOPIN  INC     PCREG       MOVE PC PAST NEXT INSTRUCTION

0689   0056 C8                  INY                 BYTE
0690   0057 C49F                CPY     OPLEN       MOVED ALL OPERAND BYTES?
0691   0059 D0F4                BNE     LOOP            NO, CONTINUE
0692   005B
0693   005B 28          DONE    PLP
0694   005C 60                  RTS
0695   005D                     END


Local Symbols

CHKA       00003A   CHKX    000031   DONE    00005B   LDXI    000144
LDYI       000140   LONG    000049   LOOP    00004F   LOOPIN  000054
SHORT      00004B
```

PRINTLN

This is the output routine. In this version, an existing 6502 output routine is called, necessitating a reversion to the emulation mode. Since this is the only place a 6502 routine is called, a simpler mode-switching routine than the generalized one of the previous chapter is used. The user registers do not need to be preserved, but zero needs to be swapped into the direct page to make it address page zero.

The main loop is in the emulation mode until the null terminal byte of **LINE** is encountered; on exit, the native mode, direct page, and status are restored.

```
0696 0000
0697 0000
0698 0000            ;.........................................................
0699 0000            ;
0700 0000            ;   PRINTLN
0701 0000            ;
0702 0000            ;   MACHINE-DEPENDENT CODE TO OUTPUT
0703 0000            ;   THE STRING STORED AT 'LINE'
0704 0000            ;
0705 0000            ;   SAVES AND RESTORES MODE FLAGS
0706 0000            ;.........................................................
0707 0000            ;
0708 0000
0709 0000
0710 0000
0711 0000            PRINTLN  START
0712 0000            COUT     EQU    $FDED     APPLE CHARACTER OUTPUT ROUTINE
0713 0000
0714 0000 08                  PHP              SAVE STATUS
0715 0001 0B                  PHD              SAVE DIRECT PAGE
0716 0002 F40000              PEA    0         SWITCH TO PAGE ZERO
0717 0005 2B                  PLD                 FOR EMULATION
0718 0006
0719 0006                     LONGA  OFF
0720 0006                     LONGI  OFF
0721 0006 38                  SEC              SWITCH TO EMULATION
0722 0007 FB                  XCE
0723 0008
0724 0008 A000                LDY    #0
0725 000A
0726 000A B90080     LOOP     LDA    LINE,Y    LOOP UNTIL STRING TERMINATOR
0727 000D F006                BEQ    DONE         REACHED
0728 000F 20EDFD              JSR    COUT
```

```
0729  0012 C8                INY
0730  0013 80F5              BRA   LOOP
0731  0015
0732  0015 18      DONE      CLC                 RESTORE NATIVE MODE
0733  0016 FB                XCE
0734  0017 2B                PLD                 RESTORE DIRECT PAGE
0735  0018 28                PLP                 RESTORE MODE FLAGS
0736  0019 60                RTS
0737  001A
0738  001A                   END


Local Symbols


COUT       00FDED  DONE     000015  LOOP     0000DA
```

TRACE

This is the actual entry to the trace routine. It performs initialization similar to LIST, and additionally sets up the BRK vectors, so they can point to locations within the tracer.

The e flag, direct page register and data bank register are all given initial values of zero. The program counter and program counter bank are presumed to have been initialized by the user. The first byte of the program to be traced is loaded; since indirect long addressing is used, this program can be used with the 65816 to debug programs located in any bank. It can, of course, also be used with the 65802.

The jump to TBEGIN enters the main loop of the trace routine in the middle—in other words, "between instructions."

```
0739  0000
0740  0000                    APPEND DB.TRACE
0741  0000
0743  0000            ;
0744  0000            ; TRACE
0745  0000            ;
0746  0000            ; ENTRY POINT FOR TRACER
0747  0000            ;..........................................
0748  0000            ;
0749  0000
0750  0000            TRACE    START
0751  0000            USRBRKV  GEQU   $3F0         USER BRK VECTOR FOR APPLE //
0752  0000            BRKN     GEQU   $FFE6        NATIVE MODE BRK VECTOR
0753  0000
0754  0000 08                  PHP                 SAVE CALLING STATE
0755  0001 18                  CLC
0756  0002 FB                  XCE
0757  0003 08                  PHP
0758  0004
0759  0004 C210               REP    #$10
0760  0006                     LONGI  ON
0761  0006 F40000              PEA    0            OLD STACK BOUNDARY
0762  0009
0763  0009 BA                  TSX
0764  000A 8E3D00              STX    SAVSTACK
0765  000D
0766  000D F40003              PEA    DPAGE                    INITIALIZE DIRECT PAGE
0767  0010 2B                  PLD
0768  0011
0769  0011 8691                STX    STACK
0770  0013
```

```
0771  0013 E220                 SEP      #$20
0772  0015                      LONGA    OFF
0773  0015
0774  0014 A901                 LDA      #1
0775  0017 8597                 STA      EBIT
0776  0019 6493                 STZ      DIRREG      DIRECT PAGE, DATA BANK
0777  001B 6494                 STZ      DIRREGH        TO POWER-UP DEFAULTS
0778  001D 6495                 STZ      DBREG
0779  001F 649E                 STZ      MNX+1
0780  0021
0781  0021 9C0080               STZ      STEPCNTRL
0782  0024
0783  0024 A20080               LDX      #EBRKIN     PATCH BRK VECTORS
0784  0027 8EF003               STX      USRBRKV        TO POINT TO TRACE CODE
0785  002A
0786  002A AEE6FF               LDX      BRKN        FIND OUT WHERE BRKN POINTS TO

0787  002D E000C0               CPX      #$C000      MAKE SURE IT'S RAM ON AN APPLE
0788  0030 9003                 BLT      OK
0789  0032 4C0080               JMP      QUIT        MIGHT AS WELL GIVE UP NOW...

0790  0035 8E3F00     OK        STX      USRBRKN
0791  0038
0792  0038 A780                 LDA      [PCREG]     GET FIRST OP CODE
0793  003A 4C0080               JMP      TBEGIN         BEGIN!
0794  003D
0795  003D           SAVSTACK   ENTRY
0796  003D 0000                 DS       2
0797  003F           USRBRKN    ENTRY
0798  003F 0000                 DS       2
0799  0041           SAVRAM     ENTRY



0800  0041 0000                 DS       2
0801  0043                      END




Local Symbols


OK         000035   SAVRAM     000041   SAVSTACK   00003D   USRBRKN   00003F
```

EBRKIN

This is the main loop of the tracer. It has three entry points: one each for the emulation and native mode **BRK** vectors to point to, and a third (**TBEGIN**) which is entered when the program starts tracing and there is no "last instruction." This entry provides the logical point to begin examining the tracing process.

TRACE has performed some initialization, having loaded the opcode of the first instruction to be traced into the accumulator. As with **FLIST**, **UPDATE** is called to update the program counter and copy the instruction attributes and operand into direct page memory. The routine **CHKSPCL** is then called to handle the flow-altering instructions; in these cases, it will modify **PCREG** to reflect the target address. In either case, the opcode of the *next* instruction is loaded, and a **BRK** instruction (a zero) is stored in its place, providing a means to regain control immediately after the execution of the current instruction.

The contents of the RAM pointed to by the (arbitrary) ROM values in the native mode **BRK** vector are temporarily saved, and the location is patched with a jump to the **NBRKIN** entry point.

The registers are then loaded with their user program values: these will have been preinitialized by **TRACE**, or will contain the values saved at the end of the execution of the previous instruction. Note the order in which the registers are loaded; some with direct page locations, others pushed onto the stack directly from direct page locations, then pulled into the various registers. Once the user registers have been loaded with their values, they cannot be used for data movement. The P status register must be pulled last, to prevent any other instructions from modifying the flags.

The e bit is restored by loading the P register with a mask reflecting the value it should have; e is exchanged with the carry, and a second **PLP** instruction restores the correct status register values.

The routine exits via a jump indirect long through the "old" pcreg variable, which points to the current instruction. It will be reentered (at either **EBRKIN** or **NBRKIN**) when the **BRK** instruction that immediately follows the current instruction is executed.

Before this, however, the single instruction will be executed by the processor; any memory to be loaded or stored, or any registers to be changed by the instruction, will be modified.

After the **BRK** is executed, control returns to the tracer either at **EBRKIN**, if the user program was in emulation mode, or at **NBRKIN** if the user program was in native mode. The first thing that must be done is preserve the state of the machine as it was at the end of the instruction.

The **BRK** instruction has put the program counter bank (only in native mode), the program counter, and the status register on the stack. The program already knows the address of the next instruction, so the value on the stack can be disregarded. The status register is needed, however.

Entry to **EBRKIN** is from the Apple // monitor user vector at $3F0 and $3F1. The Apple // monitor handles emulation mode **BRK** instructions by storing the register values to its own zero page locations; it pulls the program counter and status register from the stack and stores them, too. The code at **EBRKIN** dummies up a native mode post-**BRK** stack by first pushing three place-holder bytes, then loading the status register the from where the Apple Monitor stored it, and pushing it. The accumulator and **X** registers are re-loaded from monitor locations; **Y** has been left intact. A one is stored to variable **EBIT**, which will be used to restore the emulation mode when **EBRKIN** exits. The processor switches to native mode, and control falls through into **NBRKIN**, the native mode break handler.

With the stack in the correct state for both emulation mode and native mode entries, the routine proceeds to save the entire machine context. The register sizes are extended to sixteen bits to provide a standard size which encompasses the maximum size possible. The data bank and direct page registers are pushed onto the stack; the **DPAGE** value is pushed on immediately after, and pulled into the direct page, establishing the local direct page. With this in place, the **A**, **X**, and Y registers can be stored at their direct page locations. The register values pushed on the stack are picked off using stack-relative addressing. Since control is not returned by execution of an RTI (as is usual for interrupt processing), but instead is returned by means of a JMP, the stack must be cleaned up. Since seven bytes have been pushed, seven is added to the current stack pointer, and then saved at the direct page variable **STACK**. This being done, a small local stack region at $140 can be allocated.

The memory borrowed as a RAM native-mode **BRK** vector is restored.

The current line is then disassembled in the same manner as **LIST**. The register values just stored into memory are also displayed via the routine **DUMPREGS**.

Once this is done, the effect has been achieved and the contents of the registers between instructions has been made visible. Before resuming execution of the program being traced, a check is made to see if the user wishes to quit, pause or step, or toggle between tracing and stepping.

Before returning to the **TBEGIN** entry, the **BRK** instruction stored at the location of the new "current" instruction is replaced with the saved opcode, the current program counter is moved to the old program counter, and the cycle begins again at **TBEGIN**.

```
0802  0000
0803  0000              ;....................................................
0804  0000              ;
0805  0000              ;   EBRKIN, NBRKIN, TBEGIN
0806  0000              ;
0807  0000              ;   ENTRY POINTS FOR TRACER MAIN LOOP
0808  0000              ;   EBRKIN AND NBRKIN RECOVER CONTROL AFTER
0809  0000              ;   'BRK' INSTRUCTION EXECUTED
0810  0000              ;   TBEGIN IS INITIAL ENTRY FROM 'TRACE'
0811  0000              ;
0812  0000              ;....................................................
0813  0000              ;
0814  0000
0815  0000
0816  0000        EBRKIN   START             ENTRY FROM EMULATION MODE
0817  0000              ;                    FOR TRACER
0818  0000
0819  0000                 LONGA OFF
0820  0000                 LONGI OFF
0821  0000
0822  0000 F40000          PEA   0
0823  0003 48              PHA
0824  0004 A548            LDA   $48         APPLE // MONITOR
0825  0006 48              PHA                 LOCATIONS
0826  0007 A545            LDA   $45           FOR P, AA
0827  0009 A646            LDX   $46           AND X
0828  000B
0829  000B              ;   note that if direct page is relocated
0830  000B              ;   in emulation mode, these locations
0831  000B              ;   will be used by monitor brk handler
0832  000B
0833  000B EE9703          INC   EBIT+DPAGE  MARK AS EMULATION MODE
0834  000E
0835  000E 18              CLC               GO NATIVE
0836  000F FB              XCE
0837  0010
0838  0010        NBRKIN   ENTRY             ENTRY FROM NATIVE MODE
0839  0010              ;                    FOR TRACER
0840  0010
0841  0010 C230            REP   #M+X        USE LONG WORD SIZES
0842  0012                 LONGA ON
0843  0012                 LONGI ON
0844  0012
0845  0012 8B              PHB               SAVE DATA BANK
0846  0013 0B              PHD               DIRECT PAGE
0847  0014 F40003          PEA   DPAGE       SWITCH TO APPLICATION
```

```
0848  0017 2B           PLD                    DIRECT PAGE
0849  0018
0850  0018 858F         STA    AREG            STASH USER REGISTERS
0851  001A 868B         STX    XREG
0852  001C 848D         STY    YREG
0853  001E
0854  001E A301         LDA    1,S             GET DIRECT PAGE VALUE
0855  0020 8593         STA    DIRREG             SAVED
0856  0022
0857  0022 3B           TSC                    CALCULATE TRUE STACK
0858  0023 18           CLC                      (BEFORE BRK)
0859  0024 690700       ADC    #7
0860  0027 8591         STA    STACK           SAVE AS STACK
0861  0029
0862  0029 A303         LDA    3,S             SAVE DATA BANK, STATUS
0863  002B 8595         STA    DBREG              STATUS REGISTER
0864  002D
0865  002D A94001       LDA    #$140           SET UP SMALL STACK
0866  0030 1B           TCS
0867  0031
0868  0031 4B           PHK                    MAKE DATA BANK = PROGRAM BANK
0869  0032 AB           PLB
0870  0033 AE0080       LDX    USRBRKN         RESTORE BORROWED RAM
0871  0036 AD0180       LDA    SAVRAM+1
0872  0039 9D0100       STA    !1,X
0873  003C AD0080       LDA    SAVRAM
0874  003F 9D0000       STA    !0,X
0875  0042 200080       JSR    FLIST           FORMAT DISASSEMBLY LINE
0876  0045 200080       JSR    FRMOPRND
0877  0048
0878  0048 200080       JSR    PRINTLN         PRINT IT
0879  004B
0880  004B 200080       JSR    CLRLN
0881  004E 200080       JSR    DUMPREGS        OUTPUT REGISTER VALUES
0882  0051 200080       JSR    PRINTLN
0883  0054
0884  0054 E220         SEP    #M
0885  0056         LONGA OFF
0886  0056
0887  0056 C210         REP    #X
0888  0058         LONGI ON
0889  0058
0890  0058 2CE000       BIT    STEPCNTRL
0891  005B 300E         BMI    DOPAUSE
0892  005D
0893  005D 200080       JSR    STEP            STEP ONE AT A TIME
```

```
0894  0060 9068              BCC   QUIT          USER WANTS TO QUIT
0895  0062 5011              BVC   RESUME        WANTS TO KEEP STEPPING
0896  0064 A980              LDA   #$80          HIT CR; WANTS TO TRACE, NOT
0897  0066 8DE000            STA   STEPCNTRL      STEP -- SET FLAG
0898  0069 800A              BRA   RESUME
0899  006B
0900  006B 200080  DOPAUSE   JSR   PAUSE         TRACING; ONLY WAIT IF USER
0901  006E 905A              BCC   QUIT           HITS KEY
0902  0070 5003              BVC   RESUME        WANTS TO KEEP TRACING
0903  0072 9CE000            STZ   STEPCNTRL     HIT CR; WANTS TO STEP, NOT
0904  0075             ;                          TRACE -- CLEAR FLAG
0905  0075
0906  0075 A583    RESUME    LDA   NCODE         RESTORE OLD 'NEXT'; IT'S ABOUT
0907  0077 8780              STA   [PCREG]        TO BE EXECUTED
0908  0079
0909  0079    TBEGIN   ENTRY
0910  0079 A8                TAY                 SAVE THE CURRENT (ABOUT TO BE
0911  007A             ;                          EXECUTED) OPCODE
0912  007A
0913  007A A680              LDX   PCREG         REMEMBER WHERE YOU GOT IT FROM
0914  007C 8684              STX   OPCREG         PCREG POINTED TO IT AFTER
0915  007E A582              LDA   PCREGB         PREVIOUS CALL TO UPDATE
0916  0080 8586              STA   OPCREGB
0917  0082
0918  0082 98                TYA
0919  0083
0920  0083 8587              STA   CODE          SAVE CURRENT OPCODE
0921  0085 200080            JSR   UPDATE        UPDATE PC TO POINT PAST THIS
0922  0088             ;                          INSTRUCTION
0923  0088             ;                          UPDATE ATTRIBUTE VARIABLES
0924  0088
0925  0088 200080            JSR   CHKSPCL       CHECK TO SEE IF THIS CAUSES A
0926  008B             ;                          TRANSFER
0927  008B A780              LDA   [PCREG]       GET NEXT OPCODE TO BE EXECUTED
0928  008D             ;                          (ON NEXT LOOP THROUGH)
0929  008D 8583              STA   NCODE         SAVE IT
0930  008F A900              LDA   #0            PUT A BREAK ($00) THERE TO
0931  0091             ;                          REGAIN CONTROL
0932  0091 8780              STA   [PCREG]
0933  0093
0934  0093      GO     ENTRY
0935  0093 C230              REP   #M+X
0936  0095              LONGA ON
0937  0095              LONGI ON
0938  0095 AE0080            LDX   USRBRKN       BORROW THIS RAM FOR A SECOND
0939  0098 BD0000            LDA   !0,X
```

```
0940   009B 8D0080            STA    SAVRAM
0941   009E BD0100            LDA    !1,X
0942   00A1 8D0180            STA    SAVRAM+1
0943   00A4 A94C00            LDA    #$4C
0944   00A7 9D0000            STA    !0,X
0945   00AA A91000            LDA    #NBRKIN
0946   00AD 9D0100            STA    !1,X
0947   00B0 A591             LDA    STACK        RESTORE STACK
0948   00B2 1B               TCS
0949   00B3 D495             PEI    (DBREG)      GET THIS STUFF ON STACK
0950   00B5 D496             PEI    (EBIT-1)
0951   00B7 D493             PEI    (DIRREG)
0952   00B9
0953   00B9 6497             STZ    EBIT         ASSUME NATIVE MODE ON RETURN
0954   00BB
0955   00BB A58F             LDA    AREG         RESTORE USER REGISTERS
0956   00BD A48D             LDY    YREG
0957   00BF A68B             LDX    XREG
0958   00C1
0959   00C1 2B               PLD                 POP IT AWAY!
0960   00C2
0961   00C2 28               PLP
0962   00C3 28               PLP
0963   00C4 FB               XCE
0964   00C5
0965   00C5 AB               PLB
0966   00C6 28               PLP
0967   00C7
0968   00C7 DC8403           JMP    [DPAGE+OPCREG]      ON TO THE NEXT!
0969   00CA
0970   00CA           QUIT   ENTRY
0971   00CA E220             SEP    #$20
0972   00CC                  LONGA  OFF
0973   00CC
0974   00CC A583             LDA    NCODE        CLEAN UP OLD PATCH
0975   00CE 8780             STA    [PCREG]
0976   00D0
0977   00D0 C210             REP    #$10
0978   00D2                  LONGI  ON
0979   00D2
0980   00D2 AE0080           LDX    SAVSTACK     GET ORIGINAL STACK POINTER
0981   00D5 E8               INX
0982   00D6 E8               INX
0983   00D7 9A               TXS
0984   00D8
0985   00D8 F40000           PEA    0            RESTORE ZERO PAGE
```

```
0986   00DB 2B              PLD
0987   00DC
0988   00DC 28              PLP
0989   00DD FB              XCE
0990   00DE 28              PLP
0991   00DF 60              RTS
0992   00E0
0993   00E0          STEPCNTRL ENTRY
0994   00E0 00              DS    1
0995   00E1                 END



Local  Symbols

DOPAUSE   00006B   GO          000093   NBRKIN   000010   QUIT   0000CA
RESUME    000075   STEPCNTRL   0000E0   TBEGIN   000079
```

CHKSPCL

This routine checks the opcode about to be executed to see if it will cause a transfer of control. Is it a branch, a jump, or a call? If it is any of the three, the destination of the transfer must be calculated and stored at **PCREG** so that a **BRK** instruction can be stored there to maintain control after the current instruction is executed.

A table that contains all of the opcodes which can cause a branch or jump (**SCODES**) is scanned. If a match with the current instruction is not found, the routine exits and tracing resumes.

If a match is found, the value of the index into the table is checked. The opcodes for all the branches are stored at the beginning of **SCODES**, so if the value of the index is less than 9, the opcode was a branch and can be handled by the same general routine.

The first thing that must be determined if the opcode is a branch is whether or not the branch will be taken. By shifting the index right (dividing by two), an index for each pair of different types of branches is obtained. This index is used to get a mask for the bit in the status register to be checked. The value shifted into the carry determines whether the branch is taken if the status bit is set or clear.

If a branch is not taken, the routine exits. If, however, a branch is taken, the new program counter value must be calculated by sign extending the operand and adding it to the current program counter.

Each of the other opcodes (jumps and calls) are dispatched to handler routines through a jump table. Since only the new program counter values must be calculated, jumps and calls with the same addressing mode can be handled by the same routine.

Breaks, co-processor calls, and **RTI**s are not handled at all; a more robust tracer would handle **BRK**s by letting breakpoints be set and cleared. Since the software interrupts are not implemented, and software tracing of hardware interrupts is impractical, **RTI** is left unimplemented. The program counter is incremented by one, causing these instructions to be bypassed completely.

All of the jumps and calls are straightforward. Long addressing is used to force the stack and indirect addressing modes to access bank zero. Also notice the way the data bank register is copied to the program counter bank for indirect indexed addressing. Finally, note how the long addressing modes call their absolute analogs as subroutines, then handle the bank byte.

```
0996  0000
0997  0000
0998  0000              ;............................................................
0999  0000              ; CHKSPCL
1000  0000              ;
1001  0000              ; CHECK CURRENT OPCODE (IN CODE) FOR SPECIAL CASES
1002  0000              ; -- INSTRUCTIONS WHICH TRANSFER CONTROL (JMP, BRA, ETC.)
                        ;
1003  0000              ;
1004  0000              ; ASSUMES SHORTA, LONGI -- CALLED BY EBRKIN
1005  0000              ;............................................................
1006  0000              ;
1007  0000
1008  0000
1009  0000       CHKSPCL  START
1010  0000                LONGA OFF
1011  0000                LONGI ON
1012  0000
1013  0000 A20000        LDX   #SCX-SCODES
1014  0003 A587          LDA   CODE
1015  0005
1016  0005 DD0080  LOOP  CMP   SCODES,X    CHECK TO SEE IF CURRENT OPCODE
1017  0008 F004          BEQ   HIT         IS IN EXCEPTION TABLE
1018  000A CA            DEX
1019  000B 10F8          BPL   LOOP
1020  000D 60            RTS               EXIT IF NOT
1021  000E
1022  0003
1023  0003 E210    HIT   SEP   #X
1024  0010                LONGI OFF
1025  0010
1026  0010 8A            TXA               IF INDEX WAS LESS THAN 9, IT'S
1027  0011 C909          CMP   #9          A BRANCH
1028  0013 B00F          BGE   NOTBR
1029  0015
1030  0015 4A            LSR   A           SEE IF 'ODD OR EVEN'
1031  0016 AA            TAX
1032  0017 BD0080        LDA   PMASK,X     GET MASK TO SELECT CORRECT
1033  001A         ;                       PREG BIT
1034  001A 2596          AND   PREG        IS IT SET?
1035  001C
1036  001C B003          BCS   BBS         IF INDEX WAS ODD, BRANCH IF
1037  001E         ;                       PREG BIT IS SET
1038  001E F00B          BEQ   DOBRANCH    ELSE IF EVEN, BRANCH IF CLEAR

1039  0020 60            RTS
```

15 DEBUG16—A 65816 Programming Tool

```
1040   0021
1041   0021 D008       BBS       BNE     DOBRANCH    "BRANCH IF BIT SET"
1042   0023 60                   RTS
1043   0024
1044   0024 0A         NOTBR     ASL     A           NOT A BRANCH INSTRUCTION;
1045   0025            ;                             MULTIPLY BY TWO
1046   0025 AA                   TAX                 AND INDEX INTO HANDLER JUMP
1047   0026                                          TABLE
1048   0026 C210                 REP     #X
1049   0028 7CEE7F               JMP     (SPJMP-18,X)  BIAS JUMP TABLE BY 9
1050   0028
1051   0028       DOBRANCH ENTRY
1052   002B A9FF                 LDA     #$FF        SET ACCUMULATOR BYTE HIGH
1053   002D           ;                              (ANTICIPATE NEGATIVE)
1054   002D EB                   XBA                 AND SIGN EXTEND INTO X
1055   002E


1056   002E A588                 LDA     OPRNDL
1057   0030
1058   0030 C231                 REP     #M+X+C      MAKE REGS LONG; CLEAR CARRY
1059   0032                      LONGA ON              (ANTICIPATE ADC)
1060   0032                      LONGI ON
1061   0032
1062   0032 3003                 BMI     OK          NUMBER WAS NEGATIVE; ALL IS OK
1063   0034
1064   0034 297F00               AND     #$7F        CLEAR HIGH BYTE OF ACCUM
1065   0037           ;                              (POSITIVE NUMBER)
1066   0037 6580       OK        ADC     PCREG
1067   0039 8580                 STA     PCREG
1068   003B E220                 SEP     #M          RETURN WITH ACCUM SHORT
1069   003D 60                   RTS
1070   003E                      END



Local Symbols
BBS       000021   DOBRANCH   00002B   HIT   00000E   LOOP   000005
NOTBR     000024   OK         000037



1071   0000
1072   0000        SBRK     START              THESE ARE NOT IMPLEMENTED!
1073   0000        SRTI     ENTRY              (AN EXERCISE FOR READER)
```

```
1074  0000                SCOP     ENTRY
1075  0000 60                      RTS
1076  0001
1077  0001                SJSRABS  ENTRY            ABSOLUTES --
1078  0001                SJMPABS  ENTRY
1079  0001 A688                    LDX     OPRNDL   MOVE OPERAND TO PC
1080  0003 8680                    STX     PCREG
1081  0005 60                      RTS
1082  0006
1083  0006                SBRL     ENTRY            LONG BRANCH
1084  0006 C221                    REP     #M+C     LONG ACCUM AND CLEAR CARRY
1085  0008                         LONGA   ON
1086  0008 A588                    LDA     OPRNDL   ADD DISPLACEMENT TO
1087  000A 6580                    ADC     PCREG    PROGRAM COUNTER
1088  000C 8580                    STA     PCREG
1089  000E E220                    SEP     #M
1090  0010                         LONGA   OFF
1091  0010 60                      RTS
1092  0011
1093  0011                SJSRABSL ENTRY            ABSOLUTE LONGS
1094  0011                SJMPABSL ENTRY
1095  0011 A688                    LDX     OPRNDL   MOVE OPERAND, INCLUDING BANK,
1096  0013 8680                    STX     PCREG      TO PROGRAM COUNTER
1097  0015 A58A                    LDA     OPRNDB
1098  0017 8582                    STA     PCREGB
1099  0019 60                      RTS
1100  001A
1101  001A                SRTS     ENTRY            RETURN
1102  001A A691                    LDX     STACK    PEEK ON STACK
1103  001C EC0080                  CPX     SAVSTACK IF ORIGINAL STACK...
1104  001F D003                    BNE     CONT
1105  0021 4C0080                  JMP     QUIT     RETURN TO MONITOR
1106  0024 E8         CONT         INX
1107  0025
1108  0025 C220                    REP     #M
1109  0027 BF000000                LDA     >0,X     ALWAYS IN BANK ZERO
1110  002B 1A                      INC     A        ADD ONE TO GET TRUE RETURN
1111  002C 8580                    STA     PCREG      VALUE
1112  002E E220                    SEP     #M
1113  0030
1114  0030 60                      RTS
1115  0031
1116  0031
1117  0031                SRTL     ENTRY            RETURN LONG
1118  0031 201A00                  JSR     SRTS     DO NORMAL RETURN,
1119  0034
```

```
1120  0034 E8                    INX              THEN GET BANK BYTE
1121  0035 E8                    INX
1122  0036 BF000000      LDA     >0,X             A IS NOW SHORT FOR BANK BYTE
1123  003A 8582          STA     PCREGB
1124  003C 60            RTS
1125  003D
1126  003D
1127  003D        SJMPIND ENTRY                   INDIRECT
1128  003D A688          LDX     OPRNDL           GET THE OPERAND
1129  003F
1130  003F C220          REP     #M


1131  0041 BF000000      LDA     >0,X             JMP IND ALWAYS IN BANK ZERO
1132  0045 8580          STA     PCREG
1133  0047 E220          SEP     #M
1134  0049 60            RTS
1135  004A
1136  004A
1137  004A        SJMPINDL ENTRY
1138  004A 203D00        JSR     SJMPIND          SAME AS JMP INDIRECT,
1139  004D E8            INX                        PLUS BANK BYTE
1140  004E E8            INX
1141  004F BF000000      LDA     >0,X             ACCUM IS SHORT NOW
1142  0053 8582          STA     PCREGB
1143  0055 60            RTS
1144  0056
1145  0056
1146  0056        SJMPINDX ENTRY                  INDEX JUMPS
1147  0056        SJSRINDX ENTRY
1148  0056 A48B          LDY     XREG             LET CPU DO ADDITION
1149  0058 A688          LDX     OPRNDL           GET INDIRECT POINTER
1150  005A 8699          STX     TEMP
1151  005C A582          LDA     RCREGB           INDEXED JUMPS ARE IN PROGRAM
1152  005E 859B          STA     TEMP+2             BANK
1153  0060
1154  0060 C220          REP     #M
1155  0062 B799          LDA     [TEMP],Y         'Y IS X'
1156  0064 8680          STA     PCREG
1157  0066 E220          SEP     #M
1158  0068
1159  0068 60            RTS
1160  0069
1161  0069
1162  0069                       END
```

Local Symbols

CONT	000024	SBRL	000006	SCOP	000000	SJMPABS	000001
SJMPABSL	000011	SJMPIND	00003D	SJMPINDL	00004A	SJMPINDX	000056
SJSRABS	000001	SJSRABSL	000011	SJSRINDX	000056	SRTI	000000
SRTL	000031	SRTS	00001A				

DUMPREGS

This routine forms an output line that will display the contents of the various registers. The routine is driven in a loop by a table containing single-character register names ("A," "X," and so on) and the address of the direct page variable that contains the corresponding register value. It is interesting in that a direct page pointer to a direct page address is used, since the two index registers are occupied with accessing the table entries and pointing to the next available location in the output buffer.

```
1163  0000
1164  0000
1165  0000              ;..............................................
1166  0000              ;
1167  0000              ; DUMPREGS
1168  0000              ;
1169  0000              ; DISPLAYS CONTENTS OF REGISTER VARIABLES IN 'LINE'
1170  0000              ;
1171  0000              ; SAVES AND RESTORES MODE
1172  0000              ;..............................................
1173  0000              ;
1174  0000
1175  0000              DUMPREGS START
1176  0000 08                   PHP
1177  0001 E230                 SEP     #M+X
1178  0003                      LONGA   OFF
1179  0003                      LONGI   OFF
1180  0003
1181  0003 A000                 LDY     #0
1182  0005
1183  0005 A903                 LDA     #>DPAGE    STORE DPAGE HIGH IN TEMP HIGH
1184  0007 859A                 STA     TEMPH
1185  0009
1186  0009 A209                 LDX     #ENDTABLE-TABLE  LENGTH OF COMMAND TABLE
1187  000B
1188  000B BD4400       LOOP    LDA     TABLE,X    GET ADDRESS OF NEXT REGISTER
1189  000E 8599                 STA     TEMP
1190  0010 CA                   DEX
1191  0011 BD4400               LDA     TABLE,X    GET REGISTER 'NAME'
1192  0014 200080               JSR     PUTREG16
1193  0017 CA                   DEX
1194  0018 10F1                 BPL     LOOP
1195  001A
1196  001A 1995                 LDA     #DBREG     NOW ALL THE 8-BIT REGISTERS
1197  001C 8599                 STA     TEMP
```

```
1198   001E A9C2                  LDA     #'B'
1199   0020 200080                JSR     PUTREG8
1200   0023 A996                  LDA     #PREG
1201   0025 8599                  STA     TEMP
1202   0027 A9D0                  LDA     #'P'
1203   0029 200080                JSR     PUTREG8
1204   002C A9C5                  LDA     #'E'
1205   002E 990080                STA     LINE,Y
1206   0031 C8                    INY
1207   0032 A9BA                  LDA     #':'
1208   0034 990080                STA     LINE,Y
1209   0037 C8                    INY
1210   0038
1211   0038 A9B0                  LDA     #'0'
1212   003A A697                  LDX     EBIT
1213   003C F001                  BEQ     OK
1214   003E 1A                    INC     A          '0' BECOMES '1'
1215   003F 990080       OK       STA     LINE,Y
1216   0042
1217   0042
1218   0042 28                    PLP
1219   0043 60                    RTS
1220   0044
1221   0044 C494        TABLE     DC      C'D',I1'DIRREGH'      DIRECT PAGE
1222   0046 D392                  DC      C'S',I1'STACKH'       ADDRESS OF
1223   0048 D98E                  DC      C'Y',I1'YREGH'        REGISTER
1224   004A D88C                  DC      C'X',I1'XREGH'        VARIABLES
1225   004C C1                    DC      C'A'
1226   004D 90        ENDTABLE DC         I1'AREGH'
1227   004E                       END




Local Symbols

ENDTABLE   00004D   LOOP      00000B   OK      00003F   TABLE      000044
```

PUTREG8

This routine, along with **PUTREG16**, is called by **DUMPREGS** to actually output a register value once its label and storage location have been loaded from the table. Naturally, it calls **PUTHEX** to convert the register values to hexadecimal.

```
1228  0000
1229  0000
1230  0000            ;..........................................................
1231  0000            ;
1232  0000            ;  PUTREGS
1233  0000            ;
1234  0000            ;..........................................................
1235  0000            ;
1236  0000
1237  0000
1238  0000
1239  0000         PUTREG8   START
1240  0000 990080            STA    LINE,Y    A CONTAINS REGISTER 'NAME'
1241  0003 C8                INY
1242  0004 A9BC              LDA    #'='      EQUALS . .
1243  0006 990080            STA    LINE,Y
1244  0009 C8                INY
1245  000A 8012              BRA    PRIN      USE PUTREG16 CODE
1246  000C
1247  000C         PUTREG16  ENTRY
1248  000C 990080            STA    LINE,Y    A CONTAINS REGISTER 'NAME'
1249  000F C8                INY
1250  0010 A9BD              LDA    #'='      EQUALS . .
1251  0012 990080            STA    LINE,Y
1252  0015 C8                INY
1253  0016 C8                INY
1254  0017 B299              LDA    (TEMP)    TEMP POINTS TO REGISTER
1255  0019 C699              DEC    TEMP         VARIABLE HIGH
1256  001B 200080            JSR    PUTHEX
1257  001E
1258  001E C8       PRIN     INY
1259  001F B299              LDA    (TEMP)    TEMP POINTS TO REGISTER
1260  0021 200080            JSR    PUTHEX    VARIABLE LOW (OR 8 BIT)
1261  0024 C8                INY
1262  0025 60                RTS
1263  0026                   END

Local Symbols

PRIN       00001E   PUTREG16   00000C
```

Tables

The next several pages list the tables used by the program—SPJMP, PMASK, SCODES, MN, MODES, LENS, and ATRIBL.

SPJMP is a jump table of entry points to the trace handlers for those instructions which modify the flow of control.

PMASK contains the masks used to check the status of individual flag bits to determine if a branch will be taken.

SCODS is a table containing the opcodes of the special (flow-altering) instructions.

ATRBL is the attribute table for all 256 opcodes. Each table entry is two bytes, one is an index into the mnemonic table, the other the address mode. This information is the key to the other tables, all used by the **UPDATE** routine, which puts a description of the current instruction's attributes into the respective direct page variables. **MN** is the table of instruction mnemonics that the 'mnemonic index' attribute points into. **MODES** is a jump table with addresses of the disassembly routine for each addressing mode, and **LENS** contains the length of instructions for each addressing mode. Both of these tables are indexed into directly with the 'address mode' attribute.

```
1264 0000
1265 0000                ;............................................................
1266 0000                ;
1267 0000                ;   SPJMP
1268 0000                ;   JUMP TABLE FOR 'SPECIAL' OPCODE HANDLERS
1269 0000                ;............................................................
1270 0000                ;
1271 0000
1272 0000        SPJMP   START                       JUMP TABLE FOR
1273 0000 0080           DC      A'SBRK'             NON-BRANCH HANDLERS
1274 0002 0080           DC      A'SJSRABS'
1275 0004 0080           DC      A'SRTI'
1276 0006 0080           DC      A'SRTS'
1277 0008 0080           DC      A'SCOP'
1278 000A 0080           DC      A'SJSRABSL'
1279 000C 0080           DC      A'SBRL'
1280 000E 0080           DC      A'SRTL'
1281 0010 0080           DC      A'SJMPABS'
1282 0012 0080           DC      A'SJMPABSL'
1283 0014 0080           DC      A'SJMPIND'
1284 0016 0080           DC      A'SJMPINDX'
1285 0018 0080           DC      A'SJMPINDL'
1286 001A 0080   SCT     DC      A'SJSRINDX'
```

```
1287 001C
1288 001C                            END


Local Symbols

SCT        00001A



1289 0000
1290 0000
1291 0000
1292 0000              ;..................................................
1293 0000              ;
1294 0000              ;  PMASK
1295 0000              ;  STATUS REGISTER MASKS FOR BRANCH HANDLING CODE
1296 0000              ;..................................................
1297 0000              ;
1298 0000
1299 0000     PMASK    START                MASKS FOR STATUS REGISTER
1300 0000 80           DC      H'80'        N FLAG
1301 0001 40           DC      H'40'        V FLAG
1302 0002 01           DC      H'01'        C FLAG
1303 0003 02           DC      H'02'        Z FLAG
1304 0004 00           DC      H'00'        BRA
1305 0005             END



1306 0000
1307 0000
1308 0000
1309 0000
1310 0000
1311 0000     SCODES   START                SPECIAL OPCODES
1312 0000
1313 0000 10           DC      H'10'                BPL
1314 0001 30           DC      H'30'                BMI
1315 0002 50           DC      H'50'                BVC
1316 0003 70           DC      H'70'                BVS
1317 0004 90           DC      H'90'                BCC
1318 0005 B0           DC      H'B0'                BCS
1319 0006 D0           DC      H'D0'                BNE
1320 0007 F0           DC      H'F0'                BEQ
1321 0008 80           DC      H'80'                BRA
1322 0009 00           DC      H'00'                BRK
1323 000A 20           DC      H'20'                JSR    ABS
```

```
1324  000B 40             DC    H'40'        RTI
1325  000C 60             DC    H'60'        RTS
1326  000D 02             DC    H'02'        COP
1327  000E 22             DC    H'22'        JSR   ABSL
1328  000F 82             DC    H'82'        BRL
1329  0010 6B             DC    H'6B'        RTL
1330  0011 4C             DC    H'4C'        JMP   ABS
1331  0012 5C             DC    H'5C'        JMP   ABSL
1332  0013 6C             DC    H'6C'        JMP   ()
1333  0014 7C             DC    H'7C'        JMP   (,X)
1334  0015 DC             DC    H'DC'        JMP   []
1335  0016       SCX      ENTRY
1336  0016 FC             DC    H'FC'        JSR   (,X)
1337  0017               END
```

Local Symbols

SCX   000016


```
1138  0000                      APPEND DB.TABLE
1139  0000
1340  0000
1341  0000       MN       DATA
1342  0000 000000         DX    3
1343  0003 C1C4C3         DC    C'ADC'   1
1344  0006 C1C3C4         DC    C'AND'   2
1345  0009 C1D3CC         DC    C'ASL'   3
1346  000C C2C3C3         DC    C'BCC'   4
1347  000F C2C3D3         DC    C'BCS'   5
1348  0012 C2C5D1         DC    C'BEQ'   6
1349  0015 C2C9D4         DC    C'BIT'   7
1359  0018 C2CDC9         DC    C'BMI'   8
1351  001B C2C3C5         DC    C'BNE'   9
1352  001E C2D0CC         DC    C'BPL'   10
1353  0021 C2D2CB         DC    C'BRK'   11
1354  0024 C2D6C3         DC    C'BVC'   12
1355  0027 C2D6D3         DC    C'BVS'   13
1356  002A C3CCC3         DC    C'CLC'   14
1357  002D C3CCC4         DC    C'CLD'   15
1358  0030 C3CCC9         DC    C'CLI'   16
1359  0033 C3CCD6         DC    C'CLV'   17
1360  0036 C3CDD0         DC    C'CMP'   18
1361  0039 C3D0D8         DC    C'CPX'   19
```

```
1362  003C C3D0D9         DC    C'CPY'    20
1363  003F C4C5C3         DC    C'DEC'    21
1364  0042 C4C5D8         DC    C'DEX'    22
1365  0045 C4C5D9         DC    C'DEY'    23
1366  0048 C5CFD2         DC    C'EOR'    24
1367  004B C9CEC3         DC    C'INC'    25
1368  004E C9C3D8         DC    C'INX'    26
1369  0051 C9C3D9         DC    C'INY'    27
1370  0054 CACDD0         DC    C'JMP'    28
1371  0057 CAD3D2         DC    C'JSR'    29
1372  005A CCC4C1         DC    C'LDA'    30
1373  005D CCC4D8         DC    C'LDX'    31
1374  0060 CCC4D9         DC    C'LDY'    32
1375  0063 CCD3D2         DC    C'LSR'    33
1376  0066 CECFD0         DC    C'NOP'    34
1377  0069 CFD2C1         DC    C'ORA'    35
1378  006C D0C8C1         DC    C'PHA'    36
1379  006F D0C8D0         DC    C'PHP'    37
1380  0072 D0CCC1         DC    C'PLA'    38
1381  0075 D0CCD0         DC    C'PLP'    39
1382  0078 D2CFCC         DC    C'ROL'    40
1383  007B D2CFD2         DC    C'ROR'    41
1384  007E D2D4C9         DC    C'RIT'    42
1385  0081 D2D4D3         DC    C'RTS'    43
1386  0084 D3C2C3         DC    C'SBC'    44
1387  0087 D3C5C3         DC    C'SEC'    45
1388  008A D3C5C4         DC    C'SED'    46
1389  008D D3C5C9         DC    C'SEI'    47
1390  0090 D3D4C1         DC    C'STA'    48
1391  0093 D3D4D8         DC    C'STX'    49
1392  0096 D3D4D9         DC    C'STY'    50
1393  0099 D4C1D8         DC    C'TAX'    51
1394  009C D4C1D9         DC    C'TAY'    52
1395  009F D4D3D8         DC    C'TSX'    53
1396  00A2 D4D8C1         DC    C'TXA'    54
1397  00A5 D4D8D3         DC    C'TXS'    55
1398  00A8 D4D9C1         DC    C'TYA'    56
1399  00AB C2D2C1         DC    C'BRA'    57
1400  00AE D0CCD8         DC    C'PLX'    58
1401  00B1 D0CCD9         DC    C'PLY'    59
1402  00B4 D0C8D8         DC    C'PHX'    60
1403  00B7 D0C8D0         DC    C'PHY'    61
1404  00BA D3D4DA         DC    C'STZ'    62
1405  00BD D4D2C2         DC    C'TRB'    63
1406  00C0 D4D3C2         DC    C'TSB'    64
1407  00C3
1408  00C3 D0C5C1         DC    C'PEA'    65
1409  00C6 D0C5C9         DC    C'PEI'    66
```

```
1410   00C9 D0C5D2         DC    C'PER'     67
1411   00CC D0CCC2         DC    C'PLB'     68
1412   00CF D0CCC4         DC    C'PLD'     69
1413   00D2 D0C8C2         DC    C'PHB'     70
1414   00D5 D0C8C4         DC    C'PHD'     71
1415   00D8 D0C8CB         DC    C'PHK'     72
1416   00DB
1417   00DB D2C5D0         DC    C'REP'     73
1418   00DE D3C5D0         DC    C'SEP'     74
1419   00E1
1420   00E1 D4C3C4         DC    C'TCD'     75
1421   00E4 D4C4C3         DC    C'TDC'     76
1422   00E7 D4C3D3         DC    C'TCS'     77
1423   00EA D4D3C3         DC    C'TSC'     78
1424   00ED D4D8D9         DC    C'TXY'     79
1425   00F0 D4D9D8         DC    C'TYX'     80
1426   00F3 D8C2C1         DC    C'XBA'     81
1427   00F6 D8C3C5         DC    C'XCE'     82
1428   00F9
1429   00F9 C2D2CC         DC    C'BRL'     83
1430   00FC CAD3CC         DC    C'JSL'     84
1431   00FF D2D4CC         DC    C'RTL'     85
1432   0102 CDD6CE         DC    C'MVN'     86
1433   0105 CDD6D0         DC    C'MVP'     87
1434   0108 C3CFD0         DC    C'COP'     88
1435   010B D7C1C9         DC    C'WAI'     89
1436   010E D3D4D0         DC    C'STP'     100
1437   0111 D7C4CD         DC    C'WDM'     101
1438   0114                END


1439   0000
1440   0000         MODES  DATA
1441   0000 0000           DS    2
1442   0002 0080           DC    A'FIMM'       1
1443   0004 0080           DC    A'FABS'       2
1444   0006 0080           DC    A'FABSL'      3
1445   0008 0080           DC    A'FDIR'       4
1446   000A 0080           DC    A'FACC'       5
1447   000C 0080           DC    A'FIMP'       6
1448   000E 0080           DC    A'FINDINX'    7
1449   0010 0080           DC    A'FINDINXL'   8
1450   0012 0080           DC    A'FINXIND'    9
1451   0014 0080           DC    A'FDIRINXX'  10
1452   0016 0080           DC    A'FDIRINXY'  11
1453   0018 0080           DC    A'FABSX'     12
1454   001A 0080           DC    A'FABSLX'    13
```

```
1455  001C 0080              DC      A'FABSY'         14
1456  001E 0080              DC      A'FPCR'          15
1457  0020 0080              DC      A'FPCRL'         16
1458  0022 0080              DC      A'FABSIND'       17
1459  0024 0080              DC      A'FIND'          18
1460  0026 0080              DC      A'FINDL'         19
1461  0028 0080              DC      A'FABSINXIND'    20
1462  002A 0080              DC      A'FSTACK'        21
1463  002C 0080              DC      A'FSTACKREL'     22
1464  002E 0080              DC      A'FSRINDINX'     23
1465  0030 0080              DC      A'FBLOCK'        24
1466  0032
1467  0032                   END


1468  0000
1469  0000         LENS      START
1470  0000 02                DC      H'02'            IMM
1471  0001 03                DC      H'03'            ABS
1472  0002 04                DC      H'04'            ABS LONG
1473  0003 02                DC      H'02'            DIRECT
1474  0004 01                DC      H'01'            ACC
1475  0005 01                DC      H'01'            IMPLIED
1476  0006 02                DC      H'02'            DIR IND INX
1477  0007 02                DC      H'02'            DIR IND INX L
1478  0008 02                DC      H'02'            DIR INX IND
1479  0009 02                DC      H'02'            DIR INX X
1480  000A 02                DC      H'02'            DIR INX Y
1481  000B 03                DC      H'03'            ABS X
1482  000C 04                DC      H'04'            ABS L X
1483  000D 03                DC      H'03'            ABS Y
1484  000E 02                DC      H'02'            PCR
1485  000F 03                DC      H'03'            PCR L
1486  0010 03                DC      H'03'            ABS IND
1487  0011 02                DC      H'02'            DIR IND
1488  0012 02                DC      H'02'            DIR IND L
1489  0013 03                DC      H'03'            ABS INX IND
1490  0014 01                DC      H'01'            STACK
1491  0015 02                DC      H'02'            SR
1492  0016 02                DC      H'02'            SR INX
1493  0017 03                DC      H'03'            MOV
1494  0018                   END
1495  0000
1496  0000                   APPEND DB.ATRIB
1497  0000
1498  0000         ATRIBL    DATA
1499  0000
```

1500	0000 0B06	DC	I1'11,6'	BRK		00
1501	0002 2309	DC	I1'35,9'	ORA D,X		01
1502	0004 5804	DC	I1'88,4'	COP	(REALLY 2)	02
1503	0006 2316	DC	I1'35,22'	ORA -,X		03
1504	0008 4004	DC	I1'64,4'	TSB D		04
1505	000A 2304	DC	I1'35,4'	ORA D		05
1506	000C 0304	DC	I1'3,4'	ASL D		06
1507	000E 2313	DC	I1'35,19'	ORA [D]		07
1508	0010 2515	DC	I1'37,21'	PHP		08
1509	0012 2301	DC	I1'35,1'	ORA IMM		09
1510	0014 0305	DC	I1'3,5'	ASL ACC		0A
1511	0016 4715	DC	I1'71,21'	PHD		0B
1512	0018 4002	DC	I1'64,2'	TSB ABS		0C
1513	001A 2302	DC	I1'35,2'	ORA ABS		0D
1514	001C 0302	DC	I1'3,2'	ASL ABS		0E
1515	001E 2303	DC	I1'35,3'	ORA ABS L		0F
1516	0020 0A0F	DC	I1'10,15'	BPL		10
1517	0022 2307	DC	I1'35,7'	ORA (D),Y		11
1518	0024 2312	DC	I1'35,18'	ORA (D)		12
1519	0026 2317	DC	I1'35,23'	ORA S,Y		13
1520	0028 3F04	DC	I1'63,4'	TRB D		14
1521	002A 230A	DC	I1'35,10'	ORA D,X		15
1522	002C 030A	DC	I1'3,10'	ASL D,X		16
1523	002E 2308	DC	I1'35,8'	ORA (DL),Y		17
1524	0030 0E06	DC	I1'14,6'	CLC		18
1525	0032 230E	DC	I1'35,14'	ORA ABS,Y		19
1526	0034 1905	DC	I1'25,5'	INC ACC		1A
1527	0036 4D06	DC	I1'77,6'	TCS		1B
1528	0038 3F02	DC	I1'63,2'	TRB ABS		1C
1529	003A 230C	DC	I1'35,12'	ORA ABS,X		1D
1530	003C 030C	DC	I1'3,12'	ASL ABS,X		1E
1531	003E 230D	DC	I1'35,13'	ORA ABSL,X		1F
1532	0040 1D02	DC	I1'29,2'	JSR ABS		20
1533	0042 0207	DC	I1'2,7'	AND (D,X)		21
1534	0044 1D03	DC	I1'29,3'	JSL ABS L		22
1535	0046 0216	DC	I1'2,22'	AND SR		23
1536	0048 0704	DC	I1'7,4'	BIT D		24
1537	004A 0204	DC	I1'2,4'	AND D		25
1538	004C 2804	DC	I1'40,4'	ROL D		26
1539	004E 0213	DC	I1'2,19'	AND (DL)		27
1540	0050 2706	DC	I1'39,6'	PLP		28
1541	0052 0201	DC	I1'2,1'	AND IMM		29
1542	0054 2805	DC	I1'40,5'	ROL ACC		2A
1543	0056 4515	DC	I1'69,21'	PLD		2B
1544	0058 0705	DC	I1'7,2'	BIT ABS		2C
1545	005A 0202	DC	I1'2,2'	AND ABS		2D
1546	005C 2805	DC	I1'40,5'	ROL A		2E
1547	005E 0203	DC	I1'2,3'	AND ABS L		2F

15 DEBUG16—A 65816 Programming Tool

```
1548   0060 080F        DC      I1'8,15'        BMI             30
1549   0062 020B        DC      I1'2,11'        AND D,Y         31
1550   0064 0212        DC      I1'2,18'        AND (D)         32
1551   0066 0217        DC      I1'2,23'        AND (SR),Y      33
1552   0068 070A        DC      I1'7,10'        BIT D,X         34
1553   006A 020A        DC      I1'2,10'        AND D,X         35
1554   006C 280A        DC      I1'40,10'       ROL D,X         36
1555   006E 0208        DC      I1'2,8'         AND (DL),Y      37
1556   0070 2D06        DC      I1'45,6'        SEC             38
1557   0072 020E        DC      I1'2,14'        AND ABS,Y       39
1558   0074 1505        DC      I1'21,5'        DEC             3A
1559   0076 4E06        DC      I1'78,6'        TSC             3B
1560   0078 070C        DC      I1'7,12'        BIT A,X         3C
1561   007A 020C        DC      I1'2,12'        AND ABS,X       3D
1562   007C 280C        DC      I1'40,12'       ROL A,X         3E
1563   007E 020D        DC      I1'2,13'        AND AL,X        3F
1564   0080 2A06        DC      I1'42,6'        RTI             40
1565   0082 1809        DC      I1'24,9'        EOR (D,X)       41
1566   0084 6506        DC      I1'101,6'       WDM             42
1567   0086 1816        DC      I1'24,22'       EOR (D,X)       43
1568   0088 5718        DC      I1'87,24'       MVP             44
1569   008A 1804        DC      I1'24,4'        EOR D           45
1570   008C 2104        DC      I1'33,4'        LSR D           46
1571   008E 1813        DC      I1'24,19'       EOR (DL)        47
1572   0090 2406        DC      I1'36,6'        PHA             48
1573   0092 1801        DC      I1'24,1'        EOR IMM         49
1574   0094 2105        DC      I1'33,5'        LSR ABS L       4A
1575   0096 4806        DC      I1'72,6'        PHK             4B
1576   0098 1C02        DC      I1'28,2'        JMP ABS         4C
1577   009A 1802        DC      I1'24,2'        EOR ABS         4D
1578   009C 2102        DC      I1'33,2'        LSR ABS         4E
1579   009E 1805        DC      I1'24,5'        EOR ABS L       4F
1580   00A0 0C0F        DC      I1'12,15'       BVC             50
1581   00A2 1807        DC      I1'24,7'        EOR (D),Y       51
1582   00A4 1812        DC      I1'24,18'       EOR (D)         52
1583   00A6 1817        DC      I1'24,23'       EOR (SR),Y      53
1584   00A8 5618        DC      I1'86,24'       MVN             54
1585   00AA 180A        DC      I1'24,10'       EOR D,X         55
1586   00AC 210A        DC      I1'33,10'       LSR D,X         56
1587   00AE 1808        DC      I1'24,8'        EOR (DL),Y      57
1588   00B0 1006        DC      I1'16,6'        CLI             58
1589   00B2 180E        DC      I1'24,14'       EOR             59
1590   00B4 3D15        DC      I1'61,21'       PHY             5A
1591   00B6 4B06        DC      I1'75,6'        TCD             5B
1592   00B8 1C03        DC      I1'28,3'        JMP ABSL        5C
1593   00BA 180C        DC      I1'24,12'       EOR ABS,X       5D
1594   00BC 210C        DC      I1'33,12'       LSR ABS,X       5E
1595   00BE 180D        DC      I1'24,13'       EOR ABSL,X      5F
```

```
1596  00C0 2B06           DC    I1'43,6'    RTS           60
1597  00C2 0109           DC    I1'1,9'     ADC (D,X)     61
1598  00C4 4310           DC    I1'67,16'   PER           62
1599  00C6 0116           DC    I1'1,22'    ADC SR        63
1600  00C8 3E04           DC    I1'62,4'    STZ D         64
1601  00CA 0104           DC    I1'1,4'     ADC D         65
1602  00CC 2904           DC    I1'41,4'    ROR D         66
1603  00CE 0113           DC    I1'1,19'    ADC (DL)      67
1604  00D0 2615           DC    I1'38,21'   PLA           68
1605  00D2 0101           DC    I1'1,1'     ADC           69
1606  00D4 2905           DC    I1'41,5'    ROR ABSL      6A
1607  00D6 5506           DC    I1'85,6'    RTL           6B
1608  00D8 1C11           DC    I1'28,17'   JMP (A)       6C
1609  00DA 0102           DC    I1'1,2'     ADC ABS       6D
1610  00DC 2902           DC    I1'41,2'    ROR ABS       6E
1611  00DE 0103           DC    I1'1,3'     ADC ABSL      6F
1612  00E0 0D0F           DC    I1'13,15'   BVS           70
1613  00E2 0108           DC    I1'1,8'     ADC (D),Y     71
1614  00E4 0112           DC    I1'1,18'    ADC (D)       72
1615  00E6 0117           DC    I1'1,23'    ADC (SR),Y    73
1616  00E8 3E0A           DC    I1'62,10'   STZ D,X       74
1617  00EA 010A           DC    I1'1,10'    ADC D,X       75
1618  00EC 290A           DC    I1'41,10'   ROR D,X       76
1619  00EE 0108           DC    I1'1,8'     ADC (DL),Y    77
1620  00F0 2F06           DC    I1'47,6'    SEI           78
1621  00F2 010E           DC    I1'1,14'    ADC ABS,Y     79
1622  00F4 3B15           DC    I1'59,21'   PLY           7A
1623  00F6 4C06           DC    I1'76,6'    TDC           7B
1624  00F8 1C14           DC    I1'28,20'   JMP (A,X)     7C
1625  00FA 010C           DC    I1'1,12'    ADC ABS,X     7D
1626  00FC 290C           DC    I1'41,12'   ROR ABS,X     7E
1627  00FE 010D           DC    I1'1,13'    ADC ABSL,X    7F
1628  0100
1629  0100                END

1630  0000
1631  0000       ATRIBH   START
1632  0000 390F           DC    I1'57,15'   BRA           80
1633  0002 3009           DC    I1'48,9'    STA (D,X)     81
1634  0004 5310           DC    I1'83,16'   BRL           82
1635  0006 3016           DC    I1'48,22'   STA -,S       83
1636  0008 3204           DC    I1'50,4'    STY D         84
1637  000A 3004           DC    I1'48,4'    STA D         85
1638  000C 3104           DC    I1'49,4'    STX D         86
1639  000E 3013           DC    I1'48,19'   STA [D]       87
1640  0010 1706           DC    I1'23,6'    DEY           88
```

1641	0012 0701	DC	I1'7,1'	BIT IMM	89
1642	0014 3606	DC	I1'54,6'	TXA	8A
1643	0016 4615	DC	I1'70,21'	PHB	8B
1644	0018 3203	DC	I1'50,2'	STY ABS	8C
1645	001A 3002	DC	I1'48,2'	STA ABS	8D
1646	001C 3102	DC	I1'49,2'	STX ABS	8E
1647	001E 3003	DC	I1'48,3'	STA ABS L	8F
1648	0020 040F	DC	I1'4,15'	BC	90
1649	0022 3007	DC	I1'48,7'	STA (D),Y	91
1650	0024 3012	DC	I1'48,18'	STA (D)	92
1651	0026 3017	DC	I1'48,23'	STA (SR),Y	93
1652	0028 320A	DC	I1'50,10'	STY D,X	94
1653	002A 300A	DC	I1'48,10'	STA D,X	95
1654	002C 310B	DC	I1'49,11'	STX D,Y	96
1655	002E 3008	DC	I1'48,8'	STA (DL),Y	97
1656	0030 3806	DC	I1'56,6'	TYA	98
1657	0032 300E	DC	I1'48,14'	STA ABS,Y	99
1658	0034 3706	DC	I1'55,6'	TXS D	9A
1659	0036 4F06	DC	I1'79,6'	TXY	9B
1660	0038 3E02	DC	I1'62,2'	STZ ABS	9C
1661	003A 300C	DC	I1'48,12'	STA ABS,X	9D
1662	003C 3E0C	DC	I1'62,12'	STZ ABS,X	9E
1663	003E 300D	DC	I1'48,13'	STA ABSL,X	9F
1664	0040 2001	DC	I1'32,1'	LDY IMM	A0
1665	0042 1E09	DC	I1'30,9'	LDA (D,X)	A1
1666	0044 1F01	DC	I1'31,1'	LDX IMM	A2
1667	0046 1E16	DC	I1'30,22'	LDA SR	A3
1668	0048 2004	DC	I1'32,4'	LDY D	A4
1669	004A 1E04	DC	I1'30,4'	LDA D	A5
1670	004C 1F04	DC	I1'31,4'	LDX D	A6
1671	004E 1E13	DC	I1'30,19'	LDA (DL)	A7
1672	0050 3406	DC	I1'52,6'	TAY	A8
1673	0052 1E01	DC	I1'30,1'	LDA IMM	A9
1674	0054 3306	DC	I1'51,6'	TAX	AA
1675	0056 4415	DC	I1'68,21'	PLB	AB
1676	0058 2002	DC	I1'32,2'	LDY ABS	AC
1677	005A 1E02	DC	I1'30,2'	LDA ABS	AD
1678	005C 1F02	DC	I1'31,2'	LDX ABS	AE
1679	005E 1E03	DC	I1'30,3'	LDA ABS L	AF
1680	0060 050F	DC	I1'5,15'	BCS	B0
1681	0062 1E07	DC	I1'30,7'	LDA (D),Y	B1
1682	0064 1E12	DC	I1'30,18'	LDA (D)	B2
1683	0066 1E17	DC	I1'30,23'	LDA (SR),Y	B3
1684	0068 200A	DC	I1'32,10'	LDY D,X	B4
1685	006A 1E0A	DC	I1'30,10'	LDA D,X	B5
1686	006C 1E0B	DC	I1'30,11'	LDX D,Y	B6
1687	006E 1E08	DC	I1'30,8'	LDA (DL),Y	B7
1688	0070 1106	DC	I1'17,6'	CLV	B8

1689	0072 1E0E	DC	I1'30,14'	LDA ABS,Y		B9
1690	0074 3506	DC	I1'53,6'	TSX		BA
1691	0076 5006	DC	I1'80,6'	TYX		BB
1692	0078 200C	DC	I1'32,12'	LDY ABS,X		BC
1693	007A 1E0C	DC	I1'30,12'	LDA ABS,X		BD
1694	007C 1F0E	DC	I1'31,14'	LDX ABS,Y		BE
1695	007E 1E0D	DC	I1'30,13'	LDA ABSL,X		BF
1696	0080 1401	DC	I1'30,13'	CPY		C0
1697	0082 1209	DC	I1'18,9'	CMP (D,X)		C1
1698	0084 4901	DC	I1'73,1'	REP		C2
1699	0086 1216	DC	I1'18,22'	CMP		C3
1700	0088 1404	DC	I1'20,4'	CPY D		C4
1701	008A 1204	DC	I1'18,4'	CMP D		C5
1702	008C 1504	DC	I1'21,4'	DEC D		C6
1703	008E 1213	DC	I1'18,19'	CMP (DL)		C7
1704	0090 1B06	DC	I1'27,6'	INY		C8
1705	0092 1201	DC	I1'18,1'	CMP IMM		C9
1706	0094 1606	DC	I1'22,6'	DEX		CA
1707	0096 5906	DC	I1'89,6'	WAI		CB
1708	0098 1402	DC	I1'20,2'	CPY ABS		CC
1709	009A 1202	DC	I1'18,2'	CMP ABS		CD
1710	009C 1502	DC	I1'21,2'	DEC ABS		CE
1711	009E 1203	DC	I1'18,3'	CMP ABSL		CF
1712	00A0 090F	DC	I1'9,15'	BNE		D0
1713	00A2 1207	DC	I1'18,7'	CMP (D),Y		D1
1714	00A4 1212	DC	I1'18,18'	CMP (D)		D2
1715	00A6 1217	DC	I1'18,23'	CMP		D3
1716	00A8 4204	DC	I1'66,4'	PEI D		D4
1717	00AA 120A	DC	I1'18,10'	CMP D,X		D5
1718	00AC 150A	DC	I1'21,10'	DEC D,X		D6
1719	00AE 1208	DC	I1'18,8'	CMP (DL),Y		D7
1720	00B0 0F06	DC	I1'15,6'	CLD		D8
1721	00B2 120E	DC	I1'18,14'	CMP ABS,Y		D9
1722	00B4 3C15	DC	I1'60,21'	PHX		DA
1723	00B6 6406	DC	I1'100,6'	STP		DB
1724	00B8 1C11	DC	I1'28,17'	JMP (A)		DC
1725	00BA 120C	DC	I1'18,12'	CMP ABS,X		DD
1726	00BC 150C	DC	I1'21,12'	DEC ABS,X		DE
1727	00BE 120D	DC	I1'18,13'	CMP ABSL,X		DF
1728	00C0 1301	DC	I1'19,1'	CPX IMM		E0
1729	00C2 2C09	DC	I1'44,9'	SBC (D,X)		E1
1730	00C4 4A01	DC	I1'74,1'	SEP IMM		E2
1731	00C6 2C16	DC	I1'44,22'	SBC SR		E3
1732	00C8 1F04	DC	I1'31,4'	LDX D		E4
1733	00CA 2C04	DC	I1'44,4'	SBC D		E5
1734	00CC 1904	DC	I1'25,4'	INC D		E6
1735	00CE 2C13	DC	I1'44,19'	SBD (DL)		E7
1736	00D0 1A06	DC	I1'26,6'	INX D		E8

```
1737    00D2 2C01           DC      I1'44,1'        SBC IMM         E9
1738    00D4 2206           DC      I1'34,6'        NOP             EA
1739    00D6 5106           DC      I1'81,6'        XBA             EB
1740    00D8 1302           DC      I1'19,2'        CPX ABS         EC
1741    00DA 2C02           DC      I1'44,2'        SBC ABS         ED
1742    00DC 1902           DC      I1'25,2'        INC ABS         EE
1743    00DE 2C03           DC      I1'44,3'        SBC ABSL        EF
1744    00E0 060F           DC      I1'6,15'        BEQ             F0
1745    00E2 2C07           DC      I1'44,7'        SBC (D),Y       F1
1746    00E4 2C12           DC      I1'44,18'       SBC (D)         F2
1747    00E6 2C17           DC      I1'44,23'       SBC (SR),Y      F3
1748    00E8 4102           DC      I1'65,2'        PEA             F4
1749    00EA 2C0A           DC      I1'44,10'       SBC D,X         F5
1750    00EC 190A           DC      I1'25,10'       INC D,X         F6
1751    00EE 2C08           DC      I1'44,8'        SBC (DL),Y      F7
1752    00F0 2E06           DC      I1'46,6'        SED             F8
1753    00F2 2C0E           DC      I1'44,14'       SBC ABS,Y       F9
1754    00F4 3A15           DC      I1'58,21'       PLX             FA
1755    00F6 5206           DC      I1'82,6'        XCE             FB
1756    00F8 1D14           DC      I1'29,20'       JSR (A,X)       FC
1757    00FA 2C0C           DC      I1'44,12'       SBC ABS,X       FD
1758    00FC 190C           DC      I1'25,12'       INC ABS,X       FE
1759    00FE 2C0D           DC      I1'44,13'       SBC ABSL,X      FF
1760    0100                END
```

Global Symbols

ADDRMODE	00009C	AREG	00008F	AREGH	000090	BRKN	00FFE6
C	000001	CODE	000087	CR	00008D	DBREG	000095
DIRREG	000093	DIRREGH	000094	DPAGE	000300	EBIT	000097
M	000020	MNX	00009D	NCODE	000083	OPCREG	000084
OPCREGB	000086	OPCREGH	000085	OPLEN	00009F	OPRNDB	00008A
OPRNDH	000089	OPRNDL	000088	PCREG	000080	PCREGB	000082
PCREGH	000081	PREG	000096	STACK	000091	STACKH	000092
TEMP	000099	TEMPB	00009B	TEMPH	00009A	USRBRKV	0003F0
X	000010	XREG	00008B	XREGH	00008C	YREG	00008D
YREGH	00008E

```
1760 source lines
0 macros expanded
0 lines generated
0 page faults

Link Editor 4.0

00008000  00000037  Code:  MAIN
00008037  000000CF  Code:  EBRKIN
```

```
00008106  00000048  Code:  FLIST
0000814E  00000120  Code:  FRMOPRND
0000826E  00000019  Code:  POB
00008287  0000002F  Code:  STEP
00008286  00000026  Code:  PUTHEX
000082DC  0000005A  Code:  CLRLN
00008336  0000005D  Code:  UPDATE
00008393  0000001A  Code:  PRINTLN
000083AD  00000043  Code:  TRACE
000083F0  0000003E  Code:  CHKSPCL
0000842E  00000069  Code:  SBRK
00008497  0000004E  Code:  DUMPREGS
000084E5  00000026  Code:  PUTREG8
0000850B  0000001C  Code:  SPJMP
00008527  00000005  Code:  PMASK
0000852C  00000017  Code:  SCODES
00008543  00000114  Data:  MN
00008657  00000032  Data:  MODES
00008689  00000018  Code:  LENS
000086A1  00000100  Data:  ATRIBL
000087A1  00000100  Code:  ATRIBH


Global symbol table:

ADDRMODE    0000009C 00  AREG       0000008F 00  AREGH     00000090 00
ATRIBH      000087A1 00  ATRIBL     000086A1 03  BRKN      0000FFE6 00
C           00000001 00  CHKSPCL    00008DF0 00  CLRLN     000082DC 00
CODE        00000087 00  CR         0000008D 00  DBREG     00000095 00
DIRREG      00000093 00  DIRREGH    00000094 00  DOBRANCH  0000841B 00
DPAGE       00000300 00  DUMPREGS   00008497 00  EBIT      00000097 00
EBRXIN      00008037 00  FABS       0000816B 00  FABSIND   000081F5 00
FABSINXIND  00008224 00  FABSL      0000816E 00  FABSLX    000081C1 00
FABSX       000081BB 00  FABSY      000081C7 00  FACC      00008174 00
FBLOCK      00008526 00  FDIR       00008171 00  FDIRINXX  000081A2 00
FDIRINXY    000081A8 00  FIMM       00008159 00  FIMP      0000817A 00
FIND        00008204 00  FINDINX    0000817B 00  FINDINXL  0000818A 00
FINDL       00008214 00  FINX       000081AE 00  FINXIND   00008190 00
FINY        0000817E 00  FLIST      00008106 00  FPCR      000081CD 00
FPCRL       000081E4 00  FRMOPRND   0000814E 00  FSRINDINX 00008244 00
FSTACK      00008233 00  FSTACKREL  00008234 00  GO        000080C4 00
LENS        00008689 00  LINE       000082EE 00  LIST      00008003 00
M           00000020 00  MAIN       00008000 00  MN        00008543 01
MNX         0000009D 00  MODES      00008657 02  MOVE      0000814A 00
NBRKIN      00008047 00  NCODE      00000083 00  OPCREG    00000084 00
OPCREGB     00000086 00  OPCREGH    00000085 00  OPLEN     0000009F 00
```

16 Design and Debugging

Design and debugging stand on either side of the central coding phase of the development cycle. Good techniques for both are as important as skill in actual coding. This chapter provides a checklist of some commonly encountered bugs—ones you should immediately suspect—as well as some words of advice about program design and good coding practice, which may help you avoid some of the bugs to begin with.

Debugging Checklist

Program bugs fall into two categories: those specific to the particular processor you're writing assembly code for, and those that are generic problems which can crop up in any assembly program for almost any processor. This chapter will primarily consider bugs specific to the 65x processors, but will also discuss some generic bugs as they specifically apply in 65x assembly programs.

You may want to put a checkmark beside the bugs listed here each time you find them in your programs, giving you a personalized checklist of problems to look for. You may also want to add to the list other bugs that you write frequently.

Decimal Flag

Seldom does the **d** decimal flag get misset, but when it does, arithmetic results may seem to inexplicably go south. This can be the result of a typo, attempting to execute data, or some other execution error. Or it can result from coding errors in which the decimal flag is set to enable decimal arithmetic, then never reset. If branching occurs before the decimal flag is reset, be sure all paths ultimately result in the flag being cleared. Branching while in decimal mode is almost as dangerous as branching after temporarily pushing a value onto the stack; equal care must be taken to clear **d** and clean the stack.

This bug may be doubly hard to find on the 6502, which does not clear **d** on interrupt or, worse, on reset. An instruction inadvertently or mistakenly executed which sets **d** (only **SED**, **RTI**, or **PLP** have the capability on the 6502) would require you to specifically reclear the decimal flag or to power off and power back on again. As a result, it is always a good idea to clear the decimal flag at the beginning of every 6502 program.

Adjusting Carry Prior to Add/Subtract

If you're not used to 65x processors (and even for many programmers who are), you may tend to write an **ADC** instruction without first writing a **CLC**, or an **SBC** without first an **SEC**. After all, other processors have add and subtract instructions that do not involve the carry. But the 65x processors do not; so notice the "C" in each of the instructions each time you code them and be sure the carry has the appropriate value.

65x Left-to-Right Syntax

Unlike some other processors' instructions, 65x mnemonics read from left to right, just like English: **TAX**, for example, means to transfer the **A** accumulator to the **X** index register, not the opposite.

65x Branches

There are eight 65x conditional branches, each based on one of the two states of four condition code flags. Remembering how to use them for arithmetic is necessary to code branches that work.

Keep in mind that compare instructions cannot be used for signed comparisons: they don't affect the overflow flag. Only the subtract instruction can be used to compare two signed numbers directly (except for the relationships equal and not equal).

Remember that if the z flag is set (one), then the result was zero; and if the zero flag is clear (zero), then the result was other than zero—the opposite of most first guesses about it.

A common code sequence is to test a value, then branch on the basis of the result of the test. A common mistake is to code an instruction between the test and the branch that also affects the very flag your branch is based on (often because an instruction you don't expect to affect the flags does indeed do so).

Note that 65x pull instructions set the negative and zero flags, unlike 68xx and 8088/8086 processors; that store instructions do *not* set any flags, unlike 68xx processors; that transfer and exchange instructions *do* set flags, unlike Motorola and Intel processors; that load instructions do set flags, unlike the 8088; and increment and decrement instructions do not affect the carry flag.

Also, in decimal mode on the 6502, the negative, overflow and zero flags are not valid.

6502 Jump Bug

There's a hardware bug on the 6502 that causes jump indirect, with an operand which ends in $FF (such as $11FF), to bomb: the new high program counter value is taken incorrectly from $1100, not the correct $1200.

Interrupt-Handling Code

To correctly handle 65x interrupts, you should generally, at the outset, save all registers and, on the 6502 and in emulation mode, clear the decimal flag (to provide a consistent binary approach to arithmetic in the interrupt handler). Returning from the interrupt restores the status register, including the previous state of the decimal flag.

During interrupt handling, once the previous environment has been saved and the new one is solid, interrupts may be reenabled.

At the end of handling interrupts, restore the registers in the correct order. **RTI** will pull the program counter and status register from the stack, finishing the return to the previous environment, except that in 65802/65816 native mode it also pulls the program bank register from the stack. This means you *must* restore the mode in which the interrupt occurred (native or emulation) before executing an RTI.

65802/65816: Emulation Versus Native Mode

Emulation mode has been provided on the 65802 and 65816 to provide continuity with existing applications. Native mode provides the powerful sixteen-bit data handling registers. But mixing emulation and native modes requires careful attention to detail. You should deal with modes systematically.

Will you limit subroutines to be called only from a certain mode? All subroutines? You must carefully document each for which mode it expects.

You must be in emulation mode on the Apple // or other 6502-based system to use the monitor and operating system 6502 routines. Furthermore, you must put 0000 into D (the direct page register) before return to the monitor or operating system, because zero page addressing now addresses the direct page, but the 6502 firmware left its variables in page zero before your program switched to native mode.

Any high bytes in the index registers are lost in the switch to emulation mode.

While native mode lets you set the stack anywhere, a non-page-one stack location is lost on return to emulation mode (the high byte is thrown away, replaced by the obligatory page one high byte of emulation mode). Furthermore, when setting the stack with the TCS instruction, only the low accumulator byte is transferred to the stack pointer in emulation mode, but in native mode, the high accumulator byte, even if it is hidden, is transferred to the high stack pointer byte.

65802/65816: Eight-Bit Versus Sixteen-Bit Registers

Almost as potentially confusing as mixing emulation and native modes is mixing eight-bit and sixteen-bit modes. Again, you should deal with modes systematically.

Will you limit subroutines to be called only from a certain mode setting? You must carefully document each for the mode it expects.

Because instructions using immediate addressing are different lengths in eight- and sixteen-bit modes, being in the wrong mode will cause the processor to grab the wrong number of operand bytes, followed by a fetch for the next opcode which will miss by one and cause it to execute, as though it were an opcode, either the last operand byte of the immediate instruction, or the first operand byte of the next instruction. Either way is sure program failure.

65802/65816: The Direct Page

Avoid inadvertently branching from code written to access one direct page to code written to access another without executing an instruction to reset the direct page register to the second location first (and resetting it to the original location before returning). Remember, too, that programs run faster when the direct page register is set to a page boundary.

Pay particular attention to the peculiarities of the direct page in the emulation mode: as with the 6502 and 65C02, instructions which use direct page addressing modes will "wrap" to stay within the zero page, *but only when the direct page register is equal to zero.* Opcodes which are not found on the 6502 or 65C02 will not wrap at all, even when the direct page is equal to zero in the emulation mode.

65802/65816: Stack Overruns Program or Data

No longer limited to a single page, the native-mode stack will grow downward as far as your program pushes bytes onto it. Large programs should either retrieve every byte pushed on or reset the stack periodically (using TCS or TXS). The potential danger is when a stack grows uncontrollably until it overwrites variables, your program, or the operating system.

In this connection it is important to be aware that, although the high byte of the stack register is consistently forced to one, new 65816 opcodes executed in the emulation mode will not wrap the stack if the low byte over- or underflowed in the middle of an instruction. For example, if the stack pointer is equal to $101, and a JSL is executed, the final byte of the three bytes pushed on the stack will be at $FF, not $1FF; but the stack pointer at the end of the instruction will point to $1FE. However, if JSR (a 6502 instruction) is executed in the emulation mode with the stack pointer equal to $100, the second of the two bytes pushed will be stored at $1FF.

65802/65816: JSR/JSL and RTS/RTL

RTL pulls one more byte off the stack than RTS: it requires that a long jump-to-subroutine (JSL) or its equivalent pushed a full 24-bit return address, not just a sixteen-bit one. Equally important is that a JSL not be made to a subroutine ended by an RTS, which pulls only sixteen of the 24 bits of return address pushed.

65802/65816: MVN/MVP

MVN and MVP require two operands, usually code or data labels from which the assembler strips the bank bytes, in **sourcebank,destbank** order (opposite of object code order). Eight-bit index registers will cause these two instructions to move only zero page memory. But eight-bit accumulator mode is irrelevant to the count value; the accumulator is expanded to sixteen bits using the hidden **B** accumulator as the high byte of the count. Finally, the count in the accumulator is one less than the count of bytes to be moved: five in the accumulator means six bytes will be moved.

Return Address

If your program removes the return address from the stack in order to use it in some fashion other than using an **RTS** or **RTL** instruction to return, remember that you must add one to the stacked value to form the true return address (an operation the return-from-subroutine instructions execute automatically).

Inconsistent Assembler Syntax

6502 assemblers have been wildly inconsistent in their syntax, and early 65802 assemblers have not set standards either. This book describes syntax recommended by the designers of the 65816, the Western Design Center, as implemented in the ORCA/M assembler. Others, however, do and will differ. For example, while many assemblers use the syntax of a pound sign (#) in front of a sixteen-bit immediate value to specify that the low byte be accessed, with the greater-than sign (>) being used to represent the high byte, at least one 6502 assembler uses the same two signs to mean just the opposite. Syntax for the new block move instructions will undoubtedly vary from the recommended standard in many assemblers. Beware and keep your assembler's manual handy.

Generic Bugs: They Can Happen Anywhere

Uninitialized Variables

Failing to initialize variables may be the most common bug committed by programmers. Its symptom is often a program which operates strangely only the first time it is run (after which the variable has at some point been given a suitable value which remains in memory for the program's second try), or only after running a certain other program. Sometimes the symptom appears only on computers with one brand of memory chips, and not another; they happen to power up with different initial values.

Missing Code

The code you wrote on paper is perfect. The problem is one or more lines that never got typed in, or were typed in wrong. The solution is to compare your original handwritten code with the typed-in version, or compare a disassembly with your original code.

More enigmatically, a line may be accidentally deleted or an opcode or operand inadvertently changed by a keypress during a subsequent edit (usually in a section of code which has just been proven to work flawlessly). Regular source backups and a program that can compare text to spot changes will often solve the problem. Or you can compare a disassembly with the previous source listing.

Failure to Increment the Index in a Loop

The symptom are: everything stops, and typing at the keyboard has no effect. The problem is an endless loop—your branch out of the loop is waiting for an index to reach some specified value, but the index is never decremented or incremented and thus never reaches the target value.

Failure to Clean Up Stack

This problem is typically found in code in which first a value is pushed, then there is a conditional branch, but all paths do not pull the value still on the stack. It may result in a return address being pulled off the stack which is not really a return address (one or more bytes of it are really previously pushed data bytes).

Immediate Data Versus Memory Location

Failure to use the '#' sign to signify a constant (or whatever other syntax a particular assembler requires) will instruct the assembler to load, not the constant, but data from a memory location that it assumes the constant specifies. That is, **#VAR** means access a constant (or the address of a variable); **VAR**, on the other hand, means access its contents.

Initializing the Stack Pointer from a Subroutine

It won't take much thought to realize that you can't just reset the stack pointer from within a subroutine and expect the return-from-subroutine instruction to work. The return address was pointed to by the previous stack pointer. Who knows where it is in relation to the newly set one?

Top–Down Design and Structured Programming

It's wise to carefully consider the design of a program before beginning to write any of it. The goals of design are to minimize program errors, or **bugs**; to reduce complexity; to maximize readability; and to increase the speed and ease of coding and testing and thus the productivity of programmers.

The top–down approach to structured programming combines two major design concepts. This approach is generally recognized as the method of design which best achieves these goals, particularly when coding large programs. Top–down design suggests that programs should be broken into levels: at the top level is a statement of the goal of the program; beneath it are second-level modules, which are the main control sections of the program; the sections can be broken into their parts; and so on.

A blackjack game (twenty-one), for example, might be broken down into four second-level modules, the goals of which are to deal the cards, take and place bets on the hands dealt, respond to requests for more cards, and finally compare each player's hand with the dealer's to determine winnings. The dealing module might be broken down into two third-level modules, the goals of which are to shuffle the cards, and to deliver a card to each player (executed twice so that each player gets two cards). The shuffling module might be broken into two fourth-level modules which assign a number to each card and then create a random order to the numbers.

The makeup of each level is clear. At the top level, the makeup describes the program itself. At lower levels, the makeup describes the subprocess. At the lowest levels, the work is actually done.

A top–down design is then implemented using subroutines. The top level of the program is a very short straight-line execution routine (or loop in the case of programs that start over when they reach the end), that does nothing more than call a set of subroutines, one for each second-level module of the program. The second-level subroutines may call third-level subroutines which may call fourth-level subroutines, and so on.

Structured programming is a design concept which calls for modules to have only one entry point; jumping into the middle of a module is not permitted. (A structured approach to the problem of needing an entry point to the middle of a module is to make that portion of the module a sub-module with its own single entry and exit points.) A second rule is that all exits return control to the calling module; all branches (selections) are internal; no branches are permitted to code outside the module.

One of the side benefits of modular programming is the ability to reuse previously coded modules in other programs: the dealing module could be dropped into any card game program that calls for shuffling followed by the dealing of one card at a time to each player. And its shuffling sub-module could be borrowed for other card game programs which only need shuffling. This use of the modularity principle should not be confused with the top-down structured design; they are distinct but related concepts. Modular programming in itself is not the same as top-down design.

A software development team could, using top-down design, readily assign one programmer the task of coding the deck-shuffling routine, another programmer the betting module, another responsibility for the dealing routines, and a fourth with writing the code for the end-of-game comparison of hands and determination of the winner.

A new programmer trying to understand a top-down program avoids becoming mired in detail while trying to get an understanding of the structure, yet can very easily figure how to get to the degree of detail which interests him.

Finally **debugging,** the process of finding and removing programming mistakes, is exceptionally straightforward with top-down design: on seeing that, after shuffling, one of the 52 cards seems to be missing, the programmer can go directly to the shuffling subroutines to fix the problem.

Top-down design sometimes seems like a waste of time to programmers anxious to get the bytes flying; complex programs can take days or weeks of concerted thinking to break down into the subparts which fit together most logically and efficiently. But the savings in time spent coding—and recoding—and in being able to understand, debug, and modify the program later well justify the time spent on design.

Documentation

One of the most important elements of good programming practice is **documentation.** It is remarkable how little one can recall about the nitty-gritty details of a program written just last month (or sometimes even yesterday)—the names of the key variables, their various settings and what each means and how each interacts with other variables in various routines, and so on. "Clever" programmers, those who bend programming principles to ends never anticipated, too often find they (not to mention their co-workers) can no longer discover the meaning behind their cleverness when it comes time to debug or modify that code.

The first principle of documentation is to make the program document itself. Choose labels which are meaningful: **DEALOOP** is a much better label for the beginning of a loop which deals cards in a card game than is **LAB137**. Substitute a label for all constants: branching if there's a 1 in some register after writing a byte to disk is, by itself, meaningless; branching because there's a constant named **DISKFULL** in the register provides clear documentation. When your program needs to determine if an ASCII value is an upper-case letter, it's much clearer to compare with "greater than or equal to 'A' " than with "greater than '@' ". Who remembers that '@' precedes 'A' in the ASCII chart?

Variables should be **commented** when they're declared with a description of their purpose, their potential settings, and any default states. And if any of that information changes during the development of the program, the comment should be changed to match.

Routines should be commented when they're written: Note the purpose of the routine, the variables or parameters which need to be set before entry into the routine, and the variables or parameters which will be passed back. If other data structures will be affected by the routine, this, too, should be commented.

Nothing is as important both to debugging of code and to continuing development of programs as documentation: self-documentation; a comment on every important line of code that explains and expands it; a comment header on every routine; and a comment on every variable. While some languages are said to be automatically "self-documenting," no language can create documentation which is half adequate compared to what the original programmer can provide while the program is being written.

Part V
Reference

17 The Addressing Modes

There are fourteen addressing modes available to the 6502, all of those plus two more on the 65C02, and another nine categories available on the 65802 and 65816. Each mode allows the location of the data being referenced by a given instruction to be specified in a different manner. The availability of many different addressing modes on the 65x processors is one key to their power.

The data found in operand bytes of an instruction is only one part of the effective address specification; the addressing modes, expressed using the correct address-mode syntax in the operand field of an assembly-language statement, cause the assembler to choose from among the instruction's possible opcodes to one specific to the addressing mode. Not all addressing modes are available for all instructions; but there is one unique opcode for each combination of addressing mode and operation.

The addressing mode is the determinant of the effective address for an operation—the memory address that the instruction will access for data or to transfer control within the program. For a few of the 65x addressing modes, the effective address is provided in the operand field of the instruction. But for most of them, formation of the effective address involves an address calculation, that is, the addition of two or more values. The addressing mode used with a given instruction indicates where these values are to come from and how they are to be added together to form the effective address. This effective address calculation has as many forms as there are addressing modes.

An important aspect of effective address calculation on the 65802 and 65816, to be considered in addition to the addressing modes themselves, is the state of the x index-register select flag and, to a lesser extent, the m memory/accumulator select flag, both in the status register. In a sense, the x flag, for example, extends the addressing mode specification part of an instruction, which uses an indexed addressing mode, by determining whether or not an eight-bit or sixteen-bit index register is to be used. For every one of the indexed addressing modes, there are two similar methods of forming an effective address, depending on the setting of the index-register select flag. Pay special attention to the status and effects of the select flags.

In the following pages are graphic and written presentations of each of the addressing modes, illustrating the effective address formation, complete with a listing of the processors on which, and the instructions to which, each addressing mode is available. A sample of the assembler syntax used to invoke each one is included as well.

The descriptions are the complete set available on the 65816. The differences between the four processors, with their various modes, are graphically noted whenever possible.

The 65816's native mode features index registers and an accumulator which may be either eight bits or sixteen, depending on the settings of two mode select flags (x sets the index registers to eight or sixteen bits; m sets the accumulator and memory to eight or sixteen).

The 65802's native mode differs in that, while the bank registers are part of effective address formation, bank values are not propagated to the bus, so long addressing modes have no bank effect. The bank accessed is always bank zero, so there is, essentially, no bank portion to the effective address generated.

The 6502 emulation mode on the 65802 and 65816 processors (e = 1) differs in that the stack pointer's high byte is always $01; direct page indexed addressing always wraps around to remain in the direct page rather than crossing over into the next page (so the high direct page byte remains the high byte of all direct page addresses formed). The exception to this is that zero page stack wrapping is only enforced for 6502 and 65C02 instructions, and only when DP = 0 in the case of page zero wrapping. New opcodes will cause effective addresses to be generated *outside* of the zero page or the emulation mode stack page if an effective address calculation overflows the low byte.

Additionally, the index registers and the A accumulator are limited to eight bits. (There remains, however, a hidden eight-bit B accumulator, as well as a 16-bit C accumulator which is the concatenation of B and A but which is generally not accessible except to special instructions.)

The 65C02 and 6502 differ from 6502 emulation in that there are no bank registers whatsoever; direct page addressing is, instead, zero page addressing ($0000 is the zero page base to which offsets and, sometimes, index values are added; there is no direct page register); and there is no hidden B accumulator nor concatenated C accumulator.

The symbols in Table 17.1 are used to describe the kinds of operands that are used with the various addressing modes.

Figures 17.1 through 17.4 repeat the illustrations of the programming models for the four possible processor configurations: 6502/65C02, 65802 native mode, 65816 native mode, and 65816 emulation mode. The programming model for the native mode 65816 is used in the addressing mode figures that follow; for different processors or modes, compare the addressing mode figure with the processor-mode programming model for clarification of the operation of the addressing mode for that model.

17 The Addressing Modes

Table 17.1. Operand Symbols.

addr	two-byte address
addr/const	two-byte value: either an address or a constant
const	one- or two-byte constant
destbk	64K bank to which string will be moved
dp	one-byte direct page offset (6502/65C02: zero page)
label	label of code in same 64K bank as instruction
long	three-byte address (includes bank byte)
nearlabel	label of code close enough to instruction to be reachable by a one-byte signed offset
sr	one-byte stack relative offset
srcebk	64K bank from which string will be moved

6502/65C02 Programming Model

```
                    7                               0
                    ┌───────────────────────────────┐
                    │       Accumulator (A)         │
                    ├───────────────────────────────┤
                    │     X Index Register (X)      │
                    ├───────────────────────────────┤
                    │     Y Index Register (Y)      │
         15         ├───────────────────────────────┤
    ┌ ─ ─ ─ ─ ─ ─ ─ ┼───────────────────────────────┤
    │ 0 0 0 0 0 0 0 1│      Stack Pointer (S)       │
    ├───────────────┼───────────────────────────────┤
    │    Program    │      Counter (PC)             │
    └───────────────┴───────────────────────────────┘
```

Processor Status Register (P)

n	v		b	d	i	z	c

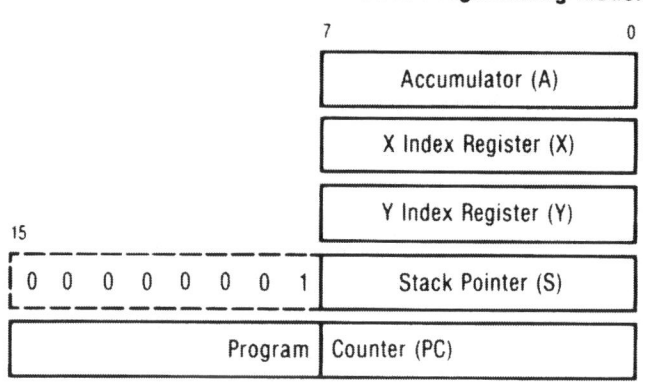

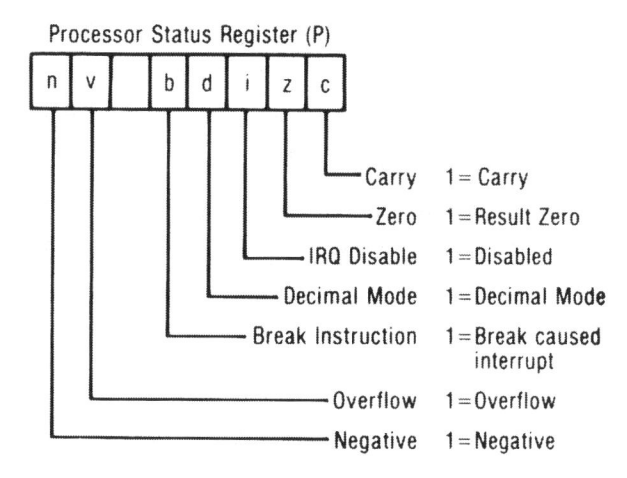

- Carry — 1 = Carry
- Zero — 1 = Result Zero
- IRQ Disable — 1 = Disabled
- Decimal Mode — 1 = Decimal Mode
- Break Instruction — 1 = Break caused interrupt
- Overflow — 1 = Overflow
- Negative — 1 = Negative

Figure 17.1. 6502/65C02 Programming Model.

65802 Native Mode Programming Model
(16-bit accumulator & index register modes: m=0 & x=0)

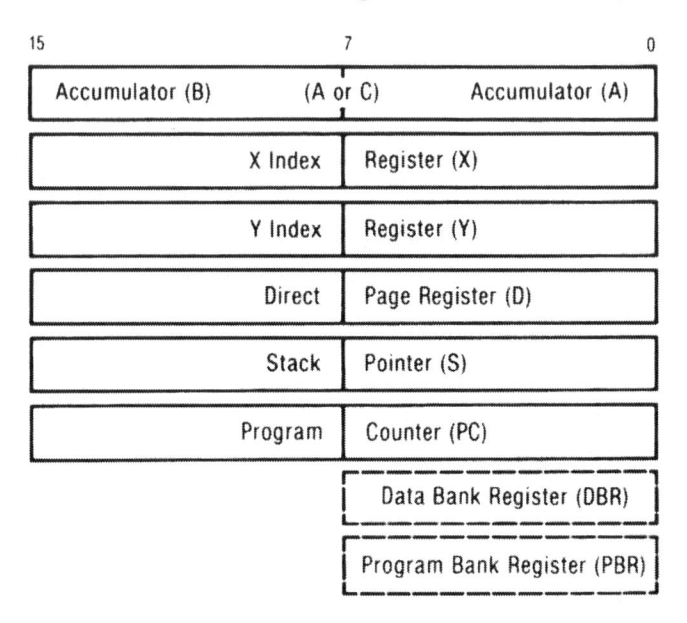

```
 15                      7                       0
┌────────────────────────┬────────────────────────┐
│    Accumulator (B)     │   (A or C)   Accumulator (A)  │
├────────────────────────┴────────────────────────┤
│         X Index        │    Register (X)        │
├────────────────────────┼────────────────────────┤
│         Y Index        │    Register (Y)        │
├────────────────────────┼────────────────────────┤
│         Direct         │   Page Register (D)    │
├────────────────────────┼────────────────────────┤
│         Stack          │    Pointer (S)         │
├────────────────────────┼────────────────────────┤
│        Program         │    Counter (PC)        │
└────────────────────────┴────────────────────────┘
                         ┌────────────────────────┐
                         │  Data Bank Register (DBR)  │
                         ├────────────────────────┤
                         │ Program Bank Register (PBR)│
                         └────────────────────────┘
```

Processor Status Register (P)

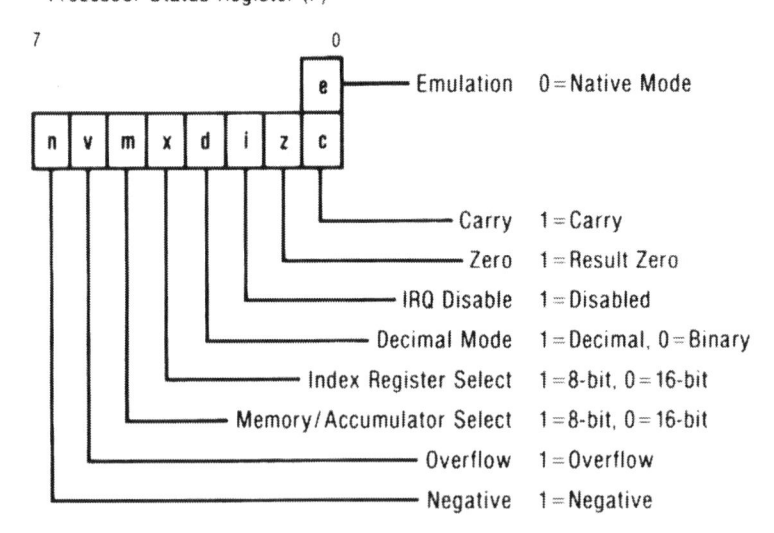

```
                              0
                             ┌─┐
                             │e│  — Emulation        0 = Native Mode
 7                           └─┘
┌─┬─┬─┬─┬─┬─┬─┬─┐
│n│v│m│x│d│i│z│c│
└─┴─┴─┴─┴─┴─┴─┴─┘
             │ └— Carry                    1 = Carry
             └— Zero                       1 = Result Zero
           └— IRQ Disable                  1 = Disabled
         └— Decimal Mode                   1 = Decimal, 0 = Binary
       └— Index Register Select            1 = 8-bit, 0 = 16-bit
     └— Memory/Accumulator Select          1 = 8-bit, 0 = 16-bit
   └— Overflow                             1 = Overflow
 └— Negative                               1 = Negative
```

Figure 17.2. 65802 Native Mode Programming Model.

17 The Addressing Modes 377

65816 Native Mode Programming Model
(16-bit accumulator & index register modes: m=0 & x=0)

```
 23                    15                 7                    0
                       | Accumulator (B) | (A or C) | Accumulator (A) |
 | Data Bank Register (DBR) |
                       | X Index | Register (X) |
                       | Y Index | Register (Y) |
 | 0 0 0 0 0 0 0 0 |   | Direct  | Page Register (D) |
 | 0 0 0 0 0 0 0 0 |   | Stack   | Pointer (S) |
 | Program Bank Register (PBR) | Program | Counter (PC) |
```

Processor Status Register (P)

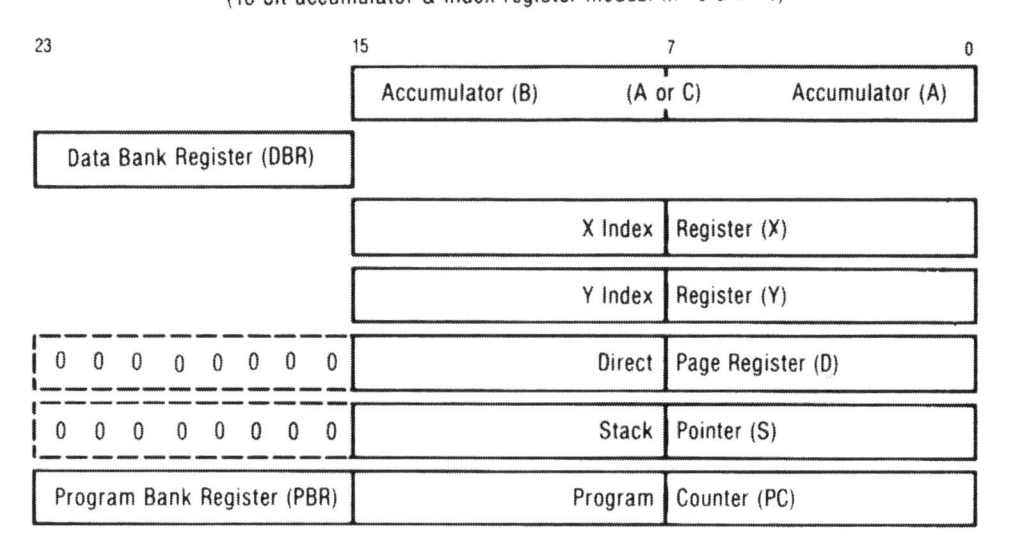

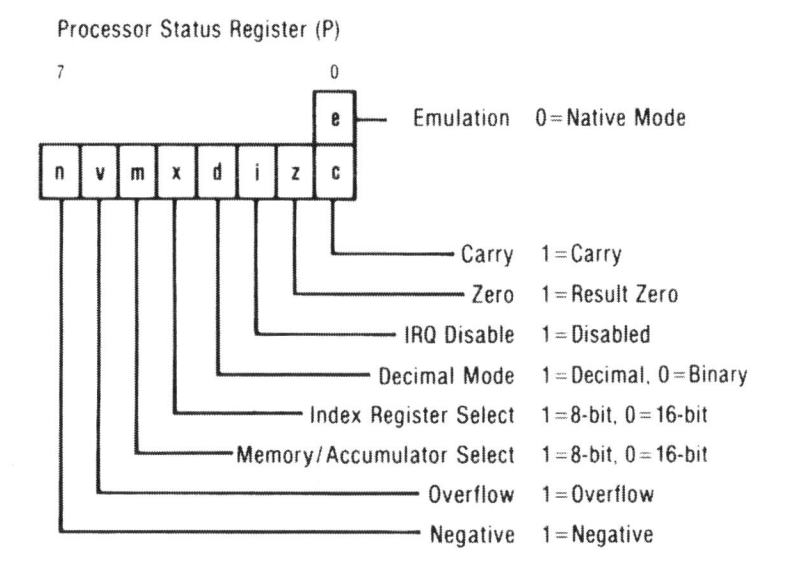

```
 7                           0
                             e  — Emulation    0 = Native Mode
 | n | v | m | x | d | i | z | c |
```

- Carry — 1 = Carry
- Zero — 1 = Result Zero
- IRQ Disable — 1 = Disabled
- Decimal Mode — 1 = Decimal, 0 = Binary
- Index Register Select — 1 = 8-bit, 0 = 16-bit
- Memory/Accumulator Select — 1 = 8-bit, 0 = 16-bit
- Overflow — 1 = Overflow
- Negative — 1 = Negative

Figure 17.3. 65816 Native Mode Programming Model.

65816 Emulation Mode Programming Model

```
23                    15                    7                    0
                      ┌─────────────────────┬─────────────────────┐
                      │   Accumulator (B)   │(C)│ Accumulator (A) │
                      └─────────────────────┴─────────────────────┘
┌─────────────────────┐
│ Data Bank Register (DBR) │
└─────────────────────┘
                                            ┌─────────────────────┐
                                            │ X Index Register (X)│
                                            └─────────────────────┘
                                            ┌─────────────────────┐
                                            │ Y Index Register (Y)│
                                            └─────────────────────┘
┌─ ─ ─ ─ ─ ─ ─ ─ ─ ─ ─┬─────────────────────┬─────────────────────┐
│ 0 0 0 0 0 0 0 0     │      Direct         │   Page Register (D) │
└─ ─ ─ ─ ─ ─ ─ ─ ─ ─ ─┴─────────────────────┴─────────────────────┘
┌─ ─ ─ ─ ─ ─ ─ ─ ─ ─ ─┬─ ─ ─ ─ ─ ─ ─ ─ ─ ─ ─┬─────────────────────┐
│ 0 0 0 0 0 0 0 0     │ 0 0 0 0 0 0 0 1     │  Stack Pointer (S)  │
└─────────────────────┴─────────────────────┴─────────────────────┘
┌─────────────────────┬───────────────────────────────────────────┐
│ Program Bank Register (PBR) │  Program     │   Counter (PC)     │
└─────────────────────┴───────────────────────────────────────────┘
```

Processor Status Register (P)

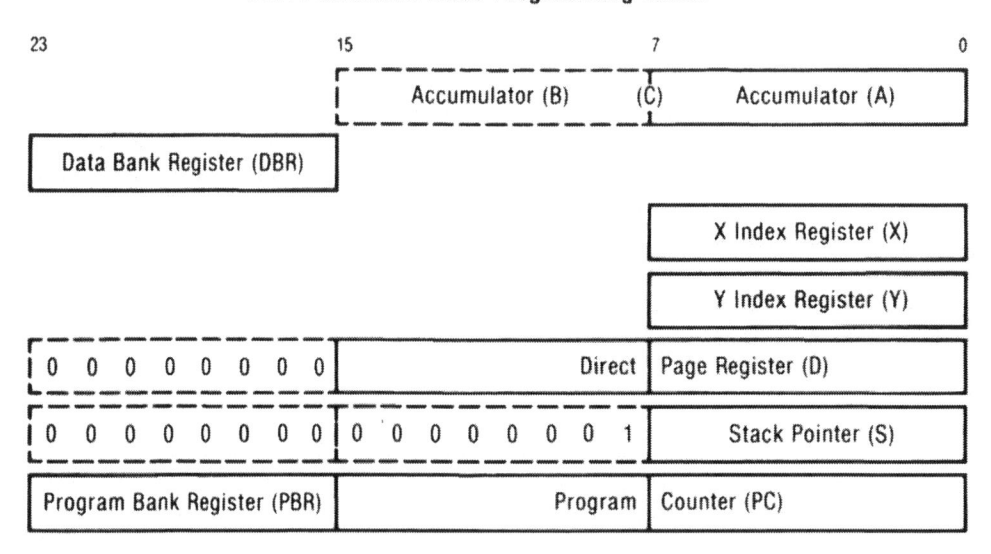

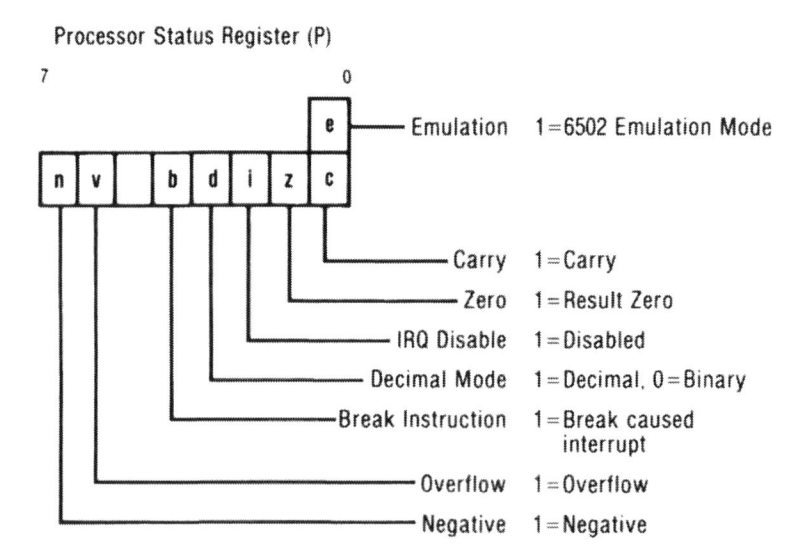

```
7                 0
              ┌───┐
              │ e │ ── Emulation    1 = 6502 Emulation Mode
┌─┬─┬─┬─┬─┬─┬─┼───┤
│n│v│ │b│d│i│z│ c │
└─┴─┴─┴─┴─┴─┴─┴───┘
 │ │   │ │ │ │ └── Carry           1 = Carry
 │ │   │ │ │ └──── Zero            1 = Result Zero
 │ │   │ │ └────── IRQ Disable     1 = Disabled
 │ │   │ └──────── Decimal Mode    1 = Decimal, 0 = Binary
 │ │   └────────── Break Instruction 1 = Break caused
 │ │                                     interrupt
 │ └────────────── Overflow        1 = Overflow
 └──────────────── Negative        1 = Negative
```

Figure 17.4. 65816 Emulation Mode Programming Model.

Absolute Addressing

Effective Address:
Bank: Data Bank Register (DBR) if locating data; Program Bank Register (PBR) if transferring control.
High: Second operand byte.
Low: First operand byte.

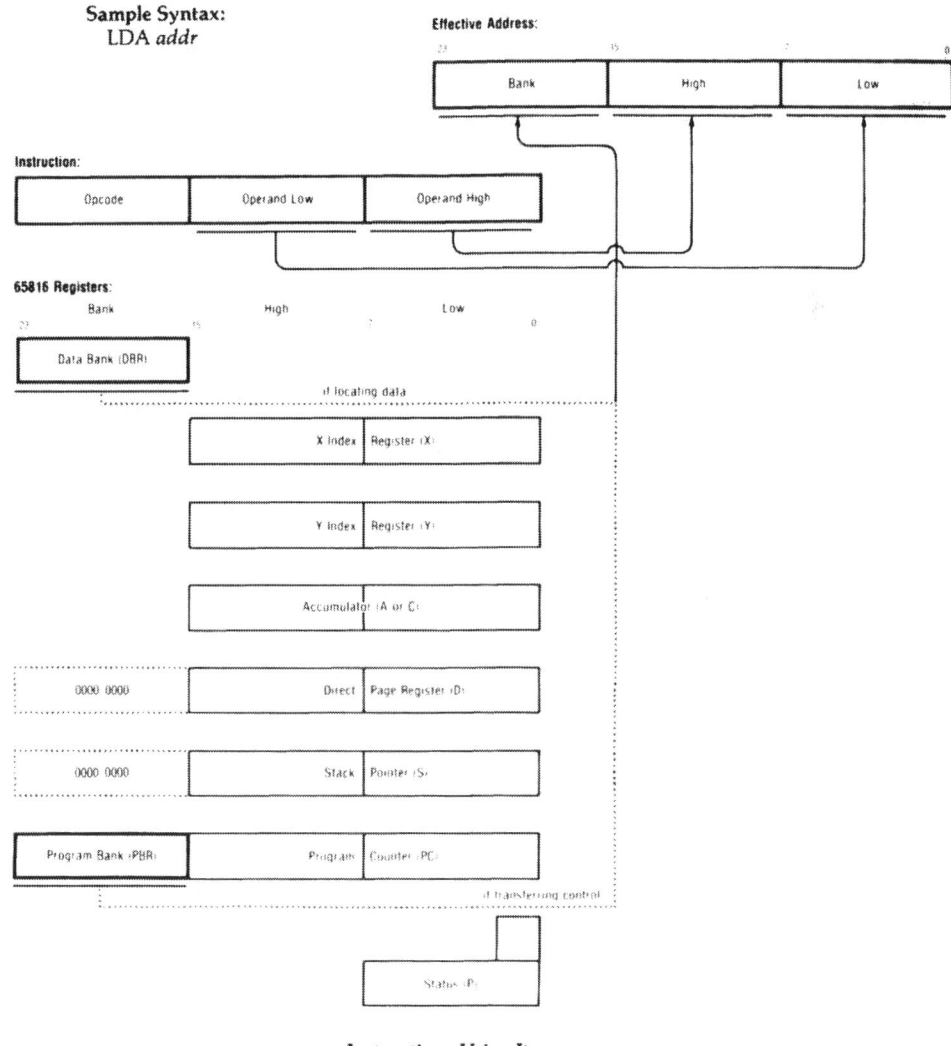

Sample Syntax:
LDA *addr*

Instructions Using It:

Effective Address Locates Data

ADC	CPY	LDY	STA
AND	DEC	LSR	STX
ASL	EOR	ORA	STY
BIT	INC	ROL	STZ[1]
CMP	LDA	ROR	TRB[1]
CPX	LDX	SBC	TSB[1]

Transfer Control to Effective Address

JMP   JSR

1 65C02 and 65802/65815 only.

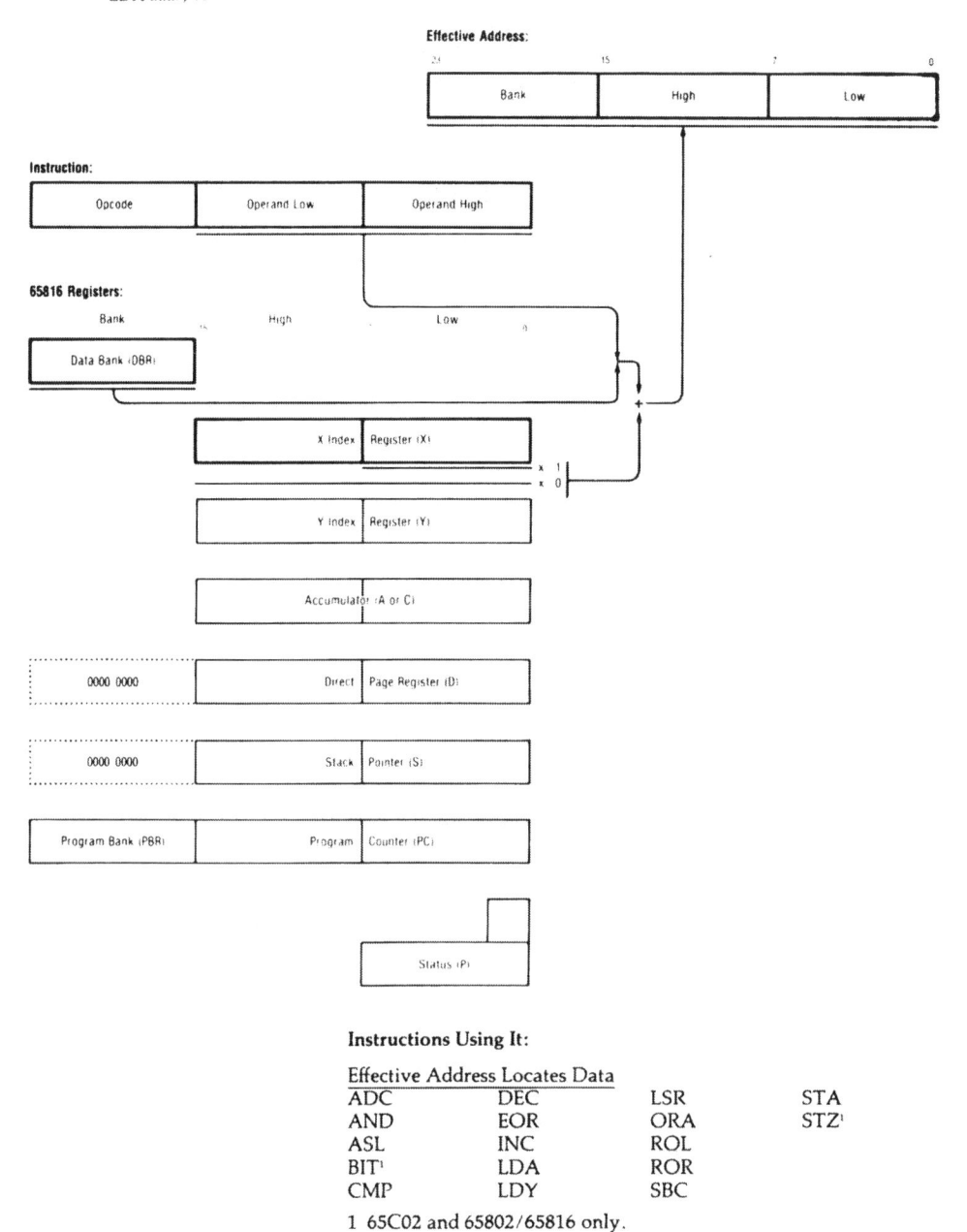

Absolute Indexed, X Addressing

Effective Address: The Data Bank Register is concatenated with the 16-bit Operand: the 24-bit result is added to X (16 bits if 65802/65816 native mode, x=0; else 8).

Sample Syntax:
 LDA *addr*, X

Instructions Using It:

Effective Address Locates Data

ADC	DEC	LSR	STA
AND	EOR	ORA	STZ[1]
ASL	INC	ROL	
BIT[1]	LDA	ROR	
CMP	LDY	SBC	

1 65C02 and 65802/65816 only.

Absolute Indexed, Y Addressing

Effective Address: The Data Bank Register is concatenated to the 16-bit Operand: the 24-bit result is added to Y (16 bits if 65802/65816 native mode, x=0; else 8).

Sample Syntax:
LDA *addr*, Y

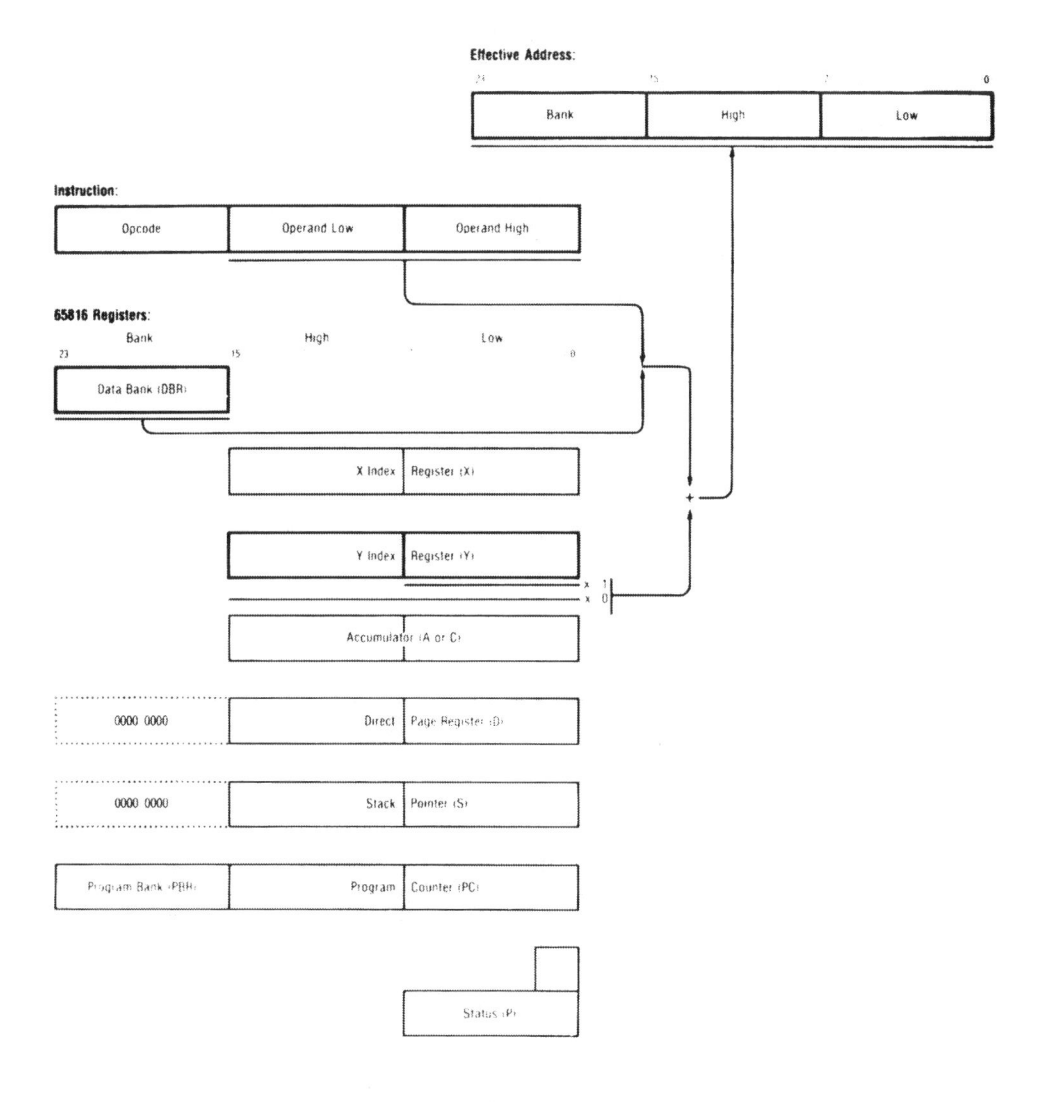

Instructions Using It:

Effective Address Locates Data

ADC	EOR	ORA
AND	LDA	SBC
CMP	LDX	STA

Absolute Indexed Indirect Addressing

Effective Address:

Bank: Program Bank Register (PBR).

High/Low: The Indirect Address.

Indirect Address: Located in the Program Bank at the sum of the Operand double byte and X (16 bits if 65802/65816 native mode, x=0; else 8 bits).

Sample Syntax:
JMP (addr, X)

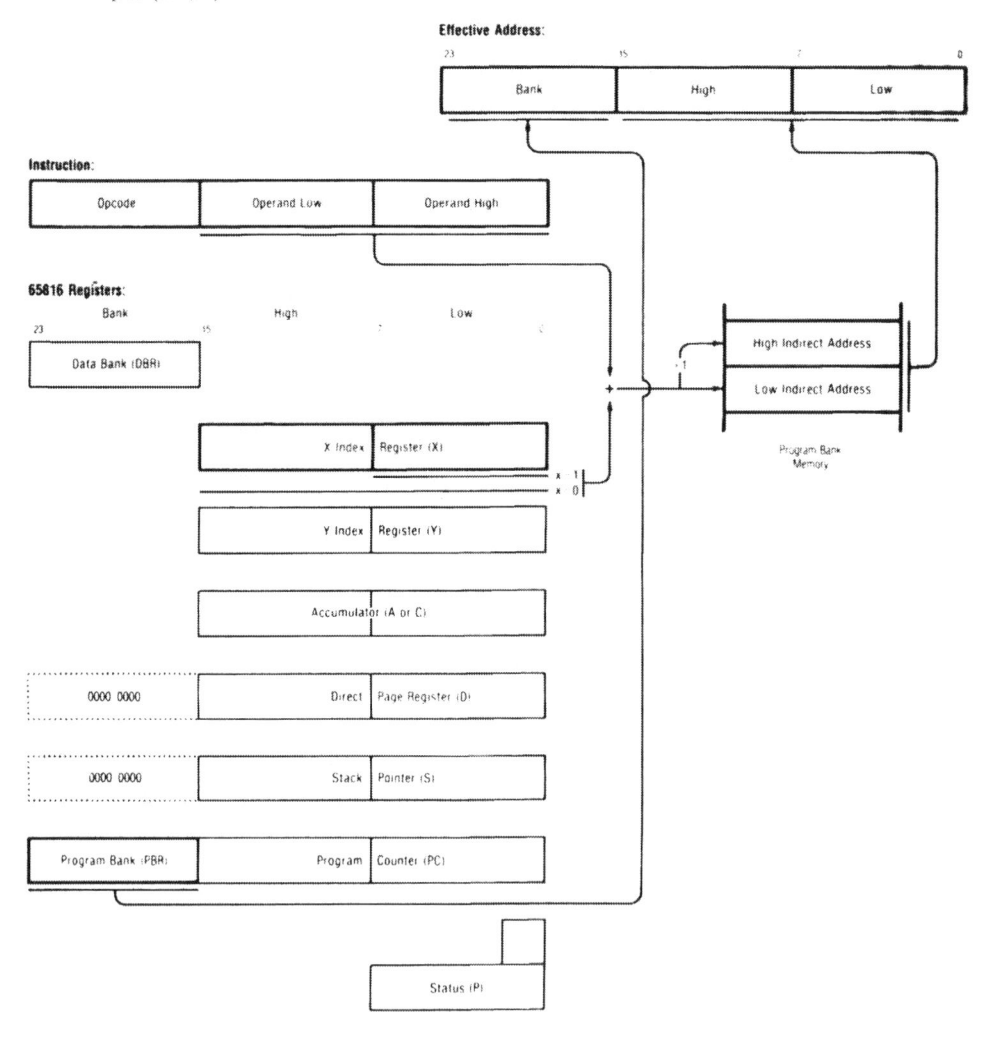

Instructions Using It:

Transfer Control to Effective Address
JMP[1]   JSR[2]

1 65C02 and 65802/65816 only.
2 65802/65816 only.

Absolute Indirect Addressing

Effective Address:

Bank: Program Bank Register (PBR).

High/Low: The Indirect Address.

Indirect Address: Located in Bank Zero, at the Operand double byte.

Sample Syntax:
JMP (addr)

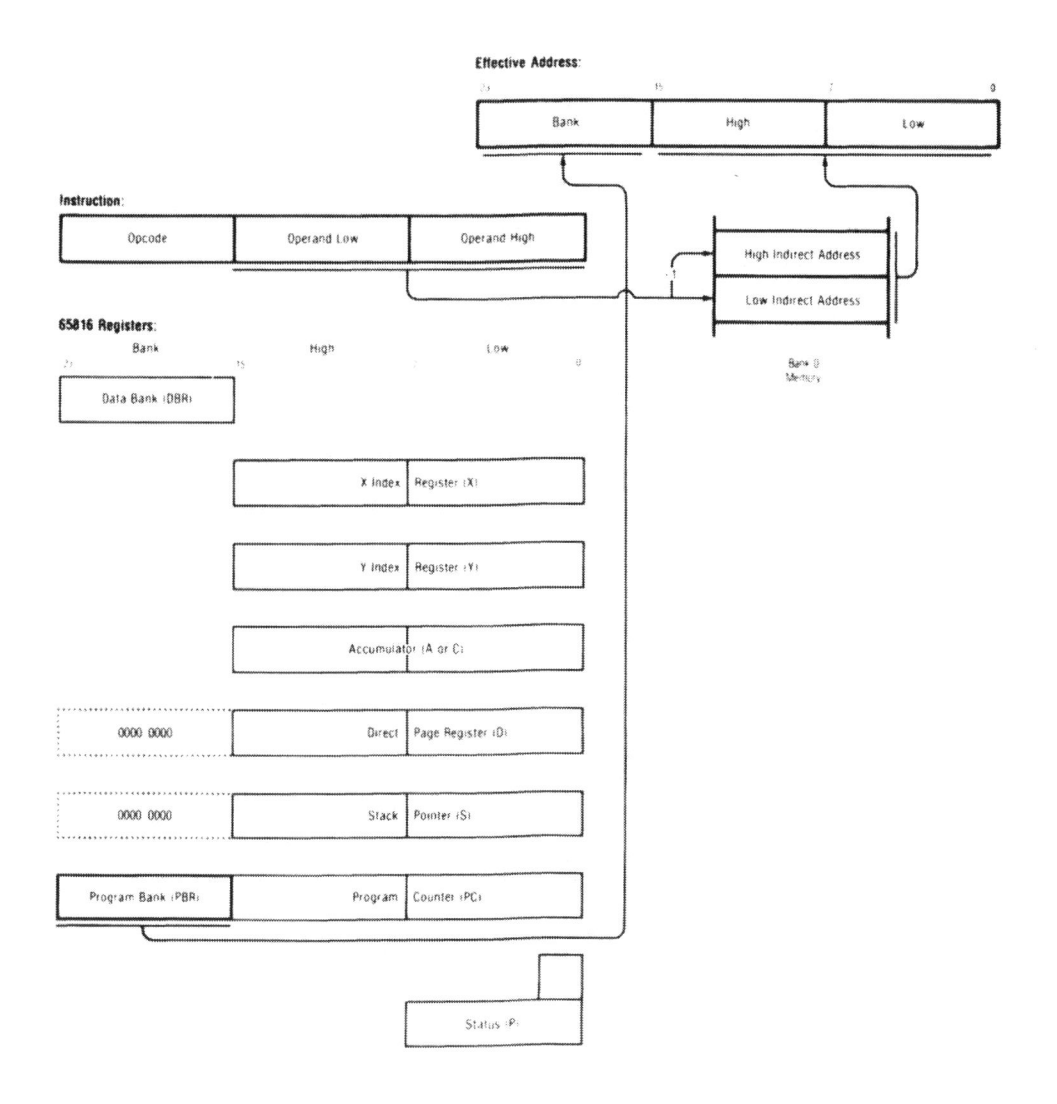

Instructions Using It:

Transfer Control to Effective Address
JMP

Absolute Indirect Long Addressing

Effective Address:

Bank/High/Low: The 24-bit Indirect Address.

Indirect Address: Located in Bank Zero, at the Operand double byte.

Sample Syntax:
JMP [addr]

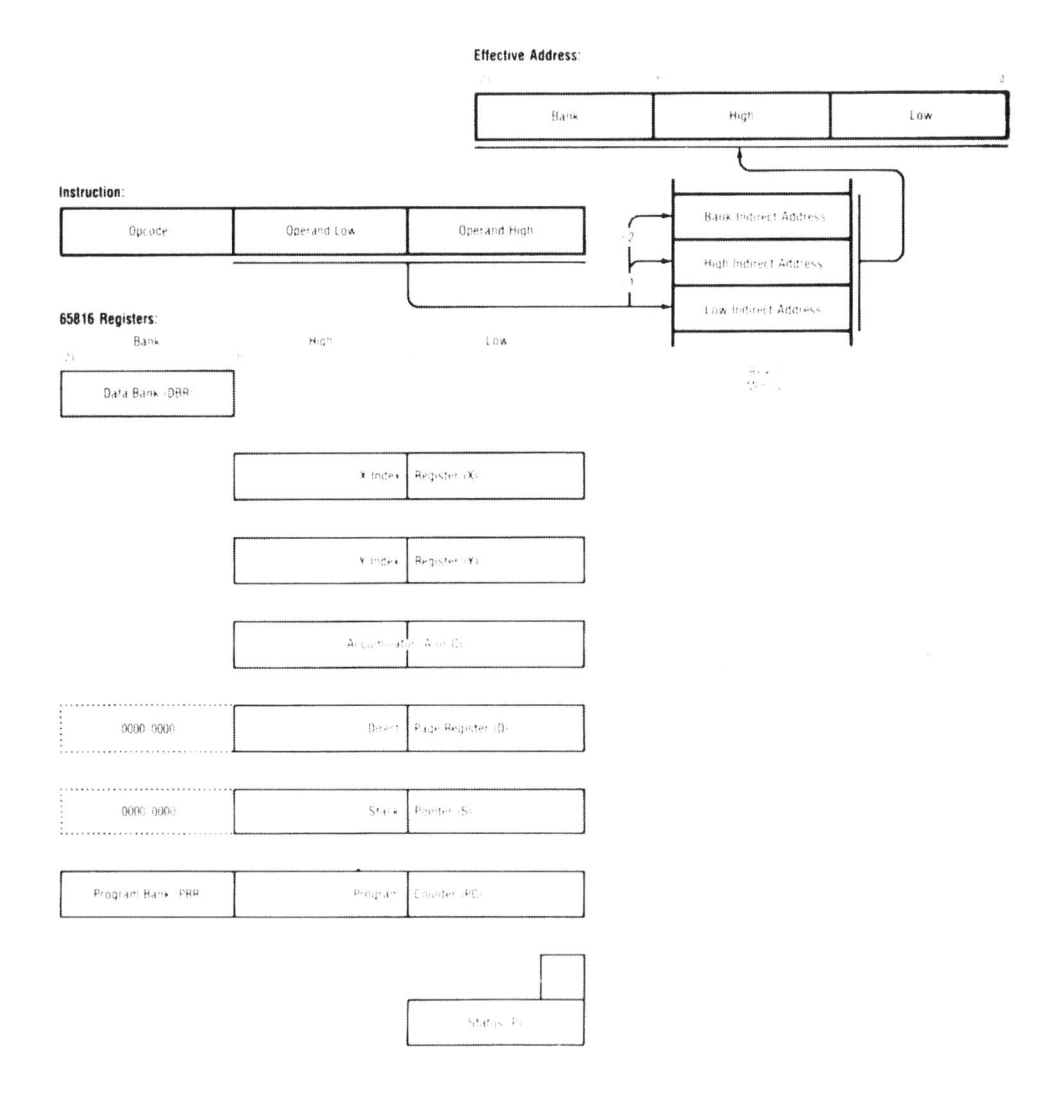

Instructions Using It:

Transfer Control to Effective Address
JMP/JML

Note: 65802/65816 only;
65802: Data bank value is not propagated to the bus (bank accessed is always bank 0).

Absolute Long Addressing

Effective Address:

Bank: Third operand byte.
High: Second operand byte.
Low: First operand byte.

Sample Syntax:
 LDA *long*

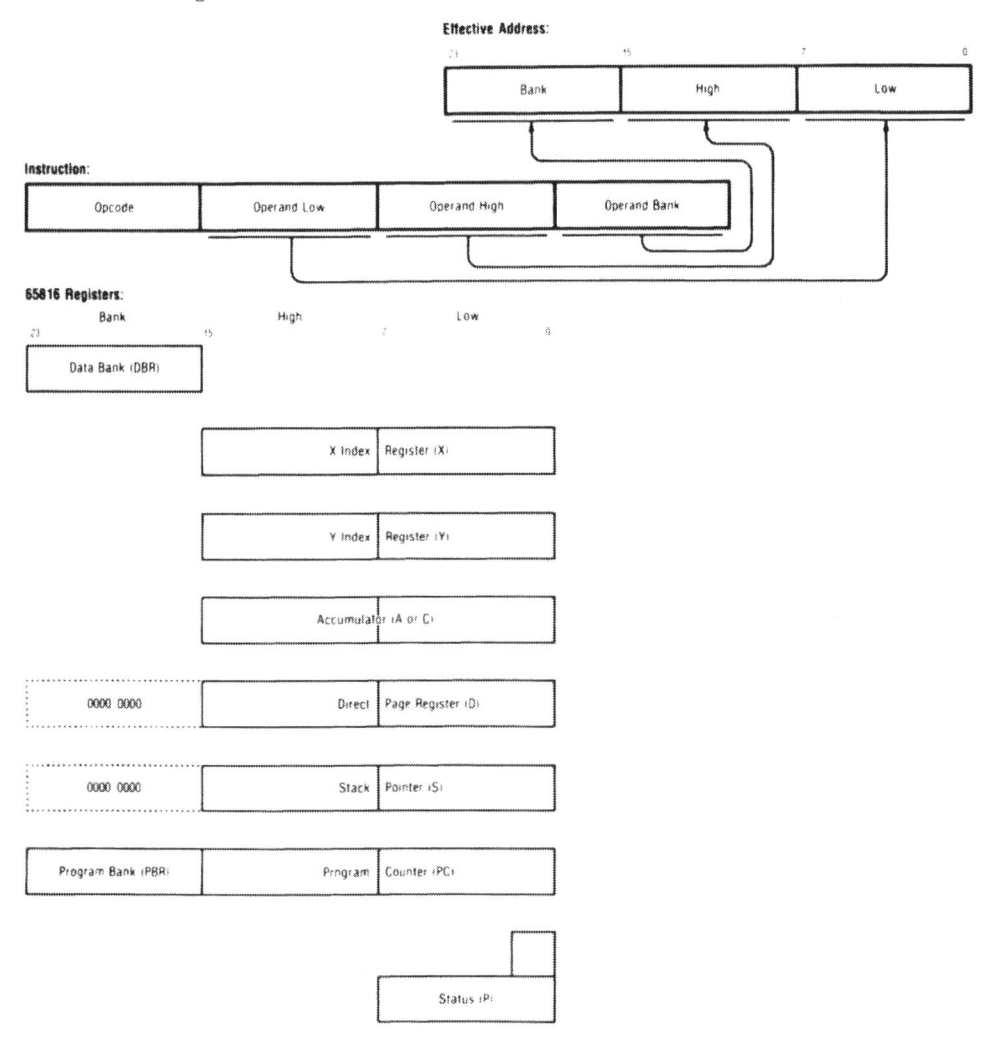

Instructions Using It:

Effective Address Locates Data

ADC	CMP	LDA	SBC
AND	EOR	ORA	STA

Transfer Control to Effective Address
JMP(JML)   JSR(JSL)

Note: All are 65802/65816 only;
65802: Data bank value is not propagated to the bus (bank accessed is always bank 0).

Absolute Long Indexed, X Addressing

Effective Address: The 24-bit Operand is added to X (16 bits if 65802/65816 native mode, x = 0; else 8 bits)

Sample Syntax:
  LDA long, X

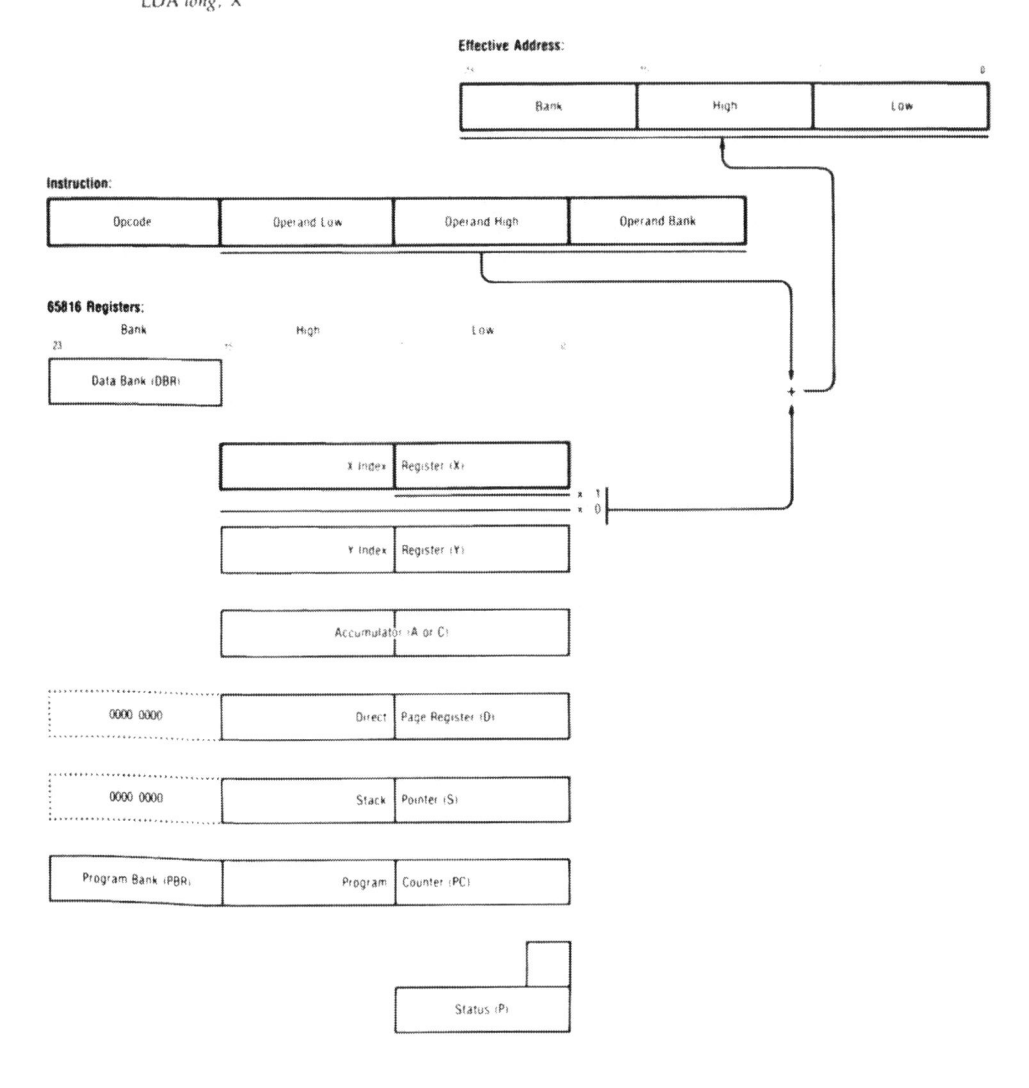

Instructions Using It:

Effective Address Locates Data

ADC	CMP	LDA	SBC
AND	EOR	ORA	STA

Note: All are 65802/65816 only;
65802: Data bank value is not propagated to the bus (bank accessed is always bank 0).

Accumulator Addressing

8-Bit Data (all processors): Data: Byte in accumulator A.

16-Bit Data (65802/65816, native mode. 16-bit accumulator (m = 0):
Data High: High byte in accumulator A.
Data Low: Low byte in accumulator A.

Sample Syntax:
ASL A

Instruction:
Opcode

65816 Registers:
Data Bank (DBR)
X Index Register (X)
Y Index Register (Y)
Accumulator (A or C)
Direct Page Register (D)
Stack Pointer (S)
Program Bank (PBR) Program Counter (PC)
Status (P)

Instructions Using It:

| ASL | INC[1] | ROL |
| DEC[1] | LSR | ROR |

1 65C02 and 65802/65816 only.

Block Move Addressing

Source Effective Address:
Bank: Second operand byte.
High/Low: The 16-bit value in X; if X is only 8 bits (mode flag x=1), the high byte is 0.
Destination Effective Address:
Bank: First operand byte.
High/Low: The 16-bit value in Y; if Y is only 8 bits (mode flag x=1), the high byte is 0.
Count:
Number of bytes to be moved: 16-bit value in Accumulator C plus 1.
Sample Syntax:
   MVN   srcebk, destbk

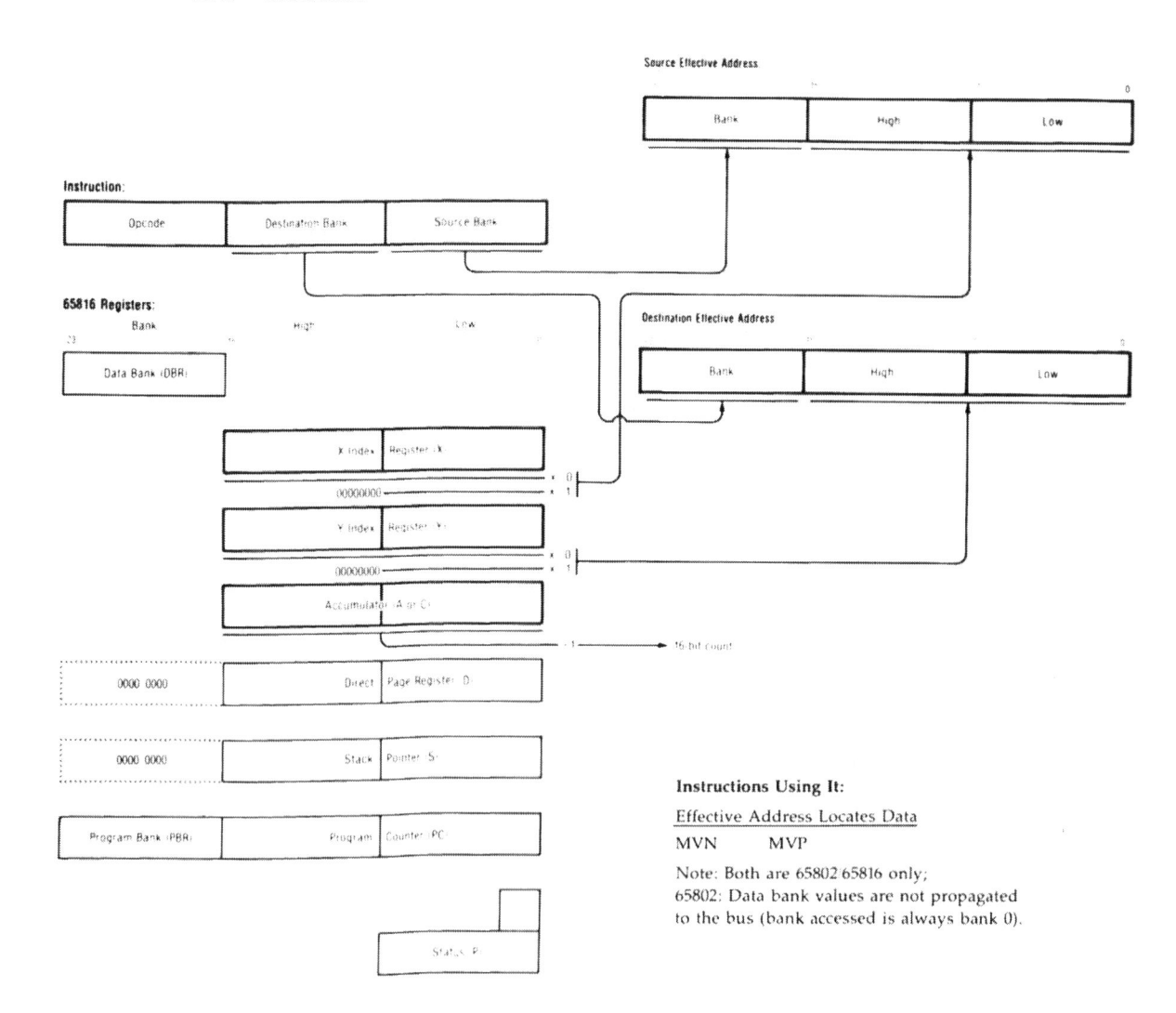

Instructions Using It:

Effective Address Locates Data
MVN   MVP

Note: Both are 65802/65816 only;
65802: Data bank values are not propagated to the bus (bank accessed is always bank 0).

Direct Page Addressing

Effective Address:
Bank: Zero
High/Low: Direct Page Register plus Operand byte.

Sample Syntax:
  LDA *dp*

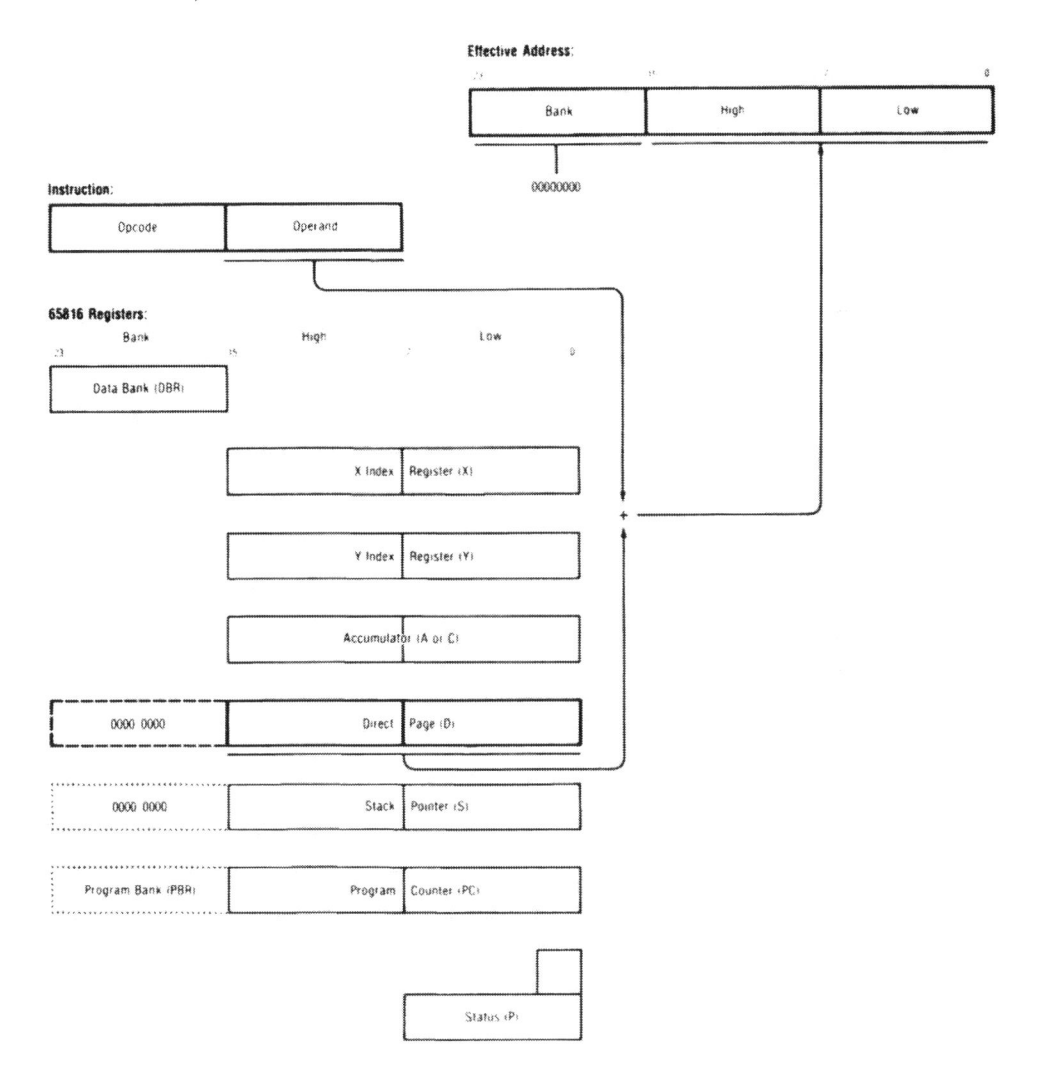

Instructions Using It:

Effective Address Locates Data

ADC	CPY	LDY	STA
AND	DEC	LSR	STX
ASL	EOR	ORA	STY
BIT	INC	ROL	STZ[1]
CMP	LDA	ROR	TRB[1]
CPX	LDX	SBC	TSB[1]

1 65C02 and 65802/65816 only.

Direct Page Indexed, X Addressing

Effective Address:

Bank: Zero
High/Low: Direct Page Register plus Operand byte plus X (16 bits if 65802/65816 native mode, x=0; else 8 bits).

Sample Syntax:
   LDA dp, X

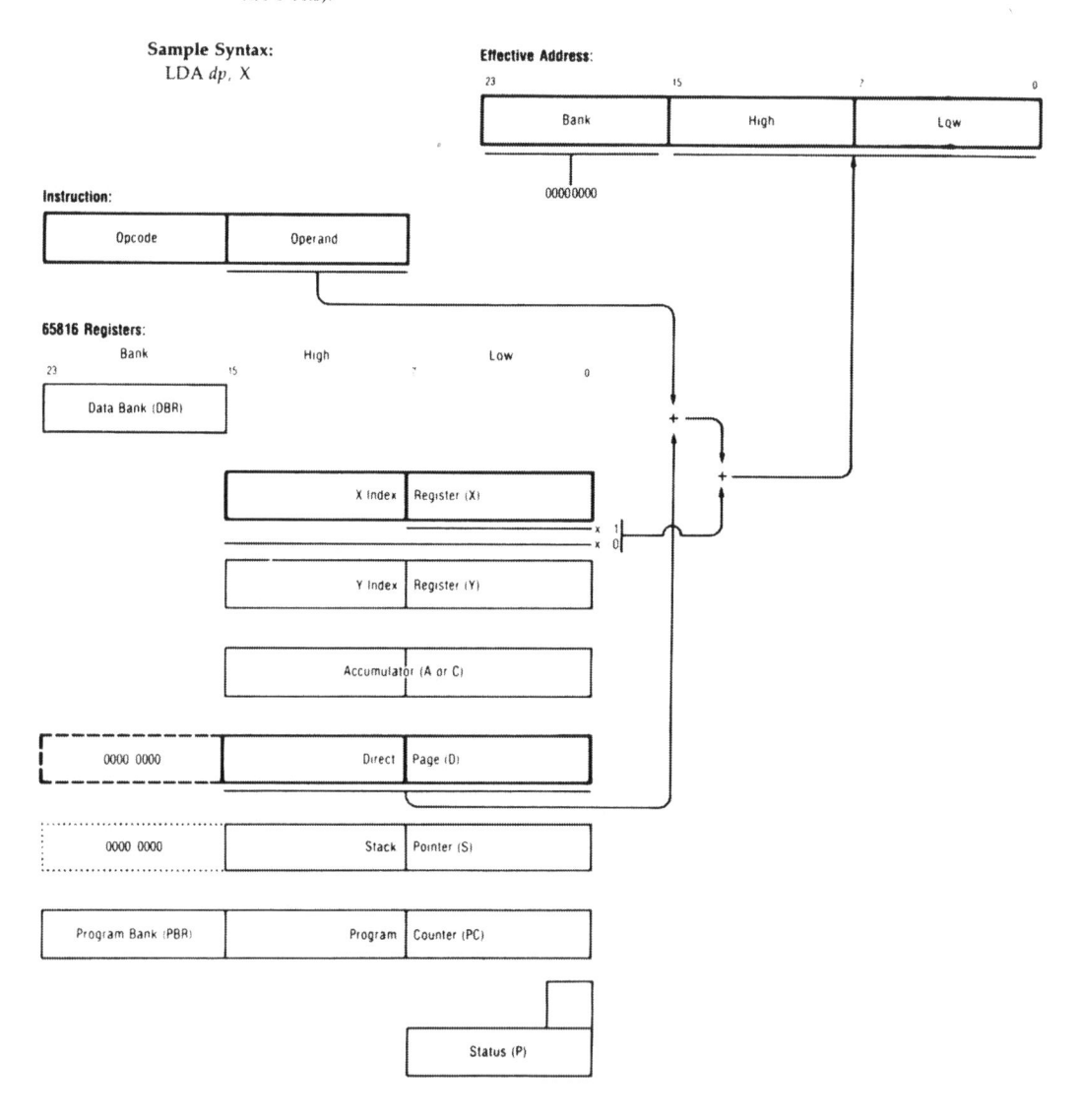

Instructions Using It:
Effective Address Locates Data

ADC	DEC	LSR	STA
AND	EOR	ORA	STY
ASL	INC	ROL	STZ[1]
BIT[1]	LDA	ROR	
CMP	LDY	SBC	

1 65C02 and 65802/65816 only.

Direct Page Indexed, Y Addressing

Effective Address:

Bank: Zero

High/Low: Direct Page Register plus Operand byte plus Y (16 bits if 65802/65816 native mode, x=0; else 8 bits).

Sample Syntax:
  LDX *dp*, Y

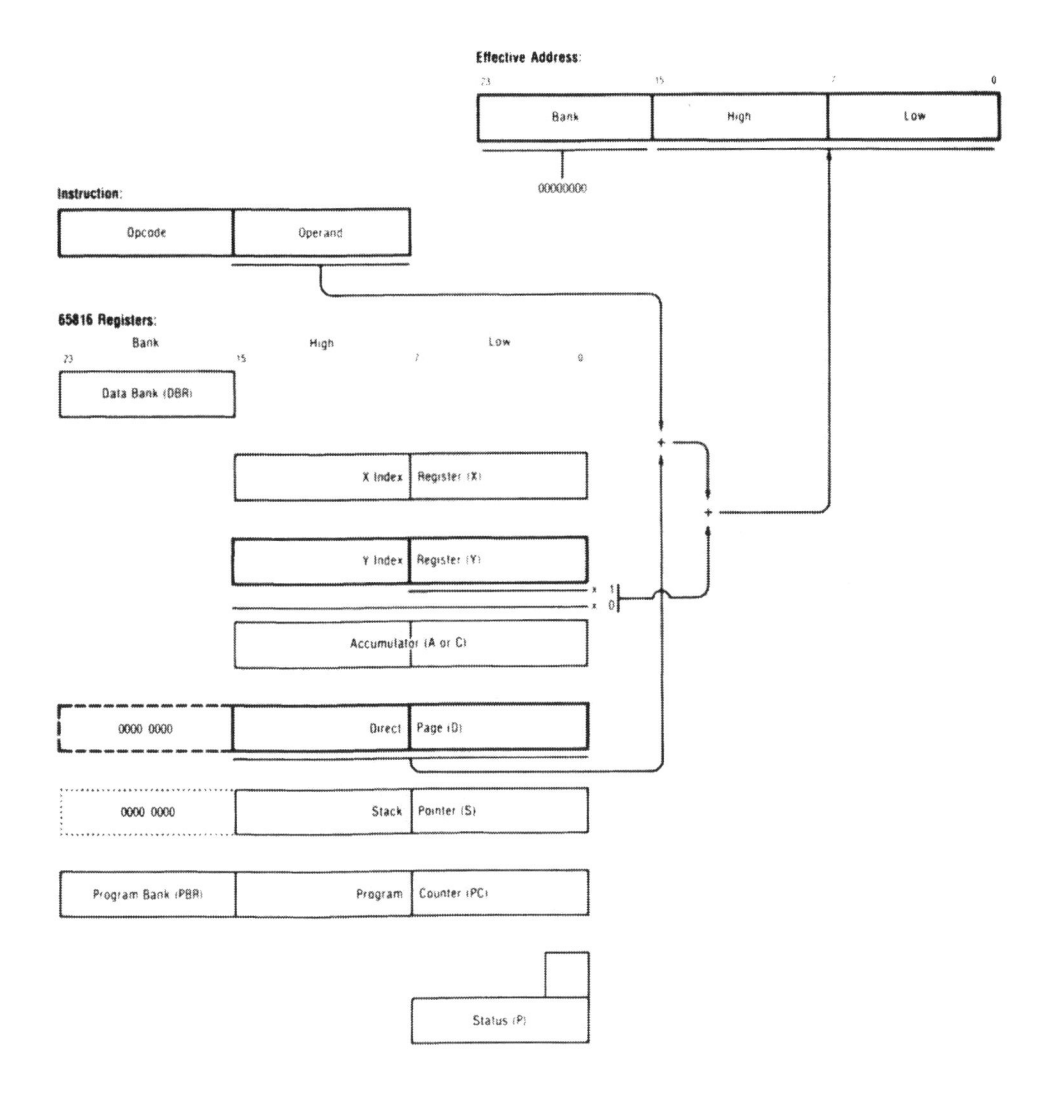

Instructions Using It:

<u>Effective Address Locates Data</u>
LDX   STX

Direct Page Indexed Indirect, X Addressing

Effective Address:

Bank: Data bank register

High/Low: The indirect address

Indirect Address: Located in the direct page at the sum of the direct page register, the operand byte, and X (16 bits if 65802/65816 native mode, x=0; else 8), in bank 0.

Sample Syntax:
LDA (dp, X)

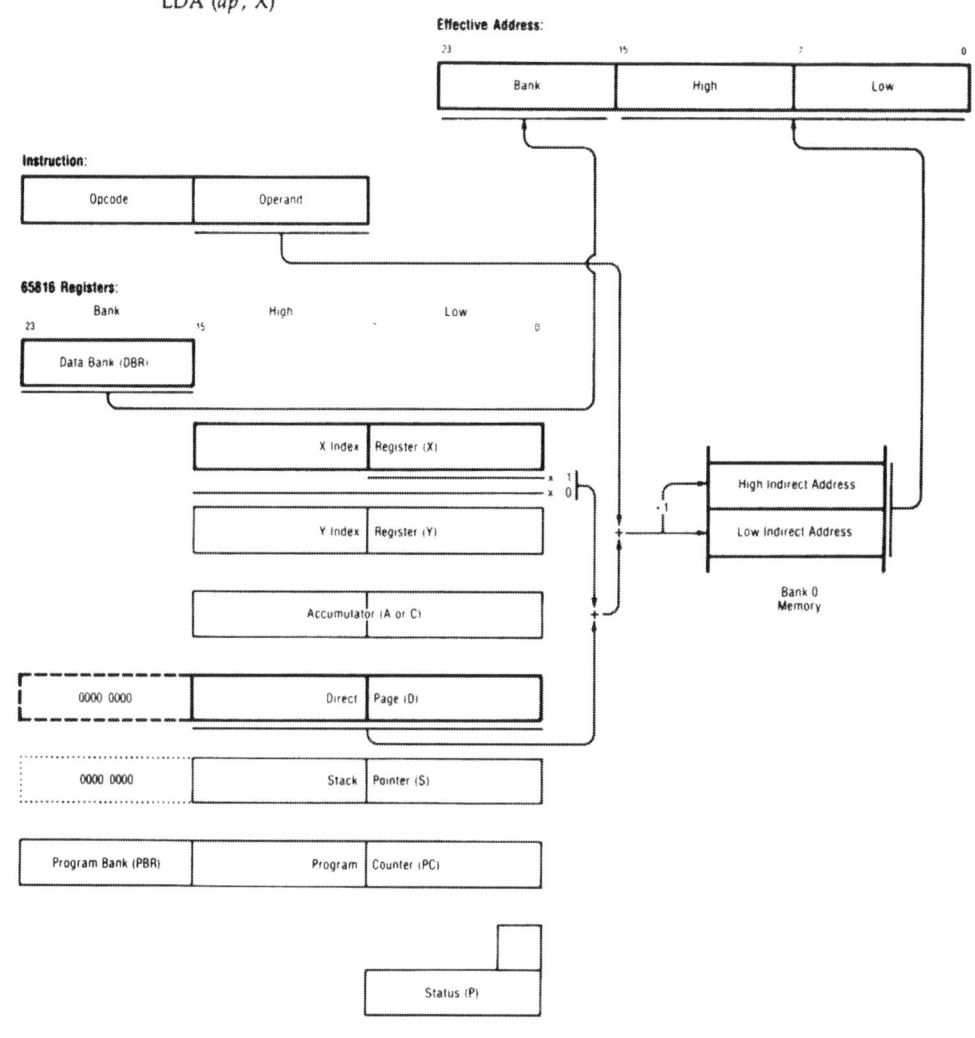

Instructions Using It:

Effective Address Locates Data

ADC	CMP	LDA	SBC
AND	EOR	ORA	STA

Direct Page Indirect Addressing

Effective Address:

Bank: Data Bank Register (DBR)

High/Low: The 16-bit Indirect Address

Indirect Address: The Operand byte plus the Direct Page Register, in Bank Zero

Sample Syntax:
 LDA (*dp*)

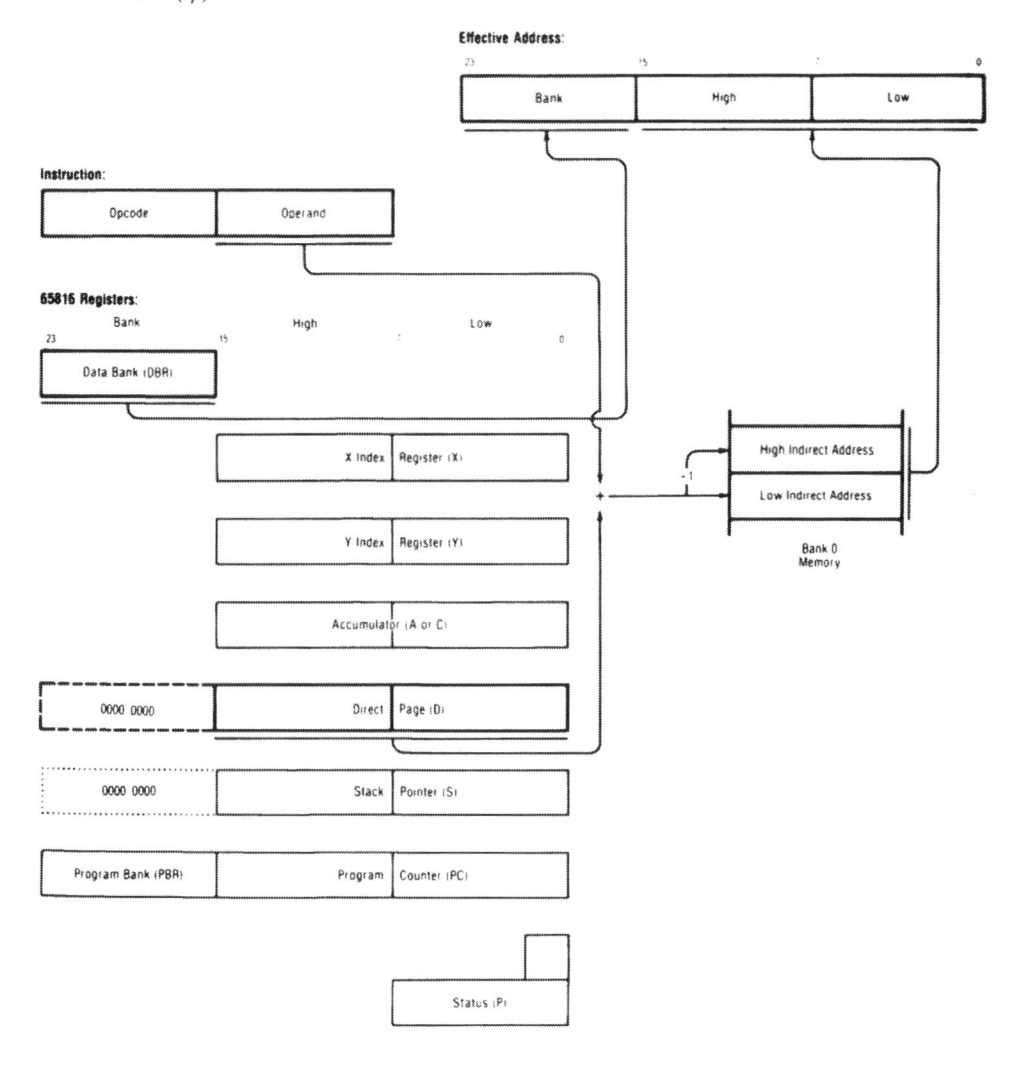

Instructions Using It:

Effective Address Locates Data

| ADC | CMP | LDA | SBC |
| AND | EOR | ORA | STA |

Note: All are 65C02 and 65802/65816 only.

Direct Page Indirect Long Addressing

Effective Address:

Bank/High/Low: The 24-bit Indirect Address

Indirect Address: The Operand byte plus the Direct Page Register, in Bank Zero

Sample Syntax:
LDA [dp]

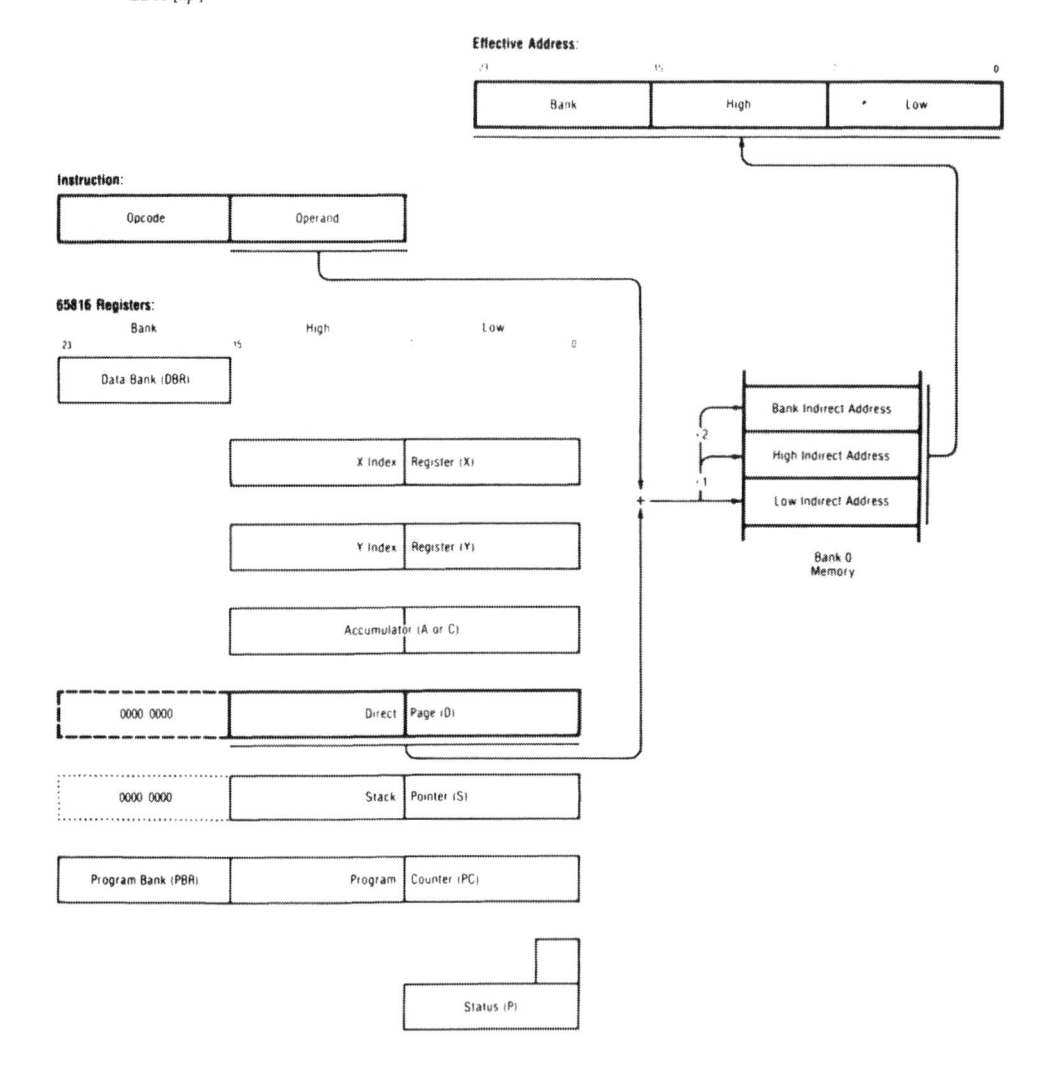

Instructions Using It:

Effective Address Locates Data

ADC	CMP	LDA	SBC
AND	EOR	ORA	STA

Note: All are 65802/65816 only;
65802: Data bank value is not propagated to the bus
(bank accessed is always bank 0)

Direct Page Indirect Indexed, Y Addressing

Effective Address: Found by concatenating the data bank to the double-byte indirect address, then adding Y (16 bits if 65802/65816 native mode, x=0; else 8).

Indirect Address: Located in the Direct Page at the sum of the direct page register and the operand byte, in bank zero.

Sample Syntax:
LDA (dp), Y

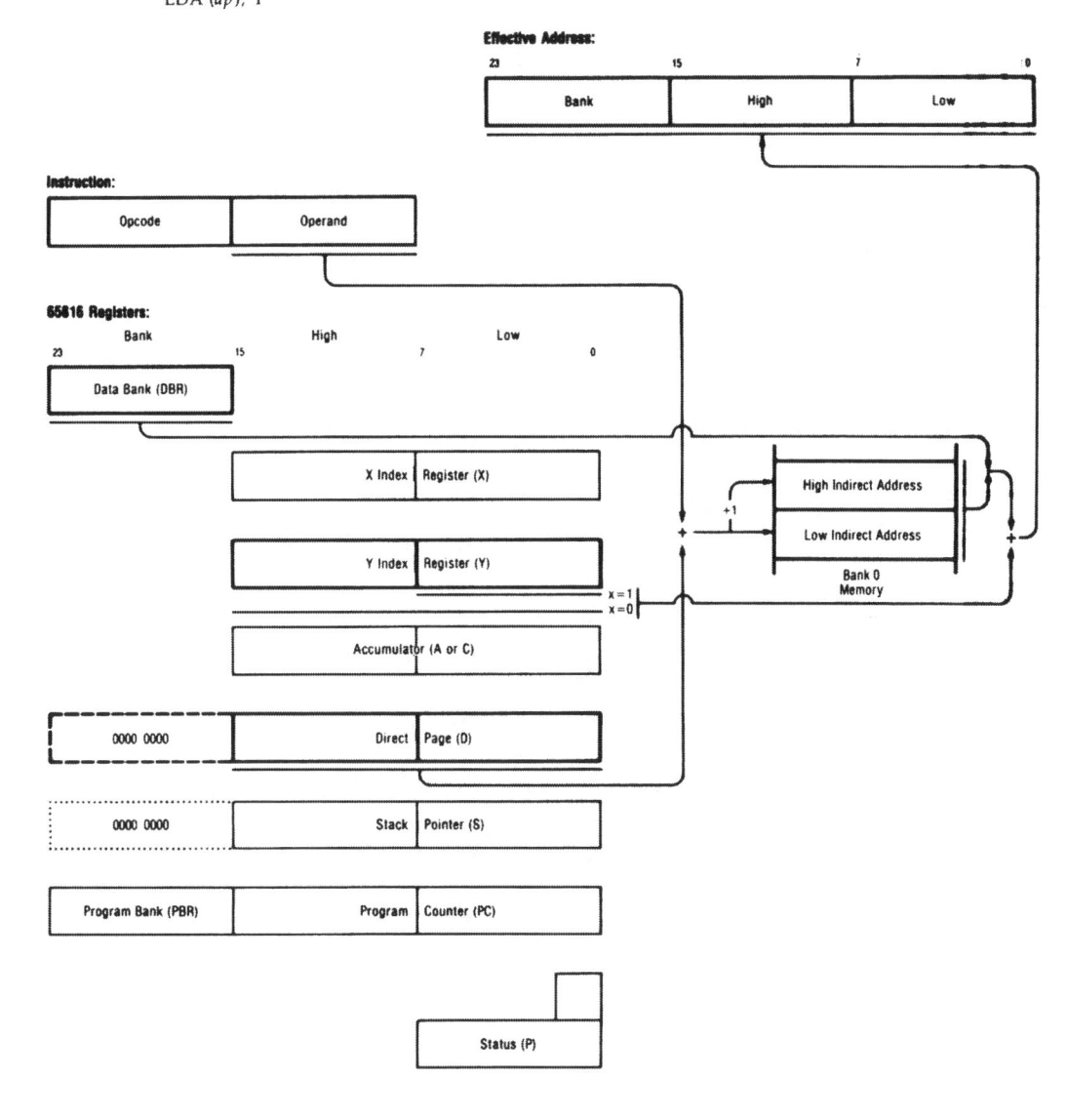

Instructions Using It:

Effective Address Locates Data
ADC	CMP	LDA	SBC
AND	EOR	ORA	STA

Direct Page Indirect Long Indexed, Y Addressing

Effective Address: Found by adding to the triple-byte indirect address Y (16 bits if 65802/65816 native mode, x = 0; else 8 bits).

Indirect Address: Located in the Direct Page at the sum of the direct page register and the operand byte in bank zero.

Sample Syntax:
   LDA (dp),Y

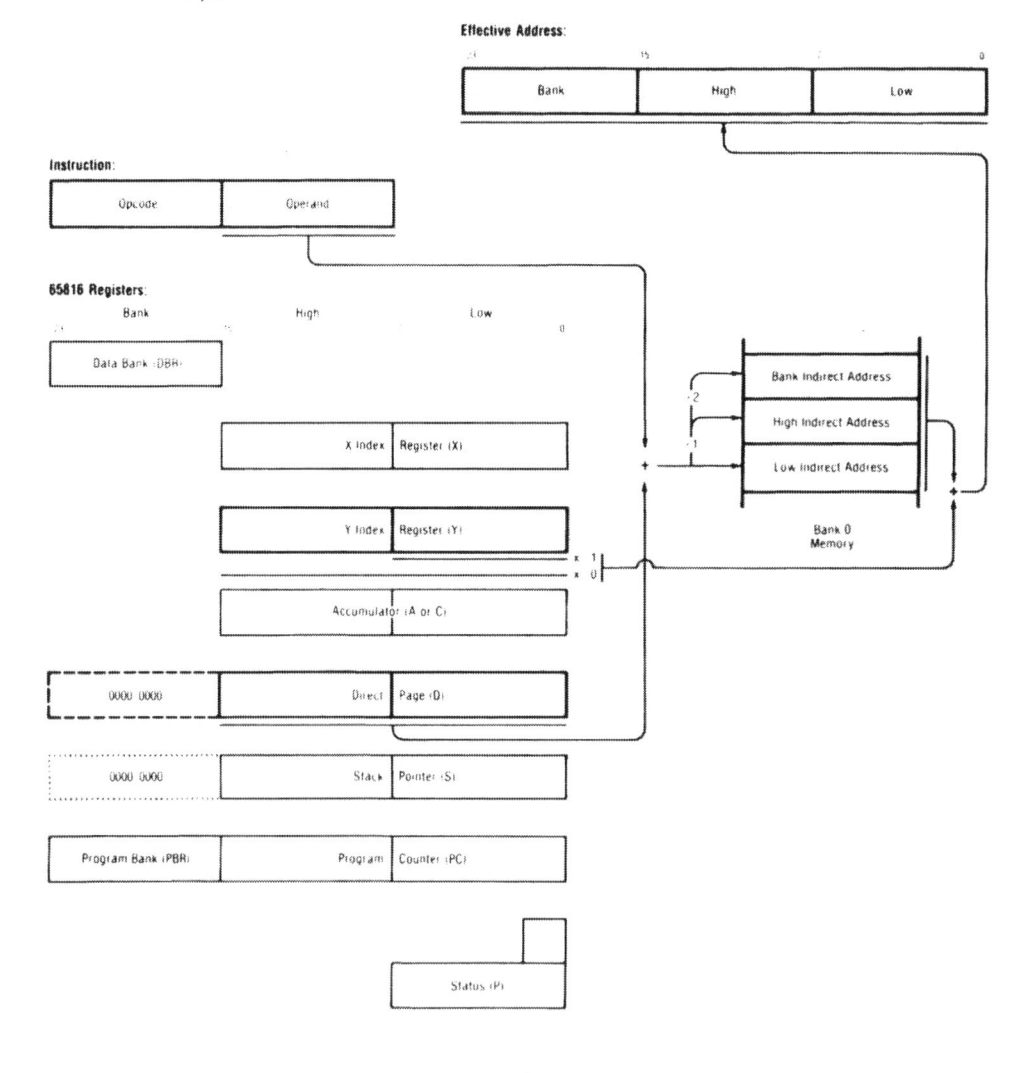

Instructions Using It:

Effective Address Locates Data

ADC	CMP	LDA	SBC
AND	EOR	ORA	STA

Note: All are 65802/65816 only;
65802: Data bank value is not propagated to the bus
(bank accessed is always bank 0)

Immediate Addressing

8-Bit Data (all processors): Data Operand byte

16-Bit Data (65802/65816, native mode, applicable mode flag m or x = 0):

Data High: Second operand byte.
Data Low: First operand byte.

Sample Syntax:
  LDA *const*.

Instruction:

Opcode	Data Low = Operand Low	Data High = Operand High

Instruction:

Opcode	Data - Operand

65816 Registers:

- Data Bank (DBR) [bits 23–16]
- X Index Register (X)
- Y Index Register (Y)
- Accumulator (A or C)
- 0000 0000 | Direct Page Register (D)
- 0000 0000 | Stack Pointer (S)
- Program Bank (PBR) | Program Counter (PC)
- Status (P)

Instructions Using It:

ADC	CPX	LDX	SBC
AND	CPY	LDY	SEP[2]
BIT[1]	EOR	ORA	
CMP	LDA	REP[1]	

1 65C02 and 65802/65816 only.
2 65802/65816 only.

Implied Addressing

Type 1: Mnemonic specifies register(s) to be operated on
Type 2: Mnemonic specifies flag bit(s) to be operated on
Type 3: Mnemonic specifies operation; no data involved

Sample Syntax:
   NOP

Instruction:
[Opcode]

65816 Registers:

Data Bank (DBR)

X Index Register (X)

Y Index Register (Y)

Accumulator (A or C)

0000 0000 | Direct Page Register (D)

0000 0000 | Stack Pointer (S)

Program Bank (PBR) | Program Counter (PC)

Status (P)

Instructions Using It:

Mnemonic Specifies Register(s)

DEX	TAY	TSX	TYX[1]
DEY	TCD[1]	TXA	XBA[1]
INX	TCS[1]	TXS	
INY	TDC[1]	TXY[1]	
TAX	TSC[1]	TYA	

Mnemonic Specifies Flag Bit(s)

CLC	CLI	SEC	SEI
CLD	CLV	SED	XCE[1]

Mnemonic Specifies Operation

NOP	STP[1]	WAI[1]

1 65802/65816 only.

Program Counter Relative Addressing

Effective Address:

Bank: Program Bank Register (PBR).

High/Low: The Operand byte, a two's complement signed value, is sign-extended to 16 bits, then added to the Program Counter (its value is the address of the opcode <u>following</u> this one).

Sample Syntax:
   BRA *nearlabel*

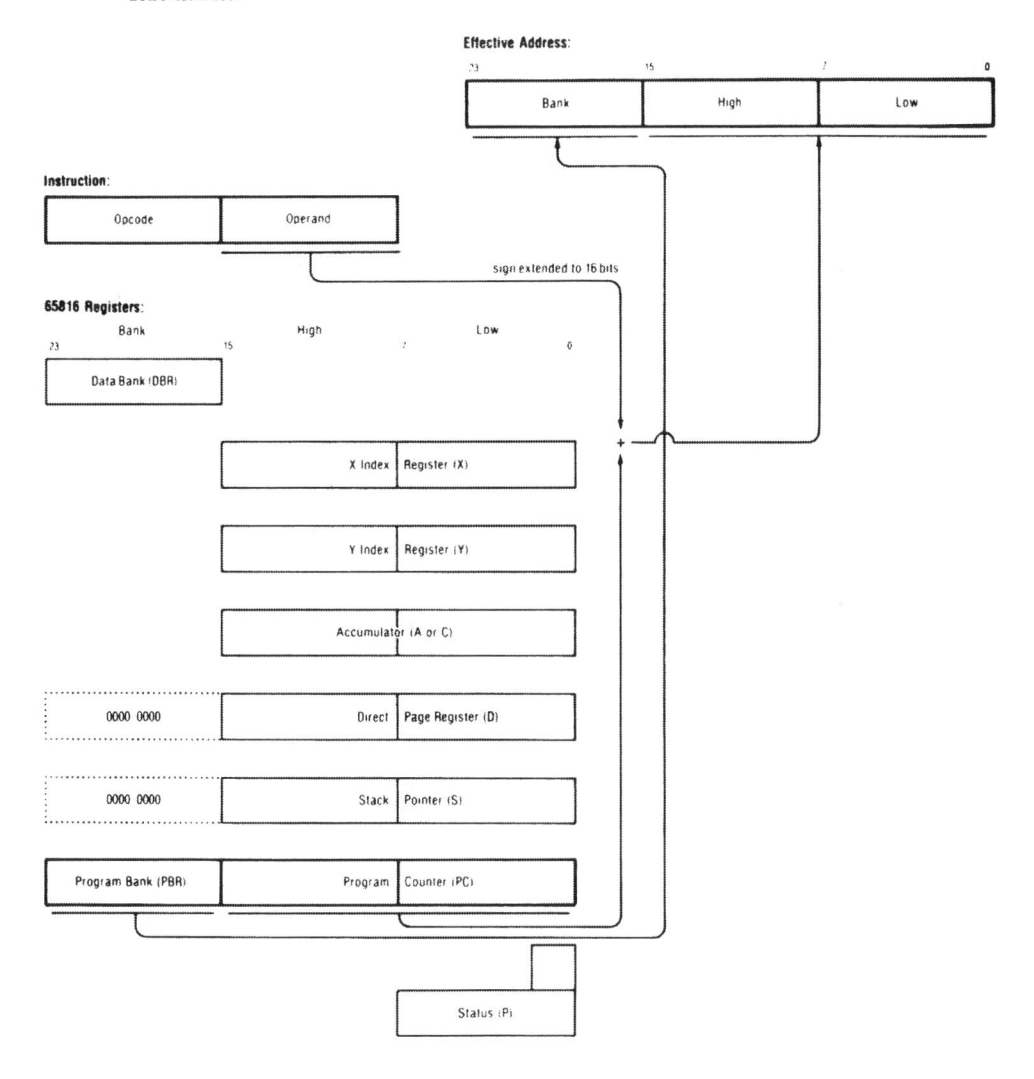

Instructions Using It:

Transfer Control to Effective Address

BCC	BMI	BRA[1]
BCS	BNE	BVC
BEQ	BPL	BVS

1 65C02 and 65802/65816 only.

Program Counter Relative Long Addressing

Effective Address:

Bank: Program Bank Register (PBR).

High/Low: The Operand double byte, a two's complement signed value, is added to the Program Counter (its value is the address of the opcode following this one).

Sample Syntax:
  BRL *label*

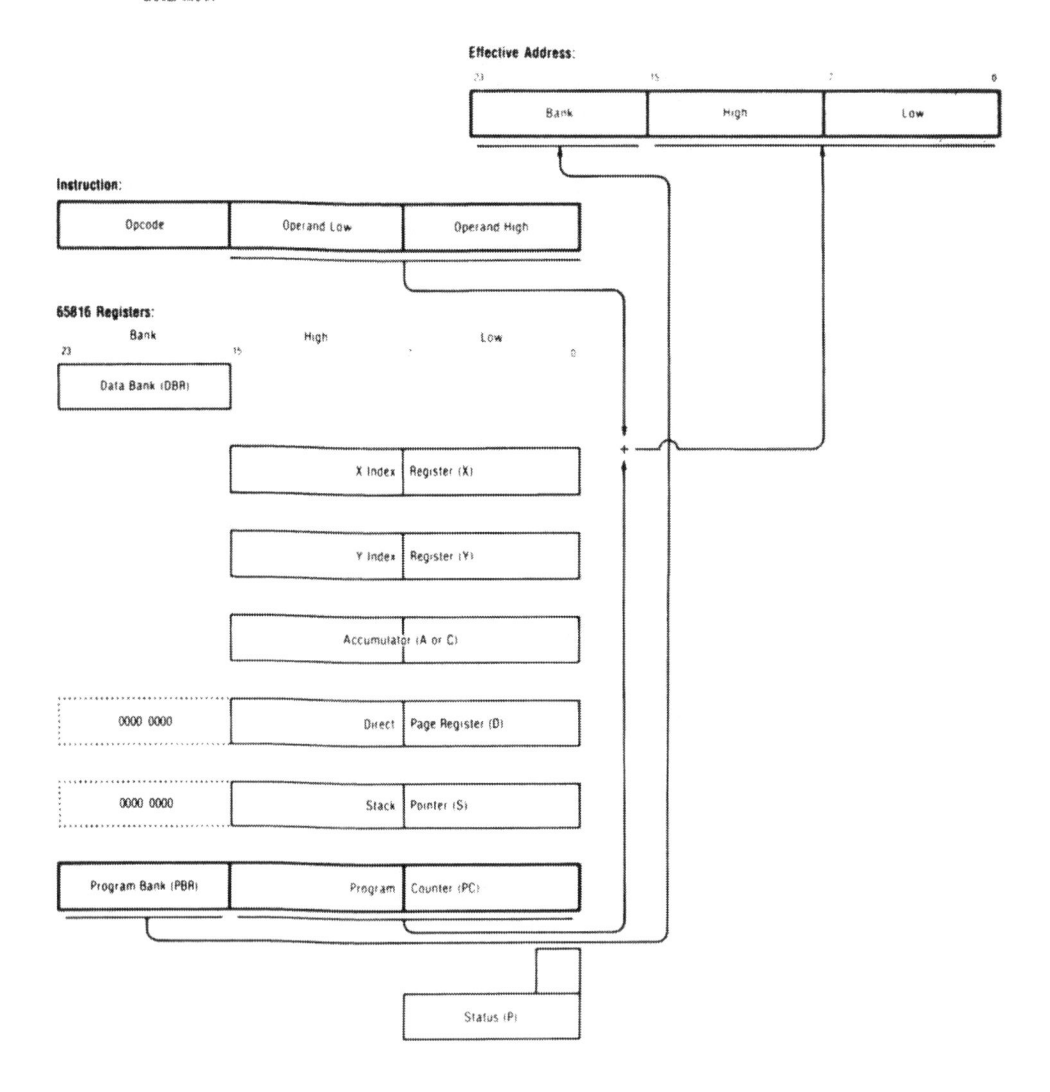

Instructions Using It:

Transfer Control to Effective Address
BRL

Note: 65802/65816 only.

Stack (Absolute) Addressing

Source of data to be pushed: The 16-bit operand, which can be either an absolute address or immediate data.

Destination effective address: Provided by Stack Pointer.

Sample Syntax:
 PEA *addr/const*

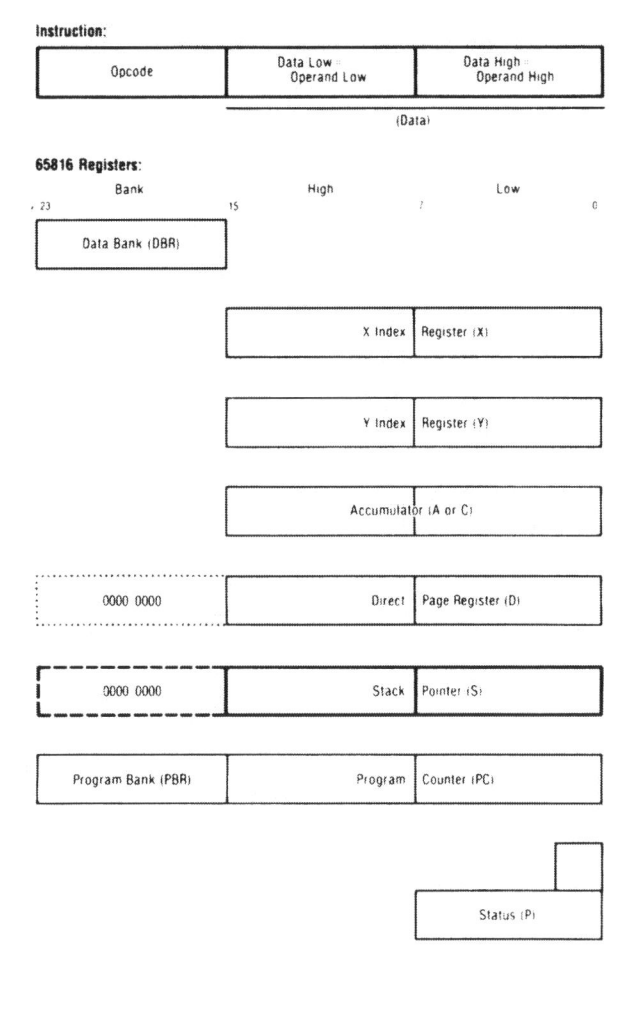

Instruction:

Opcode	Data Low Operand Low	Data High Operand High
	(Data)	

65816 Registers:

- Data Bank (DBR)
- X Index Register (X)
- Y Index Register (Y)
- Accumulator (A or C)
- 0000 0000 — Direct Page Register (D)
- 0000 0000 — Stack Pointer (S)
- Program Bank (PBR) — Program Counter (PC)
- Status (P)

Instructions Using It:
PEA
Note: 65802/65816 only.

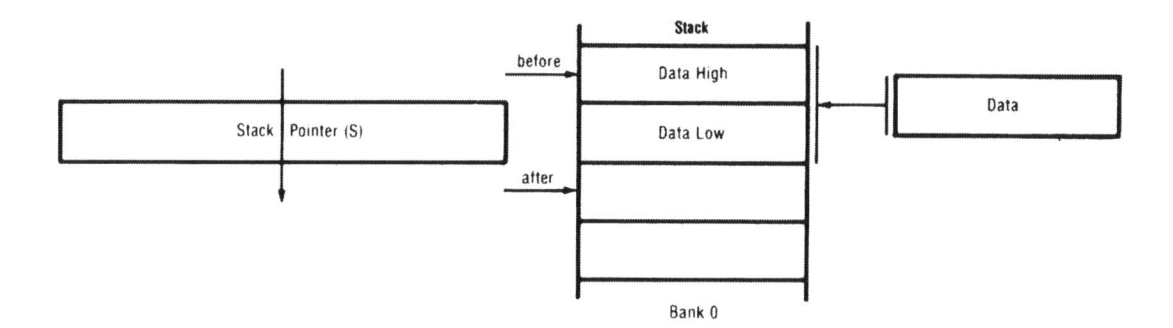

```
                              Stack
                 before  ┌─────────────┐
                  ───→   │  Data High  │ ←───┐  ┌──────┐
┌──────────────────────┐ ├─────────────┤     ├──│ Data │
│  Stack │ Pointer (S) │ │  Data Low   │     │  └──────┘
└──────────┬───────────┘ ├─────────────┤
           │       after │             │
           ↓       ───→  │             │
                         └─────────────┘
                            Bank 0
```

Stack (Direct Page Indirect) Addressing

Source of data to be pushed: The 16-bit indirect address (or double-byte data) located at the sum of the Operand byte plus the Direct Page Register, in Bank Zero.

Destination effective address: Provided by Stack Pointer.

Sample Syntax:
 PEI *dp*

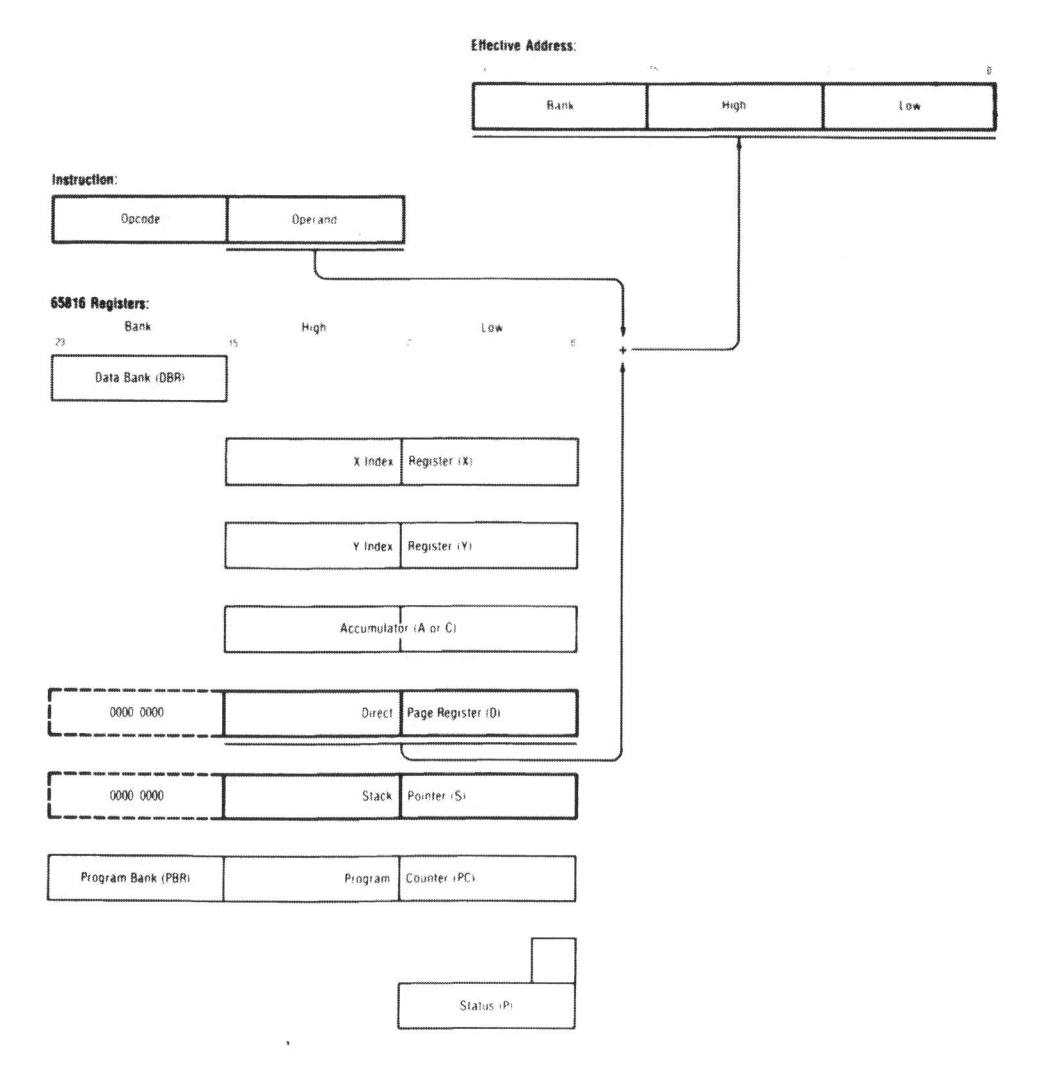

Instructions Using It:
Effective Address Locates Data
PEI
Note: 65802/65816 only.

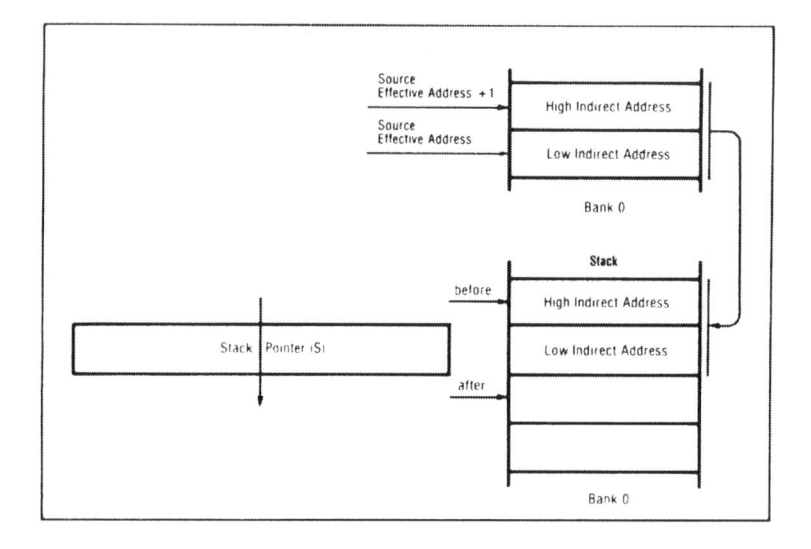

Stack (Interrupt) Addressing

Effective Address: After pushing the Program Bank (65802/816 native mode only), followed by the Program Counter and the Status Register, the Effective Address is loaded into the Program Counter and Program Bank Register, transferring control there.

Bank: Zero

High/Low: The contents of the instruction- and processor-specific interrupt vector.

Data: Source: Program Bank, Program Counter and Status Register.
  Destination Effective Address: Provided by Stack Pointer.

Sample Syntax:
  BRK

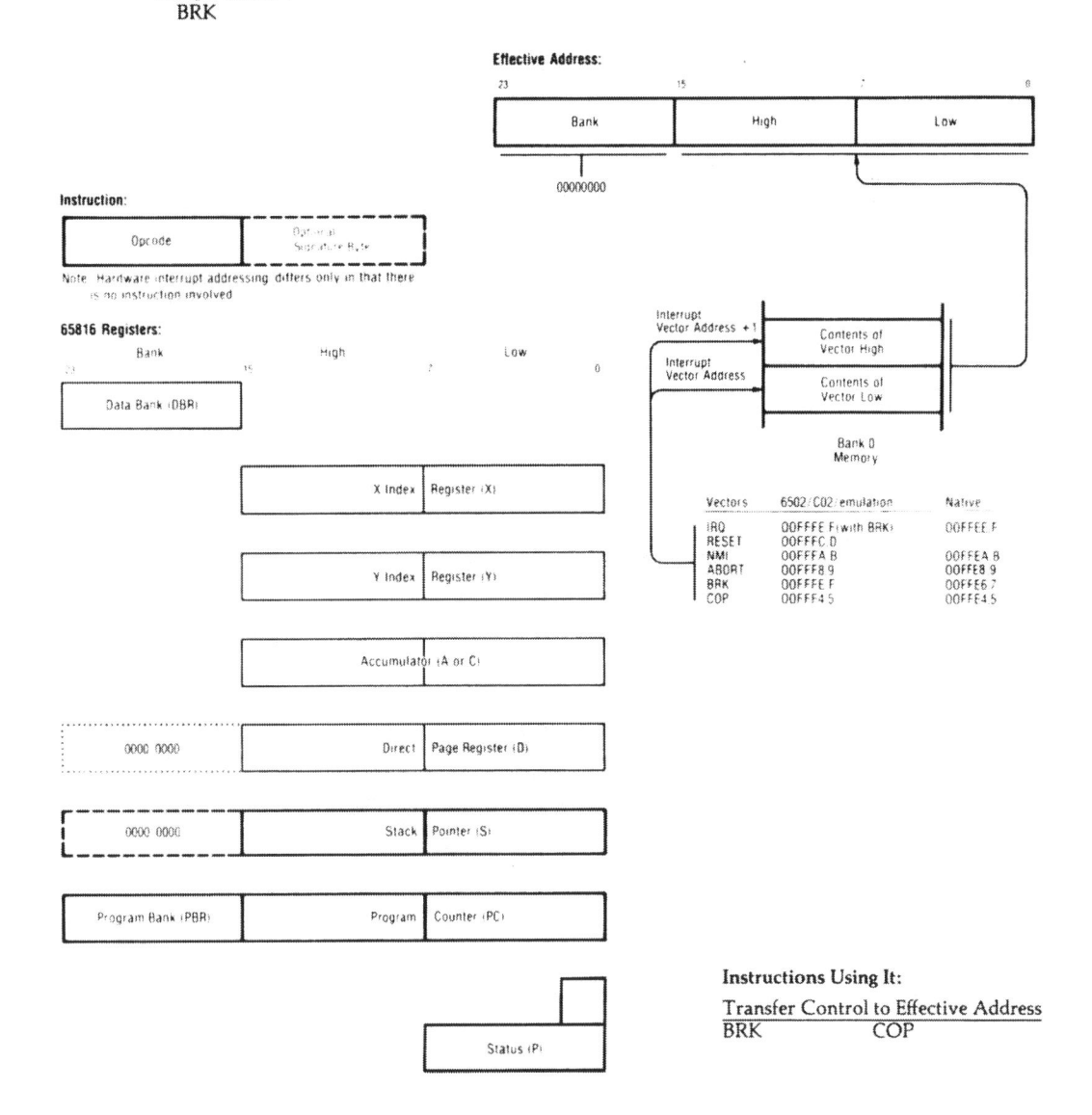

Note: Hardware interrupt addressing differs only in that there is no instruction involved.

Vectors	6502/C02/emulation	Native
IRQ	00FFFE F (with BRK)	00FFEE F
RESET	00FFFC D	
NMI	00FFFA B	00FFEA B
ABORT	00FFF8 9	00FFE8 9
BRK	00FFFE F	00FFE6 7
COP	00FFF4 5	00FFE4 5

Instructions Using It:

Transfer Control to Effective Address
BRK   COP

Stack (Interrupt) Addressing

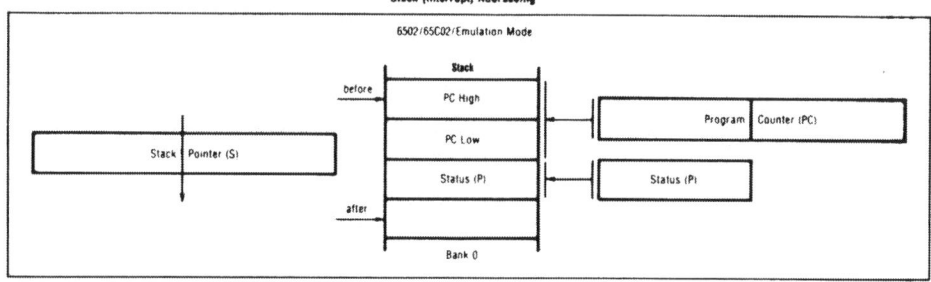

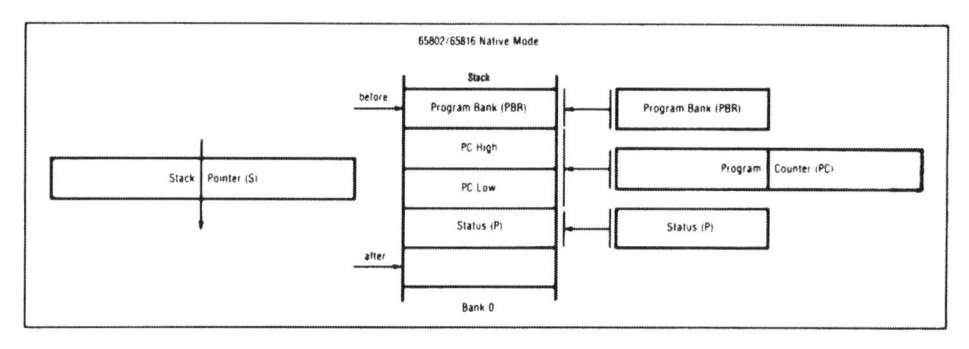

6502/65C02/Emulation Mode

Stack before: PC High, PC Low, Status (P); after pointer moves down.
Program Counter (PC) → PC High, PC Low
Status (P) → Status (P)
Bank 0

65802/65816 Native Mode

Stack before: Program Bank (PBR), PC High, PC Low, Status (P); after pointer moves down.
Program Bank (PBR) → Program Bank (PBR)
Program Counter (PC) → PC High, PC Low
Status (P) → Status (P)
Bank 0

Stack (Program Counter Relative) Addressing

Source of data to be pushed: The 16-bit sum of the 16-bit Operand plus the 16-bit Program Counter. (Note that the 16-bit Operand which is added is the object code operand; the operand used in the instruction's syntax required by most assemblers is a label which is converted to the object operand.)

Destination Effective Address: Provided by Stack Pointer.

Sample Syntax:
PER *label*

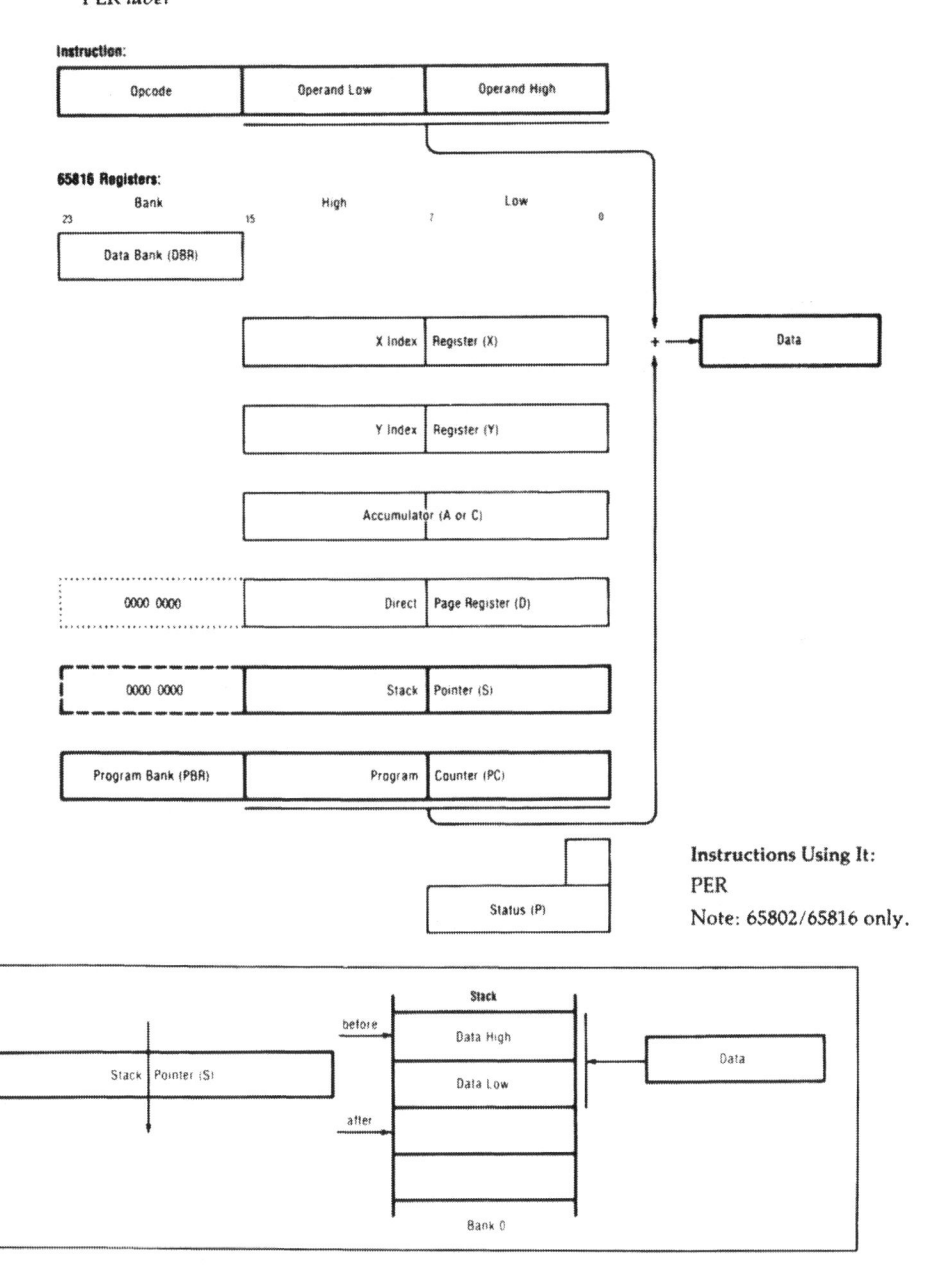

Instructions Using It:
PER
Note: 65802/65816 only.

Stack (Pull) Addressing

Source Effective Address: Provided by Stack Pointer.

Destination of data to be pulled: Register specified by the opcode.

The Stack Pointer (S) is incremented, specifying the location from which an 8-bit register—or the low byte of a 16-bit register—will be loaded. If the register is 16 bits, the Stack Pointer will be incremented a second time, and the register's high byte will be loaded from this second new Stack Pointer location.

Sample Syntax:
PLA

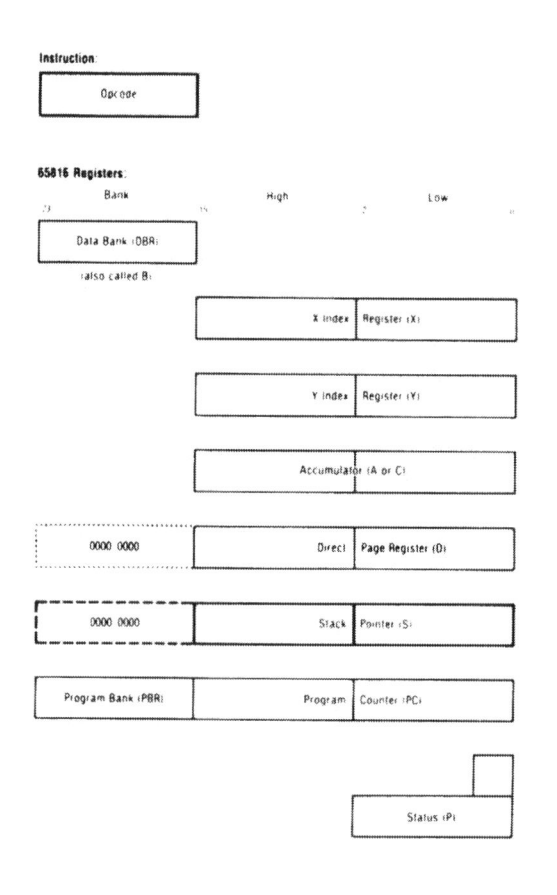

Instructions Using It:

Effective Address Locates Data

PLA[2]	PLD[1,4]	PLX[3]
PLB[1,5]	PLP[5]	PLY[3]

1 65802/65816 only.
2 8 bit register, except on 65802/816 may be either 8 or 16 bits, dependent on flag m.
3 8 bit register, except on 65802/816 may be either 8 or 16 bits, dependent on flag x.
4 16 bits always.
5 8 bits always.

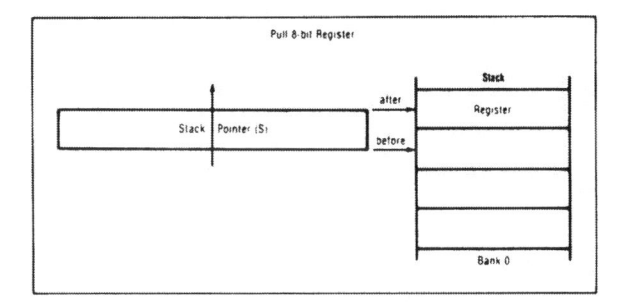

17 The Addressing Modes

Pull 8-bit Register

Stack Pointer (S)

after / before → Stack: Register

Bank 0

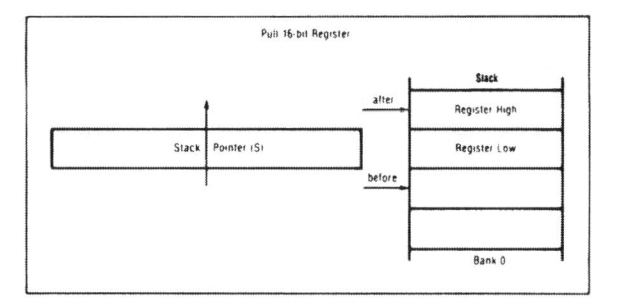

Pull 16-bit Register

Stack Pointer (S)

after / before → Stack: Register High / Register Low

Bank 0

Stack (Push) Addressing

Source of data to be pushed: Register specified by the opcode.

Destination Effective Address: Provided by Stack Pointer.

The Stack Pointer (S) specifies the location to which an 8-bit register—or the high byte of a 16-bit register—will be stored. The low byte of a 16-bit register will be stored to the Stack Pointer location minus one. After storage of an 8-bit register, S is decremented by 1; after a 16-bit register, S is decremented by 2.

Sample Syntax:
PHA

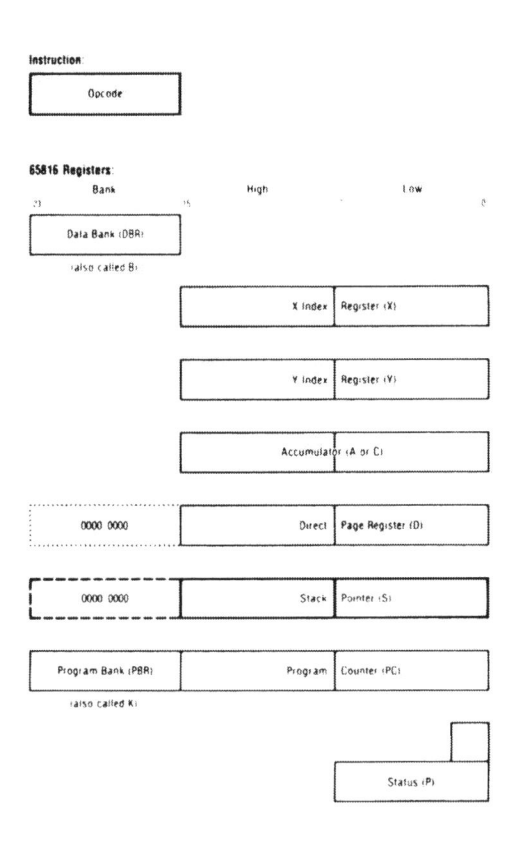

Instructions Using It:

Effective Address Locates Data

PHA[2]	PHD[1,4]	PHP[5]	PHY[3]
PHB[1,5]	PHK[1,5]	PHX[3]	

1 65802/65816 only.
2 8 bit register, except on 65802/816, may be either 8 or 16 bits, dependent on flag m.
3 8 bit register, except on 65802/816, may be either 8 or 16 bits, dependent on flag x.
4 16 bits always.
5 8 bits always.

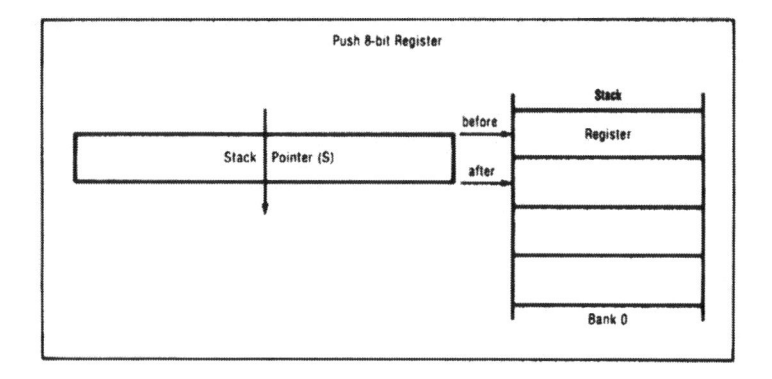

17 The Addressing Modes

Push 8-bit Register

Stack Pointer (S) → before → Stack: Register
after
Bank 0

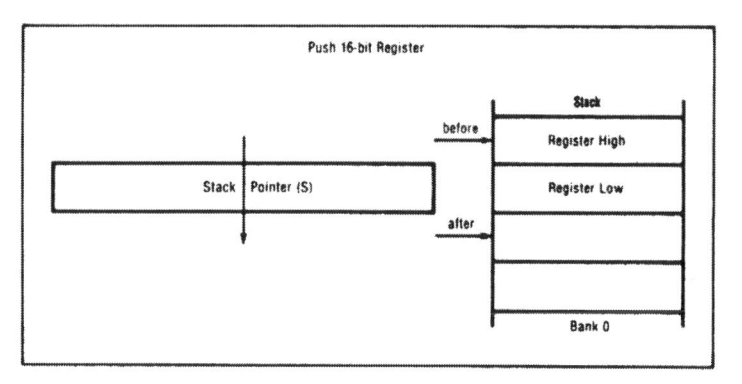

Push 16-bit Register

Stack Pointer (S) → before → Stack: Register High / Register Low
after
Bank 0

Stack (RTI) Addressing

Source Effective Address: Provided by Stack Pointer.

Destination of values to be pulled: First the Status Register, then the Program Counter is pulled, followed (65802/65816 native mode only) by the Program Bank.

Control is transferred to the new Program Counter (and Program Bank) value(s).

Sample Syntax:
RTI

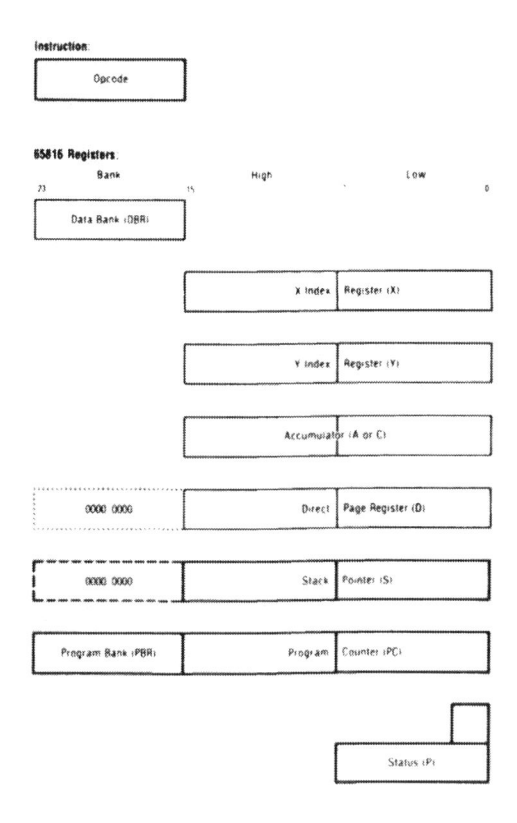

Instructions Using It:
RTI

17 The Addressing Modes

Stack (RTI) Addressing

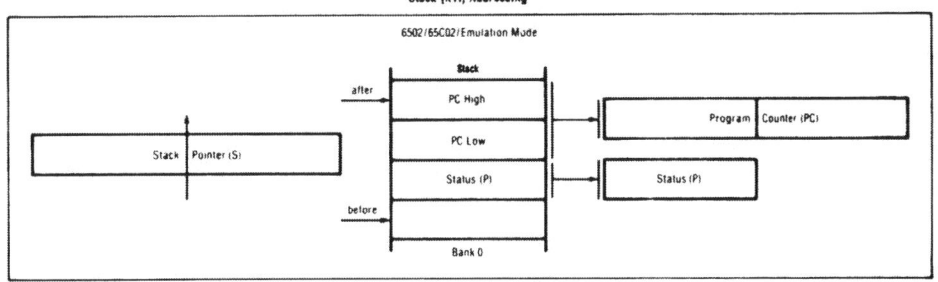

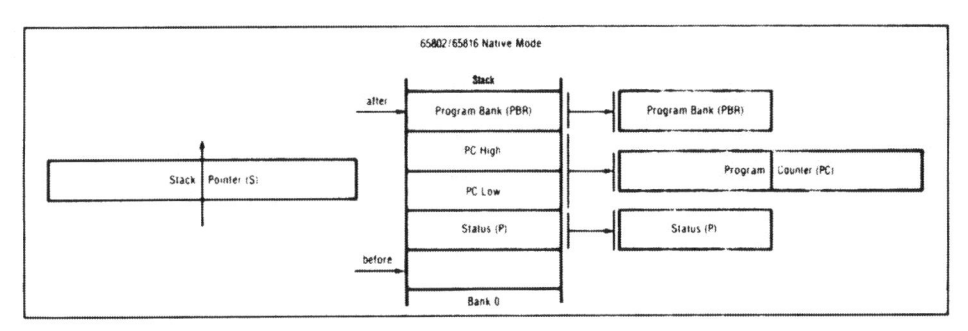

6502/65C02/Emulation Mode

65802/65816 Native Mode

Stack (RTL) Addressing

Source Effective Address: Provided by Stack Pointer.

Destination of values to be pulled: First the Program Counter is pulled and incremented by one. Then the Program Bank is pulled.

Control is transferred to the new Program Counter and Program Bank values.

Sample Syntax:
RTL

Instruction:

| Opcode |

65816 Registers:

Data Bank (DBR)

X Index Register (X)

Y Index Register (Y)

Accumulator (A or C)

Direct Page Register (D)

Stack Pointer (S)

Program Bank (PBR) | Program Counter (PC)

Status (P)

Instructions Using It:

RTL

Note: 65802/65816 only;
65802: Program Bank value is not propagated to be bus (bank accessed is always bank 0).

17 The Addressing Modes

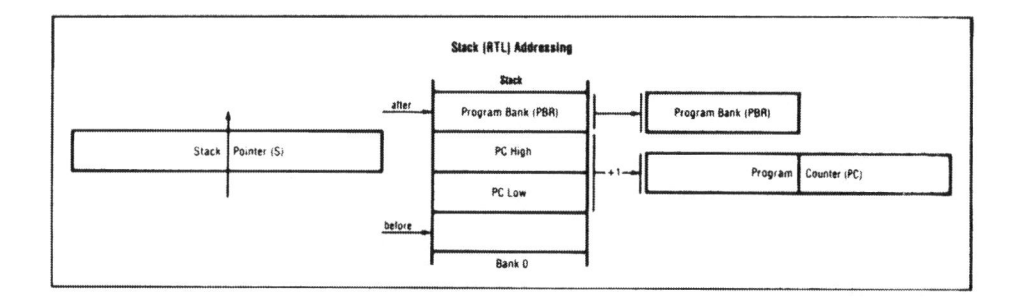

Stack (RTL) Addressing

	Stack	
after →	Program Bank (PBR)	→ Program Bank (PBR)
Stack Pointer (S)	PC High	+1 → Program Counter (PC)
	PC Low	
before →		
	Bank 0	

Stack (RTS) Addressing

Source Effective Address: Provided by Stack Pointer.

Destination of values to be pulled: The Program Counter is pulled and incremented by one. The Program Bank remains unchanged.

Control is transferred to the new Program Counter value.

Sample Syntax:
  RTS

Instruction:
[Opcode]

65816 Registers:

Instructions Using It:
  RTS

17 The Addressing Modes

Stack (RTS) Addressing

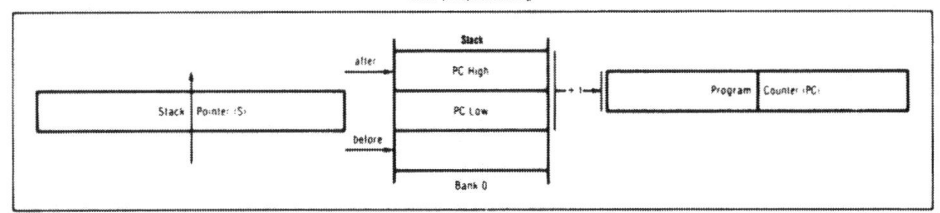

Stack Relative Addressing

Effective Address:

Bank: Zero.

High/Low: The 16-bit sum of the 8-bit Operand and the 16-bit Stack Pointer.

Sample Syntax:
 LDA sr,S

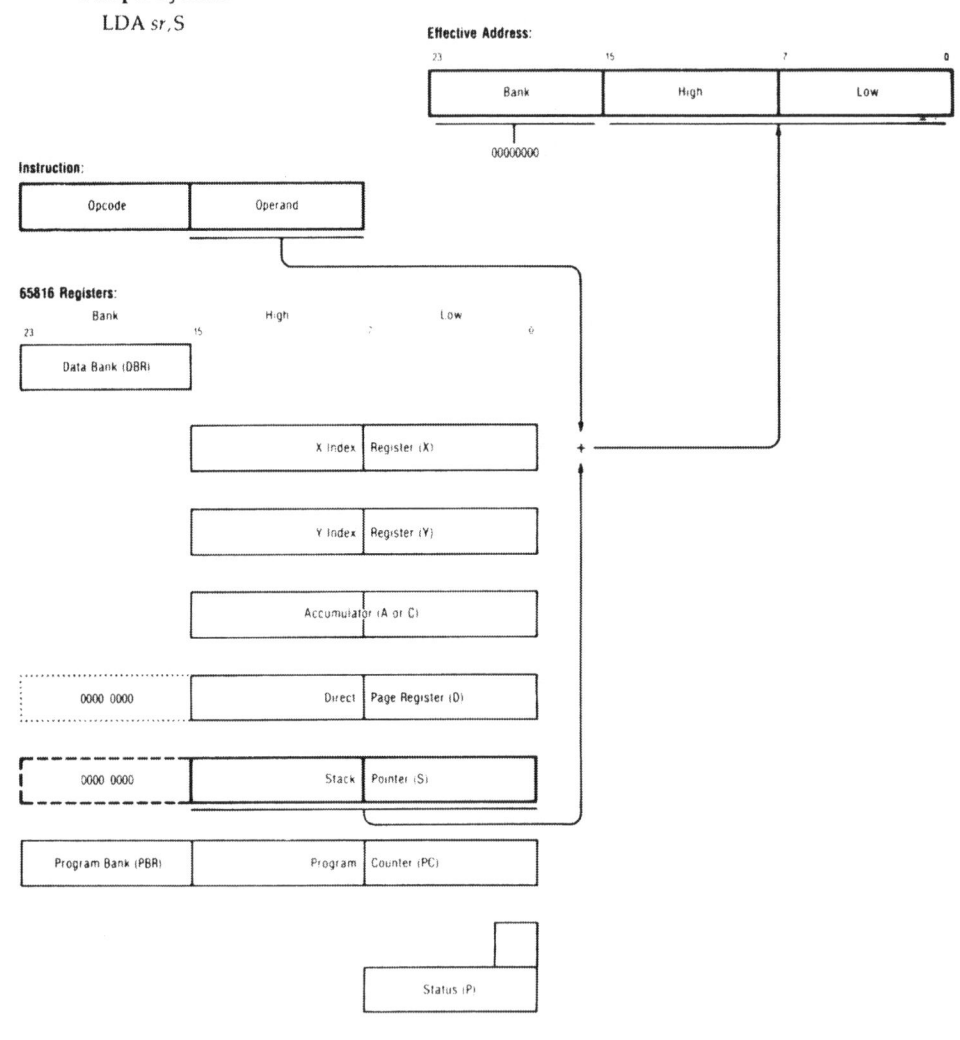

Instructions Using It:

Effective Address Locates Data

ADC	CMP	LDA	SBC
AND	EOR	ORA	STA

Note: All are 65802/65816 only.

Stack Relative Indirected Indexed, Y Addressing

Effective Address: The Data Bank Register is concatenated to the Indirect Address; the 24-bit result is added to Y (16 bits if 65802/65816 native mode, x = 0; else 8 bits).

Indirect Address: Located at the 16-bit sum of the 8-bit Operand and the 16-bit Stack Pointer.

Sample Syntax:
 LDA (sr,S), Y

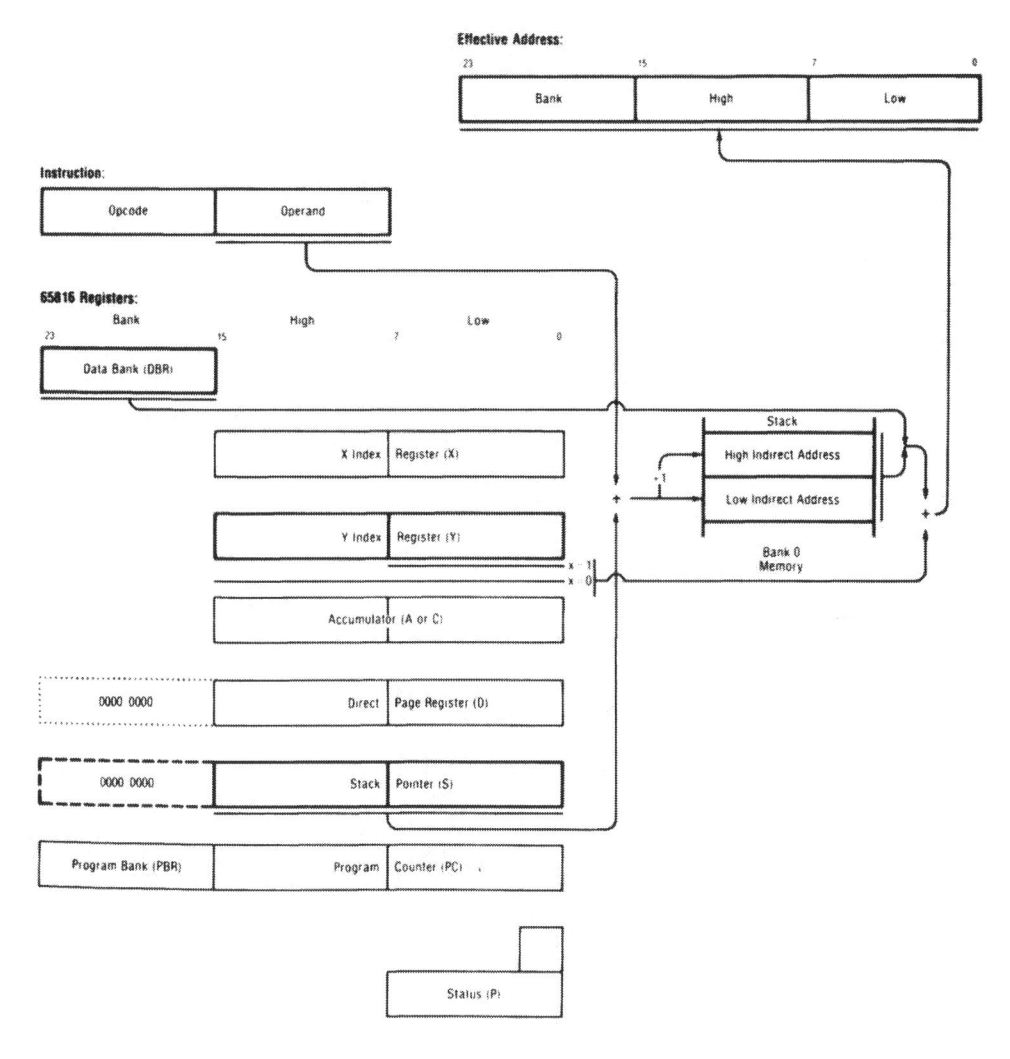

Instructions Using It:

Effective Address Locates Data
| ADC | CMP | LDA | SBC |
| AND | EOR | ORA | STA |

Note: All are 65802/65816 only;
65802: Data bank value is not propagated to the bus (bank accessed is always bank 0).

18 The Instruction Sets

This chapter devotes a page to each of the 94 different 65816 operations. Each operation may have more than one addressing mode available to it; these are detailed for each instruction. The symbols in Table 18.1 are used to express the different kinds of values that instruction operands may have. The effect of each operation on the status flags varies. The symbols in Table 18.2 are used to indicate the flags that are affected by a given operation.

Table 18.1. Operand Symbols.

addr	two-byte address
addr/const	two-byte value: either an address or a constant
const	one- or two-byte constant
destbk	64K bank to which string will be moved
dp	one-byte direct page offset (6502/65C02: zero page)
label	label of code in same 64K bank as instruction
long	three-byte address (includes bank byte)
nearlabel	label of code close enough to instruction to be reachable by a one-byte signed offset
sr	one-byte stack relative offset
srcebk	64K bank from which string will be moved

Table 18.2. 65x Flags.

Flags:

bits:	7 6 5 4 3 2 1 0
6502/65C02/6502 emulation:	n v - b d i z c
65802/65816 native:	n v m x d i z c

n — negative result
v — overflow
m — 8-bit memory/accumulator
x — 8-bit index registers
b — BRK caused interrupt
d — decimal mode
i — IRQ interrupt disable
z — zero result
c — carry

Add With Carry   ADC

Add the data located at the effective address specified by the operand to the contents of the accumulator; add one to the result if the carry flag is set, and store the final result in the accumulator.

The 65x processors have no add instruction which does not involve the carry. To avoid adding the carry flag to the result, you must either be sure that it is already clear, or you must explicitly clear it (using **CLC**) prior to executing the **ADC** instruction.

In a multi-precision (multi-word) addition, the carry should be cleared before the low-order words are added; the addition of the low word will generate a new carry flag value based on that addition. This new value in the carry flag is added into the next (middle-order or high-order) addition; each intermediate result will correctly reflect the carry from the previous addition.

d flag clear: Binary addition is performed.

d flag set: Binary coded decimal (BCD) addition is performed.

8-bit accumulator (all processors): Data added from memory is eight-bit.

16-bit accumulator (65802/65816 only, m = 0): Data added from memory is sixteen-bit: the low-order eight bits are located at the effective address; the high-order eight bits are located at the effective address plus one.

Flags Affected: n v - - - - z c

    n Set if most-significant bit of result is set; else cleared.
    v Set if signed overflow; cleared if valid signed result.
    z Set if result is zero; else cleared.
    c Set if unsigned overflow; cleared if valid unsigned result.

Codes:

Addressing Mode++	Syntax	Opcode (hex)	Available on: 6502	65C02	65802/816	# of Bytes	# of Cycles
Immediate	ADC #const	69	x	x	x	2*	$2^{1,4}$
Absolute	ADC addr	6D	x	x	x	3	$4^{1,4}$
Absolute Long	ADC long	6F			x	4	$5^{1,4}$
Direct Page (DP)	ADC dp	65	x	x	x	2	$3^{1,2,4}$
DP Indirect	ADC (dp)	72		x	x	2	$5^{1,2,4}$
DP Indirect Long	ADC [dp]	67			x	2	$6^{1,2,4}$
Absolute Indexed,X	ADC addr,X	7D	x	x	x	3	$4^{1,3,4}$
Absolute Long Indexed,X	ADC long,X	7F			x	4	$5^{1,4}$
Absolute Indexed,Y	ADC addr,Y	79	x	x	x	3	$4^{1,3,4}$
DP Indexed,X	ADC dp,X	75	x	x	x	2	$4^{1,2,4}$
DP Indexed Indirect,X	ADC (dp,X)	61	x	x	x	2	$6^{1,2,4}$
DP Indirect Indexed,Y	ADC (dp),Y	71	x	x	x	2	$5^{1,2,3,4}$
DP Indirect Long Indexed,Y	ADC [dp],Y	77			x	2	$6^{1,2,4}$
Stack Relative (SR)	ADC sr,S	63			x	2	$4^{1,4}$
SR Indirect Indexed,Y	ADC (sr,S),Y	73			x	2	$7^{1,4}$

++ ADC, a Primary Group Instruction, has available all of the Primary Group addressing modes and bit patterns
* Add 1 byte if m = 0 (16-bit memory/accumulator)
1 Add 1 cycle if m = 0 (16-bit memory/accumulator)
2 Add 1 cycle if low byte of Direct Page register is other than zero (DL < >0)
3 Add 1 cycle if adding index crosses a page boundary
4 Add 1 cycle if 65C02 and d = 1 (decimal mode, 65C02)

And Accumulator with Memory   AND

Bitwise logical AND the data located at the effective address specified by the operand with the contents of the accumulator. Each bit in the accumulator is ANDed with the corresponding bit in memory, with the result being stored in the respective accumulator bit.

The truth table for the logical AND operation is:

	Second Operand	
	0	1
First Operand		
0	0	0
1	0	1

Figure 18.1. AND Truth Table.

That is, a 1 or logical true results in a given bit being true only if both elements of the respective bits being ANDed are 1s, or logically true.

8-bit accumulator (all processors): Data ANDed from memory is eight-bit.

16-bit accumulator (65802/65816 only, m = 0): Data ANDed from memory is sixteen-bit: the low-order byte is located at the effective address; the high-order byte is located at the effective address plus one.

Flags Affected: n - - - - - z -
                      n Set if most significant bit of result is set; else cleared.
                      z Set if result is zero; else cleared.

Codes:

Addressing Mode++	Syntax	Opcode (hex)	6502	65C02	65802/816	# of Bytes	# of Cycles
Immediate	AND #*const*	29	x	x	x	2*	2^1
Absolute	AND *addr*	2D	x	x	x	3	4^1
Absolute Long	AND *long*	2F			x	4	5^1
Direct Page (DP)	AND *dp*	25	x	x	x	2	$3^{1,2}$
DP Indirect	AND (*dp*)	32		x	x	2	$5^{1,2}$
DP Indirect Long	AND [*dp*]	27			x	2	$6^{1,2}$
Absolute Indexed,X	AND *addr*,X	3D	x	x	x	3	$4^{1,3}$
Absolute Long Indexed,X	AND *long*,X	3F			x	4	5^1
Absolute Indexed,Y	AND *addr*,Y	39	x	x	x	3	$4^{1,3}$
DP Indexed,X	AND *dp*,X	35	x	x	x	2	$4^{1,2}$
DP Indexed Indirect,X	AND (*dp*,X)	21	x	x	x	2	$6^{1,2}$
DP Indirect Indexed,Y	AND (*dp*),Y	31	x	x	x	2	$5^{1,2,3}$
DP Indirect Long Indexed,Y	AND [*dp*],Y	37			x	2	$6^{1,2,0}$
Stack Relative (SR)	AND *sr*,S	23			x	2	4^1
SR Indirect Indexed,Y	AND (*sr*,S),Y	33			x	2	7^1

++ AND, a Primary Group Instruction, has available all of the Primary Group addressing modes and bit patterns
* Add 1 byte if m = 0 (16-bit memory/accumulator)
1 Add 1 cycle if m = 0 (16-bit memory/accumulator)
2 Add 1 cycle if low byte of Direct Page register is other than zero (DL < > 0)
3 Add 1 cycle if adding index crosses a page boundary

Shift Memory or Accumulator Left — ASL

Shift the contents of the location specified by the operand left one bit. That is, bit one takes on the value originally found in bit zero, bit two takes the value originally in bit one, and so on; the leftmost bit (bit 7 on the 6502 and 65C02 or if **m** = 1 on the 65802/65816, or bit 15 if **m** = 0) is transferred into the carry flag; the rightmost bit, bit zero, is cleared. The arithmetic result of the operation is an unsigned multiplication by two.

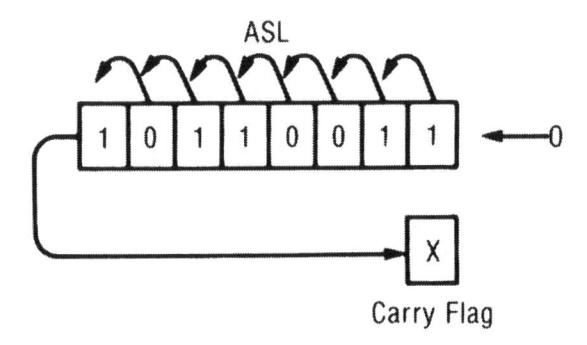

Figure 18.2. ASL.

8-bit accumulator/memory (all processors): Data shifted is eight bits.

16-bit accumulator/memory (65802/65816 only, m = 0): Data shifted is sixteen bits: if in memory, the low-order eight bits are located at the effective address; the high-order eight bits are located at the effective address plus one.

Flags Affected: n - - - - z c

- n Set if most significant bit of result is set; else cleared.
- z Set if result is zero; else cleared.
- c High bit becomes carry: set if high bit was set; cleared if high bit was zero.

Codes:

Addressing Mode	Syntax	Opcode (hex)	6502	65C02	65802/816	# of Bytes	# of Cycles
Accumulator	ASL A	0A	x	x	x	1	2
Absolute	ASL addr	0E	x	x	x	3	6[1]
Direct Page (DP)	ASL dp	06	x	x	x	2	5[1,2]
Absolute Indexed,X	ASL addr,X	1E	x	x	x	3	7[1,3]
DP Indexed,X	ASL dp,X	16	x	x	x	2	6[1,2]

1 Add 2 cycles if m = 0 (16-bit memory/accumulator)
2 Add 1 cycle if low byte of Direct Page register is other than zero (DL < >0)
3 Subtract 1 cycle if 65C02 and no page boundary crossed

BCC   Branch if Carry Clear

The carry flag in the P status register is tested. If it is clear, a branch is taken; if it is set, the instruction immediately following the two-byte BCC instruction is executed.

If the branch is taken, a one-byte signed displacement, fetched from the second byte of the instruction, is sign-extended to sixteen bits and added to the program counter. Once the branch address has been calculated, the result is loaded into the program counter, transferring control to that location.

The allowable range of the displacement is -128 to $+127$ (from the instruction immediately following the branch).

BCC may be used in several ways: to test the result of a shift into the carry; to determine if the result of a comparison is either *less than* (in which case a branch will be taken), or *greater than or equal* (which causes control to fall through the branch instruction); or to determine if further operations are needed in multi-precision arithmetic.

Because the BCC instruction causes a branch to be taken after a comparison or subtraction if the accumulator is less than the memory operand (since the carry flag will always be cleared as a result), many assemblers allow an alternate mnemonic for the BCC instruction: **BLT**, or *Branch if Less Than*.

Flags Affected: - - - - - - - -

Codes:

Addressing Mode++	Syntax	Opcode (hex)	6502	65C02	65802/816	# of Bytes	# of Cycles
Program Counter Relative	**BCC** nearlabel (or **BLT** nearlabel)	90	x	x	x	2	$2^{1,2}$

1 Add 1 cycle if branch is taken
2 Add 1 more cycle if branch taken crosses page boundary on 6502, 65C02, or 65816/65802's 6502 emulation mode (e = 1)

Branch if Carry Set   BCS

The carry flag in the P status register is tested. If it is set, a branch is taken; if it is clear, the instruction immediately following the two-byte BCS instruction is executed.

If the branch is taken, a one-byte signed displacement, fetched from the second byte of the instruction, is sign-extended to sixteen bits and added to the program counter. Once the branch address has been calculated, the result is loaded into the program counter, transferring control to that location.

The allowable range of the displacement is -128 to $+127$ (from the instruction immediately following the branch).

BCS is used in several ways: to test the result of a shift into the carry; to determine if the result of a comparison is either *greater than or equal* (which causes the branch to be taken) or *less than*; or to determine if further operations are needed in multi-precision arithmetic operations.

Because the BCS instruction causes a branch to be taken after a comparison or subtraction if the accumulator is greater than or equal to the memory operand (since the carry flag will always be set as a result), many assemblers allow an alternate mnemonic for the BCS instruction: BGE or *Branch if Greater or Equal*.

Flags Affected: - - - - - - - -

Codes:

Addressing Mode	Syntax	Opcode (hex)	6502	65C02	65802/816	# of Bytes	# of Cycles
Program Counter Relative	**BCS** *nearlabel* (or **BGE** *nearlabel*)	B0	x	x	x	2	$2^{1,2}$

1 Add 1 cycle if branch is taken
2 Add 1 more cycle if branch taken crosses page boundary on 6502, 65C02, or 65816/65802's 6502 emulation mode (e = 1)

BEQ   Branch if Equal

The zero flag in the **P** status register is tested. If it is set, meaning that the last value tested (which affected the zero flag) was zero, a branch is taken; if it is clear, meaning the value tested was non-zero, the instruction immediately following the two-byte **BEQ** instruction is executed.

If the branch is taken, a one-byte signed displacement, fetched from the second byte of the instruction, is sign-extended to sixteen bits and added to the program counter. Once the branch address has been calculated, the result is loaded into the program counter, transferring control to that location.

The allowable range of the displacement is -128 to $+127$ (from the instruction immediately following the branch).

BEQ may be used in several ways: to determine if the result of a comparison is zero (the two values compared are equal), for example, or if a value just loaded, pulled, shifted, incremented or decremented is zero; or to determine if further operations are needed in multi-precision arithmetic operations. Because testing for equality to zero does not require a previous comparison with zero, it is generally most efficient for loop counters to count downwards, exiting when zero is reached.

Flags Affected: - - - - - - - -

Codes:

Addressing Mode	Syntax	Opcode (hex)	Available on: 6502	65C02	65802/816	# of Bytes	# of Cycles
Program Counter Relative	**BEQ** *nearlabel*	F0	x	x	x	2	$2^{1,2}$

1 Add 1 cycle if branch is taken
2 Add 1 more cycle if branch taken crosses page boundary on 6502, 65C02, or 65816/65802's 6502 emulation mode (e = 1)

Test Memory Bits against Accumulator   BIT

BIT sets the P status register flags based on the result of two different operations, making it a dual-purpose instruction:

First, it sets or clears the **n** flag to reflect the value of the high bit of the data located at the effective address specified by the operand, and sets or clears the **v** flag to reflect the contents of the next-to-highest bit of the data addressed.

Second, it logically ANDs the data located at the effective address with the contents of the accumulator; it changes neither value, but sets the **z** flag if the result is zero, or clears it if the result is non-zero.

BIT is usually used immediately preceding a conditional branch instruction: to test a memory value's highest or next-to-highest bits; with a mask in the accumulator, to test any bits of the memory operand; or with a constant as the mask (using immediate addressing) or a mask in memory, to test any bits in the accumulator. All of these tests are non-destructive of the data in the accumulator or in memory. When the **BIT** instruction is used with the immediate addressing mode, the **n** and **v** flags are unaffected.

8-bit accumulator/memory (all processors): Data in memory is eight-bit; bit 7 is moved into the **n** flag; bit 6 is moved into the **v** flag.

16-bit accumulator/memory (65802/65816 only, m = 0): Data in memory is sixteen-bit: the low-order eight bits are located at the effective address; the high-order eight bits are located at the effective address plus one. Bit 15 is moved into the **n** flag; bit 14 is moved into the **v** flag.

Flags Affected: n v - - - - z - (Other than immediate addressing)
                 - - - - - - z - (Immediate addressing only)

   n Takes value of most significant bit of memory data.
   v Takes value of next-to-highest bit of memory data.
   z Set if logical AND of memory and accumulator is zero; else cleared.

Codes:

Addressing Mode	Syntax	Opcode (hex)	6502	65C02	65802/816	# of Bytes	# of Cycles
Immediate	BIT #*const*	89		x	x	2*	2^1
Absolute	BIT *addr*	2C	x	x	x	3	4^1
Direct Page (DP)	BIT *dp*	24	x	x	x	2	$3^{1,2}$
Absolute Indexed,X	BIT *addr*,X	3C		x	x	3	$4^{1,3}$
DP Indexed,X	BIT *dp*,X	34		x	x	2	$4^{1,2}$

* Add 1 byte if m = 0 (16-bit memory/accumulator)
1 Add 1 cycle if m = 0 (16-bit memory/accumulator)
2 Add 1 cycle if low byte of Direct Page register is other than zero (DL < > 0)
3 Add 1 cycle if adding index crosses a page boundary

BMI — Branch if Minus

The negative flag in the P status register is tested. If it is set, the high bit of the value which most recently affected the n flag was set, and a branch is taken. A number with its high bit set may be interpreted as a negative two's-complement number, so this instruction tests, among other things, for the sign of two's-complement numbers. If the negative flag is clear, the high bit of the value which most recently affected the flag was clear, or, in the two's-complement system, was a positive number, and the instruction immediately following the two-byte BMI instruction is executed.

If the branch is taken, a one-byte signed displacement, fetched from the second byte of the instruction, is sign-extended to sixteen bits and added to the program counter. Once the branch address has been calculated, the result is loaded into the program counter, transferring control to that location.

The allowable range of the displacement is -128 to $+127$ (from the instruction immediately following the branch).

BMI is primarily used to either determine, in two's-complement arithmetic, if a value is negative or, in logic situations, if the high bit of the value is set. It can also be used when looping down through zero (the loop counter must have a positive initial value) to determine if zero has been passed and to effect an exit from the loop.

Flags Affected: - - - - - - - -

Codes:

Addressing Mode	Syntax	Opcode (hex)	Available on: 6502	65C02	65802/816	# of Bytes	# of Cycles
Program Counter Relative	BMI nearlabel	30	x	x	x	2	$2^{1,2}$

1 Add 1 cycle if branch is taken
2 Add 1 more cycle if branch taken crosses page boundary on 6502, 65C02, or 65816/65802's 6502 emulation mode (e = 1)

Branch if Not Equal   BNE

The zero flag in the P status register is tested. If it is clear (meaning the value just tested is non-zero), a branch is taken; if it is set (meaning the value tested is zero), the instruction immediately following the two-byte **BNE** instruction is executed.

If the branch is taken, a one-byte signed displacement, fetched from the second byte of the instruction, is sign-extended to sixteen bits and added to the program counter. Once the branch address has been calculated, the result is loaded into the program counter, transferring control to that location.

The allowable range of the displacement is −128 to +127 (from the instruction immediately following the branch).

BNE may be used in several ways: to determine if the result of a comparison is non-zero (the two values compared are not equal), for example, or if the value just loaded or pulled from the stack is non-zero, or to determine if further operations are needed in multi-precision arithmetic operations.

Flags Affected: - - - - - - - -

Codes:

Addressing Mode	Syntax	Opcode (hex)	6502	65C02	65802/816	# of Bytes	# of Cycles
Program Counter Relative	**BNE** *nearlabel*	D0	x	x	x	2	$2^{1,2}$

1 Add 1 cycle if branch is taken

2 Add 1 more cycle if branch taken crosses page boundary on 6502, 65C02, or 65816/65802's 6502 emulation mode (e = 1)

BPL   Branch if Plus

The negative flag in the P status register is tested. If it is clear—meaning that the last value which affected the zero flag had its high bit clear—a branch is taken. In the two's-complement system, values with their high bit clear are interpreted as positive numbers. If the flag is set, meaning the high bit of the last value was set, the branch is not taken; it is a two's-complement negative number, and the instruction immediately following the two-byte **BPL** instruction is executed.

If the branch is taken, a one-byte signed displacement, fetched from the second byte of the instruction, is sign-extended to sixteen bits and added to the program counter. Once the branch address has been calculated, the result is loaded into the program counter, transferring control to that location.

The allowable range of the displacement is -128 to $+127$ (from the instruction immediately following the branch).

BPL is used primarily to determine, in two's-complement arithmetic, if a value is positive or not or, in logic situations, if the high bit of the value is clear.

Flags Affected: - - - - - - - -

Codes:

Addressing Mode	Syntax	Opcode (hex)	6502	65C02	65802/816	# of Bytes	# of Cycles
Program Counter Relative	**BPL** *nearlabel*	10	x	x	x	2	$2^{1,2}$

1 Add 1 cycle if branch is taken
2 Add 1 more cycle if branch taken crosses page boundary on 6502, 65C02, or 65816/65802's 6502 emulation mode (e = 1)

Branch Always   BRA

A branch is always taken, and no testing is done: in effect, an unconditional JMP is executed, but since signed displacements are used, the instruction is only two bytes, rather than the three bytes of a JMP. Additionally, using displacements from the program counter makes the **BRA** instruction relocatable. Unlike a JMP instruction, the **BRA** is limited to targets that lie within the range of the one-byte signed displacement of the conditional branches: -128 to $+127$ bytes from the first byte following the **BRA** instruction.

To branch, a one-byte signed displacement, fetched from the second byte of the instruction, is sign-extended to sixteen bits and added to the program counter. Once the branch address has been calculated, the result is loaded into the program counter, transferring control to that location.

Flags Affected: – – – – – – – –

Codes:

Addressing Mode	Syntax	Opcode (hex)	6502	65C02	65802/816	# of Bytes	# of Cycles
Program Counter Relative	**BRA** *nearlabel*	80		x	x	2	3[1]

1 Add 1 cycle if branch crosses page boundary on 65C02 or in 65816/65802's 6502 emulation mode (e = 1)

BRK   Software Break

Force a software interrupt. **BRK** is unaffected by the **i** interrupt disable flag.

Although **BRK** is a one-byte instruction, the program counter (which is pushed onto the stack by the instruction) is incremented by two; this lets you follow the break instruction with a one-byte signature byte indicating which break caused the interrupt. Even if a signature byte is not needed, either the byte following the **BRK** instruction must be padded with some value or the break-handling routine must decrement the return address on the stack to let an **RTI** (return from interrupt) instruction execute correctly.

6502, 65C02, and Emulation Mode (e = 1): The program counter is incremented by two, then pushed onto the stack; the status register, with the **b** break flag set, is pushed onto the stack; the interrupt disable flag is set; and the program counter is loaded from the interrupt vector at $FFFE-FFFF. It is up to the interrupt handling routine at this address to check the **b** flag in the stacked status register to determine if the interrupt was caused by a software interrupt (**BRK**) or by a hardware **IRQ**, which shares the **BRK** vector but pushes the status register onto the stack with the **b** break flag clear. For example,

```
0000 68          PLA                 copy status from
0001 48          PHA                   top of stack
0002 2910        AND    #$10         check BRK bit
0004 D007        BNE    ISBRK        branch if set
```

Fragment 18.1.

65802/65816 Native Mode (e = 0): The program counter bank register is pushed onto the stack; the program counter is incremented by two and pushed onto the stack; the status register is pushed onto the stack; the interrupt disable flag is set; the program bank register is cleared to zero; and the program counter is loaded from the break vector at $00FFE6-00FFE7.

6502: The **d** decimal flag is not modified after a break is executed.

65C02 and 65816/65802: The **d** decimal flag is reset to 0 after a break is executed.

18   The Instruction Sets

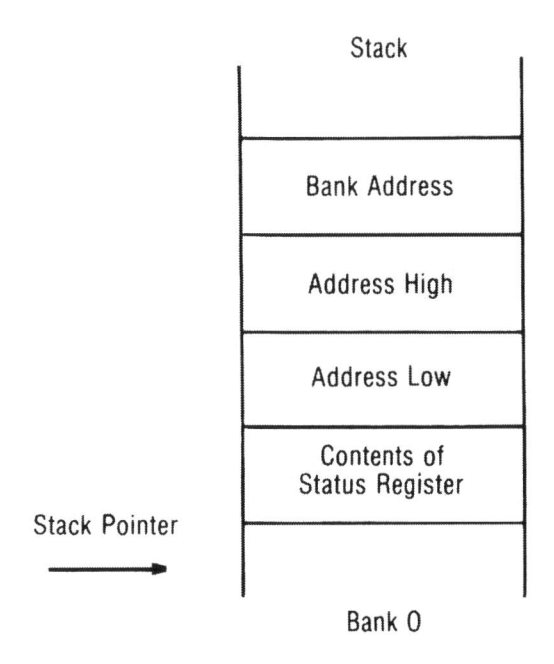

```
                    Stack
                |          |
                |          |
                |----------|
                |          |
                | Bank Address |
                |----------|
                | Address High |
                |----------|
                | Address Low |
                |----------|
                | Contents of |
                | Status Register |
Stack Pointer   |----------|
    ──▶         |          |
                |          |
                    Bank 0
```

Figure 18.3. 65802/65816 Stack After BRK.

Flags Affected: - - - b - i - -   (6502)
                 - - - b d i - -   (65C02, 65802/65816 emulation mode $e = 1$)
                 - - - - d i - -   (65802/65816 native mode $e = 0$)

  b b in the P register value pushed onto the stack is set.
  d d is reset to 0, for binary arithmetic.
  i The interrupt disable flag is set, disabling hardware IRQ interrupts.

Codes:

Addressing Mode	Syntax	Opcode (hex)	Available on: 6502	65C02	65802/816	# of Bytes	# of Cycles
Stack/Interrupt	BRK	00	x	x	x	2*	7[1]

* BRK is 1 byte, but program counter value pushed onto stack is incremented by 2 allowing for optional signature byte
1 Add 1 cycle for 65802/65816 native mode ($e = 0$)

BRL Branch Always Long

A branch is always taken, similar to the **BRA** instruction. However, **BRL** is a three-byte instruction; the two bytes immediately following the opcode form a *sixteen-bit* signed displacement from the program counter. Once the branch address has been calculated, the result is loaded into the program counter, transferring control to that location.

The allowable range of the displacement is anywhere within the current 64K program bank.

The long branch provides an unconditional transfer of control similar to the **JMP** instruction, with one major advantage: the branch instruction is relocatable while jump instructions are not. However, the (non-relocatable) jump absolute instruction executes one cycle faster.

Flags Affected: - - - - - - - -

Codes:

Addressing Mode	Syntax	Opcode (hex)	Available on: 6502	65C02	65802/816	# of Bytes	# of Cycles
Program Counter Relative Long	BRL *label*	82			x	3	4

Branch if Overflow Clear   BVC

The overflow flag in the P status register is tested. If it is clear, a branch is taken; if it is set, the instruction immediately following the two-byte **BVC** instruction is executed.

If the branch is taken, a one-byte signed displacement, fetched from the second byte of the instruction, is sign-extended to sixteen bits and added to the program counter. Once the branch address has been calculated, the result is loaded into the program counter, transferring control to that location.

The allowable range of the displacement is -128 to $+127$ (from the instruction immediately following the branch).

The overflow flag is altered by only four instructions on the 6502 and 65C02—addition, subtraction, the **CLV** clear-the-flag instruction, and the **BIT** bit-testing instruction. In addition, all the flags are restored from the stack by the **PLP** and **RTI** instructions. On the 65802/65816, however, the **SEP** and **REP** instructions can also modify the v flag.

BVC is used almost exclusively to check that a two's-complement arithmetic calculation has not overflowed, much as the carry is used to determine if an unsigned arithmetic calculation has overflowed. (Note, however, that the compare instructions do not affect the overflow flag.) You can also use **BVC** to test the second-highest bit in a value by using it after the **BIT** instruction, which moves the second-highest bit of the tested value into the v flag.

The overflow flag can also be set by the Set Overflow hardware signal on the 6502, 65C02, and 65802; on many systems, however, there is no connection to this pin.

Flags Affected: $- - - - - - - -$

Codes:

Addressing Mode	Syntax	Opcode (hex)	Available on: 6502	65C02	65802/816	# of Bytes	# of Cycles
Program Counter Relative	**BVC** *nearlabel*	50	x	x	x	2	$2^{1,2}$

1 Add 1 cycle if branch is taken
2 Add 1 more cycle if branch taken crosses page boundary on 6502, 65C02, or 65816/65802's 6502 emulation mode (e = 1)

BVS   Branch if Overflow Set

The overflow flag in the P status register is tested. If it is set, a branch is taken; if it is clear, the instruction immediately following the two-byte **BVS** instruction is executed.

If the branch is taken, a one-byte signed displacement, fetched from the second byte of the instruction, is sign-extended to sixteen bits and added to the program counter. Once the branch address has been calculated, the result is loaded into the program counter, transferring control to that location.

The allowable range of the displacement is -128 to $+127$ (from the instruction immediately following the branch).

The overflow flag is altered by only four instructions on the 6502 and 65C02—addition, subtraction, the **CLV** clear-the-flag instruction, and the **BIT** bit-testing instruction. In addition, all the flags are restored from the stack by the **PLP** and **RTI** instructions. On the 65802/65816, the **SEP** and **REP** instructions can also modify the v flag.

BVS is used almost exclusively to determine if a two's-complement arithmetic calculation has overflowed, much as the carry is used to determine if an unsigned arithmetic calculation has overflowed. (Note, however, that the compare instructions do not affect the overflow flag.) You can also use **BVS** to test the second-highest bit in a value by using it after the **BIT** instruction, which moves the second-highest bit of the tested value into the v flag.

The overflow flag can also be set by the Set Overflow hardware signal on the 6502, 65C02, and 65802; on many systems, however, there is no hardware connection to this signal.

Flags Affected: - - - - - - - -

Codes:

Addressing Mode	Syntax	Opcode (hex)	6502	65C02	65802/816	# of Bytes	# of Cycles
Program Counter Relative	**BVS** *nearlabel*	70	x	x	x	2	$2^{1,2}$

1 Add 1 cycle if branch is taken
2 Add 1 more cycle if branch taken crosses page boundary on 6502, 65C02, or 65816/65802's 6502 emulation mode (e = 1)

Clear Carry Flag   CLC

Clear the carry flag in the status register.

CLC is used prior to addition (using the 65x's **ADC** instruction) to keep the carry flag from affecting the result; prior to a **BCC** (branch on carry clear) instruction on the 6502 to force a branch-always; and prior to an **XCE** (exchange carry flag with emulation bit) instruction to put the 65802 or 65816 into native mode.

Flags Affected: – – – – – – – c
    c carry flag cleared always.

Codes:

Addressing Mode	Syntax	Opcode (hex)	6502	65C02	65802/816	# of Bytes	# of Cycles
Implied	CLC	18	x	x	x	1	2

CLD   Clear Decimal Mode Flag

Clear the decimal mode flag in the status register.

CLD is used to shift 65x processors back into binary mode from decimal mode, so that the **ADC** and **SBC** instructions will correctly operate on binary rather than BCD data.

Flags Affected: - - - d - - -

                    d decimal mode flag cleared always.

Codes:

Addressing Mode	Syntax	Opcode (hex)	Available on: 6502	65C02	65802/816	# of Bytes	# of Cycles
Implied	CLD	D8	x	x	x	1	2

Clear Interrupt Disable Flag   CLI

Clear the interrupt disable flag in the status register.

CLI is used to re-enable hardware interrupt (IRQ) processing. (When the i bit is set, hardware interrupts are ignored.) The processor itself sets the i flag when it begins servicing an interrupt, so interrupt handling routines must re-enable interrupts with CLI if the interrupt-service routine is designed to service interrupts that occur while a previous interrupt is still being handled; otherwise, the RTI instruction will restore a clear i flag from the stack, and CLI is not necessary. CLI is also used to re-enable interrupts if they have been disabled during the execution of time-critical or other code which cannot be interrupted.

Flags Affected: - - - - - i - -
                         i   interrupt disable flag cleared always.

Codes:

Addressing Mode	Syntax	Opcode (hex)	6502	65C02	65802/816	# of Bytes	# of Cycles
Implied	CLI	58	x	x	x	1	2

CLV — Clear Overflow Flag

Clear the overflow flag in the status register.

CLV is sometimes used prior to a **BVC** (branch on overflow clear) to force a branch-always on the 6502. Unlike the other clear flag instructions, there is no complementary "set flag" instruction to set the overflow flag, although the overflow flag can be set by hardware via the Set Overflow input pin on the processor. This signal, however, is often unconnected. The 65802/65816 **REP** instruction can, of course, clear the overflow flag; on the 6502 and 65C02, a **BIT** instruction with a mask in memory that has bit 6 set can be used to set the overflow flag.

Flags Affected: – v – – – – – –

    v overflow flag cleared always.

Codes:

Addressing Mode	Syntax	Opcode (hex)	6502	65C02	65802/816	# of Bytes	# of Cycles
Implied	CLV	B8	x	x	x	1	2

Compare Accumulator with Memory   CMP

Subtract the data located at the effective address specified by the operand from the contents of the accumulator, setting the carry, zero, and negative flags based on the result, but without altering the contents of either the memory location or the accumulator. That is, the result is not saved. The comparison is of unsigned binary values only.

The **CMP** instruction differs from the **SBC** instruction in several ways. First, the result is not saved. Second, the value in the carry prior to the operation is irrelevant to the operation; that is, the carry does not have to be set prior to a compare as it is with 65x subtractions. Third, the compare instruction does not set the overflow flag, so it cannot be used for signed comparisons. Although decimal mode does not affect the **CMP** instruction, decimal comparisons are effective, since the equivalent binary values maintain the same magnitude relationships as the decimal values have, for example, $99 > $04 just as 99 > 4.

The primary use for the compare instruction is to set the flags so that a conditional branch can then be executed.

8-bit accumulator (all processors): Data compared is eight-bit.

16-bit accumulator (65802/65816 only, m = 0): Data compared is sixteen-bit: the low-order eight bits of the data in memory are located at the effective address; the high-order eight bits are located at the effective address plus one.

Flags Affected: n - - - - - z c
                       n Set if most significant bit of result is set; else cleared.
                       z Set if result is zero; else cleared.
                       c Set if no borrow required (accumulator value higher or same); cleared if borrow required (accumulator value lower).

Codes:

Addressing Mode++	Syntax	Opcode (hex)	6502	65C02	65802/816	# of Bytes	# of Cycles
Immediate	CMP #const	C9	x	x	x	2*	2^1
Absolute	CMP addr	CD	x	x	x	3	4^1
Absolute Long	CMP long	CF			x	4	5^1
Direct Page (also DP)	CMP dp	C5	x	x	x	2	$3^{1,2}$
DP Indirect	CMP (dp)	D2		x	x	2	$5^{1,2}$
DP Indirect Long	CMP [dp]	C7			x	2	$6^{1,2}$
Absolute Indexed, X	CMP addr, X	DD	x	x	x	3	$4^{1,3}$
Absolute Long Indexed, X	CMP long, X	DF			x	4	5^1
Absolute Indexed, Y	CMP addr, Y	D9	x	x	x	3	$4^{1,3}$
DP Indexed, X	CMP dp, X	D5	x	x	x	2	$4^{1,2}$
DP Indexed Indirect, X	CMP (dp, X)	C1	x	x	x	2	$6^{1,2}$
DP Indirect Indexed, Y	CMP (dp), Y	D1	x	x	x	2	$5^{1,2,3}$
DP Indirect Long Indexed, Y	CMP [dp], Y	D7			x	2	$6^{1,2}$
Stack Relative (also SR)	CMP sr, S	C3			x	2	4^1
SR Indirect Indexed, Y	CMP (sr, S), Y	D3			x	2	7^1

++ CMP, a Primary Group Instruction, has available all of the Primary Group addressing modes and bit patterns
* Add 1 byte if m = 0 (16-bit memory/accumulator)
1 Add 1 cycle if m = 0 (16-bit memory/accumulator)
2 Add 1 cycle if low byte of Direct Page register is other than zero (DL < >0)
3 Add 1 cycle if adding index crosses a page boundary

Co-Processor Enable   COP

Execution of **COP** causes a software interrupt, similarly to **BRK**, but through the separate **COP** vector. Alternatively, **COP** may be trapped by a co-processor, such as a floating point or graphics processor, to call a co-processor function. **COP** is unaffected by the **i** interrupt disable flag.

COP is much like **BRK**, with the program counter value pushed on the stack being incremented by two; this lets you follow the co-processor instruction with a signature byte to indicate to the co-processor or co-processor handling routine which operation to execute. Unlike the **BRK** instruction, 65816 assemblers require you to follow the **COP** instruction with such a signature byte. Signature bytes in the range $80 - $FF are reserved by the Western Design Center for implementation of co-processor control; signatures in the range $00 - $7F are available for use with software-implemented **COP** handlers.

6502 Emulation Mode (65802/65816, e = 1): The program counter is incremented by two and pushed onto the stack; the status register is pushed onto the stack; the interrupt disable flag is set; and the program counter is loaded from the emulation mode co-processor vector at $FFF4-FFF5. The **d** decimal flag is cleared after a **COP** is executed.

65802/65816 Native Mode (e = 0): The program counter bank register is pushed onto the stack; the program counter is incremented by two and pushed onto the stack; the status register is pushed onto the stack; the interrupt disable flag is set; the program bank register is cleared to zero; and the program counter is loaded from the native mode co-processor vector at $00FFE4-00FFE5. The **d** decimal flag is reset to 0 after a **COP** is executed.

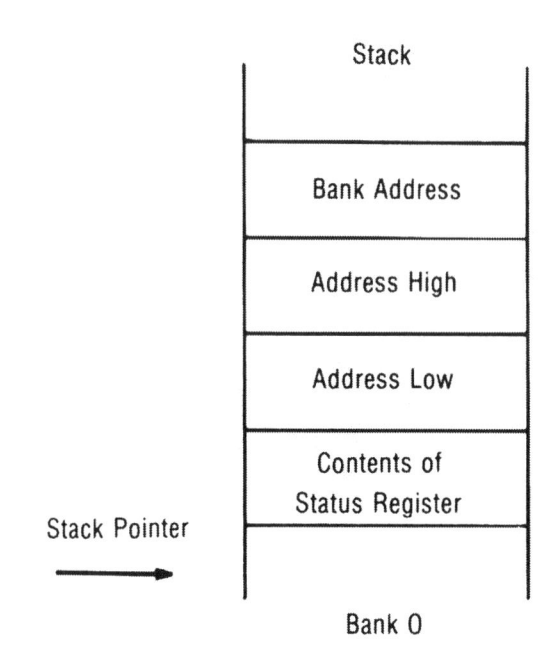

Figure 18.4. Stack after COP.

Flags Affected: − − − − d i − −
    d d is reset to 0.
    i The interrupt disable flag is set, disabling hardware interrupts.

Codes:

Addressing Mode	Syntax	Opcode (hex)	Available on: 6502	65C02	65802/816	# of Bytes	# of Cycles
Stack/Interrupt	COP const	02			x	2*	7[1]

* COP is 1 byte, but program counter value pushed onto stack is incremented by 2 allowing for optional code byte
1 Add 1 cycle for 65816/65802 native mode (e = 0)

Compare Index Register X with Memory   CPX

Subtract the data located at the effective address specified by the operand from the contents of the X register, setting the carry, zero, and negative flags based on the result, but without altering the contents of either the memory location or the register. The result is not saved. The comparison is of unsigned values only (except for signed comparison for equality).

The primary use for the **CPX** instruction is to test the value of the X index register against loop boundaries, setting the flags so that a conditional branch can be executed.

8-bit index registers (all processors): Data compared is eight-bit.

16-bit index registers (65802/65816 only, x = 0): Data compared is sixteen-bit: the low-order eight bits of the data in memory are located at the effective address; the high-order eight bits are located at the effective address plus one.

Flags Affected: n - - - - - z c

  n Set if most significant bit of result is set; else cleared.
  z Set if result is zero; else cleared.
  c Set if no borrow required (X register value higher or same); cleared if borrow required (X register value lower).

Codes:

Addressing Mode	Syntax	Opcode (hex)	6502	65C02	65802/816	# of Bytes	# of Cycles
Immediate	**CPX** #*const*	E0	x	x	x	2*	2¹
Absolute	**CPX** *addr*	EC	x	x	x	3	4¹
Direct Page (also DP)	**CPX** *dp*	E4	x	x	x	2	3¹,²

* Add 1 byte if x = 0 (16-bit index registers)

1 Add 1 cycle if x = 0 (16-bit index registers)

2 Add 1 cycle if low byte of Direct Page register is other than zero (DL < >0)

CPY — Compare Index Register Y with Memory

Subtract the data located at the effective address specified by the operand from the contents of the Y register, setting the carry, zero, and negative flags based on the result, but without altering the contents of either the memory location or the register. The comparison is of unsigned values only (except for signed comparison for equality).

The primary use for the CPY instruction is to test the value of the Y index register against loop boundaries, setting the flags so that a conditional branch can be executed.

8-bit index registers (all processors): Data compared is eight-bit.

16-bit index registers (65802/65816 only, x = 0): Data compared is sixteen-bit: the low-order eight bits of the data in memory is located at the effective address; the high-order eight bits are located at the effective address plus one.

Flags Affected: n - - - - - z c

  n Set if most significant bit of result is set; else cleared.
  z Set if result is zero; else cleared.
  c Set if no borrow required (Y register value higher or same); cleared if borrow required (Y register value lower).

Codes:

Addressing Mode[++]	Syntax	Opcode (hex)	Available on: 6502	65C02	65802/816	# of Bytes	# of Cycles
Immediate	CPY #const	C0	x	x	x	2[*]	2[1]
Absolute	CPY addr	CC	x	x	x	3	4[1]
Direct Page (also DP)	CPY dp	C4	x	x	x	2	3[1,2]

  [*] Add 1 byte if x = 0 (16-bit index registers)
  [1] Add 1 cycle if x = 0 (16-bit index registers)
  [2] Add 1 cycle if low byte of Direct Page register is other than zero (DL< >0)

Decrement DEC

Decrement by one the contents of the location specified by the operand (subtract one from the value).

Unlike subtracting a one using the **SBC** instruction, the decrement instruction is neither affected by nor affects the carry flag. You can test for wraparound only by testing after every decrement to see if the value is zero or negative. On the other hand, you don't need to set the carry before decrementing.

DEC is unaffected by the setting of the **d** (decimal) flag.

8-bit accumulator/memory (all processors): Data decremented is eight-bit.

16-bit accumulator/memory (65802/65816 only, m = 0): Data decremented is sixteen-bit: if in memory, the low-order eight bits are located at the effective address; the high-order eight bits are located at the effective address plus one.

Flags Affected: n - - - - z -
- n Set if most significant bit of result is set; else cleared.
- z Set if result is zero; else cleared.

Codes:

Addressing Mode	Syntax	Opcode (hex)	6502	65C02	65802/816	# of Bytes	# of Cycles
Accumulator	DEC A	3A		x	x	1	2
Absolute	DEC addr	CE	x	x	x	3	6[1]
Direct Page (also DP)	DEC dp	C6	x	x	x	2	5[1,2]
Absolute Indexed,X	DEC addr,X	DE	x	x	x	3	7[1,3]
DP Indexed,X	DEC dp,X	D6	x	x	x	2	6[1,2]

1 Add 2 cycles if m = 0 (16-bit memory/accumulator)
2 Add 1 cycle if low byte of Direct Page register is other than zero (DL < >0)
3 Subtract 1 cycle if 65C02 and no page boundary crossed

DEX — Decrement Index Register X

Decrement by one the contents of index register **X** (subtract one from the value). This is a special purpose, implied addressing form of the **DEC** instruction.

Unlike using **SBC** to subtract a one from the value, the **DEX** instruction does not affect the carry flag; you can test for wraparound only by testing after every decrement to see if the value is zero or negative. On the other hand, you don't need to set the carry before decrementing.

DEX is unaffected by the setting of the **d** (decimal) flag.

8-bit index registers (all processors): Data decremented is eight-bit.

16-bit index registers (65802/65816 only, x = 0): Data decremented is sixteen-bit.

Flags Affected: n - - - - z -

n Set if most significant bit of result is set; else cleared.
z Set if result is zero; else cleared.

Codes:

Addressing Mode	Syntax	Opcode (hex)	Available on: 6502	65C02	65802/816	# of Bytes	# of Cycles
Implied	DEX	CA	x	x	x	1	2

Decrement Index Register Y   DEY

Decrement by one the contents of index register Y (subtract one from the value). This is a special purpose, implied addressing form of the DEC instruction.

Unlike using SBC to subtract a one from the value, the DEY instruction does not affect the carry flag; you can test for wraparound only by testing after every decrement to see if the value is zero or negative. On the other hand, you don't need to set the carry before decrementing.

DEY is unaffected by the setting of the d (decimal) flag.

8-bit index registers (all processors): Data decremented is eight-bit.

16-bit index registers (65802/65816 only, x = 0): Data decremented is sixteen-bit.

Flags Affected: n - - - - - z -
                        n Set if most significant bit of result is set; else cleared.
                        z Set if result is zero; else cleared.

Codes:

Addressing Mode	Syntax	Opcode (hex)	Available on: 6502	65C02	65802/816	# of Bytes	# of Cycles
Implied	DEY	88	x	x	x	1	2

EOR — Exclusive-OR Accumulator with Memory

Bitwise logical Exclusive-OR the data located at the effective address specified by the operand with the contents of the accumulator. Each bit in the accumulator is exclusive-ORed with the corresponding bit in memory, and the result is stored into the same accumulator bit.

The truth table for the logical exclusive-OR operation is:

	Second Operand	
	0	1
First Operand		
0	0	1
1	1	0

Figure 18.5. Exclusive OR Truth Table.

A 1 or logical true results only if the two elements of the Exclusive-OR operation are *different*.

8-bit accumulator (all processors): Data exclusive-ORed from memory is eight-bit.

16-bit accumulator (65802/65816 only, m = 0): Data exclusive-ORed from memory is sixteen-bit: the low-order eight bits are located at the effective address; the high-order eight bits are located at the effective address plus one.

Flags Affected: n - - - - z -
    n Set if most significant bit of result is set; else cleared.
    z Set if result is zero; else cleared.

Codes:

Addressing Mode++	Syntax	Opcode (hex)	6502	65C02	65802/816	# of Bytes	# of Cycles
Immediate	EOR #*const*	49	x	x	x	2*	2[1]
Absolute	EOR *addr*	4D	x	x	x	3	4[1]
Absolute Long	EOR *long*	4F			x	4	5[1]
Direct Page (also DP)	EOR *dp*	45	x	x	x	2	3[1,2]
DP Indirect	EOR (*dp*)	52		x	x	2	5[1,2]
DP Indirect Long	EOR [*dp*]	47			x	2	6[1,2]
Absolute Indexed,X	EOR *addr*,X	5D	x	x	x	3	4[1,3]
Absolute Long Indexed,X	EOR *long*,X	5F			x	4	5[1]
Absolute Indexed,Y	EOR *addr*,Y	59	x	x	x	3	4[1,3]
DP Indexed,X	EOR *dp*,X	55	x	x	x	2	4[1,2]
DP Indexed Indirect,X	EOR (*dp*,X)	41	x	x	x	2	6[1,2]
DP Indirect Indexed,Y	EOR (*dp*),Y	51	x	x	x	2	5[1,2,3]
DP Indirect Long Indexed,Y	EOR [*dp*],Y	57			x	2	6[1,2]
Stack Relative (also SR)	EOR *sr*,S	43			x	2	4[1]
SR Indirect Indexed,Y	EOR (*sr*,S),Y	53			x	2	7[1]

++ EOR, a Primary Group Instruction, has available all of the Primary Group addressing modes and bit patterns

* Add 1 byte if m = 0 (16-bit memory/accumulator)

1 Add 1 cycle if m = 0 (16-bit memory/accumulator)

2 Add 1 cycle if low byte of Direct Page register is other than zero (DL < >0)

3 Add 1 cycle if adding index crosses a page boundary

INC   Increment

Increment by one the contents of the location specified by the operand (add one to the value).

Unlike adding a one with the **ADC** instruction, however, the increment instruction is neither affected by nor affects the carry flag. You can test for wraparound only by testing after every increment to see if the result is zero or positive. On the other hand, you don't have to clear the carry before incrementing.

The **INC** instruction is unaffected by the **d** (decimal) flag.

8-bit accumulator/memory (all processors): Data incremented is eight-bit.

16-bit accumulator/memory (65802/65816 only, m = 0): Data incremented is sixteen-bit: if in memory, the low-order eight bits are located at the effective address; the high-order eight-bits are located at the effective address plus one.

Flags Affected: n - - - - z -

                    n Set if most significant bit of result is set; else cleared.
                    z Set if result is zero; else cleared.

Codes:

Addressing Mode	Syntax	Opcode (hex)	6502	65C02	65802/816	# of Bytes	# of Cycles
Accumulator	INC A	1A		x	x	1	2
Absolute	INC addr	EE	x	x	x	3	6[1]
Direct Page (also DP)	INC dp	E6	x	x	x	2	5[1,2]
Absolute Indexed,X	INC addr,X	FE	x	x	x	3	7[1,3]
DP Indexed,X	INC dp,X	F6	x	x	x	2	6[1,2]

1 Add 2 cycles if m = 0 (16-bit memory/accumulator)
2 Add 1 cycle if low byte of Direct Page register is other than zero (DL < > 0)
3 Subtract 1 cycle if 65C02 and no page boundary crossed

Increment Index Register X   INX

Increment by one the contents of index register X (add one to the value). This is a special purpose, implied addressing form of the INC instruction.

Unlike using ADC to add a one to the value, the INX instruction does not affect the carry flag. You can execute it without first clearing the carry. But you can test for wraparound only by testing after every increment to see if the result is zero or positive. The INX instruction is unaffected by the d (decimal) flag.

8-bit index registers (all processors): Data incremented is eight-bit.

16-bit index registers (65802/65816 only, x = 0): Data incremented is sixteen-bit.

Flags Affected: n - - - - z -
                      n Set if most significant bit of result is set; else cleared.
                      z Set if result is zero; else cleared.

Codes:

Addressing Mode	Syntax	Opcode (hex)	6502	65C02	65802/816	# of Bytes	# of Cycles
Implied	INX	E8	x	x	x	1	2

INY — Increment Index Register Y

Increment by one the contents of index register Y (add one to the value). This is a special purpose, implied addressing form of the INC instruction.

Unlike using ADC to add one to the value, the INY instruction does not affect the carry flag. You can execute it without first clearing the carry. But you can test for wraparound only by testing after every increment to see if the value is zero or positive. The INY instruction is unaffected by the d (decimal) flag.

8-bit index registers (all processors): Data incremented is eight-bit.

16-bit index registers (65802/65816 only, x = 0): Data incremented is sixteen-bit.

Flags Affected: n - - - - z -

    n Set if most significant bit of result is set; else cleared.
    z Set if result is zero; else cleared.

Codes:

Addressing Mode	Syntax	Opcode (hex)	6502	65C02	65802/816	# of Bytes	# of Cycles
Implied	INY	C8	x	x	x	1	2

Jump   JMP

Transfer control to the address specified by the operand field.

The program counter is loaded with the target address. If a long JMP is executed, the program counter bank is loaded from the third byte of the target address specified by the operand.

Flags Affected: - - - - - - - -

Codes:

Addressing Mode[++]	Syntax	Opcode (hex)	6502	65C02	65802/816	# of Bytes	# of Cycles
Absolute	JMP addr	4C	x	x	x	3	3
Absolute Indirect	JMP (addr)	6C	x	x	x	3	5[1,2]
Absolute Indexed Indirect	JMP (addr,X)	7C		x	x	3	6
Absolute Long	JMP long	5C			x	4	4
	(or JML long)						
Absolute Indirect Long	JMP [addr]	DC			x	3	6
	(or JML [addr])						

1 Add 1 cycle if 65C02
2 6502: If low byte of addr is $FF (i.e., addr is $xxFF): yields incorrect result

JSL   Jump to Subroutine Long (Inter-Bank)

Jump-to-subroutine with long (24-bit) addressing: transfer control to the subroutine at the 24-bit address which is the operand, after first pushing a 24-bit (long) return address onto the stack. This return address is the address of the last instruction byte (the fourth instruction byte, or the third operand byte), *not* the address of the next instruction; it is the return address minus one.

The current program counter bank is pushed onto the stack first, then the high-order byte of the return address and then the low-order byte of the address are pushed on the stack in standard 65x order (low byte in the lowest address, bank byte in the highest address). The stack pointer is adjusted after each byte is pushed to point to the next lower byte (the next available stack location). The program counter bank register and program counter are then loaded with the operand values, and control is transferred to the specified location.

Flags Affected: - - - - - - - -

Codes:

Addressing Mode	Syntax	Opcode (hex)	6502	65C02	65802/816	# of Bytes	# of Cycles
Absolute Long	JSL *long* (or JSR *long*)	22			x	4	8

Jump to Subroutine   JSR

Transfer control to the subroutine at the location specified by the operand, after first pushing onto the stack, as a return address, the current program counter value, that is, the address of the last instruction byte (the third byte of a three-byte instruction, the fourth byte of a four-byte instruction), *not* the address of the next instruction.

If an absolute operand is coded and is less than or equal to $FFFF, absolute addressing is assumed by the assembler; if the value is greater than $FFFF, absolute long addressing is used.

If long addressing is used, the current program counter bank is pushed onto the stack first. Next—or first in the more normal case of intra-bank addressing—the high order byte of the return address is pushed, followed by the low order byte. This leaves it on the stack in standard 65x order (lowest byte at the lowest address, highest byte at the highest address). After the return address is pushed, the stack pointer points to the next available location (next lower byte) on the stack. Finally, the program counter (and, in the case of long addressing, the program counter bank register) is loaded with the values specified by the operand, and control is transferred to the target location.

Flags Affected: - - - - - - - -

Codes:

Addressing Mode	Syntax	Opcode (hex)	6502	65C02	65802/816	# of Bytes	# of Cycles
Absolute	JSR *addr*	20	x	x	x	3	6
Absolute Indexed Indirect	JSR *(addr,X)*	FC			x	3	8
Absolute Long	JSR *long*	22			x	4	8
	(or JSL *long*)						

LDA — Load Accumulator from Memory

Load the accumulator with the data located at the effective address specified by the operand.

8-bit accumulator (all processors): Data is eight-bit.

16-bit accumulator (65802/65816 only, m = 0): Data is sixteen-bit; the low-order eight bits are located at the effective address; the high-order eight bits are located at the effective address plus one.

Flags Affected: n - - - - z -

    n Set if most significant bit of loaded value is set; else cleared.
    z Set if value loaded is zero; else cleared.

Codes:

Addressing Mode[++]	Syntax	Opcode (hex)	6502	65C02	65802/816	# of Bytes	# of Cycles
Immediate	LDA #const	A9	x	x	x	2*	2^1
Absolute	LDA addr	AD	x	x	x	3	4^1
Absolute Long	LDA long	AF			x	4	5^1
Direct Page (also DP)	LDA dp	A5	x	x	x	2	$3^{1,2}$
DP Indirect	LDA (dp)	B2		x	x	2	$5^{1,2}$
DP Indirect Long	LDA [dp]	A7			x	2	$6^{1,2}$
Absolute Indexed,X	LDA addr,X	BD	x	x	x	3	$4^{1,3}$
Absolute Long Indexed,X	LDA long,X	BF			x	4	5^1
Absolute Indexed,Y	LDA addr,Y	B9	x	x	x	3	$4^{1,3}$
DP Indexed,X	LDA dp,X	B5	x	x	x	2	$4^{1,2}$
DP Indexed Indirect,X	LDA (dp,X)	A1	x	x	x	2	$6^{1,2}$
DP Indirect Indexed,Y	LDA (dp),Y	B1	x	x	x	2	$5^{1,2,3}$
DP Indirect Long Indexed,Y	LDA [dp],Y	B7			x	2	$6^{1,2}$
Stack Relative (also SR)	LDA sr,S	A3			x	2	4^1
SR Indirect Indexed,Y	LDA (sr,S),Y	B3			x	2	7^1

++ LDA, a Primary Group Instruction, has available all of the Primary Group addressing modes and bit patterns
* Add 1 byte if m = 0 (16-bit memory/accumulator)
1 Add 1 cycle if m = 0 (16-bit memory/accumulator)
2 Add 1 cycle if low byte of Direct Page register is other than zero (DL< >0)
3 Add 1 cycle if adding index crosses a page boundary

Load Index Register X from Memory — LDX

Load index register X with the data located at the effective address specified by the operand.

8-bit index registers (all processors): Data is eight-bit.

16-bit index registers (65802/65816 only, x = 0): Data is sixteen-bit: the low-order eight bits are located at the effective address; the high-order eight bits are located at the effective address plus one.

Flags Affected: n - - - - z -

- n   Set if most significant bit of loaded value is set; else cleared.
- z   Set if value loaded is zero; else cleared.

Codes:

Addressing Mode	Syntax	Opcode (hex)	6502	65C02	65802/816	# of Bytes	# of Cycles
Immediate	LDX #*const*	A2	x	x	x	2*	2^1
Absolute	LDX *addr*	AE	x	x	x	3	4^1
Direct Page (also DP)	LDX *dp*	A6	x	x	x	2	$3^{1,2}$
Absolute Indexed,Y	LDX *addr*,Y	BE	x	x	x	3	$4^{1,3}$
DP Indexed,Y	LDX *dp*,Y	B6	x	x	x	2	$4^{1,2}$

* Add 1 byte if x = 0 (16-bit index registers)
1 Add 1 cycle if x = 0 (16-bit index registers)
2 Add 1 cycle if low byte of Direct Page register is other than zero (DL < >0)
3 Add 1 cycle if adding index crosses a page boundary

LDY   Load Index Register Y from Memory

Load index register Y with the data located at the effective address specified by the operand.

8-bit index registers (all processors): Data is eight-bit.

16-bit index registers (65802/65816 only, x = 0): Data is sixteen-bit: the low-order eight bits are located at the effective address; the high-order eight bits are located at the effective address plus one.

Flags Affected: n - - - - - z -
- n   Set if most significant bit of loaded value is set; else cleared.
- z   Set if value loaded is zero; else cleared.

Codes:

Addressing Mode	Syntax	Opcode (hex)	Available to: 6502	65C02	65802/816	# of Bytes	# of Cycles
Immediate	LDY #const	A0	x	x	x	2*	2^1
Absolute	LDY addr	AC	x	x	x	3	4^1
Direct Page (also DP)	LDY dp	A4	x	x	x	2	$3^{1,2}$
Absolute Indexed,X	LDY addr,X	BC	x	x	x	3	$4^{1,3}$
DP Indexed,X	LDY dp,X	B4	x	x	x	2	$4^{1,2}$

*   Add 1 byte if x = 0 (16-bit index registers)

1   Add 1 cycle if x = 0 (16-bit index registers)

2   Add 1 cycle if low byte of Direct Page register is other than zero (DL < >0)

3   Add 1 cycle if adding index crosses a page boundary

Logical Shift Memory or Accumulator Right — LSR

Logical shift the contents of the location specified by the operand right one bit. That is, bit zero takes on the value originally found in bit one, bit one takes the value originally found in bit two, and so on; the leftmost bit (bit 7 if the m memory select flag is one when the instruction is executed or bit 15 if it is zero) is cleared; the rightmost bit, bit zero, is transferred to the carry flag. This is the arithmetic equivalent of unsigned division by two.

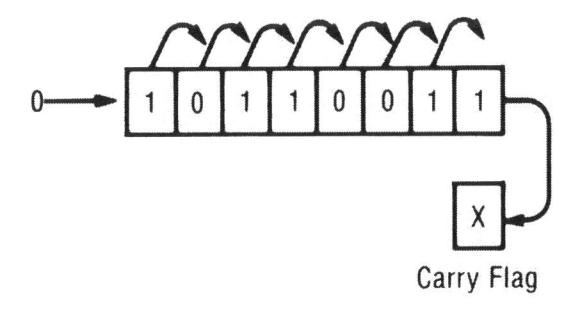

Figure 18.6. LSR.

8-bit accumulator/memory (all processors): Data shifted is eight-bit.

16-bit accumulator/memory (65802/65816 only, m = 0): Data shifted is sixteen-bit: if in memory, the low-order eight bits are located at the effective address; the high-order eight bits are located at the effective address plus one.

Flags Affected: n - - - - - z c

  n Cleared.

  z Set if result is zero; else cleared.

  c Low bit becomes carry: set if low bit was set; cleared if low bit was zero.

Codes:

Addressing Mode	Syntax	Opcode (hex)	6502	65C02	65802/816	# of Bytes	# of Cycles
Accumulator	LSR A	4A	x	x	x	1	2
Absolute	LSR addr	4E	x	x	x	3	6^1
Direct Page (also DP)	LSR dp	46	x	x	x	2	$5^{1,2}$
Absolute Indexed,X	LSR addr,X	5E	x	x	x	3	$7^{1,3}$
DP Indexed,X	LSR dp,X	56	x	x	x	2	$6^{1,2}$

1 Add 2 cycles if m = 0 (16-bit memory/accumulator)
2 Add 1 cycle if low byte of Direct Page register is other than zero (DL < >0)
3 Subtract 1 cycle if 65C02 and no page boundary crossed

MVN   Block Move Next

Moves (copies) a block of memory to a new location. The source, destination and length operands of this instruction are taken from the X, Y, and C (double accumulator) registers; these should be loaded with the correct values before executing the MVN instruction.

The source address for MVN, taken from the X register, should be the starting address (lowest in memory) of the block to be moved. The destination address, in the Y register, should be the new starting address for the moved block. The length, loaded into the double accumulator (the value in C is always used, regardless of the setting of the **m** flag) should be the length of the block to be moved *minus one*; if C contains $0005, six bytes will be moved. The two operand bytes of the MVN instruction specify the *banks* holding the two blocks of memory: the first operand byte (of object code) specifies the destination bank; the second operand byte specifies the source bank.

The execution sequence is: the first byte is moved from the address in X to the address in Y; then X and Y are incremented, C is decremented, and the *next* byte is moved; this process continues until the number of bytes specified by the value in C *plus one* is moved. In other words, until the value in C is $FFFF.

If the source and destination blocks do not overlap, then the source block remains intact after it has been copied to the destination.

If the source and destination blocks do overlap, then MVN should be used only if the destination is *lower* than the source to avoid overwriting source bytes before they've been copied to the destination. If the destination is higher, then the MVP instruction should be used instead.

When execution is complete, the value in C is $FFFF, registers X and Y each point one byte past the end of the blocks to which they were pointing, and the data bank register holds the **destination** bank value (the first operand byte).

Assembler syntax for the block move instruction calls for the operand field to be coded as two addresses, source first, then destination—the more intuitive ordering, but the opposite of the actual operand order in the object code. The assembler strips the bank bytes from the addresses (ignoring the rest) and reverses them to object code order. If a block move instruction is interrupted, it may be resumed automatically via execution of an RTI if all of the registers are restored or intact. The value pushed onto the stack when a block move is interrupted is the address of the block move instruction. The current byte-move is completed before the interrupt is serviced.

If the index registers are in eight-bit mode (x = 1), or the processor is in 6502 emulation mode (e = 1), then the blocks being specified must necessarily be in page zero since the high bytes of the index registers will contain zeroes.

18 The Instruction Sets

Flags Affected: -- -- -- -- -- -- -- --

Codes:

Addressing Mode	Syntax	Opcode (hex)	Available to: 6502	65C02	65802/816	# of Bytes	# of Cycles
Block Move	**MVN** srcbk,destbk	54			x	3	*

* 7 cycles per byte moved

MVP   Block Move Previous

Moves (copies) a block of memory to a new location. The source, destination and length operands of this instruction are taken from the X, Y, and C (double accumulator) registers; these should be loaded with the correct values before executing the MVP instruction.

The source address for MVP, taken from the X register, should be the ending address (highest in memory) of the block to be moved. The destination address, in the Y register, should be the new ending address for the moved block. The length, loaded into the double accumulator (the value in C is always used, regardless of the setting of the **m** flag) should be the length of the block to be moved *minus one;* if C contains $0005, six bytes will be moved. The two operand bytes of the MVP instruction specify the *banks* holding the two blocks of memory: the first operand byte (of object code) specifies the destination bank; the second operand byte specifies the source bank.

The execution sequence is: the first byte is moved from the address in X to the address in Y; then X and Y are decremented, C is decremented, and the *previous* byte is moved; this process continues until the number of bytes specified by the value in C *plus one* is moved. In other words, until the value in C is $FFFF.

If the source and destination blocks do not overlap, then the source block remains intact after it has been copied to the destination.

If the source and destination blocks do overlap, then MVP should be used only if the destination is *higher* than the source to avoid overwriting source bytes before they've been copied to the destination. If the destination is lower, then the MVN instruction should be used instead.

When execution is complete, the value in C is $FFFF, registers X and Y each point one byte past the beginning of the blocks to which they were pointing, and the data bank register holds the **destination** bank value (the first operand byte).

Assembler syntax for the block move instruction calls for the operand field to be coded as two addresses, source first, then destination—the more intuitive ordering, but the opposite of the actual operand order in the object code. The assembler strips the bank bytes from the addresses (ignoring the rest) and reverses them to object code order. If a block move instruction is interrupted, it may be resumed automatically via execution of an RTI if all of the registers are restored or intact. The value pushed onto the stack when a block move is interrupted is the address of the block move instruction. The current byte-move is completed before the interrupt is serviced.

If the index registers are in eight-bit mode ($x = 1$), or the processor is in 6502 emulation mode ($e = 1$), then the blocks being specified must necessarily be in page zero since the high bytes of the index registers will contain zeroes.

Flags Affected: - - - - - - - -

Codes:

Addressing Mode	Syntax	Opcode (hex)	6502	65C02	65802/816	# of Bytes	# of Cycles
Block Move	**MVP** srcbk,destbk	44			x	3	*

* 7 cycles per byte moved

NOP   No Operation

Executing a NOP takes no action; it has no effect on any 65x registers or memory, except the program counter, which is incremented once to point to the next instruction.

Its primary uses are during debugging, where it is used to "patch out" unwanted code, or as a place-holder, included in the assembler source, where you anticipate you may have to "patch in" instructions, and want to leave a "hole" for the patch.

NOP may also be used to expand timing loops—each NOP instruction takes two cycles to execute, so adding one or more may help fine tune a timing loop.

Flags Affected: - - - - - - - -

Codes:

Addressing Mode	Syntax	Opcode (hex)	Available to: 6502	65C02	65802/816	# of Bytes	# of Cycles
Implied	NOP	EA	x	x	x	1	2

OR Accumulator with Memory ORA

Bitwise logical OR the data located at the effective address specified by the operand with the contents of the accumulator. Each bit in the accumulator is ORed with the corresponding bit in memory. The result is stored into the same accumulator bit.

The truth table for the logical OR operation is:

	Second Operand	
First Operand	0	1
0	0	1
1	1	1

Figure 18.7. Logical OR Truth Table.

A 1 or logical true results if either of the two operands of the OR operation is true.

8-bit accumulator (all processors): Data ORed from memory is eight-bit.

16-bit accumulator (65802/65816 only, m = 0): Data ORed from memory is sixteen-bit: the low-order eight bits are located at the effective address; the high-order eight bits are located at the effective address plus one.

Flags Affected: n - - - - z -

    n Set if most significant bit of result is set; else cleared.

    z Set if result is zero; else cleared.

Codes:

Addressing Mode++	Syntax	Opcode (hex)	Available to: 6502	65C02	65802/816	# of Bytes	# of Cycles
Immediate	ORA #*const*	09	x	x	x	2*	2[1]
Absolute	ORA *addr*	0D	x	x	x	3	4[1]
Absolute Long	ORA *long*	0F			x	4	5[1]
Direct Page (also DP)	ORA *dp*	05	x	x	x	2	3[1,2]
DP Indirect	ORA (*dp*)	12		x	x	2	5[1,2]
DP Indirect Long	ORA [*dp*]	07			x	2	6[1,2]
Absolute Indexed,X	ORA *addr*,X	1D	x	x	x	3	4[1,3]
Absolute Long Indexed,X	ORA *long*,X	1F			x	4	5[1]
Absolute Indexed,Y	ORA *addr*,Y	19	x	x	x	3	4[1,3]
DP Indexed,X	ORA *dp*,X	15	x	x	x	2	4[1,2]
DP Indexed Indirect,X	ORA (*dp*,X)	01	x	x	x	2	6[1,2]
DP Indirect Indexed,Y	ORA (*dp*),Y	11	x	x	x	2	5[1,2,3]
DP Indirect Long Indexed,Y	ORA [*dp*],Y	17			x	2	6[1,2]
Stack Relative (also SR)	ORA *sr*,S	03			x	2	4[1]
SR Indirect Indexed,Y	ORA (*sr*,S),Y	13			x	2	7[1]

++ORA, a Primary Group Instruction, has available all of the Primary Group addressing modes and bit patterns

* Add 1 byte if m = 0 (16-bit memory/accumulator)
1 Add 1 cycle if m = 0 (16-bit memory/accumulator)
2 Add 1 cycle if low byte of Direct Page register is other than zero (DL< >0)
3 Add 1 cycle if adding index crosses a page boundary

Push Effective Absolute Address   PEA

Push the sixteen-bit operand (typically an absolute address) onto the stack. The stack pointer is decremented twice. This operation always pushes sixteen bits of data, irrespective of the settings of the **m** and **x** mode select flags.

Although the mnemonic suggests that the sixteen-bit value pushed on the stack be considered an address, the instruction may also be considered a "push sixteen-bit immediate data" instruction, although the syntax of immediate addressing is not used. The assembler syntax is that of the absolute addressing mode, that is, a label or sixteen-bit value in the operand field. Unlike all other instructions that use this assembler syntax, the **effective address** itself, rather than the data stored at the effective address, is what is accessed (and in this case, pushed onto the stack).

Flags Affected: - - - - - - - -

Codes:

Addressing Mode	Syntax	Opcode (hex)	Available to: 6502	65C02	65802/816	# of Bytes	# of Cycles
Stack (Absolute)	PEA *addr*	F4			x	3	5

PEI   Push Effective Indirect Address

Push the sixteen-bit value located at the address formed by adding the direct page offset specified by the operand to the direct page register. The mnemonic implies that the sixteen-bit data pushed is considered an address, although it can be any sixteen-bit data. This operation always pushes sixteen bits of data, irrespective of the settings of the m and x mode select flags.

The first byte pushed is the byte at the direct page offset plus one (the high byte of the double byte stored at the direct page offset). The byte at the direct page offset itself (the low byte) is pushed next. The stack pointer now points to the next available stack location, directly below the last byte pushed.

The assembler syntax is that of direct page indirect; however, unlike other instructions which use this assembler syntax, the *effective indirect address*, rather than the data stored at that address, is what is accessed and pushed onto the stack.

Flags Affected: - - - - - - - -

Codes:

Addressing Mode	Syntax	Opcode (hex)	Available to: 6502	65C02	65802/816	# of Bytes	# of Cycles
Stack (Direct Page Indirect)	PEI (dp)	D4			x	2	6[1]

1 Add 1 cycle if low byte of Direct Page register is other than zero (DL < > 0)

Push Effective PC Relative Indirect Address   PER

Add the current value of the program counter to the sixteen-bit signed displacement in the operand, and push the result on the stack. This operation always pushes sixteen bits of data, irrespective of the settings of the **m** and **x** mode select flags.

The high byte of the sum is pushed first, then the low byte is pushed. After the instruction is completed, the stack pointer points to the next available stack location, immediately below the last byte pushed.

Because **PER**'s operand is a displacement relative to the current value of the program counter (as with the branch instructions), this instruction is helpful in writing self-relocatable code in which an address within the program (typically of a data area) must be accessed. The address pushed onto the stack will be the *run-time* address of the data area, regardless of where the program was loaded in memory; it may be pulled into a register, stored in an indirect pointer, or used on the stack with the stack relative indirect indexed addressing mode to access the data at that location.

As is the case with the branch instructions, the syntax used is to specify as the operand the label of the data area you want to reference. This location must be in the **program bank**, since the displacement is relative to the program counter. The assembler converts the assembly-time label into a displacement from the assembly-time address of the next instruction.

The value of the program counter used in the addition is the address of the *next* instruction, that is, the instruction *following* the **PER** instruction.

PER may also be used to push return addresses on the stack, either as part of a simulated branch-to-subroutine or to place the return address beneath the stacked parameters to a subroutine call; always remember that a pushed return address should be the desired return address *minus one*.

Flags Affected: - - - - - - - -

Codes:

Addressing Mode	Syntax	Opcode (hex)	6502	65C02	65802/816	# of Bytes	# of Cycles
Stack (Program Counter Relative Long)	PER label	62			x	3	6

PHA — Push Accumulator

Push the accumulator onto the stack. The accumulator itself is unchanged.

8-bit accumulator (all processors): The single byte contents of the accumulator are pushed—they are stored to the location pointed to by the stack pointer and the stack pointer is decremented.

16-bit accumulator (65802/65816 only, m = 0): Both accumulator bytes are pushed. The high byte is pushed first, then the low byte. The stack pointer now points to the next available stack location, directly below the last byte pushed.

Flags Affected: - - - - - - - -

Codes:

Addressing Mode	Syntax	Opcode (hex)	Available to: 6502	65C02	65802/816	# of Bytes	# of Cycles
Stack (Push)	PHA	48	x	x	x	1	3[1]

1 Add 1 cycle if m = 0 (16-bit memory/accumulator)

Push Data Bank Register   PHB

Push the contents of the data bank register onto the stack.

The single-byte contents of the data bank register are pushed onto the stack; the stack pointer now points to the next available stack location, directly below the byte pushed. The data bank register itself is unchanged. Since the data bank register is an eight-bit register, only one byte is pushed onto the stack, regardless of the settings of the **m** and **x** mode select flags.

While the 65816 always generates 24-bit addresses, most memory references are specified by a sixteen-bit address. These addresses are concatenated with the contents of the data bank register to form a full 24-bit address. This instruction lets the current value of the data bank register be saved prior to loading a new value.

Flags Affected: - - - - - - - -

Codes:

Addressing Mode	Syntax	Opcode (hex)	Available to: 6502	65C02	65802/816	# of Bytes	# of Cycles
Stack (Push)	PHB	8B			x	1	3

PHD — Push Direct Page Register

Push the contents of the direct page register D onto the stack.

Since the direct page register is always a sixteen-bit register, this is always a sixteen-bit operation, regardless of the settings of the m and x mode select flags. The high byte of the direct page register is pushed first, then the low byte. The direct page register itself is unchanged. The stack pointer now points to the next available stack location, directly below the last byte pushed.

By pushing the D register onto the stack, the local environment of a calling subroutine may easily be saved by a called subroutine before modifying the D register to provide itself with its own direct page memory.

Flags Affected: - - - - - - - -

Codes:

Addressing Mode	Syntax	Opcode (hex)	Available to: 6502	65C02	65802/816	# of Bytes	# of Cycles
Stack (Push)	PHD	0B			x	1	4

Push Program Bank Register   PHK

Push the program bank register onto the stack.

The single-byte contents of the program bank register are pushed. The program bank register itself is unchanged. The stack pointer now points to the next available stack location, directly below the byte pushed. Since the program bank register is an eight-bit register, only one byte is pushed onto the stack, regardless of the settings of the **m** and **x** mode select flags.

While the 65816 always generates 24-bit addresses, most jumps and branches specify only a sixteen-bit address. These addresses are concatenated with the contents of the program bank register to form a full 24-bit address. This instruction lets you determine the current value of the program bank register—for example, if you want the data bank to be set to the same value as the program bank.

Flags Affected: – – – – – – – –

Codes:

Addressing Mode	Syntax	Opcode (hex)	6502	65C02	65802/816	# of Bytes	# of Cycles
Stack (Push)	PHK	4B			x	1	3

PHP — Push Processr Status Register

Push the contents of the processor status register **P** onto the stack.

Since the status register is always an eight-bit register, this is always an eight-bit operation, regardless of the settings of the **m** and **x** mode select flags on the 65802/65816. The status register contents are not changed by the operation. The stack pointer now points to the next available stack location, directly below the byte pushed.

This provides the means for saving either the current mode settings or a particular set of status flags so they may be restored or in some other way used later.

Note, however, that the **e** bit (the 6502 emulation mode flag on the 65802/65816) is **not** pushed onto the stack or otherwise accessed or saved. The only access to the **e** flag is via the **XCE** instruction.

Flags Affected: - - - - - - - -

Codes:

Addressing Mode	Syntax	Opcode (hex)	Available to: 6502	65C02	65802/816	# of Bytes	# of Cycles
Stack (Push)	PHP	08	x	x	x	1	3

Push Index Register PHX

Push the contents of the X index register onto the stack. The register itself is unchanged.

8-bit index registers (all processors): The eight-bit contents of the index register are pushed onto the stack. The stack pointer now points to the next available stack location, directly below the byte pushed.

16-bit index registers (65802/65816 only, x = 0): The sixteen-bit contents of the index register are pushed. The high byte is pushed first, then the low byte. The stack pointer now points to the next available stack location, directly below the last byte pushed.

Flags Affected: - - - - - - - -

Codes:

Addressing Mode	Syntax	Opcode (hex)	Available to: 6502	65C02	65802/816	# of Bytes	# of Cycles
Stack (Push)	PHX	DA		x	x	1	3[1]

1 Add 1 cycle if x = 0 (16-bit index registers)

PHY — Push Index Register

Push the contents of the Y index register onto the stack. The register itself is unchanged.

8-bit index registers (all processors): The eight-bit contents of the index register are pushed onto the stack. The stack pointer now points to the next available stack location, directly below the byte pushed.

16-bit index registers (65802/65816 only, x = 0): The sixteen-bit contents of the index register are pushed. The high byte is pushed first, then the low byte. The stack pointer now points to the next available stack location, directly below the last byte pushed.

Flags Affected: - - - - - - - -

Codes:

Addressing Mode	Syntax	Opcode (hex)	6502	65C02	65802/816	# of Bytes	# of Cycles
Stack (Push)	PHY	5A		x	x	1	3[1]

1 Add 1 cycle if x = 0 (16-bit index registers)

Pull Accumulator   PLA

Pull the value on the top of the stack into the accumulator. The previous contents of the accumulator are destroyed.

8-bit accumulator (all processors): The stack pointer is first incremented. Then the byte pointed to by the stack pointer is loaded into the accumulator.

16-bit accumulator (65802/65816 only, m = 0): Both accumulator bytes are pulled. The accumulator's low byte is pulled first, then the high byte is pulled.

Note that unlike some other microprocessors, the 65x pull instructions set the negative and zero flags.

Flags Affected: n - - - - z -

n   Set if most significant bit of pulled value is set; else cleared.

z   Set if value pulled is zero; else cleared.

Codes:

Addressing Mode	Syntax	Opcode (hex)	6502	65C02	65802/816	# of Bytes	# of Cycles
Stack (Pull)	PLA	68	x	x	x	1	4[1]

1 Add 1 cycle if m = 0 (16-bit memory/accumulator)

PLB — Pull Data Bank Register

Pull the eight-bit value on top of the stack into the data bank register **B**, switching the data bank to that value. All instructions which reference data that specify only sixteen-bit addresses will get their bank address from the value pulled into the data bank register. This is the only instruction that can modify the data bank register.

Since the bank register is an eight-bit register, only one byte is pulled from the stack, regardless of the settings of the **m** and **x** mode select flags. The stack pointer is first incremented. Then the byte pointed to by the stack pointer is loaded into the register.

Flags Affected: n - - - - z -

  n Set if most significant bit of pulled value is set; else cleared.
  z Set if value pulled is zero; else cleared.

Codes:

Addressing Mode	Syntax	Opcode (hex)	Available to: 6502	65C02	65802/816	# of Bytes	# of Cycles
Stack (Pull)	PLB	AB			x	1	4

Pull Direct Page Register   PLD

Pull the sixteen-bit value on top of the stack into the direct page register D, switching the direct page to that value.

PLD is typically used to restore the direct page register to a previous value.

Since the direct page register is a sixteen-bit register, two bytes are pulled from the stack, regardless of the settings of the **m** and **x** mode select flags. The low byte of the direct page register is pulled first, then the high byte. The stack pointer now points to where the high byte just pulled was stored; this is now the next available stack location.

Flags Affected: n - - - - z -

- n   Set if most significant bit of pulled value is set; else cleared.

- z   Set if value pulled is zero; else cleared.

Codes:

Addressing Mode	Syntax	Opcode (hex)	6502	65C02	65802/816	# of Bytes	# of Cycles
Stack (Pull)	PLD	2B			x	1	5

PLP   Pull Status Flags

Pull the eight-bit value on the top of the stack into the processor status register P, switching the status byte to that value.

Since the status register is an eight-bit register, only one byte is pulled from the stack, regardless of the settings of the **m** and **x** mode select flags on the 65802/65816. The stack pointer is first incremented. Then the byte pointed to by the stack pointer is loaded into the status register.

This provides the means for restoring either previous mode settings or a particular set of status flags that reflect the result of a previous operation.

Note, however, that the **e** flag—the 6502 emulation mode flag on the 65802/65816—is not on the stack so cannot be pulled from it. The only means of setting the **e** flag is the XCE instruction.

Flags Affected: n v - b d i z c   (6502, 65C02,
                                  65802/65816 emulation mode e = 1)
                     n v m x d i z c   (65802/65816 native mode e = 0)
All flags are replaced by the values in the byte pulled from the stack.

Codes:

Addressing Mode	Syntax	Opcode (hex)	Available to: 6502	65C02	65802/816	# of Bytes	# of Cycles
Stack (Pull)	PLP	28	x	x	x	1	4

Pull Index Register X from Stack   PLX

Pull the value on the top of the stack into the X index register. The previous contents of the register are destroyed.

8-bit index registers (all processors): The stack pointer is first incremented. Then the byte pointed to by the stack pointer is loaded into the register.

16-bit index registers (65802/65816 only, x = 0): Both bytes of the index register are pulled. First the low-order byte of the index register is pulled, then the high-order byte of the index register is pulled.

Unlike some other microprocessors, the 65x instructions to pull an index register affect the negative and zero flags.

Flags Affected: n - - - - z -

        n   Set if most significant bit of pulled value is set; else cleared.

        z   Set if value pulled is zero; else cleared.

Codes:

Addressing Mode	Syntax	Opcode (hex)	Available to: 6502	65C02	65802/816	# of Bytes	# of Cycles
Stack (Pull)	PLX	FA		x	x	1	4[1]

1 Add 1 cycle if x = 0 (16-bit index registers)

PLY Pull Index Register Y from Stack

Pull the value on the top of the stack into the Y index register. The previous contents of the register are destroyed.

8-bit index registers (all processors): The stack pointer is first incremented. Then the byte pointed to by the stack pointer is loaded into the register.

16-bit index registers (65802/65816 only, x = 0): Both bytes of the index register are pulled. First the low-order byte of the index register is pulled, then the high-order byte of the index register is pulled.

Unlike some other microprocessors, the 65x instructions to pull an index register affect the negative and zero flags.

Flags Affected: n - - - - z -

n Set if most significant bit of pulled value is set; else cleared.
z Set if value pulled is zero; else cleared.

Codes:

Addressing Mode	Syntax	Opcode (hex)	Available to: 6502	65C02	65802/816	# of Bytes	# of Cycles
Stack (Pull)	PLY	7A		x	x	1	4[1]

1 Add 1 cycle if x = 0 (16-bit index registers)

Reset Status Bits   REP

For each bit set to one in the operand byte, reset the corresponding bit in the status register to zero. For example, if bit three is set in the operand byte, bit three in the status register (the decimal flag) is reset to zero by this instruction. Zeroes in the operand byte cause no change to their corresponding status register bits.

This instruction lets you reset *any* flag or flags in the status register with a single two-byte instruction. Further, it is the only direct means of resetting several of the flags, including the **m** and **x** mode select flags (although instructions that pull the P status register affect the **m** and **x** mode select flags).

6502 emulation mode (65802/65816, e = 1): Neither the break flag nor bit five (the 6502's undefined flag bit) are affected by REP.

Flags Affected: n v - - d i z c (65802/65816 emulation mode e = 1)
                      n v m x d i z c (65802/65816 native mode e = 0)
  All flags for which an operand bit is set are reset to zero.
  All other flags are unaffected by the instruction.

Codes:

Addressing Mode	Syntax	Opcode (hex)	Available to: 6502	65C02	65802/816	# of Bytes	# of Cycles
Immediate	**REP** #*const*	C2			x	2	3

ROL — Rotate Memory or Accumulator Left

Rotate the contents of the location specified by the operand left one bit. Bit one takes on the value originally found in bit zero, bit two takes the value originally in bit one, and so on; the rightmost bit, bit zero, takes the value in the carry flag; the leftmost bit (bit 7 on the 6502 and 65C02 or if **m** = 1 on the 65802/65816, or bit 15 if **m** = 0) is transferred into the carry flag.

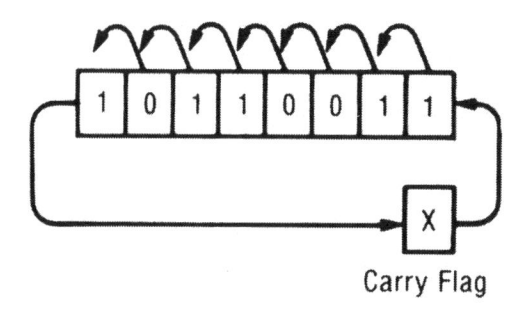

Figure 18.8. ROL.

8-bit accumulator/memory (all processors): Data rotated is eight bits, plus carry.

16-bit accumulator/memory (65802/65816 only, m = 0): Data rotated is sixteen bits, plus carry: if in memory, the low-order eight bits are located at the effective address; the high eight bits are located at the effective address plus one.

Flags Affected: n - - - - z c

- n Set if most significant bit of result is set; else cleared.
- z Set if result is zero; else cleared.
- c High bit becomes carry: set if high bit was set; cleared if high bit was clear.

Codes:

Addressing Mode	Syntax	Opcode (hex)	6502	65C02	65802/816	# of Bytes	# of Cycles
Accumulator	ROL A	2A	x	x	x	1	2
Absolute	ROL addr	2E	x	x	x	3	6[1]
Direct Page (also DP)	ROL dp	26	x	x	x	2	5[1,2]
Absolute Indexed,X	ROL addr,X	3E	x	x	x	3	7[1,3]
DP Indexed,X	ROL dp,X	36	x	x	x	2	6[1,2]

1 Add 2 cycles if m = 0 (16-bit memory/accumulator)
2 Add 1 cycle if low byte of Direct Page register is other than zero (DL< >0)
3 Subtract 1 cycle if 65C02 and no page boundary crossed

Rotate Memory or Accumulator Right ROR

Rotate the contents of the location specified by the operand right one bit. Bit zero takes on the value originally found in bit one, bit one takes the value originally in bit two, and so on; the leftmost bit (bit 7 on the 6502 and 65C02 or if $m = 1$ on the 65802/65816, or bit 15 if $m = 0$) takes the value in the carry flag; the rightmost bit, bit zero, is transferred into the carry flag.

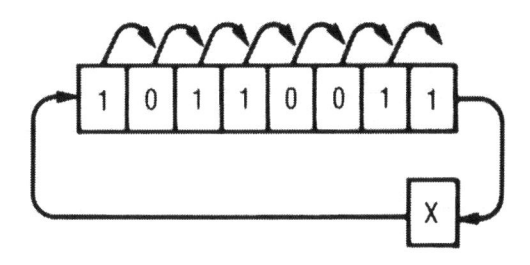

Figure 18.9. ROR.

8-bit accumulator/memory (all processors): Data rotated is eight bits, plus carry.

16-bit accumulator/memory (65802/65816 only, $m = 0$): Data rotated is sixteen bits, plus carry: if in memory, the low-order eight bits are located at the effective address; the high-order eight bits are located at the effective address plus one.

Flags Affected: n - - - - z c

    n Set if most significant bit of result is set; else cleared.

    z Set if result is zero; else cleared.

    c Low bit becomes carry: set if low bit was set; cleared if low bit was clear.

Codes:

Addressing Mode	Syntax	Opcode (hex)	6502	65C02	65802/816	# of Bytes	# of Cycles
Accumulator	ROR A	6A	x	x	x	1	2
Absolute	ROR addr	6E	x	x	x	3	6[1]
Direct Page (also DP)	ROR dp	66	x	x	x	2	5[1,2]
Absolute Indexed,X	ROR addr,X	7E	x	x	x	3	7[1,3]
DP Indexed,X	ROR dp,X	76	x	x	x	2	6[1,2]

1 Add 2 cycles if m = 0 (16-bit memory/accumulator)
2 Add 1 cycle if low byte of Direct Page register is other than zero (DL<>0)
3 Subtract 1 cycle if 65C02 and no page boundary crossed

RTI   Return from Interrupt

Pull the status register and the program counter from the stack. If the 65802/65816 is set to native mode (e = 0), also pull the program bank register from the stack.

RTI pulls values off the stack in the reverse order they were pushed onto it by hardware or software interrupts. The RTI instruction, however, has no way of knowing whether the values pulled off the stack into the status register and the program counter are valid—or even, for that matter, that an interrupt has ever occurred. It blindly pulls the first three (or four) bytes off the top of the stack and stores them into the various registers.

Unlike the **RTS** instruction, the program counter address pulled off the stack is the exact address to return to; the value on the stack is the value loaded into the program counter. It does not need to be incremented as a subroutine's return address does.

Pulling the status register gives the status flags the values they had immediately prior to the start of interrupt-processing.

One extra byte is pulled in the 65802/65816 native mode than in emulation mode, the same extra byte that is pushed by interrupts in native mode, the program bank register. It is therefore essential that the return from interrupt be executed in the same mode (emulation or native) as the original interrupt.

6502, 65C02, and Emulation Mode (e = 1): The status register is pulled from the stack, then the program counter is pulled from the stack (three bytes are pulled).

65802/65816 Native Mode (e = 0): The status register is pulled from the stack, then the program counter is pulled from the stack, then the program bank register is pulled from the stack (four bytes are pulled).

18   The Instruction Sets   **493**

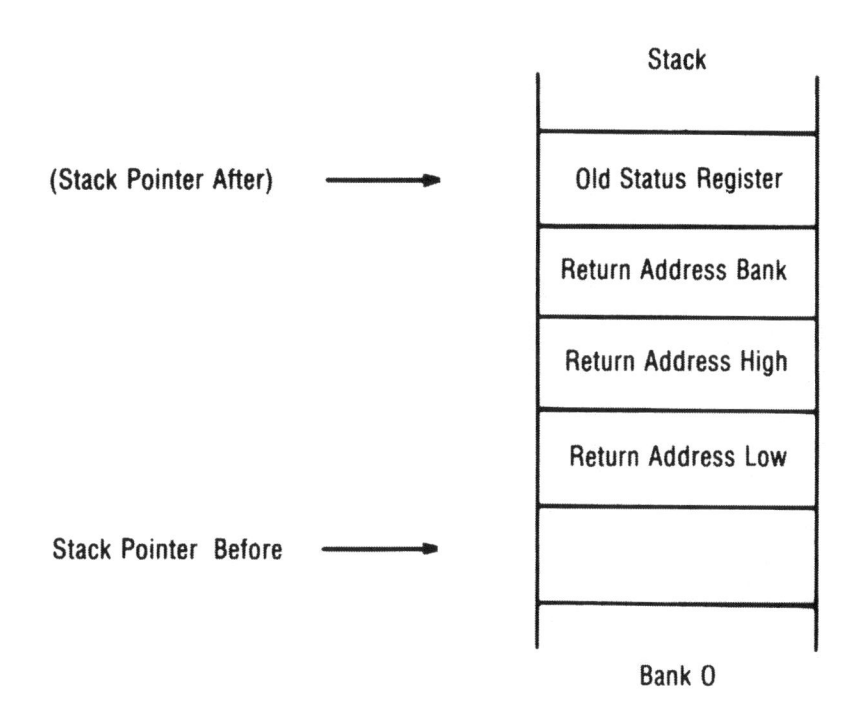

```
                                      Stack
                                  ┌──────────────────┐
                                  │                  │
(Stack Pointer After)   ──────▶   │ Old Status Register │
                                  ├──────────────────┤
                                  │ Return Address Bank │
                                  ├──────────────────┤
                                  │ Return Address High │
                                  ├──────────────────┤
                                  │ Return Address Low  │
                                  ├──────────────────┤
Stack Pointer Before    ──────▶   │                  │
                                  └──────────────────┘
                                       Bank 0
```

Figure 18.10. Native Mode Stack before RTI.

Flags Affected: n v - - d i z c   (6502, 65C02,
                            65802/65816 emulation mode e = 1)
   n v m x d i z c   (65802/65816 native mode e = 0)
   All flags are restored to their values prior to interrupt (each flag takes the value of its corresponding bit in the stacked status byte, except that the Break flag is ignored).

Codes:

Addressing Mode	Syntax	Opcode (hex)	Available to: 6502	65C02	65802/816	# of Bytes	# of Cycles
Stack (RTI)	RTI	40	x	x	x	1	6[1]

1 Add 1 cycle for 65802/65816 native mode (e = 0)

RTL — Return from Subroutine Long

Pull the program counter (incrementing the stacked, sixteen-bit value by one before loading the program counter with it), then the program bank register from the stack.

When a subroutine in another bank is called (via a jump to subroutine long instruction), the current bank address is pushed onto the stack along with the return address. To return to the calling bank, a long return instruction must be executed, which first pulls the return address from the stack, increments it, and loads the program counter with it, then pulls the calling bank from the stack and loads the program bank register. This transfers control to the instruction immediately following the original jump to subroutine long.

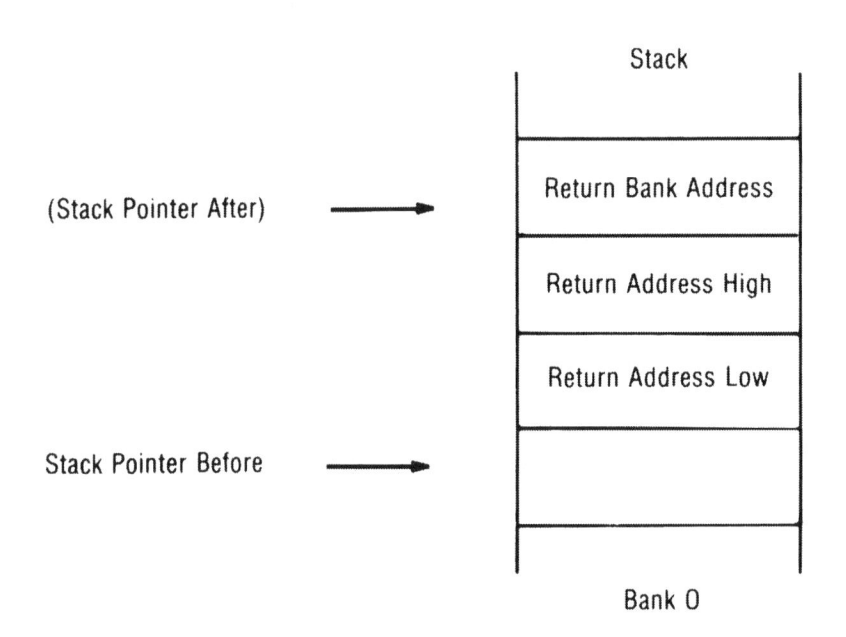

```
                                          Stack
                                     ┌──────────────────┐
                                     │                  │
                                     ├──────────────────┤
                                     │ Return Bank Addr │
(Stack Pointer After)  ──────▶       ├──────────────────┤
                                     │ Return Addr High │
                                     ├──────────────────┤
                                     │ Return Addr Low  │
                                     ├──────────────────┤
Stack Pointer Before   ──────▶       │                  │
                                     │                  │
                                     └──────────────────┘
                                            Bank 0
```

Figure 18.11. Stack before RTL.

Flags Affected: – – – – – – – –

Codes:

Addressing Mode	Syntax	Opcode (hex)	6502	65C02	65802/816	# of Bytes	# of Cycles
Stack (RTL)	RTL	6B			x	1	6

RTS   Return from Subroutine

Pull the program counter, incrementing the stacked, sixteen-bit value by one before loading the program counter with it.

When a subroutine is called (via a jump to subroutine instruction), the current return address is pushed onto the stack. To return to the code following the subroutine call, a return instruction must be executed, which pulls the return address from the stack, increments it, and loads the program counter with it, transferring control to the instruction immediately following the jump to subroutine.

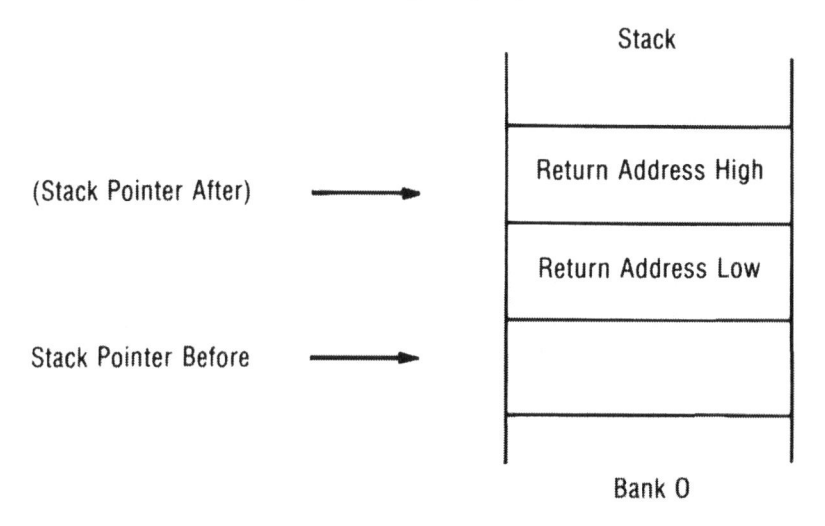

Figure 18.12. Stack before RTS.

Flags Affected: - - - - - - - -

Codes:

Addressing Mode	Syntax	Opcode (hex)	Available to: 6502	65C02	65802/816	# of Bytes	# of Cycles
Stack (RTS)	RTS	60	x	x	x	1	6

Subtract with Borrow from Accumulator   SBC

Subtract the data located at the effective address specified by the operand from the contents of the accumulator; subtract one more if the carry flag is clear, and store the result in the accumulator.

The 65x processors have no subtract instruction that does not involve the carry. To avoid subtracting the carry flag from the result, either you must be sure it is set or you must explicitly set it (using **SEC**) prior to executing the **SBC** instruction.

In a multi-precision (multi-word) subtract, you set the carry before the low words are subtracted. The low word subtraction generates a new carry flag value based on the subtraction. The carry is set if no borrow was required and cleared if borrow was required. The complement of the new carry flag (one if the carry is clear) is subtracted during the next subtraction, and so on. Each result thus correctly reflects the borrow from the previous subtraction.

Note that this use of the carry flag is the opposite of the way the borrow flag is used by some other processors, which clear (not set) the carry if no borrow was required.

d flag clear: Binary subtraction is performed.

d flag set: Binary coded decimal (BCD) subtraction is performed.

8-bit accumulator (all processors): Data subtracted from memory is eight-bit.

16-bit accumulator (65802/65816 only, m = 0): Data subtracted from memory is sixteen-bit: the low eight bits is located at the effective address; the high eight bits is located at the effective address plus one.

Flags Affected: n v - - - - z c

                     n   Set if most significant bit of result is set; else cleared.
                     v   Set if signed overflow; cleared if valid signed result.
                     z   Set if result is zero; else cleared.
                     c   Set if unsigned borrow not required; cleared if unsigned borrow.

Codes:

Addressing Mode++	Syntax	Opcode (hex)	6502	65C02	65802/816	# of Bytes	# of Cycles
Immediate	SBC #const	E9	x	x	x	2*	$2^{1,4}$
Absolute	SBC addr	ED	x	x	x	3	$4^{1,4}$
Absolute Long	SBC long	EF			x	4	$5^{1,4}$
Direct Page (also DP)	SBC dp	E5	x	x	x	2	$3^{1,2,4}$
DP Indirect	SBC (dp)	F2		x	x	2	$5^{1,2,4}$
DP Indirect Long	SBC [dp]	E7			x	2	$6^{1,2,4}$
Absolute Indexed,X	SBC addr,X	FD	x	x	x	3	$4^{1,3,4}$
Absolute Long Indexed,X	SBC long,X	FF			x	4	$5^{1,4}$
Absolute Indexed,Y	SBC addr,Y	F9	x	x	x	3	$4^{1,3,4}$
DP Indexed,X	SBC dp,X	F5	x	x	x	2	$4^{1,2,4,0}$
DP Indexed Indirect,X	SBC (dp,X)	E1	x	x	x	2	$6^{1,2,4}$
DP Indirect Indexed,Y	SBC (dp),Y	F1	x	x	x	2	$5^{1,2,3,4}$
DP Indirect Long Indexed,Y	SBC [dp],Y	F7			x	2	$6^{1,2,4}$
Stack Relative (also SR)	SBC sr,S	E3			x	2	$4^{1,4}$
SR Indirect Indexed,Y	SBC (sr,S),Y	F3			x	2	$7^{1,4}$

++ SBC, a Primary Group Instruction, has available all of the Primary Group addressing modes and bit patterns

* Add 1 byte if m = 0 (16-bit memory/accumulator)
1 Add 1 cycle if m = 0 (16-bit memory/accumulator)
2 Add 1 cycle if low byte of Direct Page register is other than zero (DL < > 0)
3 Add 1 cycle if adding index crosses a page boundary
4 Add 1 cycle if 65C02 and d = 1 (decimal mode, 65C02)

Set Carry Flag   SEC

Set the carry flag in the status register.

SEC is used prior to subtraction (using the 65x's **SBC** instruction) to keep the carry flag from affecting the result, and prior to an **XCE** (exchange carry flag with emulation bit) instruction to put the 65802 or 65816 into 6502 emulation mode.

Flags Affected: $-\ -\ -\ -\ -\ -\ c$
  c Carry flag set always.

Codes:

Addressing Mode	Syntax	Opcode (hex)	6502	65C02	65802/816	# of Bytes	# of Cycles
Implied	SEC	38	x	x	x	1	2

SED — Set Decimal Mode Flag

Set the decimal mode flag in the status register.

SED is used to shift 65x processors into decimal mode from binary mode, so that the ADC and SBC instructions will operate correctly on BCD data, performing automatic decimal adjustment.

Flags Affected: - - - - d - - -

    d Decimal mode flag set always.

Codes:

Addressing Mode	Syntax	Opcode (hex)	Available to: 6502	65C02	65802/816	# of Bytes	# of Cycles
Implied	SED	F8	x	x	x	1	2

Set Interrupt Disable Flag   SEI

Set the interrupt disable flag in the status register.

SEI is used to disable hardware interrupt processing. When the **i** bit is set, maskable hardware interrupts (IRQ') are ignored. The processor itself sets the **i** flag when it begins servicing an interrupt, so interrupt handling routines that are intended to be interruptable must reenable interrupts with **CLI**. If interrupts are to remain blocked during the interrupt service, exiting the routine via **RTI** will automatically restore the status register with the **i** flag clear, re-enabling interrupts.

Flags Affected: - - - - - i - -
　　　　　　　　　　i Interrupt disable flag set always.

Codes:

Addressing Mode	Syntax	Opcode (hex)	Available to: 6502	65C02	65802/816	# of Bytes	# of Cycles
Implied	SEI	78	x	x	x	1	2

SEP Set Status Bits

For each one-bit in the operand byte, set the corresponding bit in the status register to one. For example, if bit three is set in the operand byte, bit three in the status register (the decimal flag) is set to one by this instruction. Zeroes in the operand byte cause no change to their corresponding status register bits.

This instruction lets you set *any* flag or flags in the status register with a single two-byte instruction. Furthermore, it is the only direct means of setting the m and x mode select flags. (Instructions that pull the P status register indirectly affect the m and x mode select flags).

6502 emulation mode (65802/65816, e = 1): Neither the break flag nor bit five (the 6502's non-flag bit) is affected by SEP.

Flags Affected: n v - - d i z c (65802/65816 emulation e = 1)
   n v m x d i z c (65802/65816 native mode e = 0)
   All flags for which an operand bit is set are set to one.
   All other flags are unaffected by the instruction.

Codes:

Addressing Mode	Syntax	Opcode (hex)	Available to: 6502	65C02	65802/816	# of Bytes	# of Cycles
Immediate	SEP #*const*	E2			x	2	3

Store Accumulator to Memory   STA

Store the value in the accumulator to the effective address specified by the operand.

8-bit accumulator (all processors): Value is eight-bit.

16-bit accumulator (65802/65816 only, m = 0): Value is sixteen-bit: the low-order eight bits are stored to the effective address; the high-order eight bits are stored to the effective address plus one.

The 65x flags are unaffected by store instructions.

Flags Affected: - - - - - - - -

Codes:

Addressing Mode[++]	Syntax	Opcode (hex)	6502	65C02	65802/816	# of Bytes	# of Cycles
Absolute	STA addr	8D	x	x	x	3	4[1]
Absolute Long	STA long	8F			x	4	5[1]
Direct Page (also DP)	STA dp	85	x	x	x	2	3[1,2]
DP Indirect	STA (dp)	92		x	x	2	5[1,2]
DP Indirect Long	STA [dp]	87			x	2	6[1,2]
Absolute Indexed,X	STA addr,X	9D	x	x	x	3	5[1]
Absolute Long Indexed,X	STA long,X	9F			x	4	5[1]
Absolute Indexed,Y	STA addr,Y	99	x	x	x	3	5[1]
DP Indexed,X	STA dp,X	95	x	x	x	2	4[1,2]
DP Indexed Indirect,X	STA (dp,X)	81	x	x	x	2	6[1,2]
DP Indirect Indexed,Y	STA (dp),Y	91	x	x	x	2	6[1,2]
DP Indirect Long Indexed,Y	STA [dp],Y	97			x	2	6[1,2]
Stack Relative (also SR)	STA sr,S	83			x	2	4[1]
SR Indirect Indexed,Y	STA (sr,S),Y	93			x	2	7[1]

[++] STA, a Primary Group Instruction, has available all of the Primary Group addressing modes and bit patterns

1 Add 1 cycle if m = 0 (16-bit memory/accumulator)

2 Add 1 cycle if low byte of Direct Page register is other than zero (DL < > 0)

STP — Stop the Processor

During the processor's next phase 2 clock cycle, stop the processor's oscillator input; the processor is effectively shut down until a reset occurs (until the RES' pin is pulled low).

STP is designed to put the processor to sleep while it's not (actively) in use in order to reduce power consumption. Since power consumption is a function of frequency with CMOS circuits, stopping the clock cuts power to almost nil.

Your reset handling routine (pointed to by the reset vector, $00:FFFC-FD) should be designed to either reinitialize the system or resume control through a previously-installed reset handler.

Remember that reset is an interrupt-like signal that causes the emulation bit to be set to one. It also causes the direct page register to be reset to zero; stack high to be set to one (forcing the stack pointer to page one); and the mode select flags to be set to one (eight-bit registers; a side effect is that the high bytes of the index registers are zeroed). STP is useful only in hardware systems (such as battery-powered systems) specifically designed to support a low-power mode.

Flags Affected: - - - - - - - -

Codes:

Addressing Mode	Syntax	Opcode (hex)	6502	65C02	65802/816	# of Bytes	# of Cycles
Implied	STP	DB			x	1	3[1]

1 Uses 3 cycles to shut the processor down; additional cycles are required by reset to restart it

Store Index Register X to Memory   STX

Store the value in index register X to the effective address specified by the operand.

8-bit index registers (all processors): Value is eight-bit.

16-bit index registers (65802/65816 only, x = 0): Value is sixteen-bit: the low-order eight bits are stored to the effective address; the high-order eight bits are stored to the effective address plus one.

The 65x flags are unaffected by store instructions.

Flags Affected: - - - - - - - -

Codes:

Addressing Mode	Syntax	Opcode (hex)	6502	65C02	65802/816	# of Bytes	# of Cycles
Absolute	STX addr	8E	x	x	x	3	4[1]
Direct Page	STX dp	86	x	x	x	2	3[1,2]
Direct Page Indexed,Y	STX dp,Y	96	x	x	x	2	4[1,2]

1 Add 1 cycle if x = 0 (16-bit index registers)
2 Add 1 cycle if low byte of Direct Page register is other than zero (DL < > 0)

STY — Store Index Register Y to Memory

Store the value in index register Y to the effective address specified by the operand.

8-bit index registers (all processors): Value is eight-bit.

16-bit index registers (65802/65816 only, x = 0): Value is sixteen-bit: the low-order eight bits are stored to the effective address; the high-order eight bits are stored to the effective address plus one.

The 65x flags are unaffected by store instructions.

Flags Affected: - - - - - - - -

Codes:

Addressing Mode	Syntax	Opcode (hex)	6502	65C02	65802/816	# of Bytes	# of Cycles
Absolute	STY addr	8C	x	x	x	3	4[1]
Direct Page	STY dp	84	x	x	x	2	3[1,2]
Direct Page Indexed, X	STY dp,X	94	x	x	x	2	4[1,2]

1 Add 1 cycle if x = 0 (16-bit index registers)
2 Add 1 cycle if low byte of Direct Page register is other than zero (DL < > 0)

Store Zero to Memory   STZ

Store zero to the effective address specified by the operand.

8-bit accumulator (all processors): Zero is stored at the effective address.

16-bit accumulator/memory (65802/65816 only, m = 0): Zero is stored at the effective address and at the effective address plus one.

The 65x store zero instruction does not affect the flags.

Flags Affected: - - - - - - -

Codes:

Addressing Mode	Syntax	Opcode (hex)	6502	65C02	65802/816	# of Bytes	# of Cycles
Absolute	STZ addr	9C		x	x	3	4[1]
Direct Page	STZ dp	64		x	x	2	3[1,2]
Absolute Indexed,X	STZ addr,X	9E		x	x	3	5[1]
Direct Page Indexed,X	STZ dp,X	74		x	x	2	4[1,2]

1 Add 1 cycle if m = 0 (16-bit memory/accumulator)
2 Add 1 cycle if low byte of Direct Page register is other than zero (DL < >0)

TAX — Transfer Accumulator to Index Register X

Transfer the value in the accumulator to index register X. If the registers are different sizes, the nature of the transfer is determined by the destination register. The value in the accumulator is not changed by the operation.

8-bit accumulator, 8-bit index registers (all processors): Value transferred is eight-bit.

8-bit accumulator, 16-bit index registers (65802/65816 only, m = 1, x = 0): Value transferred is sixteen-bit; the eight-bit A accumulator becomes the low byte of the index register; the hidden eight-bit B accumulator becomes the high byte of the index register.

16-bit accumulator, 8-bit index registers (65802/65816 only, m = 0, x = 1): Value transferred to the eight-bit index register is eight-bit, the low byte of the accumulator.

16-bit accumulator, 16-bit index registers (65802/65816 only, m = 0, x = 0): Value transferred to the sixteen-bit index register is sixteen-bit, the full sixteen-bit accumulator.

Flags Affected: n - - - - z -

    n Set if most significant bit of transferred value is set; else cleared.
    z Set if value transferred is zero; else cleared.

Codes:

Addressing Mode	Syntax	Opcode (hex)	6502	65C02	65802/816	# of Bytes	# of Cycles
Implied	TAX	AA	x	x	x	1	2

Transfer Accumulator to Index Register Y TAY

Transfer the value in the accumulator to index register Y. If the registers are different sizes, the nature of the transfer is determined by the destination register. The value in the accumulator is not changed by the operation.

8-bit accumulator, 8-bit index registers (all processors): Value transferred is eight-bit.

8-bit accumulator, 16-bit index registers (65802/65816 only, m = 1, x = 0): Value transferred is sixteen-bit; the eight-bit A accumulator becomes the low byte of the index register; the hidden eight-bit B accumulator becomes the high byte of the index register.

16-bit accumulator, 8-bit index registers (65802/65816 only, m = 0, x = 1): Value transferred to the eight-bit index register is eight-bit, the low byte of the accumulator.

16-bit accumulator, 16-bit index registers (65802/65816 only, m = 0, x = 0): Value transferred to the sixteen-bit index register is sixteen-bit, the full sixteen-bit accumulator.

Flags Affected: n - - - - z -
- n Set if most significant bit of transferred value is set; else cleared.
- z Set if value transferred is zero; else cleared.

Codes:

Addressing Mode	Syntax	Opcode (hex)	Available to: 6502	65C02	65802/816	# of Bytes	# of Cycles
Implied	TAY	A8	x	x	x	1	2

TCD Transfer 16-Bit Accumulator to Direct Page Register

Transfer the value in the sixteen-bit accumulator C to the direct page register D, regardless of the setting of the accumulator/memory mode flag.

An alternate mnemonic is **TAD**, (transfer the value in the A accumulator to the direct page register).

In **TCD**, the "C" is used to indicate that sixteen bits are transferred regardless of the **m** flag. If the A accumulator is set to just eight bits (whether because the **m** flag is set, or because the processor is in 6502 emulation mode), then its value becomes the low byte of the direct page register and the value in the hidden B accumulator becomes the high byte of the direct page register.

The accumulator's sixteen-bit value is unchanged by the operation.

Flags Affected: n - - - - z -
- n Set if most significant bit of transferred value is set; else cleared.
- z Set if value transferred is zero; else cleared.

Codes:

Addressing Mode	Syntax	Opcode (hex)	Available to: 6502	65C02	65802/816	# of Bytes	# of Cycles
Implied	TCD (or TAD)	5B			x	1	2

Transfer Accumulator to Stack Pointer   TCS

Transfer the value in the accumulator to the stack pointer S. The accumulator's value is unchanged by the operation.

An alternate mnemonic is **TAS** (transfer the value in the **A** accumulator to the stack pointer).

In **TCS**, the "C" is used to indicate that, in native mode, sixteen bits are transferred regardless of the **m** flag. If the **A** accumulator is set to just eight bits (because the **m** flag is set), then its value is transferred to the low byte of the stack pointer and the value in the hidden **B** accumulator is transferred to the high byte of the stack pointer. In emulation mode, only the eight-bit **A** accumulator is transferred, since the high stack pointer byte is forced to one (the stack is confined to page one).

TCS, along with **TXS**, are the only two instructions for changing the value in the stack pointer. The two are also the only two transfer instructions not to alter the flags.

Flags Affected: - - - - - - - -

Codes:

Addressing Mode	Syntax	Opcode (hex)	6502	65C02	65802/816	# of Bytes	# of Cycles
Implied	TCS (or TAS)	1B			x	1	2

TDC Transfer Direct Page Register to 16-Bit Accumulator

Transfer the value in the sixteen-bit direct page register D to the sixteen-bit accumulator C, regardless of the setting of the accumulator/memory mode flag.

An alternate mnemonic is TDA (transfer the value in the direct page register to the A accumulator).

In TDC, the "C" is used to indicate that sixteen bits are transferred regardless of the m flag. If the A accumulator is set to just eight bits (whether because the m flag is set, or because the processor is in 6502 emulation mode), then it takes the value of the low byte of the direct page register and the hidden B accumulator takes the value of the high byte of the direct page register.

The direct page register's sixteen-bit value is unchanged by the operation.

Flags Affected: n - - - - z -

    n Set if most significant bit of transferred value is set; else cleared.
    z Set if value transferred is zero; else cleared.

Codes:

Addressing Mode	Syntax	Opcode (hex)	Available to: 6502	65C02	65802/816	# of Bytes	# of Cycles
Implied	TDC (or TDA)	7B			x	1	2

Test and Reset Memory Bits Against Accumulator TRB

Logically AND together the *complement* of the value in the accumulator with the data at the effective address specified by the operand. Store the result at the memory location.

This has the effect of clearing each memory bit for which the corresponding accumulator bit is set, while leaving unchanged all memory bits in which the corresponding accumulator bits are zeroes.

Unlike the BIT instruction, TRB is a read-modify-write instruction, not only calculating a result and modifying a flag, but also storing the result to memory as well.

The z zero flag is set based on a second and *different* operation, the ANDing of the accumulator value (not its complement) with the memory value (the same way the BIT instruction affects the zero flag). The result of this second operation is not saved; only the zero flag is affected by it.

8-bit accumulator/memory (65C02; 65802/65816, m = 1): Values in accumulator and memory are eight-bit.

16-bit accumulator/memory (65802/65816 only, m = 0): Values in accumulator and memory are sixteen-bit: the low-order eight bits are located at the effective address; the high-order eight bits are at the effective address plus one.

Flags Affected: - - - - - z -

z Set if memory value AND'ed with accumulator value is zero; else cleared.

Codes:

Addressing Mode	Syntax	Opcode (hex)	6502	65C02	65802/816	# of Bytes	# of Cycles
Absolute	TRB *addr*	1C		x	x	3	6[1]
Direct Page	TRB *dp*	14		x	x	2	5[1,2]

1 Add 2 cycles if m = 0 (16-bit memory/accumulator)
2 Add 1 cycle if low byte of Direct Page register is other than zero (DL < > 0)

TSB — Test and Set Memory Bits Against Accumulator

Logically OR together the value in the accumulator with the data at the effective address specified by the operand. Store the result at the memory location.

This has the effect of setting each memory bit for which the corresponding accumulator bit is set, while leaving unchanged all memory bits in which the corresponding accumulator bits are zeroes.

Unlike the **BIT** instruction, **TSB** is a read-modify-write instruction, not only calculating a result and modifying a flag, but storing the result to memory as well.

The z zero flag is set based on a second *different* operation, the *ANDing* of the accumulator value with the memory value (the same way the **BIT** instruction affects the zero flag). The result of this second operation is not saved; only the zero flag is affected by it.

8-bit accumulator/memory (65C02; 65802/65816, m = 1): Values in accumulator and memory are eight-bit.

16-bit accumulator/memory (65802/65816 only, m = 0): Values in accumulator and memory are sixteen-bit: the low-order eight bits are located at the effective address; the high-order eight bits are at the effective address plus one.

Flags Affected: - - - - - - z -

z Set if memory value AND'ed with accumulator value is zero; else cleared.

Codes:

Addressing Mode	Syntax	Opcode (hex)	6502	65C02	65802/816	# of Bytes	# of Cycles
Absolute	TSB *addr*	0C		x	x	3	6[1]
Direct Page	TSB *dp*	04		x	x	2	5[1,2]

1 Add 2 cycles if m = 0 (16-bit memory/accumulator)
2 Add 1 cycle if low byte of Direct Page register is other than zero (DL < > 0)

Transfer Stack Pointer to 16-Bit Accumulator   TSC

Transfer the value in the sixteen-bit stack pointer S to the sixteen-bit accumulator C, regardless of the setting of the accumulator/memory mode flag.

An alternate mnemonic is **TSA** (transfer the value in the stack pointer to the A accumulator).

In **TSC**, the "C" is used to indicate that sixteen bits are transferred regardless of the **m** flag. If the A accumulator is set to just eight bits (whether because the **m** flag is set, or because the processor is in 6502 emulation mode), then it takes the value of the low byte of the stack pointer and the hidden B accumulator takes the value of the high byte of the stack pointer. (In emulation mode, B will always take a value of one, since the stack is confined to page one.)

The stack pointer's value is unchanged by the operation.

Flags Affected: n - - - - z -

    n   Set if most significant bit of transferred value is set; else cleared.
    z   Set if value transferred is zero; else cleared.

Codes:

Addressing Mode	Syntax	Opcode (hex)	Available to: 6502	65C02	65802/816	# of Bytes	# of Cycles
Implied	TSC (or TSA)	3B			x	1	2

TSX — Transfer Stack Pointer to Index Register X

Transfer the value in the stack pointer S to index register X. The stack pointer's value is not changed by the operation.

8-bit index registers (all processors): Only the low byte of the value in the stack pointer is transferred to the X register. In the 6502, the 65C02, and the 6502 emulation mode, the stack pointer and the index registers are only a single byte each, so the byte in the stack pointer is transferred to the eight-bit X register. In 65802/65816 native mode, the stack pointer is sixteen bits, so its most significant byte is not transferred if the index registers are in eight-bit mode.

16-bit index registers (65802/65816 only, x = 0): The full sixteen-bit value in the stack pointer is transferred to the X register.

Flags Affected: n - - - - z -

    n Set if most significant bit of transferred value is set; else cleared.
    z Set if value transferred is zero; else cleared.

Codes:

Addressing Mode	Syntax	Opcode (hex)	Available to: 6502	65C02	65802/816	# of Bytes	# of Cycles
Implied	TSX	BA	x	x	x	1	2

Transfer Index Register X to Accumulator   TXA

Transfer the value in index register **X** to the accumulator. If the registers are different sizes, the nature of the transfer is determined by the destination (the accumulator). The value in the index register is not changed by the operation.

8-bit index registers, 8-bit accumulator (all processors): Value transferred is eight-bit.

16-bit index registers, 8-bit accumulator (65802/65816 only, x = 0, m = 1): Value transferred to the eight-bit accumulator is eight-bit, the low byte of the index register; the hidden eight-bit accumulator **B** is not affected by the transfer.

8-bit index registers, 16-bit accumulator (65802/65816 only, x = 1, m = 0): The eight-bit index register becomes the low byte of the accumulator; the high accumulator byte is zeroed.

16-bit index registers, 16-bit accumulator (65802/65816 only, x = 0, m = 0): Value transferred to the sixteen-bit accumulator is sixteen-bit, the full sixteen-bit index register.

Flags Affected: n - - - - z -
                   n   Set if most significant bit of transferred value is set; else cleared.
                   z   Set if value transferred is zero; else cleared.

Codes:

Addressing Mode	Syntax	Opcode (hex)	Available to: 6502	65C02	65802/816	# of Bytes	# of Cycles
Implied	TXA	8A	x	x	x	1	2

TXS — Transfer Index Register X to Stack Pointer

Transfer the value in index register X to the stack pointer, S. The index register's value is not changed by the operation.

TXS, along with TCS, are the only two instructions for changing the value in the stack pointer. The two are also the only two transfer instructions that do not alter the flags.

6502, 65C02, and 6502 emulation mode (65802/65816, e = 1): The stack pointer is only eight bits (it is concatenated to a high byte of one, confining the stack to page one), and the index registers are only eight bits. The byte in X is transferred to the eight-bit stack pointer.

8-bit index registers (65802/65816 native mode, x = 1): The stack pointer is sixteen bits but the index registers are only eight bits. A copy of the byte in X is transferred to the low stack pointer byte and the high stack pointer byte is zeroed.

16-bit index registers (65802/65816 native mode, x = 0): The full sixteen-bit value in X is transferred to the sixteen-bit stack pointer.

Flags Affected: - - - - - - - -

Codes:

Addressing Mode	Syntax	Opcode (hex)	6502	65C02	65802/816	# of Bytes	# of Cycles
Implied	TXS	9A	x	x	x	1	2

Transfer Index Registers X to Y   TXY

Transfer the value in index register X to index register Y. The value in index register X is not changed by the operation. Note that the two registers are never different sizes.

8-bit index registers (x = 1): Value transferred is eight-bit.
16-bit index registers (x = 0): Value transferred is sixteen-bit.

Flags Affected: n - - - - z -
  n Set if most significant bit of transferred value is set; else cleared.
  z Set if value transferred is zero; else cleared.

Codes:

Addressing Mode	Syntax	Opcode (hex)	Available to: 6502	65C02	65802/816	# of Bytes	# of Cycles
Implied	TXY	9B			x	1	2

TYA Transfer Index Register Y to Accumulator

Transfer the value in index register Y to the accumulator. If the registers are different sizes, the nature of the transfer is determined by the destination (the accumulator). The value in the index register is not changed by the operation.

8-bit index registers, 8-bit accumulator (all processors): Value transferred is eight-bit.

16-bit index registers, 8-bit accumulator (65802/65816 only, x = 0, m = 1): Value transferred to the eight-bit accumulator is eight-bit, the low byte of the index register; the hidden eight-bit accumulator **B** is not affected by the transfer.

8-bit index registers, 16-bit accumulator (65802/65816 only, x = 1, m = 0): The eight-bit index register becomes the low byte of the accumulator; the high accumulator byte is zeroed.

16-bit index registers, 16-bit accumulator (65802/65816 only, x = 0, m = 0): Value transferred to the sixteen-bit accumulator is sixteen-bit, the full sixteen-bit index register.

Flags Affected: n - - - - z -

    n Set if most significant bit of transferred value is set; else cleared.
    z Set if value transferred is zero; else cleared.

Codes:

Addressing Mode	Syntax	Opcode (hex)	Available to: 6502	65C02	65802/816	# of Bytes	# of Cycles
Implied	TYA	98	x	x	x	1	2

Transfer Index Registers Y to X — TYX

Transfer the value in index register Y to index register X. The value in index register Y is not changed by the operation. Note that the two registers are never different sizes.

8-bit index registers (x = 1): Value transferred is eight-bit.
16-bit index registers (x = 0): Value transferred is sixteen-bit.

Flags Affected: n - - - - z -

    n Set if most significant bit of transferred value is set; else cleared.
    z Set if value transferred is zero; else cleared.

Codes:

Addressing Mode	Syntax	Opcode (hex)	Available to: 6502	65C02	65802/816	# of Bytes	# of Cycles
Implied	TYX	BB			x	1	2

WAI   Wait for Interrupt

Pull the **RDY** pin low. Power consumption is reduced and **RDY** remains low until an external hardware interrupt (**NMI, IRQ, ABORT,** or **RESET**) is received.

WAI is designed to put the processor to sleep during an external event to reduce its power consumption, to allow it to be synchronized with an external event, and/or to reduce interrupt latency (an interrupt occurring *during* execution of an instruction is not acted upon until execution of the instruction is complete, perhaps many cycles later; **WAI** ensures that an interrupt is recognized immediately).

Once an interrupt is received, control is vectored through one of the hardware interrupt vectors; an **RTI** from the interrupt handling routine will return control to the instruction following the original **WAI**. However, if by setting the i flag, interrupts have been disabled prior to the execution of the **WAI** instruction, and **IRQ'** is asserted, the "wait" condition is terminated and control resumes with the next instruction, rather than through the interrupt vectors. This provides the quickest response to an interrupt, allowing synchronization with external events. **WAI** also frees up the bus; since **RDY** is pulled low in the third instruction cycle, the processor may be disconnected from the bus if **BE** is also pulled low.

Flags Affected: - - - - - - - -

Codes:

Addressing Mode	Syntax	Opcode (hex)	Available to: 6502	65C02	65802/816	# of Bytes	# of Cycles
Implied	WAI	CB			x	1	3[1]

1 Uses 3 cycles to shut the processor down; additional cycles are required by interrupt to restart it

Reserved for Future Expansion — WDM

The 65802 and 65816 use 255 of the 256 possible eight-bit opcodes. One was reserved; it provides an "escape hatch" for future 65x processors to expand their instruction set to sixteen bit opcodes; this opcode would signal that the next byte is an opcode in the expanded instruction set. This reserved byte for future two-byte opcodes was given a temporary mnemonic, **WDM**, which happen to be the initials of the processors' designer—William D. Mensch, Jr.

WDM should never be used in a program, since it would render the object program incompatible with any future 65x processors.

If the 65802/65816 **WDM** instruction is accidentally executed, it will act like a two-byte **NOP** instruction.

Flags Affected*: - - - - - - - -

*Flags will be affected variously by future two-byte instructions.

Codes:

Addressing Mode	Syntax	Opcode (hex)	6502	65C02	65802/816	# of Bytes	# of Cycles
	WDM	42			x	2*	*

*Byte and cycle counts subject to change in future processors which expand WDM into 2-byte opcode portions of instructions of varying lengths

XBA — Exchange the B and A Accumulators

B represents the high-order byte of the sixteen-bit C accumulator, and A in this case represents the low-order byte. XBA swaps the contents of the low-order and high-order bytes of C.

An alternate mnemonic is SWA (swap the high and low bytes of the sixteen-bit A accumulator).

XBA can be used to invert the low-order, high-order arrangement of a sixteen-bit value, or to temporarily store an eight-bit value from the A accumulator into B. Since it is an exchange, the previous contents of both accumulators are changed, replaced by the previous contents of the other.

Neither the mode select flags nor the emulation mode flag affects this operation.

The flags are changed based on the new value of the low byte, the A accumulator (that is, on the former value of the high byte, the B accumulator), even in sixteen-bit accumulator mode.

Flags Affected: n - - - - z -

- n Set if most significant bit of new 8-bit value in A accumulator is set; else cleared.
- z Set if new 8-bit value in A accumulator is zero; else cleared.

Codes:

Addressing Mode	Syntax	Opcode (hex)	Available to: 6502	65C02	65802/816	# of Bytes	# of Cycles
Implied	XBA (or SWA)	EB			x	1	3

Exchange Carry and Emulation Bits   XCE

This instruction is the only means provided by the 65802 and 65816 to shift between 6502 emulation mode and the full, sixteen-bit native mode.

The emulation mode is used to provide hardware and software compatibility between the 6502 and 65802/65816.

If the processor is in emulation mode, then to switch to native mode, first clear the carry bit, then execute an **XCE**. Since it is an exchange operation, the carry flag will reflect the previous state of the emulation bit. Switching to native mode causes bit five to stop functioning as the break flag, and function instead as the x mode select flag. A second mode select flag, **m**, uses bit six, which was unused in emulation mode. Both mode select flags are initially set to one (eight-bit modes). There are also other differences described in the text.

If the processor is in native mode, then to switch to emulation mode, you first set the carry bit, then execute an **XCE**. Switching to emulation mode causes the mode select flags (**m** and **x**) to be lost from the status register, with x replaced by the b break flag. This forces the accumulator to eight bits, but the high accumulator byte is preserved in the hidden **B** accumulator. It also forces the index registers to eight bits, causing the loss of values in their high bytes, and the stack to page one, causing the loss of the high byte of the previous stack address. There are also other differences described in the text.

Flags Affected: $- - m\ b/x - - - c$
                         e

- e Takes carry's previous value: set if carry was set; else cleared.
- c Takes emulation's previous value: set if previous mode was emulation; else cleared.
- m m is a native mode flag only; switching to native mode sets it to 1.
- x x is a native mode flag only; it becomes the b flag in emulation.
- b b is an emulation mode flag only; it is set to 1 to become the x flag in native.

Codes:

Addressing Mode	Syntax	Opcode (hex)	Available to: 6502	65C02	65802/816	# of Bytes	# of Cycles
Implied	XCE	FB			x	1	2

19 | Instruction Lists

| Opcode | | | Available on: | | | # of | # of |
Hex	Mnemonic	Addressing Mode	6502	65C02	65802/816	Bytes	Cycles
00	BRK	Stack/Interrupt	x	x	x	2**	7^9
01	ORA	DP Indexed Indirect,X	x	x	x	2	$6^{1,2}$
02	COP	Stack/Interrupt			x	2**	7^9
03	ORA	Stack Relative			x	2	4^1
04	TSB	Direct Page		x	x	2	$5^{2,5}$
05	ORA	Direct Page	x	x	x	2	$3^{1,2}$
06	ASL	Direct Page	x	x	x	2	$5^{2,5}$
07	ORA	DP Indirect Long			x	2	$6^{1,2}$
08	PHP	Stack (Push)	x	x	x	1	3
09	ORA	Immediate	x	x	x	2*	2^1
0A	ASL	Accumulator	x	x	x	1	2
0B	PHD	Stack (Push)			x	1	4
0C	TSB	Absolute		x	x	3	6^5
0D	ORA	Absolute	x	x	x	3	4^1
0E	ASL	Absolute	x	x	x	3	6^5
0F	ORA	Absolute Long			x	4	5^1
10	BPL	Program Counter Relative	x	x	x	2	$2^{7,8}$
11	ORA	DP Indirect Indexed,Y	x	x	x	2	$5^{1,2,3}$
12	ORA	DP Indirect		x	x	2	$5^{1,2}$
13	ORA	SR Indirect Indexed,Y			x	2	7^1
14	TRB	Direct Page		x	x	2	$5^{2,5}$
15	ORA	DP Indexed,X	x	x	x	2	$4^{1,2}$
16	ASL	DP Indexed,X	x	x	x	2	$6^{2,5}$
17	ORA	DP Indirect Long Indexed,Y			x	2	$6^{1,2}$
18	CLC	Implied	x	x	x	1	2
19	ORA	Absolute Indexed,Y	x	x	x	3	$4^{1,3}$
1A	INC	Accumulator		x	x	1	2
1B	TCS	Implied			x	1	2
1C	TRB	Absolute		x	x	3	6^5
1D	ORA	Absolute Indexed,X	x	x	x	3	$4^{1,3}$
1E	ASL	Absolute Indexed,X	x	x	x	3	$7^{5,6}$
1F	ORA	Absolute Long Indexed,X			x	4	5^1
20	JSR	Absolute	x	x	x	3	6
21	AND	DP Indexed Indirect,X	x	x	x	2	$6^{1,2}$

Continued.

Hex	Opcode Mnemonic	Addressing Mode	6502	65C02	65802/816	# of Bytes	# of Cycles
22	JSR	Absolute Long			x	4	8
23	AND	Stack Relative			x	2	4^1
24	BIT	Direct Page	x	x	x	2	$3^{1,2}$
25	AND	Direct Page	x	x	x	2	$3^{1,2}$
26	ROL	Direct Page	x	x	x	2	$5^{2,5}$
27	AND	DP Indirect Long			x	2	$6^{1,2}$
28	PLP	Stack (Pull)	x	x	x	1	4
29	AND	Immediate	x	x	x	2*	2^1
2A	ROL	Accumulator	x	x	x	1	2
2B	PLD	Stack (Pull)			x	1	5
2C	BIT	Absolute	x	x	x	3	4^1
2D	AND	Absolute	x	x	x	3	4^1
2E	ROL	Absolute	x	x	x	3	6^5
2F	AND	Absolute Long			x	4	5^1
30	BMI	Program Counter Relative	x	x	x	2	$2^{7,8}$
31	AND	DP Indirect Indexed,Y	x	x	x	2	$5^{1,2,3}$
32	AND	DP Indirect		x	x	2	$5^{1,2}$
33	AND	SR Indirect Indexed,Y			x	2	7^1
34	BIT	DP Indexed,X		x	x	2	$4^{1,2}$
35	AND	DP Indexed,X	x	x	x	2	$4^{1,2}$
36	ROL	DP Indexed,X	x	x	x	2	$6^{2,5}$
37	AND	DP Indirect Long Indexed,Y			x	2	$6^{1,2}$
38	SEC	Implied	x	x	x	1	2
39	AND	Absolute Indexed,Y	x	x	x	3	$4^{1,3}$
3A	DEC	Accumulator		x	x	1	2
3B	TSC	Implied			x	1	2
3C	BIT	Absolute Indexed,X		x	x	3	$4^{1,3}$
3D	AND	Absolute Indexed,X	x	x	x	3	$4^{1,3}$
3E	ROL	Absolute Indexed,X	x	x	x	3	$7^{5,6}$
3F	AND	Absolute Long Indexed,X			x	4	5^1
40	RTI	Stack/RTI	x	x	x	1	6^9
41	EOR	DP Indexed Indirect,X	x	x	x	2	$6^{1,2}$
42	WDM				x	2^{16}	16
43	EOR	Stack Relative			x	2	4^1
44	MVP	Block Move			x	3	13
45	EOR	Direct Page	x	x	x	2	$3^{1,2}$
46	LSR	Direct Page	x	x	x	2	$5^{2,5}$
47	EOR	DP Indirect Long			x	2	$6^{1,2}$
48	PHA	Stack (Push)	x	x	x	1	3^1
49	EOR	Immediate	x	x	x	2*	2^1
4A	LSR	Accumulator	x	x	x	1	2

19 Instruction Lists

	Opcode		Available on:			# of	# of
Hex	Mnemonic	Addressing Mode	6502	65C02	65802/816	Bytes	Cycles
4B	PHK	Stack (Push)			x	1	3
4C	JMP	Absolute	x	x	x	3	3
4D	EOR	Absolute	x	x	x	3	4^1
4E	LSR	Absolute	x	x	x	3	6^5
4F	EOR	Absolute Long			x	4	5^1
50	BVC	Program Counter Relative	x	x	x	2	$2^{7,8}$
51	EOR	DP Indirect Indexed, Y	x	x	x	2	$5^{1,2,3}$
52	EOR	DP Indirect		x	x	2	$5^{1,2}$
53	EOR	SR Indirect Indexed, Y			x	2	7^1
54	MVN	Block Move			x	3	13
55	EOR	DP Indexed, X	x	x	x	2	$4^{1,2}$
56	LSR	DP Indexed, X	x	x	x	2	$6^{2,5}$
57	EOR	DP Indirect Long Indexed, Y			x	2	$6^{1,2}$
58	CLI	Implied	x	x	x	1	2
59	EOR	Absolute Indexed, Y	x	x	x	3	$4^{1,3}$
5A	PHY	Stack (Push)		x	x	1	3^{10}
5B	TCD	Implied			x	1	2
5C	JMP	Absolute Long			x	4	4
5D	EOR	Absolute Indexed, X	x	x	x	3	$4^{1,3}$
5E	LSR	Absolute Indexed, X	x	x	x	3	$7^{5,6}$
5F	EOR	Absolute Long Indexed, X			x	4	5^1
60	RTS	Stack (RTS)	x	x	x	1	6
61	ADC	DP Indexed Indirect, X	x	x	x	2	$6^{1,2,4}$
62	PER	Stack (PC Relative Long)			x	3	6
63	ADC	Stack Relative			x	2	$4^{1,4}$
64	STZ	Direct Page		x	x	2	$3^{1,2}$
65	ADC	Direct Page	x	x	x	2	$3^{1,2,4}$
66	ROR	Direct Page	x	x	x	2	$5^{2,5}$
67	ADC	DP Indirect Long			x	2	$6^{1,2,4}$
68	PLA	Stack (Pull)	x	x	x	1	4^1
69	ADC	Immediate	x	x	x	2*	$2^{1,4}$
6A	ROR	Accumulator	x	x	x	1	2
6B	RTL	Stack (RTL)			x	1	6
6C	JMP	Absolute Indirect	x	x	x	3	$5^{11,12}$
6D	ADC	Absolute	x	x	x	3	$4^{1,4}$
6E	ROR	Absolute	x	x	x	3	6^5
6F	ADC	Absolute Long			x	4	$5^{1,4}$
70	BVS	Program Counter Relative	x	x	x	2	$2^{7,8}$
71	ADC	DP Indirect Indexed, Y	x	x	x	2	$5^{1,2,3,4}$
72	ADC	DP Indirect		x	x	2	$5^{1,2,4}$

Continued.

	Opcode		Available on:			# of	# of
Hex	Mnemonic	Addressing Mode	6502	65C02	65802/816	Bytes	Cycles
73	ADC	SR Indirect Indexed,Y			x	2	$7^{1,4}$
74	STZ	Direct Page Indexed,X		x	x	2	$4^{1,2}$
75	ADC	DP Indexed,X	x	x	x	2	$4^{1,2,4}$
76	ROR	DP Indexed,X	x	x	x	2	$6^{2,5}$
77	ADC	DP Indirect Long Indexed,Y			x	2	$6^{1,2,4}$
78	SEI	Implied	x	x	x	1	2
79	ADC	Absolute Indexed,Y	x	x	x	3	$4^{1,3,4}$
7A	PLY	Stack/Pull		x	x	1	4^{10}
7B	TDC	Implied			x	1	2
7C	JMP	Absolute Indexed Indirect		x	x	3	6
7D	ADC	Absolute Indexed,X	x	x	x	3	$4^{1,3,4}$
7E	ROR	Absolute Indexed,X	x	x	x	3	$7^{5,6}$
7F	ADC	Absolute Long Indexed,X			x	4	$5^{1,4}$
80	BRA	Program Counter Relative		x	x	2	3^8
81	STA	DP Indexed Indirect,X	x	x	x	2	$6^{1,2}$
82	BRL	Program Counter Relative Long			x	3	4
83	STA	Stack Relative			x	2	4^1
84	STY	Direct Page	x	x	x	2	$3^{2,10}$
85	STA	Direct Page	x	x	x	2	$3^{1,2}$
86	STX	Direct Page	x	x	x	2	$3^{2,10}$
87	STA	DP Indirect Long			x	2	$6^{1,2}$
88	DEY	Implied	x	x	x	1	2
89	BIT	Immediate		x	x	2*	2^1
8A	TXA	Implied	x	x	x	1	2
8B	PHB	Stack (Push)			x	1	3
8C	STY	Absolute	x	x	x	3	4^{10}
8D	STA	Absolute	x	x	x	3	4^1
8E	STX	Absolute	x	x	x	3	4^{10}
8F	STA	Absolute Long			x	4	5^1
90	BCC	Program Counter Relative	x	x	x	2	$2^{7,8}$
91	STA	DP Indirect Indexed,Y	x	x	x	2	$6^{1,2}$
92	STA	DP Indirect		x	x	2	$5^{1,2}$
93	STA	SR Indirect Indexed,Y			x	2	7^1
94	STY	Direct Page Indexed,X	x	x	x	2	$4^{2,10}$
95	STA	DP Indexed,X	x	x	x	2	$4^{1,2}$
96	STX	Direct Page Indexed,Y	x	x	x	2	$4^{2,10}$
97	STA	DP Indirect Long Indexed,Y			x	2	$6^{1,2}$
98	TYA	Implied	x	x	x	1	2
99	STA	Absolute Indexed,Y	x	x	x	3	5^1
9A	TXS	Implied	x	x	x	1	2
9B	TXY	Implied			x	1	2

19 Instruction Lists

Hex	Opcode Mnemonic	Addressing Mode	6502	65C02	65802/816	# of Bytes	# of Cycles
9C	STZ	Absolute		x	x	3	4^1
9D	STA	Absolute Indexed,X	x	x	x	3	5^1
9E	STZ	Absolute Indexed,X		x	x	3	5^1
9F	STA	Absolute Long Indexed,X			x	4	5^1
A0	LDY	Immediate	x	x	x	2+	2^{10}
A1	LDA	DP Indexed Indirect,X	x	x	x	2	$6^{1,2}$
A2	LDX	Immediate	x	x	x	2+	2^{10}
A3	LDA	Stack Relative			x	2	4^1
A4	LDY	Direct Page	x	x	x	2	$3^{2,10}$
A5	LDA	Direct Page	x	x	x	2	$3^{1,2}$
A6	LDX	Direct Page	x	x	x	2	$3^{2,10}$
A7	LDA	DP Indirect Long			x	2	$6^{1,2}$
A8	TAY	Implied	x	x	x	1	2
A9	LDA	Immediate	x	x	x	2*	2^1
AA	TAX	Implied	x	x	x	1	2
AB	PLB	Stack (Pull)			x	1	4
AC	LDY	Absolute	x	x	x	3	4^{10}
AD	LDA	Absolute	x	x	x	3	4^1
AE	LDX	Absolute	x	x	x	3	4^{10}
AF	LDA	Absolute Long			x	4	5^1
B0	BCS	Program Counter Relative	x	x	x	2	$2^{7,8}$
B1	LDA	DP Indirect Indexed,Y	x	x	x	2	$5^{1,2,3}$
B2	LDA	DP Indirect		x	x	2	$5^{1,2}$
B3	LDA	SR Indirect Indexed,Y			x	2	7^1
B4	LDY	DP Indexed,X	x	x	x	2	$4^{2,10}$
B5	LDA	DP Indexed,X	x	x	x	2	$4^{1,2}$
B6	LDX	DP Indexed,Y	x	x	x	2	$4^{2,10}$
B7	LDA	DP Indirect Long Indexed,Y			x	2	$6^{1,2}$
B8	CLV	Implied	x	x	x	1	2
B9	LDA	Absolute Indexed,Y	x	x	x	3	$4^{1,3}$
BA	TSX	Implied	x	x	x	1	2
BB	TYX	Implied			x	1	2
BC	LDY	Absolute Indexed,X	x	x	x	3	$4^{3,10}$
BD	LDA	Absolute Indexed,X	x	x	x	3	$4^{1,3}$
BE	LDX	Absolute Indexed,Y	x	x	x	3	$4^{3,10}$
BF	LDA	Absolute Long Indexed,X			x	4	5^1
C0	CPY	Immediate	x	x	x	2+	2^{10}
C1	CMP	DP Indexed Indirect,X	x	x	x	2	$6^{1,2}$
C2	REP	Immediate			x	2	3
C3	CMP	Stack Relative			x	2	4^1

Continued.

Hex	Opcode Mnemonic	Addressing Mode	6502	65C02	65802/816	# of Bytes	# of Cycles
C4	CPY	Direct Page	x	x	x	2	$3^{2,10}$
C5	CMP	Direct Page	x	x	x	2	$3^{1,2}$
C6	DEC	Direct Page	x	x	x	2	$5^{2,5}$
C7	CMP	DP Indirect Long			x	2	$6^{1,2}$
C8	INY	Implied	x	x	x	1	2
C9	CMP	Immediate	x	x	x	2*	2^1
CA	DEX	Implied	x	x	x	1	2
CB	WAI	Implied			x	1	3^{15}
CC	CPY	Absolute	x	x	x	3	4^{10}
CD	CMP	Absolute	x	x	x	3	4^1
CE	DEC	Absolute	x	x	x	3	6^5
CF	CMP	Absolute Long			x	4	5^1
D0	BNE	Program Counter Relative	x	x	x	2	$2^{7,8}$
D1	CMP	DP Indirect Indexed, Y	x	x	x	2	$5^{1,2,3}$
D2	CMP	DP Indirect		x	x	2	$5^{1,2}$
D3	CMP	SR Indirect Indexed, Y			x	2	7^1
D4	PEI	Stack (Direct Page Indirect)			x	2	6^2
D5	CMP	DP Indexed, X	x	x	x	2	$4^{1,2}$
D6	DEC	DP Indexed, X	x	x	x	2	$6^{2,5}$
D7	CMP	DP Indirect Long Indexed, Y			x	2	$6^{1,2}$
D8	CLD	Implied	x	x	x	1	2
D9	CMP	Absolute Indexed, Y	x	x	x	3	$4^{1,3}$
DA	PHX	Stack (Push)		x	x	1	3^{10}
DB	STP	Implied			x	1	3^{14}
DC	JMP	Absolute Indirect Long			x	3	6
DD	CMP	Absolute Indexed, X	x	x	x	3	$4^{1,3}$
DE	DEC	Absolute Indexed, X	x	x	x	3	$7^{5,6}$
DF	CMP	Absolute Long Indexed, X			x	4	5^1
E0	CPX	Immediate	x	x	x	2+	2^{10}
E1	SBC	DP Indexed Indirect, X	x	x	x	2	$6^{1,2,4}$
E2	SEP	Immediate			x	2	3
E3	SBC	Stack Relative			x	2	$4^{1,4}$
E4	CPX	Direct Page	x	x	x	2	$3^{2,10}$
E5	SBC	Direct Page	x	x	x	2	$3^{1,2,4}$
E6	INC	Direct Page	x	x	x	2	$5^{2,5}$
E7	SBC	DP Indirect Long			x	2	$6^{1,2,4}$
E8	INX	Implied	x	x	x	1	2
E9	SBC	Immediate	x	x	x	2*	$2^{1,4}$
EA	NOP	Implied	x	x	x	1	2
EB	XBA	Implied			x	1	3
EC	CPX	Absolute	x	x	x	3	4^{10}

	Opcode		Available on:			# of	# of
Hex	Mnemonic	Addressing Mode	6502	65C02	65802/816	Bytes	Cycles
ED	SBC	Absolute	x	x	x	3	$4^{1,4}$
EE	INC	Absolute	x	x	x	3	6^5
EF	SBC	Absolute Long			x	4	$5^{1,4}$
F0	BEQ	Program Counter Relative	x	x	x	2	$2^{7,8}$
F1	SBC	DP Indirect Indexed, Y	x	x	x	2	$5^{1,2,3,4}$
F2	SBC	DP Indirect		x	x	2	$5^{1,2,4}$
F3	SBC	SR Indirect Indexed, Y			x	2	$7^{1,4}$
F4	PEA	Stack (Absolute)			x	3	5
F5	SBC	DP Indexed, X	x	x	x	2	$4^{1,2,4}$
F6	INC	DP Indexed, X	x	x	x	2	$6^{2,5}$
F7	SBC	DP Indirect Long Indexed, Y			x	2	$6^{1,2,4}$
F8	SED	Implied	x	x	x	1	2
F9	SBC	Absolute Indexed, Y	x	x	x	3	$4^{1,3,4}$
FA	PLX	Stack/Pull		x	x	1	4^{10}
FB	XCE	Implied			x	1	2
FC	JSR	Absolute Indexed Indirect			x	3	8
FD	SBC	Absolute Indexed, X	x	x	x	3	$4^{1,3,4}$
FE	INC	Absolute Indexed, X	x	x	x	3	$7^{5,6}$
FF	SBC	Absolute Long Indexed, X			x	4	$5^{1,4}$

* Add 1 byte if m = 0 (16-bit memory/accumulator)

** opcode is 1 byte, but program counter value pushed onto stack is incremented by 2 allowing for optional signature byte

+ Add 1 byte if x = 0 (16-bit index registers)

[1] Add 1 cycle if m = 0 (16-bit memory/accumulator)
[2] Add 1 cycle if low byte of Direct Page register is other than zero (DL < > 0)
[3] Add 1 cycle if adding index crosses a page boundary
[4] Add 1 cycle if 65C02 and d = 1 (decimal mode, 65C02)
[5] Add 2 cycles if m = 0 (16-bit memory/accumulator)
[6] Subtract 1 cycle if 65C02 and no page boundary crossed
[7] Add 1 cycle if branch is taken
[8] Add 1 more cycle if branch taken crosses page boundary on 6502, 65C02, or 65816/65802's 6502 emulation mode (e = 1)
[9] Add 1 cycle for 65802/65816 native mode (e = 0)
[10] Add 1 cycle if x = 0 (16-bit index registers)
[11] Add 1 cycle if 65C02
[12] 6502: If low byte of operand is $FF (i.e., operand is $xxFF): yields incorrect result
[13] 7 cycles per byte moved
[14] Uses 3 cycles to shut the processor down; additional cycles are required by reset to restart it
[15] Uses 3 cycles to shut the processor down; additional cycles are required by interrupt to restart it
[16] Byte and cycle counts subject to change in future processors which expand WDM into 2-byte opcode portions of instructions of varying lengths

Opcodes Reference Chart

Mnemonic	Operation		Immediate # const	Absolute addr	Absolute Long long	Direct Page (DP) dp	Accumulator A	Implied	DP Indirect Indexed,Y (dp), Y	DP Indirect Long Indexed,Y [dp], Y	DP Indexed Indirect,X (idp,X)	DP Indexed,X dp, X	DP Indexed,Y dp, Y	Absolute Indexed,X addr, X
			1 — #	2 — #	3 — #	4 —² #	5 — #	6 — #	7 —² #	8 —² #	9 —² #	10 —² #	11 —² #	12 — #
ADC	A + M + C → A	(1)(4)	69 2 2*	6D 4 3	6F 5 4	65 3 2			71 5³ 2	77 6 2	61 6 2	75 4 2		7D 4³ 3
AND	A∧M → A	(1)	29 2 2*	2D 4 3	2F 5 4	25 3 2			31 5³ 2	37 6 2	21 6 2	35 4 2		3D 4³ 3
ASL	C← 15/7 0 ←0			0E 6 3		06 5⁵ 2	0A 2 1					16 6⁵ 2		1E 7⁵,⁶ 3
BCC	Branch if C = 0 (BLT)	(7)												
BCS	Branch if C = 1 (BGE)	(7)												
BEQ	Branch if Z = 1	(7)												
BIT	A∧M	(1)	89* 2 2*	2C 4 3		24 3 2						34* 4 2		3C* 4³ 3
BMI	Branch if N = 1	(7)												
BNE	Branch if Z = 0	(7)												
BPL	Branch if N = 0	(7)												
BRA	Branch always													
BRK	Break	(9)												
BRL	Branch long always													
BVC	Branch if V = 0	(7)												
BVS	Branch if V = 1	(7)												
CLC	0→C							18 2 1						
CLD	0→D							DB 2 1						
CLI	0→I							58 2 1						
CLV	0→V							B8 2 1						
CMP	A − M	(1)	C9 2 2*	CD 4 3	CF 5 4	C5 3 2			D1 5³ 2	D7 6 2	C1 6 2	D5 4 2		DD 4³ 3
COP	Co-processor	(9)												
CPX	X − M	(10)	E0 2 2⁺	EC 4 3		E4 3 2								
CPY	Y − M	(10)	C0 2 2⁺	CC 4 3		C4 3 2								
DEC	Decrement			CE 6 3		C6 5⁵ 2	3A* 2 1					D6 6⁵ 2		DE 7⁵,⁶ 3
DEX	X − 1 → X							CA 2 1						
DEY	Y − 1 → Y							88 2 1						
EOR	A∀M → A	(1)	49 2 2*	4D 4 3	4F 5 4	45 3 2			51 5³ 2	57 6 2	41 6 2	55 4 2		5D 4³ 3
INC	Increment			EE 6 3		E6 5⁵ 2	1A* 2 1					F6 6⁵ 2		FE 7⁵,⁶ 3
INX	X + 1 → X							E8 2 1						
INY	Y + 1 → Y							C8 2 1						
JMP	Jump to new location			4C 3 3	5C 4 4									
JSL	Jump long to subroutine				22 8 4									
JSR	Jump to subroutine			20 6 3										
LDA	M → A	(1)	A9 2 2*	AD 4 3	AF 5 4	A5 3 2			B1 5³ 2	B7 6 2	A1 6 2	B5 4 2		BD 4³ 3
LDX	M → X	(10)	A2 2 2⁺	AE 4 3		A6 3 2							B6 4 2	BC 4³ 3
LDY	M → Y	(10)	A0 2 2⁺	AC 4 3		A4 3 2						B4 4 2		
LSR	0→ 15/7 0 →C			4E 6 3		46 5⁵ 2	4A 2 1					56 6⁵ 2		5E 7⁵,⁶ 3
MVN	M→M Backward (start byte first)													
MVP	M→M Forward (end byte first)													
NOP	No operation							EA 2 1						
ORA	A∀M → A	(1)	09 2 2*	0D 4 3	0F 5 4	05 3 2			11 5³ 2	17 6 2	01 6 2	15 4 2		1D 4³ 3
PEA	M(pc + 2)→M(s); M(pc + 1)→M(s − 1) S − 2 → S													
PEI	M(d + 1)→M(s); M(d)→M(s − 1) S − 2 → S	(2)												
PER	PC + rl + 3→M(s), M(s − 1) S − 2 → S													
PHA	A→M(s); S − 2 → S or S − 1 → S	(1)												
PHB	DBR→M(s); S − 1 → S													
PHD	D→M(s), M(s − 1); S − 2 → S													
PHK	PBR→M(s); S − 1 → S													
PHP	P→M(s); S − 1 → S													
PHX	X→M(s); S − 1 → S or S − 2 → S	(10)												
PHY	Y→M(s); S − 1 → S or S − 2 → S	(10)												
PLA	S + 1 → S or S + 2 → S, M(s)→A	(1)												
PLB	S + 1 → S; M(s)→DBR													
PLD	S + 2 → S; M(s − 1), M(s)→D													
PLP	S + 1 → S; M(s)→P													
PLX	S + 1 → S or S + 2 → S; M(s)→X	(10)												
PLY	S + 1 → S or S + 2 → S; M(s)→Y	(10)												
REP	M(pc + 1)∧P → P		C2 3 2											
ROL	← 15/7 0 ←C ←			2E 6⁵ 3		26 5⁵ 2	2A 2 1					36 6⁵ 2		3E 7⁵,⁶ 3
ROR	→C→ 15/7 0 →			6E 6⁵ 3		66 5⁵ 2	6A 2 1					76 6⁵ 2		7E 7⁵,⁶ 3
RTI	Return from interrupt	(9)												
RTL	Return from subroutine long													
RTS	Return from subroutine													
SBC	A − M − C̄ → A	(1)(4)	E9 2 2*	ED 4 3	EF 5 4	E5 3 2			F1 5³ 2	F7 6 2	E1 6 2	F5 4 2		FD 4³ 3
SEC	1 → C							38 2 1						
SED	1 → D							F8 2 1						
SEI	1 → I							78 2 1						
SEP	M(pc + 1) V P → P		E2 3 2											
STA	A → M	(1)		8D 4 3	8F 5 4	85 3 2			91 6 2	97 6 2	81 6 2	95 4 2		9D 5 3

19 Instruction Lists

Opcodes Reference Chart

Absolute Long Indexed,X long,X	Absolute Indexed,Y addr,Y	PC Relative label	Absolute Indirect Long [addr]	Absolute Indirect (addr)	DP Indirect (dp)	DP Indirect Long [dp]	Absolute Indexed Indirect (addr,X)	Stack	Stack Relative (SR) sr,S	SR Indirect Indexed,Y (sr,S),Y	Block Move srcbk,destbk	Processor Status Code N V M X D I Z C (E=0) / N V 1 B D I Z C (E=1)	Mnemonic
13 - #	14 - #	15 -8 3	17 - #	17 - #	18 -2 #	19 -2 #	20 - #	21 - #	22 - #	23 - #	24 -13 #		
7F 5 4	79 4³ 3				72 5 2	67 6 2			83 4 2	73 7 2		N V . . . . Z C	ADC
3F 5 4	39 4³ 3				32 5 2	27 6 2			23 4 2	33 7 2		N . . . . . Z .	AND
												N . . . . . Z C	ASL
		90 2 2										. . . .	BCC
		B0 2 2										. . . .	BCS
		F0 2 2										. . . .	BEQ
												M₇/₁₅ M₆/₁₄ . . . . Z .	(17) BIT
		30 2 2										. . . .	BMI
		D0 2 2										. . . .	BNE
		10 2 2										. . . .	BPL
		80 3 2										. . . .	● BRA
								00 7 2**				. . . B 0 1 . .	(18) BRK
		82 4 3										. . . .	★ BRL
		50 2 2										. . . .	BVC
		70 2 2										. . . .	BVS
												 0	CLC
												. . . . 0 . . .	CLD
												. . . . . 0 . .	CLI
												. 0	CLV
DF 5 4	D9 4³ 3				D2 5 2	C7 6 2			C3 4 2	D3 7 2		N . . . . . Z C	CMP
								02 7 2**				. . . . 0 1 . .	★ COP
												N . . . . . Z C	CPX
												N . . . . . Z C	CPY
												N . . . . . Z .	DEC
												N . . . . . Z .	DEX
												N . . . . . Z .	DEY
5F 5 4	59 4³ 3				52 5 2	47 6 2			43 4 2	53 7 2		N . . . . . Z .	EOR
												N . . . . . Z .	INC
												N . . . . . Z .	INX
												N . . . . . Z .	INY
			DC 6 3	6C 5¹¹,¹² 3			7C● 6 3					. . . .	JMP
							FC★ 8 3					. . . .	★ JSL
												. . . .	JSR
BF 5 4	B9 4³ 3				B2 5 2	A7 6 2			A3 4 2	B3 7 2		N . . . . . Z .	LDA
	BE 4³ 3											N . . . . . Z .	LDX
												N . . . . . Z .	LDY
												0 . . . . . Z C	LSR
											54 7/n 3	. . . .	★ MVN
											44 7/n 3	. . . .	★ MVP
												. . . .	NOP
1F 5 4	19 4³ 3				12 5 2	07 6 2			03 4 2	13 7 2		N . . . . . Z .	ORA
								F4 5 3				. . . .	★ PEA
								D4 6 2				. . . .	★ PEI
								62 6 3				. . . .	★ PER
								48 3 1				. . . .	PHA
								8B 3 1				. . . .	★ PHB
								0B 4 1				. . . .	★ PHD
								4B 3 1				. . . .	★ PHK
								08 3 1				. . . .	PHP
								DA 3 1				. . . .	● PHX
								5A 3 1				. . . .	● PHY
								68 4 1				N . . . . . Z .	PLA
								AB 4 1				N . . . . . Z .	★ PLB
								2B 5 1				N . . . . . Z .	★ PLD
								28 4 1				N V M X D I Z C	PLP
								FA 4 1				N . . . . . Z .	● PLX
								7A 4 1				N . . . . . Z .	● PLY
												N V M X D I Z C	★ REP
												N . . . . . Z C	ROL
												N . . . . . Z C	ROR
								40 6 1				N V M X D I Z C	RTI
								6B 6 1				. . . .	★ RTL
								60 6 1				. . . .	RTS
FF 5 4	F9 4³ 3				F2 5 2	E7 6 2			E3 4 2	F3 7 2		N V . . . . Z C	SBC
												 1	SEC
												. . . . 1 . . .	SED
												. . . . . 1 . .	SEI
												N V M X D I Z C	★ SEP
9F 5 4	99 5 3				92 5 2	87 6 2			83 4 2	93 7 2		. . . .	STA

Opcodes Reference Chart—(continued)

Mnemonic	Operation		Immediate # const 1 ~ #	Absolute addr 2 ~ #	Absolute* Long long 3 ~ #	Direct Page (DP) dp 4 ~² #	Accumulator A 5 ~ #	Implied 6 ~ #	DP Indirect Indexed,Y (dp),Y 7 ~² #	DP* Indirect Long Indexed,Y [dp],Y 8 ~² #	DP Indexed Indirect,X (dp,X) 9 ~² #	DP Indexed,X dp,X 10 ~² #	DP Indexed,Y dp,Y 11 ~² #	Absolute Indexed,X addr,X 12 ~ #
STP	Stop (1 → ϕ2)	(14)						DB 3 1						
STX	X → M	(10)		8E 4 3		86 3 2							96 4 2	
STY	Y → M	(10)		8C 4 3		84 3 2						94 4 2		
STZ	00 → M	(1)		9C 4 3		64 3 2						74 4 2		9E 5 3
TAX	A → X							AA 2 1						
TAY	A → Y							A8 2 1						
TCD	C → D							5B 2 1						
TCS	C → S							1B 2 1						
TDC	D → C							7B 2 1						
TRB	Ā∧M → M	(5)		1C 6 3		14 5 2								
TSB	AVM → M	(5)		0C 6 3		04 5 2								
TSC	S → C							3B 2 1						
TSX	S → X							BA 2 1						
TXA	X → A							8A 2 1						
TXS	X → S							9A 2 1						
TXY	X → Y							9B 2 1						
TYA	Y → A							98 2 1						
TYX	Y → X							BB 2 1						
WAI	0 → RDY	(15)						CB 3 1						
WDM	No operation (reserved)	(16)						42 2^{16}						
XBA	B ↔ A							EB 3 1						
XCE	C ↔ E							FB 2 1						

Processor
● Opcode or instruction first introduced on the 65C02
* Opcode or instruction first introduced on the 65816/65802
 (not marked: first introduced on the NMOS 6502)

Addressing mode box:

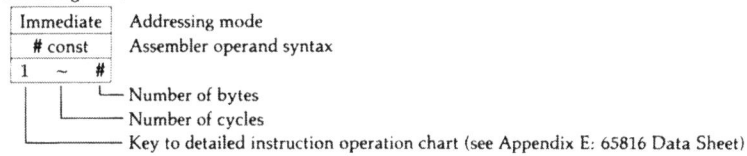

```
| Immediate |    Addressing mode
|  # const  |    Assembler operand syntax
|  1  ~  #  |
         └── Number of bytes
       └──── Number of cycles
   └──────── Key to detailed instruction operation chart (see Appendix E: 65816 Data Sheet)
```

Operation column:

- A   Accumulator
- X   Index register X
- Y   Index register Y
- M   Contents of memory location specified by effective address
- M(d)   Contents of direct page memory location pointed to by operand
- M(s)   Contents of memory location pointed to by stack pointer
- M(pc)   Current opcode pointed to by the program counter
- PC   Memory location of current opcode pointed to by the program counter
- rl   Two-byte operand of relative long addressing mode instruction
- +   Add
- −   Subtract
- ∧   And
- ∨   Or
- ⊻   Exclusive Or
- —   Logical complement of a value or status bit ($\overline{A}$ indicates the complement of the value in the accumulator)
- $\phi 2$ Phase 2 clock (hardware signal)
- RDY   Ready (hardware signal)

Opcodes Reference Chart—(continued)

Absolute Long Indexed,X	Absolute Indexed,Y	PC Relative	Absolute Indirect Long	Absolute Indirect	DP Indirect	DP Indirect Long	Absolute Indexed Indirect	Stack	Stack Relative (SR)	SR Indirect Indexed,Y	Block Move	Processor Status Code 7 6 5 4 3 2 1 0								Mnemonic
long,X	addr,Y	label	[addr]	(addr)	(dp)	[dp]	(addr,X)		sr,S	(sr,S),Y	srcbk,destbk	N	V	M	X	D	I	Z	C	E=0
13 - #	14 - #	15 -⁸ #	16 - #	17 - #	18 -² #	19 -² #	20 - #	21 - #	22 - #	23 - #	24 -¹³ #	N	V	1	B	D	I	Z	C	E=1
												.	.	.	.	.	.	.	.	• STP
												.	.	.	.	.	.	.	.	STX
												.	.	.	.	.	.	.	.	STY
												.	.	.	.	.	.	.	.	• STZ
												N	.	.	.	.	.	Z	.	TAX
												N	.	.	.	.	.	Z	.	TAY
												N	.	.	.	.	.	Z	.	• TCD
												.	.	.	.	.	.	.	.	• TCS
												N	.	.	.	.	.	Z	.	• TDC
												.	.	.	.	.	.	Z	.	• TRB
												.	.	.	.	.	.	Z	.	TSB
												N	.	.	.	.	.	Z	.	• TSC
												N	.	.	.	.	.	Z	.	TSX
												N	.	.	.	.	.	Z	.	TXA
												.	.	.	.	.	.	.	.	TXS
												N	.	.	.	.	.	Z	.	TXY
												N	.	.	.	.	.	Z	.	TYA
												N	.	.	.	.	.	Z	.	TYX
												.	.	.	.	.	.	.	.	• WAI
												.	.	.	.	.	.	.	.	• WDM
												N	.	.	.	.	.	Z	.	• XBA
												.	.	.	.	.	.	.	E	• XCE

Bytes, cycles, and status codes:

*   Add 1 byte if M=0 (16-bit memory/accumulator)

**   opcode is 1 byte, but program counter value pushed onto stack is incremented by 2 allowing for optional signature byte

\+   Add 1 byte if x=0 (16-bit index registers)

n   number of bytes moved

1. Add 1 cycle if m=0 (16-bit memory/accumulator)
2. Add 1 cycle if low byte of Direct Page register is other than zero (DL<>0)
3. Add 1 cycle if adding index crosses a page boundary
4. Add 1 cycle if 65C02 and d=1 (decimal mode, 65C02)
5. Add 2 cycles if m=0 (16-bit memory/accumulator)
6. Subtract 1 cycle if 65C02 and no page boundary crossed
7. Add 1 cycle if branch is taken
8. Add 1 more cycle if branch taken crosses page boundary on 6502, 65C02, or 65816/65802's 6502 emulation mode (e=1)
9. Add 1 cycle for 65802/65816 native mode (e=0)
10. Add 1 cycle if x=0 (16-bit index registers)
11. Add 1 cycle if 65C02
12. 6502: If low byte of *addr* is $FF (i.e., *addr* is $xxFF): yields incorrect result
13. 7 cycles per byte moved
14. Uses 3 cycles to shut the processor down; additional cycles are required by reset to restart it
15. Uses 3 cycles to shut the processor down; additional cycles are required by interrupt to restart it
16. Byte and cycle counts subject to change in future processors which expand WDM into 2-byte opcode portions of instructions of varying lengths
17. BIT: immediate n and v flags not affected; if m=0, m(15) →n and M(14) →v; if m=1, M(7) →n and M(6) →v
18. BRK: if b=1 in pushed status register (6502, 65C02 and emulation mode e=1), then interrupt was caused by software BRK;
    if 6502, d is unaffected by BRK; if 65C02 or 65816/65802, d is 0 after BRK

Opcode Matrix

MSD\LSD	0	1	2	3	4	5	6	7	8	9	A	B	C	D	E	F
0	BRK s 2●7	ORA (d,x) 2 6	COP s 2★7	ORA d,s 2 4	TSB d 2 5	ORA d 2 3	ASL d 2 5	ORA [d] 2★6	PHP s 1 3	ORA # 2 2	ASL A 1 2	PHD s 1★4	TSB a 3 6	ORA a 3 4	ASL a 3 6	ORA al 4★5
1	BPL r 2 2	ORA (d),y 2 5	ORA (d) 2★5	ORA (d,s),y 2★7	TRB d 2 5	ORA d,x 2 4	ASL d,x 2 6	ORA [d],y 2★6	CLC i 1 2	ORA a,y 3 4	INC A 1●2	TCS s 1★2	TRB a 3 6	ORA a,x 3 4	ASL a,x 3 7	ORA al,x 4★5
2	JSR a 3 6	AND (d,x) 2 6	JSL al 4★8	AND d,s 2★4	BIT d 2 3	AND d 2 3	ROL d 2 5	AND [d] 2★6	PLP s 1 4	AND # 2 2	ROL A 1 2	PLD s 1★5	BIT a 3 4	AND a 3 4	ROL a 3 6	AND al 4★5
3	BMI r 2 2	AND (d),y 2 5	AND (d) 2★5	AND (d,s),y 2★7	BIT d,x 2●4	AND d,x 2 4	ROL d,x 2 6	AND [d],y 2★6	SEC i 1 2	AND a,y 3 4	DEC A 1 2	TSC s 1★2	BIT a,x 3●4	AND a,x 3 4	ROL a,x 3 7	AND al,x 4★5
4	RTI s 1 6	EOR (d,x) 2 6	WDM 2	EOR d,s 2★4	MVP xyc 3★7	EOR d 2 3	LSR d 2 5	EOR [d] 2★6	PHA s 1 3	EOR # 2 2	LSR A 1 2	PHK s 1★3	JMP a 3 3	EOR a 3 4	LSR a 3 6	EOR al 4★5
5	BVC r 2 2	EOR (d),y 2 5	EOR (d) 2★5	EOR (d,s),y 2★7	MVN xyc 3★7	EOR d,x 2 4	LSR d,x 2 6	EOR [d],y 2★6	CLI i 1 2	EOR a,y 3 4	PHY s 1●3	TCD s 1★2	JMP al 4★4	EOR a,x 3 4	LSR a,x 3 7	EOR al,x 4★5
6	RTS s 1 6	ADC (d,x) 2 6	PER s 3★6	ADC d,s 2★4	STZ d 2 3	ADC d 2 3	ROR d 2 5	ADC [d] 2★6	PLA s 1 4	ADC # 2 2	ROR A 1 2	RTL s 1★6	JMP (a) 3 5	ADC a 3 4	ROR a 3 6	ADC al 4★5
7	BVS r 2 2	ADC (d),y 2 5	ADC (d) 2★5	ADC (d,s),y 2★7	STZ d,x 2●4	ADC d,x 2 4	ROR d,x 2 6	ADC [d],y 2★6	SEI i 1 2	ADC a,y 3 4	PLY s 1●4	TDC s 1★2	JMP (a,x) 3●6	ADC a,x 3 4	ROR a,x 3 7	ADC al,x 4★5
8	BRA r 2●3	STA (d,x) 2 6	BRL rl 3★4	STA d,s 2★4	STY d 2 3	STA d 2 3	STX d 2 3	STA [d] 2★6	DEY i 1 2	BIT # 2●2	TXA i 1 2	PHB s 1★3	STY a 3 4	STA a 3 4	STX a 3 4	STA al 4★5
9	BCC r 2 2	STA (d),y 2 6	STA (d) 2●5	STA (d,s),y 2★7	STY d,x 2 4	STA d,x 2 4	STX d,y 2 4	STA [d],y 2★6	TYA i 1 2	STA a,y 3 5	TXS i 1 2	TXY i 1★2	STZ a 3●4	STA a,x 3 5	STZ a,x 3●5	STA al,x 4★5
A	LDY # 2 2	LDA (d,x) 2 6	LDX # 2 2	LDA d,s 2★4	LDY d 2 3	LDA d 2 3	LDX d 2 3	LDA [d] 2★6	TAY i 1 2	LDA # 2 2	TAX i 1 2	PLB s 1★4	LDY a 3 4	LDA a 3 4	LDX a 3 4	LDA al 4★5
B	BCS r 2 2	LDA (d),y 2 5	LDA (d) 2●5	LDA (d,s),y 2★7	LDY d,x 2 4	LDA d,x 2 4	LDX d,y 2 4	LDA [d],y 2★6	CLV i 1 2	LDA a,y 3 4	TSX i 1 2	TYX i 1★2	LDY a,x 3 4	LDA a,x 3 4	LDX a,y 3 4	LDA al,x 4★5
C	CPY # 2 2	CMP (d,x) 2 6	REP # 2★3	CMP d,s 2★4	CPY d 2 3	CMP d 2 3	DEC d 2 5	CMP [d] 2★6	INY i 1 2	CMP # 2 2	DEX i 1 2	WAI i 1★3	CPY a 3 4	CMP a 3 4	DEC a 3 6	CMP al 4★5
D	BNE r 2 2	CMP (d),y 2 5	CMP (d) 2●5	CMP (d,s),y 2★7	PEI s 2★6	CMP d,x 2 4	DEC d,x 2 6	CMP [d],y 2★6	CLD i 1 2	CMP a,y 3 4	PHX s 1●3	STP i 1★3	JML (a) 3★6	CMP a,x 3 4	DEC a,x 3 7	CMP al,x 4★5
E	CPX # 2 2	SBC (d,x) 2 6	SEP # 2★3	SBC d,s 2★4	CPX d 2 3	SBC d 2 3	INC d 2 5	SBC [d] 2★6	INX i 1 2	SBC # 2 2	NOP i 1 2	XBA i 1★3	CPX a 3 4	SBC a 3 4	INC a 3 6	SBC al 4★5
F	BEQ r 2 2	SBC (d),y 2 5	SBC (d) 2●5	SBC (d,s),y 2★7	PEA s 3★5	SBC d,x 2 4	INC d,x 2 6	SBC [d],y 2★6	SED i 1 2	SBC a,y 3 4	PLX s 1●4	XCE i 1★2	JSR (a,x) 3★8	SBC a,x 3 4	INC a,x 3 7	SBC al,x 4★5

Op Code Matrix Legend

```
INSTRUCTION                                    ADDRESSING
MNEMONIC        ★ = New W65C816/802 Opcodes    MODE
                ● = New W65C02 Opcodes
   BASE         Blank = NMOS 6502 Opcodes         BASE
 NO. BYTES                                      NO. CYCLES
```

symbol	addressing mode
#	immediate
A	accumulator
r	program counter relative
rl	program counter relative long
i	implied
s	stack
d	direct
d,x	direct indexed (with x)
d,y	direct indexed (with y)
(d)	direct indirect
(d,x)	direct indexed indirect
(d),y	direct indirect indexed

symbol	addressing mode
[d]	direct indirect long
[d],y	direct indirect long indexed
a	absolute
a,x	absolute indexed (with x)
a,y	absolute indexed (with y)
al	absolute long
al,x	absolute long indexed
d,s	stack relative
(d,s),y	stack relative indirect indexed
(a)	absolute indirect
(a,x)	absolute indexed indirect
xyc	block move

Appendices

A | 65x Signal Description

The four standard 65x parts considered in this book—the 6502, 65C02, 65802, and 65816—are each housed in a 40-pin dual in-line package. There are also a number of special versions of the basic parts, versions with external clocks, fewer address pins, one-chip computers with on-board RAM and ROM, and with quadrature clocks. These are not considered here; refer to the appropriate manufacturer's literature for details about these special chips.

This appendix describes the pin signals found on the four standard parts—the pins that connect the processor to the external system. Many of them are common to all processors, some are unique to each.

The descriptions are meant to satisfy the programmer with a general interest in the system implementation; the engineer implementing a 65x system should consult the manufacturer's data sheets for more detailed information.

To begin with, refer to Figure A.1, which illustrates the pin configurations of the four different processors.

W65C816 pinout (left):

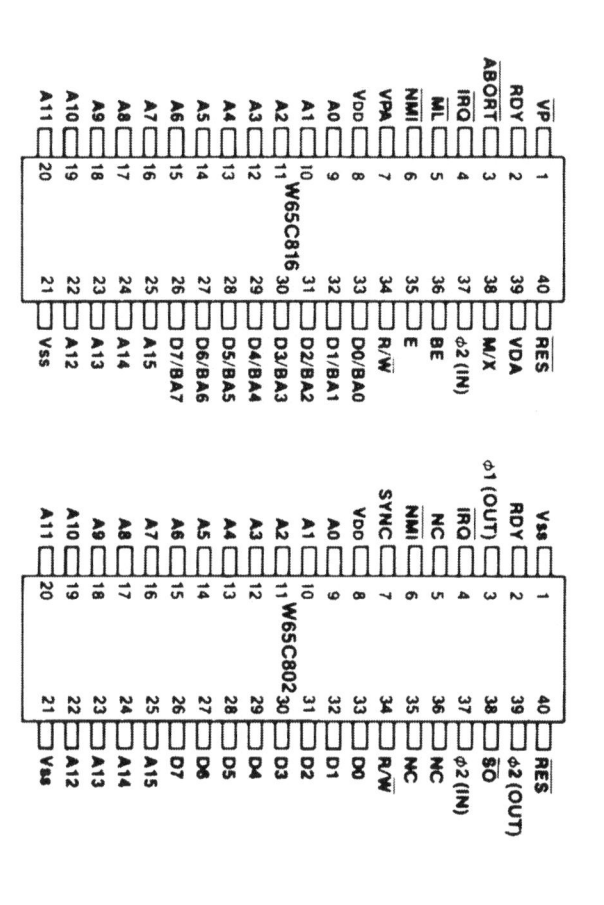

Pin	Name	Pin	Name
1	VP	40	RES
2	RDY	39	VDA
3	ABORT	38	M/X
4	IRQ	37	φ2 (IN)
5	ML	36	BE
6	NMI	35	E
7	VPA	34	R/W
8	VDD	33	D0/BA0
9	A0	32	D1/BA1
10	A1	31	D2/BA2
11	A2	30	D3/BA3
12	A3	29	D4/BA4
13	A4	28	D5/BA5
14	A5	27	D6/BA6
15	A6	26	D7/BA7
16	A7	25	A15
17	A8	24	A14
18	A9	23	A13
19	A10	22	A12
20	A11	21	Vss

W65C802 pinout (right):

Pin	Name	Pin	Name
1	Vss	40	RES
2	RDY	39	φ2 (OUT)
3	φ1 (OUT)	38	SO
4	IRQ	37	φ2 (IN)
5	NC	36	NC
6	NMI	35	R/W
7	SYNC	34	D0
8	VDD	33	D1
9	A0	32	D2
10	A1	31	D3
11	A2	30	D4
12	A3	29	D5
13	A4	28	D6
14	A5	27	D7
15	A6	26	A15
16	A7	25	A14
17	A8	24	A13
18	A9	23	A12
19	A10	22	Vss
20	A11	21	—

Figure A.1. 65x Pinouts.

6502

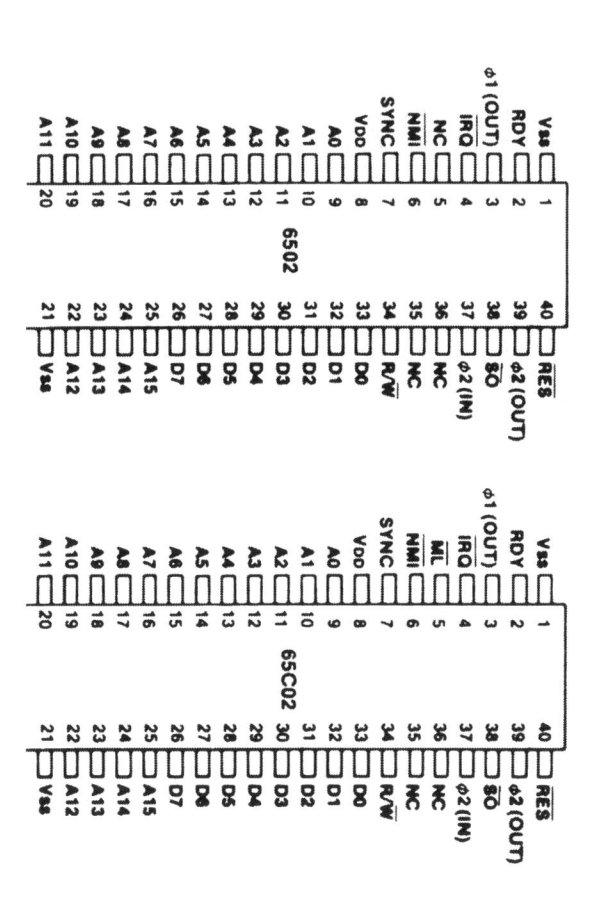

Pin	Signal	Pin	Signal
1	Vss	40	RES
2	RDY	39	φ2 (OUT)
3	φ1 (OUT)	38	SO
4	IRQ	37	φ2 (IN)
5	NC	36	NC
6	NMI	35	NC
7	SYNC	34	R/W
8	VDD	33	D0
9	A0	32	D1
10	A1	31	D2
11	A2	30	D3
12	A3	29	D4
13	A4	28	D5
14	A5	27	D6
15	A6	26	D7
16	A7	25	A15
17	A8	24	A14
18	A9	23	A13
19	A10	22	A12
20	A11	21	Vss

65C02

Pin	Signal	Pin	Signal
1	Vss	40	RES
2	RDY	39	φ2 (OUT)
3	φ1 (OUT)	38	SO
4	IRQ	37	φ2 (IN)
5	ML	36	NC
6	NMI	35	NC
7	SYNC	34	R/W
8	VDD	33	D0
9	A0	32	D1
10	A1	31	D2
11	A2	30	D3
12	A3	29	D4
13	A4	28	D5
14	A5	27	D6
15	A6	26	D7
16	A7	25	A15
17	A8	24	A14
18	A9	23	A13
19	A10	22	A12
20	A11	21	Vss

6502 Signals

The 6502 defines the basic set of signals.

Address Bus

Pins A0 - A15 are the **address lines**. Every time an address is generated—opcode fetch, operand read, intermediate address, or effective address of a read or write operation—the binary value of the address appears on these pins, **A0** representing the low-order bit of the address, and **A15** representing the high-order bit. These outputs are TTL compatible.

Clock Signals

All of the 65x series processors operate on a two-phase external cycle; a 65x processor's frequency, expressed in **Megahertz**, or millions of cycles per second, is also its memory-access cycle time. The 6502 has an internal clock generator based on the **phase zero** input signal, a time base typically provided by a crystal oscillator. The two output signals, **phase one** and **phase two**, are derived from this signal. Phase one goes high when phase zero is low; phase two goes low on the rising edge of phase one.

Data Bus

Pins **D0–D7** are the **data lines;** these eight pins form a bi-directional data bus to read and write data between the processor and memory and the peripheral devices. Like the address lines, the outputs can drive one standard TTL load.

Data Bus Enable

This controls the three-state output buffers of the processor; it normally is enabled by the phase two output, effectively disabling the output buffers during phase one; this frees the bus for access by other devices during phase one. By pulling **DBE** low, the buffers may be disabled externally.

Read/Write

R/W' is high when data is being read from memory or peripherals into the processor, low when the processor is writing data. When in the low state, data and address lines have valid data and addresses.

Ready

The **RDY** signal enables the processor to be single-stepped on all cycles except write cycles. When enabled during phase one, the processor is halted and the address lines maintain the current address; this lets the processor interface with lower-speed read-only memory devices, and can also be used in direct memory access implementations.

Interrupt Request

The IRQ' signal requests that an interrupt-service cycle be initiated. This signal is connected to peripheral devices that are designed to be interrupt-driven. This is the maskable interrupt signal, so the interrupt disable flag in the status register must be zero for the interrupt to be effective. The RDY signal must be high for an interrupt to be recognized. IRQ' is sampled during phase 2.

Non-maskable Interrupt

NMI' is basically identical to IRQ', except that it causes an unconditional interrupt when it is asserted, and control vectors through the NMI' vector rather than IRQ'.

Set Overflow

When this line goes low on the trailing edge of phase one, the overflow flag in the processor status register is set.

Sync

This line goes high during phase one of those cycles that are opcode fetches. When used with the RDY signal, this allows hardware implementation of a single-step debugging capability.

Reset

RESET' reinitializes the processor, either at power-up or to restart the system from a known state. RESET' must be held low for at least two cycles after a power down. When it is asserted, an interrupt-like service routine begins (although the status and program counter are not stacked), with the result that control is transferred through the RESET' vector.

65C02 Signals

The 65C02 pinout is identical to the 6502, with the exception of memory lock and notes described below.

Memory Lock

The ML' output signal assures the integrity of read-modify-write instructions by signaling other devices, for example, other processors in a multiprocessor environment, that the bus may not be claimed until completion of the read-modify-write operation. This signal goes low during the execution of the memory-referencing (non-register operand) ASL, DEC, INC, LSR, ROL, ROR, TRB, and TSB instructions.

Notes

The 65C02, unlike the 6502, responds to **RDY** during a write cycle as well as a read, halting the processor.

Response of the 65C02 to a reset is different from the 6502 in that the 65C02's program counter and status register are written to the stack. Additionally, the 65C02 decimal flag is cleared after reset or interrupt; its value is indeterminate after reset and not modified after interrupt on the 6502.

When an interrupt occurs immediately after the fetch of a **BRK** instruction on the 6502, the **BRK** is ignored; on the 65C02, the **BRK** is executed, then the interrupt is executed.

Finally, the 65C02 R/W' line is high during the modify (internal operation) cycle of the read-modify-write operations; on the 6502, it is low.

65802 Signals

The 65802 signals are by definition 6502 pin-compatible. The 65C02 ML' (memory lock) signal is not on the standard pin-out, although it is available as a special-order mask option. Like the 6502, and unlike the 65C02, the 65802 does not write to the stack during a reset.

Some of the enhancements of the 65C02 are available on the 65802 in the native mode, while in emulation mode the system behaves as a 6502. R/W' is low during the modify cycle of read-modify-write cycles in the emulation mode; high in the native mode.

65816 Signals

Most of the signals behave as on the 65802, with the following additions and changes:

Bank Address

The most important difference on the 65816 is the multiplexing of the bank address (**BA0–BA7**) with the data pins (**D0–D7**). During phase two low, the bank address is valid; during phase two high, data is read or written on the same pins. The bank address must be latched during phase one to provide a valid twenty-four bit address when concatenated with A0–A15.

Vector Pull

The **VP'** signal is asserted whenever any of the vector addresses ($00:FFE4-FFEF, $00:FFF4-FFFF) are being accessed as part of an interrupt-type service cycle. This lets external hardware modify the interrupt vector, eliminating the need for software polling for interrupt sources.

Abort

The **ABORT'** input pin, when it is asserted, causes the current instruction to be aborted. Unlike an interrupt, none of the registers are updated and the instruction quits execution from the cycle where the ABORT' signal was received. No registers are modified. In other words, the processor is left in the state it was in before the instruction that was aborted. Control is shifted to the ABORT' vector after an interrupt-like context-saving cycle.

The ABORT' signal lets external hardware abort instructions on the basis of undesirable address bus conditions; memory protection and paged virtual memory systems can be fully implemented using this signal.

ABORT' should be held low for only one cycle; if held low during the ABORT interrupt sequence, the ABORT interrupt will be aborted.

Valid Program Address and Valid Data Address

The **VPA** and **VDA** signals extend the concept of the SYNC signal. Together, these two pins encode one of four possible internal processor states, based on the type of memory being accessed:

VPA	VDA	
0	0	–Internal operation
0	1	–Valid program address
1	0	–Valid data address
1	1	–Opcode fetch

During internal operations, the output buffers may be disabled by external logic, making the address bus available for transparent direct memory access. Also, since the 65816 sometimes generates a false read during instructions that cross page boundaries, these may be trapped via these two signals if this is desirable. Note, however, that addresses should not be qualified in emulation mode if hardware such as the Apple // disk controller is used, which requires false read to operate.

The other states may be used for virtual memory implementation and high-speed data or instruction cache control. VPA and VDA high together are equivalent to the 6502 SYNC output.

Memory and Index

These two signals are multiplexed on pin 38. M is available during phase zero, X during phase one. These signals reflect the contents of the status register m and x flags, allowing (along with E described below) external logic to fully decode opcode fetches.

As a mask option, the 65816 may be specified with the 6502 SET OVERFLOW signal instead of the M/X signal.

M and X are invalid for the instruction cycle following the **REP**, **SEP**, and **PLP** instruction execution; this cycle is the opcode fetch cycle of the next instruction.

Emulation

The E signal reflects the state of the processor's e flag; depending on whether or not the processor is in emulation mode or not, external system compatibility features (such as memory mapping or system speed) could be enabled or disabled.

Bus Enable

This signal replaces the data bus enable signal of the 6502; when asserted, it disables the address buffers and R/W' as well as the data buffers.

B | 65x Series Support Chips

There are a plethora of companion chips for the 65x processors. The ones every assembly language programmer runs into eventually are serial and parallel input/output (I/O) chips. The 65x family serial I/O controller is the 6551 Asynchronous Communication Interface Adapter (ACIA), while the the simplest parallel I/O controller is the 6521 Peripheral Interface Adapter (PIA).

As the architecture section of this book has already noted, the 65x microprocessors have memory-mapped I/O, not special I/O opcodes. That is, they assign each input and each output device one or more memory locations. An output device's status registers can be tested to determine if the device is ready to send a unit of data. Conversely, an input device's status registers can be tested to determine if a unit of data has arrived and can be read. Writing data is accomplished by storing it to one of the output device's memory locations; reading it is accomplished with a load-register instruction, with its operand one of the input device's memory locations.

One caution: Don't attempt to use *any* peripheral chips without calling or writing the chip's manufacturer for a data sheet, usually provided for little or no charge. While data sheets are no joy to read, they contain enough information to sooner or later explain the programming problems you will run into, if not on your current project, then on the next one.

The 6551 Serial Chip

You may already be familiar with the 6551 ACIA. There is one controlling the serial port on every Apple //c, and one on the plug-in Apple //e Super Serial Card.

The 6551 features an on-chip baud-rate generator, which lets your program set any of fifteen baud rates from 50 to 19,200. Like most other serial chips, word length, number of stop bits, and parity bit generation and detection can also be set under program control.

As an example, if the Super Serial Card were located, as it commonly is, in the Apple //e's port two, four consecutive memory locations are allocated to the 6551 beginning at $C0A8. The 6551's Transmit/Receive Data Register is located at $C0A8. The current status of the chip (for example, indicating it has received a byte of data) is indicated in the Status Register, located at $C0A9 (see Figure B.1). Two registers are used to initialize the chip. The Command Register, located at $C0AA, is used to set up parity and several other parameters. As Figure B.2 indicates, writing $0B to the Command Register sets up a commonly used set of parameters—no parity, and both the RTS and the DTR lines enabled. The Control Register, located at $C0AB, is used to set up stop bits, word length, and baud rate; as Figure B.3 indicates, writing $1E to the Control Register sets up a commonly used set of parameters—one stop bit, eight-bit data, and communications running at 9600 baud.

So the 6551 is initialized by the 65816 code shown in Fragment B.1.

```
0000            COMPORT GEQU    $C0A8       6551 located at $C0A8,9,A,B
0000
0000 E220               SEP     #$20        use 8-bit accumulator
0002                    LONGA   OFF
0002
0002 A900               LDA     #0
0004 8DA9C0             STA     COMPORT+1   StatusReg: programmed reset first
0007 A91E               LDA     #$1E
0009 8DABC0             STA     COMPORT+3   CtrlReg:1 stop bit/8-bit data/960
000C A90B               LDA     #$0B
000E 8DAAC0             STA     COMPORT+2   CmdReg: no parity/RTS,DTR enabled
0011 60                 RTS
```

Fragment B.1.

Actually, *any* value can be written to the status register to cause a programmed reset; this operation is done to reinitialize the I/O registers—the three figures each show the effects on the non-data registers on each of their status bits.

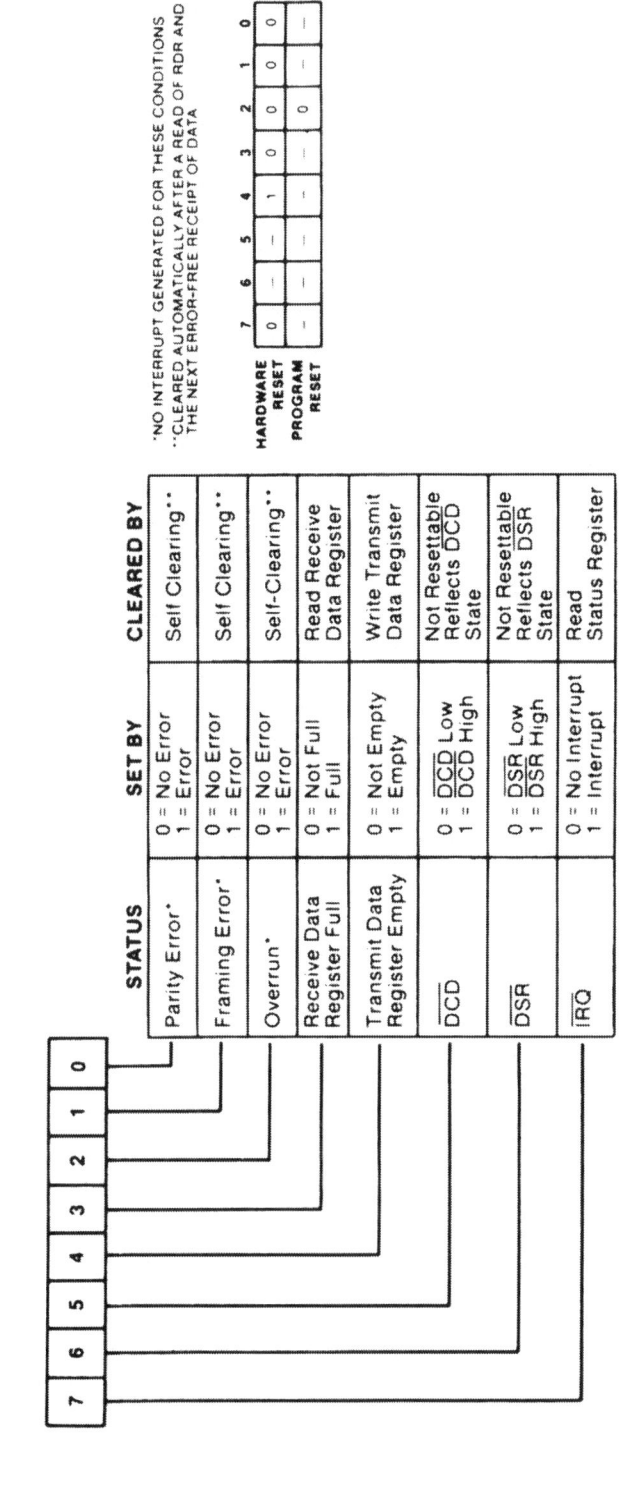

STATUS	SET BY	CLEARED BY
Parity Error*	0 = No Error 1 = Error	Self Clearing**
Framing Error*	0 = No Error 1 = Error	Self Clearing**
Overrun*	0 = No Error 1 = Error	Self-Clearing**
Receive Data Register Full	0 = Not Full 1 = Full	Read Receive Data Register
Transmit Data Register Empty	0 = Not Empty 1 = Empty	Write Transmit Data Register
$\overline{DCD}$	0 = $\overline{DCD}$ Low 1 = $\overline{DCD}$ High	Not Resettable Reflects $\overline{DCD}$ State
$\overline{DSR}$	0 = $\overline{DSR}$ Low 1 = $\overline{DSR}$ High	Not Resettable Reflects $\overline{DSR}$ State
$\overline{IRQ}$	0 = No Interrupt 1 = Interrupt	Read Status Register

*NO INTERRUPT GENERATED FOR THESE CONDITIONS
**CLEARED AUTOMATICALLY AFTER A READ OF RDR AND THE NEXT ERROR-FREE RECEIPT OF DATA

	7	6	5	4	3	2	1	0
HARDWARE RESET	0	-	-	1	0	0	0	0
PROGRAM RESET	-	-	-	-	-	0	0	-

Figure B.1. 6551 Status Register.

COMMAND REGISTER

Bits: 7 6 5 4 3 2 1 0

Bit 0 — DATA TERMINAL READY
- 0 = Disable Receiver and All Interrupts (DTR high)
- 1 = Enable Receiver and All Interrupts (DTR low)

Bit 1 — RECEIVER INTERRUPT ENABLE
- 0 = IRQ Interrupt Enabled from Bit 3 of Status Register
- 1 = IRQ Interrupt Disabled

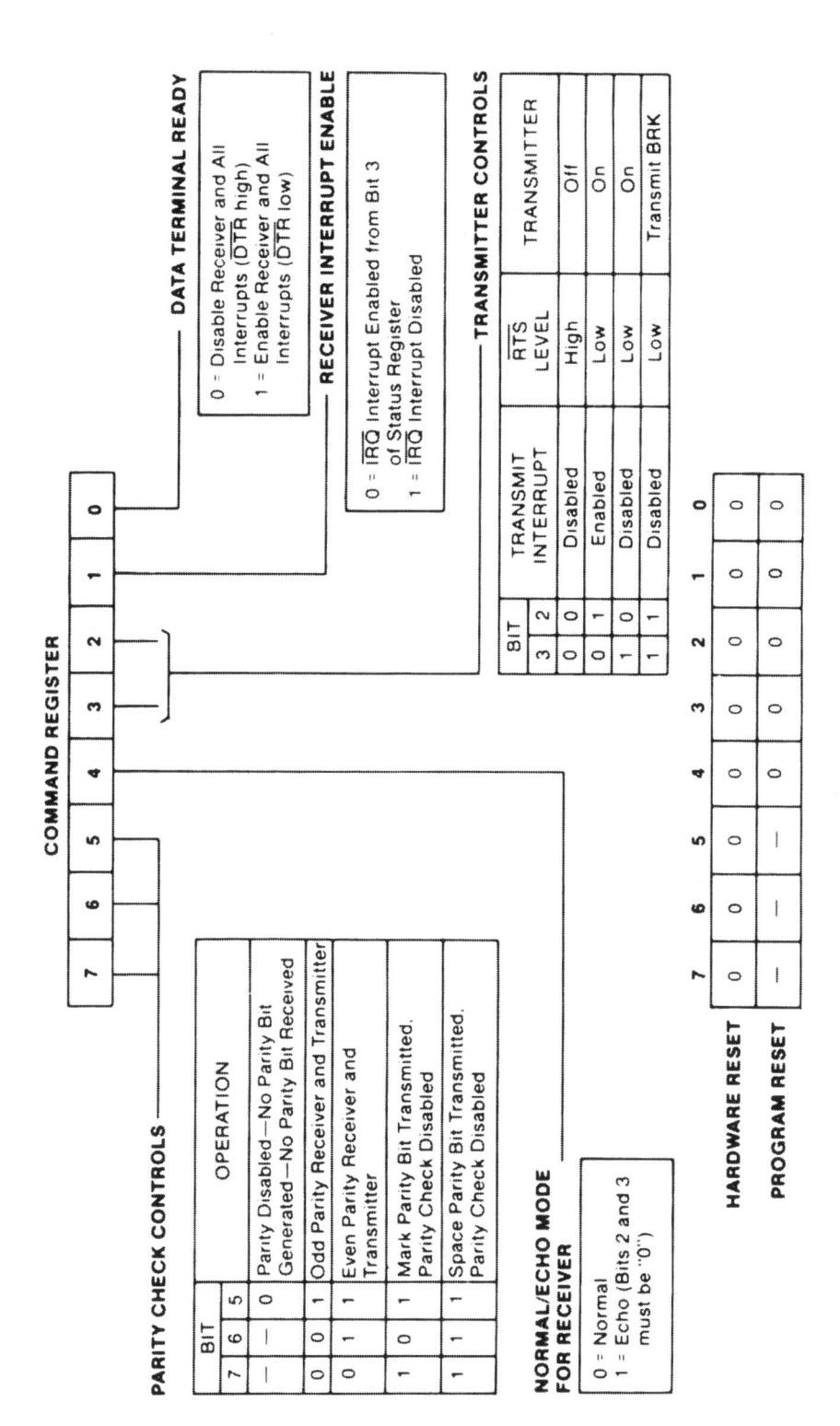

Bits 2, 3 — TRANSMITTER CONTROLS

BIT 3	BIT 2	TRANSMIT INTERRUPT	RTS LEVEL	TRANSMITTER
0	0	Disabled	High	Off
0	1	Enabled	Low	On
1	0	Disabled	Low	On
1	1	Disabled	Low	Transmit BRK

Bits 5, 6, 7 — PARITY CHECK CONTROLS

BIT 7	BIT 6	BIT 5	OPERATION
—	—	0	Parity Disabled—No Parity Bit Generated—No Parity Bit Received
0	0	1	Odd Parity Receiver and Transmitter
0	1	1	Even Parity Receiver and Transmitter
1	0	1	Mark Parity Bit Transmitted, Parity Check Disabled
1	1	1	Space Parity Bit Transmitted, Parity Check Disabled

Bit 4 — NORMAL/ECHO MODE FOR RECEIVER
- 0 = Normal
- 1 = Echo (Bits 2 and 3 must be "0")

Reset states:

	7	6	5	4	3	2	1	0
HARDWARE RESET	0	0	0	0	0	0	0	0
PROGRAM RESET	—	—	—	0	0	0	0	0

Figure B.2. 6551 Command Register.

CONTROL REGISTER

7	6	5	4	3	2	1	0	BAUD RATE GENERATOR
				0	0	0	0	16x EXTERNAL CLOCK
				0	0	0	1	50 BAUD
				0	0	1	0	75
				0	0	1	1	109.92
				0	1	0	0	134.58
				0	1	0	1	150
				0	1	1	0	300
				0	1	1	1	600
				1	0	0	0	1200
				1	0	0	1	1800
				1	0	1	0	2400
				1	0	1	1	3600
				1	1	0	0	4800
				1	1	0	1	7200
				1	1	1	0	9600
				1	1	1	1	19,200

	7	6	5	4	3	2	1	0
HARDWARE RESET	0	0	0	0	0	0	0	0
PROGRAM RESET	—	—	—	—	—	—	—	—

STOP BITS

0 = 1 Stop Bit
1 = 2 Stop Bits
    = 1 Stop Bit if Word Length
      = 8 Bits and Parity*
    = 1½ Stop Bits if Word Length
      = 5 Bits and No Parity

WORD LENGTH

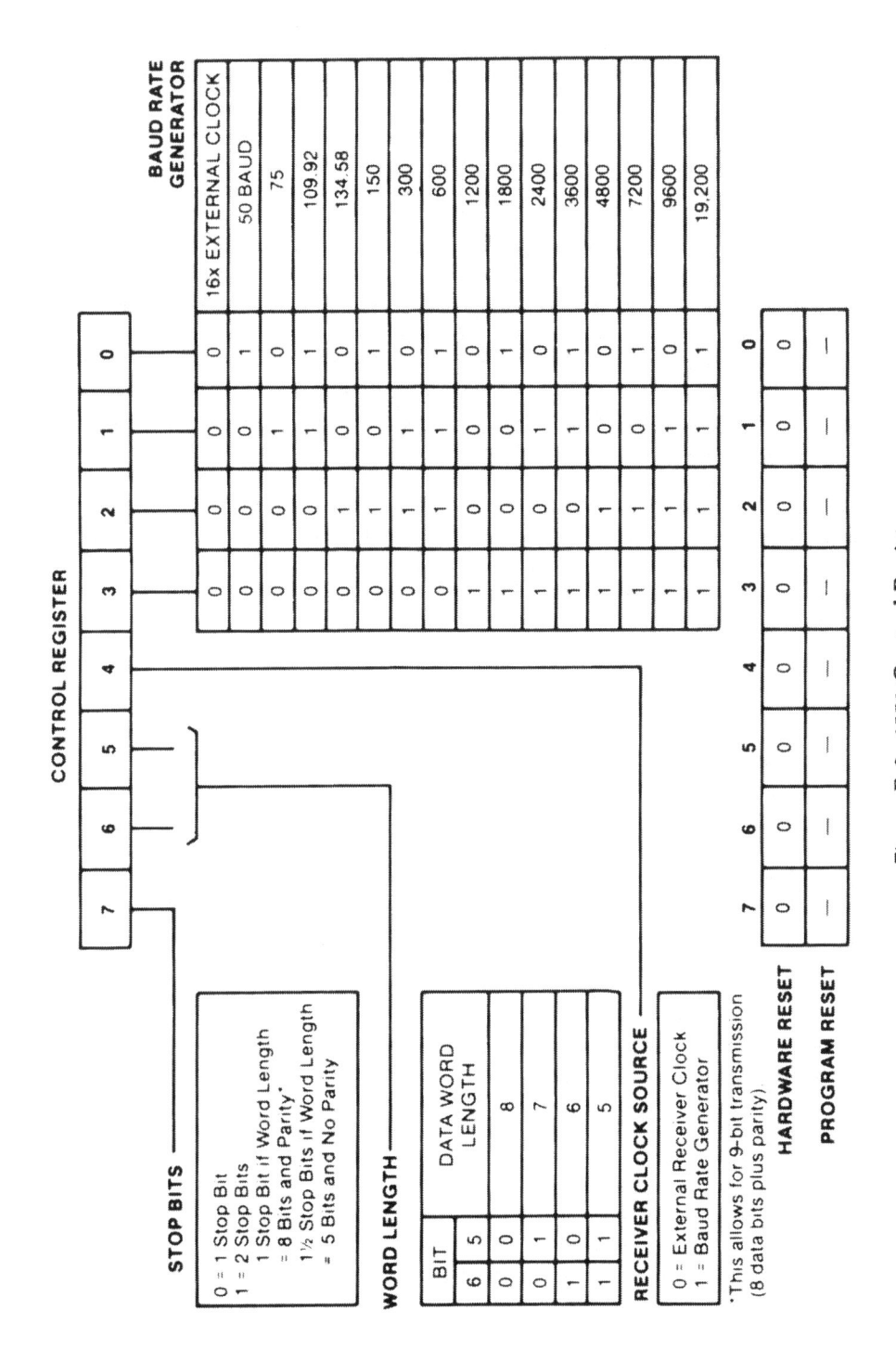

BIT		DATA WORD LENGTH
6	5	
0	0	8
0	1	7
1	0	6
1	1	5

RECEIVER CLOCK SOURCE

0 = External Receiver Clock
1 = Baud Rate Generator

*This allows for 9-bit transmission (8 data bits plus parity)

Figure B.3. 6551 Control Register.

When the 6551 connects a computer to a communications line—whether twisted-pair wire at 9600 baud or a modem at 300 baud—reading a byte from the communications line is a matter of (once the 6551 has been initialized) waiting until the status register bit three (receiver data register full) is set, then reading the byte from the data register, as shown in Fragment B.2.

```
0000                    ; code to read a byte from the communications line (6551)
0000                    ; returns byte in 8-bit A
0000
0000            COMPORT GEQU    $C0A8       6551 located at $C0A8,9,A,B
0000
0000 E220               SEP     #$20        use 8-bit accumulator
0002                    LONGA   OFF
0002
0002 AD A9 C0   AWAITCH LDA     COMPORT+1   read Status Reg
0005 2908               AND     #8          single out bit 3 (rcvr data reg full)
0007 F0F9               BEQ     AWAITCH     loop until bit 3 set
0009
0009 AD A8 C0           LDA     COMPORT     read the byte from Receive Data Reg
000C 60                 RTS                 and return with it
```

Fragment B.2.

Similarly, as Fragment B.3 shows, writing a byte out to the communications line is a matter of (once the 6551 has been initialized) waiting until the status register bit four (transmitter data register empty) is set, then writing the byte to the data register.

Neither routine does any error checking using the other status register bits.

The 6521 Parallel Chip

The 6521 parallel I/O peripheral interface adapter is used to interface 65x microprocessors with printers, matrix-type keyboards, and other devices. It features two programmable eight-bit bidirectional parallel I/O ports (Ports A and B), any lines of which can be individually set for either reading or writing via a Data Direction Register. Provided all eight lines are set one way, you can either read or write a byte at a time (as opposed to a bit at a time via a serial chip) through the port. For fancy I/O, the 6521 has several "handshake" lines for greater control of I/O.

Like the 6551, the 6521 occupies four address locations (those dependent on the hardwiring of the two Register Select lines). But it has six reg-

B 65x Series Support Chips

```
0000                    ; routine to write a byte to the communications line (6551)
0000                    ; enter with byte in 8-bit A
0000
0000            COMPORT GEQU    $C0A8       6551 located at $C0A8,9,A,B
0000
0000 48                 PHA                 save byte to write; free accum
0001
0001 ADA9C0    WAITRDY  LDA    COMPORT+1    read Status Reg
0004 291000             AND    #$10         get bit 4 (trnsmt data reg empty)
0007 F0F8               BEQ    WAITRDY      loop until bit 4 set
0009
0009 68                 PLA                 retrieve byte to write
000A 8DA8C0             STA    COMPORT      write the byte to Transmit Data Reg
000D 60                 RTS
```

Fragment B.3.

isters, three for each port: a control register, a data register, and a data direction register. Each port's data register and data direction register are addressed at the same location. Bit two of the port's control register determines which register is connected to that address at any one time: if control register bit two is set, the data register is connected; if control register bit two is clear, the data direction register is connected.

The data direction register is generally initialized for an application just once; then the data register is selected. Each data direction register bit controls the same-numbered bit in the data register: if a data direction register bit is set, the corresponding data register bit becomes an output line; if a data direction register bit is clear, the corresponding data register bit becomes an input line.

Imagine an application in which a printer is wired through a Centronics-compatible printer port to a 6521's port A: the 6521's eight Port A bits are connected to Centronics pins two through nine. Port B is used to control the interface between computer and printer: the 6521's Port B bit zero is connected to the printer's Data Strobe (Centronics pin one); the 6521's Port B bit seven is connected to the printer Busy Line (Centronics pin 11).

The 6521 PIA is automatically initialized on power-up and reset to all be inputs (all registers are cleared). So every program should initialize all the lines it will use, either as inputs or as outputs, every time it is run. In this case, setting up output to the printer means all of Port A needs to be set up as inputs, while Port B bit zero must be initialized as an output and bit seven as an input. Setting up the rest of Port B as inputs is a good habit to protect outside peripherals, as seen in Fragment B.4.

```
0000 E220              SEP     #$20         use 8-bit accumulator
0002                   LONGA   OFF
0002
0002             ; set up Port A as entirely output
0002
0002 AD0080            LDA     PORTACTRL    get byte in Port A Control Reg
0005 29FB              AND     #%11111011   clear bit 2: select Data Direction Reg
0007 8D0080            STA     PORTACTRL    and store it back
000A
000A A9FF              LDA     #$FF
000C 8D0080            STA     PORTA        store all 1's to make Port A an output
000F
000F AD0080            LDA     PORTACTRL    get byte in Port A Control Reg
0012 0904              ORA     #%00000100   set bit 2: select Data Reg
0014 8D0080            STA     PORTACTRL    and store it back
0017
0017             ; set up Port B: bit 0 as output; bit 7 as input
0017
0017 AD0080            LDA     PORTBCTRL    get byte in Port B Control Reg
001A 29FB              AND     #%11111011   clear bit 2: select Data Direction Reg
001C 8D0080            STA     PORTBCTRL    and store it back
001F
001F A901              LDA     #1
0021 8D0080            STA     PORTB        store 1 to bit 0 (output); 0 to bit 7
0024
0024 AD0080            LDA     PORTBCTRL    get byte in Port B Control Reg
0027 0904              ORA     #%00000100   set bit 2: select Data Reg
0029 8D0080            STA     PORTBCTRL    and store it back
002C
002C A901              LDA     #1           write 1 to printer's Data Strobe
002E 8D0080            STA     PORTB        to initialize Data Strobe to 1 (high)
0031
0031 60                RTS
```

Fragment B.4.

PORTACTRL, PORTA, PORTBCTRL, and **PORTB** must be elsewhere equated to the addresses at which each is located. The value in the control register is loaded and bit two is ANDed out with the mask, then stored back to choose the data direction register as the chosen register in each port. All ones are stored to Port A's data direction register, selecting all eight lines as outputs. One is stored to Port B's data direction register, selecting bit zero as an output and the rest of the port as inputs. Then the control registers are loaded again, this time ORing bit two back on before re-storing them, to choose the data register as the chosen register in each port. Finally, one is written out Port B to the printer's Data Strobe to initialize the line.

Now bytes can be written to the printer by waiting for a zero on the Printer Busy Line (bit seven of Port B was chosen so that a positive/negative test could be made to test the bit), then storing the byte to be written to Port A, and finally toggling the Data Strobe to zero and then back to one to inform the printer that a new character is ready to be printed.

```
0000              ; write character in eight-bit accumulator to the printer
0000
0000 2C0080  POUT  BIT   PORTB   move Port B bit 7 (Busy Line) to n flag
0003 30FB          BMI   POUT    wait until printer is not busy
0005
0005 8D0080        STA   PORTA   write char in accum to printer
0008
0008 A90000        LDA   #0      tell the printer to get and print it:
000B 8D0080        STA   PORTB   strobe the printer: write a 0 to bit 0
000E EA            NOP           allow a wait cycle
000F A90100        LDA   #1
0012 8D0080        STA   PORTB   then toggle Strobe back to high (normal)
0015
0015 60            RTS
```

Fragment B.5.

You must be sure, in toggling the Strobe by writing to it, that the zero written to bit seven (zeroes are written to bits one through seven during both writes to Port B) not be read back as though it is a value being sent by the printer's Busy Line indicating the printer is not busy.

Remember that it is always important to have a data sheet for each peripheral support chip you attempt to write code for.

C | The Rockwell 65C02

Rockwell International Corporation has a family of CPUs which it calls the R65C00 family. It includes their R65C02; while the designation would lead you to believe it is the 65C02 to which a part of this book is devoted, in fact its instruction set is a superset of the 65C02 instruction set discussed earlier. It is the 65C02 described earlier, not the Rockwell part, which Apple employed in its //c computer and the 1985 upgrade to its //e computer.

Furthermore, the R65C02's superset adds 32 instructions with opcodes that are the same as 32 very different instructions on the 65816, making the Rockwell R65C02 incompatible with the 65802 and 65816. For this reason, the R65C02 has been relegated to this appendix. If these additional instructions are disregarded and left unused, the remaining available instructions correspond to the standard 65C02 instruction set.

This is not to say the additional instructions are without merit. Rockwell's R65C02 has two additional operations for manipulating a single zero page bit at a time, Reset Memory Bit (**RMB**) and Set Memory Bit (**SMB**), and two additional operations for testing a single zero page bit and branching if it is clear or set, Branch on Bit Reset (**BBR**) and Branch on Bit Set (**BBS**). All four have eight versions—one for each bit—which are specified by adding a bit number (0 through 7) to the mnemonic. So there are 32 total additional instructions.

The operand to the bit-manipulating instructions is a zero page address (specified as **dp**, for "direct page", in the following pages to be consistent with the instructions chapter, although the direct page is actually limited to the zero page). The operand to the bit-testing instructions is a compound operand: a zero page address to test, a comma, and a nearby label to which to branch (which an assembler turns into a program counter relative offset).

While incompatible with the 65802/65816 family expansion, the Rockwell 65C02's bit manipulation and testing instructions can be valuable for control applications, in which single bits are used to store boolean true/false values and to send signals to external devices.

BBR   Branch on Bit Reset

The specified bit in the zero page location specified in the operand is tested. If it is clear (reset), a branch is taken; if it is set, the instruction immediately following the two-byte **BBRx** instruction is executed. The bit is specified by a number (0 through 7) concatenated to the end of the mnemonic.

If the branch is performed, the third byte of the instruction is used as a signed displacement from the program counter; that is, it is added to the program counter: a positive value (numbers less than or equal to $80; that is, numbers with the high-order bit clear) results in a branch to a higher location; a negative value (greater than $80, with the high-order bit set) results in a branch to a lower location. Once the branch address is calculated, the result is loaded into the program counter, transferring control to that location.

Most assemblers calculate the displacement for you: you must specify as the operand, not the displacement but rather the label to which you wish to branch. The assembler then calculates the correct offset.

Flags Affected: - - - - - - - -

Codes:

Addressing Mode	Syntax	Opcode (hex)	Available to: 6502	65C02	R65C02	65802	# of Bytes	# of Cycles
Direct Page/Program Counter Relative	**BBR0** *dp,nearlabel*	0F			x		3	5
Direct Page/Program Counter Relative	**BBR1** *dp,nearlabel*	1F			x		3	5
Direct Page/Program Counter Relative	**BBR2** *dp,nearlabel*	2F			x		3	5
Direct Page/Program Counter Relative	**BBR3** *dp,nearlabel*	3F			x		3	5
Direct Page/Program Counter Relative	**BBR4** *dp,nearlabel*	4F			x		3	5
Direct Page/Program Counter Relative	**BBR5** *dp,nearlabel*	5F			x		3	5
Direct Page/Program Counter Relative	**BBR6** *dp,nearlabel*	6F			x		3	5
Direct Page/Program Counter Relative	**BBR7** *dp,nearlabel*	7F			x		3	5

BBS — Branch on Bit Set

The specified bit in the zero page location specified in the operand is tested. If it is set, a branch is taken; if it is clear (reset), the instruction immediately following the two-byte **BBSx** instruction is executed. The bit is specified by a number (0 through 7) concatenated to the end of the mnemonic.

If the branch is performed, the third byte of the instruction is used as a signed displacement from the program counter; that is, it is added to the program counter: a positive value (numbers less than or equal to $80; that is, numbers with the high-order bit clear) results in a branch to a higher location; a negative value (greater than $80, with the high-order bit set) results in a branch to a lower location. Once the branch address is calculated, the result is loaded into the program counter, transferring control to that location.

Most assemblers calculate the displacement for you: you must specify as the operand, not the displacement but rather the label to which you wish to branch. The assembler then calculates the correct offset.

Flags Affected: d - - - - - - -

Codes:

Addressing Mode	Syntax	Opcode (hex)	Available to: 6502	65C02	R65C02	65802	# of Bytes	# of Cycles
Direct Page/Program Counter Relative	BBS0 *dp,nearlabel*	8F			x		3	5
Direct Page/Program Counter Relative	BBS1 *dp,nearlabel*	9F			x		3	5
Direct Page/Program Counter Relative	BBS2 *dp,nearlabel*	AF			x		3	5
Direct Page/Program Counter Relative	BBS3 *dp,nearlabel*	BF			x		3	5
Direct Page/Program Counter Relative	BBS4 *dp,nearlabel*	CF			x		3	5
Direct Page/Program Counter Relative	BBS5 *dp,nearlabel*	DF			x		3	5
Direct Page/Program Counter Relative	BBS6 *dp,nearlabel*	EF			x		3	5
Direct Page/Program Counter Relative	BBS7 *dp,nearlabel*	FF			x		3	5

RMB   Reset Memory Bit

Clear the specified bit in the zero page memory location specified in the operand. The bit to clear is specified by a number (0 through 7) concatenated to the end of the mnemonic.

Flags Affected: - - - - - - - -

Codes:

Addressing Mode	Syntax	Opcode (hex)	6502	65C02	R65C02	65802	# of Bytes	# of Cycles
Direct Page	RMB0 dp	07			x		2	5
Direct Page	RMB1 dp	17			x		2	5
Direct Page	RMB2 dp	27			x		2	5
Direct Page	RMB3 dp	37			x		2	5
Direct Page	RMB4 dp	47			x		2	5
Direct Page	RMB5 dp	57			x		2	5
Direct Page	RMB6 dp	67			x		2	5
Direct Page	RMB7 dp	77			x		2	5

SMB — Set Memory Bit

Set the specified bit in the zero page memory location specified in the operand. The bit to set is specified by a number (0 through 7) concatenated to the end of the mnemonic.

Flags Affected: - - - - - - - -

Codes:

Addressing Mode	Syntax	Opcode (hex)	6502	65C02	R65C02	65802	# of Bytes	# of Cycles
Direct Page	SMB0 dp	87			x		2	5
Direct Page	SMB1 dp	97			x		2	5
Direct Page	SMB2 dp	A7			x		2	5
Direct Page	SMB3 dp	B7			x		2	5
Direct Page	SMB4 dp	C7			x		2	5
Direct Page	SMB5 dp	D7			x		2	5
Direct Page	SMB6 dp	E7			x		2	5
Direct Page	SMB7 dp	F7			x		2	5

D | Instruction Groups

The 65x instructions can be divided into three groups, on the basis of both the types of actions of each instruction and the addressing modes each can use. The opcodes in the first group and some in the second have similar bit patterns, the same addressing modes available, and regularity which can make remembering the capabilities of a particular instruction—or creating a compiler code generator—much easier.

Group I instructions are the most commonly used load, store, logic, and arithmetic instructions, and have by far the most addressing modes available to them. Group II instructions are mostly **read-modify-write** instructions, such as increment, decrement, shift, and rotate, which both access and change one and only one register or memory location.

Group III is a catch-all for the remaining instructions, such as index register comparisons and stack operations.

Group I Instructions

The 65x Group I instructions, with their opcode's bit patterns, are shown in Table D.1. The 'aaaaa's are filled with addressing mode bit patterns—there is one pattern for each addressing mode available to Group I instructions.

Table D.1. Group I Instructions Opcode Patterns.

Add with Carry to the Accumulator (ADC)	011a aaaa
And the Accumulator (AND)	001a aaaa
Compare the Accumulator (CMP)	110a aaaa
Exclusive Or the Accumulator (EOR)	010a aaaa
Load the Accumulator (LDA)	101a aaaa
Or the Accumulator (ORA)	000a aaaa
Subtract with Borrow from the Accumulator (SBC)	111a aaaa
Store the Accumulator (STA)	100a aaaa

The 6502 addressing modes available to the Group I instructions have bit patterns that all end in '01'. These bit patterns are found in Table D.2. The exception to this scheme is **STA** immediate; since it is not possible to use immediate addressing with a store instruction, its logical opcode 1000 1001 is used by a non-Group-I instruction.

Table D.2. Address Mode Patterns for Group I Instructions.

Immediate	0 1001
Direct (Zero) Page	0 0101
Absolute	0 1101
Direct (Zero) Page Indexed by X	1 0101
Absolute Indexed by X	1 1101
Absolute Indexed by Y	1 1001
Direct (Zero) Page Indexed Indirect with X (pre-indexed)	0 0001
Direct (Zero) Page Indirect Indexed with Y (post-indexed)	1 0001

The 65C02 adds one more addressing mode for Group I instructions; it has the only Group I addressing mode bit pattern to end in a zero:

Direct (Zero) Page Indirect   10010

The 65802 and 65816 add the six addressing modes for Group I instructions found in Table D.3.

Table D.3. 65802/65816 Group I Addressing Mode Patterns.

Direct Page Indirect Long Indexed with Y (post-indexed long)	1 0111
Direct Page Indirect Long	0 0111
Absolute Long	0 1111
Absolute Long Indexed with X	1 1111
Stack Relative	0 0011
Stack Relative Indirect Indexed with Y	1 0011

Group II Instructions

Group II instructions are an amalgam of mostly read-modify-write instructions with very similar addressing modes (differing only whether they have accumulator addressing available to them on the 6502). The instructions, with their opcode bit patterns, are listing in Table D.4.

There are either four or five addressing modes available to these instructions on the 6502—five if the missing bits are 'bbc' rather than just 'bb', the fifth addressing mode being accumulator addressing.

Table D.5 shows the five addressing modes with their bit patterns. All three bits in this table are filled into the 'bbc' missing bits in Table D.4; only the first two bits of each Table D.5 set are filled into 'bb' missing bits in Table D.4.

Table D.4. Group II Opcode Patterns.

Arithmetic Shift Left (ASL)	000b bc10
Decrement (DEC)	110b b110
Increment (INC)	111b b110
Logical Shift Right (LSR)	010b bc10
Rotate Left through Carry (ROL)	001b bc10
Rotate Right through Carry (ROR)	011b bc10
Store Index Register X (STX)	100b b110
Store Index Register Y (STY)	100b b100

Table D.5. Address Mode Patterns for Group II Instructions.

Accumulator	0 10
Direct (Zero) Page	0 01
Absolute	0 11
Direct (Zero) Page Indexed by X	1 01
Absolute Indexed by X	1 11

Notice how the four 'bb1' addressing modes have the same bit patterns as the first three bits of their corresponding bit patterns for the Group I instruction addressing modes.

There are a few exceptions.

Absolute indexing is not available for storing either index register. Furthermore, since the register cannot use itself to store itself, the **STX** instruction can't use direct page,X; instead, direct page,Y substitutes for this instruction's direct page, indexed store.

The two 65C02 instructions to increment and decrement the accumulator do not follow this scheme at all; giving these instructions that addressing mode clearly was not planned when the 6502 was designed, since their opcodes were assigned to other instructions. Nor does the 65C02's **STZ** (store zero to memory) instruction, which uses the main four addressing modes, follow the scheme, even though it seems clearly to be a Group II instruction of this type. But four of the five addressing modes of the **BIT** instruction on the 65C02, 65802, and 65816 (the 6502 has only two addressing modes for this instruction)—the four 'bb1' addressing modes above—follow this scheme (its bit pattern is 001b b100). It also has an immediate addressing mode, however, which is in no way regular.

Loading the Index Registers

The two index registers can be loaded with regular opcodes:

Load Index Register X (LDX)   101d dd10
Load Index Register Y (LDY)   101d dd00

Available to them are the five addressing modes in table D.6.

Table D.6. Address Mode Patterns for Load Index Register Instructions.

Immediate	0 00
Direct Page	0 01
Absolute	0 11
Direct Page Indexed	1 01
Absolute Indexed	1 11

The two indexed modes use the Y index register for indexing when loading the X register and vice versa.

Index Register Compares

The two instructions to compare an index register to memory have three addressing modes available to them.

The instructions are:

Compare Index Register X with Memory (CPX) 1110 ee00
Compare Index Register Y with Memory (CPY) 1100 ee00

Table D.7 lists the three addressing modes available.

Table D.7. Address Mode Patterns for Compare Index Register Instructions.

Immediate	00
Direct Page	01
Absolute	11

Test-and-Change-Bits Instructions

The two test-and-change-bits instructions each have two addressing modes that they use in a regular manner.

The two instructions are:

Test and Reset Memory Bits (TRB)	0001 x100
Test and Set Memory Bits (TSB)	0000 x100

The two addressing modes are:

Direct Page	$x = 0$
Absolute	$x = 1$

W65C816 Data Sheet

CMOS W65C816 and W65C802 16-Bit Microprocessor Family

Features

- Advanced CMOS design for low power consumption and increased noise immunity
- Single 3-6V power supply, 5V specified
- Emulation mode allows complete hardware and software compatibility with 6502 designs
- 24-bit address bus allows access to 16 MBytes of memory space
- Full 16-bit ALU, Accumulator, Stack Pointer, and Index Registers
- Valid Data Address (VDA) and Valid Program Address (VPA) output allows dual cache and cycle steal DMA implementation
- Vector Pull (VP) output indicates when interrupt vectors are being addressed. May be used to implement vectored interrupt design
- Abort (ABORT) input and associated vector supports virtual memory system design
- Separate program and data bank registers allow program segmentation or full 16-MByte linear addressing
- New Direct Register and stack relative addressing provides capability for re-entrant, re-cursive and re-locatable programming
- 24 addressing modes — 13 original 6502 modes, plus 11 new addressing modes with 91 instructions using 255 opcodes
- New Wait for Interrupt (WAI) and Stop the Clock (STP) instructions further reduce power consumption, decrease interrupt latency and allows synchronization with external events
- New Co-Processor instruction (COP) with associated vector supports co-processor configurations, i.e., floating point processors
- New block move ability

General Description

WDC's W65C802 and W65C816 are CMOS 16-bit microprocessors featuring total software compatibility with their 8-bit NMOS and CMOS 6500-series predecessors. The W65C802 is pin-to-pin compatible with 8-bit devices currently available, while the W65C816 extends addressing to a full 16 megabytes. These devices offer the many advantages of CMOS technology, including increased noise immunity, higher reliability, and greatly reduced power requirements. A software switch determines whether the processor is in the 8-bit "emulation" mode, or in the native mode, thus allowing existing systems to use the expanded features.

As shown in the processor programming model, the Accumulator, ALU, X and Y Index registers, and Stack Pointer register have all been extended to 16 bits. A new 16-bit Direct Page register augments the Direct Page addressing mode (formerly Zero Page addressing). Separate Program Bank and Data Bank registers allow 24-bit memory addressing with segmented or linear addressing.

Four new signals provide the system designer with many options. The ABORT input can interrupt the currently executing instruction without modifying internal register, thus allowing virtual memory system design. Valid Data Address (VDA) and Valid Program Address (VPA) outputs facilitate dual cache memory by indicating whether a data segment or program segment is accessed. Modifying a vector is made easy by monitoring the Vector Pull (VP) output.

Note: To assist the design engineer, a Caveat and Application Information section has been included within this data sheet.

W65C816 Processor Programming Model

8 BITS	8 BITS	8 BITS
Data Bank Reg (DBR)	X Register Hi (XH) (X)	X Register Low (XL)
Data Bank Reg (DBR)	Y Register Hi (YH) (Y)	Y Register Low (YL)
00	Stack Register Hi (SH) (S)	Stack Reg. Low (SL)
= 6502 Registers	Accumulator (B) (C)	Accumulator (A)
Program Bank Reg (PBR)	Program (PCH) (PC)	Counter (PCL)
00	Direct Reg Hi (DH) (D)	Direct Reg Low (DL)

Status Register Coding

```
STATUS REG (P)
[1 B]                E  → EMULATION 1 = 6502
N V M X D I Z C            0 = NATIVE
        │ │ │ │ └── CARRY         1 = TRUE
        │ │ │ └──── ZERO          1 = RESULT ZERO
        │ │ └────── IRQ DISABLE   1 = DISABLE
        │ └──────── DECIMAL MODE  1 = TRUE
        └────────── INDEX REG SELECT  1 = 8 BIT, 0 = 16 BIT
└──────────────── MEMORY SELECT   1 = 8 BIT 0 = 16 BIT
└────────────── OVER FLOW       1 = TRUE
└──────────── NEGATIVE         1 = NEGATIVE
```

Design Engineer: William D. Mensch, Jr.

Pin Configuration

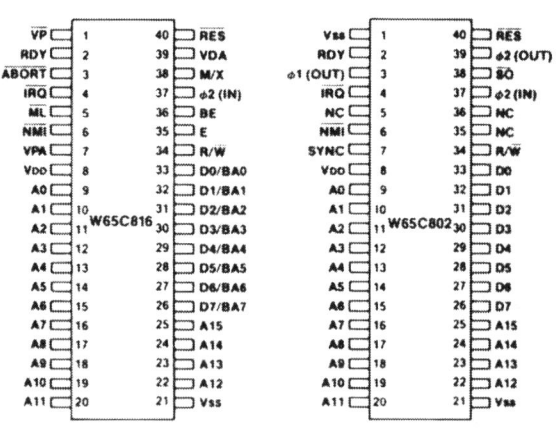

W65C816

Pin	Signal	Pin	Signal
1	VP	40	RES
2	RDY	39	VDA
3	ABORT	38	M/X
4	IRQ	37	φ2 (IN)
5	ML	36	BE
6	NMI	35	E
7	VPA	34	R/W
8	VDD	33	D0/BA0
9	A0	32	D1/BA1
10	A1	31	D2/BA2
11	A2	30	D3/BA3
12	A3	29	D4/BA4
13	A4	28	D5/BA5
14	A5	27	D6/BA6
15	A6	26	D7/BA7
16	A7	25	A15
17	A8	24	A14
18	A9	23	A13
19	A10	22	A12
20	A11	21	Vss

W65C802

Pin	Signal	Pin	Signal
1	Vss	40	RES
2	RDY	39	φ2 (OUT)
3	φ1 (OUT)	38	SO
4	IRQ	37	φ2 (IN)
5	NC	36	NC
6	NMI	35	NC
7	SYNC	34	R/W
8	VDD	33	D0
9	A0	32	D1
10	A1	31	D2
11	A2	30	D3
12	A3	29	D4
13	A4	28	D5
14	A5	27	D6
15	A6	26	D7
16	A7	25	A15
17	A8	24	A14
18	A9	23	A13
19	A10	22	A12
20	A11	21	Vss

WDC — THE WESTERN DESIGN CENTER, INC.
2166 East Brown Road • Mesa, Arizona 85203 • 602-962-4545

Advance Information Data Sheet:

This is advanced information and specifications are subject to change without notice.

Absolute Maximum Ratings: (Note 1)

Rating	Symbol	Value
Supply Voltage	V_{DD}	-0.3V to +7.0V
Input Voltage	V_{IN}	-0.3V to V_{DD} +0.3V
Operating Temperature	T_A	0°C to +70°C
Storage Temperature	T_S	-55°C to +150°C

This device contains input protection against damage due to high static voltages or electric fields, however, precautions should be taken to avoid application of voltages higher than the maximum rating.

Notes

1. Exceeding these ratings may cause permanent damage. Functional operation under these conditions is not implied.

DC Characteristics (All Devices): V_{DD} = 5.0V ±5%, V_{SS} = 0V, T_A = 0°C to +70°C

Parameter	Symbol	Min	Max	Unit
Input High Voltage RES, RDY, IRQ, Data, SO, BE, φ2 (IN), NMI, ABORT	V_{IH}	2.0 0.7 V_{DD}	V_{DD} + 0.3 V_{DD} + 0.3	V V
Input Low Voltage RES, RDY, IRQ, Data, SO, BE, φ2 (IN), NMI, ABORT	V_{IL}	-0.3 -0.3	0.8 0.2	V V
Input Leakage Current (V_{IN} = 0 to V_{DD}) RES, NMI, RDY, IRQ, SO, BE, ABORT (Internal Pullup) φ2 (IN) Address, Data, R/W (Off State, BE = 0)	I_{IN}	-100 -1 -10	1 1 10	μA μA μA
Output High Voltage (I_{OH} = -100μA) SYNC, Data, Address, R/W, ML, VP, M/X, E, VDA, VPA, φ1 (OUT), φ2 (OUT)	V_{OH}	0.7 V_{DD}	—	V
Output Low Voltage (I_{OL} = 1.6mA) SYNC, Data, Address, R/W, ML, VP, M/X, E, VDA, VPA, φ1 (OUT), φ2 (OUT)	V_{OL}	—	0.4	V
Supply Current (No Load)	I_{DD}	—	4	mA/MHz
Standby Current (No Load, Data Bus = V_{SS} or V_{DD} RES, NMI, IRQ, SO, BE, ABORT, φ2 = V_{DD})	I_{SB}	—	10	μA
Capacitance (V_{IN} = 0V, T_A = 25°C, f = 2 MHz) Logic, φ2 (IN) Address, Data, R/W (Off State)	C_{IN} C_{TS}	— —	10 15	pF pF

Pin Function Table

Pin	Description
A0–A15	Address Bus
ABORT	Abort Input
BE	Bus Enable
φ2 (IN)	Phase 2 In Clock
φ1 (OUT)	Phase 1 Out Clock
φ2 (OUT)	Phase 2 Out Clock
D0–D7	Data Bus (G65SC802)
D0/BA0–D7/BA7	Data Bus, Multiplexed (G65SC816)
E	Emulation Select
IRQ	Interrupt Request
ML	Memory Lock
M/X	Mode Select (P_M or P_X)

Pin	Description
NC	No Connection
NMI	Non-Maskable Interrupt
RDY	Ready
RES	Reset
R/W	Read/Write
SO	Set Overflow
SYNC	Synchronize
VDA	Valid Data Address
VP	Vector Pull
VPA	Valid Program Address
V_{DD}	Positive Power Supply (+5 Volts)
V_{SS}	Internal Logic Ground

E W65C816 Data Sheet

AC Characteristics (W65C816): V_DD = 5.0V ±5%, V_SS = 0V, T_A = 0°C to +70°C

Parameter	Symbol	2 MHz Min	2 MHz Max	4 MHz Min	4 MHz Max	6 MHz Min	6 MHz Max	8 MHz Min	8 MHz Max	Unit
Cycle Time	tCYC	500	DC	250	DC	167	DC	125	DC	nS
Clock Pulse Width Low	tPWL	0.240	10	0.120	10	0.080	10	0.060	10	µS
Clock Pulse Width High	tPWH	240	∞	120	∞	80	∞	60	∞	nS
Fall Time, Rise Time	tF, tR	—	10	—	10	—	5	—	5	nS
A0-A15 Hold Time	tAH	10	—	10	—	10	—	10	—	nS
A0-A15 Setup Time	tADS	—	100	—	75	—	60	—	40	nS
BA0-BA7 Hold Time	tBH	10	—	10	—	10	—	10	—	nS
BA0-BA7 Setup Time	tBAS	—	100	—	90	—	65	—	45	nS
Access Time	tACC	365	—	130	—	87	—	70	—	nS
Read Data Hold Time	tDHR	10	—	10	—	10	—	10	—	nS
Read Data Setup Time	tDSR	40	—	30	—	20	—	15	—	nS
Write Data Delay Time	tMDS	—	100	—	70	—	60	—	40	nS
Write Data Hold Time	tDHW	10	—	10	—	10	—	10	—	nS
Processor Control Setup Time	tPCS	40	—	30	—	20	—	15	—	nS
Processor Control Hold Time	tPCH	10	—	10	—	10	—	10	—	nS
E,MX Output Hold Time	tEH	10	—	10	—	5	—	5	—	nS
E,MX Output Setup Time	tES	50	—	50	—	25	—	15	—	nS
Capacitive Load (Address, Data, and R/W)	CEXT	—	100	—	100	—	35	—	35	pF
BE to High Impedance State	tBHZ	—	30	—	30	—	30	—	30	nS
BE to Valid Data	tBVD	—	30	—	30	—	30	—	30	nS

Timing Diagram (W65C816)

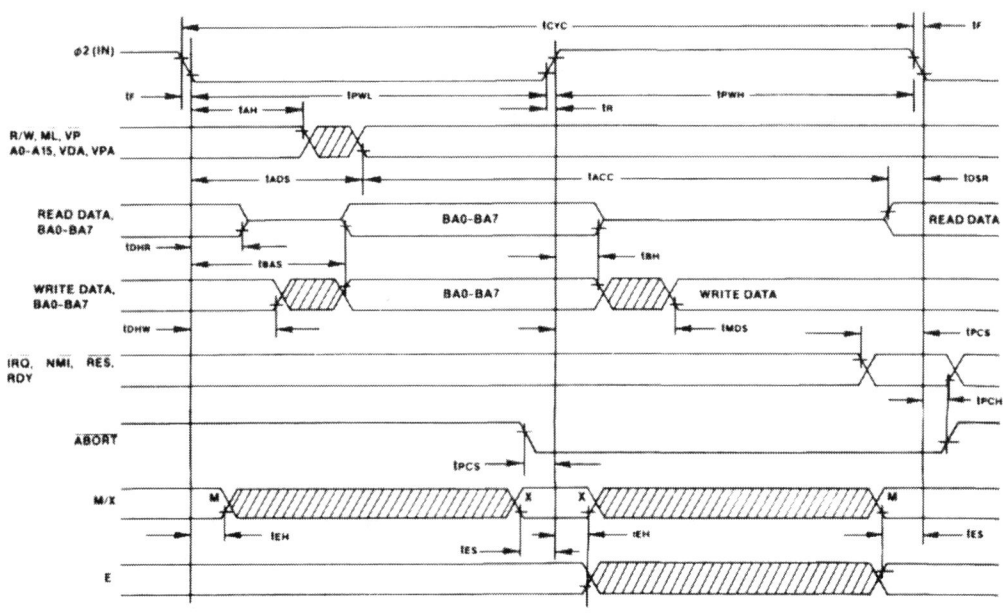

Timing Notes:
1. Voltage levels are V_L = 0.4V, V_H = 2.4V
2. Timing measurement points are 0.8V and 2.0V

AC Characteristics (W65C802): $V_{DD} = 5.0V \pm 5\%$, $V_{SS} = 0V$, $T_A = 0°C$ to $+70°C$

Parameter	Symbol	2 MHz Min	2 MHz Max	4 MHz Min	4 MHz Max	6 MHz Min	6 MHz Max	8 MHz Min	8 MHz Max	Unit
Cycle Time	t_{CYC}	500	DC	250	DC	167	DC	125	DC	nS
Clock Pulse Width Low	t_{PWL}	0.240	10	0.120	10	0.080	10	0.060	10	µS
Clock Pulse Width High	t_{PWH}	240	∞	120	∞	80	∞	60	∞	nS
Fall Time, Rise Time	t_F, t_R	—	10	—	10	—	5	—	5	nS
Delay Time, φ2 (IN) to φ1 (OUT)	$t_{D\phi1}$	—	20	—	20	—	20	—	20	nS
Delay Time, φ2 (IN) to φ2 (OUT)	$t_{D\phi2}$	—	40	—	40	—	40	—	40	nS
Address Hold Time	t_{AH}	10	—	10	—	10	—	10	—	nS
Address Setup Time	t_{ADS}	—	100	—	75	—	60	—	40	nS
Access Time	t_{ACC}	365	—	130	—	87	—	70	—	nS
Read Data Hold Time	t_{DHR}	10	—	10	—	10	—	10	—	nS
Read Data Setup Time	t_{DSR}	40	—	30	—	20	—	15	—	nS
Write Data Delay Time	t_{MDS}	—	100	—	70	—	60	—	40	nS
Write Data Hold Time	t_{DHW}	10	—	10	—	10	—	10	—	nS
Processor Control Setup Time	t_{PCS}	40	—	30	—	20	—	15	—	nS
Processor Control Hold Time	t_{PCH}	10	—	10	—	10	—	10	—	nS
Capacitive Load (Address, Data, and R/W)	C_{EXT}	—	100	—	100	—	35	—	35	pF

Timing Diagram (W65C802)

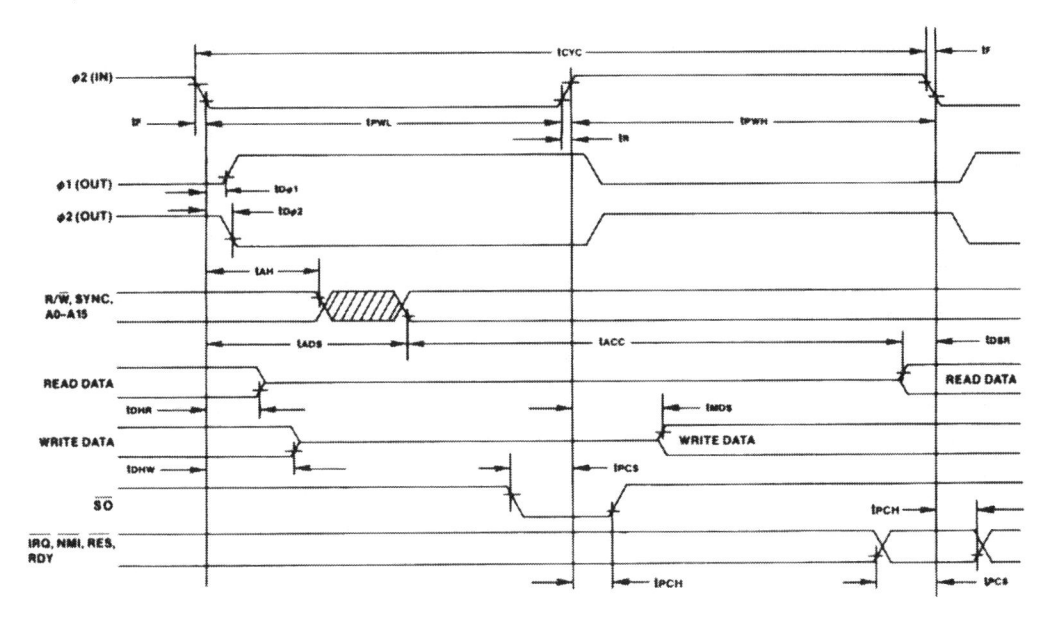

Timing Notes:
1. Voltage levels are $V_L < 0.4V$, $V_H > 2.4V$
2. Timing measurement points are 0.8V and 2.0V

Functional Description

The W65C802 offers the design engineer the opportunity to utilize both existing software programs and hardware configurations, while also achieving the added advantages of increased register lengths and faster execution times. The W65C802's "ease of use" design and implementation features provide the designer with increased flexibility and reduced implementation costs. In the Emulation mode, the W65C802 not only offers software compatibility, but is also hardware (pin-to-pin) compatible with 6502 designs. plus it provides the advantages of 16-bit internal operation in 6502-compatible applications. The W65C802 is an excellent direct replacement microprocessor for 6502 designs.

The W65C816 provides the design engineer with upward mobility and software compatibility in applications where a 16-bit system configuration is desired. The W65C816's 16-bit hardware configuration, coupled with current software allows a wide selection of system applications. In the Emulation mode, the W65C816 offers many advantages, including full software compatibility with 6502 coding. In addition, the W65C816's powerful instruction set and addressing modes make it an excellent choice for new 16-bit designs.

Internal organization of the W65C802 and W65C816 can be divided into two parts: 1) The Register Section, and 2) The Control Section. Instructions (or opcodes) obtained from program memory are executed by implementing a series of data transfers within the Register Section. Signals that cause data transfers to be executed are generated within the Control Section. Both the W65C802 and the W65C816 have a 16-bit internal architecture with an 8-bit external data bus.

Instruction Register and Decode

An opcode enters the processor on the Data Bus, and is latched into the Instruction Register during the instruction fetch cycle. This instruction is then decoded, along with timing and interrupt signals, to generate the various Instruction Register control signals.

Timing Control Unit (TCU)

The Timing Control Unit keeps track of each instruction cycle as it is executed. The TCU is set to zero each time an instruction fetch is executed, and is advanced at the beginning of each cycle for as many cycles as is required to complete the instruction. Each data transfer between registers depends upon decoding the contents of both the Instruction Register and the Timing Control Unit.

Arithmetic and Logic Unit (ALU)

All arithmetic and logic operations take place within the 16-bit ALU. In addition to data operations, the ALU also calculates the effective address for relative and indexed addressing modes. The result of a data operation is stored in either memory or an internal register. Carry, Negative, Overflow and Zero flags may be updated following the ALU data operation.

Internal Registers (Refer to Programming Model)

Accumulators (A, B, C)

The Accumulator is a general purpose register which stores one of the operands, or the result of most arithmetic and logical operations. In the Native mode (E=0), when the Accumulator Select Bit (M) equals zero, the Accumulator is established as 16 bits wide (A + B = C). When the Accumulator Select Bit (M) equals one, the Accumulator is 8 bits wide (A). In this case, the upper 8 bits (B) may be used for temporary storage in conjunction with the Exchange Accumulator (XBA) instruction.

Data Bank Register (DBR)

During modes of operation, the 8-bit Data Bank Register holds the default bank address for memory transfers. The 24-bit address is composed of the 16-bit instruction effective address and the 8-bit Data Bank address. The register value is multiplexed with the data value and is present on the Data/Address lines during the first half of a data transfer memory cycle for the W65C816. The Data Bank Register is initialized to zero during Reset.

Direct (D)

The 16-bit Direct Register provides an address offset for all instructions using direct addressing. The effective bank zero address is formed by adding the 8-bit instruction operand address to the Direct Register. The Direct Register is initialized to zero during Reset.

Index (X and Y)

There are two Index Registers (X and Y) which may be used as general purpose registers or to provide an index value for calculation of the effective address. When executing an instruction with indexed addressing, the microprocessor fetches the opcode and the base address, and then modifies the address by adding the Index Register contents to the address prior to performing the desired operation. Pre-indexing or post-indexing of indirect addresses may be selected. In the Native mode (E=0), both Index Registers are 16 bits wide (providing the Index Select Bit (X) equals zero). If the Index Select Bit (X) equals one, both registers will be 8 bits wide, and the high byte is forced to zero.

Processor Status (P)

The 8-bit Processor Status Register contains status flags and mode select bits. The Carry (C), Negative (N), Overflow (V), and Zero (Z) status flags serve to report the status of most ALU operations. These status flags are tested by use of Conditional Branch instructions. The Decimal (D), IRQ Disable (I), Memory/Accumulator (M), and Index (X) bits are used as mode select flags. These flags are set by the program to change microprocessor operations.

The Emulation (E) select and the Break (B) flags are accessible only through the Processor Status Register. The Emulation mode select flag is selected by the Exchange Carry and Emulation Bits (XCE) instruction. Table 1, W65C802 and W65C816 Mode Comparison, illustrates the features of the Native (E=0) and Emulation (E=1) modes. The M and X flags are always equal to one in the Emulation mode. When an interrupt occurs during the Emulation mode, the Break flag is written to stack memory as bit 4 of the Processor Status Register.

Program Bank Register (PBR)

The 8-bit Program Bank Register holds the bank address for all instruction fetches. The 24-bit address consists of the 16-bit instruction effective address and the 8-bit Program Bank address. The register value is multiplexed with the data value and presented on the Data/Address lines during the first half of a program memory read cycle. The Program Bank Register is initialized to zero during Reset. The PHK instruction pushes the PBR register onto the Stack.

Program Counter (PC)

The 16-bit Program Counter Register provides the addresses which are used to step the microprocessor through sequential program instructions. The register is incremented each time an instruction or operand is fetched from program memory.

Stack Pointer (S)

The Stack Pointer is a 16-bit register which is used to indicate the next available location in the stack memory area. It serves as the effective address in stack addressing modes as well as subroutine and interrupt processing. The Stack Pointer allows simple implementation of nested subroutines and multiple-level interrupts. During the Emulation mode, the Stack Pointer high-order byte (SH) is always equal to one. The bank address for all stack operations is Bank zero.

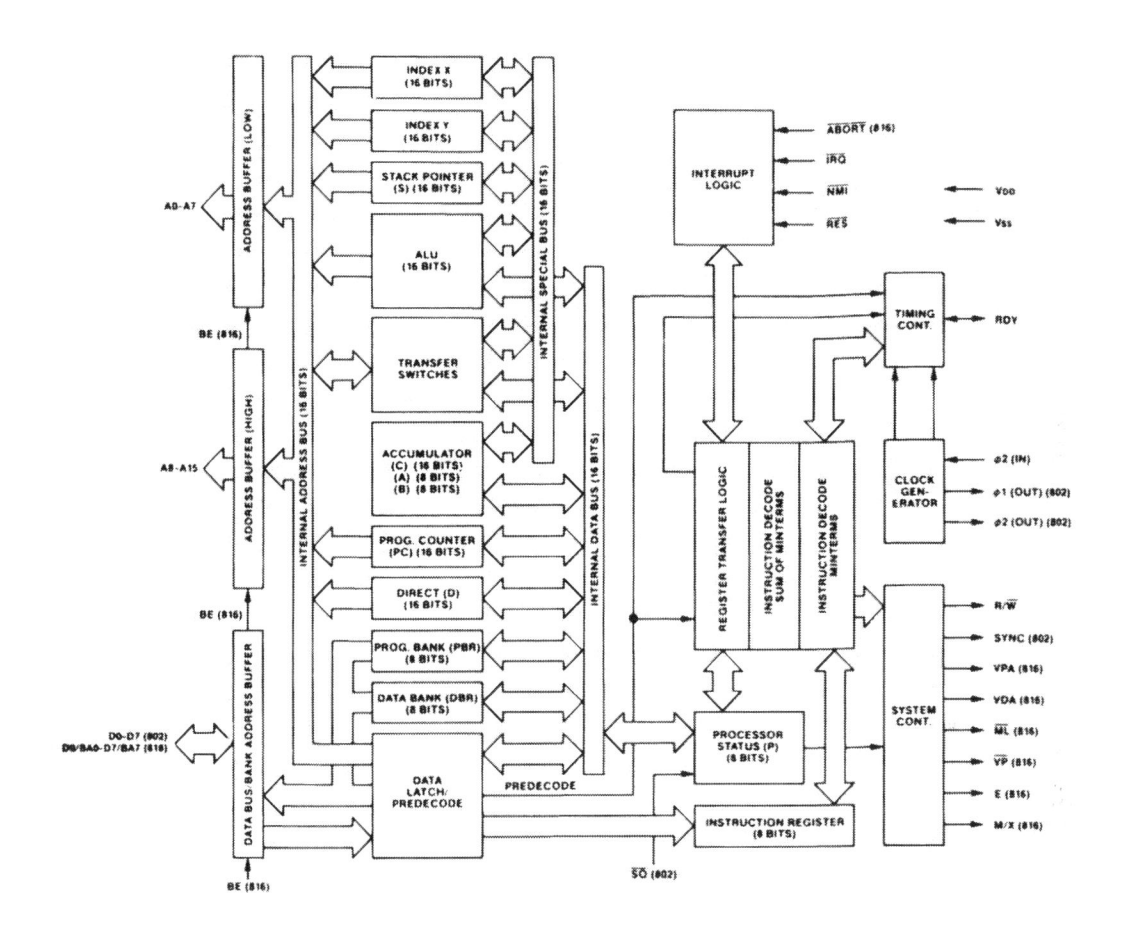

Figure 1. Block Diagram — Internal Architecture

Signal Description

The following Signal Description applies to both the G65SC802 and the G65SC816 except as otherwise noted.

Abort (ABORT)—G65SC816
The Abort input is used to abort instructions (usually due to an Address Bus condition). A negative transition will inhibit modification of any internal register during the current instruction. Upon completion of this instruction, an interrupt sequence is initiated. The location of the aborted opcode is stored as the return address in stack memory. The Abort vector address is 00FFF8,9 (Emulation mode) or 00FFE8,9 (Native mode). Note that ABORT is a pulse-sensitive signal, i.e., an abort will occur whenever there is a negative pulse (or level) on the ABORT pin during a ø2 clock.

Address Bus (A0-A15)
These sixteen output lines form the Address Bus for memory and I/O exchange on the Data Bus. When using the G65SC816, the address lines may be set to the high impedance state by the Bus Enable (BE) signal.

Bus Enable (BE)—W65C816
The Bus Enable input signal allows external control of the Address and Data Buffers, as well as the R/W signal. With Bus Enable high, the R/W and Address Buffers are active. The Data/Address Buffers are active during the first half of every cycle and the second half of a write cycle. When BE is low, these buffers are disabled. Bus Enable is an asynchronous signal.

Data Bus (D0-D7)—W65C802
The eight Data Bus lines provide an 8-bit bidirectional Data Bus for use during data exchanges between the microprocessor and external memory or peripherals. Two memory cycles are required for the transfer of 16-bit values.

Data/Address Bus (D0/BA0-D7/BA7)—W65C816
These eight lines multiplex address bits BA0-BA7 with the data value. The

address is present during the first half of a memory cycle, and the data value is read or written during the second half of the memory cycle. Two memory cycles are required to transfer 16-bit values. These lines may be set to the high impedance state by the Bus Enable (BE) signal.

Emulation Status (E)—W65C816
The Emulation Status output reflects the state of the Emulation (E) mode flag in the Processor Status (P) Register. This signal may be thought of as an opcode extension and used for memory and system management.

Interrupt Request ($\overline{IRQ}$)
The Interrupt Request input signal is used to request that an interrupt sequence be initiated. When the IRQ Disable (I) flag is cleared, a low input logic level initiates an interrupt sequence after the current instruction is completed. The Wait for Interrupt (WAI) instruction may be executed to ensure the interrupt will be recognized immediately. The Interrupt Request vector address is 00FFFE,F (Emulation mode) or 00FFEE,F (Native mode). Since $\overline{IRQ}$ is a level-sensitive input, an interrupt will occur if the interrupt source was not cleared since the last interrupt. Also, no interrupt will occur if the interrupt source is cleared prior to interrupt recognition.

Memory Lock ($\overline{ML}$)—W65C816
The Memory Lock output may be used to ensure the integrity of Read-Modify-Write instructions in a multiprocessor system. Memory Lock indicates the need to defer arbitration of the next bus cycle. Memory Lock is low during the last three or five cycles of ASL, DEC, INC, LSR, ROL, ROR, TRB, and TSB memory referencing instructions, depending on the state of the M flag.

Memory/Index Select Status (M/X)—W65C816
This multiplexed output reflects the state of the Accumulator (M) and Index (X) select flags (bits 5 and 4 of the Processor Status (P) Register. Flag M is valid during the Phase 2 clock negative transition and Flag X is valid during the Phase 2 clock positive transition. These bits may be thought of as opcode extensions and may be used for memory and system management.

Non-Maskable Interrupt ($\overline{NMI}$)
A negative transition on the $\overline{NMI}$ input initiates an interrupt sequence. A high-to-low transition initiates an interrupt sequence after the current instruction is completed. The Wait for Interrupt (WAI) instruction may be executed to ensure that the interrupt will be recognized immediately. The Non-Maskable Interrupt vector address is 00FFFA,B (Emulation mode) or 00FFEA,B (Native mode). Since $\overline{NMI}$ is an edge-sensitive input, an interrupt will occur if there is a negative transition while servicing a previous interrupt. Also, no interrupt will occur if $\overline{NMI}$ remains low.

Phase 1 Out (ϕ1 (OUT))—W65C802
This inverted clock output signal provides timing for external read and write operations. Executing the Stop (STP) instruction holds this clock in the low state.

Phase 2 In (ϕ2 (IN))
This is the system clock input to the microprocessor internal clock generator (equivalent to ϕ0 (IN) on the 6502). During the low power Standby Mode, ϕ2 (IN) should be held in the high state to preserve the contents of internal registers.

Phase 2 Out (ϕ2 (OUT))—W65C802
This clock output signal provides timing for external read and write operations. Addresses are valid (after the Address Setup Time (TADS)) following the negative transition of Phase 2 Out. Executing the Stop (STP) instruction holds Phase 2 Out in the High state.

Read/Write (R/$\overline{W}$)
When the R/$\overline{W}$ output signal is in the high state, the microprocessor is reading data from memory or I/O. When in the low state, the Data Bus contains valid data from the microprocessor which is to be stored at the addressed memory location. When using the W65C816, the R/$\overline{W}$ signal may be set to the high impedance state by Bus Enable (BE).

Ready (RDY)
This bidirectional signal indicates that a Wait for Interrupt (WAI) instruction has been executed allowing the user to halt operation of the microprocessor. A low input logic level will halt the microprocessor in its current state (note that when in the Emulation mode, the W65C802 stops only during a read cycle). Returning RDY to the active high state allows the microprocessor to continue following the next Phase 2 In Clock negative transition. The RDY signal is internally pulled low following the execution of a Wait for Interrupt (WAI) instruction, and then returned to the high state when a $\overline{RES}$, $\overline{ABORT}$, $\overline{NMI}$, or $\overline{IRQ}$ external interrupt is provided. This feature may be used to eliminate interrupt latency by placing the WAI instruction at the beginning of the $\overline{IRQ}$ servicing routine. If the $\overline{IRQ}$ Disable flag has been set, the next instruction will be executed when the $\overline{IRQ}$ occurs. The processor will not stop after a WAI instruction if RDY has been forced to a high state. The Stop (STP) instruction has no effect on RDY.

Reset ($\overline{RES}$)
The Reset input is used to initialize the microprocessor and start program execution. The Reset input buffer has hysteresis such that a simple R-C timing circuit may be used with the internal pullup device. The $\overline{RES}$ signal must be held low for at least two clock cycles after VDD reaches operating voltage. Ready (RDY) has no effect while $\overline{RES}$ is being held low. During this Reset conditioning period, the following processor initialization takes place:

Registers

D	=	0000					SH	=	01
DBR	=	00					XH	=	00
PBR	=	00					YH	=	00

	N	V	M	X	D	I	Z	C/E
P	*	*	1	1	0	1	*	*/1

* = Not Initialized

STP and WAI instructions are cleared.

Signals

E	= 1		VDA	= 0
M/X	= 1		$\overline{VP}$	= 1
R/$\overline{W}$	= 1		VPA	= 0
SYNC	= 0			

When Reset is brought high, an interrupt sequence is initiated.
- R/$\overline{W}$ remains in the high state during the stack address cycles
- The Reset vector address is 00FFFC,D.

Set Overflow ($\overline{SO}$)—W65C802
A negative transition on this input sets the Overflow (V) flag, bit 6 of the Processor Status (P) Register.

Synchronize (SYNC)—W65C802
The SYNC output is provided to identify those cycles during which the microprocessor is fetching an opcode. The SYNC signal is high during an opcode fetch cycle, and when combined with Ready (RDY), can be used for single instruction execution.

Valid Data Address (VDA) and
Valid Program Address (VPA)—G65SC816
These two output signals indicate valid memory addresses when high (logic 1), and must be used for memory or I/O address qualification:

VDA	VPA	
0	0	Internal Operation—Address and Data Bus available. The Address Bus may be invalid
0	1	Valid program address—may be used for program cache control
1	0	Valid data address—may be used for data cache control
1	1	Opcode fetch—may be used for program cache control and single step control

VDD and VSS
VDD is the positive supply voltage and VSS is system logic ground. Pin 21 of the two VSS pins on the W65C802 should be used for system ground.

Vector Pull ($\overline{VP}$)—W65C816
The Vector Pull output indicates that a vector location is being addressed during an interrupt sequence. $\overline{VP}$ is low during the last two interrupt sequence cycles, during which time the processor reads the interrupt vector. The $\overline{VP}$ signal may be used to select and prioritize interrupts from several sources by modifying the vector addresses.

Table 1. W65C816 Compatibility Issues

	W65C816/802	W65C02	NMOS 6502
1. S (Stack)	Always page 1 (E = 1), 8 bits 16 bits when (E = 0)	Always page 1, 8 bits	Always page 1, 8 bits
2. X (X Index Register)	Indexed page zero always in page 0 (E = 1), Cross page (E = 0)	Always page 0	Always page 0
3. Y (Y Index Register)	Indexed page zero always in page 0 (E = 1), Cross page (E = 0)	Always page 0	Always page 0
4. A (Accumulator)	8 bits (M = 1), 16 bits (M = 0)	8 bits	8 bits
5. P (Flag Register)	N, V, and Z flags valid in decimal mode. D = 0 after reset or interrupt	N, V, and Z flags valid in decimal mode. D = 0 after reset and interrupt	N, V, and Z flags invalid in decimal mode. D = unknown after reset. D not modified after interrupt.
6. Timing A. ABS, X ASL, LSR, ROL, ROR With No Page Crossing	7 cycles	6 cycles	7 cycles
B. Jump Indirect Operand = XXFF	5 cycles	6 cycles	5 cycles and invalid page crossing
C. Branch Across Page	4 cycles (E = 1) 3 cycles (E = 0)	4 cycles	4 cycles
D. Decimal Mode	No additional cycle	Add 1 cycle	No additional cycle
7. BRK Vector	00FFFE,F (E = 1) BRK bit = 0 on stack if IRQ, NMI, ABORT. 00FFE6, 7 (E = 0) X = X on Stack always.	FFFE,F BRK bit = 0 on stack if IRQ, NMI.	FFFE,F BRK bit = 0 on stack if IRQ, NMI.
8. Interrupt or Break Bank Address	PBR not pushed (E = 1) RTI PBR not pulled (E = 1) PBR pushed (E = 0) RTI PBR pulled (E = 0)	Not available	Not available
9. Memory Lock (ML)	ML = 0 during Read, Modify and Write cycles	ML = 0 during Modify and Write.	Not available
10. Indexed Across Page Boundary (d),y, a,x, a,y	Extra read of invalid address (Note 1)	Extra read of last instruction fetch	Extra read of invalid address
11. RDY Pulled During Write Cycle	Ignored (E = 1) for W65C802 only. Processor stops (E = 0).	Processor stops	Ignored
12. WAI and STP Instructions	Available	Available	Not available
13. Unused OP Codes	One reserved OP Code specified as WDM will be used in future systems. The W65C816 performs a no-operation.	No operation	Unknown and some "hang up" processor
14. Bank Address Handling	PBR = 00 after reset or interrupts.	Not available	Not available
15. R/W During Read-Modify-Write Instructions	E = 1, R/W = 0 during Modify and Write cycles. E = 0, R/W = 0 only during Write cycle	R/W = 0 only during Write cycle	R/W = 0 during Modify and Write cycles
16. Pin 7	W65C802 = SYNC W65C816 = VPA	SYNC	SYNC
17. COP Instruction Signatures 00-7F user defined Signatures 80-FF reserved	Available	Not available	Not available

Note 1. See Caveat section for additional information.

W65C802 and W65C816
Microprocessor Addressing Modes

The W65C816 is capable of directly addressing 16 MBytes of memory. This address space has special significance within certain addressing modes, as follows:

Reset and Interrupt Vectors
The Reset and Interrupt vectors use the majority of the fixed addresses between 00FFE0 and 00FFFF.

Stack
The Stack may use memory from 000000 to 00FFFF. The effective address of Stack and Stack Relative addressing modes will always be within this range.

Direct
The Direct addressing modes are usually used to store memory registers and pointers. The effective address generated by Direct, Direct,X and Direct,Y addressing modes is always in Bank 0 (000000-00FFFF).

Program Address Space
The Program Bank register is not affected by the Relative, Relative Long, Absolute, Absolute Indirect, and Absolute Indexed Indirect addressing modes or by incrementing the Program Counter from FFFF. The only instructions that affect the Program Bank register are: RTI, RTL, JML, JSL, and JMP Absolute Long. Program code may exceed 64K bytes although code segments may not span bank boundaries.

Data Address Space
The data address space is contiguous throughout the 16 MByte address space. Words, arrays, records, or any data structures may span 64 KByte bank boundaries with no compromise in code efficiency. The following addressing modes generate 24-bit effective addresses.
- Direct Indexed Indirect (d,x)
- Direct Indirect Indexed (d),y
- Direct Indirect (d)
- Direct Indirect Long [d]
- Direct Indirect Long Indexed [d],y
- Absolute a
- Absolute a,x
- Absolute a,y
- Absolute Long al
- Absolute Long Indexed al,x
- Stack Relative Indirect Indexed (d,s),y

The following addressing mode descriptions provide additional detail as to how effective addresses are calculated.

Twenty-four addressing modes are available for use with the W65C802 and W65C816 microprocessors. The "long" addressing modes may be used with the W65C802, however, the high byte of the address is not available to the hardware. Detailed descriptions of the 24 addressing modes are as follows:

1. Immediate Addressing—#
The operand is the second byte (second and third bytes when in the 16-bit mode) of the instruction.

2. Absolute—a
With Absolute addressing the second and third bytes of the instruction form the low-order 16 bits of the effective address. The Data Bank Register contains the high-order 8 bits of the operand address.

Instruction:	opcode	addrl	addrh
Operand Address:	DBR	addrh	addrl

3. Absolute Long—al
The second, third, and fourth byte of the instruction form the 24-bit effective address.

Instruction:	opcode	addrl	addrh	baddr
Operand Address:	baddr	addrh	addrl	

4. Direct—d
The second byte of the instruction is added to the Direct Register (D) to form the effective address. An additional cycle is required when the Direct Register is not page aligned (DL not equal 0). The Bank register is always 0.

Instruction:	opcode	offset

```
             Direct Register
           +             offset
Operand
Address:   00     effective address
```

5. Accumulator—A
This form of addressing always uses a single byte instruction. The operand is the Accumulator.

6. Implied—i
Implied addressing uses a single byte instruction. The operand is implicitly defined by the instruction.

7. Direct Indirect Indexed—(d),y
This address mode is often referred to as Indirect,Y. The second byte of the instruction is added to the Direct Register (D). The 16-bit contents of this memory location is then combined with the Data Bank register to form a 24-bit base address. The Y Index Register is added to the base address to form the effective address.

Instruction:	opcode	offset

```
                 Direct Register
               +             offset
                 00    direct address
then:
                 00    (direct address)
               + DBR
                 base address
               +             Y Reg
Operand
Address:         effective address
```

8. Direct Indirect Long Indexed—[d],y
With this addressing mode, the 24-bit base address is pointed to by the sum of the second byte of the instruction and the Direct Register. The effective address is this 24-bit base address plus the Y Index Register.

Instruction:	opcode	offset

```
                 Direct Register
               +             offset
                 00    direct address
then
                 (direct address)
               +             Y Reg
Operand
Address:         effective address
```

9. Direct Indexed Indirect—(d,x)
This address mode is often referred to as Indirect,X. The second byte of the instruction is added to the sum of the Direct Register and the X Index Register. The result points to the low-order 16 bits of the effective address. The Data Bank Register contains the high-order 8 bits of the effective address.

Instruction:	opcode	offset
		Direct Register
	+	offset
		direct address
	+	X Reg
then	00	address
	00	(address)
	+	DBR
Operand Address:		effective address

10. Direct Indexed With X—d,x
The second byte of the instruction is added to the sum of the Direct Register and the X Index Register to form the 16-bit effective address. The operand is always in Bank 0.

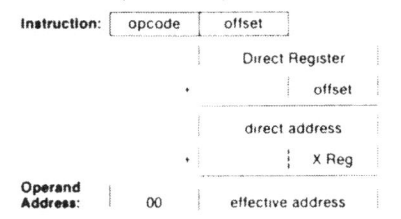

Instruction:	opcode	offset
		Direct Register
	+	offset
		direct address
	+	X Reg
Operand Address:	00	effective address

11. Direct Indexed With Y—d,y
The second byte of the instruction is added to the sum of the Direct Register and the Y Index Register to form the 16-bit effective address. The operand is always in Bank 0.

Instruction:	opcode	offset
		Direct Register
	+	offset
		direct address
	+	Y Reg
Operand Address:	00	effective address

12. Absolute Indexed With X—a,x
The second and third bytes of the instruction are added to the X Index Register to form the low-order 16 bits of the effective address. The Data Bank Register contains the high-order 8 bits of the effective address.

Instruction:	opcode	addrl	addrh
	DBR	addrh	addrl
	+		X Reg
Operand Address:		effective address	

13. Absolute Long Indexed With X—al,x
The second, third and fourth bytes of the instruction form a 24-bit base address. The effective address is the sum of this 24-bit address and the X Index Register.

Instruction:	opcode	addrl	addrh	baddr
	baddr	addrh	addrl	
	+		X Reg	
Operand Address:		effective address		

14. Absolute Indexed With Y—a,y
The second and third bytes of the instruction are added to the Y Index Register to form the low-order 16 bits of the effective address. The Data Bank Register contains the high-order 8 bits of the effective address.

Instruction:	opcode	addrl	addrh
	DBR	addrh	addrl
	+		Y Reg
Operand Address:		effective address	

15. Program Counter Relative—r
This address mode, referred to as Relative Addressing, is used only with the Branch instructions. If the condition being tested is met, the second byte of the instruction is added to the Program Counter, which has been updated to point to the opcode of the next instruction. The offset is a signed 8-bit quantity in the range from -128 to 127. The Program Bank Register is not affected.

16. Program Counter Relative Long—rl
This address mode, referred to as Relative Long Addressing, is used only with the Unconditional Branch Long instruction (BRL) and the Push Effective Relative instruction (PER). The second and third bytes of the instruction are added to the Program Counter, which has been updated to point to the opcode of the next instruction. With the branch instruction, the Program Counter is loaded with the result. With the Push Effective Relative instruction, the result is stored on the stack. The offset is a signed 16-bit quantity in the range from -32768 to 32767. The Program Bank Register is not affected.

17. Absolute Indirect—(a)
The second and third bytes of the instruction form an address to a pointer in Bank 0. The Program Counter is loaded with the first and second bytes at this pointer. With the Jump Long (JML) instruction, the Program Bank Register is loaded with the third byte of the pointer.

Instruction:	opcode	addrl	addrh
Indirect Address =		00	addrh	addrl

New PC = (indirect address)
with JML:
New PC = (indirect address)
New PBR = (indirect address +2)

18. Direct Indirect—(d)
The second byte of the instruction is added to the Direct Register to form a pointer to the low-order 16 bits of the effective address. The Data Bank Register contains the high-order 8 bits of the effective address.

Instruction:	opcode	offset
		Direct Register
	+	offset
	00	direct address
then	00	(direct address)
	+	DBR
Operand Address:		effective address

19. Direct Indirect Long—[d]

The second byte of the instruction is added to the Direct Register to form a pointer to the 24-bit effective address.

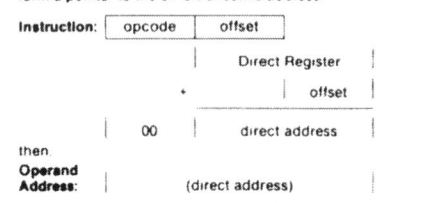

```
Instruction:   | opcode | offset |

                         | Direct Register |
                       + |      offset     |

               |   00   |  direct address  |
then:
Operand
Address:       |        (direct address)   |
```

20. Absolute Indexed Indirect—(a,x)

The second and third bytes of the instruction are added to the X Index Register to form a 16-bit pointer in Bank 0. The contents of this pointer are loaded in the Program Counter. The Program Bank Register is not changed.

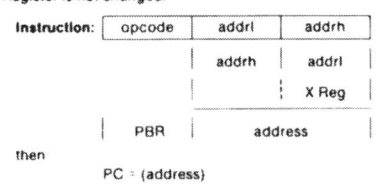

```
Instruction:   | opcode | addrl | addrh |

                        | addrh | addrl |
                      + |       | X Reg |

               |  PBR   |   address     |
then:
               PC = (address)
```

21. Stack—s

Stack addressing refers to all instructions that push or pull data from the stack, such as Push, Pull, Jump to Subroutine, Return from Subroutine, Interrupts, and Return from Interrupt. The bank address is always 0. Interrupt Vectors are always fetched from Bank 0.

22. Stack Relative—d,s

The low-order 16 bits of the effective address is formed from the sum of the second byte of the instruction and the Stack Pointer. The high-order 8 bits of the effective address is always zero. The relative offset is an unsigned 8-bit quantity in the range of 0 to 255.

```
Instruction:   | opcode | offset |

                         | Stack Pointer |
                       + |     offset    |

Operand
Address:       |   00   | effective address |
```

23. Stack Relative Indirect Indexed—(d,s),y

The second byte of the instruction is added to the Stack Pointer to form a pointer to the low-order 16-bit base address in Bank 0. The Data Bank Register contains the high-order 8 bits of the base address. The effective address is the sum of the 24-bit base address and the Y Index Register.

```
Instruction:   | opcode |  offset  |

                        | Stack Pointer |
                      + |    offset     |

               |   00   |   S + offset   |
then:
                        |   S + offset   |
             + |  DBR   |                |

               |       base address      |

                      + |      Y Reg     |
Operand
Address:       |     effective address   |
```

24. Block Source Bank, Destination Bank—xyc

This addressing mode is used by the Block Move instructions. The second byte of the instruction contains the high-order 8 bits of the destination address. The Y index Register contains the low-order 16 bits of the destination address. The third byte of the instruction contains the high-order 8 bits of the source address. The X Index Register contains the low-order 16 bits of the source address. The C Accumulator contains one less than the number of bytes to move. The second byte of the block move instructions is also loaded into the Data Bank Register.

```
Instruction:   | opcode | dstbnk | srcbnk |

                         dstbnk  →  DBR
Source
Address:                | scrbnk | X Reg |
Destination
Address:                |  DBR   | Y Reg |
```

Increment (MVN) or decrement (MVP) X and Y.
Decrement C (if greater than zero), then PC+3 → PC

Table 2. W65C802 and W65C816 Instruction Set—Alphabetical Sequence

ADC	Add Memory to Accumulator with Carry		PHA	Push Accumulator on Stack
AND	"AND" Memory with Accumulator		PHB	Push Data Bank Register on Stack
ASL	Shift One Bit Left, Memory or Accumulator		PHD	Push Direct Register on Stack
BCC	Branch on Carry Clear (Pc = 0)		PHK	Push Program Bank Register on Stack
BCS	Branch on Carry Set (Pc = 1)		PHP	Push Processor Status on Stack
BEQ	Branch if Equal (Pz = 1)		PHX	Push Index X on Stack
BIT	Bit Test		PHY	Push Index Y on Stack
BMI	Branch if Result Minus (PN = 1)		PLA	Pull Accumulator from Stack
BNE	Branch if Not Equal (Pz = 0)		PLB	Pull Data Bank Register from Stack
BPL	Branch if Result Plus (PN = 0)		PLD	Pull Direct Register from Stack
BRA	Branch Always		PLP	Pull Processor Status from Stack
BRK	Force Break		PLX	Pull Index X from Stack
BRL	Branch Always Long		PLY	Pull Index Y form Stack
BVC	Branch on Overflow Clear (Pv = 0)		REP	Reset Status Bits
BVS	Branch on Overflow Set (Pv = 1)		ROL	Rotate One Bit Left (Memory or Accumulator)
CLC	Clear Carry Flag		ROR	Rotate One Bit Right (Memory or Accumulator)
CLD	Clear Decimal Mode		RTI	Return from Interrupt
CLI	Clear Interrupt Disable Bit		RTL	Return from Subroutine Long
CLV	Clear Overflow Flag		RTS	Return from Subroutine
CMP	Compare Memory and Accumulator		SBC	Subtract Memory from Accumulator with Borrow
COP	Coprocessor		SEC	Set Carry Flag
CPX	Compare Memory and Index X		SED	Set Decimal Mode
CPY	Compare Memory and Index Y		SEI	Set Interrupt Disable Status
DEC	Decrement Memory or Accumulator by One		SEP	Set Processor Status Bite
DEX	Decrement Index X by One		STA	Store Accumulator in Memory
DEY	Decrement Index Y by One		STP	Stop the Clock
EOR	"Exclusive OR" Memory with Accumulator		STX	Store Index X in Memory
INC	Increment Memory or Accumulator by One		STY	Store Index Y in Memory
INX	Increment Index X by One		STZ	Store Zero in Memory
INY	Increment Index Y by One		TAX	Transfer Accumulator to Index X
JML	Jump Long		TAY	Transfer Accumulator to Index Y
JMP	Jump to New Location		TCD	Transfer C Accumulator to Direct Register
JSL	Jump Subroutine Long		TCS	Transfer C Accumulator to Stack Pointer Register
JSR	Jump to New Location Saving Return Address		TDC	Transfer Direct Register to C Accumulator
LDA	Load Accumulator with Memory		TRB	Test and Reset Bit
LDX	Load Index X with Memory		TSB	Test and Set Bit
LDY	Load Index Y with Memory		TSC	Transfer Stack Pointer Register to C Accumulator
LSR	Shift One Bit Right (Memory or Accumulator)		TSX	Transfer Stack Pointer Register to Index X
MVN	Block Move Negative		TXA	Transfer Index X to Accumulator
MVP	Block Move Positive		TXS	Transfer Index X to Stack Pointer Register
NOP	No Operation		TXY	Transfer Index X to Index Y
ORA	"OR" Memory with Accumulator		TYA	Transfer Index Y to Accumulator
PEA	Push Effective Absolute Address on Stack (or Push Immediate Data on Stack)		TYX	Transfer Index Y to Index X
			WAI	Wait for Interrupt
PEI	Push Effective Indirect Address on Stack (or Push Direct Data on Stack)		WDM	Reserved for Future Use
			XBA	Exchange B and A Accumulator
PER	Push Effective Program Counter Relative Address on Stack		XCE	Exchange Carry and Emulation Bits

For alternate mnemonics, see Table 7.

Table 3. Vector Locations

E = 1
00FFFE,F	—IRQ/BRK	Hardware/Software
00FFFC,D	—RESET	Hardware
00FFFA,B	—NMI	Hardware
00FFF8,9	—ABORT	Hardware
00FFF6,7	—(Reserved)	
00FFF4,5	—COP	Software

E = 0
00FFEE,F	—IRQ	Hardware
00FFEC,D	—(Reserved)	
00FFEA,B	—NMI	Hardware
00FFE8,9	—ABORT	Hardware
00FFE6,7	—BRK	Software
00FFE4,5	—COP	Software

The VP output is low during the two cycles used for vector location access
When an interrupt is executed, D = 0 and I = 1 in Status Register P

E W65C816 Data Sheet

Opcode Matrix

MSD\LSD	0	1	2	3	4	5	6	7	8	9	A	B	C	D	E	F	MSD
0	BRK s 2 8	ORA (d,x) 2 6	COP s 2*8	ORA d,s 2*4	TSB d 2 5	ORA d 2 3	ASL d 2 5	ORA [d] 2*6	PHP s 1 3	ORA # 2 2	ASL A 1 2	PHD s 1*4	TSB a 3 6	ORA a 3 4	ASL a 3 6	ORA al 4*5	0
1	BPL r 2 2	ORA (d),y 2 5	ORA (d) 2*5	ORA (d,s),y 2*7	TRB d 2 5	ORA d,x 2 4	ASL d,x 2 6	ORA [d],y 2*6	CLC i 1 2	ORA a,y 3 4	INC A 1*2	TCS i 1*2	TRB a 3 6	ORA a,x 3 4	ASL a,x 3 7	ORA al,x 4*5	1
2	JSR a 3 6	AND (d,x) 2 6	JSL al 4*8	AND d,s 2*4	BIT d 2 3	AND d 2 3	ROL d 2 5	AND [d] 2*6	PLP s 1 4	AND # 2 2	ROL A 1 2	PLD s 1*5	BIT a 3 4	AND a 3 4	ROL a 3 6	AND al 4*5	2
3	BMI r 2 2	AND (d),y 2 5	AND (d) 2*5	AND (d,s),y 2*7	BIT d,x 2*4	AND d,x 2 4	ROL d,x 2 6	AND [d],y 2*6	SEC i 1 2	AND a,y 3 4	DEC A 1*2	TSC i 1*2	BIT a,x 3*4	AND a,x 3 4	ROL a,x 3 7	AND al,x 4*5	3
4	RTI s 1 7	EOR (d,x) 2 6	WDM 2*2	EOR d,s 2*4	MVP xyc 3*7	EOR d 2 3	LSR d 2 5	EOR [d] 2*6	PHA s 1 3	EOR # 2 2	LSR A 1 2	PHK s 1*3	JMP a 3 3	EOR a 3 4	LSR a 3 6	EOR al 4*5	4
5	BVC r 2 2	EOR (d),y 2 5	EOR (d) 2*5	EOR (d,s),y 2*7	MVN xyc 3*7	EOR d,x 2 4	LSR d,x 2 6	EOR [d],y 2*6	CLI i 1 2	EOR a,y 3 4	PHY s 1*3	TCD i 1*2	JMP al 4*4	EOR a,x 3 4	LSR a,x 3 7	EOR al,x 4*5	5
6	RTS s 1 6	ADC (d,x) 2 6	PER s 3*6	ADC d,s 2*4	STZ d 2*3	ADC d 2 3	ROR d 2 5	ADC [d] 2*6	PLA s 1 4	ADC # 2 2	ROR A 1 2	RTL s 1*6	JMP (a) 3 5	ADC a 3 4	ROR a 3 6	ADC al 4*5	6
7	BVS r 2 2	ADC (d),y 2 5	ADC (d) 2*5	ADC (d,s),y 2*7	STZ d,x 2*4	ADC d,x 2 4	ROR d,x 2 6	ADC [d],y 2*6	SEI i 1 2	ADC a,y 3 4	PLY s 1*4	TDC i 1*2	JMP (a,x) 3*6	ADC a,x 3 4	ROR a,x 3 7	ADC al,x 4*5	7
8	BRA r 2*2	STA (d,x) 2 6	BRL rl 3*3	STA d,s 2*4	STY d 2 3	STA d 2 3	STX d 2 3	STA [d] 2*6	DEY i 1 2	BIT # 2*2	TXA i 1 2	PHB s 1*3	STY a 3 4	STA a 3 4	STX a 3 4	STA al 4*5	8
9	BCC r 2 2	STA (d),y 2 5	STA (d) 2*5	STA (d,s),y 2*7	STY d,x 2 4	STA d,x 2 4	STX d,y 2 4	STA [d],y 2*6	TYA i 1 2	STA a,y 3 5	TXS i 1 2	TXY i 1*2	STZ a 3*4	STA a,x 3 5	STZ a,x 3*5	STA al,x 4*5	9
A	LDY # 2 2	LDA (d,x) 2 6	LDX # 2 2	LDA d,s 2*4	LDY d 2 3	LDA d 2 3	LDX d 2 3	LDA [d] 2*6	TAY i 1 2	LDA # 2 2	TAX i 1 2	PLB s 1*4	LDY a 3 4	LDA a 3 4	LDX a 3 4	LDA al 4*5	A
B	BCS r 2 2	LDA (d),y 2 5	LDA (d) 2*5	LDA (d,s),y 2*7	LDY d,x 2 4	LDA d,x 2 4	LDX d,y 2 4	LDA [d],y 2*6	CLV i 1 2	LDA a,y 3 4	TSX i 1 2	TYX i 1*2	LDY a,x 3 4	LDA a,x 3 4	LDX a,y 3 4	LDA al,x 4*5	B
C	CPY # 2 2	CMP (d,x) 2 6	REP # 2*3	CMP d,s 2*4	CPY d 2 3	CMP d 2 3	DEC d 2 5	CMP [d] 2*6	INY i 1 2	CMP # 2 2	DEX i 1 2	WAI i 1*3	CPY a 3 4	CMP a 3 4	DEC a 3 6	CMP al 4*5	C
D	BNE r 2 2	CMP (d),y 2 5	CMP (d) 2*5	CMP (d,s),y 2*7	PEI s 2*6	CMP d,x 2 4	DEC d,x 2 6	CMP [d],y 2*6	CLD i 1 2	CMP a,y 3 4	PHX s 1*3	STP i 1*3	JML (a) 3*6	CMP a,x 3 4	DEC a,x 3 7	CMP al,x 4*5	D
E	CPX # 2 2	SBC (d,x) 2 6	SEP # 2*3	SBC d,s 2*4	CPX d 2 3	SBC d 2 3	INC d 2 5	SBC [d] 2*6	INX i 1 2	SBC # 2 2	NOP i 1 2	XBA i 1*3	CPX a 3 4	SBC a 3 4	INC a 3 6	SBC al 4*5	E
F	BEQ r 2 2	SBC (d),y 2 5	SBC (d) 2*5	SBC (d,s),y 2*7	PEA s 3*5	SBC d,x 2 4	INC d,x 2 6	SBC [d],y 2*6	SED i 1 2	SBC a,y 3 4	PLX s 1*4	XCE i 1*2	JSR (a,x) 3*6	SBC a,x 3 4	INC a,x 3 7	SBC al,x 4*5	F

symbol	addressing mode	symbol	addressing mode
#	immediate	[d]	direct indirect long
A	accumulator	[d],y	direct indirect long indexed
r	program counter relative	a	absolute
rl	program counter relative long	a,x	absolute indexed (with x)
i	implied	a,y	absolute indexed (with y)
s	stack	al	absolute long
d	direct	al,x	absolute long indexed
d,x	direct indexed (with x)	d,s	stack relative
d,y	direct indexed (with y)	(d,s),y	stack relative indirect indexed
(d)	direct indirect	(a)	absolute indirect
(d,x)	direct indexed indirect	(a,x)	absolute indexed indirect
(d),y	direct indirect indexed	xyc	block move

Op Code Matrix Legend

INSTRUCTION MNEMONIC		ADDRESSING MODE
	★ = New W65C816/802 Opcodes	
	● = New W65C02 Opcodes	
BASE NO BYTES	Blank = NMOS 6502 Opcodes	BASE NO CYCLES

Table 5. Operation, Operation Codes, and Status Register

MNEMONIC	OPERATION	#	s	a	d	-	(d),y	[d],y	(d,x)	d,x	d,y	a,x	al,x	a,y	r	(a)	(d)	[d]	(a,x)	a	d,s	(d,s),y	xyc	PROCESSOR STATUS CODE 7 6 5 4 3 2 1 0 N V M X B D I Z C E	MNEMONIC
		1	2	3	4	5	6	7	8	9	10	11	12	13	14	15	16	17	18	19	20	21	22	23	24	N V M X B D I Z C E	
ADC	A + M + C → A	69	6D	6F	65		71	77	61	75		7D	7F	79							72	67		63	73		N V Z C	ADC
AND	A∧M → A	29	2D	2F	25		31	37	21	35		3D	3F	39							32	27		23	33		N Z	AND
ASL	C ← [15/7 0] ← 0		0E		06	0A				16		1E															N Z C	ASL
BCC	BRANCH IF C = 0															90													BCC
BCS	BRANCH IF C = 1															B0													BCS
BEQ	BRANCH IF Z = 1															F0													BEQ
BIT	A∧M (NOTE 1)	89	2C		24					34		3C															M-M7 Z	BIT
BMI	BRANCH IF N = 1															30													BMI
BNE	BRANCH IF Z = 0															D0													BNE
BPL	BRANCH IF N = 0															10													BPL
BRA	BRANCH ALWAYS															80													BRA
BRK	BREAK (NOTE 2)																									00	• • 0 1	BRK
BRL	BRANCH LONG ALWAYS																	82										★	BRL
BVC	BRANCH IF V = 0															50													BVC
BVS	BRANCH IF V = 1															70													BVS
CLC	0 → C									18																	0	CLC
CLD	0 → D									D8																	0	CLD
CLI	0 → I									58																	0	CLI
CLV	0 → V									B8																	0	CLV
CMP	C - M	C9	CD	CF	C5		D1	D7	C1	D5		DD	DF	D9							D2	C7		C3	D3		N Z C	CMP
COP	CO-PROCESSOR																									02	• 0 1 ★	COP
CPX	X - M	E0	EC		E4																						N Z C	CPX
CPY	Y - M	C0	CC		C4																						N Z C	CPY
DEC	DECREMENT		CE		C6	3A				D6		DE															N Z	DEC
DEX	X - 1 → X					CA																					N Z	DEX
DEY	Y - 1 → Y					88																					N Z	DEY
EOR	A∨M → A	49	4D	4F	45		51	57	41	55		5D	5F	59							52	47		43	53		N Z	EOR
INC	INCREMENTS		EE		E6	1A				F6		FE															N Z	INC
INX	X + 1 → X					E8																					N Z	INX
INY	Y + 1 → Y					C8																					N Z	INY
JML	JUMP LONG TO NEW LOC																		DC								★	JML
JMP	JUMP TO NEW LOC		4C	5C														6C		7C								JMP
JSL	JUMP LONG TO SUB			22																							★	JSL
JSR	JUMP TO SUB		20																	FC								JSR
LDA	M → A	A9	AD	AF	A5		B1	B7	A1	B5		BD	BF	B9							B2	A7		A3	B3		N Z	LDA
LDX	M → X	A2	AE		A6						B6			BE													N Z	LDX
LDY	M → Y	A0	AC		A4					B4		BC															N Z	LDY
LSR	0 → [15/7 0] → C		4E		46	4A				56		5E															0 Z C	LSR
MVN	M → M BACKWARD																							54			★	MVN
MVP	M → M FORWARD																							44			★	MVP
NOP	NO OPERATION									EA																		NOP
ORA	A∨M → A	09	0D	0F	05		11	17	01	15		1D	1F	19							12	07		03	13		N Z	ORA
PEA	Mpc+1, Mpc+2 → Ms, 1 Ms S - 2 → S																				F4						★	PEA
PEI	M(d), M(d+1) → Ms, 1 Ms S - 2 → S																				D4						★	PEI
PER	Mpc+rl, Mpc+rl+1 → Ms, 1 Ms S - 2 → S																				62						★	PER
PHA	A → Ms, S - 1 → S									48																		PHA
PHB	DBR → Ms, S - 1 → S									8B																		PHB
PHD	D → Ms, S - 1, S - 2 → S									0B																	★	PHD
PHK	PBR → Ms, S - 1 → S									4B																		PHK
PHP	P → Ms, S - 1 → S									08																		PHP
PHX	X → Ms, S - 1 → S									DA																	•	PHX
PHY	Y → Ms, S - 1 → S									5A																	•	PHY
PLA	S + 1 → S, Ms → A									68																	N Z	PLA
PLB	S + 1 → S, Ms → DBR									AB																	N Z	PLB
PLD	S + 2 → S, Ms, 1, Ms → D									2B																	N Z	PLD
PLP	S + 1 → S, Ms → P									28																	N V M X D I Z C	PLP
PLX	S + 1 → S, Ms → X									FA																	N Z	PLX
PLY	S + 1 → S, Ms → Y									7A																	N Z	PLY
REP	MAP → P	C2																									N V M X D I Z C ★	REP
ROL	C ← [15/7 0] ← C		2E		26	2A				36		3E															N Z C	ROL
ROR	C → [15/7 0] → C		6E		66	6A				76		7E															N Z C	ROR
RTI	RTRN FROM INT									40																	N V M X D I Z C	RTI
RTL	RTRN FROM SUB LONG									6B																	★	RTL
RTS	RTRN SUBROUTINE									60																		RTS
SBC	A - M - C̄ → A	E9	ED	EF	E5		F1	F7	E1	F5		FD	FF	F9							F2	E7		E3	F3		N V Z C	SBC
SEC	1 → C									38																	1	SEC
SED	1 → D									F8																	1	SED
SEI	1 → I									78																	1	SEI
SEP	MVP → P	E2																									N V M X D I Z C ★	SEP
STA	A → M		8D	8F	85		91	97	81	95		9D	9F	99							92	87		83	93			STA
STP	STOP (1 → φ2)									DB																	•	STP
STX	X → M		8E		86						96																	STX
STY	Y → M		8C		84					94																		STY
STZ	00 → M		9C		64					74		9E															•	STZ
TAX	A → X					AA																					N Z	TAX
TAY	A → Y					A8																					N Z	TAY
TCD	C → D					5B																					N Z ★	TCD
TCS	C → S					1B																					★	TCS
TDC	D → C					7B																					N Z ★	TDC
TRB						1C		14																			•	TRB
TSB	A∨M → M		0C		04																						N Z •	TSB
TSC	S → C					3B																					N Z ★	TSC
TSX	S → X					BA																					N Z	TSX
TXA	X → A					8A																					N Z	TXA
TXS	X → S					9A																						TXS
TXY	X → Y					9B																					N Z ★	TXY
TYA	Y → A					98																					N Z	TYA
TYX	Y → X					BB																					N Z ★	TYX
WAI	0 → RDY					CB																					•	WAI
WDM	NO OPERATION (RESERVED)					42																					•	WDM
XBA	B ↔ A					EB																					N Z	XBA
XCE	C ↔ E					FB																						E	XCE

Notes
1 Bit immediate N and V flags not affected. When M = 0, M15 → N and M14 → V
2 Break Bit (B) in Status register indicates hardware or software break

3 ★ = New W65C816/802 Instructions
  • = New W65C02 Instructions
  Blank = NMOS 6502

· = Add
- = Subtract
∀ = Exclusive OR
∧ = AND

∨ = OR

Table 6. Detailed Instruction Operation

	ADDRESS MODE		CYCLE	VP	ML	VDA	VPA	RDY	ADDRESS BUS	DATA BUS	R/W
1	Immediate #		1	1	1	1	1		PBR,PC	Op Code	1
	(LDY CPY CPX LDX ORA		2	1	1	0	1		PBR,PC+1	IDL	1
	AND EOR ADC BIT LDA	(1)(8)	2a	1	1	0	1		PBR,PC+2	IDH	1
	CMP SBC REP SEP)										
	(14 Op Codes)										
	(2 and 3 bytes)										
	(2 and 3 cycles)										
2a	Absolute a		1	1	1	1	1		PBR,PC	Op Code	1
	(BIT STY STZ LDY		2	1	1	0	1		PBR,PC+1	AAL	1
	CPY CPX STX LDX		3	1	1	0	1		PBR,PC+2	AAH	1
	ORA AND EOR ADC		4	1	1	1	0		DBR,AA	Data Low	1/0
	STA LDA CMP SBC)	(1)	4a	1	1	1	0		DBR,AA+1	Data High	1/0
	(18 Op Codes)										
	(3 bytes)										
	(4 and 5 cycles)										
2b	Absolute (R-M-W) a		1	1	1	1	1		PBR,PC	Op Code	1
			2	1	1	0	1		PBR,PC+1	AAL	1
	(ASL ROL LSR ROR		3	1	1	0	1		PBR,PC+2	AAH	1
	DEC INC TSB TRB)		4	1	0	1	0		DBR,AA	Data Low	1
	(6 Op Codes)	(1)	4a	1	0	1	0		DBR,AA+1	Data High	1
	(3 bytes)	(3)	5	1	0	0	0		DBR,AA+1	IO	1
	(6 and 8 cycles)	(1)	6a	1	0	1	0		DBR,AA+1	Data High	0
			6	1	0	1	0		DBR,AA	Data Low	0
2c	Absolute (JUMP) a		1	1	1	1	1		PBR,PC	Op Code	1
	(JMP)(4C)		2	1	1	0	1		PBR,PC+1	NEW PCL	1
	(1 Op Code)		3	1	1	0	1		PBR,PC+2	NEW PCH	1
	(3 bytes)		1	1	1	1	1		PBR,NEW PC	Op Code	1
	(3 cycles)										
2d	Absolute (Jump to subroutine) a		1	1	1	1	1		PBR,PC	Op Code	1
	(JSR)		2	1	1	0	1		PBR,PC+1	NEW PCL	1
	(1 Op Code)		3	1	1	0	1		PBR,PC+2	NEW PCH	1
	(3 bytes)		4	1	1	0	0		PBR,PC+2	IO	1
	(6 cycles)		5	1	1	1	0		0,S	PCH	0
	(different order from N6502)		6	1	1	1	0		0,S-1	PCL	0
			1	1	1	1	1		PBR,NEW PC	Next Op Code	1
*3a	Absolute Long al		1	1	1	1	1		PBR,PC	Op Code	1
	(ORA AND EOR ADC		2	1	1	0	1		PBR,PC+1	AAL	1
	STA LDA CMP SBC)		3	1	1	0	1		PBR,PC+2	AAH	1
	(8 Op Codes)		4	1	1	0	1		PBR,PC+3	AAB	1
	(4 bytes)		5	1	1	1	0		AAB,AA	Data Low	1/0
	(5 and 6 cycles)	(1)	5a	1	1	1	0		AAB,AA+1	Data High	1/0
*3b	Absolute Long (JUMP) al		1	1	1	1	1		PBR,PC	Op Code	1
	(JMP)		2	1	1	0	1		PBR,PC+1	NEW PCL	1
	(1 Op Code)		3	1	1	0	1		PBR,PC+2	NEW PCH	1
	(4 bytes)		4	1	1	0	1		PBR,PC+3	NEW BR	1
	(4 cycles)		1	1	1	1	1		NEW PBR,PC	Op Code	1
*3c	Absolute Long (Jump to Subroutine Long) al		1	1	1	1	1		PBR,PC	Op Code	1
	(JSL)		2	1	1	0	1		PBR,PC+1	NEW PCL	1
	(1 Op Code)		3	1	1	0	1		PBR,PC+2	NEW PCH	1
	(4 bytes)		4	1	1	1	0		0,S	PBR	0
	(7 cycles)		5	1	1	0	0		0,S	IO	1
			6	1	1	0	1		PBR,PC+3	NEW PBR	1
			7	1	1	1	0		0,S-1	PCH	0
			8	1	1	1	0		0,S-2	PCL	0
			1	1	1	1	1		NEW PBR,PC	Next Op Code	1
4a	Direct d		1	1	1	1	1		PBR,PC	Op Code	1
	(BIT STZ STY LDY		2	1	1	0	1		PBR,PC+1	DO	1
	CPY CPX STX LDX	(2)	2a	1	1	0	0		PBR,PC+1	IO	1
	ORA AND EOR ADC		3	1	1	1	0		0,D+DO	Data Low	1/0
	STA LDA CMP SBC)	(1)	3a	1	1	1	0		0,D+DO+1	Data High	1/0
	(18 Op Codes)										
	(2 bytes)										
	(3,4 and 5 cycles)										
4b	Direct (R-M-W) d		1	1	1	1	1		PBR,PC	Op Code	1
	(ASL ROL LSR ROR		2	1	1	0	1		PBR,PC+1	DO	1
	DEC INC TSB TRB)	(2)	2a	1	1	0	0		PBR,PC+1	IO	1
	(6 Op Codes)		3	1	0	1	0		0,D+DO	Data Low	1
	(2 bytes)	(1)	3a	1	0	1	0		0,D+DO+1	Data High	1
	(5,6,7 and 8 cycles)	(3)	4	1	0	0	0		0,D+DO+1	IO	1
		(1)	5a	1	0	1	0		0,D+DO+1	Data High	0
			5	1	0	1	0		0,D+DO	Data Low	0
5	Accumulator A		1	1	1	1	1		PBR,PC	Op Code	1
	(ASL INC ROL DEC LSR ROR)		2	1	1	0	0		PBR,PC+1	IO	1
	(6 Op Codes)										
	(1 byte)										
	(2 cycles)										
6a	Implied i		1	1	1	1	1		PBR,PC	Op Code	1
	(DEY INY INX DEX NOP		2	1	1	0	0		PBR,PC+1	IO	1
	XCE TYA TAY TXA TXS										
	TAX TSX TCS TSC TCD										
	TDC TXY TYX CLC SEC										
	CLI SEI CLV CLD SED)										
	(25 Op Codes)										
	(1 byte)										
	(2 cycles)										
*6b	Implied i		1	1	1	1	1		PBR,PC	Op Code	1
	(XBA)		2	1	1	0	0		PBR,PC+1	IO	1
	(1 Op Code)		3	1	1	0	0		PBR,PC+1	IO	1
	(1 byte)										
	(3 cycles)										
• 6c	Wait For Interrupt										
	(WAI)		1	1	1	1	1	1	PBR,PC	Op Code	1
	(1 Op Code)	(9)	2	1	1	0	0	1	PBR,PC+1	IO	1
	(1 byte)		3	1	1	0	0	0	PBR,PC+1	IO	1
	(3 cycles)	IRQ,NMI	1	1	1	1	1	1	PBR,PC+1	IRQ(BRK)	1
• 6d	Stop-The-Clock										
	(STP)		1	1	1	1	1	1	PBR,PC	Op Code	1
	(1 Op Code)		2	1	1	0	0	1	PBR,PC+1	IO	1
	(1 byte)	RES = 1	3	1	1	0	0	1	PBR,PC+1	IO	1
	(3 cycles)	RES = 0	1c	1	1	0	0	1	PBR,PC+1	RES(BRK)	1
		RES = 0	1b	1	1	0	0	1	PBR,PC+1	RES(BRK)	1
		RES = 1	1a	1	1	0	0	1	PBR,PC+1	RES(BRK)	1
	See 21a Stack (Hardware Interrupt)		1	1	1	1	1	1	PBR,PC+1	BEGIN	1
7	Direct Indirect Indexed (d),y		1	1	1	1	1		PBR,PC	Op Code	1
	(ORA AND EOR ADC		2	1	1	0	1		PBR,PC+1	DO	1
	STA LDA CMP SBC)	(2)	2a	1	1	0	0		PBR,PC+1	IO	1
	(8 Op Codes)		3	1	1	1	0		0,D+DO	AAL	1
	(2 bytes)		4	1	1	1	0		0,D+DO+1	AAH	1
	(5,6,7 and 8 cycles)	(4)	4a	1	1	0	0		DBR,AAH,AAL+YL	IO	1
			5	1	1	1	0		DBR,AA+Y	Data Low	1/0
		(1)	5a	1	1	1	0		DBR,AA+Y+1	Data High	1/0
8	Direct Indirect Indexed Long [d],y		1	1	1	1	1		PBR,PC	Op Code	1
			2	1	1	0	1		PBR,PC+1	DO	1
	(ORA AND EOR ADC	(2)	2a	1	1	0	0		PBR,PC+1	IO	1
	STA LDA CMP SBC)		3	1	1	1	0		0,D+DO	AAL	1
	(8 Op Codes)		4	1	1	1	0		0,D+DO+1	AAH	1
	(2 bytes)		5	1	1	1	0		0,D+DO+2	AAB	1
	(6,7 and 8 cycles)		6	1	1	1	0		AAB,AA+Y	Data Low	1/0
		(1)	6a	1	1	1	0		AAB,AA+Y+1	Data High	1/0
9	Direct Indexed Indirect (d,x)		1	1	1	1	1		PBR,PC	Op Code	1
	(ORA AND EOR ADC		2	1	1	0	1		PBR,PC+1	DO	1
	STA LDA CMP SBC)	(2)	2a	1	1	0	0		PBR,PC+1	IO	1
	(8 Op Codes)		3	1	1	0	0		PBR,PC+1	IO	1
	(2 bytes)		4	1	1	1	0		0,D+DO+X	AAL	1
	(6,7 and 8 cycles)		5	1	1	1	0		0,D+DO+X+1	AAH	1
			6	1	1	1	0		DBR,AA	Data Low	1/0
		(1)	6a	1	1	1	0		DBR,AA+1	Data High	1/0
10a	Direct,X d,x		1	1	1	1	1		PBR,PC	Op Code	1
	(BIT STZ STY LDY		2	1	1	0	1		PBR,PC+1	DO	1
	ORA AND EOR ADC	(2)	2a	1	1	0	0		PBR,PC+1	IO	1
	STA LDA CMP SBC)		3	1	1	0	0		PBR,PC+1	IO	1
	(11 Op Codes)		4	1	1	1	0		0,D+DO+X	Data Low	1/0
	(2 bytes)	(1)	4a	1	1	1	0		0,D+DO+X+1	Data High	1/0
	(4,5 and 6 cycles)										
10b	Direct,X(R-M-W) d,x		1	1	1	1	1		PBR,PC	Op Code	1
	(ASL ROL LSR ROR		2	1	1	0	1		PBR,PC+1	DO	1
	DEC INC)	(2)	2a	1	1	0	0		PBR,PC+1	IO	1
	(6 Op Codes)		3	1	1	0	0		PBR,PC+1	IO	1
	(2 bytes)		4	1	0	1	0		0,D+DO+X	Data Low	1
	(6,7,8 and 9 cycles)	(1)	4a	1	0	1	0		0,D+DO+X+1	Data High	1
		(3)	5	1	0	0	0		0,D+DO+X+1	IO	1
		(1)	6a	1	0	1	0		0,D+DO+X+1	Data High	0
			6	1	0	1	0		0,D+DO+X	Data Low	0
11	Direct,Y d,y		1	1	1	1	1		PBR,PC	Op Code	1
	(STX LDX)		2	1	1	0	1		PBR,PC+1	DO	1
	(2 Op Codes)	(2)	2a	1	1	0	0		PBR,PC+1	IO	1
	(2 bytes)		3	1	1	0	0		PBR,PC+1	IO	1
	(4,5 and 6 cycles)		4	1	1	1	0		0,D+DO+Y	Data Low	1/0
		(1)	4a	1	1	1	0		0,D+DO+Y+1	Data High	1/0
12a	Absolute,X a,x		1	1	1	1	1		PBR,PC	Op Code	1
	(BIT LDY STZ		2	1	1	0	1		PBR,PC+1	AAL	1
	ORA AND EOR ADC		3	1	1	0	1		PBR,PC+2	AAH	1
	STA LDA CMP SBC)	(4)	3a	1	1	0	0		DBR,AAH,AAL+XL	IO	1
	(11 Op Codes)		4	1	1	1	0		DBR,AA+X	Data Low	1/0
	(3 bytes)	(1)	4a	1	1	1	0		DBR,AA+X+1	Data High	1/0
	(4,5 and 6 cycles)										
12b	Absolute,X(R-M-W) a,x		1	1	1	1	1		PBR,PC	Op Code	1
	(ASL ROL LSR ROR		2	1	1	0	1		PBR,PC+1	AAL	1
	DEC INC)		3	1	1	0	1		PBR,PC+2	AAH	1
	(6 Op Codes)		4	1	1	0	0		DBR,AAH,AAL+XL	IO	1
	(3 bytes)		5	1	0	1	0		DBR,AA+X	Data Low	1
	(7 and 9 cycles)	(1)	5a	1	0	1	0		DBR,AA+X+1	Data High	1
		(3)	6	1	0	0	0		DBR,AA+X+1	IO	1
		(1)	7a	1	0	1	0		DBR,AA+X+1	Data High	0
			7	1	0	1	0		DBR,AA+X	Data Low	0
*13	Absolute Long,X al,x		1	1	1	1	1		PBR,PC	Op Code	1
	(ORA AND EOR ADC		2	1	1	0	1		PBR,PC+1	AAL	1
	STA LDA CMP SBC)		3	1	1	0	1		PBR,PC+2	AAH	1
	(8 Op Codes)		4	1	1	0	1		PBR,PC+3	AAB	1
	(4 bytes)		5	1	1	1	0		AAB,AA+X	Data Low	1/0
	(5 and 6 cycles)	(1)	5a	1	1	1	0		AAB,AA+X+1	Data High	1/0
14	Absolute,Y a,y		1	1	1	1	1		PBR,PC	Op Code	1
	(LDX ORA AND EOR ADC		2	1	1	0	1		PBR,PC+1	AAL	1
	STA LDA CMP SBC)		3	1	1	0	1		PBR,PC+2	AAH	1
	(9 Op Codes)	(4)	3a	1	1	0	0		DBR,AAH,AAL+YL	IO	1
	(3 bytes)		4	1	1	1	0		DBR,AA+Y	Data Low	1/0
	(4,5 and 6 cycles)	(1)	4a	1	1	1	0		DBR,AA+Y+1	Data High	1/0
15	Relative r		1	1	1	1	1		PBR,PC	Op Code	1
	(BPL BMI BVC BVS BCC		2	1	1	0	1		PBR,PC+1	Offset	1
	BCS BNE BEQ BRA)	(5)	2a	1	1	0	0		PBR,PC+1	IO	1
	(9 Op Codes)	(6)	2b	1	1	0	0		PBR,PC+1	IO	1
	(2 bytes)		1	1	1	1	1		PBR,PC+Offset	Op Code	1
	(2,3 and 4 cycles)										
*16	Relative Long rl		1	1	1	1	1		PBR,PC	Op Code	1
	(BRL)		2	1	1	0	1		PBR,PC+1	Offset Low	1
	(1 Op Code)		3	1	1	0	1		PBR,PC+2	Offset High	1
	(3 bytes)		4	1	1	0	0		PBR,PC+2	IO	1
	(4 cycles)		1	1	1	1	1		PBR,PC+Offset	Op Code	1
17a	Absolute Indirect (a)		1	1	1	1	1		PBR,PC	Op Code	1
	(JMP)		2	1	1	0	1		PBR,PC+1	AAL	1
	(1 Op Code)		3	1	1	0	1		PBR,PC+2	AAH	1
	(3 bytes)		4	1	1	1	0		0,AA	NEW PCL	1
	(5 cycles)		5	1	1	1	0		0,AA+1	NEW PCH	1
			1	1	1	1	1		PBR,NEW PC	Op Code	1
*17b	Absolute Indirect [a]		1	1	1	1	1		PBR,PC	Op Code	1
			2	1	1	0	1		PBR,PC+1	AAL	1
	(JML)		3	1	1	0	1		PBR,PC+2	AAH	1
	(1 Op Code)		4	1	1	1	0		0,AA	NEW PCL	1
	(3 bytes)		5	1	1	1	0		0,AA+1	NEW PCH	1
	(6 cycles)		6	1	1	1	0		0,AA+2	NEW PBR	1
			1	1	1	1	1		NEW PBR,PC	Op Code	1
• 18	Direct Indirect (d)		1	1	1	1	1		PBR,PC	Op Code	1
	(ORA AND EOR ADC		2	1	1	0	1		PBR,PC+1	DO	1
	STA LDA CMP SBC)	(2)	2a	1	1	0	0		PBR,PC+1	IO	1
	(8 Op Codes)		3	1	1	1	0		0,D+DO	AAL	1
	(2 bytes)		4	1	1	1	0		0,D+DO+1	AAH	1
	(5,6 and 7 cycles)		5	1	1	1	0		DBR,AA	Data Low	1/0
		(1)	5a	1	1	1	0		DBR,AA+1	Data Low	1/0

Table 6. Detailed Instruction Operation (continued)

	ADDRESS MODE		CYCLE	$\overline{VP}$	$\overline{ML}$	VDA	VPA	ADDRESS BUS	DATA BUS	R/$\overline{W}$
*19	Direct Indirect Long [d]		1	1	1	1	1	PBR,PC	Op Code	1
	(ORA AND EOR ADC		2	1	1	0	1	PBR,PC+1	DO	1
	STA LDA CMP SBC)	(2)	2a	1	1	0	0	PBR,PC+1	IO	1
	(8 Op Codes)		3	1	1	1	0	0,D+DO	AAL	1
	(2 bytes)		4	1	1	1	0	0,D+DO+1	AAH	1
	(6, 7 and 8 cycles)		5	1	1	1	0	0,D+DO+2	AAB	1
			6	1	1	1	0	AAB,AA	Data Low	1/0
		(1)	6a	1	1	1	0	AAB,AA+1	Data High	1/0
20a	Absolute Indexed Indirect (a,x)		1	1	1	1	1	PBR,PC	Op Code	1
	(JMP)		2	1	1	0	1	PBR,PC+1	AAL	1
	(1 Op Code)		3	1	1	0	1	PBR,PC+2	AAH	1
	(3 bytes)		4	1	1	0	0	PBR,PC+2	IO	1
	(6 cycles)		5	1	1	0	1	PBR,AA+X	NEW PCL	1
			6	1	1	0	1	PBR,AA+X+1	NEW PCH	1
			1	1	1	1	1	PBR,NEW PC	Op Code	1
*20b	Absolute Indexed Indirect		1	1	1	1	1	PBR,PC	Op Code	1
	(Jump to Subroutine Indexed		2	1	1	0	1	PBR,PC+1	AAL	1
	Indirect) (a,x)		3	1	1	1	0	0,S	PCH	0
	(JSR)		4	1	1	1	0	0,S-1	PCL	0
	(1 Op Code)		5	1	1	0	1	PBR,PC+2	AAH	1
	(3 bytes)		6	1	1	0	0	PBR,PC+2	IO	1
	(8 cycles)		7	1	1	0	1	PBR,AA+X	NEW PCL	1
			8	1	1	0	1	PBR,AA+X+1	NEW PCH	1
			1	1	1	1	1	PBR,NEW PC	Next Op Code	1
21a	Stack (Hardware		1	1	1	1	1	PBR,PC	IO	1
	Interrupts) s	(3)	2	1	1	0	0	PBR,PC	IO	1
	(IRQ NMI ABORT RES)	(7)	3	1	1	1	0	0,S	PBR	0
	(4 hardware interrupts)		4	1	1	1	0	0,S-1	PCH	0
	(0 bytes)		5	1	1	1	0	0,S-2	PCL	0
	(7 and 8 cycles)		6	1	1	1	0	0,S-3	P	0
			7	0	1	1	0	0,VA	AAVL	1
			8	0	1	1	0	0,VA+1	AAVH	1
			1	1	1	1	1	0,AAV	Next Op Code	1
21b	Stack (Software		1	1	1	1	1	PBR,PC	Op Code	1
	Interrupts) s	(3)	2	1	1	0	1	PBR,PC+1	Signature	1
	(BRK COP)	(7)	3	1	1	1	0	0,S	PBR	0
	(2 Op Codes)		4	1	1	1	0	0,S-1	PCH	0
	(2 bytes)		5	1	1	1	0	0,S-2	PCL	0
	(7 and 8 cycles)		6	1	1	1	0	0,S-3 (COP Latches)	P	0
			7	0	1	1	0	0,VA	AAVL	1
			8	0	1	1	0	0,VA+1	AAVH	1
			1	1	1	1	1	0,AAV	Next Op Code	1
21c	Stack (Return from		1	1	1	1	1	PBR,PC	Op Code	1
	Interrupt) s		2	1	1	0	0	PBR,PC+1	IO	1
	(RTI)	(3)	3	1	1	0	0	PBR,PC+1	IO	1
	(1 Op Code)		4	1	1	1	0	0,S+1	P	1
	(1 byte)		5	1	1	1	0	0,S+2	PCL	1
	(6 and 7 cycles)		6	1	1	1	0	0,S+3	PCH	1
	(different order from N6502)	(7)	7	1	1	1	0	0,S+4	PBR	1
			1	1	1	1	1	PBR,PC	New Op Code	1
21d	Stack (Return from		1	1	1	1	1	PBR,PC	Op Code	1
	Subroutine) s		2	1	1	0	0	PBR,PC+1	IO	1
	(RTS)		3	1	1	0	0	PBR,PC+1	IO	1
	(1 Op Code)		4	1	1	1	0	0,S+1	PCL	1
	(1 byte)		5	1	1	1	0	0,S+2	PCH	1
	(6 cycles)		6	1	1	0	0	0,S+2	IO	1
			1	1	1	1	1	PBR,PC	Op Code	1
*21e	Stack (Return from		1	1	1	1	1	PBR,PC	Op Code	1
	Subroutine Long) s		2	1	1	0	0	PBR,PC+1	IO	1
	(RTL)		3	1	1	0	0	PBR,PC+1	IO	1
	(1 Op Code)		4	1	1	1	0	0,S+1	NEW PCL	1
	(1 byte)		5	1	1	1	0	0,S+2	NEW PCH	1
	(6 cycles)		6	1	1	1	0	0,S+3	NEW PBR	1
			1	1	1	1	1	NEW PBR,PC	Next Op Code	1
21f	Stack (Push) s		1	1	1	1	1	PBR,PC	Op Code	1
	(PHP PHA PHY PHX		2	1	1	0	0	PBR,PC+1	IO	1
	PHD PHK PHB)	(1)	3a	1	1	1	0	0,S	Register High	1
	(7 Op Codes)		3	1	1	1	0	0,S-1	Register Low	1
	(1 byte)									
	(3 and 4 cycles)									
21g	Stack (Pull) s		1	1	1	1	1	PBR,PC	Op Code	1
	(PLP PLA PLY PLX PLD PLB)		2	1	1	0	0	PBR,PC+1	IO	1
	(Different than N6502)		3	1	1	0	0	PBR,PC+1	IO	1
	(6 Op Codes)		4	1	1	1	0	0,S+1	Register Low	1
	(1 byte)	(1)	4a	1	1	1	0	0,S+2	Register High	1
	(4 and 5 cycles)									
*21h	Stack (Push Effective		1	1	1	1	1	PBR,PC	Op Code	1
	Indirect Address) s		2	1	1	0	1	PBR,PC+1	DO	1
	(PEI)	(2)	2a	1	1	0	0	PBR,PC+1	IO	1
	(1 Op Code)		3	1	1	1	0	0,D+DO	AAL	1
	(2 bytes)		4	1	1	1	0	0,D+DO+1	AAH	1
	(6 and 7 cycles)		5	1	1	1	0	0,S	AAH	0
			6	1	1	1	0	0,S-1	AAL	0
*21i	Stack (Push Effective		1	1	1	1	1	PBR,PC	Op Code	1
	Absolute Address) s		2	1	1	0	1	PBR,PC+1	AAL	1
	(PEA)		3	1	1	0	1	PBR,PC+2	AAH	1
	(1 Op Code)		4	1	1	1	0	0,S	AAH	0
	(3 bytes)		5	1	1	1	0	0,S-1	AAL	0
	(5 cycles)									
*21j	Stack (Push Effective		1	1	1	1	1	PBR,PC	Op Code	1
	Program Counter Relative		2	1	1	0	1	PBR,PC+1	Offset Low	1
	Address) s		3	1	1	0	1	PBR,PC+2	Offset High	1
	(PER)		4	1	1	0	0	PBR,PC+2	IO	1
	(1 Op Code)		5	1	1	1	0	0,S	PCH+OFF+ CARRY	0
	(3 bytes)									
	(6 cycles)		6	1	1	1	0	0,S-1	PCL+OFFSET	0
*22	Stack Relative d,s		1	1	1	1	1	PBR,PC	Op Code	1
	(ORA AND EOR ADC		2	1	1	0	1	PBR,PC+1	SO	1
	STA LDA CMP SBC)		3	1	1	0	0	PBR,PC+1	IO	1
	(8 Op Codes)		4	1	1	1	0	0,S+SO	Data Low	1/0
	(2 bytes)	(1)	4a	1	1	1	0	0,S+SO+1	Data High	1/0
	(4 and 5 cycles)									
*23	Stack Relative Indirect		1	1	1	1	1	PBR,PC	Op Code	1
	Indexed (d,s),y		2	1	1	0	1	PBR,PC+1	SO	1
	(ORA AND EOR ADC		3	1	1	0	0	PBR,PC+1	IO	1
	STA LDA CMP SBC)		4	1	1	1	0	0,S+SO	AAL	1
	(8 Op Codes)		5	1	1	1	0	0,S+SO+1	AAH	1
	(2 bytes)		6	1	1	0	0	0,S+SO+1	IO	1
	(7 and 8 Cycles)		7	1	1	1	0	DBR,AA+Y	Data Low	1/0
		(1)	7a	1	1	1	0	DBR,AA+Y+1	Data High	1/0
*24a	Block Move Positive		1	1	1	1	1	PBR,PC	Op Code	1
	(forward) xyc		2	1	1	0	1	PBR,PC+1	DBA	1
	(MVP)		3	1	1	0	1	PBR,PC+2	SBA	1
	(1 Op Code)	N-2	4	1	1	1	0	SBA,X	Source Data	1
	(3 bytes)	Byte	5	1	1	1	0	DBA,Y	Dest Data	0
	(7 cycles)	C-2	6	1	1	0	0	DBA,Y	IO	1
	x Source Address		7	1	1	0	0	DBA,Y	IO	1
	y Destination		1	1	1	1	1	PBR,PC	Op Code	1
	c Number of Bytes to Move -1		2	1	1	0	1	PBR,PC+1	DBA	1
	x,y Decrement		3	1	1	0	1	PBR,PC+2	SBA	1
	MVP is used when the	N-1	4	1	1	1	0	SBA,X-1	Source Data	1
	destination start address	Byte	5	1	1	1	0	DBA,Y-1	Dest Data	0
	is higher (more positive)	C-1	6	1	1	0	0	DBA,Y-1	IO	1
	than the source start address		7	1	1	0	0	DBA,Y-1	IO	1
			1	1	1	1	1	PBR,PC	Op Code	1
	FFFFFF		2	1	1	0	1	PBR,PC+1	DBA	1
	↑ Dest Start	N Byte	3	1	1	0	1	PBR,PC+2	SBA	1
		Last	4	1	1	1	0	SBA,X-2	Source Data	1
	Source Start	C-0	5	1	1	1	0	DBA,Y-2	Dest Data	0
	Dest End		6	1	1	0	0	DBA,Y-2	IO	1
	Source End		7	1	1	0	0	DBA,Y-2	IO	1
	000000		1	1	1	1	1	PBR,PC+3	Next Op Code	1
*24b	Block Move Negative		1	1	1	1	1	PBR,PC	Op Code	1
	(backward) xyc		2	1	1	0	1	PBR,PC+1	DBA	1
	(MVN)	N-2	3	1	1	0	1	PBR,PC+2	SBA	1
	(1 Op Code)	Byte	4	1	1	1	0	SBA,X	Source Data	1
	(3 bytes)	C-2	5	1	1	1	0	DBA,Y	Dest Data	0
	(7 cycles)		6	1	1	0	0	DBA,Y	IO	1
	x Source Address		7	1	1	0	0	DBA,Y	IO	1
	y Destination									
	c Number of Bytes to Move -1		1	1	1	1	1	PBR,PC	Op Code	1
	x,y Increment		2	1	1	0	1	PBR,PC+1	DBA	1
	FFFFFF	N-1	3	1	1	0	1	PBR,PC+2	SBA	1
	Source End	Byte	4	1	1	1	0	SBA,X+1	Source Data	1
		C-1	5	1	1	1	0	DBA,Y+1	Dest Data	0
	Dest End		6	1	1	0	0	DBA,Y+1	IO	1
	Source Start		7	1	1	0	0	DBA,Y+1	IO	1
	Dest Start		1	1	1	1	1	PBR,PC	Op Code	1
	↓		2	1	1	0	1	PBR,PC+1	DBA	1
		N Byte	3	1	1	0	1	PBR,PC+2	SBA	1
	000000	C-0	4	1	1	1	0	SBA,X+2	Source Data	1
	MVN is used when the		5	1	1	1	0	DBA,Y+2	Dest Data	0
	destination start address		6	1	1	0	0	DBA,Y+2	IO	1
	is lower (more negative)		7	1	1	0	0	DBA,Y+2	IO	1
	than the source start address		1	1	1	1	1	PBR,PC+3	Next Op Code	1

Notes

(1) Add 1 byte (for immediate only) for M=0 or X=0 (i.e. 16 bit data); add 1 cycle for M=0 or X=0.
(2) Add 1 cycle for direct register low (DL) not equal 0.
(3) Special case for aborting instruction. This is the last cycle which may be aborted or the Status, PBR or DBR registers will be updated.
(4) Add 1 cycle for indexing across page boundaries, or write, or X=0. When X=1 or in the emulation mode, this cycle contains invalid addresses.
(5) Add 1 cycle if branch is taken.
(6) Add 1 cycle if branch is taken across page boundaries in 6502 emulation mode (E=1).
(7) Subtract 1 cycle for 6502 emulation mode (E=1).
(8) Add 1 cycle for REP, SEP.
(9) Wait at cycle 2 for 2 cycles after $\overline{NMI}$ or $\overline{IRQ}$ active input.

Abbreviations

AAB Absolute Address Bank
AAH Absolute Address High
AAL Absolute Address Low
AAVH Absolute Address Vector High
AAVL Absolute Address Vector Low
C Accumulator
D Direct Register
DBA Destination Bank Address
DBR Data Bank Register
DO Direct Offset
IDH Immediate Data High
IDL Immediate Data Low
IO Internal Operation
P Status Register
PBR Program Bank Register
PC Program Counter
R-M-W Read-Modify-Write
S Stack Address
SBA Source Bank Address
SO Stack Offset
VA Vector Address
x, y Index Registers
* New W65C816/802 Addressing Modes
• New W65C02 Addressing Modes
Blank NMOS 6502 Addressing Modes

Recommended W65C816 and W65C802 Assembler Syntax Standards

Directives
Assembler directives are those parts of the assembly language source program which give directions to the assembler; this includes the definition of data area and constants within a program. This standard excludes any definitions of assembler directives.

Comments
An assembler should provide a way to use any line of the source program as a comment. The recommended way of doing this is to treat any blank line, or any line that starts with a semi-colon or an asterisk as a comment. Other special characters may be used as well.

The Source Line
Any line which causes the generation of a single W65C816 or W65C802 machine language instruction should be divided into four fields: a label field, the operation code, the operand, and the comment field.

The Label Field — The label field begins in column one of the line. A label must start with an alphabetic character, and may be followed by zero or more alphanumeric characters. An assembler may define an upper limit on the number of characters that can be in a label, so long as that upper limit is greater than or equal to six characters. An assembler may limit the alphabetic characters to upper-case characters if desired. If lower-case characters are allowed, they should be treated as identical to their upper-case equivalents. Other characters may be allowed in the label, so long as their use does not conflict with the coding of operand fields.

The Operation Code Field — The operation code shall consist of a three character sequence (mnemonic) from Table 3. It shall start no sooner than column 2 of the line, or one space after the label if a label is coded.

Many of the operation codes in Table 3 have duplicate mnemonics; when two or more machine language instructions have the same mnemonic, the assembler resolves the difference based on the operand.

If an assembler allows lower-case letters in labels, it must also allow lower-case letters in the mnemonic. When lower-case letters are used in the mnemonic, they shall be treated as equivalent to the upper-case counterpart. Thus, the mnemonics LDA, lda, and LdA must all be recognized, and are equivalent.

In addition to the mnemonics shown in Table 3, an assembler may provide the alternate mnemonics shown in Table 6.

Table 7. Alternate Mnemonics

Standard	Alias
BCC	BLT
BCS	BGE
CMP A	CMA
DEC A	DEA
INC A	INA
JSL	JSR
JML	JMP
TCD	TAD
TCS	TAS
TDC	TDA
TSC	TSA
XBA	SWA

JSL should be recognized as equivalent to JSR when it is specified with a long absolute address. JML is equivalent to JMP with long addressing forced.

The Operand Field — The operand field may start no sooner than one space after the operation code field. The assembler must be capable of at least twenty-four bit address calculations. The assembler should be capable of specifying addresses as labels, integer constants, and hexadecimal constants. The assembler must allow addition and subtraction in the operand field. Labels shall be recognized by the fact that they start with alphabetic characters. Decimal numbers shall be recognized as containing only the decimal digits 0-9. Hexadecimal constants shall be recognized by prefixing the constant with a "$" character, followed by zero or more of either the decimal digits or the hexadecimal digits "A" - "F". If lower-case letters are allowed in the label field, then they shall also be allowed as hexadecimal digits.

All constants, no matter what their format, shall provide at least enough precision to specify all values that can be represented by a twenty-four bit signed or unsigned integer represented in two's complement notation.

Table 8 shows the operand formats which shall be recognized by the assembler. The symbol d is a label or value which the assembler can recognize as being less than $100. The symbol a is a label or value which the assembler can recognize as greater than $FF but less than $10000; the symbol al is a label or value that the assembler can recognize as being greater than $FFFF. The symbol EXT is a label which cannot be located by the assembler at the time the instruction is assembled. Unless instructed otherwise, an assembler shall assume that EXT labels are two bytes long. The symbols r and rl are 8 and 16 bit signed displacements calculated by the assembler.

Note that the operand does not determine whether or not immediate addressing loads one or two bytes; this is determined by the setting of the status register. This forces the requirement for a directive or directives that tell the assembler to generate one or two bytes of space for immediate loads. The directives provided shall allow separate settings for the accumulator and index registers.

The assembler shall use the <, >, and ^ characters after the # character in immediate address to specify which byte or bytes will be selected from the value of the operand. Any calculations in the operand must be performed before the byte selection takes place. Table 7 defines the action taken by each operand by showing the effect of the operator on an address. The column that shows a two byte immediate value show the bytes in the order in which they appear in memory. The coding of the operand is for an assembler which uses 32 bit address calculations, showing the way that the address should be reduced to a 24 bit value.

Table 8. Byte Selection Operator

Operand	One Byte Result	Two Byte Result	
#$01020304	04	04	03
#<$01020304	04	04	03
#>$01020304	03	03	02
#^$01020304	02	02	01

In any location in an operand where an address, or expression resulting in an address, can be coded, the assembler shall recognize the prefix characters <, |, and >, which force one byte (direct page), two byte (absolute) or three byte (long absolute) addressing. In cases where the addressing mode is not forced, the assembler shall assume that the address is two bytes unless the assembler is able to determine the type of addressing required by context, in which case that addressing mode will be used. Addresses shall be truncated without error if an addressing mode is forced which does not require the entire value of the address. For example,

LDA $0203   LDA |$010203

are completely equivalent. If the addressing mode is not forced, and the type of addressing cannot be determined from context, the assembler shall assume that a two byte address is to be used. If an instruction does not have a short addressing mode (as in LDA, which has no direct page indexed by Y) and a short address is used in the operand, the assembler shall automatically extend the address by padding the most significant bytes with zeroes in order to extend the address to the length needed. As with immediate addressing, any expression evaluation shall take place before the address is selected; thus, the address selection character is only used once, before the address of expression.

The ! (exclamation point) character should be supported as an alternative to the | (vertical bar).

A long indirect address is indicated in the operand field of an instruction by surrounding the direct page address where the indirect address is found by square brackets; direct page addresses which contain sixteen-bit addresses are indicated by being surrounded by parentheses.

The operands of a block move instruction are specified as source bank, destination bank — the opposite order of the object bytes generated.

Comment Field — The comment field may start no sooner than one space after the operation code field or operand field depending on instruction type.

Table 9. Address Mode Formats

Addressing Mode	Format	Addressing Mode	Format	
Immediate	#d	Absolute Indexed by Y	!d,y	
	#a		d,y	
	#al		a,y	
	#EXT		!a,y	
	#<d		!al,y	
	#<a		!EXT,y	
	#<al		EXT,y	
	#<EXT	Absolute Long Indexed	>d,x	
	#>d	by X	>a,x	
	#>a		>al,x	
	#>al		al,x	
	#>EXT		>EXT,x	
	#^d	Program Counter	d	(the assembler calculates
	#^a	Relative and	a	r and rl)
	#^al	Program Counter	al	
	#^EXT	Relative Long	EXT	
Absolute	!d	Absolute Indirect	(d)	
	!a		(!d)	
	a		(a)	
	!al		(!a)	
	!EXT		(!al)	
	EXT		(EXT)	
Absolute Long	>d	Direct Indirect	(d)	
	>a		(<a)	
	>al		(<al)	
	al		(<EXT)	
	>EXT	Direct Indirect Long	[d]	
Direct Page	d		[<a]	
	<d		[<al]	
	<a		[<EXT]	
	<al	Absolute Indexed	(d,x)	
	<EXT		(!d,x)	
Accumulator	A		(a,x)	
Implied Addressing	(no operand)		(!a,x)	
Direct Indirect	(d),y		(!al,x)	
Indexed	(<d),y		(EXT,x)	
	(<a),y		(!EXT,x)	
	(<al),y	Stack Addressing	(no operand)	
	(<EXT),y	Stack Relative	(d,s),y	
Direct Indirect	[d],y	Indirect Indexed	(<d,s),y	
Indexed Long	[<d],y		(<a,s),y	
	[<a],y		(<al,s),y	
	[<al],y		(<EXT,s),y	
	[<EXT],y	Block Move	d,d	
Direct Indexed	(d,x)		d,a	
Indirect	(<d,x)		d,al	
	(<a,x)		d,EXT	
	(<al,x)		a,d	
	(<EXT,x)		a,a	
Direct Indexed by X	d,x		a,al	
	<d,x		a,EXT	
	<a,x		al,d	
	<al,x		al,a	
	<EXT,x		al,al	
Direct Indexed by Y	d,y		al,EXT	
	<d,y		EXT,d	
	<a,y		EXT,a	
	<al,y		EXT,al	
	<EXT,y		EXT,EXT	
Absolute Indexed by X	d,x			
	!d,x			
	a,x			
	!a,x			
	!al,x			
	!EXT,x			
	EXT,x			

Note: The alternate ! (exclamation point) is used in place of the | (vertical bar).

E W65C816 Data Sheet

Table 10. Addressing Mode Summary

Address Mode	Instruction Times In Memory Cycles		Memory Utilization In Number of Program Sequence Bytes	
	Original 8 Bit NMOS 6502	New W65C816	Original 8 Bit NMOS 6502	New W65C816
1 Immediate	2	2(3)	2	2(3)
2 Absolute	4(5)	4(3,5)	3	3
3 Absolute Long	—	5(3)	—	4
4 Direct	3(5)	3(3,4,5)	2	2
5 Accumulator	2	2	1	1
6 Implied	2	2	1	1
7 Direct Indirect Indexed (d),y	5(1)	5(1,3,4)	2	2
8 Direct Indirect Indexed Long [d],y	—	6(3,4)	—	2
9 Direct Indexed Indirect (d,x)	6	6(3,4)	2	2
10 Direct, X	4(5)	4(3,4,5)	2	2
11 Direct, Y	4	4(3,4)	2	2
12 Absolute, X	4(1,5)	4(1,3,5)	3	3
13 Absolute Long, X	—	5(3)	—	4
14 Absolute, Y	4(1)	4(1,3)	3	3
15 Relative	2(1,2)	2(2)	2	2
16 Relative Long	—	3(2)	—	3
17 Absolute Indirect (Jump)	5	5	3	3
18 Direct Indirect	—	5(3,4)	—	2
19 Direct Indirect Long	—	6(3,4)	—	2
20 Absolute Indexed Indirect (Jump)	—	6	—	3
21 Stack	3-7	3-8	1-3	1-4
22 Stack Relative	—	4(3)	—	2
23 Stack Relative Indirect Indexed	—	7(3)	—	2
24 Block Move X, Y, C (Source, Destination, Block Length)	—	7	—	3

NOTES
1. Page boundary, add 1 cycle if page boundary is crossed when forming address.
2. Branch taken, add 1 cycle if branch is taken.
3. M = 0 or X = 0, 16 bit operation, add 1 cycle, add 1 byte for immediate.
4. Direct register low (DL) not equal zero, add 1 cycle.
5. Read-Modify-Write, add 2 cycles for M = 1, add 3 cycles for M = 0.

Caveats and Application Information

Stack Addressing
When in the Native mode, the Stack may use memory locations 000000 to 00FFFF. The effective address generated by Stack, Stack Relative, and Stack Relative Indirect Indexed addressing modes will always be within this range. In the Emulation mode, the Stack address range is 000100 to 0001FF. The following opcodes and addressing modes will increment or decrement beyond this range when accessing two or three bytes.

JSL, JSR(a,x), PEA, PEI, PER, PHD, PLD, RTL, d,s, (d,s),y

Direct Addressing
The Direct Addressing modes are often used to access memory registers and pointers. The effective address generated by Direct, Direct,X and Direct,Y addressing modes will always be in the Native mode range 000000 to 00FFFF. When in the Emulation mode, the direct addressing range is 000000 to 0000FF, except for [Direct] and [Direct],Y addressing modes and the PEI instruction which will increment from 0000FE or 0000FF into the Stack area.

When in the Emulation mode and DH is not equal to zero, the direct addressing range is 00DH00 to 00DHFF, except for [Direct] and [Direct],Y addressing modes and the PEI instruction which will increment from 00DHFE or 00DHFF into the next higher page.

When in the Emulation mode and DL in not equal to zero, the direct addressing range is 000000 to 00FFFF.

Absolute Indexed Addressing (W65C816 Only)
The Absolute Indexed addressing modes are used to address data outside the direct addressing range. The W65C02 and W65C802 addressing range is 0000 to FFFF. Indexing from page FFXX may result in a 00YY data fetch when using the W65C02 or W65C802. In contrast, indexing from page ZZFFXX may result in ZZ+1,00YY when using the W65C816.

Future Microprocessors (i.e., W65C832)
Future WDC microprocessors will support all current W65C816 operating modes for both index and offset address generation.

ABORT Input (W65C816 Only)
ABORT should be held low for a period not to exceed one cycle. Also, if ABORT is held low during the Abort Interrupt sequence, the Abort Interrupt will be aborted. It is not recommended to abort the Abort Interrupt. The ABORT internal latch is cleared during the second cycle of the Abort Interrupt. Asserting the ABORT input after the following instruction cycles will cause registers to be modified.
- **Read-Modify-Write:** Processor status modified if ABORT is asserted after a modify cycle.
- **RTI:** Processor status will be modified if ABORT is asserted after cycle 3.
- **IRQ, NMI, ABORT BRK, COP:** When ABORT is asserted after cycle 2, PBR and DBR will become 00 (Emulation mode) or PBR will become 00 (Native mode)

The Abort Interrupt has been designed for virtual memory systems. For this reason, asynchronous ABORT's may cause undesirable results due to the above conditions.

VDA and VPA Valid Memory Address Output Signals (W65C816 Only)
When VDA or VPA are high and during all write cycles, the Address Bus is always valid. VDA and VPA should be used to qualify all memory cycles. Note that when VDA and VPA are both low, invalid addresses may be generated. The Page and Bank addresses could also be invalid. This will be due to low byte addition only. The cycle when only low byte addition occurs is an optional cycle for instructions which read memory when the Index Register consists of 8 bits. This optional cycle becomes a standard cycle for the Store instruction, all instructions using the 16-bit Index Register mode, and the Read-Modify-Write instruction when using 8- or 16-bit Index Register modes.

Apple II, IIe, IIc and II+ Disk Systems (W65C816 Only)
VDA and VPA should not be used to qualify addresses during disk operation on Apple systems. Consult your Apple representative for hardware/software configurations.

DB/BA Operation when RDY is Pulled Low (W65C816 Only)
When RDY is low, the Data Bus is held in the data transfer state (i.e., φ2 high). The Bank address external transparent latch should be latched when the φ2 clock or RDY is low.

M/X Output (W65C816 Only)
The M/X output reflects the value of the M and X bits of the processor Status Register. The REP, SEP and PLP instructions may change the state of the M and X bits. Note that the M/X output is invalid during the instruction cycle following REP, SEP and PLP instruction execution. This cycle is used as the opcode fetch cycle of the next instruction.

All Opcodes Function in All Modes of Operation
It should be noted that all opcodes function in all modes of operation. However, some instructions and addressing modes are intended for W65C816 24-bit addressing and are therefore less useful for the W65C802. The following is a list of instructions and addressing modes which are primarily intended for W65C816 use:

JSL, RTL, [d]; [d],y, JMP al, JML, al; al,x

The following instructions may be used with the W65C802 even though a Bank Address is not multiplexed on the Data Bus:

PHK, PHB; PLB

The following instructions have "limited" use in the Emulation mode:
- The REP and SEP instructions cannot modify the M and X bits when in the Emulation mode. In this mode the M and X bits will always be high (logic 1).
- When in the Emulation mode, the MVP and MVN instructions use the X and Y Index Registers for the memory address. Also, the MVP and MVN instructions can only move data within the memory range 0000 (Source Bank) to 00FF (Destination Bank) for the W65C816, and 0000 to 00FF for the W65C802.

Indirect Jumps
The JMP (a) and JML (a) instructions use the direct Bank for indirect addressing, while JMP (a,x) and JSR (a,x) use the Program Bank for indirect address tables.

Switching Modes
When switching from the Native mode to the Emulation mode, the X and M bits of the Status Register are set high (logic 1), the high byte of the Stack is set to 01, and the high bytes of the X and Y Index Registers are set to 00. To save previous values, these bytes must always be stored before changing modes. Note that the low byte of the S, X and Y Registers and the low and high byte of the Accumulator (A and B) are not affected by a mode change.

How Hardware Interrupts, BRK, and COP Instructions Affect the Program Bank and the Data Bank Registers
When in the Native mode, the Program Bank register (PBR) is cleared to 00 when a hardware interrupt, BRK or COP is executed. In the Native mode, previous PBR contents is automatically saved on Stack.

In the Emulation mode, the PBR and DBR registers are cleared to 00 when a hardware interrupt, BRK or COP is executed. In this case, previous contents of the PBR are not automatically saved.

Note that a Return from Interrupt (RTI) should always be executed from the same "mode" which originally generated the interrupt.

Binary Mode
The Binary mode is set whenever a hardware or software interrupt is executed. The D flag within the Status Register is cleared to zero.

WAI Instruction
The WAI instruction pulls RDY low and places the processor in the WAI "low power" mode. NMI, IRQ or RESET will terminate the WAI condition and transfer control to the interrupt handler routine. Note that an ABORT input will abort the WAI instruction, but will not restart the processor. When the Status Register I flag is set (IRQ disabled), the IRQ interrupt will cause the next instruction (following the WAI instruction) to be executed without going to the IRQ interrupt handler. This method results in the highest speed response to an IRQ input. When an interrupt

is received after an $\overline{\text{ABORT}}$ which occurs during the WAI instruction, the processor will return to the WAI instruction. Other than $\overline{\text{RES}}$ (highest priority), $\overline{\text{ABORT}}$ is the next highest priority, followed by $\overline{\text{NMI}}$ or $\overline{\text{IRQ}}$ interrupts.

STP Instruction
The STP instruction disables the $\phi 2$ clock to all circuitry. When disabled, the $\phi 2$ clock is held in the high state. In this case, the Data Bus will remain in the data transfer state and the Bank address will not be multiplexed onto the Data Bus. Upon executing the STP instruction, the $\overline{\text{RES}}$ signal is the only input which can restart the processor. The processor is restarted by enabling the $\phi 2$ clock, which occurs on the falling edge of the $\overline{\text{RES}}$ input. Note that the external oscillator must be stable and operating properly before $\overline{\text{RES}}$ goes high.

COP Signatures
Signatures 00-7F may be user defined, while signatures 80-FF are reserved for instructions on future microprocessors (i.e., W65C832). Contact WDC for software emulation of future microprocessor hardware functions.

WDM Opcode Use
The WDM opcode will be used on future microprocessors. For example, the new W65C832 uses this opcode to provide 32-bit floating-point and other 32-bit math and data operations. Note that the W65C832 will be a plug-to-plug replacement for the W65C816, and can be used where high-speed, 32-bit math processing is required. The W65C832 will be available in the near future.

RDY Pulled During Write
The NMOS 6502 does not stop during a write operation. In contrast, both the W65C02 and the W65C816 do stop during write operations. The W65C802 stops during a write when in the Native mode, but does not stop when in the Emulation mode.

MVN and MVP Affects on the Data Bank Register
The MVN and MVP instructions change the Data Bank Register to the value of the second byte of the instruction (destination bank address).

Interrupt Priorities
The following interrupt priorities will be in effect should more than one interrupt occur at the same time.

$\overline{\text{RES}}$	Highest Priority
$\overline{\text{ABORT}}$	
$\overline{\text{NMI}}$	
$\overline{\text{IRQ}}$	Lowest Priority

Transfers from 8-Bit to 16-Bit, or 16-Bit to 8-Bit Registers
All transfers from one register to another will result in a full 16-bit output from the source register. The destination register size will determine the number of bits actually stored in the destination register and the values stored in the processor Status Register. The following are always 16-bit transfers, regardless of the accumulator size.

TCS, TSC, TCD, TDC

Stack Transfers
When in the Emulation mode, a 01 is forced into SH. In this case, the B Accumulator will not be loaded into SH during a TCS instruction. When in the Native mode, the B Accumulator is transferred to SH. Note that in both the Emulation and Native modes, the full 16 bits of the Stack Register are transferred to the A, B and C Accumulators, regardless of the state of the M bit in the Status Register.

Packaging Information

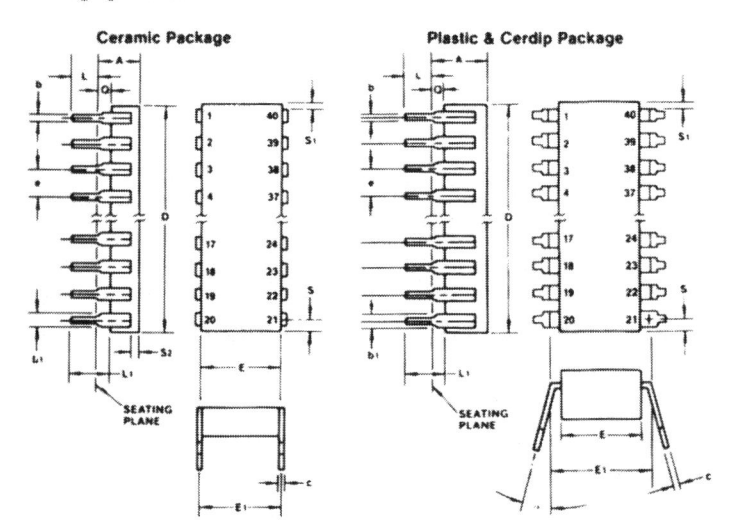

Ceramic Package

Plastic & Cerdip Package

SYM BOL	40-PIN PACKAGE			
	INCHES		MILLIMETERS	
	MIN	MAX	MIN	MAX
A		0.225		5.72
b	0.014	0.023	0.36	0.58
b1	0.030	0.070	0.76	1.78
c	0.008	0.015	0.20	0.38
D		2.096		53.24
E	0.510	0.620	12.95	15.75
E1	0.520	0.630	13.21	16.00
e	0.100 BSC		2.54 BSC	
L	0.125	0.200	3.18	5.08
L1	0.150		3.81	
Q	0.020	0.060	0.51	1.52
S		0.098		2.49
S1	0.005		0.13	
S2	0.005		0.13	
α	0°	15°	0°	15°

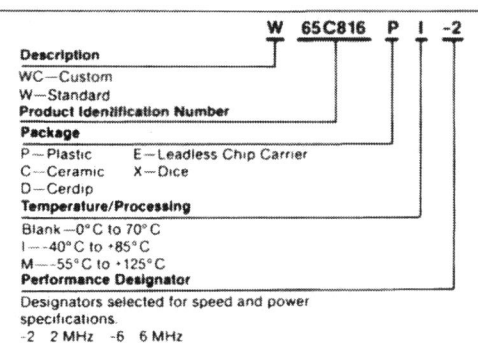

```
            W 65C816 P I -2
Description ─┘    │    │ │ │
WC—Custom         │    │ │ │
W—Standard        │    │ │ │
Product Identification Number ┘ │ │
Package ──────────────┘      │ │
  P—Plastic    E—Leadless Chip Carrier
  C—Ceramic    X—Dice
  D—Cerdip
Temperature/Processing ──────┘ │
  Blank—0°C to 70°C
  I—-40°C to +85°C
  M—-55°C to +125°C
Performance Designator ────────┘
Designators selected for speed and power
specifications.
  -2  2 MHz    -6  6 MHz
  -4  4 MHz    -8  8 MHz
```

Sales Offices:
Technical or sales assistance may be requested from:
The Western Design Center, Inc.
2166 East Brown Road
Mesa, Arizona 85203
602/962-4545
TLX 6835057

WARNING:
MOS CIRCUITS ARE SUBJECT TO DAMAGE FROM STATIC DISCHARGE
Internal static discharge circuits are provided to minimize part damage due to environmental static electrical charge build ups. Industry established recommendations for handling MOS circuits include:
1. Ship and store product in conductive shipping tubes or in conductive foam plastic. Never ship or store product in non conductive plastic containers or non conductive plastic foam material.
2. Handle MOS parts only at conductive work stations.
3. Ground all assembly and repair tools.

Represented in your area by:

WDC reserves the right to make changes at any time and without notice.
Information contained herein is provided gratuitously and without liability, to any user. Reasonable efforts have been made to verify the accuracy of the information but no guarantee whatsoever is given as to the accuracy or as to its applicability to particular uses. In every instance, it must be the responsibility of the user to determine the suitability of the products for each application. WDC products are not authorized for use as critical components in life support devices or systems. Nothing contained herein shall be construed as a recommendation to use any product in violation of existing patents or other rights of third parties. The sale of any WDC product is subject to all WDC Terms and Conditions of Sale and Sales Policies, copies of which are available upon request.
©The Western Design Center, Inc. 1985

The Western Design Center, Inc.   2166 E. Brown Rd./Mesa, AZ 85203   602/962-4545/TLX 6835057

Revised November 1985   Published in U.S.A   November 1983

F | The ASCII Character Set

Low Bit Set: High Bit Set:

Decimal	Hex	Decimal	Hex	Character	Names
0	00	128	80	Control-@	NUL, null
1	01	129	81	Control-A	
2	02	130	82	Control-B	
3	03	131	83	Control-C	Break
4	04	132	84	Control-D	
5	05	133	85	Control-E	
6	06	134	86	Control-F	
7	07	135	87	Control-G	BEL, bell
8	08	136	88	Control-H	BS, backspace
9	09	137	89	Control-I	HT, horizontal tab
10	0A	138	8A	Control-J	LF, line feed
11	0B	139	8B	Control-K	VT, vertical tab
12	0C	140	8C	Control-L	FF, form feed, Page
13	0D	141	8D	Control-M	CR, carriage return
14	0E	142	8E	Control-N	
15	0F	143	8F	Control-O	
16	10	144	90	Control-P	
17	11	145	91	Control-Q	XON, resume
18	12	146	92	Control-R	
19	13	147	93	Control-S	XOFF, screen pause
20	14	148	94	Control-T	
21	15	149	95	Control-U	
22	16	150	96	Control-V	
23	17	151	97	Control-W	
24	18	152	98	Control-X	CAN, cancel line
25	19	153	99	Control-Y	
26	1A	154	9A	Control-Z	End of file
27	1B	155	9B	Control-[	ESC, escape
28	1C	156	9C	Control-\	
29	1D	157	9D	Control-]	
30	1E	158	9E	Control-^	

Continued.

Low Bit Set: High Bit Set:

Decimal	Hex	Decimal	Hex	Character	Names
31	1F	159	9F	Control-__	
32	20	160	A0		Space
33	21	161	A1	!	Exclamation point
34	22	162	A2	"	Quote
35	23	163	A3	#	Pound sign
36	24	164	A4	$	Dollar sign
37	25	165	A5	%	Percent sign
38	26	166	A6	&	Ampersand
39	27	167	A7	'	Apostrophe
40	28	168	A8	(	Left parenthesis
41	29	169	A9	)	Right parenthesis
42	2A	170	AA	*	Asterisk
43	2B	171	AB	+	Plus sign
44	2C	172	AC	,	Comma
45	2D	173	AD	-	Minus sign, dash
46	2E	174	AE	.	Period
47	2F	175	AF	\	Backslash
48	30	176	B0	0	
49	31	177	B1	1	
50	32	178	B2	2	
51	33	179	B3	3	
52	34	180	B4	4	
53	35	181	B5	5	
54	36	182	B6	6	
55	37	183	B7	7	
56	38	184	B8	8	
57	39	185	B9	9	
58	3A	186	BA	:	Colon
59	3B	187	BB	;	Semicolon
60	3C	188	BC	<	Less than
61	3D	189	BD	=	Equal
62	3E	190	BE	>	Greater than
63	3F	191	BF	?	Question mark
64	40	192	C0	@	At sign
65	41	193	C1	A	
66	42	194	C2	B	
67	43	195	C3	C	
68	44	196	C4	D	
69	45	197	C5	E	
70	46	198	C6	F	
71	47	199	C7	G	

F The ASCII Character Set

Low Bit Set: High Bit Set:

Decimal	Hex	Decimal	Hex	Character	Names
72	48	200	C8	H	
73	49	201	C9	I	
74	4A	202	CA	J	
75	4B	203	CB	K	
76	4C	204	CC	L	
77	4D	205	CD	M	
78	4E	206	CE	N	
79	4F	207	CF	O	
80	50	208	D0	P	
81	51	209	D1	Q	
82	52	210	D2	R	
83	53	211	D3	S	
84	54	212	D4	T	
85	55	213	D5	U	
86	56	214	D6	V	
87	57	215	D7	W	
88	58	216	D8	X	
89	59	217	D9	Y	
90	5A	218	DA	Z	
91	5B	219	DB	[	Left bracket
92	5C	220	DC	\	Backslash
93	5D	221	DD	]	Right bracket
94	5E	222	DE	^	Caret
95	5F	223	DF	_	Underscore
96	60	224	E0	`	Accent grave
97	61	225	E1	a	
98	62	226	E2	b	
99	63	227	E3	c	
100	64	228	E4	d	
101	65	229	E5	e	
102	66	230	E6	f	
103	67	231	E7	g	
104	68	232	E8	h	
105	69	233	E9	i	
106	6A	234	EA	j	
107	6B	235	EB	k	
108	6C	236	EC	l	
109	6D	237	ED	m	
110	6E	238	EE	n	
111	6F	239	EF	o	

Continued.

Low Bit Set:		High Bit Set:			
Decimal	Hex	Decimal	Hex	Character	Names
112	70	240	F0	p	
113	71	241	F1	q	
114	72	242	F2	r	
115	73	243	F3	s	
116	74	244	F4	t	
117	75	245	F5	u	
118	76	246	F6	v	
119	77	247	F7	w	
120	78	248	F8	x	
121	79	249	F9	y	
122	7A	250	FA	z	
123	7B	251	FB	{	Left brace
124	7C	252	FC	|	Vertical line
125	7D	253	FD	}	Right brace
126	7E	254	FE	~	Tilde
127	7F	255	FF	DEL	delete, rubout

Index

!, see |
#, 109, 367
$, 8, 78
%, 78, 181
<, 109, 201–203
>, 109, 132, 134, 143, 201–203
|, 117, 122, 201–202

A register, see Accumulator
Abort signal, 64, 65, 261, 522, 548
Accumulator, 15, 26–27, 56, 91
  16-bit, 51
  A, 58, 96, 102
    in emulation mode, 69
  B, 58, 95–97, 100, 102
    in emulation mode, 69
  C, 58, 100, 102, 103–104
    in emulation mode, 69
Accumulator/Memory select flag, 56, 67, 71, 109, 112
Addition, 30, 151–165, 423
Address 5
  lines, 545
  notation, 81
  space, 6502, 27
Addresses, direct page, 81, 116
Addressing Modes, 26
  6502, 34
  6502 addressing modes on the 65816, 59
  65C02, 46
  65C02 on the 65816, 59
  65816/65802, 61
  absolute, 34, 35, 61, 108, 111–114
  absolute indexed, 29, 46
  absolute indexed indirect, 197, 210–212
    with JSR, 230–231
  absolute indexed with X, 34, 120–123, 187
  absolute indexed with Y, 34, 197, 120–123
  absolute indirect, 34, 141, 142
  absolute indirect long, 61, 62
  absolute long, 61, 62, 108, 130–135
  absolute long indexed with X, 61, 62, 134–135, 197
  accumulator, 34, 35, 108, 126–127
  block move, 61, 62, 108, 137
  complex, 197–223
  direct page, 34, 108, 114–117, 197
  direct page indexed indirect with X, 34, 197, 206–210
  direct page indexed with X, 34, 197, 123–126
  direct page indexed with Y, 34, 197, 123–126
  direct page indexed, 29
  direct page indirect indexed with Y, 34, 197, 203–206
  direct page indirect long indexed with Y, 61, 62, 197, 212–214
  direct page indirect long, 61, 62, 108, 135–137
  direct page indirect, 46, 108, 128–130
  for accumulator operations, 28
  immediate, 34, 35, 61, 108–111
    implications of, 109–111
  implied, 34, 35, 108, 127
  indexed, 61, 122
  indexed indirect, 29
  indirect indexed, 29
  postindexed, see Addressing Modes, direct page indirect indexed with Y
  postindexed long, see Addressing Modes, direct page indirect long indexed with Y
  preindexed, see Addressing Modes, direct page indexed indirect with X
  program counter relative long, 61, 62
  program counter relative, 34, 35
  simple, 107–138
  stack, 34, 35, 108, 127
  stack relative indirect indexed with Y, 61, 62, 197, 216–217
  stack relative, 61, 62, 197, 213–215
  syntax summary, 108, 197
  zero page, see Addressing Modes, direct page
Addressing
  direct page, 55, 198
  long, 130–138
    used with the 65802, 132
And, 9–10, 181–183, 187, 189, 193

Apple II, 45, 48, 71, 75, 78, 278, 301, 302, 319, 333, 552
  40-column screen, 205
  keyboard, 149
  screen memory, 183–184
Architecture,
  6502, 25–44
  65C02, 45–48
  65816/65802, 49–72
Arithmetic instructions, 156
Arithmetic, 155–178
  multiple precision, 15, 30, 163–166
  signed, 170–174
  unsigned, 161–166
Array, 117
ASCII, 3, 8
  chart, 595–598
Assembler
  addressing mode assumptions, overriding, 200–203
  macro, 17
  special syntax, immediate addressing, 109
Assembler, ORCA/M, 78, 366
Assembler directives, 18
  ANOP, 81
  DS, 80
  GEQU, 79
  LONGA, 110–111, 112
  LONGI, 110–111, 112
  ORG, 79
Assembler syntax, 117, 132, 134, 366
Assemblers, 16
Assembly language, 16
Asserted, 179

b, *see* Break flag
B register, *see* Data bank register
Back space, 8
Bank, memory, 6, 53, 114
Bank address lines, 547
Bank byte, 53, 132
Bank change, as result of indexing, 119–120
Bank-independent, 132
Bank registers, 65
  see also Data bank register or Program bank register
Bank zero, 55, 141, 143
  interrupt vectors, 251

  use for direct page, 199
BASIC, 15

BBR, R65C02 instruction, 561, 562
BBS, R65C02 instruction, 561, 563
Benchmarks, 293–298
Binary Coded Decimal (BCD) numbers, 3, 14, 31, 176, 284, 442
Binary
  arithmetic, 15
  digit, 4
  division, 273
  number systems, 3
Bit, 4
  inversion, 185
  manipulation, 187–189, 193
  numbering, 6, 179
  testing, 431, 513–514
Bit-field, 179
Bit-manipulation instructions, 180
Bit-reset, 513
Bit-set, 514
Bitwise, 9, 181
Block move, 69, 103, 466–467, 468–469
  see also Addressing Modes, block move
  see also Instructions, MVN
  see also Instructions, MVP
Boolean logic, *see* Logical operations
Borrow, 30–31, 165
Branch
  conditional, 20, 29, 1143–1151
  branch always, synthesis, 148
  branch to subroutine, synthesis, 232, 234–235
  instructions, 20, 139, 140, 143–153
  limitations, 150–151
  timing of, 144
  unconditional, 47, 151–153
Break flag, 29, 30, 42, 58, 67, 71, 253–254, 436
BRK, used in debugging, 300, 332
BRK vector, 253
Bugs
  6502, 43
  65C02, 48
  65816/65802, 72
Bus enable signal, 549
Byte, 5, 56
Byteworks, 78

c, *see* Carry flag
C accumulator, 374
C programming language, 285, 287
Carriage return, 8
Carry, 30
Carry bit, 15
Carry flag, 29, 144, 147–148, 174, 189,
    428, 429, 441, 497, 499
  as source of error, 362
  effect of comparison on, 167
  in decimal mode, 176
  use in arithmetic, 162–166
Chip packaging, 543
Clearing memory, 507
Clock signal, 40
CMOS, 43, 45, 47
Comments, in source code, 17, 370
Compare instructions, 156
Comparison, 166–170, 445, 449, 450
  signed, 174–175
Compatibility, 65816 with 6502, 67
Compilers, 16, 285
Complement, 11
Constant data, 108
Context-saving, 277
Control codes, 8
COP vector, 253
Co-processor, 447
Cycle count,
  branch instructions, 144
  reduced on some 65816 instructions, 165

d, *see* Decimal flag
D register, *see* Direct page register
Data bank register, 53, 55, 114, 130, 477,
    484
Data Bus Enable signal, 545
Data lines, 545
DBR, *see* Data bank register
DEBUG16, 299–359
Debuggers, 299
Debugging, 369
  checklist, 362–370
Decimal adjustment, 176–177
Decimal flag, 31, 176, 262, 442, 500
  as source of error, 362
  effect of interrupt, 251
Decimal mode, 31, 176–177, 284
Decimal numbers, 13

Decrement, 28, 156–161, 451, 452, 453
Differences between processors and
    modes, 68
Direct page, 49, 124, 374
  addresses, 81, 116
  addressing, 55, 198
  addressing modes, *see* Addressing
    modes, direct page
  as pointer to stack, 281
  direct page offset, 116
  errors in using, 365
  relocating, 198–200
  set to page boundary, 199–200
  vs. zero page, 60
Direct page register, 53, 55, 116, 124,
    478, 485
Disassembly, 299
Division, 183, 272–277
  binary, 273
  by powers of two, 191, 193
  not built in, 155
  on 6502, 273
  on 65C02, 275
  on 65802 and 65816, 275–277
Documentation, 369
  of subroutines, 236
Double byte, 5, 56

e, *see* Emulation flag
Effective address, 26
Eight-bit registers, 364
Emulation flag, 58, 69, 148, 480, 486
Emulation mode, 50, 61, 64, 67, 148,
    364, 374
  switching to native mode from, 525
Emulation signal, 549
Eratosthenes sieve program, 293–298
Error messages, 18
Exchanges, 102–103
Exclusive or, 9–11, 185–187, 454
Execution
  selection between paths, 19
  straight-line, 18
External events, synchronization, 522

False, 179
Flags, status, 29–31, 53–54, 56–57,
    58–59
Flow of control, 139–153

Group I instructions, 122, 567, 568–569
Group II instructions, 567, 569–570

Hardware signals, *see* Signals
Hexadecimal, 7
    notation, 321
    number systems, 3
High-order
    bit, 171
    byte, 53, 131
    value, 4

i, *see* Interrupt Flag
Increment, 28, 156–161, 456, 457, 458
    instructions, 156
    sixteen-bits, 158
Index register mode select flag, 56, 71, 77, 109, 112
Index registers, 27–28, 51
Index signal, 549
Indexed addressing, 61, 122
Indexing, 35, 36, 117–119, 156
    across banks, 119–120, 126
    past end of direct page 124–126, 209–210
    step value, 156
Indirect address, 118, 128, 130
Indirection, 35, 37
Input/Output, 42, 250
Instruction groups, 567–571
Instruction sets, 421–525
Instructions
    ADC, 156, 161, 163–165, 172, 176, 423–424
    AND, 180, 426
    ASL, 180, 189, 427
    BCC, 147–148, 167–168, 428
    BCS, 147–148, 167–168, 429
    BEQ, 140, 146–147, 166, 430
    BGE, 168, 429
    BIT, 180, 187–188, 431, 439, 440
    BLT, 168, 428
    BMI, 149, 171, 432
    BNE, 146–147, 433
    BPL, 149, 171, 434
    BRA, 140, 151–153, 435
    BRK, 64, 139, 249, 255, 436–437
    BRL, 140, 153, 438
    BVC, 150, 439
    BVS, 150, 440

CLC, 249, 262, 423, 441
    use in addition, 163
CLD, 249, 262, 442
CLI, 249, 262–263, 443
CLV, 249, 263, 439, 440, 444
CMP, 156, 167–170, 174, 176, 445–446
COP, 64, 65, 139, 249, 255, 261, 447–448
CPX, 156, 170, 449
CPY, 156, 170, 450
DEC, 156–161, 451
DEX, 156–161, 452
DEY, 156–161, 453
EOR, 180, 454–455
INC, 156–161, 456
INX, 156–161, 457
INY, 156–161, 458
JML, 139, 143, 459
JMP, 139, 140–143, 459
JSL, 140, 226, 231–232, 460
JSR, 140, 225–248, 461
LDA, 84, 462
LDX, 84, 463
LDY, 84, 464
LSR, 180, 189, 465
MVN, 104–105, 466–467, 85
MVP, 105–106, 468–469, 85
NOP, 249, 263–264, 470
ORA, 180, 471
PEA, 84, 94, 218–219, 473
PEI, 84, 94, 218, 220, 474
PER, 64, 84, 94, 218, 221–223, 232, 234–235, 475
PHA, 84, 91, 476
PHB, 84, 91, 93, 477
PHD, 84, 94, 478
PHK, 84, 93, 479
PHP, 84, 480
PHX, 84, 91, 481
PHY, 84, 91, 482
PLA, 84, 91
PLB, 84, 91, 94, 484
PLD, 84, 94, 198, 485
PLP, 84, 91, 486
PLX, 84, 91, 487
PLY, 84, 91, 488
REP, 58, 75, 77, 86, 112, 249, 262, 489
ROL, 180, 189, 490
ROR, 180, 189, 491
RTI, 139, 249, 251, 254–255, 259, 262, 492–493

RTL, 139, 140, 226, 231–233, 254–255, 494–495
RTS, 77, 140, 225–248, 254–255, 496
SBC, 156, 161, 166–167, 172, 174, 176, 497–498
SEC, 166–167, 249, 262, 497, 499
SED, 176, 249, 262, 500
SEI, 249, 262–263, 501
SEP, 58, 75, 77, 86, 112, 249, 262, 502
STA, 84, 108, 503
STP, 249, 260–261, 504
STX, 84, 108, 505
STY, 84, 108, 506
STZ, 85, 103, 507
SWA, 524
TAD, 510
TAS, 511
TAX, 84, 95, 508
TAY, 84, 95, 509
TCD, 84, 99, 198, 510
TCS, 84, 100, 511
TDA, 512
TDC, 84, 99, 512
TRB, 180, 188–189, 513
TSA, 515
TSB, 180, 188–189, 514
TSC, 85, 100, 515, 516
TSX, 84, 95, 516
TXA, 84, 95, 517
TXS, 84, 95, 518
TXY, 85, 101, 519
TYA, 84, 95, 520
TYX, 85, 101, 521
WAI, 249, 260, 522
WDM, 249, 264, 523
XBA, 85, 95, 102, 524
XCE, 58, 85, 102, 441, 525
Instructions
  6502, 38–39, 65C02, 47
  65816/65802, 63
  arithmetic, 156
  bit manipulation, 180
  data movement, 84
  flow of control, 140
  interrupts, 249
  logic, 180
  R65C02, 561–565
  subroutines, 226
  system control, 249
  unimplemented, 44, 48, 72, 264

Intel, 41, 42, 88, 91
Interpreters, 16
Interrupt, 30, 32, 42, 58, 64, 65, 249–253, 300, 363
  hardware, 250, 253, 443
  instructions, 139
  latency, 43, 260, 522
  maskable, 42
  nonmaskable, 43, 251
  processing, 251, 256–259
  response time, 259–260
  service routine, 42
  software, 42, 251, 253, 436–437, 447
  vector locations, 42, 64, 69, 251, 253
Interrupt flag, 31, 262–263, 436, 443, 501
  effect of interrupt, 251
  flag, effect upon IRQ, 251
I/O, memory-mapped, 42
IRQ signal, 31, 64, 250, 253, 436, 443, 501, 522, 546
IRQ vector, 253
Iteration, 20

Jump, 20, 139
  indexed indirect, 210–212
  indirect, using RTS, 228, 230
  indirect long, 54
  indirect vs. indexed indirect, bank assumptions, 212
  long, 54
  subroutine, 21, 93
Jump instructions, 140–143
Jump long instructions, 139

K register, *see* Program bank register
Kilobyte, 6

Labels, 17, 79, 112
Line feed, 8
Linked list, 147
Logic, 9
Logic instructions, 180–181
Logical false, 9
Logical operations, 179–189
Logical true, 9
Loop control, 160
Looping, 20, 139, 146
Low-order, 4

m, *see* Accumulator/memory select flag
Machine language, 15

Macro instructions, 17
Mask, 77, 181
Maskable interrupt, 42
Masking bit fields, 180
Megahertz, 40, 545
Memory, 26
 addressable, 65802, 49
 addressable, 65816, 49
 bank, 6, 53, 114
 high-low order, 41
 low-high order, 41
 order of multi-byte values, 41
 page, 35, 53, 114
 stack, 90
Memory Lock signal, 544-545
Memory-mapped I/O, 42
Memory models, 286
Memory signal, 549
Mensch, William D., Jr., 64
Mixing
 eight- and sixteen-bit registers, 364
 emulation and native code, 364
 6502 and 65816 code, 277
Mnemonic, 16
Mode
 8-bit, 112
 16-bit, 112
 differences, 68
 flags, 98
 select, 31
Modular programming, 368-369
Modulus, 183, 193
Motorola, 41, 42, 88, 91
Move block, see Block move
Multiple precision arithmetic, 15, 30, 163-166
Multiplication, 183, 268-272
 by powers of two, 191-193
 by ten, 192
 not built in, 155
 on 6502, 269
 on 65C02, 269, 270
 on 65802 and 65816, 269, 271
 signed, 185-187
MVN/MVP, errors in using, 365-366

n, see Negative flag
Native mode, 50, 51, 61, 64, 67, 148, 364
 differences on 65802 and 65816, 374
 register size combinations, 57
 switching to emulation, 525

Negated, 179
Negation, subroutine, 235-237
Negative flag, 29, 144, 157-161, 171, 187, 188, 431, 432, 434
 effect of comparison on, 167
Nibble, 321
NMI signal, 64, 251, 522, 546
NMI vector, 253
NMOS, 43
Nonmaskable interrupt, 43, 251
Number systems, 3

Object code, 17
Off, 179
On, 179
Opcode, 16
Opcode, reserved, 523
Opcodes, unimplemented, 51
Operand, 16
Operand symbols, 375
Operation code, see Opcode
Operations,
 6502, 36
 65C02, 46
Or, 9-10, 183-185, 188
ORCA/M assembler, 78, 366
Overflow,
 arithmetic, 30
 two's complement, 30
Overflow flag, 29, 144, 150, 172-175, 187, 188, 263, 431, 439, 440, 444
 decimal mode, 176
Overflow signal, 150

P register, see Status register
Packaging, chip, 543
Page, memory, 35, 53, 114
Page wraparound, 60
Page zero, see Zero page
Parameter passing, 237-248, 283
Pascal, 15, 287
PBR, see Program bank register
PC, see Program counter
Phase one signal, 545
Phase two signal, 545
Phase zero signal, 545
Pinout, 544
 6502, 49, 544
 65802, 49, 544
Pipelining, 40, 41

Pointers, in C, 285
Polling, 256
Position independence, 151–153
Positional notation, 4, 7
Power consumption, 64, 260–261, 504, 522
Processor status register, see Status register
Processor type, 284–285
Processors,
  16-bit, 49
  differences, 68
Program bank register, 53–54, 114, 139, 479
Program counter, 19, 27, 33
Program counter relative, 144
Program loop, 159–161
Programming, structured, 225
Programming model,
  6502, 27, 375
  65C02, 375
  65802 native mode, 66, 376
  65816 emulation mode, 70, 378
  65816 native mode, 52, 377
Pull, 31, 91
Push, 31, 89, 92
Push effective address instructions, 94, 216, 218–222

R65C02, 561–565
RDY signal, 260, 522, 545
Read-modify-write instructions, 126, 157
Read/Write signal, 545
Recursion, 228, 247, 287
Reentrancy, 228, 230, 247, 259
Register-oriented machines, 26
Register size, switching, 58
Register transfers, 94
Registers, 15, 26
Relocatable code, 151–153, 222–223, 232, 234–235, 435, 475
Relocatable module, 17
Remainder, 193
Reset signal, 4, 42, 64, 161, 179, 253, 262, 504, 522, 546
Reset vector, 253
Return, 21, 32
  long, 54
Return address, 460, 461

RMB, R65C02 instruction, 561, 564
Rockwell, see R65C02
Rotates and shifts, 30, 61, 180, 189–195, 427, 465
  in multiplication, 269

S register, see Stack pointer
Selection between paths, 139, 144
Sequential execution, 139
Set, 4, 179
Set Overflow signal, 263, 439, 440, 444, 546
Shifts and rotates, see Rotates and shifts
Sieve of Eratosthenes, 293–298
Sign extension, 174, 187–188
Sign flag, 171, 179, 284
Signals,
  abort, 64, 65, 261, 522, 548
  bus enable, 549
  clock, 40
  data Bus Enable, 545
  emulation, 549
  index, 549
  IRQ, 31, 64, 250, 253, 436, 443, 501, 522, 546
  memory, 549
  memory lock, 544–545
  NMI, 64, 251, 522, 546
  overflow, 150
  phase one, 545
  phase two, 545
  phase zero, 545
  RDY, 260, 522, 545
  read/write, 545
  reset, 4, 42, 64, 161, 179, 253, 262, 504, 522, 546
  set overflow, 263, 439, 440, 444, 546
  valid data address, 548
  valid program address, 548
  vector pull, 256–257, 548
Signed arithmetic, 170–174
Signed comparisons, 174–175
  as source of error, 363
Signed numbers, 12, 171
Significance, 4
Single-stepping, 300
Sixteen-bit registers, 364
Small C programming language, 285
SMB, R65C02 instruction, 561, 565
Sorting routine, 168–170

Source program, 17, 18
Stack, 6502, 31, 277
Stack memory, 90
Stack pointer, 27, 31, 49, 55, 89, 100, 511, 518
   6502, 31, 277
   errors in initialization, 367
   relocating, 281
   overflow, 365
Status flags, routine to display, 193-195
Status register, 27, 29, 58, 480, 486, 489, 502
   control instructions, 249, 262-264
   emulation mode, 69
   flags, 144
   native mode, 53-54, 58-59
Step-and-trace, 299
Structured programming, 368-369
Subroutine, 140, 225-248, 460, 461, 494, 496
   branch-to, synthesis, 232, 234-235
Subroutines, 20, 32
   documentation, 236
   libraries, 21, 235
   parameter-passing, 237-248
   when to use, 235-237
Subtraction, 30, 161, 165-167, 497
Support chips, 551-559
Switching between native and emulation modes, 71, 76, 283
Switching register size, 58
Switching to emulation mode, 283
Symbolic labels, *see* Labels
Synchronization with external events, 522

Test and set instruction, 188-189
Timing, 51
   65816 instruction execution improvements, 165
   branch instructions, 144
Top-down programming, 368-369
Transfers, 94
True, 179
Truth table, 10
   and, 10, 425
   complement, 12
   exclusive or, 11, 454
   or, 11, 471

Two's complement, 12
   notation, 171
   number, 148-149
   overflow, 30

Unary operations, 126
Unsigned arithmetic, 161-166

v, *see* Overflow flag
Valid data address signal, 548
Valid program address signal, 548
Vector pull signal, 256-257, 548

Western Design Center, 78, 366
Word size, 5, 49, 56

x, *see* Index register mode select flag
X register, 27-28, 56, 91, 103-104

Y register, 27-28, 56, 91, 103-104

z, *see* Zero flag
Z80 processor, 40, 41
Zero bank, *see* Bank zero
Zero flag, 29, 144, 146-147, 157-161, 166, 187, 188, 430, 433
   effect of comparison on, 167
Zero page, 15, 35, 277
   no longer special on 65816/65802, 200-202
   vs. direct page, 60
Zeroing memory, 507
Zilog, 41, 42

65x support chips, 551-559
6502
   address space, 27
   architecture, 25-44
   bugs, 43
   difference from emulation mode, 374
   division routine, 273-275
   existing 6502 applications running on 65816, 277-284, 308, 319
   instructions, 38-39
   Jump bug, 363
   multiplication routine, 269, 270
   operations, 36
   pinout, 49, 544
   programming model, 27-28, 375
   signals, 545
   stack, 31, 277

Index

6502 emulation mode on 65816/65802, *see* Emulation mode
65C02
  architecture, 45–48
  bugs, 48
  difference from emulation mode, 374
  division routine, 275
  instructions, 47
  multiplication routine, 269
  operations, 46
  pinout, 544, 546
  programming model, 375
  Rockwell version, 561–565
  signals, 546
6521 PIA IC, 551, 556–558
6522 Versatile Interface Adapter, 257–259
6551 ACIA IC, 551, 552–556
65802/65816,
  16-bit accumulator, 51
  16-bit index registers, 51
  architecture, 49–72
  bugs, 72
  compatibility with 6502, 67
  division routine, 275–277
  instructions, 63
  multiplication routine, 269, 271
  native mode, *see* Native mode
65802
  addressable memory, 49
  pinout, 49
  programming model, native mode, 66, 376
  signals, 547
65816
  addressable memory, 49
  compiler-generated code, 285–291
  programming model
    emulation mode, 70, 378
    native mode, 52, 377
  signals, 547

68xx processors, 88, 91, 363
6800 processor, 35, 41, 53
6809 processor, 41, 53
68000 processor, 40, 41

80xx processors, 88, 91, 363
  MOV instruction, 88
8080 processor, 40, 41
8086 processor, 41

Made in the USA
Monee, IL
20 January 2024